# URBAN
# GEOGRAPHY

# URBAN GEOGRAPHY

## RAY M. NORTHAM
OREGON STATE UNIVERSITY

JOHN WILEY & SONS, INC., NEW YORK LONDON SYDNEY TORONTO

*Library of Congress Cataloging in Publication Data*

Northam, Ray M
  Urban geography.

  Includes bibliographical references.
  1.  Cities and towns.  2.  Cities and towns — United
States.  I.  Title.
HT151.N64    301.36'3'09    74–14900
ISBN 0–471–65135–4

Printed in the United States of America

10 9 8 7 6 5 4 3

# preface

Even the most casual of observer is aware of the many population centers in the settlement pattern of the world today — hamlets, villages, towns, and cities. A person who knows history realizes the importance of these population centers in the course of world events, and a person who is interested in the political scene is aware of the impact of the world's cities on the political structure of different areas. A social worker realizes that many of the social problems of the past and present are most acute in cities, while a student of economics considers the urban center as a unique microcosm within which general economic concerns are reflected. The engineer believes that many of today's engineering challenges involve urban centers, and the practitioner of planning also views the city in terms of meeting challenges and problems that beset much of the world's population. Furthermore, many geographers are interested in the spatial aspects of the above mentioned concerns and the occupance of land area by cities. Thus, there is an unbounded, common interest in cities that transcends many disciplines and extends to the citizen, the observer, the academic, the student, and the technician. This widespread interest is understandable and warranted, since the largest portion of the population of many nations resides in cities, and significant parts of the population of most nations live in urban agglomerations (large or small). Although many people do not live in these centers, they depend on them and, therefore, have urban interests.

The people that live in urban centers total about one third of the world population. The centers provide them with living space, livelihoods, and goods and services. There are thousands of urban centers in various spatial settings and diverse cultures, and the centers are a complex, baffling, and not easily understood creation of man. No one can claim to have a complete knowledge or understanding of this creation, which evolved during several millennia. I, like others, do not profess to have an unusual understanding or insight of the urban phenomenon, but I do have helpful knowledge and understanding that is included here.

Although this book is my work, the effort was shared by many people. I must make a major acknowledgment to the many authors of books, professional articles, monographs, and reports that provided basic the facts and ideas incorporated here. I thank the publisher's editorial staff, especially Gary Brahms, for providing encouragement during the book's development. I also appreciate the comments of the manuscript's reviewers whose suggestions were of great value. I am grateful to Ruth Weller Thompson, Joyce Northam, Rosemary McLeod, and Judith Cichowicz who helped in preparation of illustrations. Without an understanding, patient wife and children, Joyce, Amy, and Paul, this book would have been much harder to write. To all of these people and to others unnamed, I sincerely say "Thank you."

*Ray M. Northam*

v

# contents

## 1 Introduction

## 2 Terminology and Classifications

## 3 The City in History

## 4 Recent Urbanization: World Regions and the United States

# 5 The Urban Environment and the Livability of Cities

# 6 Urban Hierarchies and Urban Regions

# 7 Central Place Concepts

# 8 The Labor Force and Economic Base of the City

## 9 Land Use in the City

## 10 Land Values and Land Use Zoning

## 11 Commercial Activities and Centers in the City

## 12 Residential Land in the City: Its Characteristics and Its Use

## 13  Manufacturing in the City

## 14  Transportation in the City

## 15  Other Land Components of the City

# 16   Spatial Movements, Areal Expansion, and Urban Governments

# 17   Urban Land Policy, Urban Planning, and New Towns

# Index

# 1
# introduction

This book, written primarily for university students, has the purpose of presenting factual information, hypotheses, concepts, and theory pertaining to the subject of cities. These objectives are presented in accord with the points of view of the discipline of geography which provides the organizational framework of the book.

The author intends to present the material contained herein in a succinct and orderly manner in which one section blends into others and in which each section builds on those preceding it. Although the organization is that of an urban geographer, the author does not choose to be bound by the artificial dogmatic bounds often discussed in academic circles. The concern essentially is to present a given subject, and less attention is paid to whether or not the content remains within the supposed bounds of a given discipline.

## The Nature of Geographic Study

Geographers, for the most part, consider that they are in that science that deals with the earth as the habitat of man. Still, one knowledgeable in the nature of geography realizes that many different types of inquiry and study come under this broad umbrella. As a result, one is aware that there is no singly accepted definition or approach of geography, but that a number of them exist, depending on the interests of the individual geographer.

This matter has been explicitly approached by one geographer who identified four traditions of geography that embrace virtually all of the diverse thrusts of geography that might be put forward, those four traditions are (1) the spatial tradition, (2) the area studies tradition, (3) the man-land tradition, and (4) the earth science tradition.[1] The spatial tradition has to do with the geometry or positioning of geographic phenomena associated with a given spatial system and the interrelationships within this spatial system. Considering the city as the geographic phenomenon in question, its location or position in two dimensional space, relative to other cities or other geographic phenomena, is one aspect of inquiry in the spatial tradition of geography. Movement to and from a given

[1]William D. Pattison, "The Four Traditions of Geography," *The Journal of Geography,* Vol. LXIII, No. 5 (May, 1964).

city or among a number of cities for acquisition of goods and services by persons living in outlying areas is another topic of study in the spatial tradition.

Geographers may be interested in those aspects of a specific segment of the earth's surface that serve to give it distinct character and that provide a basis for differentiation of the selected area from other earth areas. Within this tradition of area studies, the surface segment may be of large size, in which case one is dealing with world regions, arid regions, polar regions, and the like. By changing the scale of inquiry, one might consider the city as the area of study and here too, would attempt to establish the characteristics of the city that provide its physical, economic, and/or social character and which make it identifiably different from other cities. Within this tradition, attention is focused more on the uniqueness of a given area than on similarities or relationships among areas.

Another of the traditions of geography, the man-land tradition, deals with the adjustment of man to the physical earth and, carried to an extreme, the shaping of human settlement and spatial behavior by the physical environment. This tradition can be extended to the study of cities, since urban settlements do adjust to a physical setting, although this can be modified to some degree, for example, rivers are bridged, slopes are leveled, and depressions are filled. Still, one cannot forget that cities, like other terrestrial phenomena, occupy land area and, therefore, the physical setting of the city would be a factor in understanding a specific city. At a more basic level, however, one might postulate a hypothetical earth surface as physically homogeneous as a tabletop, that is, there would be no variation in the physical characteristics. If people were placed on such a surface, would they not form cities or some such agglomeration, and would not these cities be arranged in some type of spatial pattern with each dominant in its own territory? The answer to the above question

likely is "yes," which tends to refute somewhat the influence of purely physical factors in city formation and spatial patterns of cities.

In any case, the geographers' interest in urban phenomena is varied, but tends to be mainly within the context of one or more of three of the four stated traditions of geography. Conceivably, geographic study of cities might be in the earth science tradition as well, but this is somewhat less likely.

One should realize fully that a given inquiry of an urban nature may not fall completely within one of the above traditions, but might have aspects of two or more of them. For example, how would one identify a study of land use in a given city? It would be concerned with a single area, the specific city, and thus would be in the area studies tradition. However, it also would be concerned with man's use of urban land and logically would be in the man-land tradition as well. In attempting to explain the land use pattern, the researcher might consider travel distances regularly traveled by the urban population, thus introducing a spatial dimension to the study. Also, if the study included sections on the relative locations of different land use zones or subareas within the city and attempted an explanation of the spatial pattern formed, it also would be dealing with spatial relationships and would be within the spatial tradition of geography.

## The Approaches of Urban Geographers

The urban geographer traditionally has been most interested in populated places on the earth's surface and the relationships that exist within such places and among these population centers that collectively constitute a spatial system of places. These relationships exist, not only within and among places, but also between a place and the people inhabiting that place, with these relationships also of interest to the urban geographer.

In Figure 1–1, the different thrusts of study of urban centers are depicted, with barbed lines indicating the nature of inquiry of different types. There is one channel of inquiry (*A*) involving relationships between a place and its population, another channel of study (*B*) concerned with relationships among different places, a further channel (*C*) dealing with the study of relationships that exist between populations of more than one place, and still another channel of study (*D*) concerned with relationships existent in only one place or in the population of a single place. Examples might serve to clarify these different channels of inquiry within the context of urban geography.

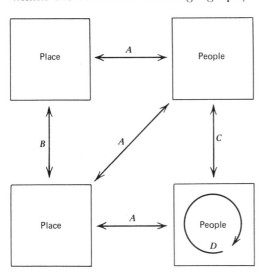

**Figure 1-1**   Thrusts of study in urban geography.

An example of type *A* studies could be one on the variations and patterns of population distribution in a city. An example of type *B* study would be one where the spacing and geometric patterns of urban settlements is the major concern or in which the spatial arrangement of places of similar types is highlighted. Type *C* studies might include one dealing with spatial aspects of the voting behavior of the populations of different urban centers, one concerned with different economic characteristics of the populations of several urban centers, or

one dealing with differences in demographic characteristics of the populations of a number of places. Examples of type *D* studies could include land use study of the single urban center, study of the commercial structure of the single city, or study of differences in residential neighborhoods within a chosen city. In general, the urban geographer is interested mainly in type *A* or type *B* channels of urban inquiry and, to a lesser degree, in type *C* and type *D* studies. It must be recognized, however, that many studies do not fit neatly into the above framework because a certain study may have aspects of several of the channels mentioned, which is true of the content of this book.

## The Approach of This Book

This book does not fit entirely into any one of the traditions or approaches of geography mentioned previously, and no attempt has been made to achieve this end. However, it deals more with two of the stated traditions than with others —the spatial tradition and the man-land tradition.

The fundamental approach of this book is one where a specific city is considered as an *intraurban system* which comprises a subsystem within a larger scale *interurban system* made up of a number of cities in a given region, with each type of system consisting of interrelated component elements. In the intraurban system, there are a number of different component elements comprising the city, such as a residential element, a commercial element, and an industrial element. Each of these elements has functional and spatial relationships with each of the others and a degree of mutual interdependence exists among them, with each of the component elements occupying space in the city. While each type of space use or activity in the individual city comprises a component element in the intraurban system, each city in a region constitutes a component element in the interurban system. Since there are interrelationships

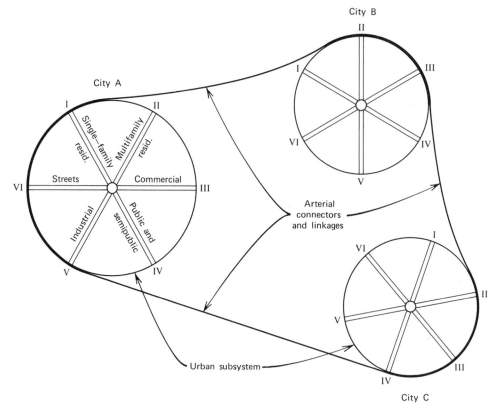

**Figure 1-2** Diagrammatic representation of an urban system and included intraurban subsystems.

among the elements of an urban subsystem, there also are relationships (spatial, functional, and social) among the cities in the interurban system of a particular region. There are interconnections and degrees of interdependence among cities in a region, as there are among component elements in a city. The above situation might be likened to a system of interacting wheels of different sizes, with spokes of each of the wheels analogous to component elements of the city (Figure 1–2). Each spoke in the wheel represents a different type of space use or activity (residential or commercial, for instance), and each is instrumental in provision of structure, support, and cohesiveness to the entire entity, the urban subsystem. Although each spoke is an essential element of the wheel as each type of space use or activity is an essential element of the city, it is the population of the city that pro-

vides the driving force to activate the urban subsystem, as an engine might activate the wheel. The individual wheel, with its array of spokes, represents a given city and the interacting parts comprise the intraurban system. In turn, the entire arrangement of wheels, large and small, is analogous to an interurban system of cities in a specific region. Still using the example of wheels to represent cities, they interact by means of a belt system, with this component, in turn, analogous to avenues of transportation and communication among cities in the region.

In the above process, a regional system of cities which interact and which have interrelationships of the component entities making up the system is recognized. In turn, each of the entities making up the interurban system is comprised of component elements which interact and are interrelated in a different manner, and these individual entities (the individual city) are considered as well.

## The Structure of This Book

The first part of this book deals with the clarification of terms and classifications pertaining to cities, the bases and regions of city formation, the evolution of cities to their present form, general growth trends and patterns in the rise of urbanism in the world and in major world regions, stages in the urbanization process and present levels of urbanization, projected levels of urbanization to the year 2000, and degradation of the urban environment where about one-third of the world's people now live.

The next section of the book is concerned with cities as parts of spatial systems or interurban systems. The various concepts and hypotheses having to do with the spatial arrangement of cities are included, as are concepts dealing with the relationships between cities and the regions they serve. Further, concepts of hierarchies of cities are considered, including rank-size relationships and spatial hierarchies. This section recognizes that the individual city is but one component element in a system of cities and that the region served by the individual city is but one component element in a system of such regional units. Included in this part of the book is coverage of the regions served by cities—their delimitation, identification, and differences.

The section of the book that follows focuses on the elements comprising the intraurban system; the subsystem represented by the individual city. Since the spatial expression or manifestation of each of the functional component elements is a type of land use, this section includes coverage of land uses in the city, the manner in which they are identified and represented, patterns and concepts dealing with their spatial arrangement, and concepts having to do with patterns they exhibit. Since each land use is distinctly different from others, with each serving a different role in the operation of the whole city, each land use and associated activity in the city is explored in some depth. Transportation is an element of the urban subsystem somewhat different from others in that it serves as a means of activating the entire intraurban system, as well as being a land use component in its own right.

The remaining section of the book includes coverage of the areal expansion of cities or "urban sprawl," and the political organization of urban areas which is conducive to such uncontrolled expansion. Furthermore, this section contains coverage of different urban land policies in different parts of the world, as well as the nature of efforts made in the realm of urban planning. The latter includes coverage of the planning and development of "new towns" or self-contained, free-standing new communities.

In summary, the content of this book might be stated with a series of phrases: (1) establishment of a working background, (2) evolution and dispersal of urban centers, (3) recent world trends, patterns of urbanization, and future estimates, (4) spatial hierarchies and spatial systems, (5) functional elements of the city, and (6) current and future problems, policies, and programs. The purpose, overall, is to impart some appreciation for and knowledge of the above topics, with special concern for cities in the United States.

# 2
# urban terminology and classifications

In any body of organized knowledge, there is a certain vocabulary and classification that is developed or employed, and urban geography is no exception. This vocabulary aids in communication and understanding of the subject matter of the discipline. Some of the words and phrases that are commonly used in urban geography have originated within geography, while others have originated in other fields of study and have been adopted by geographers. Much of this terminology has been utilized in this book and the purpose at this point is to clarify the meanings of frequently used terms, at least in a manner suitable to the content of this book. Many of the terms have no single meaning that is acceptable to all persons, but at least the definitions put forward have meaning to the content of this book, if not to others.

Also included in this chapter is coverage of some basic types of classifications used in urban study. These also involve definition of a type, but not of an isolated term. Here the definition is of a term that is used in conjunction with others and which has meaning when used in the perspective of a number of other terms.

The overall objective here is to present basic, often used terminology, but not to provide a glossary of all terms used in the book. It is more appropriate to clarify the meaning of terms used in a particular context at the time the pertinent material is presented. The same qualification applies to classifications as well.

## General Terminology

*Urban.* The sociologist, Nels Anderson, implies that urban or urbanism is a way of life of man or the condition of man characterized by certain attitudes, such as transiency, superficiality, and anonymity.[1] This type of definition may suffice for recognition of differences in social types, but does not serve well as a working definition for geographers.

Geographers are more inclined toward a definition of "urban" that recognizes, not a mode of behavior, but a place of occupance. Certainly, man in a certain locational setting may adopt certain indentifiable behavior traits, but the geographer is more concerned with his locational setting than with his life style.

Most geographers would accept a definition of "urban" that would essentially state that urban is a locational set-

[1]Nels Anderson, *The Urban Community: A World Perspective*, Henry Holt and Co., New York, 1959.

ting in which (1) the density of settlement is considerably higher than that of the general population, (2) the people in that setting mainly are engaged in nonagricultural activities, not in economic activities normally placed in the primary economic sector, and (3) the locational setting serves as a cultural, administrative, and economic center for a region peripheral to the center in question. Urban, as used here, refers to the activities of a human agglomeration at a specific location or place.

*City.* The meaning of this word also is somewhat unclear, although it is very often used. The problem of definition is made more difficult by the use of the term "city" in different contexts. One meaning refers to a discrete area with a discrete population that has legal status and the margins of this discrete area, the "city limits," have legal definition and recognition. This legalistic definition is more of a formal one than a general definition, and is employed in much usage of the word "city."

Another, but more general, definition of "city" is one that holds the city to be a locale with a sizable agglomeration of people having the characteristics of an urban being. This definition may or may not incorporate the legal boundaries consistent with the legalistic meaning of the word. Often, the use of the word "city" is a quite general one, such as in the term "city limits" when referring to the margin of the built-up area with population densities greater than those prevailing in rural areas.

An interesting concept dealing with the use of the term "city" has arisen in urban geography. One aspect of this concept concerns the case where urban settlement is confined to the area within the legal limits of the city and virtually all of this area is occupied by urban residents. Such cities are known as "truebounded" cities (Figure 2–1). Another situation exists where urban settlement occupies only a portion of the area included within the legal limits of the city which is termed the "over-bounded" city. Still another situation is one in which urban settlement has spread beyond the legal limits of the city—a situation very common to large urban centers. These cities are known as "underbounded" cities and are a very prevalent type, since legal limits of cities tend to be relatively static, while urban settlement is spatially dynamic.

*Agglomerated Settlement.* This is a term used in geography and other disciplines and infers a settlement form in which there is a density of population greater than those of rural areas. The agglomerated settlement consists of a cluster of population in which the people are not engaged in rural economic activities for

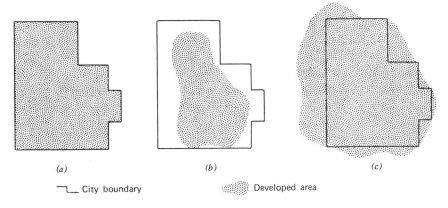

(a)                    (b)                    (c)

⌐⌐⌐ City boundary          ⣿⣿⣿ Developed area

**Figure 2-1** Types of "bounded" cities. (*a*) Truebounded. (*b*) Overbounded. (*c*) Underbounded.

the most part. The agglomerated settlement may or may not have legal status
and fixed boundaries.

## Formalized Terminology

In addition to the general terminology
discussed above, there is a body of terminology that is, at least in the United
States, given a more explicit meaning by
public agencies involved in the process of
data accumulation and reporting. The
following section deals with the major
terms of this type.

*Places: Incorporated, Unincorporated, and
Urban.*   The Bureau of the Census uses
the term "place" in reference to a concentration of population regardless of
the existence of legally prescribed limits,
powers, or functions. Thus, the term has
a meaning essentially the same as that of
"agglomerated settlement" mentioned
earlier.

Of "places" identified by the Bureau of
the Census, some are incorporated places
and some are unincorporated places. Incorporated places are those legally char-
tered as cities, towns, villages, or
boroughs. They have established limits or
boundaries which approximate the areas
of high density settlement. Unincorporated places are those population concentrations that have no fixed corporate
limits and do not have the legal powers of
incorporated places (Table 2–1). Prior to
1970, an urban town or township was
recognized, this being a minor civil division of a county with a population dense
enough to be declared an urban town (as
in New England) or an urban township
(as in the American Midwest). Such units
are now included as unincorporated
places.

A variation of the use of the term
"place" is the "urban place" as designated
by the Bureau of the Census. An urban
place is a concentration of population including 2500 people or more and may be
an incorporated place or an unincorporated place. In general, an urban place is
a subdivision of the minor civil division

**Table 2–1**   "Places" Classified by the
Bureau of the Census, 1970

| | |
|---|---:|
| Incorporated places | |
| Number | 18,666 |
| Percent of total places | 89.9 |
| Population (millions) | 131.9 |
| | |
| Unincorporated places | |
| Number | 2,102 |
| Percent of total places | 10.0 |
| Population (millions) | 12.8 |

SOURCE:   U.S. Bureau of the Census, Census
of Population, 1970. *Number of Inhabitants.*
Final Report PC(1) A1, United States Summary.

within which it is located such as a county.
There are some instances, however,
where the urban place is considered a
minor civil division in its own right and is
independent of any county organization.
Such is the case of St. Louis, Missouri,
Baltimore, Maryland, and a number of
smaller cities in Virginia. In the United
States in 1970, there were 6435 urban
places, each with a population of over
2500.

Notice that, although a population of
2500 is the distinction on which urban
places are recognized in the United
States, other standards are used in other
nations. In Denmark, an urban place is
an agglomeration of 250 or more people.
In   Greece,   urban   places   include
municipalities and communes with agglomerations of 10,000 or more people,
while Guatemala has considered places as
urban if they have 2000 or more inhabitants, plus places with 1500 or more inhabitants if running water service is provided in the houses. These are only a few
of the variety of ways in which urban
places are defined in different countries;
it is unusual to find two national
definitions that are exactly the same.

But is there not a formal or organized
way of distinguishing between large and
small urban places? In the United States
there is, and this takes the form of the
"central city" which is a large urban place,

normally incorporated, with a population of at least 50,000 people. In cases of twin cities, twin central city status is afforded if the combined population of the two is at least 50,000 and the smaller of the two has at least 15,000 people. In 1970 in the United States, there were 310 incorporated cities having central city status, although quite often two or more of these were combined into a single entity, for example, Albany, Schenectady, and Troy, New York or San Francisco, and Oakland, California. The 310 cities of central city status, either singly or in combination, formed 248 urban entities in 1970 and had a combined population of nearly 64 million or 31 percent of the total population of the nation. Of the 248 urban concentrations comprised of one or more central cities, 50 had twin-city, tri-city, or quad-city status.

It usually is true that urban settlement does not cease at the legal limits of a central city, for many places and people just beyond the boundaries of the large city are functionally tied to the central city to which they are adjacent and they share many common problems with the central city. This peripheral zone, including much of what is popularly known as "suburbia," has been formally recognized as the "urban fringe" by the Bureau of the Census. This zone includes the nearby incorporated and unincorporated places, plus other areas that meet specified criteria. The criteria used and areas included in delimiting the urban fringe include:

1.  Incorporated places with 2500 or more people.

2.  Incorporated places with less than 2500 inhabitants, providing each has a closely settled area with 100 dwelling units or more.

3.  Small land parcels normally less than one square mile in area with a population density of 1000 inhabitants or more per square mile.

4.  Other small areas in unincorporated territory with lower population

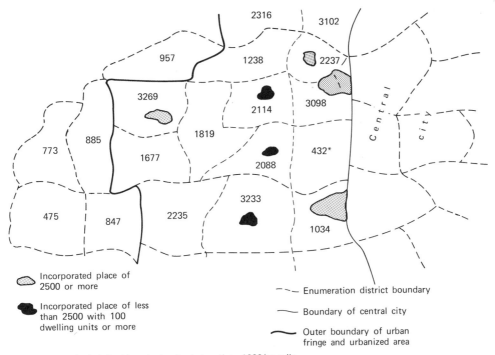

Incorporated place of 2500 or more

Incorporated place of less than 2500 with 100 dwelling units or more

‒ ‒ ‒ Enumeration district boundary

——— Boundary of central city

——— Outer boundary of urban fringe and urbanized area

*Enclave included, although density is less than 1000/sq mile

**Figure 2-2**  Portion of a hypothetical central city and urban fringe. (Numbers are population densities of enumeration districts.)

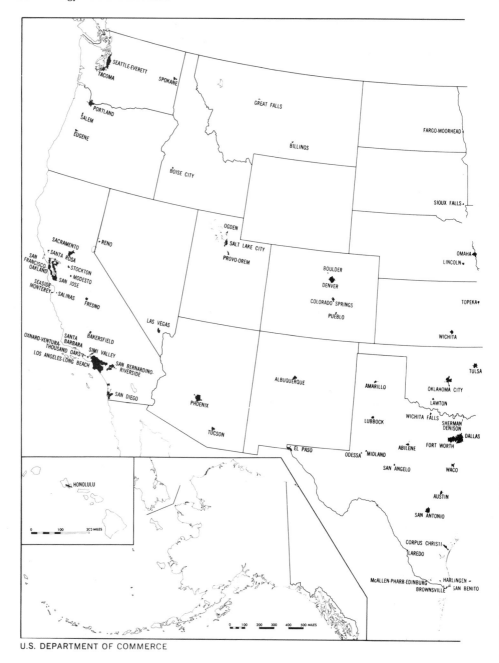

U.S. DEPARTMENT OF COMMERCE

**Figure 2–3** Urbanized areas of the United States: 1970.

density providing that they serve one of the following purposes:

    a.  To eliminate enclaves.

    b.  To close indentations in the urbanized area of one mile or less across the open end.

    c.  To link outlying enumeration districts of qualifying density that

are no more than 1½ miles from the main body of the urbanized area.

Since the outer boundary of the urban fringe tends to follow census enumeration district borders, it normally follows such features as roads, streets, railroads, streams, and other clearly defined lines

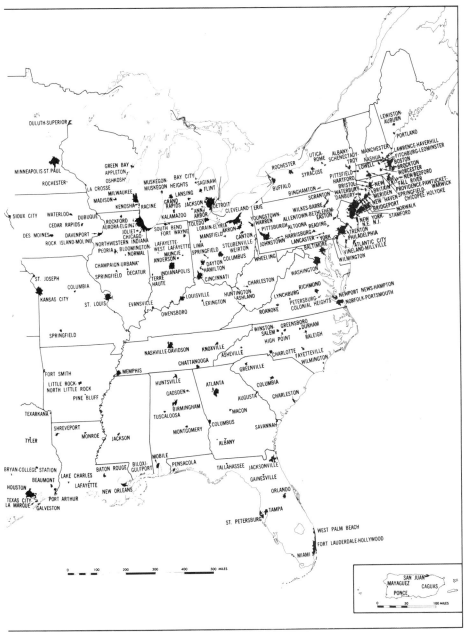

SOCIAL AND ECONOMIC STATISTICS ADMINISTRATION    BUREAU OF THE CENSUS

for ease in census enumeration in the field. Often, the outer boundary of the fringe area does not conform to the boundaries of political units, such as counties (Figure 2–2).

Now that we have two urban settlement types—the central city and the urban fringe—the next step is to combine them into a single entity which is done to form the urbanized area. To provide a better separation of urban and rural population in the vicinity of larger cities, the Bureau of the Census formalized the concept of the urbanized area which includes the major population center (or centers in the cases of twin-, tri-, or quad-cities) in an area, the central city, and the surrounding built-up area that is associated with the central city or cities (the urban fringe). Urbanized areas were first formally identified in 1950 and correspond generally to what are known as "conurbations" in Great Britain. In 1970, there were 248 urbanized areas in the United States and these included over 118 million people, or 58 percent of the national population (Figure 2–3). The areal spread of an urban agglomeration is not confined to a single political jurisdiction, however, and of the 248 urbanized areas, 32 include portions of two adjacent states, and 1 includes small portions of three adjacent states (Sioux City, Iowa-Nebraska-South Dakota).

For some purposes, such as ease of data collection, it is useful to consider an urban region the limits of which conform to existing political boundaries, such as county boundaries. Not only would such a move facilitate data collection and use, it would also deal with an areal unit that is less likely to contract or expand over time than is the urbanized area, where enumeration district borders are subject to periodic change. In response to this need, the Bureau of the Census has recognized an areal unit known as the Standard Metropolitan Statistical Area (the S.M.S.A.). This is but another type of urban region, the definition of which has been institutionally formalized.

The attempt here is to consider an areal unit in which the greatest share of the population is engaged in activities that form an integrated social and economic system. Except in New England, a S.M.S.A. is a county or group of contiguous counties containing at least one city of 50,000 inhabitants or twin cities with at least 50,000 inhabitants. In addition to the county or counties containing the central city or cities, contiguous counties are included in the S.M.S.A. if they meet certain criteria, are metropolitan in character, and are socially and economically integrated with the central city. The criteria of metropolitan

character relate primarily to the attributes of the outlying county as a place of work or residence for a concentration of nonagricultural inhabitants. Specifically, these criteria include:[2]

1.   At least 75 percent of the labor force of the county must be in the nonagricultural labor force.

2.   In addition to the above criterion, the county must meet at least one of these conditions:

   a.   It must have 50 percent or more of its population living in contiguous minor civil divisions with a density of at least 150 persons per square mile, in an unbroken chain of minor civil divisions with such density radiating from a central city in the area.

   b.   The number of nonagricultural workers employed in the county must equal at least 10 percent of the number of nonagricultural workers employed in the county containing the largest city in the area, or the outlying county must be the place of employment of at least 10,000 nonagricultural workers.

   c.   The nonagricultural labor force living in the county must equal at least 10 percent of the number of nonagricultural labor force living in the county containing the largest city in the area, or the outlying county must be the place of residence of a nonagricultural labor force of at least 10,000.

In addition to the above criteria which have to do with the structure of the labor force, there are several others that have to do with relationships between county of residence and county of employment, and the regularity of commutation between the two. Further, there are criteria that have to do with the degree of social integration. These include telephone calls between the county containing the

[2]In New England states, S.M.S.A.'s consist of towns and cities instead of counties.

central city and an outlying county, newspaper circulation, analysis of charge accounts in retail stores in the central city, delivery service from central city establishments, traffic counts, and extent of public transportation facilities between the central city and points in the contiguous county. In New England, where the city and town are administratively more important than the county, a population density of at least 100 persons per square mile is used as a measure of metropolitan character.

In the form of the Standard Metropolitan Statistical Area (S.M.S.A.), there is created an urban region that serves well for data compilation, since it is based on counties, and which suffices for a rather general frame of reference where one might conduct investigations of a metropolitan nature. One reservation concerning this type of urban region, however, is the fact that entire counties are brought into an S.M.S.A., even though many sections or even a major part of the county area may be rural in character. Therefore, treatment of the entire county as a metropolitan unit is misleading. Moreover, there are many unusually large counties, especially in western parts of the United States, and if entire county units are considered as parts of an S.M.S.A., many rural or sparsely populated sections are again included in the metropolitan area. Prime examples of this situation are San Bernadino County, California (20,117 sq. mi.) in the San Bernadino-Riverside-Ontario S.M.S.A., Washoe County, Nevada (6366 sq. mi.) in the Reno S.M.S.A., Clark County, Nevada (7874 sq. mi.) in the Las Vegas S.M.S.A., Lane County, Oregon (4552 sq. mi.) in the Eugene S.M.S.A., and St. Louis County, Minnesota (6092 sq. mi.) in the Duluth S.M.S.A. (Figure 2–4). These counties include such sparsely populated or uninhabited sections as the Mojave Desert, the Smoke Creek Desert, parts of the Lake Mead National Recreation Area and Hoover Dam, and parts of large national forests on the west slope of

the Cascade Mountains. To consider such areas as metropolitan is to test one's imagination.

## Urban Classifications

Classification is a means of organizing diverse information so that it might be more easily comprehended. It is a manner of grouping like or similar items into a single entity. In this manner, generalizations can be made concerning a single group comprised of like items, or one group can be compared and contrasted with one or more other groups. Classifications are made in an urban context for these basic reasons and have proven useful to many. Some of these classifications are fairly general and involve relatively few, broad classes, while others are somewhat more involved and are more rigorously established and tend to deal with more classes or with classes that are less broad. There are various approaches used in urban classifications and this section touches on a number of these.

*The Genetic Classification.* A genetic classification of cities deals mainly with the historical origins of urban centers or the chronological sequencing of city beginnings. One author, using a genetic classification, recognized five separate classes of cities based on the time or era of city development. The classes recognized are (1) the Prehistoric Town, (2) the Classical Greek Town, (3) the Roman Town, (4) the Medieval City, and (5) the Modern City.[3] Each of these classes includes cities developed during the period identified and considers the identifying characteristics of each that sets it apart from other classes of cities recognized. The value of such a classification is that it provides a time frame within which different cities can be placed, with similar properties of character and form typifying cities formed during the same interval in the time frame.

[3]Griffith Taylor, *Urban Geography,* London: Methuen, 1949.

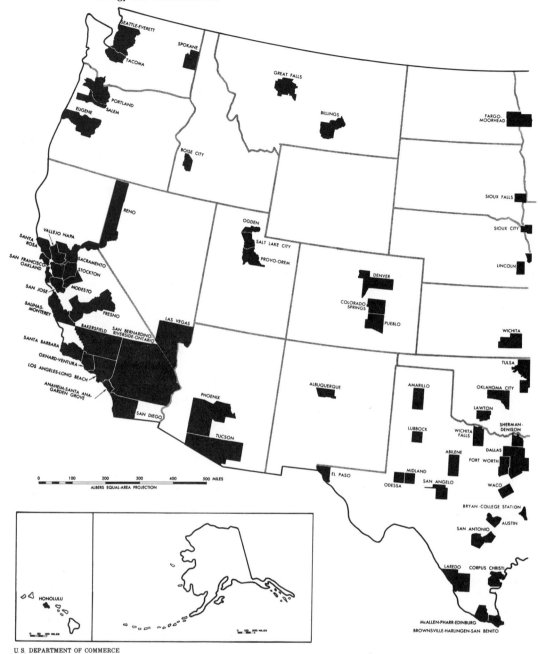

U.S. DEPARTMENT OF COMMERCE

**Figure 2–4**  Standard metropolitan statistical areas of the United States: 1970.

*The Locational or Site Classification.* This type of classification is one that groups cities with particular reference to some common characteristic in their positioning or location on the earth's surface. The criteria on which class differences are based have to do mostly with the nature of the physical site

occupied by the specific city. Classes that might be included in such a classification are (1) towns in plains, (2) towns located on rivers, (3) ports on seas or lakes, (4) mountain towns, and (5) resort towns. Each of these examples makes reference to a common physical association between the location of the city and one or

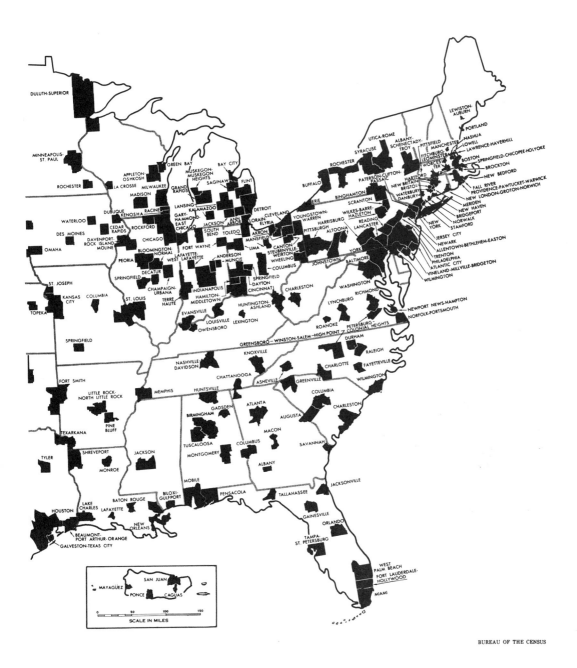

more physical characteristics of the space it occupies, that is, the location on the physical landscape. In the broad use of this type of classification, it would not appear to lead to significant distinctions among cities. When a finer classification is developed, however, it can be a very meaningful type of classification. As an example of this, one might develop a class of cities to be known simply as "cities on floodplains" with sub-classes developed that would recognize the incidence, severity, areal extent, and duration of flooding. Some cities might experience minor flooding of a river or rivers in the city that would inundate a relatively small part of the city and for only a few days at the most. Other cities might experience more frequent flooding of large sections of the city and the floodwaters might cause a great deal of property damage and remain for longer periods of time. Differences in cities based on the locational setting in this example could be very pertinent and meaningful in classifying cities and in dealing with their problems.

*The Morphological Classification.* A morphological classification deals with the similarities and differences in the spatial form that cities might take. The concern might be for two-dimensional differences in form, that is, the surface configuration of the city. In this type of classification, one might recognize the linear or attenuated city, the compact city with no particular elongation, and the composite city with aspects of both compactness and linearity (Figure 2–5). Cities, especially smaller ones, in mountain valleys or located along major transportation arteries often are of the linear type and could be called "ribbon" type cities. Cities developed in plains often are of the compact type and have a relatively even areal spread outward from the core of the city which often is the point of intersection of transportation arterials. Perhaps, the bulk of cities, however, are of a composite form that originally may have been compact, but evolved into an irregular configuration or shape due to annexation of additional land area. Another morphological class of cities might be the fragmented city, meaning that one or more of the parts are physically detached from others. This fragmentation often results from different parts of the city being relatively isolated from others, at least at the time of origin of the city, by physical features, such as rivers. An example of this situation is Budapest, Hungary, which originally consisted of two sections on opposite sides of the Danube River, Buda on the heights on the west bank and Pest on the low eastern bank. Such fragmented cities, including Budapest, have often become

more unified through bridges or tunnel construction, as in the case of New York City.

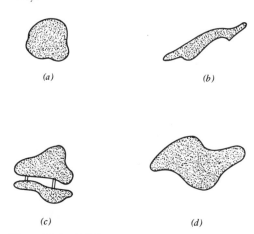

(a)          (b)

(c)          (d)

**Figure 2-5**   Different morphological types of cities. (*a*) The compact form. (*b*) The linear form. (*c*) The fragmented form (with linkages). (*d*) The composite form.

Another version of a morphological classification of cities is one that takes into account the internal structure of the city based upon the spatial arrangement of the component parts. Different arrangements result in different city forms. Often, the spatial arrangement of land use zones in a given city is established and compared with the land use zonation of other cities. This is a form of study utilizing a morphological classification. Still another version of such a classification is one that considers variations and similarities in the use of three dimensional space. Some parts of the city are developed relatively near the surface, such as areas with one or two story construction. Still other parts of the city are users of three, four, or five story construction or its equivalent, while other parts of the city use still more third dimensional space, with extremes extending to 100 or more stories or more than 1000 feet of third dimensional space. As these differences occur, there are obvious morphological differences in the city, with different structure heights comprising different morphological classes. One might consider a classification of the type presented in Table 2–2.

**Table 2–2**  A Suggested Morphological Classification, Based upon Structure Heights

| | |
|---|---|
| Class I | No structures: vacant or undeveloped land |
| Class II | One or two story structures or the equivalent (app. 25 feet) |
| Class III | Three to five story structures or the equivalent (elevators or escalators may be unnecessary) |
| Class IV | Five to 25 story structures (elevators or escalators necessary) |
| Class V | Over 25 stories (elevators necessary; many times express elevators are employed) |

One example of a morphological classification that has been developed combines aspects of form (morphology) with aspects of a genetic classification (Table 2–3). Notice from this table that the names of the classes have to do with chronological stages in the evolution of cities, but the characteristics of each class deal with the form developed by cities of that class or stage.

**Table 2–3**  A Classification of Cities, Combining Morphology and Genesis

| Class | Major Characteristics |
|---|---|
| Infantile towns | Haphazard distribution of shops and houses; no factories |
| Juvenile towns | Differentiation of zones begins; shops are separated |
| Adolescent towns | Scattered factories, but no definite zone of first-class houses |
| Early mature towns | A clear segregation of first-class houses |
| Mature towns | Separate commercial and industrial area; four zones of houses, ranging from mansions to shacks |

Source:  After Griffith Taylor, *Urban Geography*, 1949.

*The Hierarchical Classification.*   A hierarchical classification is one that deals with different orders or levels of cities, with each hierarchy based on stated criteria, such as population size, city area, or number of functions performed. In such an ordering, each class recognized is not based on criteria different from the others, but it has a different level or order of magnitude of the same criterion.

An example of a hierarchical classification of urban centers is presented in Table 2–4. The single criterion on which this classification is based is population size. Implied in this classification is the fact that each class is a discrete entity at a given point in time, yet a specific city can well change its hierarchical order or standing with the passage of time. In this sense, a hierarchical classification is a *dynamic type* of classification as opposed to a *static type* of classification in which a given urban center usually remains in a given class. Genetic and locational classifications tend to be of the latter type.

A further type of hierarchical classification is one based on a hierarchy of functional bases of cities. This applies particularly to the ordering of places based on their roles as trade centers dispensing goods and services to a surrounding trade area, tributary area, or hinterland. A given city may dispense a limited number of goods and services to a limited trade area peripheral to the trade center, while another city might dispense a greater number of goods and services to a larger trade area that will include the trade area of the first city. This progression could be extended to include more cities, each successively distributing a greater array of goods and services to increasingly larger trade or tributary areas. Each of the cities dispensing the same general number and mix of goods and services to areas of the same general size would be in the same functional order in a functional hierarchy and, as in the given situation, there would be a number of different orders in the same functional hierarchy. Functional hierarchies of this

**Table 2–4**  A Hierarchical Classification of Urban Centers, Based upon Population

| Order or Class Number | Class Name | Approximate Population |
|---|---|---|
| I | Hamlet | 16–150 |
| II | Village | 150–1,000 |
| III | Town | 1,000–2,500 |
| IV | Small city | 2,500–25,000 |
| V | Medium sized city | 25,000–100,000 |
| VI | Large city | 100,000–800,000 |
| VII | Metropolis | 800,000–Indefinite |
| VIII | Megalopolis | Indefinite, but at least several million |
| IX | Ecumenopolis | Indefinite, but likely tens of millions |

SOURCE:  Adapted from R. M. Highsmith and Ray M. Northam, *World Economic Activities*, 1968, Table 16–3.

type are discussed at length in Chapter 6 and again in Chapter 11, though at a different scale. It suffices here to say only that this is but another type of hierarchical classification of cities.

*The Functional Classification.*  This is a type of classification of cities that recognizes that different cities have different functions and, based on the dominant function or functions performed, the city is included in a certain functional class. Generally, this type of classification is based on different types of employment of the urban work force, perhaps because such data are relatively easy to acquire.

This type of classification of cities is not to be confused with the functional-hierarchical classification discussed above, since (1) it does not have aspects of functional orders included within it, and (2) it is more of a static type of classification. In this type of classification, each functional class is a discrete entity not concerned with other functional classes.

There are several different, but similar, functional classifications of cities in the United States that have been developed. One of the better known and earliest was developed by Chauncy D. Harris.[4] He used employment data for

988 cities and, based on rather arbitrary criteria, identified eight different functional types of cities. Again, it might be noted that the classification by Harris involves a number of arbitrary decisions based on personal insight and bias, for example, the choice of values such as 74, 60, 50, and 25 percent of persons in a given employment group, as criteria for classification of cities by functional class.

Another functional classification of cities in the United States was that developed by Howard Nelson.[5] He used employment data in 24 industry groups for 897 urban concentrations of 10,000 or more people. For each industry group, the average (mean) proportion of the labor force engaged in that activity was determined. Few, if any, cities would have the average employment in a given industry, thus, most would exhibit some degree of variation from the mean or average relative employment. For example, the average employment in a given industry group might be 10.0 percent, yet a certain city might have 25.0 percent of its labor force employed in this industry group. A key matter, then, becomes that of identifying significant deviations or degrees of variation from the average. The method used by Nelson was to em-

[4]Chauncy D. Harris, "A Functional Classification of Cities in the United States," *Geographical Review*, V. 33 No. 1, January, 1943.

[5]Howard Nelson, "A Service Classification of American Cities," *Economic Geography*, Vol. 31, No. 3; July, 1955.

ploy standard deviations to establish degrees of functional specialization in a given industry group. Standard deviation is a formalized and relatively simple measurement of levels of variation from a mean or average. One standard deviation includes just over 68 percent of the items included (in this case, cities), or the 34 percent immediately above the mean and the 34 percent just below the mean (Figure 2–6). Two standard deviations include slightly over 95 percent of the items included and three standard deviations include over 99 percent. Nelson computed three standard deviations above the mean of each industry group, since he was concerned with levels of employment that were unusually high, in order to identify a functional emphasis in a chosen city. The specific city then might be within one, two, or three standard deviations above the mean employment in a given industry group. This would identify the functional specialization of the city and also the degree of emphasis in this industry group. For example, if the mean employment in a particular industry group is 25 percent of the total urban labor force and one standard deviation is 10 percent, city A with 32 percent of its labor force in this industry, would be within one standard deviation above the mean, while city B, with 40 percent of its labor force in this industry group, would

be within two standard deviations of the mean. Both would have the same general specialty in this industry group, but city B would have a greater degree of specialization of this type than would city A. In this manner, degrees of functional emphasis in a specific city were established and it could be assigned to one or more classes making up the classification. As an example, Portland, Oregon is within one standard deviation above the mean for wholesale trade and for finance, insurance, and real estate. By contrast, Atlanta, Georgia is not above the mean for wholesale trade, but is within two standard deviations for finance, insurance, and real estate. In a functional classification, Portland emerges as a wholesale trade and financial center of a minor level, while Atlanta is not a wholesale trade center of any level, but is a financial center of a level higher than Portland.

In evaluating this classification, one can note that it allows for a multifunctional city and that distinctions between functional classes are made in a more systematic manner in which personal judgements have been largely removed. One might question, however, the use of standard deviations for data of the type used. If we consider the nature of these data, we note that they are not normal distributions, but that they are skewed, mostly to

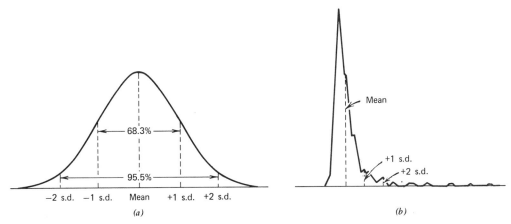

**Figure 2–6** Types of distribution curves. (a) Normal distribution. (b) Skewed distribution. Means, one standard deviation ( ± 1 s.d.) and two standard deviations ( ± 2 s.d.), are indicated.

the left (Figure 2–6). Therefore, one standard deviation above the mean includes a greater range of city values than does one standard deviation below the mean. Further, the nature of the distribution may not lead to any "natural breaks" in the distribution curve, but the use of standard deviations imposes a "statistical break."

Still another example of a functional classification of cities is the one developed by Gunnar Alexandersson.[6] In essence, this system considered that the labor force of a city can be divided between the "city-forming" employment sector and the "city-serving" employment sector. The former includes employment in the city devoted to production of goods and services for consumption or use outside the city, while the latter includes employment in the city concerned with the production of goods and services for consumption by the people residing in that city. This distinction is pursued at greater length in a later chapter, but an example might serve well to illustrate this point.

serving employment. Another employee in the same city is employed in an industrial concern producing goods for a national market and, thus, is engaged in city-forming employment that generates wealth from outside the city, not just recirculation of wealth within the city. Alexandersson arrayed 864 cities in a cumulative manner, beginning with the lowest percent employed in a given industry and ranging upward to the highest percent employed in that industry. He considered throughout his analysis that there was a certain level of employment that served as the minimum amount needed to support the needs of residents of the city (city-serving employment) and that the functional character of the city emerged once this minimal level was surpassed. This is to say the functional class of a city would be based on city-forming employment, not total employment in a given industry group. He considered that this distinction could be based on employment levels of the city at a point 5 percent from the bottom of the array of

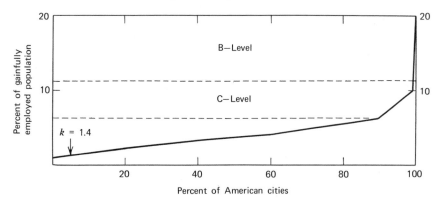

**Figure 2-7**   Cumulative distribution curve and class levels: wholesale trade, as developed by G. Alexandersson. Based on Gunnar Alexandersson *The Industrial Structure of American Cities,* Figure 25.

Teachers in an urban school are rendering their services to children who, together with their parents, are residents of the city in which the school is located. Thus, the teacher is engaged in city-

[6]Gunnar Alexandersson, *The Industrial Structure of American Cities,* Lincoln, University of Nebraska Press, 1956.

864 cities (Figure 2–7). Thus, the employment in a certain industry of the 43rd city from the point of origin in the cumulative distribution was taken as the critical level for all industry types and this value was identified as the "$k$" value. As one example of this system, with education being the employment type consid-

ered, the k value is 2.6 percent. This means, according to Alexandersson, that 2.6 percent of the gainfully employed urban labor force is necessary to satisfy the education needs of the urban center and that any employment greater than this adds to the city-forming employment and provides a basis for a functional class of cities based on employment of this type greater than the minimal level of 2.6 percent. By contrast, the k value for electrical machinery manufacture is 0.0, meaning that there is no minimal employment of this type that is essential to the needs of the city, that is, all such employment is city-forming.

Once the amount of city-forming employment is isolated from city-serving employment, three levels of magnitude of each function were identified as follows: "C town" (5–10 percent beyond the k value), "B town" (10–20 percent beyond the k value), and "A town" (more than 20 percent greater than the k value). These class distinctions differ, of course, among the various industry groups considered, as exemplified in Table 2–5.

This classification, like that of Nelson, has much of the subjectivity removed although it still employs rather arbitrary divisions between different levels of magnitude within each of the classes recognized, even though the classes are quite explicitly formulated. Its prime attribute, perhaps, is the distinction made between city-forming and city-serving

employment and the recognition that a minimal amount of employment exists in the city to maintain the needs of that city. Amounts greater than these minima are those considered as valid in establishing the distinctive economic function of the city. Another attribute of this classification is that a given city can have more than one city-forming function, as exemplified by Bridgeport, Connecticut, which is a B-type center of machinery manufacture (other than electrical), and a C-type center for the manufacture of electrical machinery, fabricated metal products, and primary metal manufacture.

*Other Possible Classifications.*  There are other functional classifications that have been or could be developed, but those discussed above serve to illustrate some of the most widely accepted ones and present some of the different methodology used in their development. One point here is that all or nearly all functional classifications developed deal with *economic function,* as based upon employment of the urban labor force. It is reasonable to consider that there may be (1) some economic functions existent or even dominant in the city that are not recognized by usual data gathering methods or data handling techniques, and (2) some urban functions exist that are not essentially economic activities, meaning they do not deal primarily with the labor force.

**Table 2–5**  Selected Examples of Divisions Between Class Levels, Based Upon Differing *K* Values

| Industry | k Value (%) | C Type (k plus 5–9.9%) | B Type (k plus 10–19.9%) | C Type (k plus 20% or more) |
|---|---|---|---|---|
| Education | 2.6 | 7.6–12.5 | 12.5–22.5 | 22.6 or more |
| Electrical machinery | 0.0 | 5.0– 9.9 | 10.0–19.9 | 20.0 or more |
| Chemicals | 0.1 | 5.1–10.0 | 10.1–20.0 | 20.1 or more |
| Food manufacture | 0.7 | 5.7–10.6 | 10.7–20.6 | 20.7 or more |
| Wholesale trade | 1.4 | 6.4–11.3 | 11.4–21.3 | 21.4 or more |
| Finance, insurance, and real estate | 1.8 | 6.8–11.7 | 11.8–21.7 | 21.8 or more |

SOURCE:  Adapted from Gunnar Alexandersson, *The Industrial Structure of American Cities,* 1956.

Examples of the unrecognized economic functions of cities might include the function of public administration at the state or federal levels. Some urban centers have an economic structure that is dominated by the presence of large federal agencies or state agencies headquartered in that city. This type of economic function, however, is not generally recognized in functional classifications of cities. Another example of an unrecognized economic function is in the realm of transportation centers. If employment data are used as the basis for classification of such centers, employment in all forms of transportation are grouped together, which tends to obscure the specific type of transportation center represented. Is the urban center so classified a port city, a terminal center for truck transport, a rail center, or is it a major center of air transportation? When the general designation is used, one does not know the specific functional type of city represented.

With respect to the functions of the city that do not easily lend themselves to analysis based on standard data sources, such as employment data, there are several examples. One of these is recognition that an important function, and perhaps the major function, of a city is serving as the place of residence of large numbers of retired and elderly people.

Such individuals add to the character of the city, but are not engaged, at least to any great degree, in any productive effort or economic activity that would be reported in standard data sources. Therefore, they are not likely to be included in any functional classification of cities. Another example of noneconomic urban functions might be that of serving as a cultural center for the urban population and for people in adjacent areas as well. Facilities such as a large urban zoo, an art museum, a museum of science and industry, a civic auditorium, or a coliseum serve to attract large numbers of people. This might be a function of the city having these facilities of such magnitude or importance as to comprise one of the major city functions, yet it would not be identified as such from standard data sources, especially employment data.

Realize, then, that no matter how carefully terms are defined, how many are defined, or how many and how carefully classifications are made of urban centers, there are still inadequacies and shortcomings in urban terminology and classification. However, the major terminology and classifications developed and used in urban geography have been presented in this chapter. Others will be presented as the need arises.

# 3
# the city
# in history

Terminology and classifications pertaining to cities, as discussed in the previous chapter, deal mainly with the contemporary city and those of recent history. Such considerations do not apply to cities of past millenia and of the future, nor could they be expected to. They represent the urban condition as it exists for one relatively short period of time; not a time span that covers thousands of years of human experience. To fully grasp the nature of cities during this short time period that we call the present, it is important to provide some historical

framework and setting of the development of agglomerated settlements to gain greater understanding and appreciation for cities as we know them today. This chapter attempts to trace the historical evolution of cities and considers the conditions that led to their genesis, the process of their formation, the regions within which they originated, their form and functions, and their gradual refinement and transformation into the urban centers of today.

## Development of Early Campsites and Villages

Paleolithic man had a nomadic existence largely based on his quest for sustenance by hunting, gathering, and fishing. He had needs, however, that attracted family groups, clans, and tribes together on a seasonal basis at a number of campsites. The campsites tended to be located on a solid rise of land with a year-around supply of fresh water and access to rivers, swamps, or estuaries from which supplies of fish and shellfish could be taken.[1] These early campsites satisfied needs in regard to physical survival and also needs of a spiritual or sacred nature. Reverence of the dead was a common practice and ceremonies or rituals concerned with the dead acted as a motivation for migration to a common campsite, however temporary. Most likely, such campsites represented the first resident groupings of people, although they were only seasonal. Given the conditions of existence of paleolithic man, these were not conducive to formation of large or permanent settlements, for hunting and gathering usually supports fewer than ten people per square mile.

Several prerequisites had to be met, therefore, before there could be a transition from a system of temporary campsites of nomadic groups of hunters and gatherers to one of longer lasting villages.

[1]Lewis Mumford, *The City In History*, New York, Harcourt, Brace, and World, 1961.

There had to be a physical environment, especially a favorable climate and soil resource, that would support plant and animal life, even to the point of providing agricultural surpluses.[2] In this manner, a relatively large share of the population could be supported by only a segment of the population on relatively little of the land area. Also, a fairly abundant water supply was needed to support agricultural production. The need for an ample, reliable food supply arose in the mesolithic period about fifteen thousand years ago, and it was about this time the first domestication of plants and animals took place. The first reproduction of food plants involved cuttings such as from the date palm, the olive, the fig, the apple, and the grape and this tended to reduce the dependence on gathering such foods from natural stands. A second stage in the domestication of plants was entered about ten or twelve thousand years ago with the systematic gathering and planting of seeds, including those of certain grasses, and the utilization of herd animals such as the ox, the sheep, and later, the donkey and the horse. These developments in the production of a food supply necessitated a degree of permanence of settlement that previously was lacking; at least the settlement had to remain in place enough to prepare ground for cultivation and to see through the life cycle of the domesticated plants. Especially important in the realm of plant domestication was that of the grains, for this resulted in production of a staple food that could be easily stored to provide a year-around food supply and one that could be easily transported. Each of the early cultures giving rise to a village settlement pattern utilized a domesticated grain as a dietary staple—wheat and barley in the Middle East and China, and maize in Meso-America.

Another prerequisite to the rise of village settlement was the development of a

relatively advanced technology in agriculture and in other pursuits. The advances made over long periods of time included large scale irrigation works, including the canalization of water, metallurgy, the wheel, rudimentary agricultural equipment, and storage facilities.

As these prerequisites were met, the system of villages slowly emerged, each perhaps but a clustering of mud huts in the midst of garden plots and irregular shaped fields. There may have been enclosures for containment of the domesticated animals—another sign of permanence. It is suggested that in the early village in the period from about 9000 to 4000 B.C., there was some provision made for storage of surplus foods, if nothing more than woven baskets placed in the ground. In these villages of from maybe six to sixty families, each household had its own god, its own shrine, and its own burial plot—all indicative of the ritualistic and spiritual overtones of society of that period. A further element of the village that may have developed was a social structuring in which a group of elders may have had responsibilities for collection and distribution of agricultural surpluses, to oversee the division of labor that slowly developed, and to pass judgement on morality and justice. If so, the beginnings of local government may have been developed then; it is known that such beginnings were in evidence in villages in the fourth millennium B.C. in Mesopotamia.

## Transformation From Village to City

From a blending of the paleolithic culture with the neolithic, there slowly emerged a new settlement form, the city, in which the old components of the village were incorporated into the new urban unit. The new settlement form was based on a mobilization of manpower, development of long distance transportation and communications, a burst of new invention, and considerable increase in

[2]Gideon Sjoberg, *The Preindustrial City,* New York, The Free Press, 1960.

agricultural productivity. There was more concern given to common gods and the local chieftains were elevated to almost divine positions. Villagers no longer labored to provide for family and village needs alone; they had to produce to support a royal and priestly stratum of society. Many functions that heretofore had been scattered and unorganized were gathered within a limited area often enclosed by a confining wall. Considering that technology, politics, and religion were codominant in the rise of cities, by the time cities were clearly established, religion had become the dominant force shaping the activities of the people, with technology and politics more in supporting roles. The power was more and more concentrated within the massive walls of cities and in this sense, there was implosion, rather than an explosion, in which the power was centralized in a relatively small area. There was continued assumption of powers by the priestly caste, with the gradual evolution of something akin to a kingship. This gave rise to construction of large imposing temples within which the wealth of the city was stored, much in the form of food that was collected with the aid of armed representatives of the king. With the accumulation of more and more wealth, each city became potential booty for others and armed guards were developed to protect against invasion by adjacent city-states. Although populations of the cities grew and the area needed to support them increased, there arose an attitude in which the armies would be used to subdue surrounding areas or adjacent cities, that is, the armies became instruments of divine destruction, rather than benign protection.

With the founding of cities came a pronounced division of the labor of their inhabitants, although there may have been some development of special castes and occupations before this time. However, with the coming of cities, there came occupational specialization for the entire population. Concentration in a single activity was, however, for the benefit of king, god, and city—not for the benefit of the worker. Not only was there a stratification by occupation, but also one by caste, with the priestly and warrior castes at the peak of the social pyramid, merchants and craftsmen at the next level, peasants, sailors, house servants, and freed men at the next level, with slaves forming the lowest stratum of the pyramid.

## Areas of City Origin

Before discussing the areas of the world in which the earliest cities came into being, the matter of origin and dispersal of culture and technological traits might be examined. There is considerable scholarly debate as to whether a given trait found in the world today had a single place or area of origin with subsequent dispersal to other areas, or a spontaneous or independent origin in several areas with dispersal taking place from each of the places of origin. For example, did the stirrup have one place of origin or was it developed independently in a number of areas? Did chivalry develop in one area from which it spread or were there a number of source areas of this cultural characteristic? The origins and dispersal of human attitudes, institutions, and technology are not easily determined and much is left to speculation, conjecture, and extrapolation; at least the historical record is not always sufficiently complete to produce definitive answers to such perplexing questions.

The human institution considered here is the city, and we should examine the area or areas of origin of this creation. There are at least two points of view. One follows the thinking that there was a single area of origin of cities, a single culture-hearth. The argument is that cities originated in the Fertile Crescent of Mesopotamia and that the concept of city formation was diffused from this area to the Nile Valley, the Indus Valley, the Hwang Ho Valley, and perhaps to

Meso-America. In many respects, there is a parallel collection of cultural traits, such as a number of deities, an exalted rule and a central authority, great temples, division of castes and division of labor, the beginnings of writing, and a calendar. The argument is that these traits were too specific to have been spontaneously developed and must have originated in a common culture hearth and modified to suit each area to which they were diffused. A counter argument is that cities originated spontaneously in different regions without external influence, even though the indications are that cities in different regions were formed as much as several millenia apart. The lines of

communications between the various areas involved were supposedly nonexistent and transportation was not developed at the scale needed for migration or travel between these areas. While the environments within which cities were first developed in Mesopotamia, Egypt, the Indus Valley, and the Hwang Ho Valley were generally similar—level floodplains and soils and climate favoring surplus agricultural production—the cities of Meso-America were first developed in what might be considered a harsh environment. In this instance, agriculture was difficult at best, transportation was crude, and many elements of the technology of the Old World were ab-

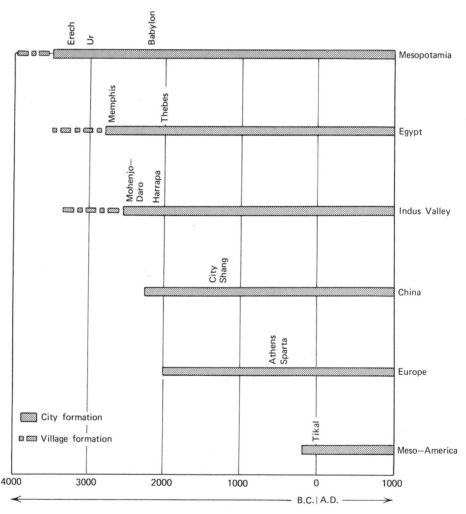

**Figure 3-1**   Approximate times of city formation in different world regions.

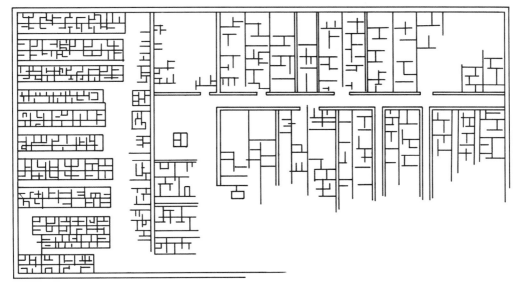

**Figure 3-2** Kahun (Kahune), Egypt about 3000 B.C. Built for the slaves and artisans assigned to work on the Illahun pyramid. Adapted from *The Urban Pattern* by A. B. Gallion. Copyright © 1950. By permission of Van Nostrand, Reinholt.

sent. Although the argument continues, the greatest body of evidence supports the contention that the area of origin of cities was Mesopotamia, and in some manner the notion of forming sizable population agglomerations was extended to other regions of the world (Figure 3–1).

In Mesopotamia, a system of villages was developed first, with these communities of about 200 to 500 individuals especially concentrated in the hills and piedmont of the Tigris-Euphrates river system and not on the floodplains proper. A second area of early development of agglomerated settlements was the valley of the lower Nile River, with these dating from about 3500 to 4000 B.C. These early settlements were crude walled clusterings with the dwellings like huge barracks and narrow lanes between that served as sewers as well. One such settlement was Kahune (about 3000 B.C.) which was built to house workers on the pyramid of Illahun (Figure 3–2). A third area in which population agglomerations originated was the upper Indus River Valley. Evidence indicates there were numerous towns and villages in this region based on a highly productive system

of agriculture. Also, there most likely was a fairly sophisticated system of irrigation and water impoundment. The beginnings of village settlements in this area date from about 3300 B.C., although cities as such date from about 1500–2500 B.C. Another area of origin of towns was the Wei Valley, not far from the Hwang Ho River in China.[3] Towns were established about 2250 B.C. in this region, although the level of technology was lower than in other areas of city origin. Although the inhabitants appeared to produce surpluses of food, especially millet, and had domesticated animals, they left no evidence of a knowledge of metallurgy. An additional area of origin of cities was Meso-America in the centuries preceding the Christian era. Quite advanced communities had been developed in pre-Columbian times by the peoples indigenous to this region, notably the Maya, Zapotecs, Mixtecs, and Aztecs. Even though, there may be some strong doubt concerning the independent development of cities and towns in other regions mentioned, there is less question at this

[3]Jean Comhaire, *How Cities Grew,* Madison, N. J., The Florham Park Press, 1959.

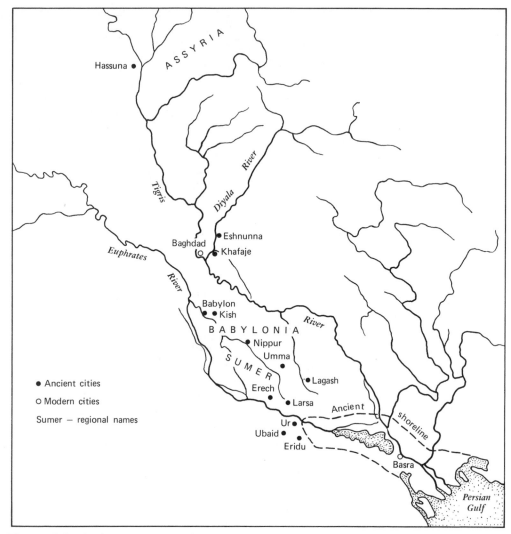

**Figure 3-3** Ancient Mesopotamia.

time concerning a possible independent origin of cities in Meso-America.

The antecedents of these cities stimulated the formation of larger population concentrations more in keeping with present definitions of cities. By virtue of population size alone, there developed a number of concentrations that might be called cities. Also, there was a more pronounced division of labor in the population of the areas involved and an increased share of the population dependent on nonagricultural pursuits. During this period, some of the villages matured into cities; many of them disappeared, and others were formed, but only some of the earlier villages and some of the newer ones developed into distinguishable cities. The objective at this time is to trace through the evolution of the earliest of cities in various areas of origin in the world.

Among the earliest cities of Mesopotamia were Erech, Eridu, Ur, Lagash, and Larsa in the southernmost part of the Tigris-Euphrates River valley and Kish and Jemdet Nasr in the midsection of the same river valley (Figure 3–3).[4] It is reported that of these cities, Ur was formed later than the others, but all of

[4]Sjoberg, *Op. Cit.*

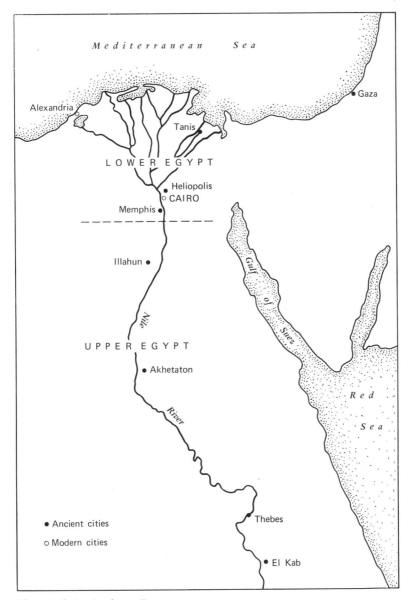

**Figure 3-4**  Ancient Egypt.

them were transformations of older village settlements into cities. This transformation process consumed centuries, however, before it was complete.

The setting within which these early cities of Mesopotamia were developed was one of a number of city-states with similar language, religion, social organization, and material culture. Each city-state was ruled by a king, although the term likely was unknown at the time, who also was its chief priest. Since the land

that supported the city was considered the domain of the chief religious figure, the farming population was expected to return to him part of the surplus agricultural output. This surplus, stored in the main temple of the city, provided the sustenance of the ruling group of the city. Generally, the cities founded at this time were on sites located on the low interfluves between channels of the Tigris-Euphrates River system where they were afforded the greatest protection from floods that occurred frequently. In this manner, the people and their surplus food supplies received some protection from floodwaters.

In the Nile River Valley, as in Mesopotamia, there was first the development of walled villages in the delta area of the lower river valley about 3500 B.C. These villages were clustered into politically independent units, each with its own cooperative irrigation systems for cultivation of staple grains, especially wheat and barley. Not only was irrigation practiced and agricultural surpluses produced as in Mesopotamia, there was also an established metallurgy and use of domesticated animals. Also, there were a social stratification and an emerging division of labor—additional preconditions to city formation. The earliest cities emerged in this region about 3100 B.C. and included Memphis, This, Heliopolis, Nekheb (El Kab), and later, Thebes (Figure 3–4).[5] The remains of these cities have mostly been covered by silt deposited in the annual floods of the Nile River, as well as by settlements of later periods. There appears to be considerable doubt among scholars as to a spontaneous development of cities in the Nile Valley, in favor of a theory that there was diffusion of characteristics from Mesopotamia. Certain artifacts found on the sites of ancient Nile River cities are thought to have been borrowed from Mesopotamia, as well as the concept of writing itself.

From a background of village formation in the Indus Valley, the cities of Mohenjo-Daro and Harappa developed into major cities by 2500 B.C. Harappa was in the Punjab in the headwaters of the Indus and Mohenjo-Daro was about 350 miles to the south in the valley of the Indus and these cities rose to the status of capitals of an empire that flourished between 1500 and 2500 B.C.[6] Before the obliteration by invaders of the early

Indus Valley civilization about 1500 B.C., there had developed a system of villages and towns with Mohenjo-Daro and Harappa as the focal points. This system was based on productive types of agriculture and likely, systems of irrigation. Surpluses of wheat and barley likely were produced in this area and the use of tools was known, as was the employment of domesticated animals and wheeled vehicles.

The first cities to be developed in China seem to have been in the Hwang Ho Valley, with the earliest being the City Shang (or Yin), on the Hwang Ho at Anyang. Shang civilization was based on agriculture that included wheat, barley, millet, and perhaps, rice. There appears to have been water impoundment measures and canalization to produce greater volumes of staple foodstuffs. Also, domesticated animals were in use, as were wheeled vehicles. In these early cities of China, there appeared to be a well-defined power structure with a hereditary political leader and a nobility.

The early cities of Meso-America, such as Tikal and Uaxactun, and the later ones including Chichen Itza, Mayapan, Copan, and Palenque, supposedly were developed by a society that produced surpluses of maize. Apparently, these communities were foci of small city-states that occasionally combined into loose confederations. There was development of a class structure in which the leadership was provided by the priestly class. Another social class maintained order in the cities and villages and collected tribute from the farmers to support the urban population.

Of the cities developed in these regions, virtually all are nonexistent today. Some were submerged beneath flood waters, some gradually disintegrated, and others were buried by accumulations of sand and silt. They existed long enough, however, to constitute a fundamental change in the spatial distribution of population and to provide the first ripple that was to become a wave of city

[5]Sjoberg, *Op. Cit.*
[6]Sjoberg, *Op. Cit.*

formation that spread over most of the world and continues to the present day.

## Characteristics of the Earliest Cities

Having discussed the areas of origin of cities and the transformation from village to city formation, we now examine the characteristics of the earliest of agglomerations of people that might be called cities. Cities in each region were expressions of the culture of the region and of the people forming them and, as might be expected, they had similarities in the manner in which the culture was expressed. Also, there were differences between cities in the same culture region, but more striking are the differences between cities in different culture areas. The factors of similarity or difference considered here include population, area included in the city, pattern or layout of the city, sites occupied, social order, and special features of a particular city.

Early cities of Mesopotamia grew up within a walled section that included the temples characteristic of such cities, especially in Babylon which rose to prominence by 1900 B.C. The priestly class dominated the social structure and guided both economic and ritualistic aspects of the society. Special attention was given to construction of temples and palaces, and it is likely that thousands of laborers who were first captives, then slaves, worked on their building. The temples were the most prominent elements of the cities in which they were built, and one such temple at Erech was built on an artificial mound about forty feet in height and covered about ten acres, making it prominent indeed, considering it was probably surrounded by huts of less than ten feet in height.[7] Invariably, the section containing the temple-palace complex was surrounded by a wall, although the reason for this is debated; it may have been a defensive

measure to afford protection from marauders from adjacent city-states or it may have provided a measure of protection against recurring floods in the Tigris-Euphrates Valley. In the case of Babylon, after it emerged as the seat of power of the reigning dynasty, a second wall was built around the first, with the latter in the shape of a square with a perimeter of about 55 to 80 miles. The city of Erech had a mud brick wall enclosing an area of about two square miles, while the city of Ur had a wall that enclosed about one-fifth of a square mile.

The walls, like the palaces, temples, and houses, were built of fired or unfired mud brick. Houses were jumbled together in an irregular mass that was interrupted by open spaces in the vicinity of temples and other public buildings. Streets were narrow lanes without surfacing or drainage. These lanes became the places of accumulation of refuse and the extreme of this condition probably existed in Ur where excavations disclosed that refuse had gradually raised the level of the streets to such a point that houses had to have entrances cut on the second level since the original ground floor was below street level.[8] Interspersed among the clusters of houses were chapels, small shops, and lines of booths that probably were used by merchants and artisans. Near the outer margin of the city was a zone of the poorest elements of the population living in mud and reed huts. An interesting point concerning the structure of early Mesopotamian cities is the existence within or on the periphery of the city of a large number of agriculturalists. The cultivation of crops within or near the margin of these cities was beneficial in that it facilitated the movement of produce to markets in the heart of the city, as well as providing a more assured food supply.

The earliest cities did not occupy large amounts of land area, nor did they have populations that today would be consid-

---

[7]Sjoberg, *Op. Cit.*

[8]Sjoberg, *Op. Cit.*

ered large. Karkemish on the Euphrates River covered 240 acres and Mohenjo-Daro on the Indus River covered but 600 acres.[9] Ur, with its canals, harbors, and temples, occupied 200 acres and the walls of Uruk included about two square miles, or 1200 acres. Somewhat later, Khorsabad in Assyria enclosed about 740 acres and Nineveh included about 1800 acres.

Regarding the populations of the earliest cities, there is no concensus. For cities of the late fourth millennium B.C., estimates range between 5000 and 20,000, although estimates are especially difficult since it is not known how many agriculturalists were residents of the respective cities. In the third millennium B.C., when cities were more firmly established, the population of Ur is put at about 24,000 people, Lagash 19,000, Umma 16,000, and Khafaje 12,000. By the beginning of the next millennium, the population of Ur was put at 34,000 in the inner walled city and that of "Greater Ur" at 360,000, although the latter figure surely includes agriculturalists who were not part of the urban society. With relatively little land area included within the walled cities and given the population estimates above, the population densities must have been in excess of 10,000 per square mile which is considerably higher than urban densities in cities of comparable size in the Western world today. Crowdedness, congestion, slums, and pollution have been urban problems since cities were first formed.

The transition from village to city appeared to be more gradual in the Nile Valley area than in Mesopotamia; at least the traces of large cities before about 2000 B.C. are few. It could be that large cities were not developed early due to the practice of changing the site of the capital, usually the largest settlement, with the ascendancy of a new pharaoh. Around 2900 B.C., Thinis became the first capital, with Memphis enjoying this role after 2700 B.C. After about 2000 B.C., Thebes became a large city and Akhetaton served as the capital for a short period.

Part of the reason why traces of earlier cities in the Nile Valley are lacking may have to do with the building materials used. Sun dried clay bricks supplemented with wattle and daub were used widely, and these materials do not readily withstand the weathering of time. Even later, when stone was used for construction of the pyramids, the houses of the people were made of perishable materials. In the cities developed after about 2000 B.C., the remains indicate that multistoried houses were fairly common, as was the broad processional avenue. The structure of cities of this time seemed to be one of a social stratification, with a slum area, a workingman's section (handicrafts), and a core area including a palace, temples, storehouses for surplus food, and public buildings. Here, as in Mesopotamia, streets were unsurfaced and no drainage was provided.

## Dispersal of City Formation

In the centuries following the development of the first cities in Mesopotamia about 3500 B.C., the various city-states vied for dominance, with Lagash, Umma, Eshnunna, Kish, and Ur gaining, in turn, dominance over the others. Babylon was formed about 2200 B.C. and had attained a dominant position by about 1800 B.C. in the lower reaches of the Tigris-Euphrates Valley. At about the same time, the Assyrians to the north had strengthened the position of Assur while Hittites established new cities such as Khattushashboghazkoy and Carchemish.[10] By 2500 B.C., numerous cities were developed on the island of Crete, with Knossos and Mallia the best known. By 1600 B.C., the cities of Mycenae on the Greek mainland and

---

[9]Mumford, *Op. Cit.*

[10]Sjoberg, *Op. Cit.*

Troy in Asia Minor were established, although they were to disappear within a few centuries.

The older capital cities of the Nile Valley, such as Heliopolis, Abydos, and Nekheb (El Kab) were thriving and about 2000 B.C., Thebes, Akhentaten, Tanis, Heraclepolis, and Bubastis rose to important positions. In the Nile region, city formation slowed appreciably until about 400 B.C., after which new cities were formed again.

The eastern end of the Mediterranean Sea experienced a wave of city formation about 2000 B.C. Some of the more significant city-states developed were Tyre, Beirut, Sidon, Jericho, Gaza, Halap (Aleppo), and Damascus, the latter being one of the oldest continuously inhabited cities in the world today. Numerous other cities were established by different culture groups in Asia Minor and the Levant by about 1200 B.C. By the seventh century B.C., city formation had been extended into Central Asia, with some founded at this time persisting to the present time.

After the explosion of Islam about the seventh century A.D., many of the older empires were demolished and a host of new cities were established, except in Central Asia where the earlier cities escaped the turmoil of the times. As part of the Arab extension of city building, there was a rise in cities in North Africa and later, along the east African coast, with cities formed during this period including Timbuktu, Kano, Kilwa, Mombasa, and Gedi.

In Europe, there were cities formed that were the creations of the Greeks who moved into the hostile coastal pockets in the Aegean region and, drawing on the city-building expertise of others, formed the cities of Sparta, Corinth, Megara, Byzantium, and Athens by the eighth century B.C. During the same general period, the Etruscans developed the centers of Veii, Pisa, and Siena, among others. On the heels of the Etruscan city

formation, the Greek city-states were developing colonies on the north side of the Mediterranean in Italy, Spain, and Gaul, plus north of the Black Sea as well. Since some of the Greek cities, especially Athens, had outgrown their limited food supplies and could only exist by trade, colonies could provide them with foodstuffs in exchange for certain manufactured goods such as woolens, wine, silver, pottery, and metal articles.[11] Noncolonies also could provide food based, not on trade, but on plunder.

Rome overthrew the Etruscan dominance about 500 B.C. and became the seat of an empire that advanced the urban frontier to the north and west. City formation by the Romans was extended into England and to the Rhine River in western Europe, into central Europe and the Balkans, and in much of the Near East. Many of the major contemporary cities had their origins during this era of Roman city-building, including York, London, Brussels, Utrecht, Granada, Seville, Cologne, Strasbourg, Paris, Bordeaux, Vienna, Zagreb, and Belgrade. City life in western Europe declined after the collapse of Roman rule, however, and only portions of Europe under Byzantine or Muslim influence had a viable urban life.

The cities of western Europe declined still more as their trade routes were obliterated by Germanic invaders. However, a number of Roman cities were sustained as bishoprics, with cathedrals built within the walls of old Roman cities. There emerged a religious-administrative center that was ringed by settlements of merchants and artisans and these evolved into vigorous cities once again. Members of the nobility established themselves on old Roman sites and built fortified strongholds that attracted people to them. Such was the genesis of cities such as Bruges, Antwerp, Frankfurt-Am-

[11]Arthur E. Smailes, *The Geography of Towns*, London: Hutchinson's University Library, 1953.

Main, Hamburg, Prague, Warsaw, and Buda (later combined with Pest to form Budapest). After the ninth and tenth centuries, there was greater political stability and kingdoms were consolidated; these factors were conducive to an acceleration of city formation during this period. Cities achieving a new prominence at this time included Venice, Genoa, Milan, and Florence, plus what was essentially a rebirth of Ypres, Ghent, Liege, Cologne, Utrecht, Paris and Toulouse.

In northern Europe that had remained free of Roman domination, the first appearance of cities was delayed until about the twelfth century. City life in European Russia had originated in about the eighth century B.C. as a result of Greek colonization, but it was not until the centuries between 600 and 1100 A.D. that any cities of consequence were founded, such as Kiev, Novgorod, and Rostov. The development of Moscow did not assume urban proportions until the thirteenth century, although earlier it had a citadel, the Kremlin, as its nucleus.

In the Indus Valley, there was a demise of cities for about a millennium and a reappearance of city formation under Aryan control about the sixth century B.C. By the fourth century B.C., cities included Taxila, Kasi (Benares), Champa, Kampila, and Pataliputra (Patna). By the end of the fourth century B.C., urbanization had been extended to the south of the subcontinent, although few new cities were formed until the era of Muslim rule beginning in the eighth century. By the seventeenth century, the Muslim empire was fading and new cities arose under the influence of European colonists, such as Bombay, Calcutta, and Madras. The same type of colonial origin led to the rise of Singapore, Rangoon, and Manila in Southeast Asia, although earlier cities had been established in Burma and Cambodia by Hindu and Buddist groups.

In China, the City Shang, discussed earlier, was destroyed in the twelfth century B.C. and the invaders spread urban life east and south of the Yangtze River in founding the major cities of Loyang and Ch'angan. The major wave of city formation in China and most of East Asia occurred in the period from the third century B.C. to the third century A.D. To the north, the cities formed included Liangchow, Suchow, Khotan (Hotien) and Anhsi and, to the south, Canton, Nanking, and Chengtu emerged as urban centers. At about the time of the Mongol invasions, after a period of quiescence, city formation began anew and cities such as Hangchow, Yunanfu (Kunming), and Shenyang (Mukden) took shape. By the end of the thirteenth century, the major cities of China had been established, except for Shanghai and Hong Kong which were formed during the time of European colonization. Japan is said to owe its urbanization to diffusion from the Chinese mainland. City formation began about 400 A.D. with Osaka as the major center. After an early burst of city formation, there was a decline of city life that was replaced in the late fourteenth century by a renewal of urban activity. By about the sixteenth century, the landscape was dotted with "castletowns" such as Edo (Tokyo) and Hiroshima, each with populations of 10,000 or more.

In Meso-America, the early groups, such as the Mayas and Zapotecs, continued to spread the development of urban centers at the same time that other groups to the north and west were doing the same, although the cities formed in the latter case were of relatively short duration. After the Spanish conquest in the sixteenth century, there was a drastic cultural change in the remaining cities of earlier eras and cities formed were established in the European tradition.

## The Bases of City Development, Diffusion, and Decline

Two factors mentioned previously as being instrumental in providing the bases for city development or formation are (1) technology, and (2) social structure. Certainly, there had to be a means of providing surplus food supplies and raw materials to support a nonagricultural population and this factor was basic to the formation of the earliest of true cities. One of the most vital technological advances made later that expedited development of an urban society was the invention of iron-working techniques about 1200 B.C. which provided for a shift from copper and bronze implements to ones made of iron. The use of iron provided for cheaper implements and the availability of iron tools likely was first evidenced in agriculture where the iron plow replaced those of bronze, stone, or wood, and improved wheeled vehicles provided for better transportation to ship food and other goods to markets in the cities. It has been observed that urbanization in the first five centuries after the onset of the iron age expanded at a greater rate than it had in the previous fifteen centuries of the bronze age.[12] Of course, the iron age did not begin at the same time in all parts of the world, with its start about 1200 B.C. in western Asia, about 600 B.C. in China, and still later in Europe.

Not only were agricultural implements and wheeled vehicles improved with the coming of the iron age, so were there advances in irrigation, weaving techniques, and coined money. The former development facilitated expansion of agricultural areas and increases in food surpluses, which meant more territory under control of the early city-states and increased ability to support a nonagricultural population. It should be remembered that in each of the culture hearths of cities, Mesopotamia, the Nile Valley, and the Indus Valley, irrigation was necessary to support production of domesticated staple crops.

In addition to advances in technology, it was necessary to have a power structure that could organize, channel, and exploit these advances. Furthermore, this power structure had to be concentrated areally.

As stated by Sjoberg, ". . . a power group in the feudal society can sustain itself only if its members concentrate in the kinds of settlements we call urban."[13] Very often, these were fortified places to protect the ruling class from marauders and invaders and invariably these were focal points of transportation and communication. The existence of a power structure was of prime importance in (1) the expansion of cities, both in size and number, (2) the diffusion of cities into new areas, and (3) the decline and sometimes a resurgence of cities. As a society broadens its political control, it also broadens its economic support. Cities can then tap the resource base of an enlarged hinterland and can maintain and expand trade routes, permitting a more active and versatile economy. City life was extended to new areas since the extension of the domain of the power structure is empire building in which new cities followed in the wake of waves of conquest. Perhaps, the extension of the Roman Empire into England and northwestern Europe is a prime example of such a situation—city building following in the wake of conquest. Not only does the establishment of a sophisticated power structure stimulate the process of city formation and the diffusion of city-building, the withdrawal or collapse of this power structure can well lead to the decline and perhaps, the demise of cities. This is especially true of political capitals and administrative centers which become prime targets for invading armies, such as did Babylon, Nineveh, Anuradhapura, and Angkor. To be sure, however, the rise or decline of a given city could be based on factors other than a flourishing technology or an entrenched power structure. The value system of a people can lead to the continuation or reestablishment of a city when other advantages have been diminished or lost, as in the case of Jerusalem. Also, the vagaries of the physical environment can lead to the sudden or prolonged de-

---

[12]Sjoberg, *Op. Cit.*

[13]Sjoberg, *Op. Cit.*, p. 67.

mise of a city, as in the case of Pompeii obliterated by a volcanic eruption and Kish that was submerged by a change in the course of the Euphrates River.

## Structural Components of The Ancient City

One of the earliest structural elements of the ancient city was the walled citadel, often ringed by one or more settlements, with the wall providing protection to the ruling group contained within its confines. The wall, however, did not express the limits of city expansion, for much of the population lived outside of its protection. The citadel consisted of prominent structures containing the treasures of the society and surplus foods and provided the living space for the powerful and revered leadership class. Quite often, the citadel was located on a mound of earth or debris giving it a more imposing appearance. In early cities of Mesopotamia, the development of the "religious quarter" provided the most prominent structural component, as it often did in the early cities of the Nile Valley.

Although the religious or temple enclave of the early city with its surrounding wall developed, there was in Mesopotamian cities the scattered residential development on the outer fringe and outside the wall. This, perhaps, might be considered the forerunner of modern day suburbia or at least the outer residential zone of the city, but without the commutation characteristic of modern suburbia.

Considering the complex of public buildings and temples forming a prominent, if not the dominant component of the ancient city, the term *acropolis* might be appropriate. Reference is sometimes made to an acropolis in ancient cities of Mesopotamia, although it was best exemplified by the Acropolis of Athens. The Acropolis of Athens is located atop a rugged cliff and surrounded by a wall and was the focus of ritualistic events involving processions winding their way up the cliff to the Acropolis. Although the Acropolis was outstanding in architectural splendor, the homes outward from its base were little more than mud huts. They were arrayed in a disorganized manner along narrow lanes which did double duty, since the homes did not enjoy the benefits of sanitary sewers.

Even though the acropolis served as a lofty meeting place dedicated to sacrifice and prayer to the gods, there was need of a meeting place for secular transactions and assembly. As originally developed, this district, the *agora,* was a place of assembly for the townspeople and for settlement of minor judicial matters. The early agora had an irregular form, sometimes an open square and other times a widening of a street. Above all, the original agora was an open space, publicly owned and used for public purposes, but not enclosed. Quite often, the agora was ringed by temporary stalls and craftsmen's workshops. From the seventh century on, with the introduction of stamped coins, commerce became a more important element of city life and the economic functions of the agora expanded significantly. As the agora became a type of market place, it also retained its role as an open place and the social function of the agora was retained in later cities, but with new names such as *plaza, piazza,* and *campo.* At best, the agora occupied less than five percent of the area of the ancient city, although its social and economic role was very considerable. It is interesting to speculate that the agora, with its dual social and economic functions, was the earliest form of a commercial district and the antecedent of the central business district of contemporary cities.

Another element of some early cities of the Greek culture that has endured over the centuries is the gridiron plan. The gridiron plan was employed by Hippodamus, a Greek planner of about 500

B.C., in the development of several Greek cities. This type of spatial pattern, discussed in greater detail in the following section, involved two major thoroughfares intersecting in the center of the city, with the agora, major public buildings, and temples placed around this intersection. Although not especially suited to the rugged settings of many Greek cities, the grid still was developed and likely provided the stimulus for its duplication in later cities the world over.

Roman cities utilized many components from cities of earlier cultures and developed some new ones as well. The acropolis was a common component and usually was situated on a hill or prominent height. The wall around the city also was common in Roman towns, although it was not in Greek cities. The gridiron plan was common to many Roman cities and towns, with major thoroughfares crossing at right angles in the middle of the city. This intersection was selected as the place for the forum, the Roman equivalent of the acropolis and the agora conceived as one. Quite likely, the orientation of the streets was based on religious grounds and not the cardinal points of the compass, although concessions to comfort were made later by orientation of streets and alleys to shut out unpleasant cold or hot winds. It was said by Strabo, the Greek geographer (63 B.C.?–24 A.D.?), that Greeks turned their attention to beauty and fortification, to harbors and fertile soils, in building their cities, while the Romans were concerned with the pavement of streets, the water supply, and the sewers.[14]

One component of the Roman city not found in Greek cities was the *thermae* or public bath. These tended to be lavish and luxurious buildings and the first were established as early as 33 B.C. The public bath was a vast enclosure containing several pools, massage rooms, and rooms for partaking of food. Often the public baths had attached gymnasia and playfields. With such a variety of facilities, it was suggested that the Roman bath was somewhat similar to the modern shopping center.[15] As originally conceived, there was separation of men and women in the baths, but gradually they turned into places of drunkenness and debauchery as the sexes became intermixed.

Another urban component characteristic of Rome especially resulted from the population growth of the city and the congestion that existed in the streets. This was the *insula,* the rough equivalent of the tenement of cities in the recent past as well as at present. Each insula was a group of dwelling units for the less privileged elements of Roman society. The insulae were several stories high, although height limitations were later put on them, they were poorly built, and were of wood construction which made them very vulnerable to fire as well as deterioration. By the time of Caesar, there were over 46,000 insulae in Roman cities, containing on the average about two hundred persons each, which would put the population housed in this manner in excess of nine million.[16] By contrast, there were about 1800 palaces of nobles at the same time. With the insulae developed the notion of multiple-family dwelling units of poor quality, whereas the pattern before had been one of single-family huts of poor quality, but with the house as the focal point of the family unit. The insulae tended to disrupt the basic element of society, the family, and were quick to develop into mass slums. No doubt, the heritage of cities of today that was derived from Roman cities includes the tenement and the urban slum. The structural nature of Rome about 315 A.D. is indicated by the following: there were 3323 acres within the wall and 1617 acres of built-up area outside

[14]Mumford, *Op. Cit.*

[15]Mumford, *Op. Cit.,* p. 226.
[16]Mumford, *Op. Cit.*

the wall; within the wall enclosure were 8 bridges, 11 public baths, 2 circuses, 2 amphitheaters, 3 theaters, 28 libraries, 4 gladiatorial schools, 36 marble arches, 37 gates, 290 storehouses and warehouses, 254 public bakehouses, 1790 palaces, 46,602 tenements (insulae), and 500 fountains.[17] Perhaps more important than the structural artifacts left, however, is the type of urban culture bequeathed and diffused to other parts of the world and on which were formed the medieval cities.

## Basic Types of Urban Patterns

Before turning to medieval cities, we should isolate one urban component, the pattern or layout of the city, and examine it in detail. Remembering that there are a number of structural components of the city, past and present, these can be arranged in various ways, each of which produces a different spatial pattern of the city. Perhaps, the most apparent manifestation of these different patterns is the layout of streets, but it should be realized that arrangement and placement of other components also contribute to the character of a particular spatial pattern. It behooves us to consider the basic types of urban patterns that characterize different cities or their parts and which typify different periods of city formation. Three basic systems of spatial patterns of cities are considered at this time.

*The Irregular System.* The irregular system of city pattern includes streets that are without a regular order, both in terms of direction and width. Houses are irregularly positioned with respect to each other and to any dominant focal point of the urban center—evidence of the absence of a guiding authority in development of the city. In the transformation from village to city, there are relatively few cities that have passed to the latter stage without having the irregular system of layout at the village stage; the

nucleus may have had this pattern, but later expansion generally followed some type of orderly plan.

The irregular system of city layout tends to characterize cities that grew from villages in Britain, France, the Low Countries, and western Germany.[18] Also, this pattern characterizes many Moorish cities of Spain and Moslem cities of North Africa and the Middle East, plus some older cities of eastern Europe.

The irregular layout of cities, with its jumble of houses, winding streets of different widths, and many branching cul-de-sacs, all brought together in a veritable maze, may be thought a natural response to topographic conditions. Although this may be true in a number of cases, many cities without such topographic constraints on their pattern of growth developed such an irregular pattern, more as an extension of village attitudes to city development than of the dictates of the terrain. Most cities, after all, have been developed in areas without such physical constraints, yet many developed in irregular pattern, at least in their early stages of settlement.

*The Radial-Concentric System.* There are two essential features of this system: a radial arrangement of major streets and a concentric arrangement around a central nucleus. The focal point may have been a market place, a fortress complex, a castle, or a religious complex including temples, cathedrals, etc. The system had the appearance of a spider web and in western Europe, the center of the weblike system often was the *burg*—a fortified stronghold.[19]

This system was employed in an unplanned form in a number of medieval cities, but was not adopted in a planned form until the Renaissance era in the period 1500 to 1800. The utilization of this system is discussed in more detail in

---

[17]Mumford, *Op. Cit.*, p. 235–236.

[18]Robert E. Dickinson, *The West European City,* London: Routledge & Kegan Paul, Ltd., Second Edition, 1961.

[19]Dickinson, *Ibid.*

later sections. It suffices to say that with the advent of wheeled vehicles, the radial-concentric system was better suited to city needs than was the irregular system. Many new urban settlements had this plan from their inception, and it also was employed in adapting older cities with irregular patterns to changing needs—the fabric of the radial-concentric system as an overlay on the irregular system.

*The Rectangular or Grid System.* The earliest known occurrence of the grid pattern of street layout is that of Mohenjo-Daro in the first half of the third millennium B.C.[20] The next known use of the grid pattern was in Assyria at Dur-Sarginu about the eighth century B.C. There is a continuous record of use of the grid pattern after the sixth century B.C. in Greece under the influence of Hippodamus who is attributed with the application of the grid pattern to the Piraeus (the harbor of Athens), and to Miletus. It is believed, however, that the inspiration for the grid pattern was diffused from the Indus Valley, by way of Asia Minor where Greek settlements had been made, that is, the concept did not originate with Hippodamus; however, he formalized it more than his predecessors. After the fifth and sixth centuries, the formation of towns was widespread and the grid pattern was used, not only in Greece, but in western territories as well, such as Thurii in southern Italy, Selinus in Sicily, and Naples on the Italian peninsula. Greek influence continued along the shores of the Mediterranean into lands that were to become Roman. The grid pattern as used by the Romans was not exactly the pattern used by the Greeks, being modified to suit Roman order with its intense centralization of the power structure.

The advent of the medieval period diminished the conditions supporting use of the grid pattern greatly, especially the existence of centralized control and the lack of need of the grid pattern which functioned well for trade centers, since trade during this period was restricted.

In the latter part of the Middle Ages, there was some use of the grid pattern in newly formed cities and the pattern became firmly established during the Renaissance. In the thirteenth century, this pattern was used by the Italians in Sicily and by the Germans in Slavic territory. Perhaps, the most significant application of the grid pattern during this period was in France with establishment of the *bastides,* a form of new town (Figure 3–5). These urban settlements were rigidly planned with the town site platted into rectangular blocks divided by streets that were parallel or at right angles to one another. The main streets extended from the gates on the outer margin to a large square or market place at the center of the town. In England, towns were founded somewhat later in the period that bear the imprint of those developed in France using the grid pattern.

*Summary of Types of Urban Patterns.* Each type of urban pattern, planned or unplanned, came to characterize towns and cities in different regions and in different periods. Although not all cities formed in a given region or period had the same basic pattern, there are some generalizations that might be made in which a given type of pattern is associated with a particular period of periods.

TYPE I: The Irregular System— Most characteristic of ancient towns and cities of Mesopotamia and the Nile Valley, and later, medieval cities in Europe.

TYPE II: The Radial-Concentric System—Most characteristic of baroque cities of the Renaissance.

TYPE III: The Rectangular or Grid System—Characteristic of many cities formed in the Renaissance period in Europe. More characteristic of the mercantile cities formed in the seventeenth century or later.

[20]Dan Stanislawski, "The Origin and Spread of the Grid-Pattern Town," *Geographical Review,* Vol. 36, No. 1 (January, 1946).

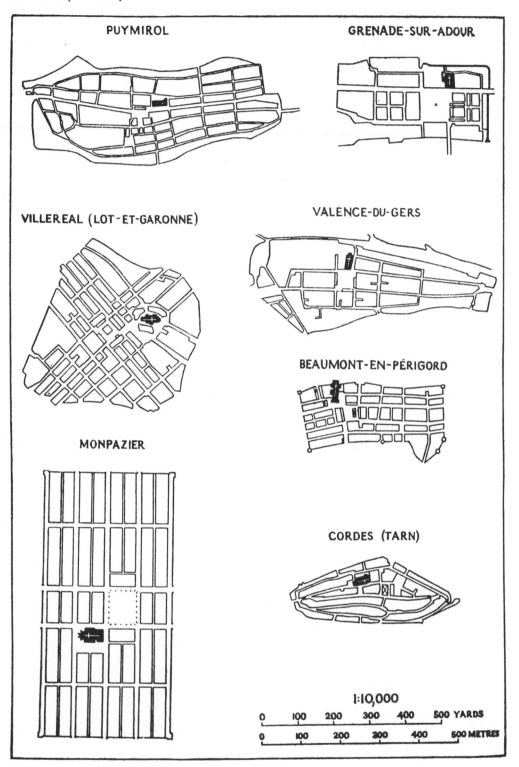

PUYMIROL

GRENADE-SUR-ADOUR

VILLEREAL (LOT-ET-GARONNE)

VALENCE-DU-GERS

BEAUMONT-EN-PÉRIGORD

MONPAZIER

CORDES (TARN)

1:10,000

**Figure 3-5**  Bastide towns in southern France with rectangular plans. From R.E. Dickinson, WESTERN EUROPEAN CITY, 1961.
*(By permission of Routledge & Kegan Paul, Ltd. and Humanities Press, Inc., New Jersey.)*

It should be pointed out again, however, that not all cities developed in a given time period had the same pattern, since there generally is a time lag in the diffusion of a cultural trait whereby patterns of cities in different regions may have been duplicated in other regions in a later time period. Also, one should note that a single city may exhibit vestiges of more than one or of all types of urban pattern discussed above. A city may have originated with an irregular pattern that was later added to or modified with a radial-concentric pattern, with a grid pattern used still later for the areas of expansion of the urban center. In this sense, a composite pattern characterizes many cities of today, if not most cities. The cities with a "pure" type of urban pattern are relatively rare.

## Medieval Cities

By the beginning of the fifth century, invasions by Germanic tribes led to the breakdown of the western part of the Roman empire and one by one, former Roman provinces were changed into Germanic kingdoms: the Vandals in Africa, the Visigoths in Aquitaine and in Spain, the Burgundians in the Rhone Valley, and the Ostrogoths in Italy. Although political structure was changed and the role of the Church altered, existent cities largely remained and municipal organization passed through the transition to a new order with little change. The economic functions of cities remained essentially as they were: market centers for agricultural surpluses produced in the surrounding countryside and as centers of commerce, the role of which decreased with distance from the Mediterranean. Inland commerce grew in importance, but was not the equal of that of the Mediterranean Sea. Therefore, some cities of western Europe had their growth stimulated greatly by the port function, especially Marseilles. Trade ties between Germanic kingdoms on the west and the Byzantine Empire on the east were abruptly broken by the invasion of Islam in the period from 571 to 711 that was to be checked in the early part of the eighth century. In their consolidation of domination over the Mediterranean, the Moslems founded new cities on the African shore, including Tunis and Cairo. Shortly after, the empire created by Charlemagne eventually crumbled since it is said to have lacked a tax system, financial control, fiscal centralization, and a treasury.[21] With the demise of the Carolingian Empire, the wealth became vested in the hands of the landed proprietors and the feudal system began to take shape.

City life and city formation continued during the turmoil of the ninth century, although the economic support was based on agriculture more than commercial activity. Two of the basic attributes of cities were present, however—a middle-class population and a communal organization. The cities at this time were centers of assembly, places for the observance of religious rites, local market centers, and political and judicial centers. Also, military needs were provided for by the cities of this era to protect refugees and the treasures of the society. The two main aspects of urban life and urban centers in western Europe at this time were (1) religious and (2) military (Figure 3–6). The towns were fortresses as well as episcopal residences and fortresses sprang up everywhere at the start of the ninth century.[22] Each of these fortifications commonly was known as a *burg, borough, bourg,* or *borgo,* depending upon the language. These burgs usually were circular in form, with a wall and a moat. In the center of the walled enclosure was the strongest structure—the last defense in event of an attack in which a permanent military garrison was stationed. The ruling authority had a residence in each of

[21]Henri Pirenne, *Medieval Cities.* First translated in 1925 and published by Princeton University Press. Later reprinted by Doubleday and Company.

[22]Pirenne, *Ibid.*

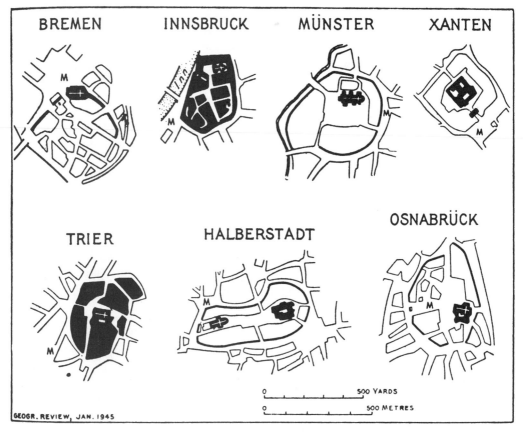

BREMEN    INNSBRUCK    MÜNSTER    XANTEN

OSNABRÜCK

TRIER    HALBERSTADT

0 _____ 500 YARDS

0 _____ 500 METRES

GEOGR. REVIEW, JAN. 1945

**Figure 3-6** Early medieval towns in the German lands. From R.E. Dickinson, WESTERN EUROPEAN CITY, 1961. *(By permission of Routledge & Kegan Paul, Ltd. and Humanities Press, Inc., New Jersey.)*

the burgs in his domain and very often a chapel or church and buildings to house the clergy were parts of this central complex. Also, there was a granary and storehouses in which to store food in case of a seige, this food being provided by surrounding peasants. Above all, the burg was a military establishment, with a secondary function of religious-administration headquarters. The burg was not really a city, but cities did begin to take shape outside their walls and served as the predecessors of larger cities to come.

Another force in urban life in the medieval period was the development of the guilds, which were, with the exception of the church, the most widespread representatives of corporate life. The antecedents of the guild existed with the formation of unions and brotherhoods in third-century Greece. The first guilds for which there are records were in Germany (Mainz in 1099), Italy (Pavia in 1010), and France (St. Omer in 1050).

A guild was an association or fellowship of persons engaged in the same type of economic activity, and it structured the productive population along occupational lines, but at the same time there were strong religious aspects of the guild system. The guild provided a cohesiveness to the productive population and a continuity that was needed for ongoing economic activity in times of upheaval and drastic social change. The merchants, tradesmen, craftsmen, shopkeepers, and others formed independent guilds under the guidance of the church and the nobility and continued to collectively make strides forward in regard to the commercial life of the city where they were most commonly found; the guild was not part of the agrarian scene. Indeed, the guilds became so pervasive in medieval urban society that even the prostitutes formed guilds.

The guilds regulated conditions of production, of distribution, and of marketing and the role of the working class was upgraded in the process. Where the objectives of the clergy and nobility were piety and power, and the motive of the military was defense and armed might, the motive of the guilds was economic strengthening and betterment.

Looking now at the living conditions in medieval cities, the houses of most people were two or three stories high in continuous rows, which is to say, common-wall dwellings, and when located on large blocks, they often had inner courts. Freestanding houses were uncommon, since they were exposed to the elements, were wasteful of land, and were harder to heat. Heating of homes became less of a problem, however, when the fireplace and chimney began to replace the open hearth. Somewhat later, fireproof roofing, stone and tile construction, and whitewashed thatch roofs came into wider use, leading to the avoidance of devastating fires, which had been quite common earlier. Until the beginning of mass production in some industries in the fourteenth century, the urban home often was the workshop, store, or counting house that provided the livelihood of the occupants. All in all, the medieval home, with its extended family, lacked two desirable attributes: privacy and comfort.

The early medieval village and town experienced little in the way of sanitation problems, but as cities began to take shape serious pollution problems arose from accumulation of human waste, from decay of accumulated corpses, and from garbage. To combat these problems, the English parliament in 1388 passed an act that forbade the discard of garbage into open waterways. It was not until 1543 in the city of Bunzlau in Silesia that the first public sewage plant and water works was developed. Although water had been piped to public fountains in the fifteenth century, piped water to individual households did not gain wide use until the seventeenth century.

There were three different types or forms of cities of this period, based on their historic origin, their geographic setting, and their type of development. The towns that remained from the time of the Roman empire usually retained their rectangular system of platting in the central area, with growth spreading outward slowly from this rectangular area in response to topographic characteristics. A second form of medieval city without a pronounced heritage from a former culture was one that developed in a spontaneous manner with an irregular, disorganized form in which, for example, circuitous, winding cowpaths developed into streets. A third form of medieval town or city was one in which the town was designed in advance of its settlement, i.e., a planned town. Most often such towns were laid out in a fairly rigid gridiron pattern with a central area reserved for the market and public assembly. It is stated that an early partiality developed for the gridiron plan, with the rectangle becoming the basic unit of land division. Many cities of the time had, however, vestiges of all three forms that were developed at different stages in the growth of the city. The key elements and those most commonly found were the castle, the Abbey, the Cathedral, the town hall, the guild hall, the market place, and the wall with one or more gates.

During the medieval period, thousands of new towns were formed and those that already existed expanded areally. A not uncommon practice was to remove the wall built to contain the population at a certain time and rebuild it in such a manner as to enclose the population that had settled outside the original wall (Figure

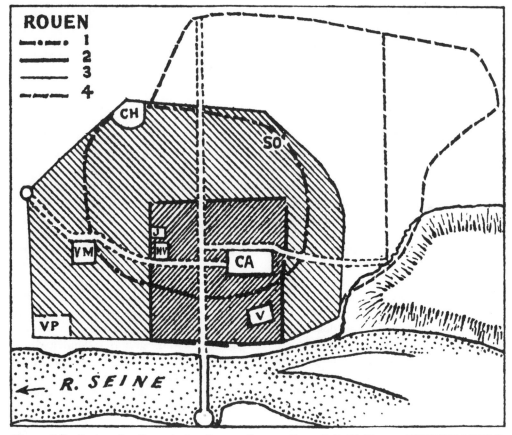

**Figure 3-7** Series of walls enclosing Rouen, France. From R.E. Dickinson, WESTERN EURO-
PEAN CITY, 1961.
*(By permission of Routledge & Kegan Paul, Ltd. and Humanities Press, Inc., New Jersey.)*

3–7). The city of Florence, for example, replaced its original wall in 1172 and about a century later built a third wall that enclosed a still greater area.[23] As suburbs developed, the wall was rebuilt to encircle them and this practice continued until about the sixteenth century, after which the wall proved to be an inadequate form of defense, except in newly colonized parts of the world.

While many cities grew in population during this period, the largest of the cities did not reach the same levels they had earlier. City population usually ranged between a few thousand to forty thousand, the latter the population of London in the fifteenth century. Populations in excess of a hundred thousand

that had been reached earlier by Paris, Venice, Milan, and Florence were unusual until the seventeenth century. The larger cities of the medieval period included, in addition to those mentioned above, Nurnberg (20,000), Ypres (10,376), and Brussels (25–40,000).[24] Of 150 larger cities in Germany at the time, the largest contained less than 35,000 people.

## Cities of the Renaissance

Between the fifteenth and the eighteenth centuries, a new form and content of urban life took shape in Europe, with trade, religion, and politics emerging as separate entities, rather than being in-

[23]Mumford, *Op. Cit.*

[24]Mumford, *Op. Cit.*, p. 314.

terwoven as they had in the medieval period. Following the social disunity at the time of the Black Death in the fourteenth century when between one-third and one-half of the population of Western Europe died, power came into the hands of those who controlled armies, trade routes, and large amounts of capital. The trend was away from medieval universality to baroque uniformity, and from medieval localism to baroque centralism—these changes occurring over a span of about four to five centuries. During the Renaissance, there was consolidation of dispersed feudal states and creation of a continuous political administration, with the more powerful cities seeking to overcome their weaker neighbors.

One result of these changes was the rise of a despotic organization and a flourishing bureaucracy along with the development of the office building that is so common in cities of today. The cities that rose to dominance after the sixteenth century were those that were seats of royal courts—the apex of economic power. At this time, London had a population of 250,000, Naples 240,000, Milan over 200,000, Palermo and Rome 100,000, Lisbon 100,000 and Paris 180,000.

With new offensive weapons and tactics developing, the old defensive measures of cities, mainly the walls, proved inadequate and new types of fortification were built, with salients and bastions in intricate arrangements built in a more substantial manner than the older masonry walls. Not only were these defenses more difficult to build, they were difficult to alter and tended to inhibit lateral expansion of the cities they were to protect. Since a growing population, including refugees from the adjacent countryside, were confined within such fortifications, there was severe overcrowding and increased population densities in the cities, along with the loss of open space that had existed. One response to these circumstances was the adoption of increased building heights—four or five story buildings replacing those of two stories. Five or six story buildings were constructed in old Geneva and in Paris, and eight or more story buildings were built in Edinburgh.[25] Cities in this period were confined within their walls and could only expand upward, while their fortifications spread laterally.

At this time, there arose a new perception of space in which perspective played a vital role and out of this rose the baroque city in which the avenue became the most important symbol of the city. There were several major broad avenues, as opposed to narrow alleys as before. The development of the linear avenue was based partially on artistic grounds, but also was due to the more widespread use of wheeled vehicles that were not suited to the narrow, winding alleys of the medieval city. The avenues were not only wanted for commercial movement but they were vital for military movement and pageantry as well. Accompanying development of the broad avenue in the baroque city of the Renaissance, was the building of magnificent palaces for the nobility, along with ornate fountains and gardens. So much of the civic activity revolved around the court that a new element arose to accommodate visitors; this was the hotel. Most cities formed between the sixteenth and nineteenth centuries in Europe, aside from overseas colonization, either were places of residence of kings and princes, such as Versailles, Karlsruhe, and Potsdam, or were garrison cities that were seats of royal power in absentia. Another development of the baroque city was the residential square, an open space surrounded by residential structures, not commercial, and perhaps a church. These squares, established after about 1600, met the upper class needs especially, although they later came to satisfy needs of all urban dwellers.

[25]Mumford, *Op. Cit.*

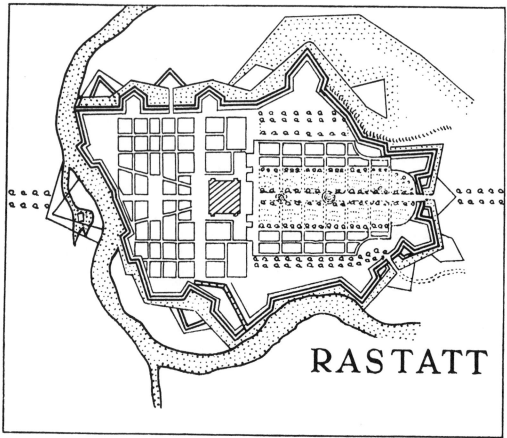

**Figures 3-8** Baroque town of the renaissance period. From R.E. Dickinson, WESTERN EUROPEAN CITY, 1961.
*(By permission of Routledge & Kegan Paul, Ltd. and Humanities Press, Inc., New Jersey.)*

The essence of the baroque city was its geometric regularity involving a number of broad diagonal avenues radiating from a given point and producing an asterisk-shaped pattern (Figure 3–8). Such a plan is a concession to geometric order, but often was implemented without regard to economic cost or to other urban functions. If the terrain was irregular, the task was one of leveling it, regardless of cost, to adhere to the plan; if a grove of trees was in the path of construction of an avenue, it was removed. Perhaps most important, however, is the inability of the baroque plan to accommodate urban life today with its plethora of wheeled vehicles. If all activity is directed by a system of radial avenues to a single focal point or even to a number of such focal points, the efficiency of

movement is seriously impaired. Further, movements between outlying points of the city is "against the grain" of the major arterials and is made more difficult as a result. Another disadvantage of the baroque plan was that it was not dynamic; it was developed completely at a certain point in time, then fixed and frozen forever. It was not the type of plan that could be added to as the city expanded areally, nor could it be altered internally.

In spite of its shortcomings, the baroque plan provided the layout of a number of large cities in the twentieth century, such as Tokyo, New Delhi, San Francisco, and Chicago. A modified form of the baroque plan was followed in the development of Washington D.C., with the only major component missing being the fortifications of the baroque city of the sixteenth century. All other components of the baroque plan were present—the complex of public buildings, broad avenues, the radial approaches, the openness and greenery, and the concession to perspective. Present day Washington has been modified from the baroque plan, however, but numerous smaller cities developed according to the same plan also have been modified greatly to adjust to changing circumstances. Perhaps, the greatest legacy of the Renaissance period was the baroque plan and many cities of today bear the imprint of this philosophy and strive to overcome some of its elements that tend to inhibit the modern commercial city.

## The Rise of the Mercantile City

From the seventeenth century on, the stimuli of urban expansion, areal and economic, were the merchants, financiers, and landlords, with the gradual development of the commercial city the result. Investment and financial gain became common goals of city dwellers and the rise of a monied class occurred. Financial transactions gave rise to new economic activities and some cities emerged as financial centers and virtually all cities took on the role of a commercial center.

One significant aspect of urban society at this time was the change in attitude toward land. Under the feudal system, land was leased for long periods (99 to 999 years) and was not sold, creating a stability and continuity in use of the land resource. After the seventeenth century, land came to be regarded as a commodity, not a stewardship, and was treated as a commodity in the market place. With the advent of the capitalistic motive in dealing with urban land, rents rose substantially and took a larger and larger share of the workers income. Furthermore, since urban housing became a means of reaping substantial profits by the monied interests and landlords, there

was little attempt made to maintain the housing, with the result that slums became increasingly widespread and common. It was true at this time, as it is at present, that the greater gain is to be made from degraded or dilapidated land use, and it was likely true in London, New York, and Paris before the middle of the nineteenth century, that the worse the dwelling, the higher the total rent of the property.[26] The exploitation of land existed in outlying areas as well as in the city proper. Farmsteads were acquired and divided into building lots resulting in a piecemeal dismemberment of the corporate city. City life during this period was subject to commercial speculation, social disintegration, and physical disorganization at the same time that cities were multiplying in number and increasing in size throughout the western world. Accompanying these trends was a multiplication of the profits to be reaped from slum housing.

With the rise of the contemporary city, individual lots and blocks became units for buying and selling without regard for historic uses, physical conditions, or social needs. The reason that this pattern appears more representative of American cities is because cities developed in the United States, with the exception of New England and a few other areas, did not inherit a heritage of urban patterns of other types.

While walls around cities of Western Europe after the seventeenth century had been made obsolete as a defensive measure and served as a deterrent to areal expansion of mercantile cities, they were still a feature of some cities being developed in early America. One study states that of over 250 major U.S. cities, eleven had walls early in their development in the seventeenth and eighteenth centuries.[27] Of these, perhaps the best

[26]Mumford, *Op. Cit.*

[27]Howard J. Nelson, "Walled Cities in the United States," *Annals of the Association of American Geographers,* Vol. 51, No. 1 (March, 1961).

**Figure 3-9**   Early New York City, showing fortifications and the wall (about 1660). From H.J. Nelson, 1961.
*(Reproduced by permission from the* Annals *of the Association of American Geographers.)*

known is the wall built in New Amsterdam (New York) on the tip of Manhattan Island. Actually, there were two walls built here, one about 1653 and the other about 1745, the earlier one following a path now occupied by present day Wall Street (Figure 3–9). Walls around cities in the U.S. were relatively crudely constructed and have long since passed from the scene, having served the purpose for which they were built—defense in a hostile environment.

The most expedient form of land division and one conducive to additions to the spread of the city by continued subdivision of outlying farmland was a type of gridiron system involving straight streets intersecting at right angles. As a derivative of this system, rectangular building lots could be formed, with the shortest dimension on the street side, thereby, giving more lots street frontage. It was also easier, with the rectangular

grid, to assemble individual lots into larger units, such as blocks, for sale to users of the land other than for single-family residences. Not only did the rectangular survey system influence the street pattern and the geometry of individual building lots, it also influenced the basic design of the dwelling unit, with the boxlike rectangular house becoming commonplace.

Cities in this period expanded areally and some new ones were formed, with the result that more of the world's people were residing in urban centers. It is stated, however, that cities at the end of the eighteenth century had fewer inhabitants than they had 300 years earlier and that the distribution of cities in Europe in 1830 was essentially the same as it had been for the previous five centuries.[28]

[28]Dickinson, *Op. Cit.*

The development that stimulated city growth at this time, perhaps more than any other, was the industrial revolution. Urbanization increased in nearly direct proportion to industrialization and more of the urban dwellers gained their livelihoods from manufacturing industries than ever before. After the 1830's, the development of factory production and new methods of transportation provided needs for more workers in developing industrial centers, stimulating migration from non-urban areas. Of prime importance in creating the rise of a factory city was the development of the steam engine, with this in turn creating new energy needs, especially for coal. The main elements of the new urban industrial complex were the factory, the railroad, and the slum, with the factory the nucleus of the new urban organization.[29] The factory generally occupied the best sites in the city, was the most powerful in shaping the work patterns of urban dwellers, and was the prime source of degradation of the urban environment, although the railroads contributed to this blight as well.

In this setting of expanding factory production in a soiled city, the thousands of workers vital to the industrial process often resided in quarters that were comparable to the lowest serfs dwelling in the medieval period. In Birmingham and Bradford, England, thousands of workers' dwellings were built back to back, so that two of the four rooms in each dwelling had no light or ventilation. In such districts, there was no open space, except the lane between rows of dwellings and this was the receptacle for accumulated rubbish. There was little in the way of toilet facilities, except the cellar, and many of these were used for dwelling places and pigsties. In one part of Manchester, England in 1843–1844, there was one toilet for every 212 persons.[30] Even with the introduction of piped water in the early nineteenth century, there still

were deplorable sanitation conditions and infectious disease was freely spread. The mortality rate was extremely high, especially the infant mortality rate. In New York City in 1810, the rate was between 120 and 145 per thousand live births, 180 by 1850, 220 in 1860, and 240 in 1870.[31] Such conditions were not peculiar to New York, however, with similar conditions existing in Berlin, Vienna, and Paris during the middle of the nineteenth century.

By the middle of the nineteenth century, progress was being made to alleviate some of the chronic ills of the city, especially those of a hygenic nature. Production of glazed drains and cast iron pipe allowed the distribution of higher quality water to increasing numbers of dwelling units, as well as the disposal of sewage. Open space in the form of small parks began to appear in minimal amounts; hospitals became more available; street cleaning became more commonplace; private toilets were common in most dwelling units; these were some of the advances made in the latter half of the nineteenth century. It is likely that hygiene was the most positive contribution to urban culture in the nineteenth century.

Another contribution to urban culture in the nineteenth century was development of the suburb. When many repressed workers gained the means needed, they tended to escape the overcrowded, unsightly, and unsanitary city by moving to an adjacent community where living conditions were better. Most certainly, embryonic forms of suburbs are known to have existed in cities developed much earlier, but with the advent of the railroad between 1850 and 1920, plus the coming of the electric trolley in the 1880's, suburbs began to develop on the margins of many large cities. These early suburbs were relatively small, however, rarely having populations over 5,000, with a number of these small nucleations strung out along the rail-

[29]Mumford, *Op. Cit.*

[30]Mumford, *Op. Cit.*

[31]Mumford, *Op. Cit.*

roads radiating from the city. So long as railroad stops and walking distance to them controlled the size of the suburb, it had a form that was quite compact.

From the beginning of the rise of suburbs in the nineteenth century, the people who took up residence in them were those with the greatest wealth, and the suburbs that developed were populated with the high and middle income groups. The workers in the industries that formed the base of the new urban wealth were not in a position to escape the dismal, debilitating, and degrading environment that characterized the central city.

The coming of the private automobile in the early twentieth century heralded the era of mass suburbia in which more and more of the people of the city fled the central city to find a better living environment in suburbia. However, the problems that they were trying to evade tended to reappear; congestion, impersonality, water problems, overcrowding, sewage disposal, pollution, and high population densities have, in minor or major forms, become problems of the suburban dwellers as they were and still are for people living in the central city. Additional aspects of suburban structure and growth are considered in the chapters that follow.

Quite clearly, during the millennia of formation and growth, the dominant functions of cities have changed considerably, and so have the concomitant forms and structures of the cities. Certain component parts came to characterize each period of city formation, with some being lost in the passage of time, while others have been retained and exist in a modified form in the cities of today.

# 4

# recent urbanization: world regions and the united states

A fact of modern life is that the population of the world has become increasingly concentrated in relatively little of the earth's surface area. Man has become more and more urbanized, especially since the middle of the twentieth century.

## Urban Growth and Urbanization

A distinction should be made, however, between an increase in urban population and a population that is becoming more urbanized. Let us assume a region or perhaps a nation, in which the population is divided between 60 percent in the rural sector and 40 percent in the urban sector (Table 4–1). Resulting from natural reproduction and immigration over a period of time, the population of the region (Region A) increases, say, from 15 million to 18 million, but the population is still divided between 60 percent in the rural sector and 40 percent in the urban sector. The urban population has increased by 1.2 million from 6 million to 7.2 million and the rural sector during the same period has increased by 1.8 million from 9.0 million to 10.8 million. The key point in this example is that the rate of change in both sectors of the population has been 20 percent over the time period considered (Table 4–1). In this case, the population structure of the region is no different at the end of the time period than at the beginning, although there has been a substantial increase in the population of the region, both urban and rural. In a second region (Region B), with the same base population (15 million) and with the same amount and rate of increase over the time period (3 million and 20 percent respectively), the urban-rural breakdown is appreciably different from that of the first hypothetical region. In the latter region, the increase has been concentrated mainly in the urban sector and, since rates of natural reproduction can be assumed to be the same in all population sectors, this would indicate a migration to urban centers from rural areas. In this case, the rural population increased by 5.6 percent and the urban population by 41.7 percent, yet the total regional population increased by 20.0 percent, as it had in the first hypothetical region (Table 4–1). In the first region, there was a continuation of the population structure that existed previously, whereas in the second region there was a restructuring of the regional population.

It is important to consider differences of these types. It is possible to have sustained growth in urban population, with this phenomenon expected as part of the

**Table 4–1**   Hypothetical Situation Illustrating the Difference Between Urban Growth and Urbanization

| Total population (Millions) | Rural Population | | Urban Population | |
| --- | --- | --- | --- | --- |
| | Amount (Millions) | Percent of Total | Amount (Millions) | Percent of Total |
| *Region A* (condition of urban growth) | | | | |
| Begining of time period              15.0 | 9.0 | 60.0 | 6.0 | 40.0 |
| Ending of time period                18.0 | 10.8 | 60.0 | 7.2 | 40.0 |
| Population increase                    3.0 | 1.8 | (20.0% increase) | 1.2 | (20.0% increase) |
| *Region B* (condition of urbanization) | | | | |
| Beginning of time period             15.0 | 9.0 | 60.0 | 6.0 | 40.0 |
| End of time period                   18.0 | 9.5 | 52.8 | 8.5 | 47.2 |
| Population increase                    3.0 | .5 | (5.6% increase) | 2.5 | (41.7% increase) |

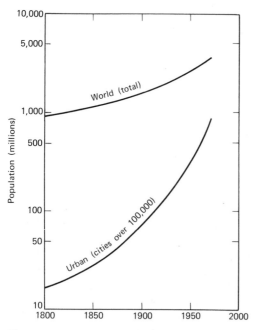

**Figure 4-1** World and urban populations 1800–1972. Adapted from Kingsley Davis in *Cities,* Alfred A. Knopf (1965) and Population Reference Bureau (1972).

natural increase in numbers of a given species. When the rates of increase in an urban population are equal to or less than the rates of increase of the population of the region of which the urban population is a part, the condition of *urban growth* exists. In cases where the rate of increase in the urban population exceeds the regional rate of increase, especially by a considerable margin, the condition of *urbanization* exists. It might be said that urbanization is an accelerated form of urban growth. In any region, it is possible to recognize the *level of urbanization* reached or the degree to which the region's population has become urban.

The world's population, as a whole, has been experiencing urbanization in that rates of increase of urban population have exceeded overall rates of population increase for at least two centuries (Figure 4–1).

Whereas the world's population is experiencing urban growth as well as ur-

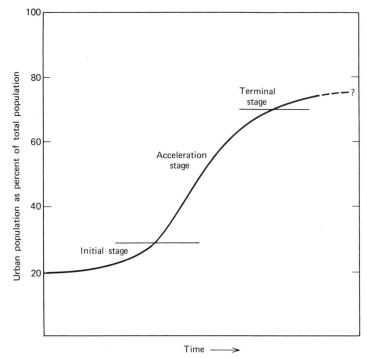

**Figure 4-2**  The urbanization curve and stages of urbanization

banization, the levels of urbanization are quite varied among the world regions, with some having reached higher levels of urbanization than others. It is estimated that in 1960, one-third of the population resided in urban centers.[1] This compares with approximately 2 percent in 1800 and 4 percent in 1900.[2] Rates of urban growth have exceeded rates of general population growth during this period and it is appropriate to say that there has been an urbanization of world population underway for at least two centuries (Figure 4–1). Further, urbanization has increased at an increasing rate, which is to say that the rate of urban growth in the world outstrips the rate of overall population growth by a greater margin as time passes.

[1]Kingsley Davis, *Cities,* New York, Alfred A. Knopf, 1965.

[2]One interested in urban growth might read *The Spatial Expression of Urban Growth,* Commission on College Geography, Association of American Geographers, Resource Paper No. 7 (1969).

## The Urbanization Curve

During the initial period of urban population growth, a curve representing the trend of urbanization rises gradually (Figure 4–2). During this period the population is fairly dispersed, as is the economic activity which is primarily rural and agricultural. This segment of the urbanization curve merges into one of steep rise, indicating a period in which an increasingly large share of the population is in urban centers. Once the greatest share of the population becomes urban, there is a gradual flattening of the curve, since there likely is some upper limit on the share of the population that can be urban. Some segment of the population will remain in rural areas to provide the goods, especially food and fiber, needed to support the urban population. Thus, the urbanization curve has the shape of an attenuated "S." Different nations and regions reach different points on the curve at different times, as exemplified by England and Wales which reached the upper portion of the curve shortly after 1900, while the the United States didn't reach the same point until approximately 1950.

It might prove useful to identify the distinct stages in the urbanization curve. The flattish, lower end of the curve depicting conditions at an early time period might be referred to as the *initial stage* of urbanization. It is characterized by an economic structure known as the "traditional society."[3] The emphasis here is on the agrarian sector of the economy which has characteristically been accompanied by a dispersed population, a relatively small share of which resides in cities. The attenuated trunk of the urbanization curve can be referred to as the *acceleration stage* during which there is a pronounced redistribution of the population such that, from less than about 25 percent of the population being urban, the urban component rises to 50, 60, or 70 percent or more of the total. During this stage, there is a decided concentration, not only of people, but of economic activity in the region and a basic restructuring of the economy and investment of social overhead capital in such sectors as transportation. Economic activity during this stage becomes more localized or less dispersed, and the secondary and tertiary economic sectors take on increased importance. Manufacturing industries and trade and service activities employ increasingly large numbers of people and become more significant, relative to employment gains in the primary sector that includes agriculture. After the acceleration stage has run its course, there comes the third stage of urbanization and this might be termed the *terminal stage*. The situation here is one in which the share of the population considered as urban is in excess of about 60 or 70 percent, with the remainder being rural farm and nonfarm inhabitants supplying the needs of the urban dwellers. As a result, once the

urbanization curve approaches 100 percent, it will invariably begin to level, thus creating a flattish upper portion of the curve. As one example, since about 1900, the urbanization curve for England and Wales has tended to flatten after the level of about 80 percent was reached.

However, the urbanization curve, based on centuries of human experience, may change in the future either by (1) a flattening of the upper portion of the curve at a lower level of urban population, or (2) a reversal of the urbanization curve resulting from an outmigration from urban centers or from greater rates of population growth in rural areas than in urban areas. In the former case, there might be a slowing or stoppage of migration to urban centers so that a condition of equilibrium would be reached such that, for example, once the population becomes 40 to 50 percent urban, it might stabilize at that level leading to an earlier beginning of the terminal stage of the urbanization curve. In the latter case, the "flight to the city" might be replaced by a "flight to the countryside," in which the outmigration from the city might more than offset inmigration and natural reproduction increases. In this instance, there would be a downturn in the urbanization curve. Either of these alternatives would be contrary to past human behavior, however, except for a few instances involving small regions and relatively few people.

## Regional and National Contrasts in Urbanization

The levels of urbanization reached in different regions of the world are presented in Table 4–2, together with 1980 estimates. Data are not available for an urban-rural breakdown of the population of many nations of the world, but the general situation can be expressed by examination of the population structure of a number of nations for which data are available. This has been done in Table 4–3, which presents rates and levels of

---

[3]W. W. Rostow, *The Stages of Economic Growth,* Cambridge University Press, 1960.

**Table 4–2**   Urban and Rural Population, by World Region: 1960 and 1980 (Estimated)

| World and Region | Urban Population (Percent of Total) | | Rural Population (Percent of Total) | |
|---|---|---|---|---|
| | 1960 | 1980 est. | 1960 | 1980 est. |
| WORLD | 33 | 46 | 67 | 54 |
| Africa | 18 | 28 | 82 | 72 |
| East Asia | 23 | 31 | 77 | 69 |
| South Asia | 18 | 25 | 82 | 75 |
| Europe | 58 | 65 | 42 | 35 |
| Northern America | 70 | 81 | 30 | 19 |
| Oceania | 64 | 75 | 36 | 25 |
| Latin America | 49 | 60 | 51 | 40 |
| U.S.S.R. | 49 | 68 | 51 | 32 |
| More developed regions | 60 | 71 | 40 | 29 |
| Less developed regions | 20 | 30 | 80 | 70 |

SOURCE: Adapted from United Nations, *Growth of the World's Urban and Rural Population, 1920–2000,* Dept. of Economic and Social Affairs, Population Studies, No. 44, New York, 1969, Table 39.

urbanization, plus rates of increase of total population for a number of countries. From this, the distinction between urban growth and urbanization is made somewhat more clear.

From Table 4–3, it can be seen that rates of urban growth have outstripped, by a considerable margin, rates of total population growth in Mexico, Venezuela, Iran, Finland, Poland, and the U.S.S.R. Considering that in these nations the share of the population viewed as urban is, with the exception of Venezuela, in the range of 35 to 60 percent, these nations might be described as being in the acceleration stage of urbanization. By contrast, Israel, the Netherlands, and England-Wales have had increases in urban population approximately equal to or somewhat less than overall rates of national population increase. Also, the urban population sector accounts for at least three-fourths of the total population in each of the latter cases. Thus, these

**Table 4–3**   Rates of Population Change and Levels of Urbanization for Selected Nations

| Nation | Rate of Change of Total Population (Percent) | Rate of Change of Urban Population (Percent) | Percent Urban at Beginning of Time Period | Percent Urban at End of Time Period |
|---|---|---|---|---|
| Mexico (1965–1969) | 14.6 | 21.6 | 55.2 | 58.7 |
| Venezuela (1965–1969) | 15.1 | 20.5 | 71.6 | 74.9 |
| Iran (1965–1969) | 12.4 | 20.2 | 37.4 | 40.0 |
| Finland (1965–1969) | 2.0 | 15.8 | 44.0 | 50.0 |
| Poland (1965–1969) | 3.4 | 7.1 | 49.5 | 51.3 |
| U.S.S.R. (1965–1969) | 4.3 | 9.0 | 53.4 | 55.8 |
| Israel (1965–1968) | 9.3 | 9.7 | 81.8 | 82.2 |
| Netherlands (1965–1968) | 3.4 | 3.2 | 78.3 | 78.2 |
| England-Wales (1965–1968) | 1.7 | 1.4 | 79.1 | 78.9 |

SOURCE: Derived from data in United Nations; *Demographic Yearbook*, 1969.

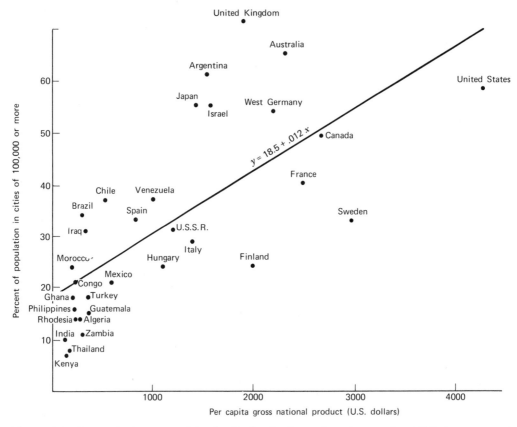

**Figure 4-3**   Per capita income and levels of urbanization, selected countries: 1972. *Source.* Based on data by Population Reference Bureau. *1972 World Population Data Sheet.*

nations are in the terminal stage of urbanization.

In general, the developed nations of the world might be considered as being in the terminal stage of urbanization, since much of their development has involved the concentration of economic activity in relatively few places and this increased localization of economic activity has been accompanied by a concomitant localization of population. The developing nations, on the other hand, tend to be somewhere in the acceleration stage of urbanization with some, such as Iran, nearer the lower part of this stage and others, such as the U.S.S.R., nearer the upper part of this stage. Still other nations, though a distinct minority, are in the initial stage of urbanization. These are the nations having a largely agrarian society.

If per capita income can be taken as a measure of economic development, it can be seen from Figure 4–3 that there is a roughly linear correlation between per capita income and level of urbanization, with the level of urbanization being greatest in nations with highest per capita income levels. Conversely, in nations where the per capita income is lowest, the levels of urbanization tend to be the lowest. A three factor correlation might be made at this point. As time passes, (1) more of the economic activity is in the secondary and tertiary sectors. As these activities are generally localized, the population engaged in them becomes more localized, and (2) per capita incomes increase. As population becomes more localized, (3) the level of urbanization becomes greater. However, as the rate of localization of population and

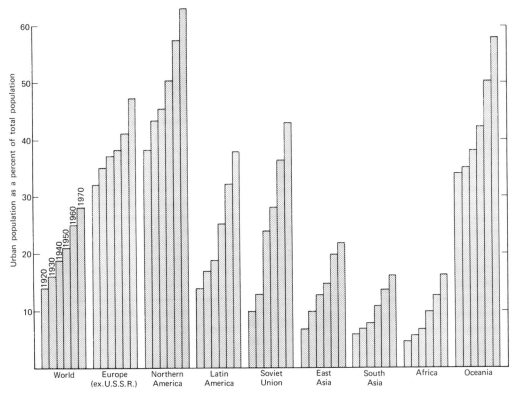

**Figure 4-4**  Urban population in major world regions: 1920–1970 (cities of 20,000 and over). *Source.* Adapted from data in *Growth of the World's Urban and Rural Population, 1920–2000,* United Nations, 1969.

economic activity slackens, incomes become relatively stabilized, lessening the pace of urbanization.

If we consider the time period 1920 to 1960, we note that the proportion of world population living in urban centers of 20,000 or more people has increased from 14 to 25 percent (compared with 33 percent in urban centers of all sizes), a percentage increase of 11 percent in 40 years (Figure 4–4).[4] Over this 40 year time span, world regions have experienced different rates of increase, although all major world regions have become more urbanized. Considering changes in levels of urbanization, based on populations in urban centers of 20,000 or more, five world regions have exceeded the world change in the period

1920 to 1960, with these being the Soviet Union, Northern America, Latin America, Oceania, and East Asia (Figure 4–4). By contrast, three world regions have experienced a change in level of urbanization less than the world average, namely Europe (except the U.S.S.R.), South Asia, and Africa. Notice the contrast among the latter regions, in that the 1960 level of urbanization in Europe was estimated to be from 58 to nearly 73 percent, while the levels in South Asia and Africa were about 18 percent. The former region has reached a high level of urbanization which is slackening, while the two latter regions have not reached this level.

For the world as a whole, in the period 1920–1960, the total population increased by about 61 percent. During this time, populations of cities of all sizes, except those under 20,000, increased by an

[4]United Nations, *Urbanization: Development Policies and Planning,* International Social Development Review, No. 1, New York, 1968.

even greater rate, with the rate of increase becoming greater as larger size cities are considered (Figure 4–5). The populations of cities of one-half million or more have increased by between two and three times during this 40 year period.

Of all types of urban centers, based on population size, the one that has grown the fastest and likely warrants the greatest attention is the one of large size. In this context, the *metropolitan area,* roughly analogous to the urbanized area as defined by the Bureau of the Census and as discussed in Chapter 2, is the appropriate unit to consider. This term is used in reference to a single functional unit with a population of at least 100,000 people. The number of metropolitan areas in the world is approximately 1374, with these distributed among world regions in the manner presented in Table 4–4.[5]

In terms of growth of individual metropolitan areas, extreme differences are provided by Southern Africa and the Middle East, as compared with Eastern and Western Europe. In the former regions, with about 3 percent of the world's metropolitan areas, the growth rates are very high—about 5 percent or more per year. In the latter regions, however, the growth rates of metropolitan areas are especially low. In these regions are about one-third of the metropolitan areas of the world, but their growth rates, on the average, are less than 2 percent per year. Notice too that the less developed world regions have higher rates of metropolitan area growth than the world average of 2.4 percent per year. Southern Africa, the Middle East, Middle America, North Africa, South America, Southern Asia, and Eastern Asia all have regional metropolitan area growth rates greater than the world average. By contrast, the more developed regions of the world with higher levels of urbanization, tend to

[5]Jack P. Gibbs, "Growth of Individual Metropolitan Areas," *Annals of the Association of American Geographers,* Vol. 51, No. 4, December, 1961.

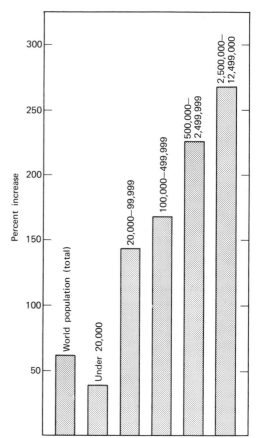

**Figure 4-5**   Percentage increase in urban and world population, by size class (1920–1960). *Source.* Adapted from *Urbanization: Development Policies and Planning,* United Nations, 1968.

have lower regional rates of metropolitan area growth. North America, Oceania, the U.S.S.R., Eastern Europe, and Western Europe have rates of metropolitan area growth equal to or less than the world average. Data are insufficient to determine whether the same contrasts occur with respect to smaller cities in the respective world regions, that is, whether rates of growth of smaller cities or agglomerations are the same as they are for large metropolitan areas in each of the world regions.

To pursue the matter of metropolitan area growth a bit further, note that there is considerable variation within a given world region, as well as among world regions. Also, remember that some me-

**Table 4–4**  Number of Metropolitan Areas and Average Annual Growth Rate: By World Region

| World Region | Number of Metropolitan Areas[a] | Average Annual Growth Rate of Metropolitan Areas (%)[b] | Percent of Regional Population in Metropolitan Areas |
|---|---|---|---|
| Southern Africa | 44 | 5.3 | 5.0 |
| Middle East | 13[b] | 4.5 | — |
| Middle America | 37 | 4.0 | 33.0 |
| North Africa | 15 | 3.7 | 22.0 |
| South America | 88 | 3.5 | 27.0 |
| Southern Asia ⎫ Eastern Asia ⎭ | 481 | ⎧ 3.4 ⎫ ⎩ 2.6 ⎭ | 14.0 |
| North America | 169 | 2.4 | 51.0 |
| Oceania | 12 | 2.4 | 50.0 |
| U.S.S.R. | 220 | 2.3 | 27.0 |
| Eastern Europe | 94 | 1.9 | 21.0 |
| Western Europe | 214 | 1.0 | 33.0 |
| WORLD | 1,387 | 2.4 | — |

SOURCE:  [a]Kingsley Davis, *Scientific American*, 1965.
[b]Jack P. Gibbs, *Annals of the Association of American Geographers*, December, 1961.

tropolitan areas are gaining population very rapidly, others are growing at only modest rates, and a small number are losing population, very likely from an exodus to smaller urban centers from larger urban agglomerations.

Clearly, there is considerable variation in rates of growth of metropolitan areas in different world regions, particularly in developed regions as compared with the developing regions. One of these contrasts is that in none of the developed regions is the upper end of the cumulative distribution curve extended beyond an annual average growth of more than 8 percent, while in several of the developing regions, the annual average growth rate is greater than 8 percent and, in fact is as great as 12–13 percent in Eastern Asia (Figure 4–6). Another contrast found is that the point of origin of the curves for the less developed world regions is, in every case, somewhere between 0 and 2 percent, while in the developed world regions the point of origin of most is between −2.0 and 0, indicating that in these regions some of the metropolitan areas are decreasing in population. Still another contrast is that the range in

growth rates of individual metropolitan areas is greater in the less developed regions than it is in the developed regions, that is, the curves in the latter cases are steeper than are those in the former.

In summary, notice that *rates* of urbanization tend to be greater in the less developed regions of the world, while the *levels* of urbanization are highest in the developed regions. The developed regions tend to be in the terminal stage of urbanization, while the developing regions of the world, by and large, tend to be in the acceleration stage of urbanization. One puzzling situation exists in the form of rates of urbanization in developed regions, especially in metropolitan areas, in which there is a population decrease rather than a population increase. This may indicate that, if this is a continued and common phenomenon, there may be yet another stage in the urbanization curve in which it eventually turns downward after reaching its apex in the terminal stage. Remember too, there may be a *regressive stage* in this curve. Still, economic activity remains concentrated in larger urban areas providing the rationale for continued con-

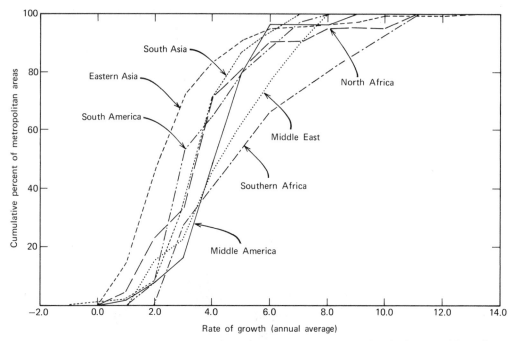

**Figure 4-6a.** Growth rates of metropolitan areas (1941–1955), developing world regions. *Source.* Adapted from data in Jack P. Gibbs, *Annals* of the AAG, December 1961.

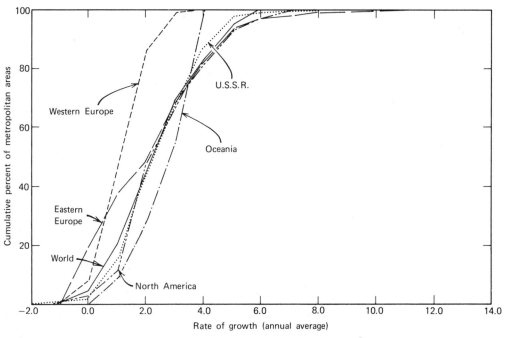

**Figure 4-6b** Growth rates of metropolitan areas (1941–1955), world and developed world regions. *Source.* Adapted from data in Jack P. Gibbs, *Annals* of the AAG, December 1961.

centration of population. There are few indications to support the proposition that economic activity is lessening in met-ropolitan areas, so one must ask what has stimulated this decrease in metropolitan area population? Is it simply a decline in

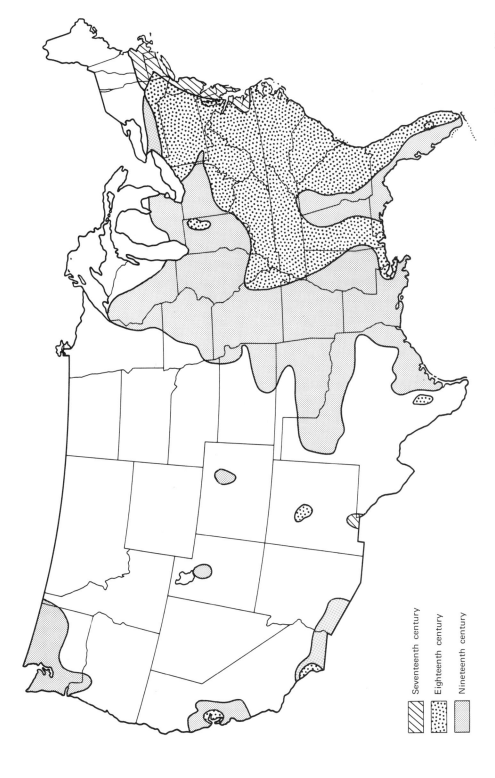

**Figure 4-7** Century of major city formation (United States) with a 1970 population of 100,000 or more. Gary, Indiana and Torrance, California, formed in the twentieth century, not shown.

Seventeenth century

Eighteenth century

Nineteenth century

birth rates and natural reproduction in metropolitan areas, rather than a flight from an increasingly untenable or unacceptable environment in the metropolitan areas? The latter possibility is pursued in more detail in the next chapter.

## Urban Growth and Urbanization in the United States

It is well known that city formation and growth have characterized the history of the United States. So it is important to observe the geographic spread of this phenomenon and the changes in degree to which the urban population has characterized the national population at certain times, that is, the degree of urbanization present at different points in the past.

The earliest urban settlements in the country were forerunners of the large metropolitan centers of today. Once founded, most cities gained in population so there is no American equivalent of Memphis, Babylon, Ur, or Mohenjo-Daro—relatively large and prominent cities of the past that withered and died.

The seventeenth century saw the formation of a number of urban centers on the eastern seaboard of the country and in areas peripheral to the seaboard. Cities founded during this period include Boston (1630), New York (1626 to 1664), and Philadelphia (1682), all of which have become major metropolitan centers (Figure 4–7). Not only were the earliest port cities founded at this time, so were some inland cities within a few hundred miles of the seaboard and a few inland garrison centers.

The eighteenth century witnessed the founding of additional cities on the eastern seaboard, as well as a large number founded in the Ohio River and Mississippi River valleys. Also, the first city formation occurred on the western seaboard during this period. Major cities of today that were formed during this period include Detroit, New Orleans, Baltimore, St. Louis, San Diego, Pittsburgh, San Francisco, Los Angeles, and Cleve-

land (Figure 4–7). Obviously, riverine sites were selected for city formation during this period, as well as seaboard sites.

The earlier founded cities had the greatest populations at the end of the eighteenth century; New York had 60,000 inhabitants, and Boston had 25,000. Other large cities in 1800 were Baltimore with 26,000 people, and Charleston with 19,000. Through new city formation and growth of existing cities, the urban population in the nation in 1800 accounted for slightly over 6 percent of the national total (Table 4–5).

By the end of the nineteenth century, city formation had been extended to all sections of the country and most of the previously founded cities continued to gain in population. Many cities were founded in the Midwest during this period, mainly on the Great Lakes or on navigable rivers. Cities formed during this time span include Chicago, Milwaukee, Houston, Atlanta, Dallas, Minneapolis, Denver, Portland, and Seattle (Figure 4–7). There was relatively little city formation on the eastern seaboard during this period, with the exceptions of Tampa and Miami in Florida. By the end of the nineteenth century, urbanization of the national population had proceeded to a point where about 40 percent of the people of the nation lived in urban centers (Table 4–5).

In the twentieth century, the pace of city formation slowed appreciably, though it did not come to an end. Some of the new cities formed were to become larger metropolitan centers at a later time, such as Gary, Indiana and Torrance, California. The major thrust during this period, however, was in population growth of already formed cities in all parts of the nation. Midway through this century, the level of urbanization had reached 64 percent and from about World War I on, the greatest share of the nations people lived in urban centers. By 1970, 74 percent of the national population was considered as urban (Figure 4–8).

**Table 4–5**  Urban and Rural Composition, and Rates of Urban and Rural Growth in the United States: 1790–1970

| Year | Percent of Total Population | | Percentage Urban Gain over Preceding Decade | Percentage Change over Preceding Census | |
|---|---|---|---|---|---|
| | Urban | Rural | | Urban | Rural |
| 1970 | 73.5 | 26.5 | 3.6 | 19.2 | −0.3 |
| 1960 | 69.9 | 30.1 | 5.9 | 29.3 | −0.8 |
| 1950 | 64.0 | 36.0 | 7.5 | 21.8 | 3.4 |
| 1940 | 56.5 | 43.5 | 0.3 | 7.9 | 6.4 |
| 1930 | 56.2 | 43.8 | 5.0 | 27.3 | 4.4 |
| 1920 | 51.2 | 48.8 | 5.5 | 29.0 | 3.2 |
| 1910 | 45.7 | 54.3 | 6.0 | 39.3 | 9.0 |
| 1900 | 39.7 | 60.3 | 4.6 | 36.4 | 12.2 |
| 1890 | 35.1 | 64.9 | 6.9 | 56.5 | 13.4 |
| 1880 | 28.2 | 71.8 | 0.7 | 42.7 | 25.7 |
| 1870 | 27.5 | 74.3 | 7.7 | 59.3 | 13.6 |
| 1860 | 19.8 | 80.2 | 4.5 | 75.4 | 28.4 |
| 1850 | 15.3 | 84.7 | 4.5 | 92.1 | 29.1 |
| 1840 | 10.8 | 89.2 | 2.0 | 63.7 | 29.7 |
| 1830 | 8.8 | 91.2 | 1.6 | 62.6 | 31.2 |
| 1820 | 7.2 | 92.8 | −0.1 | 31.9 | 33.2 |
| 1810 | 7.3 | 92.7 | 1.2 | 63.0 | 34.7 |
| 1800 | 6.1 | 93.9 | 1.0 | 59.9 | 33.8 |
| 1790 | 5.1 | 94.9 | — | — | — |

SOURCE:  Bureau of the Census, *Census of Population, United States Summary*, 1970.

To be sure, the level of urbanization varies among states, with the highest levels occurring in states in southern New England and in the Middle Atlantic regions (Figure 4–9). Levels in states in these regions often are in excess of 80 percent. States in the southwest of the country also have high levels of urbanization, generally in excess of 70 percent. By contrast, states in the northern Great

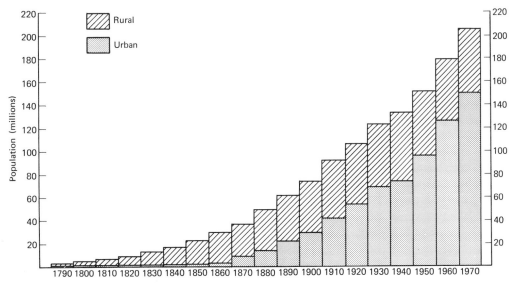

**Figure 4-8**  Urban and rural population: 1790–1970, United States. *Source.* Based on data in Bureau of Census, *Census of Population: 1970.*

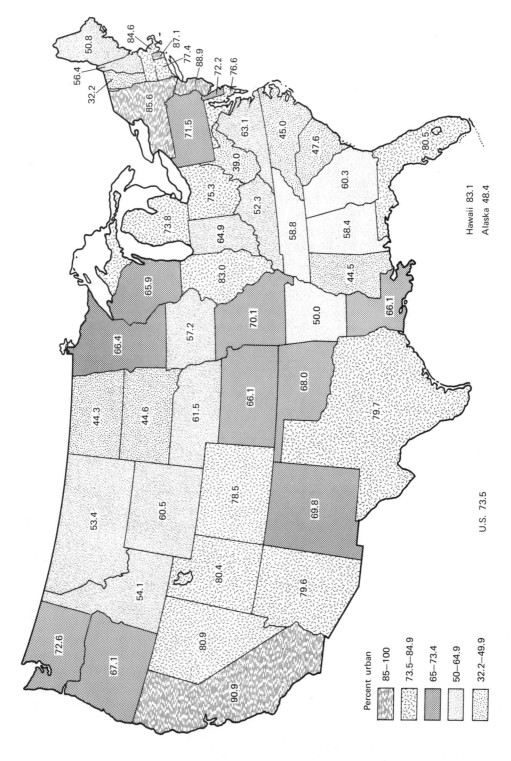

**Figure 4-9**  Percentage of urban population, by state, 1970. *Source. Census of Population: 1970.*

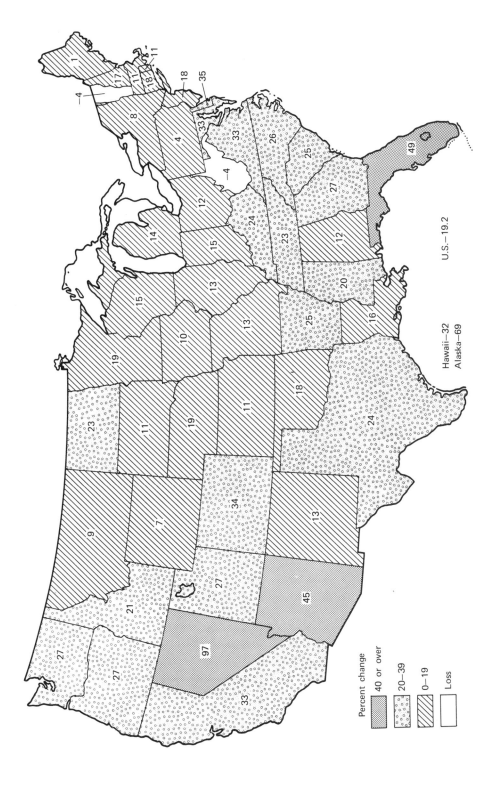

**Figures 4-10** Percent of change in urban population by state: 1960–1970. *Source: Census of Population: 1970.*

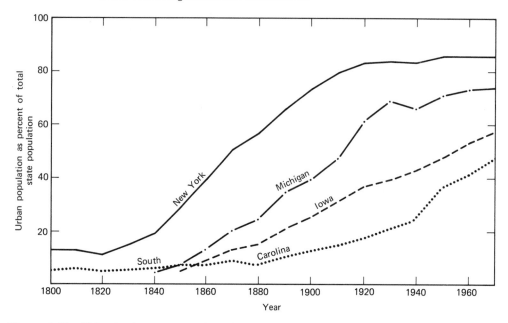

**Figure 4-11**   Urbanization curves: selected states, 1800–1970.

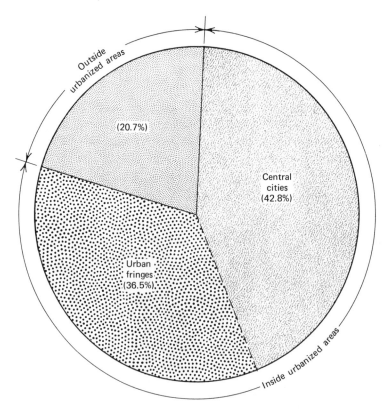

**Figure 4-12**   Composition of the U.S. urban population, 1970.
*Source*. Bureau of the Census. *Census of Population: 1970*.

**Table 4–6**  Composition of the Urban Population, 1970

| Type of Place and/or Size-Class | Number of Places | Population (Millions) | Percent of Urban Population |
|---|---|---|---|
| Total | 7,062 | 149.3 | 100.0 |
| Inside urbanized areas | 3,222 | 118.4 | 79.3 |
| Central cities | 308 | 63.9 | 42.8 |
| Cities of: | | | |
| 1,000,000 or more | 6 | 18.8 | 12.6 |
| 500,000 to 1,000,000 | 20 | 13.0 | 8.7 |
| 250,000 to 500,000 | 30 | 10.4 | 7.0 |
| 100,000 to 250,000 | 78 | 11.5 | 7.7 |
| 50,000 to 100,000 | 125 | 8.6 | 5.8 |
| Less than 50,000 | 49 | 1.6 | 1.1 |
| Urban fringe | 2,914 | 54.5 | 36.5 |
| Places of 2500 or more | 2,287 | 38.6 | 25.9 |
| 100,000 or more | 22 | 2.8 | 1.9 |
| 50,000 to 100,000 | 115 | 8.1 | 5.4 |
| 25,000 to 50,000 | 278 | 9.5 | 6.4 |
| 10,000 to 25,000 | 727 | 11.5 | 7.7 |
| 5,000 to 10,000 | 724 | 5.2 | 3.5 |
| 2,500 to 5,000 | 421 | 1.5 | 1.0 |
| Places less than 2,500 | 627 | .7 | .5 |
| 2,000 to 2,500 | 107 | .2 | .2 |
| 1,500 to 2,000 | 100 | .2 | .1 |
| 1,000 to 1,500 | 132 | .2 | .1 |
| Less than 1,000 | 288 | .2 | .1 |
| Other urban | — | 15.2 | 10.2 |
| Outside urbanized areas | 3,840 | 30.9 | 20.7 |
| Places of: | | | |
| 25,000 or more | 205 | 6.9 | 4.6 |
| 10,000 to 25,000 | 646 | 9.7 | 6.5 |
| 5,000 to 10,000 | 1,115 | 7.7 | 5.2 |
| 2,500 to 5,000 | 1,874 | 6.5 | 4.4 |

SOURCE:  Bureau of the Census, U.S. Census of Population, 1970, *Number of Inhabitants,* Final Report PC(1)–Al, *United States Summary* Government Printing Office, Washington, 1971, Table 4.

Plains and in some parts of the deep South have relatively low levels of urbanization, with the level in North and South Dakota below 45 percent, as it is in Mississippi (Figure 4–9).

Also note that there is a variation in the rate of urbanization of states, as there is in the level of urbanization. States that have the highest rates of urbanization tend to be in the Southwest (Nevada and Arizona), plus Florida and Alaska (Figure 4–10).

Considering both level of urbanization and rate of urbanization, one can place a given state into the context of the urbanization curve. Here, as in the cases of nations, the states with levels of urbanization in excess of about 75 percent have relatively low rates of urbanization. In this sense, they are in the terminal stage of the curve in which the curve is beginning to level off. By contrast, states with intermediate levels of urbanization (about 50 to 70 percent) tend to have the highest rates of urbanization. They could be placed in the acceleration stage of the urbanization curve, most likely near the upper end (Figure 4–11).

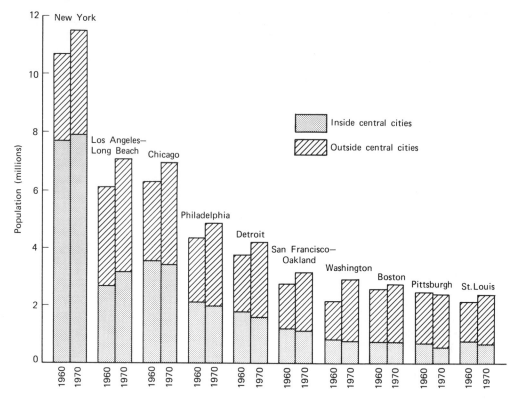

**Figure 4-13**   Population change: ten largest S.M.S.A.'s, 1960–1970. *Source.* Bureau of the Census. *Census of Population: 1970.*

## Structure and Trends in the Urban Population of the United States

The urban population of the country is found in a number of different urban settings. The greatest share, about 43 percent, lives in central cities (definition in Chapter 2), while another 37 percent lives in fringe areas peripheral to central cities. Thus, approximately four-fifths of the urban dwellers live in 248 urbanized areas in the country (Figure 4–12). The population of the fringe areas is divided among incorporated places, unincorporated places, and persons residing outside urban places yet within an urbanized area. About 21 percent or one-fifth of the urban population resides outside of urbanized areas, mostly in cities of 10,000 or more people (Table 4–6), while a smaller share resides in unincorporated places.

Various sectors of the urban population have experienced high rates of increase in recent years, others a moderate rate of increase, and some have shown a decline. The high rates of growth have mainly been in the fringes of urbanized areas, particularly in incorporated places that are suburbs of central cities that provide the residences for large numbers of people, but not the employment opportunities which remain concentrated in the central city. More and more of the urban population is comprised of daily commuters, creating several types of problems for central cities and suburbs alike. These are discussed in later chapters.

Regarding urban centers which had a population loss in recent years, there are two distinctly different types. The large central city in the midst of a metropolitan area is one of the types experiencing population loss. It is reported that 13 of the 25 largest central cities in the country

**Table 4–7**   Number of Declining Urban Centers, by Size Class (1940–1960)

| Size Class | Number of Declining Centers | Percent of Centers or Size Class | Cumulative Percent of Total Number |
|---|---|---|---|
| 1–500 | 3,789 | 57.3 | 62.8 |
| 501–1,000 | 920 | 28.2 | 78.0 |
| 1,000–1,500 | 370 | 16.5 | 84.2 |
| 1,501–2,000 | 208 | 15.6 | 87.6 |
| 2,001–3,000 | 183 ⎫ | | 90.7 ⎫ |
| 3,001–4,000 | 99 ⎬ | 11.2 | 92.3 ⎬ |
| 4,001–5,000 | 59 ⎭ | | 93.3 ⎭ |
| over 5,000 | 406 | 12.3 | 100.0 |
| Total | 6,034 | | |

SOURCE:   Modified from Ray M. Northam, *Annals* of the Association of American Geographers. March, 1963, Table 1.

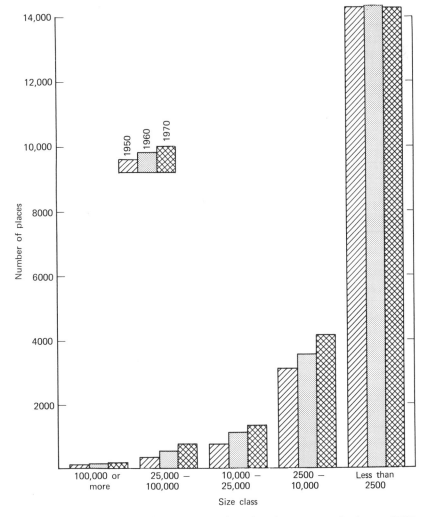

**Figure 4-14**  Number of incorporated and unincorporated places: 1950, 1960, 1970 by size class. *Source.* Bureau of the Census. *Census of Population: 1970 and 1960.*

suffered a population loss in the decade 1960 to 1970, with these including New York, Chicago, and Detroit among others (Figure 4–13). Interestingly, in cases where central cities had a loss of people, the urbanized areas of which they are parts had a population gain, a fact due to increases in the fringe areas which more than offset losses of the central city. This condition is so pronounced that fringe area residents now outnumber those living in central cities. The reasons for these happenings and their consequences are discussed later in this book.

A second type of urban center subject to population loss is the incorporated place of small size, especially one distant from a larger city of central city status. A recent study disclosed that, in the period 1940 to 1960, there were just over 6000 urban centers in the United States that experienced population decline. Of this number, nearly 88 percent had populations of 2000 or less, while only about 5 percent had more than 7000 people (Table 4–7).[6] The matter of decline of small centers is discussed more fully in Chapter 6. The overall structure of the urban population of the United States is shown graphically in Figure 4–14, which shows recent changes in the structure as well.

## Future Estimates: World and Major Regions

There are numerous methods by which population estimates for different points in the future can be made, but the longer the time period, the less reliable the estimates regardless of the method. Notwithstanding, demographers with the United Nations, using several accepted methods of making population projections, have produced estimates of future populations of the world and major world regions for different points in time to the year 2000. These estimates have

been disaggregated into (1) agglomerated population comprised of localized concentrations of 20,000 inhabitants or more, and (2) rural and small-town population, the latter consisting of localized concentrations of less than 20,000 inhabitants.

It is estimated that world population in 1980 will be about 4.3 billion and in 2000 it will be approximately 6.1 billion.[7] Of these estimated populations, it is considered that urban populations will comprise 46 percent in 1980 and 51 percent in 2000, both significant increases from the 33 percent in 1960. Two pertinent points about these increases concern the regions of the world in which they are likely to be most pronounced, and the nature of the increases projected —agglomerated population or rural and small-town population.

Regarding the first, population of the more developed regions of the world is projected to increase by approximately one-half in the forty-year period 1960 to 2000, while the population of the less developed world regions is projected to more than double (Figure 4–15). As to future increases in agglomerated population (concentrations of 20,000 people or more) in the more developed world regions, it is projected to rise from 389 million in 1960 to 784 million in 2000, a forty year increase of slightly over 100 percent, compared to a total population increase in such regions of 48 percent.[8] Projected increase in agglomerated population in less developed regions indicates a rise from 371 million in 1960 to 1553 million in 2000, for a forty year increase of well over one billion or 319 percent, contrasted with an increase in total

[6]Ray M. Northam, *Annals of the Association of American Geographers,* Vol. 53, No. 1, March, 1963.

[7]United Nations, *Growth of the World's Urban and Rural Population, 1920–2000,* Department of Economic and Social Affairs, Population Studies, No. 44, Table 32, New York, 1969. Also appears in abstract form in *Ekistics,* Vol. 29, No. 175 (June, 1970). Data included in subsequent passages of this section are taken or adapted from the United Nations publication cited.

[8]United Nations, *Ibid.*

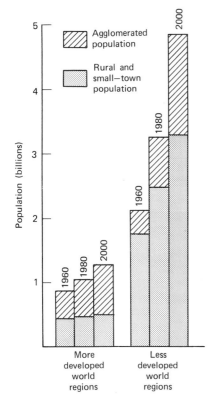

**Figure 4-15** Estimated population: 1960, 1980, 2000. *Source.* Based on data in United Nations, *Growth of the World's Urban and Rural Population, 1920–2000* (1969), Table 32.

population in less developed regions of 127 percent.

Significantly, in every one of the eight major world regions considered, the projected rate of increase of the agglomerated population outstrips the projected rate of increase of regional population. Thus, indications are that each of the major world regions will experience increased urbanization in years to come, not just urban growth. Even Europe, one of the more developed world regions, with the lowest projected rate of population increase in the period 1960 to 2000, is expected to have a rate of increase in urban population that far exceeds that of the general population (Figure 4–16). Of the more developed world regions, the Soviet Union is estimated to experience the greatest increase in degree of urbanization by the year 2000. Of the less developed world regions that include East

Asia, South Asia, Latin America, and Africa, each is projected to have an increase in agglomerated population that is twice or more than the increase in general population of the respective regions (Figure 4–16).[9] The degree of urbanization is projected to be greatest in East Asia and somewhat less so in Africa and South Asia.

To summerize remember that (1) reliable projections indicate that rates of increase in agglomerated population of the world are expected to be greater than rates of increase in general world population, that is, the process of world urbanization is expected to continue, and (2) rates of increase of agglomerated population and increase in degree of urbanization are expected to be greater in the less developed world regions than in the more developed regions.

## A Possible New Settlement Form in the Future

Given the projected increases in agglomerated populations of the world mentioned earlier where over half of the world's people likely will reside in urban concentrations by the year 2000, questions might be asked as to the types of settlements they will occupy. Certainly villages will grow into towns, towns into cities, and cities into metropolises. Also, new free-standing agglomerations likely will be formed (see Chapter 17), but there remain aspects of urban settlement forms to accommodate projected increased urbanization that might be overlooked.

As urban places grow in area and population, they also have increased contacts with other places by means of improved transportation and communications. The area within which the force or influence of the urban center is extended

[9]Treatment of urbanization in the less developed regions of the world is a major aspect of the multivolume International Survey of Urbanization conducted and published by the Ford Foundation in the period 1970–1972.

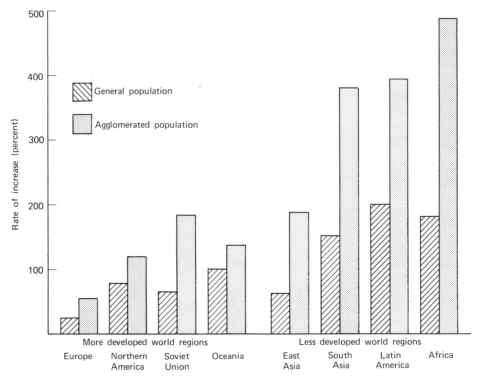

**Figure 4-16** Estimated rates of general and agglomerated population increase, 1960–2000; by world region. *Source.* Ibid., Figure 4-15.

might be referred to as the *kinetic field* of that place, with this established by the spatial expenditure of energy by the population of the place.[10] The extent of the kinetic field largely is determined by the population of the place, the energy expended by it, and by distances to other urban places, while its configuration is set by natural conditions, especially topography, and by transportation networks.

With kinetic fields expanding over time and area as a result of increased population and improvements in modes and routes of transportation, there is a gradual merging of kinetic fields of areally distributed urban settlements, both large and small, and an emergence of a complex system of interrelationships among urban centers. In this process, urban settlements that formerly were relatively free-standing, discrete entities are drawn into a complex system with each town or city becoming an integral part of the larger system. The name given to this emerging entity is *ecumenopolis*— a settlement form of great areal dimensions and population and with a number of major nodes or growth poles linked together into a network.[11]

It is suggested that in about a century, an ecumenopolis will span each of the world's inhabited continents (Figure 4–17). It is suggested that the ecumenopolis of Europe will have major nodes in northwestern Europe, northern Italy, and in the Belorussia-Ukraine area, with numerous linkages between these and other parts of the continent (Figure 4–18). Ecumenopolis of the United States will have the northeastern section as a major focus, with secondary outliers in California, Florida, and the Gulf Coast (Figure 4–19). Again, linkages in the

[10]For a discussion of kinetic fields, one might read C. A. Doxiadis' "Man's Movement and His Settlements," *Ekistics,* Vol. 29, No. 174 (May, 1970).

[11]One of the earliest formal statements on this topic was in Arnold Toynbee (Ed.), "Ecumenopolis: The Coming World-City," *Cities of Destiny,* Thames and Hudson, 1967.

ECUMENOPOLIS IN THE WORLD, 2060
Study by ACE, revised 1969

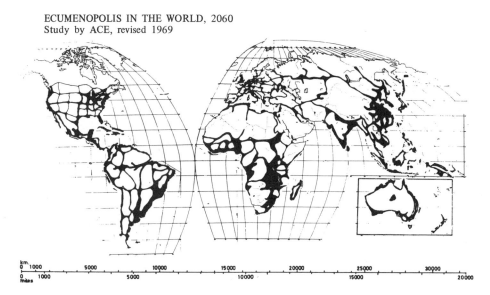

**Figure 4-17** Ecumenopolis in the world, 2060. From 'Man's Movement and His Settlements,' by C. A. Doxiadis; *Ekistics,* Vol. 29, May 1970.

ECUMENOPOLIS IN EUROPE, 2060
Study by ACE, revised 1969

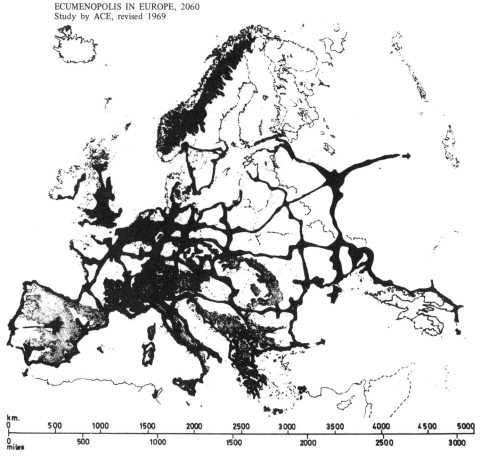

**Figure 4-18** Ecumenopolis in Europe, 2060. From 'Man's Movement and His Settlements,' by C. A. Doxiadis; *Ekistics,* Vol. 29, May 1970.

ECUMENOPOLIS IN THE USA
Study by ACE, 1968

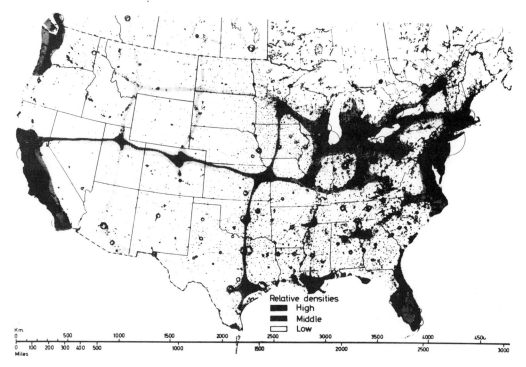

**Figure 4-19** Ecumenopolis in the U.S.A. From 'Man's Movement and His Settlements,' by C. A. Doxiadis; *Ekistics,* Vol. 29, May 1970.

form of growth corridors will tie these areas together and to outlying and intervening growth poles. In these and other land masses, the configuration of the ecumenopolis will be in accord with physical constraints on the growth pattern, such as the arid interior of Australia, and will constitute a melding of settlement outward from existing growth poles via growth corridors which also provide the transportation arteries.

Although the exact nature of ecumenopolis in the world and even the

liklihood of their formation within the next century are speculative, it may be logical to assume the evolution of such settlement forms if the projections of future urban population growth and increases in degree of urbanization are anywhere near correct. There has been an evolution of urban settlement forms in past millenia, as discussed in Chapter 3, and the concept of ecumenopolis is suggested as the next stage in this evolutionary process. However, only time will tell if such an eventuality is to occur.

# 5

# the urban environment and the livability of cities

In the past, the rationale for continued growth of population in urban centers, large and small, centered on the availability of employment opportunities and social facilities. More and more of the industrial effort came to be located in urban areas, as did the social facilities desired by an increasingly affluent population. In addition, there has been a concomitant increase in the concentration of tertiary activities in urban areas, especially trade and service industries, adding to the desirability of urban areas and to the supply of employment opportunities.

Along with the continued growth of urban centers, however, have come problems of an environmental nature and these have assumed crisis proportions in some areas. Of the gradual development of environmental problems of staggering proportions in the city, it is said by John V. Lindsay, recent mayor of New York City, that "Technology produced the crisis and technology can end it."[1] It would appear that the first hurdle to be overcome in dealing with an environmental crisis is to become aware of the existence and magnitude of the problem, the details of it, and the causes of it, before the problem can be alleviated or solved.

The general problem is that there has developed a progressively less livable urban environment that has become less attractive to present urban residents and to possible future migrants to the urban center as well. If a certain city has a marginal level of livability at present, extrapolation produces a dismal view of the livability of cities in the future, for it easily may fall below minimal levels. It is reported that livability in some cities today, based on spoilation of the urban environment, has already passed below minimal levels of livability, especially in some of the larger metropolitan centers.

## Types of Environmental Degradation

There are different ways in which the environment of cities has been degraded with some of these involving contamination of a natural resource on which the urban center depends. Other types of environmental degradation involve problems of the environment that do not involve the natural resource base, but deal with some societal aspect of the environment, rather than some physical aspect.

Of the two types of environmental degradation (physical and societal), it is

[1] John V. Lindsay, "The Plight of the Cities," *The Crisis of Survival*, Scott Foresman and Company, 1970, p. 43.

man who contributes most to the problems. Still, there is naturally occurring degradation of a physical nature, such as water pollution from vegetation or sediment in a water supply, or smoke from lightning-caused fires. In not all cases, then, is man the cause of environmental degradation, but in most cases he likely is.

Environmental degradation of a physical nature involves contamination or impairment of use of a naturally occurring element of man's environment in which the natural element is the vehicle by which the pollutant is dispersed or disseminated. Without the natural element as a vehicle of dispersal, the pollutant would be confined to a relatively small area and the adverse effects would remain more localized. Moving water is the vehicle for dispersal of water pollutants, while moving air is the vehicle for dispersal of air pollutants.

Environmental degradation of a societal nature is somewhat different because it involves environmental contamination of urban space, more than of a natural element. Furthermore, there is no vehicle involved in the dispersal of such degradation other than man himself.

Another distinction between physical and societal types of environmental degradation might be based on the hazard or effect experienced. Environmental degradation of a physical nature poses distinct threats or hazards to human health. It is not only an aggravation, it is a threat to physical health. Water pollution, air pollution, and noise pollution can all result in short-term, chronic, or fatal health problems. Societal types of environmental degradation, by contrast, are more in the realm of aggravation, nuisance, or blight and do not pose the same magnitude of problem of health that physical types do. This does not mean that societal types of degradation are unimportant, instead, it suggests differences in the severity of different types of problems. Solutions to physical problems of environmental degradation in the city are essential to survival of the population; solutions to societal problems of environmental degradation are essential to enhancement of livability for the population. Using the human body as an example, a tumor can destroy the life of the person; a wart or mole may make life less pleasant, but most likely will not destroy it.

## Physical Types of Environmental Degradation

One of the physical environmental problems of cities is the matter of water pollution, especially the pollution of surface waters. Most large cities in the United States rely on surface water supplies for municipal needs and these have become increasingly contaminated, largely through discharge of municipal and industrial wastes into adjacent rivers and lakes. Of the one-hundred largest cities in the country, sixty-seven obtain their water supplies from surface sources, nineteen from groundwater supplies, and fourteen from a combination of surface and groundwater sources (Figure 5–1). Surely, the sources of water pollution are not solely urban in nature, but with the bulk of the population now living in urban areas, urban dwellers constitute the largest population block affected by water pollution. Not only are surface water supplies endangered by water pollution, so are underground water supplies, although not likely to the same degree and as rapidly as surface supplies. Another contrast between surface and underground water supplies is that surface water supplies, in addition to withdrawal for consumptive use, have value as well for outdoor recreation, for aesthetic reasons, and for maintenance of aquatic life, and pollution lessens or destroys the utility of the water supply for all of these uses. One additional point with regard to water pollution is that the condition whereby a water supply is rendered less useable through pollution may be of short-term or a long-term nature. Because of the cyclic nature of stream

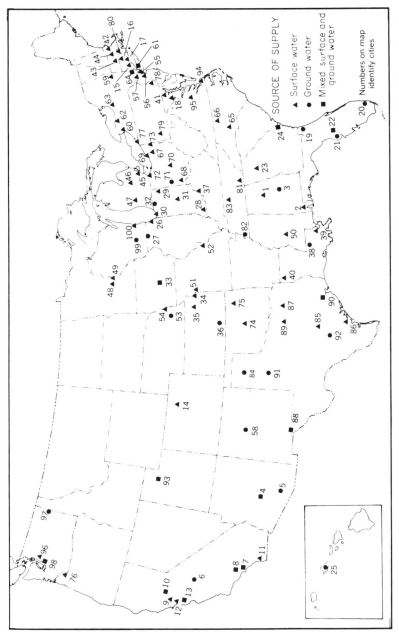

**Figure 5-1**  Sources of water for public water systems: 100 large American cities. (From U.S.G.S., Water Supply Paper 1871, 1968)

flows, the pollution levels of a stream during the time of low or minimum stream flow, usually in late summer, may reach harmful proportions. During periods of greater stream flow, however, the problem may be alleviated or reduced, which is to say that environmental degradation from water pollution may be of a seasonal nature as well as a year-around nature.

Specifically, water pollution results from the presence of substances in a body of water in sufficient amounts that they render the water less useable for most needs or, when carried to an extreme, render it unuseable for most purposes. The pollutants involved include (1) living organisms, such as bacteria and viruses, (2) oxygen-demanding organics, (3) oxygen consuming chemical materials, (4) sediments, (5) soluble minerals, and (6) heat.[2] Singly or in combination, these pollutants render the water supply less useable to man. The major sources of these water pollutants originating in or near urban areas are (1) sewered municipal wastes, (2) industrial water discharges, and (3) discharges from thermal electric generation plants (Figure 5–2).

With the increased acceptance and implementation of sewage treatment in urban areas, the volume of pollutants discharged into surface waters is progressively lessened. Still, there is substantial water pollution from this source—more from the discharge of solids than from oxygen-demanding material. However, it is reported that a greater volume of pollutant material originates from industrial waste discharge than from municipal sewer systems, both of oxygen demanding material and solid wastes (Table 5–1). Nationwide, industries discharge approximately three times the amount of each type of waste as do sewer systems of the country and, in this sense, are a more

serious cause of water pollution. Most certainly, not all the industrial waste originates in urban areas, but the greatest share likely does since industry is especially concentrated in urban areas. Furthermore, not all industries pollute water to the same degree and in the same manner, with the principal industrial offenders being the paper and allied products, the chemical and allied products, and the primary metals industries (Table 5–2). Of these industry types, paper and paper products manufacture is not generally part of urban industrial structure, while the others often are, as are the less offensive industrial polluters.

**Table 5–1**    Sources of Water Pollutants: By Major Type

| Source | Biochemical Oxygen-Demanding Material | Solids |
|--------|-----|-----|
| | (Millions of Pounds per Day) | |
| Sewered municipal wastes | 22.6 | 27.1 |
| Industrial waste discharge | 34.0 | 30.9 |

SOURCE:   Adapted from American Society of Engineering Education, *Interdisciplinary Research Topics in Urban Engineering,* Washington, D.C. (October, 1969).

To eliminate water pollution problems resulting from issuance of industrial waste, large investments must be made in waste treatment facilities. It is estimated that between one and three billion dollars of investment is needed to provide such facilities for the nation.[3] Because of regional variations in the distribution of industry, in the industrial mix, and of the severity of the problem, there are regional differences in the amount of investment needed to correct problems of industrial water pollution. The largest investments are needed in the North Atlantic, Great Lakes, Ohio River, and

[2]One interested in sources, quantity, and quality of water supplies of individual metropolitan areas should examine the following: Geological Survey, *Water Data for Metropolitan Areas,* Water Supply Paper 1871, Washington, Government Printing Office, 1968.

[3]Water Resources Council, *The Nation's Water Resources,* Washington, D.C., Government Printing Office, 1968.

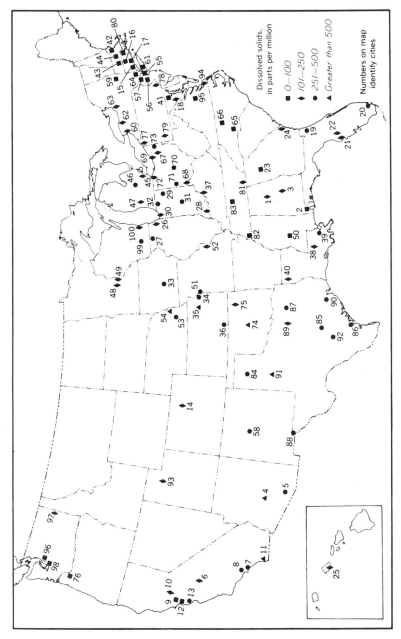

**Figure 5-2** Dissolved solids in untreated public water systems: 100 American cities. (Same source as Figure 5-1)

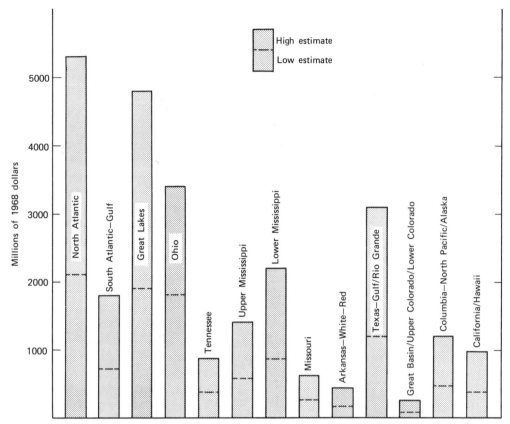

**Figure 5-3** Estimated regional investment required to eliminate industrial waste treatment deficiencies accumulated through 1968, by water resource region. *Source.* Based on data in *The Nation's Water Resources,* Water Resources Council, 1968.

Texas-Gulf/Rio Grande regions (Figure 5-3). Observe that these are estimated expenditures to correct existing problems of water pollution from industrial sources, and do not take into account the cost of eliminating problems associated with industrial expansion in the future. In other words, this is the estimated cost of corrective action, not the cost of preventative action.

Another form of water pollution is the heating of surface waters by discharges of thermal electric generating plants. The discharge of such plants is estimated to be 150 billion gallons of water per day which has been heated an average 13° above ambient (surrounding) temperatures.[4] In

addition to harm to aquatic ecosystems, there are certain undesirable results to humans from the acceleration of chemical reaction rates and increased solubility of waterborne materials by heated discharge waters.

Even if the point of discharge of pollutants of the types discussed is some distance from the urban center, if it is upstream and the urban area withdraws water at some point downstream, the burden and expense of treating the polluted water is increased if the water for the municipal system is to be rendered less harmful. Remember the saying "everyone is downstream from somewhere." Clearly, water pollution is a regional problem and not just an urban problem.

If surface waters in or adjacent to urban centers have become polluted, so

[4]American Society of Engineering Education, *Interdisciplinary Research Topics in Urban Engineering,* Washington, D.C., (October, 1969), p. 215.

**Table 5–2**   Estimated Volume of Industrial Wastes Before Treatment, 1963

| Industry | Wastewater (Billions of Gallons) | Biochemical Oxygen-Demand (Millions of Pounds) | Settleable and Suspended Solids (Millions of) Pounds |
|---|---|---|---|
| Primary metals | 4,300 | 480 | 4,700 |
| Chemicals and chemical products | 3,700 | 9,700 | 1,900 |
| Paper and allied products | 1,900 | 5,900 | 3,000 |
| Petroleum and coal | 1,300 | 500 | 460 |
| Food and kindred products | 690 | 4,300 | 6,600 |
| Transportation equipment | 240 | 120 | Not available |
| Rubber and plastics | 160 | 40 | 50 |
| Machinery (ex. electrical) | 150 | 60 | 50 |
| Textile mill products | 140 | 890 | Not available |
| Electrical machinery | 91 | 70 | 20 |
| All other manufacturing | 450 | 390 | 950 |
| All manufacturing | 13,100 | 22,000 | 18,000 |
| FOR COMPARISON: Sewered population of the U.S. | 5,300 | 7,300 | 8,800 |

SOURCE:   *The Nation's Water Resources*, Water Resources Council, 1968.

has much of the atmosphere above the urban centers. Air pollution has emerged as a major national environmental problem since it affects a large number of areas and a major part of the national population. The sources of air pollution, as with water pollution, are not confined to cities either. The major sources include automobile exhaust, emissions from industrial operations, and thermal electric generation plants and these are not limited to urban areas, but do have their greatest levels of occurrence in urban areas. Hence, the problems we attribute to them are most likely to occur in urban regions. The problems of air pollution have become so great that in some cities the amount of effluent into the atmosphere is monitored and recorded through instrumentation, and when conditions are ripe for air pollution and the pollution levels become sufficient to create a hazard to health and well-being, pollution alerts are issued. During such periods, certain industrial operations are placed on a reduced level of operation, thermal electric plants reduce their output and, in extreme cases, limits are placed on the use of motor vehicles, especially in high traffic density areas. Other controls, too, might be placed on urban

residents during periods of high air pollution or in periods when natural conditions are favorable for air pollution. These include restrictions on backyard trash burning, garbage burning, and land clearance.

It is estimated that about 173 million tons of contaminants are released into the nation's atmosphere annually.[5] These come from various sources and are of several types of which carbon monoxide is the major contributor, making up just over one-half of the total volume of contaminants (Table 5–3). Just over three-fourths (77 percent) of the carbon monoxide comes from motor vehicles such as automobiles and busses. Another major type of air contaminant is hydrocarbons which account for about 23 million tons of contaminant or just over 13 percent of the total volume (Table 5–3). The major source of this contaminant, like carbon monoxide, is the motor vehicle. Further contamination of the atmosphere comes from nitrogen oxides, nearly half of these from motor vehicles, and from particulate matter and sulfur oxides. Particulate matter refers to small

[5]American Society of Engineering Education. *Interdisciplinary Research Topics in Urban Engineering*, Washington, D.C., (October, 1969).

particles of solid material temporarily suspended in the air, while the other contaminants referred to are gasses. Particulate matter results mainly from non-vehicular sources, except in the case of lead particulate stemming from the use of motor fuels that contain amounts of lead. Sulfur oxides also come mainly from nonvehicular sources and only a small share comes from the use of motor vehicles. The highest levels of atmospheric contamination by particulate matter and sulfur oxides occur in areas where coal and residual fuel oil are the primary power sources, such as in the urbanized northeastern seaboard of the United States, otherwise known as Megalopolis. Another form of air pollution is *photochemical smog* which is a complex mixture of gasses and particulates that is produced from the interaction of sunlight and nitrogen oxides and hydrocarbons.

**Table 5–3** Major Sources of Air Contaminants in the United States

| Contaminant | Annual Volume (Millions of Tons) | Proportion of Total Volume (Percent) |
|---|---|---|
| Carbon monoxide | 87 | 50.3 |
| Hydrocarbons | 23 | 13.3 |
| Nitrogen oxides | 18 | 10.4 |
| Particulate matter | 15 | 8.7 |
| Sulfur oxides | 30 | 17.3 |
| Totals | 173 | 100.0 |

SOURCE: Adapted from American Society of Engineering Education, *Interdisciplinary Research Topics in Urban Education*, Washington, D.C., (October, 1969), Figure B–1.

Levels of air pollution, like other forms of pollution, vary from place to place and time to time. These variations reflect spatial and temporal differences in (1) population density and character, (2) concentrations of vehicular traffic, (3) agglomerations of industrial activities, (4) physiographic or landform elements, and (5) meterological conditions. Since these factors vary over large expanses of earth surface and not just within a given urban center, the problems resulting are basically regional in nature.

Even so, with regard to population densities, vehicular traffic volumes, and industrial activities as factors associated with the incidence of air pollution, it would logically follow that it is within urban regions that each of these contributors is found to the greatest degree. Moreover, thermal electric generating plants commonly are within or adjacent to urban centers (Figure 5–4). Thus, it is within or near major urban centers that the contaminants leading to air pollution are spewed into the atmosphere in the greatest volumes.

In a given large city, the highest levels of air pollution occur in the core area of the central city, gradually becoming less toward the periphery (Figure 5–5). Since pollution levels vary with location in the urban area, as does the type of pollution, they vary as well among cities depending on the nature and location of the city. Evaluating 298 cities in the United States on a scale of one through five, with five the most severe condition, over 40 percent experience the most acute levels of suspended particulates (Table 5–4).[6] On the same scale, a similar percentage of cities have the most serious degrees of incidence of sulfur dioxide and nitrogen dioxide. Large cities with highest levels of particulate matter include Los Angeles, Denver, Chicago, Indianapolis, Baltimore, Detroit, St. Louis, New York, Philadelphia, and Pittsburgh (Figure 5–6). Major cities with especially high incidence of sulfur and nitrogen dioxide include New Haven, Washington, Chicago, Indianapolis, Baltimore, Boston, St. Louis, New York, Cleveland, Pittsburgh, and Providence (Figure 5–6). By and large, the cities with the highest levels of air pollution are industrial cities in the American Manufacturing Belt,

[6]Public Health Service, *Air Pollution — A National Sample*, Washington, D.C., Govt. Printing Office, 1966.

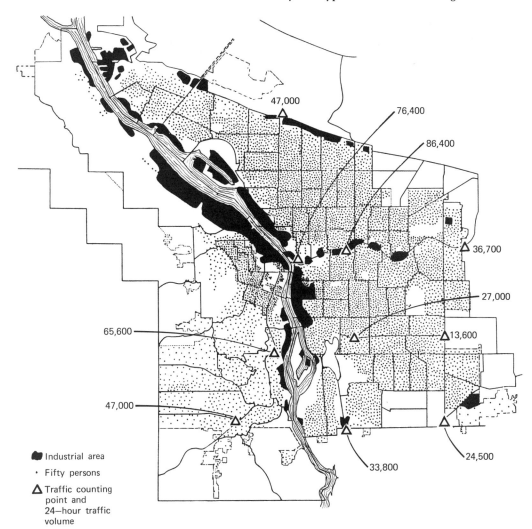

**Figure 5-4**   Association of populaltion, industrial areas, and high volumes of vehicular traffic Portland, Oregon. *Source.* Portland City Planning Commission, *Portland's Residential Areas* (October 1965); and *Portland's Industrial Areas* (April 1967). Oregon State Highway Division, *1969 Traffic Flow Map* (1969).

larger cities outside this region, and those with some unusual industrial or physical characteristic conducive to pollution buildup. There are no cities, of the many sampled with instrumentation, that are free from all sources of air pollution, although there are differences among cities in the levels and types of air pollution.

Once again, the incidence of air pollution problems is most pronounced in urban areas. Generally, the degree or level of air pollution varies with the sea-

son of the year, with the day of the week, and with certain hours of the day. There is a tendency for greater concentrations of sulfur dioxide and nitrogen dioxide in the urban atmosphere in winter, which is also true of fine particulates (Figure 5–7).[7] During this season, there is greater use of sulfur-bearing fuels for space heating and electric power production. Also, there are differences between air pollution levels on different days of the week,

[7]Public Health Service, *Ibid.*

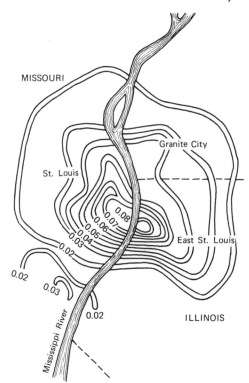

**Figure 5-5** Sulfur dioxide levels from central city outward. *Source*. United States Public Health Service Publication No. 1562.

with weekdays being worse in this respect than weekend days, especially Sunday (Figure 5–8). This basically is the result of greater use of motor vehicles in central cities on weekdays. Regardless of the day of the week, there tend to be variations in

**Table 5–4**  Pollution Levels in American Cities: By Type of Pollutant

|  | Number of Cities | | |
|---|---|---|---|
| Level of Occurrence | Suspended Particulates | Sulfur Dioxide | Nitrogen Dioxide |
| I (lowest) | 63 | 9 | 8 |
| II | 54 | 12 | 9 |
| III | 59 | 10 | 11 |
| IV | 62 | 10 | 10 |
| V (highest) | 60 | 12 | 11 |
| Totals | 298 | 53 | 49 |

SOURCE:  Adapted from Public Health Service, *Air Pollution—A National Survey*, 1966.

pollutant levels at different hours of the day (Figure 5–8). There is a tendency toward a bimodal pattern with the highest levels of pollutants occurring in the hours of mid-morning when rush hour traffic occurs, heating plants are starting up, and electric generation is increased. A secondary but broader peak period occurs in the hours of late afternoon and early evening, accompanying a second period of rush hour traffic and poor conditions of natural ventilation.

Concerning the physical conditions favorable to air pollution once the pollutants are issued into the atmosphere, no single condition is solely involved, but a combination of conditions can collectively lead to a dangerous air pollution level. Consider an urbanized area that is nestled between two parallel mountain barriers at right angles to the prevailing winds or one that occupies a basin surrounded by topographic obstructions. Prevailing winds of the region may be insufficiently strong to surmount the mountain barriers or may be deflected by the topographic barriers so they do not pass over the urban areas. In either case, *natural ventilation* will be so inadequate that buildups of atmospheric contaminants will not be carried away from the urban area producing them.

Another condition leading to high levels of air pollution exists even in urban areas without nearby topographic barriers to natural ventilation. A normal atmospheric process involves the cooling of air as it rises from the surface so that air temperatures at a level hundreds or thousands of feet above the surface are lower than those at the surface. An anomalous condition exists, however, in which a layer of air above the surface may be warmer than air beneath it and this layer may remain stagnant for a period as long as several days. This condition is known as a *temperature inversion* and the layer or lens of relatively warm air is known as the *inversion layer*. A temperature inversion has the effect of creating a type of atmospheric lid which traps the

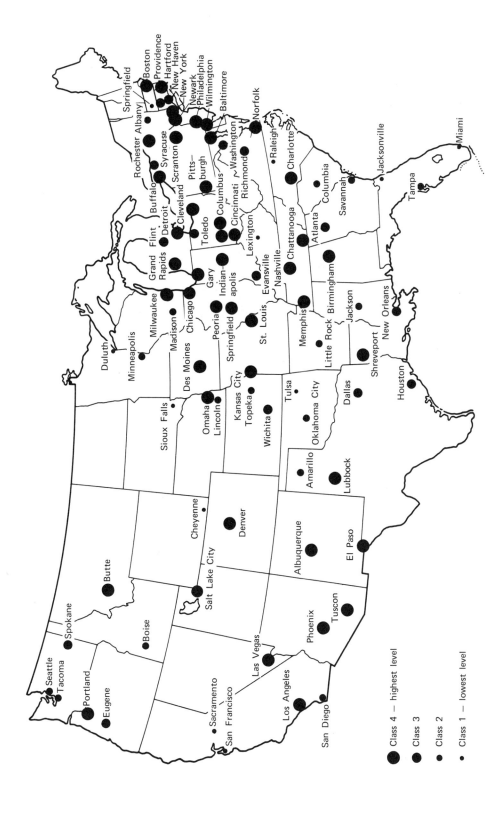

**Figure 5-6a** Suspended particulate levels in selected American cities. *Source.* Based on data in Public Health Service Publication No. 1562, 1966.

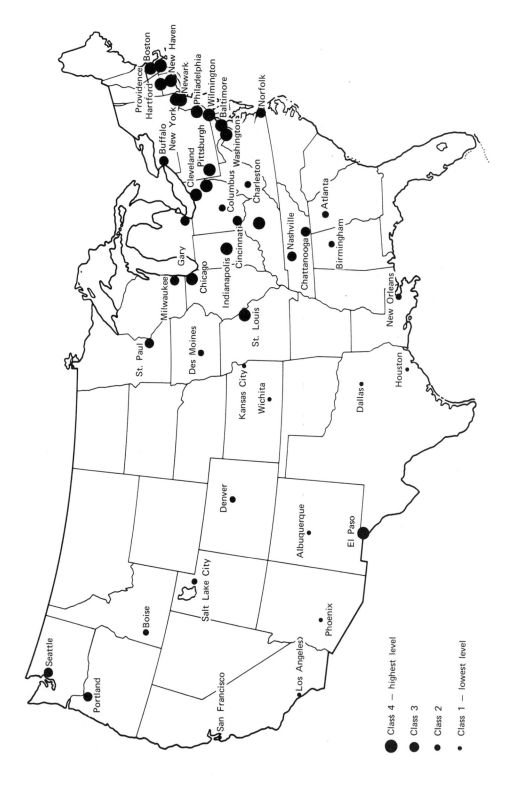

**Figure 5-6b**    Sulfur dioxide levels in selected American cities. *Sources.* Ibid., Figure 5-6a.

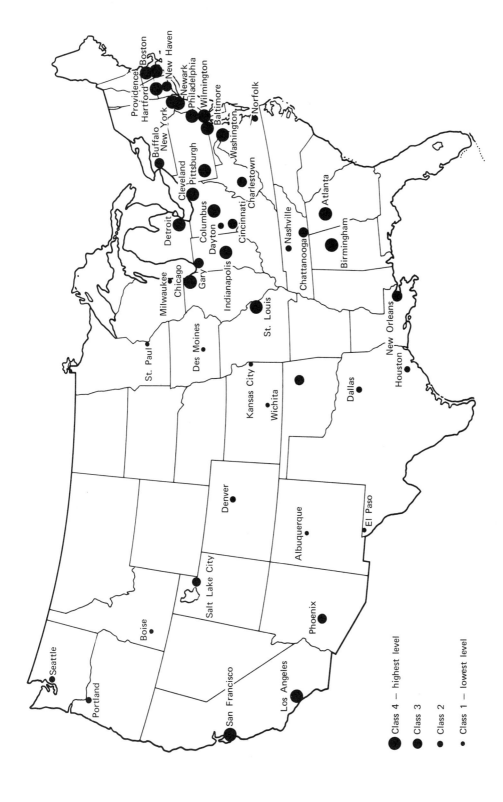

**Figure 5-6c**   Nitrogen dioxide levels in selected American cities. *Source.* Ibid., Figure 5-6a.

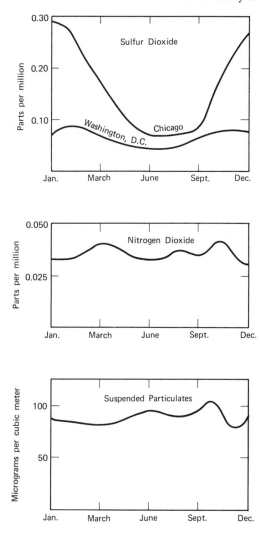

**Figure 5-7** Monthly incidence of sulfur dioxide, nitrogen dioxide, and suspended particulates. *Source.* Based on United States Public Health Service Publication No. 1562, 1966.

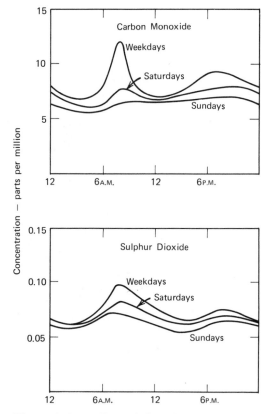

**Figure 5-8** Daily and hourly variation of selected gaseous pollutants. *Source.* Public Health Service Publication No. 1562, 1966.

air beneath it. Thus, the air beneath the inversion layer becomes increasingly polluted and will remain so until finally disseminated by an inflow of surface winds. This condition can exist during calm periods when surface winds are extremely weak or absent. In some urban areas where this condition has persisted for a number of days, the situation created has become so extreme and hazardous that a limited pollution alert has been issued, calling for a curtailment of those activities that contribute substantially to air pollution.

There are different types of temperature inversions, based on the conditions favorable to their development. One type involves the cooling of air near the surface by conduction of radiated heat back to the surface, leaving a layer of air above the cooled layer that is warm, relative to the surface layer (Figure 5–9). In this case, a *surface inversion* is produced and the inversion layer acts as a lid on atmospheric pollutants that are spewed forth into the lower atmosphere with this condition continuing until there is an influx of moving air to disperse the inversion layer. Another type of inversion is one that results from topographic conditions — the *topographic inversion.* In this instance, cool air moves downslope with the build-up of a layer of cool air near the surface of a topographic basin or valley. Above this cool layer, there is a layer of relatively warmer air that exists beneath a

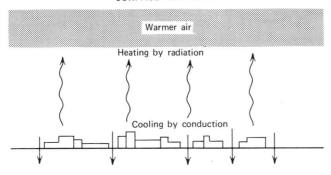

SURFACE INVERSION

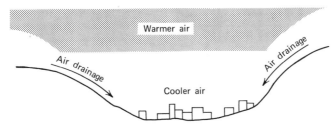

TOPOGRAPHIC INVERSION

**Figure 5-9**   Types of temperature inversions.

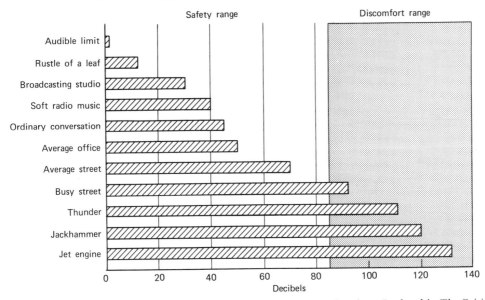

**Figure 5-10**   Levels of common noises. *Source.* Adapted from Theodore Berland in *The Crisis of Survival* Scott, Foresman & Co. (1970).

mass of cooler air, the latter serving to contain the inversion layer (Figure 5–9). Here too, the lens of warmer air acts as a lid on the lower atmosphere and normally will persist only until continued inflow of air by air drainage downslope

dissipates the conditions favorable to its formation. Many times, however, air drainage leads to the formation of the inversion layer and then ceases, so that circulation of the lower atmosphere is retarded for some time and pollutants is-

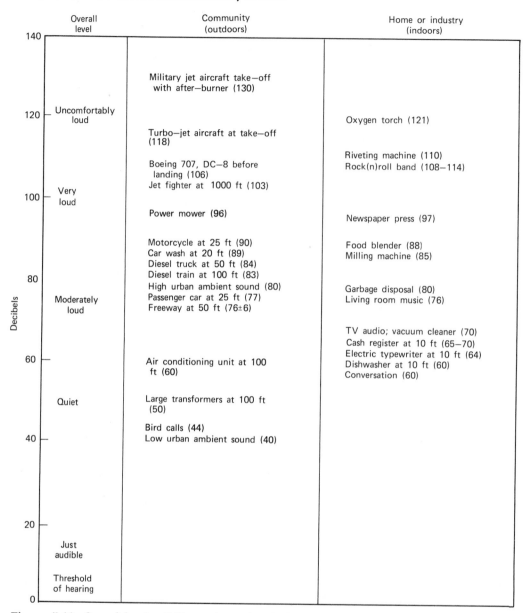

**Figure 5-11**   Sound levels of illustrative noises in indoor and outdoor enviroments. *Source.* Adapted from Melville C. Branch, *Traffic Quarterly* (April 1971).

sued into the lower levels of the atmosphere continue to accumulate, creating severe pollution conditions.

But what are the dangers of air pollution? There are forms of damage by air pollution to vegetation and property, but more important is the danger to human life and well-being. Quite commonly, air pollution leads to problems of discomfort and irritation like particulate matter that falls in small, dustlike particles on clothing or in the eyes or perhaps there is discomfort from an offensive odor that pervades the entire region. More serious, however, are the problems of air pollution that lead to disability or even death. High levels of air pollution are associated with such chronic diseases as asthma, bronchitis, emphysema, and lung cancer. When levels of air pollution are extreme and persist for an extended period, death may result. In London in 1952, protracted and extremely intense air pollution resulted in an estimated 3500 to 4000 deaths. In Danora, Pennsylvania in 1948, 20 persons died and thousands were made sick as a result of air pollution. New York City, in different periods in 1963, lost 405 persons because of atmospheric contamination. This is, of course, the ultimate consequence from creation of an unlivable urban environment.

Another form of contamination of the urban environment is excessive noise. Noise or ear pollution is an urban environmental problem that has only recently received much attention, yet it has been decades in the making. The perception of noise as a problem is different for different people. Noise at certain levels might be an aggravation or nuisance for some, while at higher levels, noise might become a more widespread or general aggravation or nuisance. At still higher levels, noise might fall within the "discomfort range" and at even higher levels, urban noise might lead to types of physical and psychological damage (Figure 5–10). Noise above 75 decibels can produce temporary changes in the physiological state of man and the same source reports that "noise is registered by and affects the unconscious mind and central nervous system as an irritant. . . ."[8]

The most popular measure of noise level is the decibel.[9] Some people feel discomfort when noise levels reach 85 decibels, but most do not until the noise level reaches 115 decibels. At about 145 decibels, people begin to experience physical pain, especially if the noise is of prolonged duration. The noise level in the American kitchen, filled with the usual array of appliances, often reaches 100 decibels. The urban environment is degraded by noise from a variety of sources, many of them vehicular. Trucks and busses generate noise as high as 100 decibels, 100 feet from the roadway, while motorcycles produce noise levels in the 95 to 120 decibel range.[10] In various forms, then, excessive noise renders the urban environment less livable.

Loudness alone is not the sole cause of noise problems, although this is the most apparent characteristic of noise that creates environmental problems. Pitch of the noise also influences the degree of annoyance—the higher the pitch, the greater the annoyance. Intermittency of noise also influences the degree of annoyance. Intermittent noises are those that change in rate of intensity or frequency and noise with the more pronounced intermittency has a higher degree of annoyance, like the blast of an automobile horn or the operation of a garbage truck with hydraulic loading devices. Duration of the noise also determines how annoying or irritating noise will be, with the degree of annoyance greater with exposure to noises of longer duration. Also influencing noise problems is the man-made environment within which the noise occurs. A given noise in an enclosed space, such as a dowtown city street surrounded by multistory buildings, will take on the dimensions of a noise problem, while the same noise occurring in an area of open space will not appear to be as serious. In the same vein, traffic noise from a depressed highway will not annoy as much as the same noise from a surface highway.

Regarding the sources of noise that bother urban dwellers, a recent study of noise problems in major cities disclosed the same general sources of noise problems, but the degree to which a given

[8]Melville C. Branch, Jr., "Outdoor Noise, Transportation, and City Planning," *Traffic Quarterly*, Vol. XXV, No. 2 (April, 1971).

[9]The decibel is the basic measure of the intensity of sound and is one-tenth of a larger unit, the bel. One decibel is the equivalent of the faintest sound that can be heard. It is not a linear unit, such as the inch, but a logarithmic unit.

[10]Theodore Berland, "Up to Our Ears in Noise," *The Crisis of Survival*, Scott Foresman and Company, 1970.

**Table 5–5**   Sources of Noise Considered as Bothersome by Respondents: Los Angeles, Boston, and New York

| Source of Bothersome Noise | Los Angeles | | | Boston | | | | New York | | | |
|---|---|---|---|---|---|---|---|---|---|---|---|
| | All Incomes | Middle Income | Low Income | All Incomes | High Income | Middle Income | Low Income | All Incomes | High Income | Middle Income | Low Income |
| | (Percent of Total) | | | (Percent of Total) | | | | (Percent of Total) | | | |
| Traffic | 13 | 13 | 13 | 17 | 13 | 21 | 17 | 14 | 19 | 13 | 14 |
| Sonic boom | 13 | 17 | 6 | — | — | — | — | — | — | — | — |
| Children/neighbors | 11 | 13 | 6 | 6 | 3 | 8 | 8 | 25 | 19 | 20 | 33 |
| Animals | 11 | 10 | 13 | 5 | 13 | 2 | 0 | 2 | 5 | 0 | 3 |
| Others | 9 | 10 | 6 | 4 | 0 | 4 | 8 | 8 | 5 | 13 | 6 |
| Planes | 4 | 7 | 0 | 9 | 15 | 8 | 0 | 2 | 0 | 5 | 0 |
| Motorcycles | 2 | 3 | 0 | 2 | 3 | 2 | 0 | 3 | 0 | 8 | 0 |
| Trains | 2 | 0 | 6 | — | — | — | — | 1 | 0 | 0 | 3 |
| Sirens/horns | — | — | — | 3 | 0 | 2 | 0 | 7 | 19 | 8 | 0 |
| Industry | — | — | — | 5 | 0 | 8 | 8 | 1 | 0 | 3 | 0 |
| Passersby | — | — | — | — | — | — | — | 6 | 5 | 13 | 0 |
| Not bothered | 35 | 27 | 50 | 50 | 54 | 43 | 58 | 30 | 29 | 20 | 42 |

SOURCE:   Department of Housing and Urban Development, *Noise in Urban and Suburban Areas*, January, 1967.

noise source was a problem varied among cities.[11] Also, the degree to which a noise source was a problem varied with different income levels (Table 5–5). Notice, for example, the difference in perception of noise from industry as a problem for high and low income groups in Boston. Also, observe the differences in perception of noise from trains as a problem for middle and low income groups in Los Angeles. And also note that vehicles of one type or another account for the greatest share of bothersome noise in New York, Los Angeles, and Boston. Thus, although it is difficult to measure and evaluate, noise from a number of sources is an urban problem because it contributes to overall environmental degradation.

Noise as an urban problem has gradually become more pronounced. Notice that ambient or background noise levels can range from 40 decibels during early morning hours to 80 decibels in the noisiest part of the day. Interestingly, but unfortunately, ambient noise levels in urban areas in the 1936 to 1963 period increased by an average of one decibel per year or 25 decibels in 25 years.[12] Remember, however, that the cost-benefit ratio for noise abatement is more favorable than it is for water and air pollution alleviation, since noise abatement does not involve large fixed capital investments.

## Societal Types of Environmental Degradation

There are other ways, besides water, air, and noise pollution, that the urban environment is made less livable. Vehicular congestion on city streets is a type of environmental contaminant of a societal nature, as is the accumulation of solid waste, including large numbers of aban-

doned automobiles. General dilapidation of structures, especially residential buildings, can be a form of environmental impairment. Certainly, this is true if the dwelling units house vermin and rodents which create a health hazard.

The form of societal environmental degradation created by abandonment of motor vehicles, although widespread, is often neglected. The approximately 828 thousand abandoned cars in the U.S. in 1965, about 10 percent of the autos retired in that year, represent a form of environmental blight in several respects.[13] The problem too is getting progressively worse as time passes with more vehicles on the streets and highways. There are areal variations in the rate of abandoned auto removal in the United States, with rates highest in the Midwest, the northern Great Plains, and the Far West (Figure 5–12). Further, there are variations in removal rates between cities of different sizes, with the rate being 1.4 vehicles removed from public property per 1,000 persons in cities with populations under 50,000, and 3.1 per 1000 persons in cities with populations of 500,000 or more.[14] In general, the removal rate increases with size of the city.

Autos are abandoned for a variety of reasons, the major ones being (1) vehicle failure or breakdown, (2) cost of disposing of vehicles in other ways, and (3) ignorance of alternate methods of disposal (Figure 5–13). About one-third of the autos abandoned in the country are left in urban centers, largely on city streets and on other city property and once left, the autos usually are removed by city removal crews or by private wrecking companies.[15] In either case, the abandoned autos may be taken to a municipal

[11]Department of Housing and Urban Development, *Noise in Urban and Suburban Areas*, Washington, D.C., (January, 1967).

[12]Melville C. Branch, Jr., *Op. Cit.*

[13]George E. Kanaan, "Debris of the Motor Age," *Traffic Quarterly*, Vol. XXIV, No. 3 (July, 1970).

[14]Department of Commerce, *Motor Vehicle Abandonment in U.S. Urban Areas*, Washington, March, 1967.

[15]Department of Commerce, *Ibid.*

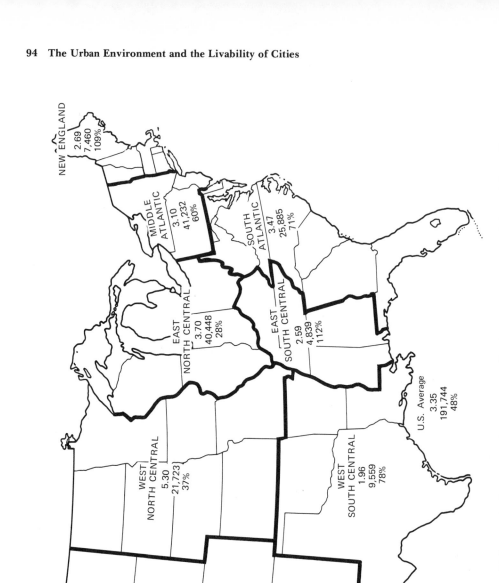

**Figure 5-12**   Removal of abandoned motor vehicles: United States and geographic divisions (1965). *Source.* Adapted from Department of Commerce, *Motor Vehicle Abandonment in U.S. Urban aAreas* (March 1967).

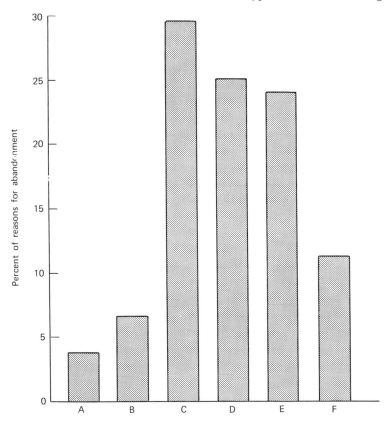

**Figure 5-13** Reasons for motor vehicle abandonment. (A) Vehicle could not be disposed of because title was lost. (B) Vehicle could not be disposed of because title was encumbered. (C) Vehicle was abandoned on street or highway because of breakdown. (D) Vehicle could have been disposed of by owner to auto wrecker or scrap processor, but it would have cost owner more than he was willing to pay. (E) Owner did not know how to dispose of vehicle other than by abandonment. (F) Other. *Source.* Based on data in Department of Commerce, *Motor Vehicle Abandonment in U.S. Urban Areas,* (March, 1967).

lot where, after a prescribed interval for retrieval by the owner, they are disposed of with wrecking yards or scrap metal dealers for sale to metal recovery operations. The average price paid for vehicles disposed of from municipal impounding lots in 1965 was approximately $32, compared with a direct municipal cost of $5 to 10 for removal to an impoundment lot where the abandoned vehicles usually are held for 30 to 90 days.[16]

In this process, there is impairment of

the urban environment by the abandoned cars and direct expense to the municipality in their removal and impoundment. Furthermore, with the fluctuations in price of scrap metal, there is no assurance that outlets for abandoned cars through recycling in steel mills will be as likely as in the past. Therefore, space needs for impounded autos and costs of removal are likely to mount as more and more vehicles are abandoned in the future.

The abandoned auto is but one form of a larger problem which is solid waste dis-

[16]Department of Commerce, *Op. Cit.*

posal. This problem is of mounting magnitude in large and small cities and essentially involves the disposal of the garbage of a modern society that is not biodegradable. Included here are the host of wornout household appliances, general machinery parts, plastic items, and general metal debris. This material accumulates in vast amounts and is difficult to dispose of. A commonly used method has been the "land-fill" in which the solid waste is mixed with earth material to fill inundated areas, depressions, and similar areas with little or no potential for development without improvement. The problems connected with land-fill are several and include the fact that there is a limited number of sites that can be used for land-fill and the movement of solid waste to the land-fill site is difficult and expensive, since the solid waste is derived from a multitude of origins. Land-fill has been used to extend shorelines in some urban areas and perhaps could be employed to fill old abandoned quarries or sand and gravel pits. The alternative of transporting solid waste by barge to some distance offshore where it is dumped is not an acceptable alternative.

The matter of urban environmental degradation by dilapidated or run-down housing is discussed in Chapter 12. Environmental degradation by garish and tasteless commercial ribbon developments and outdoor advertising is discussed in Chapter 11. It suffices at this point to mention that these are but two additional ways in which the urban environment is degraded and, in the process, is made somewhat less livable.

## Urban Growth and Environmental Degradation

Can we assume, if the urban environment becomes less livable in future years, that the populations of urban centers will become less as a consequence or at least, that they will become relatively stabilized? In other words, will there likely be a reversal of the urbanization curve or a flattening of it? There are many facets to the answer and no firm one can be given yet. To develop an answer, however, bear in mind the basic elements of population change, including birth rates, death rates, and migration.

Given a hypothetical urban center with an initial population of 100,000 persons, one might consider what the population of this center would likely be after the passage of a full decade if (1) national birth rates and death rates continue at the level at which they were in 1965, and (2) there is no inmigration or outmigration from the urban center in question. The birth rate in the United States in 1965 was 19.4 per 1000 persons and the death rate was 9.4 per 1000 persons. The numerical difference between birth rate and death rate, then, was 10.0 per 1000 persons, or ten additional persons at the end of the first year of the decade for each 1000 residents during that year. The rate of natural increase, then, is one percent per year. During this ten year span there is, in this hypothetical case, no increment or loss to the urban population through inmigration or outmigration, yet at the end of the decade the population would have increased by 10,463 persons or by 10.46 percent over the population of the urban center in the initial year. Even if birth rates were reduced substantially during the decade, the death rate also is likely to lessen due to advances in geriatrics and general health care. The end result is the inevitable increase in urban population solely through natural increases.

Thus, even if the urban environment becomes so unlivable that it loses its attractiveness to people, causing migration to urban centers to cease completely, there would still be growth of the urban centers of the nation and of the world. Would the solution be an exodus of people presently residing in urban centers? If so, to where would they go? To another urban center that would then experience urban growth from inmigration, as well as from natural increases?

Would the solution be a striking reduction in birth rates that would bring them in line with death rates, creating a rate of natural increase of zero? This is an idealistic solution; the reality is that man does not seem ready yet to follow such a course.

Or is the solution more likely to be that expoused by John Lindsay: "Technology produced the crisis and technology can end it."? [17] Environmental degradation is neither welcome nor desired, but then neither are sickness or death and famine or flood. Hopefully, however, it is within the capabilities of man to rid himself of the problems of environmental degradation.

[17] Lindsay, *op. cit.*

# 6

# urban hierarchies and urban regions

In the United States, there are no natural breaks in the size distribution curve of urban centers arrayed from smallest to largest, yet it is desirable to group urban centers of approximately the same size into discrete size-groups, for example, 50,000 to 100,000 or 250,000 to 500,000, and this is what is done by the Bureau of the Census and by those involved in study of cities. By arrangement of size-classes of progressively larger or smaller populations, an ordering of size-classes is formed, with different size-classes taking on a specified rank-size order in which the largest size-class may be referred to as rank-order I, the next highest size-class rank-order II, and so on through the entire array of size-classes. Most classifications, such as those discussed in Chapter 2, incorporate a number of variable items for assignment of a specific urban center to a certain class, for example, a high proportion of manufacturing employment as the basis for identifying manufacturing cities, or a high proportion of employment in retail and wholesale trade to identify trade centers, etc. In the case of the development of a rank-size ordering of cities, the single variable is population and differences in magnitude of population serve to distinguish different orders or levels in a *rank-size hierarchy* which is the topic explored in this chapter.

In other instances, however, an urban hierarchy may be developed using a different variable, such as the number of functions performed in the cities of the region. In this case, one is dealing with a *functional hierarchy* of cities within a spatial framework. We might have a case in which one group of cities will be identified as "low-order trade centers," and another group as "high-order trade centers." The common characteristic recognized is trade and there are different orders of cities with this function, depending on the number of functions performed. The elements of functional hierarchies of cities are detailed in Chapter 7; the purpose here is to recognize that conceptually this is a hierarchy similar to one that may be based on population.

Notice too that the terminology often used in reference to urban centers basically is a recognition of rank-size hierarchies. Terms such as "village," "town," and "city" have a connotation of a rank-size hierarchy without benefit of formal definition. Similarly, terms such as "local trade center," "regional capital," and the like have connotations of a functional hierarchy, again without benefit of clear definition.

Already, the reader has been introduced to the idea of a hierarchical nature of urban centers, so the aim here is to explore in more detail the elements of several of these hierarchies as they are evident in two dimensional space. It is important to deal with urban hierarchies; to do otherwise would be to examine a single entity without regard for the entire structure of which the single entity is a part. Only by considering the hierarchical arrangement of urban centers, can relationships among urban centers be fully dealt with. This line of study might be likened to one studying the human heart without regard for its role as a part of the physiological system of the entire body. To study the single city without regard for the urban system of which it is a part is equally limited and shortsighted.

## Rank-Size Relationships

Let us consider a hypothetical region of at least modest areal extent and with a heritage and economic structure conducive to city formation. In addition, consider that a level of urbanization has been reached in this region, if only the initial stage in the urbanization process. If the conditions are favorable for city formation, it is unlikely that just one city would

be formed in this region, and most likely, a number of cities would be formed and, in this example, let us hypothesize the formation of 120 cities. Furthermore, we will assume a grouping of cities based on population size and that there would be four such groupings or size-classes. Would you expect that the number of cities in a given size-class would equal the number in each of the other size-classes (Table 6–1, column 2), or that the number of cities in each size-class would be different (Table 6–1, columns 4, 6, and 8)? If there are different numbers of cities in each of the size-classes, would you expect that there would be a constant ratio between the number in successive size-classes (Table 6–1, column 7), or would the ratio become progressively greater or progressively smaller (Table 6–1, columns 5 and 9)? There are two facets of the above hypothetical distributions that deserve more examination. One is the distribution of urban centers among size-classes. Quite obviously, the number of cities in any size-class is dependent on the limits set for that size-class. What, for example, would be the effect, in the example presented, of making a division between size-classes at 40,000 or 60,000, rather than 50,000? One might be guided in this matter by the system of grouping cities into size-classes followed by the Bureau of the

**Table 6–1**  Different Hypothetical Distributions of Urban Centers by Size-Class

| Size Class (Population) | Distribution A | | Distribution B | | Distribution C | | Distribution D | |
|---|---|---|---|---|---|---|---|---|
| | Number | $k^a$ | Number | $k$ | Number | $k$ | Number | $k$ |
| (1) | (2) | (3) | (4) | (5) | (6) | (7) | (8) | (9) |
| Over 200,000 | 30 | | 40 | | 2 | | 3 | |
| | | 1.0 | | 0.9 | | 3.5 | | 3.5 |
| 50,000–200,000 | 30 | | 35 | | 7 | | 11 | |
| | | 1.0 | | 0.8 | | 3.5 | | 2.8 |
| 10,000–50,000 | 30 | | 27 | | 25 | | 31 | |
| | | 1.0 | | 0.7 | | 3.5 | | 2.4 |
| 1,000–10,000 | 30 | | 18 | | 86 | | 75 | |
| Totals | 120 | | 120 | | 120 | | 120 | |

$^a k$ denotes the ratio between numbers of cities in two successive size classes.

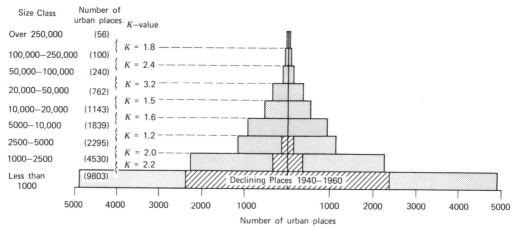

**Figure 6–1**   Urban population pyramid—1970. *Source.* Based on data in U.S. Bureau of the Census—U.S. Census of Population 1970, *Number of Inhabitant: U.S. Summary,* Washington, D.C., 1971.

Census; at least this provides a common basis for data gathering, reporting, and analysis.

A basic generalization we can make is that the number of cities in successively larger size-classes becomes progressively less. One manner of depicting this arrangement is the *urban pyramid,* such as the one presented for the United States in Figure 6–1. In this figure, note that the greater the size of the city, the lower the number of cities in the size-class. Thus, beginning with a broad base made up of numerous small urban centers, the number of cities gradually lessens until there are relatively few cities in the highest size-class. To extend this proposition a bit further than shown in Figure 6–1, at the very top of the urban pyramid would be a single urban center that, by virtue of its large population, would have no equal, i.e., the entire size-class would be made up of a single city. The city found at the peak of the urban pyramid has been termed the *primate city* and is exemplified by such cities as New York, Moscow, London, Paris and Tokyo.[1] Viewing the upper portion of the urban pyramid of the United States, we find that the New York-Northeastern

[1]Mark Jefferson, "The Law of the Primate City," *Geographical Review,* Vol. 29 (1939).

New Jersey Urbanized Area, here considered a single agglomeration with over 16 million people, has the greatest population of all urbanized areas in the country. Therefore, it has undisputed highest rank, as would New York City if the pyramid was based on single cities, rather than urbanized areas. In the next size-class, there are two urbanized areas, each with about seven or eight million people, and these share second rank. The two second rank urbanized areas are the Los Angeles-Long Beach and the Chicago-Northwestern Indiana urbanized areas. With populations of from two to five million people each are five urbanized areas sharing third rank, and so on for urbanized areas in still smaller size-classes of lower rank. This supports the statement that large metropolitan areas differ in size and rank and that one center clearly emerges as the primate city in a rank-size pyramid.

It generally is true that in any region, there is a single primate city. Most states (a political region) in the United States have one city significantly larger than any other, with this city being the primate city of the state. It may be noted, however, in only 16 of the states is the primate city also the state capital. At a smaller scale, too, there are aspects of the urban pyramid at the top of which is a primate

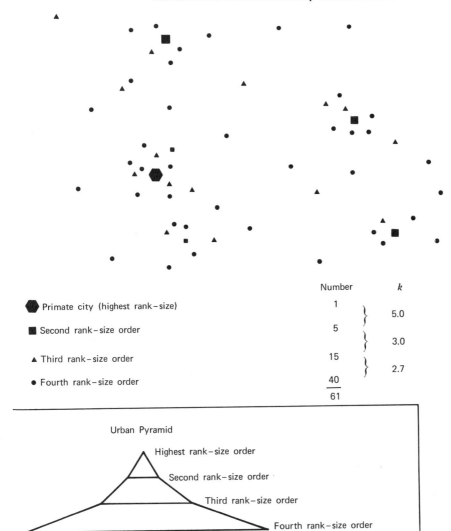

Figure 6–2   Hypothetical distribution of cities of different rank-size classes.

or dominant city, such as the case of counties where the county seat often is the primate city of the county. The major point here is that in any areal unit, there is a tendency toward an urban pyramid with a single city of the highest rank-size (Figure 6–2).

## Formalization of the Relationship Between Rank and Size of Cities

As early as 1913, Auerbach noted the regularity between the sizes of cities and their rank.[2] This concept was formalized

in the writing of G. K. Zipf who attempted to show this distribution as following an empirical rule, the *rank-size* rule.[3]

The rank-size rule can be stated with the following equation:

$$P_r = \frac{P_1}{r}$$

where:
$P_r$ is the population of a city of rank $r$, $P_1$ is the population of the largest city (the primate city), and $r$ is the rank of a given city. With all cities in a region arranged in descending order of population, the size

[2]Auerbach, F, "Das Gesetz der Bevolkerungskon- zentration," *Petermann's Mitteilungen,* V. 59 (1913).

[3]G. K. Zipf, *Human Behavior and the Principle of Least Effort,* New York, Addison-Wesley Press, 1949.

of the 4th city would be $P/r$, the size of the largest city, according to the series $P$, $P/2$, $P/3$, $P/4 \ldots P/r$. To illustrate the application of this model, the largest city in a region might have a population of 1,000,000. By applying the rank-size rule, the second ranked city would have a population of 500,000 (1,000,000/2), the third ranked city a population of 333,333 (1,000,000/3), and the fourth ranked city a population of 250,000 (1,000,000/4). Note that the application of the rank-size rule as advanced by Zipf fails to provide for more than one city of a given rank. And, even though it would be naive to expect two or more cities to have exactly the same populations, especially large cities, the amount of variation between them may be fairly small; thus, one might deal with rank of a size-class, rather than absolute populations. In the above example, there may be and likely would be more than one city with populations of approximately 250,000 (fourth ranked). However, the number of cities of a given rank in a hierarchy is a matter to be considered later.

Regarding the applicability of the rank-size rule of Zipf, Charles T. Stewart, Jr. summarizes it as follows: "The rank-size rule, although in many cases a reasonable approximation to the actual distribution of towns by size, has no logical basis. It breaks down in many areas at both extremes—the largest and the smallest towns. The rule is a better description of reality for large heterogeneous areas than for small homogeneous areas, where town size, spacing, and functions are most closely interconnected."[4] This statement, in general expresses the considerable reservation held concerning the applicability of the rank-size rule as put forward by Zipf. In one recent investigation of the applicability of the rank-size rule to cities in (1) the Athens, Georgia area and (2) to all

cities in Georgia, it was found that neither case was satisfactorily described by the rank-size rule.[5] In the respective regions, Athens and Atlanta (the highest ranked cities) were larger than called for by the rank-size rule, thus supporting the statement of Stewart.

Another theory dealing with rank-size relationships is based on the writings of W. Christaller.[6] In conjunction with development of other theoretical considerations of areal distributions of cities, Christaller considered that there were regularities in the urban pyramid that would recognize, like the concept of Zipf, a primate city with a population expressed symbolically as $P$. Other cities in the region would be arranged in a hierarchy according to the series $P/3$, $P/9$, $P/27$, etc.[7] Taking again a primate city with a population of 1,000,000 and applying the rank-size concept of Christaller, the second ranked city or cities would have a population of 333,333 ($P/3$), the third ranked city or cities, a population of 111,111 ($P/9$), and the fourth ranked city a population of 37,037 ($P/27$). In general, the relationships as stated by Christaller have greater applicability than those of Zipf.

In scrutinizing the various concepts of rank-size, it appears that none of them is universally or even widely applicable. Still, the overwhelming impression remains that there is an ordering of cities, and that there are regularities in the distribution of cities by rank-size, although different parameters might be needed to suit different types and scale of regions. One recent study discloses, however, that there are no relationships between type

[4]Charles T. Stewart, Jr., "The Size and Spacing of Cities," *Geographical Review*, Vol. 48, No. 2 (April, 1958).

[5]James B. Kenyon, "On the Relationship Between Central Function and Size of Place," *Annals of the Association of American Geographers*, Vol. 57, No. 4 (December, 1967).

[6]W. Christaller, *Central Places in Southern Germany*, C. W. Baskin (trans.), Prentice-Hall, 1966.

[7]A concise review of this and other rank-size concepts is presented by Brian J. L. Berry and William L. Garrison in "Alternative Explanations of Urban Rank-Size Relationships," *Annals of the Association of American Geographers*, Vol. 48, No. 1 (March, 1958).

of city size distribution and either level of economic development or the degree of urbanization in countries.[8]

## The Significance of the Rank-Size Concept

One might ask why the concern over the rank-ordering of cities based on their populations? What is the significance of engaging in this line of study? There are several possible answers to these questions.

Man, in his constant quest for knowledge, has sought to find regularities, orders, and patterns in distributions of many elements of his physical and cultural world. Often, the attempt is to find associations between two or more of these distributions. At other times, the attempt might be to establish causal relationships between different distributions, such as air pollution and respiratory ailments. Geographers have been concerned particularly with areal distributions, including the distributions of cities over two dimensional space. Are cities distributed within this space in a haphazard, seemingly random manner or is there some regular pattern or arrangement in which cities of different size-classes are distributed within this space? Are there regularities in the relationships between different parts of the distributions? These are the questions that involve rank-size concepts.

If it is established, within certain parameters, that rank-size regularities exist and if the nature of these regularities is determined, benefit can be derived from this knowledge. Questions on which rank-size concepts might have a bearing are numerous and include the following. When a region matures economically and experiences change in economic structure, are there concomitant changes in the urban pyramid

[8]Brian J. L. Berry, "City Size Distributions and Economic Development," *Economic Development and Cultural Change,* Vol. 9, No. 4 (1961).

(rank-size structure) of the region? If so, what is the expected nature of the change in the urban hierarchy? What, for example, happens to the urban hierarchy as growth accelerates in the secondary and tertiary economic sectors, while the primary sector remains stabilized? If there are changes in the urban pyramid or rank-size structure, what is the likely expected distribution of demand for urban land in the future, that is, what localities will experience increased demand and which localities unchanged or decreased demand? If the urban pyramid changes, what are the expanding sections of the pyramid and which are the contracting sections? With changes in the urban pyramid, what are the likely changes in spatial mobility patterns that will occur in the region and what will be the nature of the new patterns? Will the paths of migration be simply small town to metropolitan area, or will they be metropolitan area to intermediate size city, metropolitan area to small town, or intermediate-size city to metropolitan area? Do rank-size relationships that apply to a region of large size, such as a nation, also apply to smaller regions, such as drainage basins or states; that is, does scale of region have a bearing on rank-size relationships? These are a few of the questions that could benefit from application of the rank-size concepts, and once the concepts are formalized in a more acceptable manner with more widespread application, they could and should have considerable utility.

## The *k* Value

Having considered an urban pyramid that includes cities of different rank-sizes and the semblance of an ordering or hierarchy among cities in that urban pyramid, one might inquire as to possible relationships between number of cities in successive rank-orders in the hierarchy. The most convenient way of expressing such relationships is by means of a ratio between numbers of cities of two successive rank-orders (Figure 6–2). Thus, if there are 200 cities of a specific size-class and 800 cities of the next lower ranked size-class, the ratio between them would be 1:4. If this ratio, at least in general, exists between cities of the same size-classes in other distributions in other regions, it is considered as a constant relationship and is indicated with the letter $k$, a standard statistical symbol for a constant value. In the above example, the $k$ value is 4.0, although the ratio between numbers of cities in other successive rank-orders may be different (Table 6–1). If the relationship between each pair of successive size-classes remains the same throughout the urban pyramid, the $k$ value likewise remains the same (column 7, Table 6–1).

Studies by Christaller in South Germany and by Green in England and Wales, indicated that the $k$ values all fall between 3 and 4, that is, the ratio between size-classes of successive rank-orders was the same throughout the respective urban pyramids.[9] Stewart, however, concludes that "The relation $k$ between any two successive town classes starts from a high value and declines..."[10]

## Distortions of $k$ and the Urban Pyramid

We mentioned before that the number of size-classes in the urban pyramid is going to influence the $k$ values expressing relationships between numbers of cities in successive size-classes. Because of the arbitrary manner in which size-classes are defined, a form of distortion can be introduced (Table 6–2). By dividing the same number of cities in a region, say 680, into different size classes, the $k$ values are changed from a constant $k$ of 4 to values ranging from 1 through 24. This illustrates that the specific $k$ values are

[9]Christaller, *Op. Cit.*

F. H. W. Green. "Urban Hinterlands in England and Wales: Analysis of Bus Services." *Geographical Journal.* V. 96, 1961.

[10]Charles T. Stewart, *Op. Cit.*

dependent on the size-class structure used and that change in size-class structure results in one set of $k$ values being distorted, relative to the other, and that any generalizations made concerning these $k$ values are subject to the same distortion.

**Table 6–2**  Distortion of $k$ Values by Changing Size-Class Structure

| CASE A | | |
|---|---|---|
| Size-Class | Number of Cities | $k$ |
| 1,000–5,000 | 512 | 4 |
| 5,000–20,000 | 128 | 4 |
| 20,000–50,000 | 32 | 4 |
| 50,000–100,000 | 8 | |
| | 680 | |

| CASE B | | |
|---|---|---|
| Size-Class | Number of Cities | $k$ |
| 1,000–10,000 | 576 | 6 |
| 10,000–50,000 | 96 | 24 |
| 50,000–75,000 | 4 | 1 |
| 75,000–100,000 | 4 | |
| | 680 | |

It has been pointed out that $k$ values may be distorted if they are derived for a single urban hierarchy. If the hierarchy developed is based on economic functions performed by the cities in the hierarchy, a specific set of $k$ values will be derived, but if the hierarchy is an administrative one, based on different levels of administrative authority rather than on population or functions, a different set of $k$ values likely will result. In a similar vein, per capita income affects the urban pyramid, since in regions with lower per capita incomes, there is a lower demand for goods and services. Thus, urban centers whose basic function it is to provide goods and services will be fewer than in regions or nations of greater average per capita income. In this sense, differences in economic level of the region will provide a distortion of the urban pyramid and the $k$ values produced from it.

A further distortion of the urban pyramid exists in regions that have a relatively dispersed population. In these regions, the population in a given locale may be sufficient to support a low order trade and service center, resulting in a fairly dispersed number of small urban centers. But these may be so far apart that they do not have the access needed for the economic support of cities in the next larger size-class. Related to this case, is the one in which a region may have a poor regional transportation system. Again, the access will not be provided for the economic support of cities in the higher order size-classes. This would have the effect of maintaining a large number of small urban centers and if the access is provided to larger cities through such programs as rural road development, this leads to more support of nearby larger cities, perhaps at the expense of the smaller ones.

Without this access, the $k$ values in the lower part of the urban pyramid are relatively large; with the access, the $k$ values tend to become lower. In general, in a highly developed industrial and commercial society, the $k$ values at the bottom of the pyramid diminish while those toward the top of the pyramid increase.

## Current Alteration of the Urban Pyramid

Regardless of the nature of the urban pyramid and the relationships between numbers of cities in different size-classes making up that pyramid, it must be remembered that the conditions found are true only in a given period of time. Conditions in the manner in which man adjusts to the earth's surface are rarely, if ever, stable and are ever changing. Expect then that change will be experienced in urban structure, as presented in the form of the urban pyramid.

The record shows that some cities grow in population, while others lose popula-

tion, that is, experience a decline. For the United States, the record shows that declining centers are, more often than not, small urban centers that are in size-classes near the bottom of the urban pyramid. Note too in Table 6–3, in the period 1940 to 1960, that there were over 6000 declining centers in the country and slightly over nine-tenths of these had populations of 3000 or less, which would put them at or near the bottom of the urban pyramid, no matter how it was structured. Also, as shown in Figure 6–1, declining centers comprise fairly high proportions of total numbers of urban centers in size-classes near the bottom of the urban pyramid. The least viable of urban centers are those in the lowest size-classes, particularly small centers with populations less than 1000. Generally then, there is evidence that the base of the urban pyramid is experiencing contraction. Also, when you consider that numerous large central

**Table 6–3** Declining Urban Centers as a Proportion of Total Urban Centers: By Size-Class (1940–1960)

| Size-Class | Number of Urban Centers | Number of Declining Centers | Percent of Declining Centers |
|---|---|---|---|
| 1,000 or less | 9,874 | 4,709 | 47.7 |
| 1,000–2,500 | 4,471 | 683 | 15.3 |
| 2,500–5,000 | 2,152 | 236 | 11.0 |
| Over 5,000 | 3,293 | 406 | 12.3 |

Source: Adapted from Ray M. Northam, "Declining Urban Centers in the United States, 1940–1960," *Annals of the Association of American Geographers*, 1963, and from Bureau of the Census, *United States Summary, 1960*.

cities are losing population as well, there would be a contraction of number of cities in size-classes near the very apex of the pyramid. The mid-section of the pyramid, however, as represented by cities in size-classes of approximately 25,000 to 100,000 continues to expand or at least remains stable. It is not inconceivable that the future will see a transforma-

**Table 6–4**  The Probability of Declining Urban Centers, by Size-Class (1940–1960): United States.

| Size-Class | Number of Urban Centers (1940) | Number of Declining Urban Centers (1940–1960) | Probability of Declining Urban Centers (1940–1960) |
|---|---|---|---|
| 1,000,000 or more | 5 | 0 | .0000[a] |
| 500,000–1,000,000 | 9 | 5 | .5555[a] |
| 250,000–500,000 | 23 | 5 | .2173[a] |
| 100,000–250,000 | 55 | 18 | .3272[a] |
| 50,000–100,000 | 107 | 26 | 2429 |
| 25,000–50,000 | 213 | 32 | .1502 |
| 10,000–25,000 | 665 | 92 | .1383 |
| 5,000–10,000 | 965 | 175 | .1813 |
| 2,500–5,000 | 1,422 | 269 | .1891 |
| 1,000–2,500 | 3,205 | 804 | .2508 |
| Under 1,000 | 10,083 | 4,608 | .4570 |
| | 16,752 | 6,034 | |

[a]In this study, urban center was taken to mean an incorporated city or large unincorporated place. Hence, central cities within urbanized areas were considered separately from other incorporated places in the urbanized area.
SOURCE:   Ray M. Northam, *Land Economics,* August, 1969.

tion of the urban pyramid into a truncated diamond, as more of the very small centers lose population and slowly pass out of existence and the bulk of those that remain gain in population and gradually pass into higher size-classes. But it would not be realistic though to believe that all of the small centers will disappear, thereby shifting the entire pyramid upward, since there have always been and likely will always be many small centers to serve the needs of the dispersed rural population.

The point has been made that many urban centers in the lowest size-class are losing population, that is, are declining urban centers, but not all are so characterized. In a study that considered the many factors that might be associated with decline of a small urban center, several were found to be significant. One oft-stated explanation is that small centers decline because of impairment or loss of the regional economic base, such as through a decline in agriculture, mining, or forestry. This proved to be an inadequate explanation, however, since

in a given region experiencing such metamorphosis of the regional economic base, not all urban centers, not even all those of the same size-class, suffer decline. Thus, there must be factors other than general change in regional economic base that are unique to the declining centers. Two factors were isolated and examined in detail in different parts of the United States and these served to explain most of the incidence of urban center decline. The two variables involved were (1) the initial population of the urban center, and (2) distance from a major urban center of central city status (50,000 or more).[11]

The first factor found significant in urban center decline was the population of the center at the beginning of the time period during which decline occurred. The likelihood of a given center within a given size-class being a declining center is

[11]Ray M. Northam, "Population Size, Relative Location, and Declining Urban Centers, Conterminous United States, 1940–1960," *Land Economics,* Vol. XLV, No. 3 (August, 1969).

presented in Table 6–4. Thus, it can be seen that, with the exception of large central cities, the probability of a place being a declining urban center increases inversely with population size.

**Table 6–5**   The Probability of Declining Urban Centers with Increased Distance from a Central City

| Distance Zone from a Central City (Miles) | Probability of Declining Urban Centers in a Given Distance Zone |
|---|---|
| 0–10 | .1373 |
| 10–20 | .1374 |
| 20–30 | .2161 |
| 30–40 | .3190 |
| 40–50 | .4049 |
| 50–60 | .4425 |
| 60–70 | .4721 |
| 70–80 | .4812 |
| 80–90 | .4564 |
| 90–100 | .4290 |

SOURCE:   Ray M. Northam, *Land Economics*, August, 1969.

The second important variable in the decline of urban centers is a spatial variable—the distance of the declining center from a central city (a city of 50,000 or more people). The likelihood of a place being a declining center, based on increased linear distance from a central city is presented in Table 6–5. It will be seen that as distance increases, the probability of decline increases as well, until a distance of about eighty miles is reached, after which probability of decline begins to lower. The locational setting of the urban center, then, has a bearing on the likelihood of decline of the center. If a small center is in close proximity to a large central city, its inhabitants can maintain residence in the small center and, at the same time, commute daily to places of employment in the central city. A point or distance is reached, however, after which the small center is beyond the normal commuting range and, in the face of dwindling economic opportunities, people migrate to the larger centers,

producing a decline of the smaller center in the process. Thus, the small urban center retains its viability if its locational setting provides it with access to a larger urban center. The small, more isolated centers continue to lose population and, if the trend continues, might pass from existence, thereby contributing to a change in the urban pyramid.

## Nodal Regions and Urban Focal Points

In considering cities, it is important to remember that they are, regardless of rank-size, distributed over two dimensional space and that the interstices between them are populated as well, but with a much lower density (persons per square mile). The urban center might be viewed as a peak representing high population densities, as exemplified by a density of 26,343 in the City of New York within the New York-Northeastern New Jersey urbanized area. As one progresses outward from this peak, population densities become lower as a function of distance from the peak, as illustrated by a density of 2063 in the urban fringe of New York and a density of 371 in the Middle Atlantic region of which New York City is a part.

This gives rise to a profile in which the slopes may be regular, concave, or convex, but generally are concave. Gradually, the densities become less and will continue so until one slope merges with one peripheral to an adjacent peak (Figure 6–3). In reality, there often are lower secondary peaks that break up the smoothness of the slope, and these represent outlying nodes of population in the form of suburban and satellite agglomerations.

The urban center may be viewed as the primate center of the region and, as such, exerts social, economic, and administrative influence on areas marginal to the center itself. An analogy might be a mountain peak that intercepts a large amount of atmospheric moisture which, as surface water, moves outward from

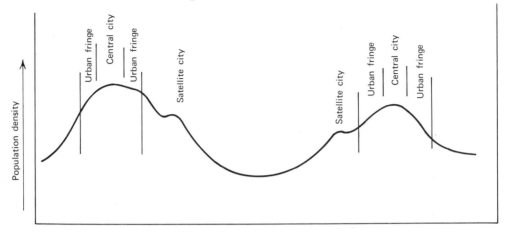

**Figure 6–3** A hypothetical profile of regional population densities; binodal region.

the peak and downslope and will continue to as long as the slope continues. In the same sense, the influence of an urban center will be exerted in areas beyond the confines of the central city or the urbanized area of which the central city is a part. It will be extended to outlying areas with a rural-farm population or to areas with a rural non-farm population, as well as to lower subsidiary peaks representing urban centers of smaller size and lower population densities. What is being said is that the influence of a city is experienced, not only in the city itself, but in areas adjacent to the city. Legal boundaries and administrative borders do not deter the diffusion of this influence, although they may alter it somewhat.

Thus, an urban center should be viewed as but one component in a regional system and, as there is an urban center which is the focal point of the region, there is an urban region that includes that center. The urban center serves all or most of the region, as the region serves the urban center. We turn, then, to consideration of the urban region.

The urban region, which is the spatial unit within which the influence of an urban center is exhibited and extended, consists of two parts, the focal point and the tributary area. Together, these parts constitute a spatial entity which has been referred to as a nodal region. D. Whittlesey and, more recently, P. Haggett, consider that there are two types of geographic regions: the *uniform region* and the *nodal region*.[12] With the uniform region, the criteria on which it is based, such as soils, surface type, vegetation type, etc., are relatively uniformly distributed within the region, although there are minor exceptions found that are considered irrelevant and are disregarded. Remaining is an areal unit within which the phenomenon considered is relatively uniform in occurrence, at least to an acceptable degree. The boundaries of such a region will be established when the occurrence of the phenomenon ceases or falls below accepted levels.

In a nodal region, it is the unity and form of spatial organization, not the spread of specific features, that differentiates it from other regions. The nodal region contains one or more focal points, most often urban centers, and these serve as nodes of organization or centers of influence. In some instances, the focal point of a nodal region may lie outside the region it serves, but in most cases the focal point is within the region and enjoys a central location within the region.[13]

[12]Derwent Whittlesey, In James, P. E., C. F. Jones and J. K. Wright (Ed.), *American Geography, Inventory and Prospect,* Syracuse, Syracuse University Press, 1954. Peter Haggett, *Locational Analysis in Human Geography,* New York, St. Martins Press, 1966.

[13]W. Siddall, "Seattle, Regional Capital of Alaska," *Annals of the Association of American Geographers,* Vol. 47, No. 3 (September, 1957).

The key to the nature of the nodal region is the complex pattern of communications that provide linkages within the region. These communications may involve physical movement through travel and transportation, or may include communications in which there is no movement, such as telephone calls and mailed communications. The physical movements may be of different types, from the compulsory, such as school attendance, to the spontaneous, like shopping trips.

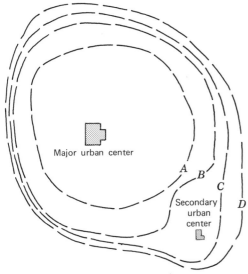

**Figure 6–4**  A focal point city and its tributary area delimited by selected criteria.
(A) Extent of toll-free phone service.
(B) Extent of regular retail trade.
(C) Extent of regular banking service.
(D) Extent of employee commuting zone.

The focal point(s) comprises but one component of the urban region; the other component is the area tributary to that focal point (Figure 6–4). The area peripheral to the focal point and that serves the urban center that is the focal point or is served by it, goes by a variety of names. Since it is tributary to the focal point, the term *tributary area* is used quite often. The term *hinterland* also is used in reference to this peripheral zone. Originally used in Europe, the latter term had reference to areas inland from ports in which commodities moving through the port originated and terminated. This

spatial concept might be extended to all urban centers on which goods movements are focused, and in this sense, every urban agglomeration has a hinterland. *Trade area* also is used to identify the area peripheral to a focal point and obviously is the zone from which customers for goods provided in the urban center (the focal point) are derived or within which these goods are distributed. *Sphere of influence* is used for the peripheral area as well, with this a more inclusive term than is "trade area," since it includes all or virtually all types of contact between the focal point and the peripheral zone. Types of contact included with use of this term are medical services, educational services, administrative services, and cultural services, among others, while the term "trade area" has reference just to retail or wholesale trade. Also, there is communication between an urban center and its peripheral zone in the form of daily commuting between the peripheral zone and places of employment in the urban center serving as regional focal point. These movements would be included with usage of the term "sphere of influence," while they would not be if the term "trade area" was used. In this vein, the term *laborshed* is sometimes used in reference to the area peripheral to the focal point from which at least some of the employees in the focal point city are derived. The outer margin of the laborshed roughly corresponds to the outer limit of daily commutation and because of this, the area is sometimes referred to as the *commuting zone*. It is from the commuting zone that much of the labor force employed in the urban center (the focal point) and many of the shoppers are derived.

These are some of the ways by which the tributary area of an urban center is identified. In this book, the terms "tributary area," "sphere of influence," and "commuting zone" are all used at various points. Others could be used as well, but some would be redundant of others, so there is little to be gained by introducing them.

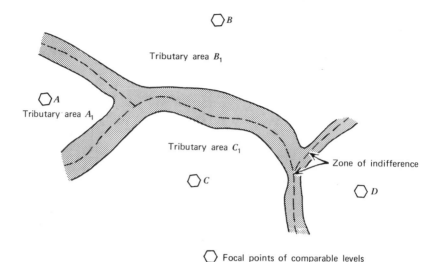

**Figure 6–5**   Hypothetical case of the zone of indifference between adjacent tributary areas.

One aspect of nodal regions is that they are formulated or delimited on the basis that interaction exists between the focal point and the tributary area and that, given a series of focal points of comparable types or orders, each with its own tributary area, all parts of a region would be included in the tributary area of one or another of the focal points. On occasion, however, there are relatively small and sparsely populated areas that are not closely linked to any focal point. The level of self-sufficiency is so high and the need for outside contacts so small that the inhabitants have little, if any, communication with any focal point. Perhaps, sections of Appalachia, the southern Rocky Mountain region, and the northern interior of Canada include examples of this situation.

The entire notion of delimitation of tributary areas of urban centers is predicated on the assumption that the urban center which is the focal point of the urban region enjoys a monopolistic position as far as serving the needs of the tributary area is concerned. It assumes that the population of the tributary area will be within the sphere of influence of only one focal point or urban center for a particular type of good, service or contact. In fact, the resident in the area

peripheral to two or more adjacent focal points of the same general type or order, may have sufficient mobility that he maintains contacts with each of the competing centers. He may travel to one for employment, but travel to another for shopping or he may conduct some of his shopping at one focal point and some at a second focal point of the same general type or order. For a specific good or service, such as the purchase of furniture or appliances, he may turn to each of the two adjacent centers, but at different times. In general, he exhibits an indifference as far as choice of urban center with which he interacts, whether it is interaction involving different types of activities or interaction involving different activities of the same general type.

There is, then, a *zone of indifference* that exists in many instances on the outer margin of the tributary areas of two adjacent focal point cities of the same general order (Figure 6–5). The expense, time, and effort expended for travel to and from adjacent focal points from locations in the zone of indifference are nearly the same, providing more alternatives for contact with focal point cities than would exist for locations near the inner margin of the tributary area. As an example, persons living in the zone of indifference often subscribe to the daily newspapers of each of the two adjacent focal point cities, while persons living near the inner margin of the tributary area generally subscribe to daily newspapers published in the focal point city nearest to them and the one where they have the most regular contact.

No doubt, it is apparent to the reader that the width of the zone of indifference, the degree to which it exists, and its very configuration are dependent on a number of factors. These include (1) a level of affluence which will allow the selection from among alternate choices, some of which may be more costly than others, (2) available time to be used in selecting from among alternate choices, (3) availability of information concerning the alternate choices, and (4) the same approximate mix of goods and services offered by the alternate choices. Since any or all of these factors might, and logically would, experience change over time, the zone of indifference is subject to areal change, expanding at some times and contracting at other times.

## Delimitation of Nodal Regions

Basically the region, whatever the type, is an abstraction, and thus has no precise boundaries that are fixed in space or time. Yet we accept the notion that the region exists as an entity. One might conclude that it would prove folly to attempt the delimitation of an abstraction in the same manner as it would prove fruitless to attempt to measure the width of a rainbow. It should be said, however, that a region can have substance within the context of an operational definition. The factors that lead to the substance of the region often lend themselves to measurement at any given time and if one clearly defines the parameters of the criteria on which he is basing the extent of the region and these criteria are measured, there can be an operational basis for regional delimitation. One might adopt, as an operational criterion, one

calling for at least weekly vehicular travel from a point in the tributary area to the focal point city. If the level of weekly contacts of this magnitude in a marginal portion of the area falls below the stated criteria, it would not be included within the nodal region peripheral to the urban center in question. Once a logical operating definition, such as the one mentioned, can be formulated providing the basis for inclusion in the nodal region, the task is made much easier. The following sections deal with different means of delimiting nodal regions, based on differing operational criteria. In some cases, the delimitation is based on empirical or observable criteria and in others on theoretical concepts that include rational criteria that cannot, in fact, be observed.

## Empirical Means of Regional Delimitation

By definition, "empirical" means something capable of being observed and, if necessary, of being measured or counted, that is, something tangible. To delimit urban nodal regions would entail using criteria that involve interaction between the focal point and the tributary area. A number of different empirical criteria have been used for this purpose.

One of the most likely forms of communication or interaction between tributary areas and focal points is some form of transportation. In this vein, vehicular traffic flow directed to the urban center from within the tributary area serves quite well in a society where possession of automobiles is commonplace and where there is a good network of highways. In the United States, traffic flow maps are available showing the magnitude and pattern of vehicular traffic movement for nearly all states (Figure 6–6). By measurement of line widths on traffic flow maps where line width is proportionate to traffic volume, or use of actual traffic counts usually noted on the map, one can determine the

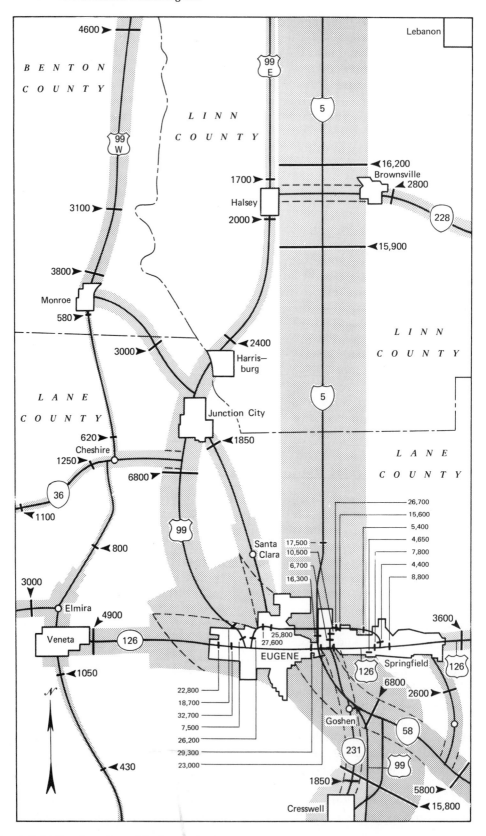

**Figure 6–6**   Portion of a vehicular traffic flow map, Willamette Valley, Oregon. Numbers are average number of vehicles per 24-hour period. *Source.* Extracted from *Traffic Flow Map:* Oregon State Highway System, 1971.

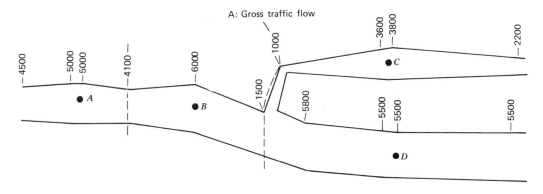

A: Gross traffic flow

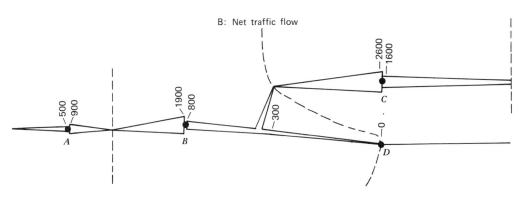

B: Net traffic flow

– – – Portion of tributary area boundary

**Figure 6–7** Delimitation of a tributary area boundary, based on traffic flow. (Numbers refer to volume of vehicles.)

point where traffic flow between two centers is at a minimum. This point can be taken as the divide between two streams of traffic, each directed toward a different urban center. Such points can be established for all highways radiating from a particular urban center and these points then can be connected with a smooth line which approximates the nodal region of the urban center to which the traffic is moving (Figure 6–7A). If the aim is to estimate the volume as well as direction of traffic flow directed to adjacent centers, one could also use traffic flow information. In this case, points of minimum traffic flow would be established along a given route, as in the previous case, and notation would be made of the actual volume in number of vehicles per day passing that point (Figure

6–7B). A record would then be kept of the actual volume of vehicles entering the city, with this usually available from the traffic flow map. It might be assumed that the minimum volume noted is daily traffic that is moving between the two centers and is not generated within the tributary area of either of the centers. The numerical difference between minimum traffic volume at the edge of the tributary area and maximum volume at the entrance to the city provides an estimate of net traffic flow generated by the tributary area of the city in question. This procedure is then repeated for each of the highway routes radiating from the particular city and the points of minimum flow connected with a smooth line, thus delimiting the tributary area as before. In this case, however, not only is the tributary area delimited, but also produced is a measure of the volume of vehicular traffic generated by the city in question when net traffic flows along all routes radiating from that city are summed (Figure 6–7B). This procedure can be expressed in the following manner:

$$Ntfi = \sum nr \ (T \ \max_{i-y} - T \ \min_{i-z})$$

where:
$Ntfi$ is the net traffic flow directed toward city $i$; $\sum nr$ is the sum of net traffic flows on a number of routes radiating from city $i$; $T \ \max_{i-y}$ is the maximum volume of traffic flow between city $i$ and $y$, with $y$ the point of minimum flow between city $i$ and an adjacent city (city $z$); $T \ \min_{i-z}$ is the minimum volume of traffic between city $i$ and an adjacent city (city $z$).

Application of the above procedure allows a measure of the degree to which the city in question attracts traffic from its tributary area, as well as the area from which the traffic is drawn.

Often, the empirical data used in regional delimitation are derived from personal interviews with consumers to determine the urban center or centers where they make certain types of purchases, usually in the realm of shopper's goods.[14] The rationale for using shopper's goods purchases is that the effort is made to determine the maximum distance to which customers travel for goods found in the urban center that is the focal point of the region, as opposed to secondary centers that are not of the highest rank-order in the region. One authority in these matters considers consumer interview methods the most accurate and most desired of all methods of

tributary area definition that might be employed.[15] It must also be considered the most time consuming, as illustrated by a survey conducted to delimit the trading area of Stillwater, Oklahoma (population 31,000 in 1970), in which it was estimated that over one thousand man hours were spent in making consumer interviews.[16] We doubt that the productivity in this type of effort has increased significantly in the years since this survey was made.

Another approach in regional delimitation using empirical techniques involves collection of data from trade and service outlets in the focal point city. One might solicit responses from major retailers as to the distance and area from which customers are derived. Here, the retail outlets contacted would usually be those dispensing shopper's goods, since these have the largest areas of distribution. The distribution of account holders in major banks or buyers of bulk fuel oil also serve as measures of the extent of the tributary area. Another method is to check addresses of patients at hospitals and clinics to determine the service area; this is done especially by checking the birth records of a hospital, since these are fairly easy to get and often are published in local papers. License plate survey or auto registration often will give the addresses of the automobile owner, thus the location of residence of persons present in the focal point city.

Another relatively simple and less expensive method of determining the extent of a tributary area is to use newspaper circulation data either from daily or weekly newspapers, depending on the size of the focal point city. The premise is that persons receiving the newspaper

---

[14]Shopper's goods are those distributed through retail outlets in which (1) there is usually comparative shopping involved, (2) the individual purchase is of relatively high value, and (3) the purchase is made infrequently. Examples of shopper's goods outlets normally include men's and women's apparel stores, furniture stores, appliance stores and jewelry stores, among others.

[15]Isadore V. Fine, *Retail Trade Area Analysis,* Wisconsin Commerce Papers, Vol. 1, No. 6 (January, 1954).

[16]Perham C. Nahl, *Application of the Interview Method to a Trading Area Survey of Stillwater, Oklahoma,* Stillwater: School of Commerce, Oklahoma Agricultural and Mechanical College, 1939.

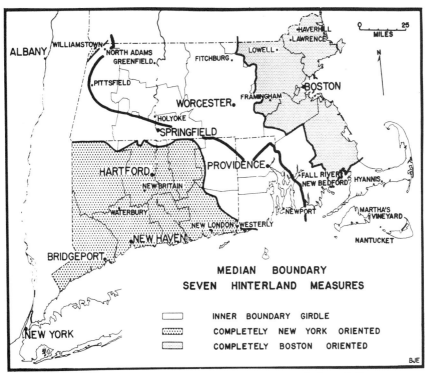

**Figure 6-8**  Composite hinterland boundaries of New York and Boston. *Source.* Howard L. Green, *Economic Geography,* Vol. 31, (1955). Reproduced by permission of *Economic Geography.*

have an interest in the economic, social, or cultural affairs of the focal point city and are free to avail themselves of what that city offers. In the United States, the Audit Bureau of Circulation (ABC) provides an audit of circulation figures for subscribing newspapers and they, in turn, may make them available to the public. Most newspapers in large and medium sized cities have such information available. Somewhat related to ABC data are published regional delimitations in the Rand McNally *Commercial Atlas and Marketing Guide,* which is updated and published annually and is generally available in any sizeable public library.

As valuable as any one of the above techniques might be, it is usually the case that a number of criteria are employed in delimiting nodal regions. For example, in a study of regional boundaries of the hinterlands of New York City and Boston, the criteria used included (1) railroad commuter traffic, (2) daily newspaper circulation, (3) telephone calls between the hinterlands and New York and Boston respectively, (4) patronage of banks, (5) truck freight movement, (6) metropolitan origin of vacationers, and (7) business addresses of directors of major industrial firms within the intervening area between the two focal points.[17] Boundaries were drawn for each of the seven criteria and these were then synthesized into a composite boundary Figure 6–9). Others too have utilized multiple criteria for regional delimitation and have then developed a single boundary that is a composite of several. Since a boundary established from a single criterion will experience changes in its configuration and in the area included, the multiple-factor boundary may be more realistic than any developed by a single criterion.

[17]Howard L. Green, "Hinterland Boundaries of New York and Boston in Southern New England," *Economic Geography,* Vol. 31, (October, 1955).

## Theoretical Methods of Regional Delimitation

These methods are based, not on observed or determined linkages between focal point and tributary area, but on logically derived expected linkages. In many instances, the level of these expected linkages or communications is derived from application of a model of one type or another, with a model taken here to be a generalized approximation of reality. The globe, as one example of a model, is an approximation of the earth, and a map, as another example, is an approximation of a segment of the earth's surface. The models employed in regional delimitation usually are symbolic models or mathematical models, in which some aspect of reality is denoted with a symbol, such as a letter or a numerical value.

(communication) between two places ($P_1$ and $P_2$);

$P_1$ is the population of the larger of two places or small areas;

$P_2$ is the population of the smaller of two places or small areas;

and $d$ is the distance (generally in miles) between the two places or small areas ($P_1$ and $P_2$).

The gravity or interaction model is patterned after the law of gravitation. It has been expressed by H. C. Carey as follows:

"The great law of Molecular Gravitation (is) the indispensable condition of the existence of the being known as man ... The greater the number collected in a given space, the greater is the attractive force that is there exerted ... Gravitation is here, as everywhere, in the direct ratio of the

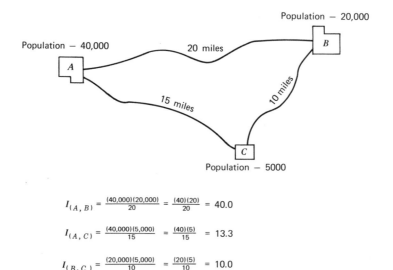

$$I_{(A,B)} = \frac{(40,000)(20,000)}{20} = \frac{(40)(20)}{20} = 40.0$$

$$I_{(A,C)} = \frac{(40,000)(5,000)}{15} = \frac{(40)(5)}{15} = 13.3$$

$$I_{(B,C)} = \frac{(20,000)(5,000)}{10} = \frac{(20)(5)}{10} = 10.0$$

**Figure 6–9**  Hypothetical application of the simple interaction or gravity model $I = P_1 P_2 / d$.

The models employed are, for the most part, variations of the *gravity or interaction model* which estimates, in a rational manner, the streams of communications between points or areas. In simplified form, the gravity model is expressed:

$$I = \frac{P_1 P_2}{d}$$

where:

$I$ is the measure of relative interation

mass, and in the inverse one of the distance."[18]

Thus, the two key factors or variables employed in the model based on Carey's work that are said to influence man's spatial movement are (1) the population (mass) of an attractive force, and (2) the distance he is from that attractive force.

[18]H. C. Carey, *Principles of Social Science,* Philadelphia, Lippincott, (1858–59).

Extending this concept, the inhabitants of one population center will interact with those of another center, based on their respective masses and the distance between them. This is the situation expressed symbolically in the gravity or interaction model presented above and graphically in Figure 6–9. This concept has been modified and applied numerous times and has, with some modification and substitution, been utilized for regional delimitation.

was developed by P. Converse who advanced the "breaking point concept."[20] The breaking point is that location that marks the division of two streams of movement, each directed to a different focal point. The breaking point concept is expressed as follows:

$$B = \frac{d}{1 + \sqrt{\dfrac{P_1}{P_2}}}$$

$B$ is the breaking point, in miles, from the

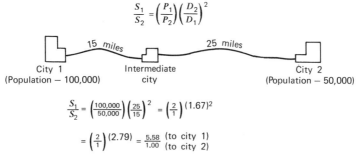

$$\frac{S_1}{S_2} = \left(\frac{P_1}{P_2}\right)\left(\frac{D_2}{D_1}\right)^2$$

15 miles    25 miles

City 1
(Population — 100,000)

Intermediate
city

City 2
(Population — 50,000)

$$\frac{S_1}{S_2} = \left(\frac{100,000}{50,000}\right)\left(\frac{25}{15}\right)^2 = \left(\frac{2}{1}\right)(1.67)^2$$

$$= \left(\frac{2}{1}\right)(2.79) = \frac{5.58}{1.00} \begin{array}{l} \text{(to city 1)} \\ \text{(to city 2)} \end{array}$$

**Figure 6–10** Hypothetical application of Reilly's "Law of Retail Gravitation."
$S_1/S_2 = (P_1/P_2)\,(D_2/D_1)^2$.

In 1931, W. J. Reilly adapted the interaction or gravity model to estimate how much of the retail sales volume of a city or small area located between two larger cities with greater retail offerings would go to each of the competing centers (Figure 6–10).[19] "Reilly's Law," as it came to be known, is expressed symbolically as:

$$\frac{S_1}{S_2} = \left(\frac{P_1}{P_2}\right)\left(\frac{D_2}{D_1}\right)^2$$

where:
$S_1$ and $S_2$ are the relative shares of sales in each of two cities, made to residents of an intermediate city or town;
$P_1$ and $P_2$ are the populations of two competing trade centers deriving customers from the intermediate town or city;
and $D_1$ and $D_2$ are the distances respectively from each of two cities ($P_1$ and $P_2$) to an intermediate city or town.
A major modification of Reilly's Law

smaller of two adjacent trade centers;
$d$ is the distance, in miles, between two competing and adjacent trade centers;
$P_1$ is the population of the largest of two competing trade centers and $P_2$ is the population of the smaller of two competing trade centers.
One can note that each of these models, Reilly's and Converse's, incorporates the same variables as put forth by Carey, that is, mass (population) and distance.
The breaking point equation provides one with an estimate of the location of the outer margins of two adjoining tributary areas or trade areas. When the breaking point is established between competing trade centers in all possible directions from a given trade center and these points are connected with a smooth line, the tributary area or trade area of the focal point city in question has been approximated (Figure 6–11). If one accepts the fact, however, that the outer margin of a tributary area is not likely to be a

[19]William J. Reilly, *The Law of Retail Gravitation,* The Knickerbocker Press, New York, 1931.

[20]P. D. Converse, "New Laws of Retail Gravitation," *Journal of Marketing,* Vol. 14 (October, 1949).

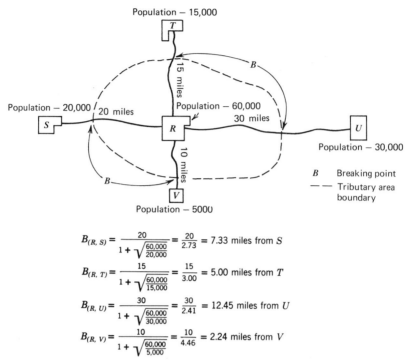

$$B_{(R, S)} = \cfrac{20}{1 + \sqrt{\cfrac{60,000}{20,000}}} = \frac{20}{2.73} = 7.33 \text{ miles from } S$$

$$B_{(R, T)} = \cfrac{15}{1 + \sqrt{\cfrac{60,000}{15,000}}} = \frac{15}{3.00} = 5.00 \text{ miles from } T$$

$$B_{(R, U)} = \cfrac{30}{1 + \sqrt{\cfrac{60,000}{30,000}}} = \frac{30}{2.41} = 12.45 \text{ miles from } U$$

$$B_{(R, V)} = \cfrac{10}{1 + \sqrt{\cfrac{60,000}{5,000}}} = \frac{10}{4.46} = 2.24 \text{ miles from } V$$

**Figure 6–11** Hypothetical application of the breaking point concept.

$$B = d/1 + \sqrt{\frac{P_1}{P_2}}$$

precisely established line, but is the zone of indifference, the precision implied by the breaking point concept is to be questioned. However, the breaking point would not be without value if one considers that it identifies, not the wall-like division between two streams of movement, but the approximate center of a zone of indifference between two or more adjacent and competing focal points, each of which is a trade center.

Before leaving the topic of the breaking point concept in regional delimitation, we should mention that various modifications of this concept have been employed. For one, the distance variable in the basic equation may be substituted for with travel time, with $B$ in the equation becoming travel time from the smaller of two competing centers. This is a plausible substitution when one considers that in many circumstances, travel time takes on a greater significance than does distance. In suburban areas, housing people who work in the core areas of central cities, the amount of time spent in commuting may be more significant than the distance to the place of employment. The distance between place of residence and place of work may be shorter via circuitous or narrow streets with many stoplights and stop signs and lower posted speed limits. An alternate route, though somewhat longer, may be a multilane arterial street with fewer impediments to smooth traffic flow and, as a result, may be somewhat faster. Considering these alternatives, the longer but faster route is the one usually followed.

The distance variable also may be weighted or modified to take into account different road conditions, route friction in the form of hazards along the route, points of congestion, and the like.

Regarding the other variable in the interaction equation, mass or population, one might substitute other measures in dealing with the attractiveness of a focal point. Volume of retail sales is one substitution that has been used, as has floor space in retail establishments, particularly in shopper's goods lines. We could also consider that employment opportunities would be a preferable expression of attractiveness based on the assumption that people are attracted to places that have greater employment possibilities, either in total number or in the array of types of possible employment. These are only a few of the modifications that might be or have been employed in formulating the gravity or interaction model. Regardless of the modification, the basic notions remain that mass and distance are the two significant factors influencing man's movements over two dimensional space.

# 7

# central place concepts

In examining the nature of cities, large and small, we recognized that each has relationships with a tributary area and the non-urban population of that area in a symbiotic manner (Chapter 6). Each has contacts and communications with a tributary area to some extent and degree. Although the particular city may have a function of a relatively uncommon nature or a function that is not especially prominent in or characteristic of other cities, such as railroad repair or servicing centers, winter recreation centers, financial centers, and the like, all cities have the common function of providing or distributing an array of goods and services to the resident population of that city and to the population of the tributary area. Cities, in their development, have all become—as many began—trade and service centers to some extent.

Consider now a region with one hundred urban centers. One of these might have the dominant function of being a railroad repair center, four might have the chief purpose of providing outdoor recreation services, five might mainly provide financial services, five might do the same with educational services, ten might offer mostly administrative services, and so on until all one hundred are accounted for. Each of the centers, though, regardless of the dominant function, has a role in fulfilling the function of a trade and service center that distributes an array of goods and services to the resident and nonresident population. Even though in some cases these goods and services might be dispensed to a population far removed from the distribution center, such as with auto assembly plants or a Federal Reserve Bank, the greatest amount or degree of interaction can be expected to take place between points of origin of the goods and services in the urban center and the resident population of the center itself and that of the surrounding tributary area.

Thus, the common function of virtually all centers is the dispensing of goods and services to a local resident population and to the population of the adjacent tributary area. These are functions carried on at centralized locations, as opposed to functions dispersed widely over area, with the former occurring at relatively few locations in a region, namely, the focal points of that region. In each case, there are spatial relationships between the functional offerings of the focal point and their distribution within the tributary area.

Now it is necessary to clarify some terms used above and in the sections to follow. *Function* has reference to the conduct of an activity of a discrete type.

There are numerous functions performed by the city and many, if not most, of these have to do with the dispensing of goods and services. The distribution of food from supermarkets, the dispensing of motor fuel at gasoline stations, and the offering of financial services at banks and other financial institutions are examples of the many functions conducted in the city. Each of the functions of the city takes place in an *establishment* which simply refers to the physical unit, usually a building, within which an activity takes place, that is, in which a function is performed. *Functional unit* is a term used to denote the single occurrence of a function. Thus, in a single establishment, two functions might be performed, as with a combination garage and gasoline station. In this case, two functions are performed, with two functional units, but there is only one establishment. If there are two establishments, one, a gasoline station, and the other, a combination gasoline station and garage, there would be two functions performed, two establishments, and three functional units. Reference will be made in the following sections to these terms and an understanding of their meanings is important at this time.

## Spatial Setting of Central Place Functions

To begin, let us consider a region where there is a self-sufficient, dispersed population, like that found in an agrarian society. The stage of self-sufficiency is passed at some point in time due to needs for specialized goods and services that cannot be provided by the consuming unit, such as a family or clan. A specialized item, like salt, might be needed yet the individual population unit is not in a position to provide it, thus, there is a demand for a good that cannot be satisfied by the individual unit. Another factor coming into play is that the people comprising the dispersed

population have rising expectations. Perhaps, infant mortality has been common among the population and each generation longs for or desires medical care for infants beyond what is forthcoming in the individual population unit. In this case, a demand for service (medical care) is produced and it cannot be satisfied by the individual population unit.

In the forms of (1) unsatisfied demands, and (2) rising expectations, a rationale is provided, then, for the occurrence of establishments that will provide the goods and services needed by the dispersed population. In other words, a rationale is provided for the occurrence of centralized functions most in demand by the dispersed population and for the development of some establishments in which these functions are performed.

Before these events can occur, however, several conditions must be met. There must be a division of labor accompanying specialization of economic activity. A given proprietor in the population must devote all or nearly all of his working effort and talents to provision of the specialized good or service, whether he is a shopkeeper or a medical practitioner. Another condition accompanying the occurrence of a specialized function is the attempt to maximize access to the population served by the establishment that provides the good or service. This involves selection of a site of operations that is fairly well centralized within the region served and with a transportation network, however rudimentary, that allows point-to-point movement within the region. In many areas in the world, such movement is by means of footpaths, wagonroads, and shallow streams, but in more economically advanced regions, this movement is via graded and surfaced roads and railroads. But whatever the means of movement, the objective is the same: to provide a means of obtaining needed goods and services.

Also needed for the occurrence of the centralized function is an adequate *threshold*. Threshold refers to the latent body of consumers of the good or service provided. The threshold population might be thought of simply as the number of people needed to provide a sufficient aggregate demand that justifies the inauguration and continuance of a centralized function, or it might be considered the aggregate purchasing power of the population available to procure a given good or service. As an example, a certain functional unit might have a latent body of 1000 customers. If their average annual disposable income is $200, there would be $200,000 available from which goods and services could be acquired. If, however, the regional average annual disposable income was $2000, there would be $2,000,000 available to acquire goods and services, even though the population is the same. Obviously, then, in dealing with regions where income levels are relatively homogeneous, one might be content to consider threshold as referring to the population serving as consumers for a specific good or service. If there are significant differences in income levels among or within regions, it would be better to consider disposable or gross income that is available for acquisition of goods and services.

Whether or not the threshold population or purchasing power is available to a certain establishment at a particular location depends, in turn, on the *range* of good or service. Range is the distance beyond which the total cost to the user becomes greater than the value of the good or service to him. A loaf of bread might serve as an example. The selling price of this good in a certain establishment might be twenty five cents. Then add to this the transportation cost of acquiring the good, either in money or time, say five cents for a nearby consumer. The total cost of the good at this close-in point of consumption becomes thirty cents. A second party, four times as distant from the establishment offering the same good, is faced with the twenty five cent purchase price, plus about twenty cents in transport cost, for a total

price of approximately forty five cents.[1] At this price, the second consumer might elect not to acquire the good and, therefore, would be beyond the range of it, since the cost to him is greater than the value received or than his ability to acquire it.

For persons beyond the range of a good or service offered at a given location, the alternatives are three. He might do without the good or service, he might substitute an alternative good or service, or he might obtain the good or service from a different source on a more favorable basis, once the alternate source comes into existence and providing he is within the range of the good distributed from this second source.

## Development of Lowest Order Central Places

A central place means the locality within which centralized functions are performed, especially the distribution of goods and services. Further, the central place offers goods and services for consumption by the population of the central place itself and also by the population of the tributary area that is within the range of the goods or services being offered by the central place. At the time of origin of the central place, the number of goods and services dispensed is limited, thus the number of functions performed is limited. Each of the functional offerings has a relatively low threshold and range in that the goods or services offered are not distributed to great distance or to a large population and large aggregate purchasing power.

In a study of hamlets in southwestern

---

[1]Transport cost, as used in this presentation, refers to the investment needed to overcome the distance between place of demand and place of supply. This might be an investment of money or of time. In the example cited, if the consumer travels to the establishment to acquire a loaf of bread, he invests money in the means of conveyance, such as a horse, a wagon, or an automobile, and he invests time as well.

**Table 7–1**  Rank-Orders of Most Frequently Occurring Central Functions in Three Spatial Settings

| Iowa | Southern Illinois | Southwest Wales |
|---|---|---|
| 1. Gasoline filling station | Gasoline filling station | Place of worship |
| 2. Church | Church | Post office branch |
| 3. Animal feed store | Food store | Grocery/general store |
| 4. Auto repair shop | Tavern | Public house |
| 5. Insurance agency | Restaurant | Petrol filling station |
| 6. Food store | Beauty shop | Junior school |
| 7. Tavern | Insurance agency | Meeting hall |
| 8. Restaurant | General store | Car repair garage |
| 9. Bulk oil distributor | Auto repair garage | Haulage/general carrier |
| 10. Meeting hall | Meeting hall | Confectioner/tobacconist |

SOURCES:  E. Thomas, *Iowa Business Digest*, Vol. 31 (1960), H. Stafford, *Economic Geography*, Vol. 39, No. 2 (April 1963), H. Carter, H. Stafford, and M. Gilbert, *Economic Geography*, Vol. 46, No. 1 (January, 1970).

Wisconsin, G. Trewartha developed a definition of hamlet that took into account the functional establishments characteristic of these very small population centers.[2] He stated that in the usual hamlet, there was a total of six active functional units and although there is no fixed number of functional units characterizing other small central places, the number likely is less than 6 to 12. Assuming that the functions are performed by residents of the small central place and not by absentees, and that the average family size is four, there would be a resident population of something less than fifty persons in such centers. In a historical context, the number of functional units in embryonic centers commonly was one, and the number of functions two—a general store and a hostelry in combination. Often, the way-station on a transportation route, with its stable and inn, served as the nucleus for the evolution of a small trade center.

The specific types of centralized functions characterizing low order central places vary among different cultures, as well as within a given culture. To a large degree, they reflect the social and economic nature of the region they serve. The four most commonly occurring functions in small trade centers in Iowa were found to be gasoline filling stations, churches, animal feed stores, and auto repair shops.[3] The four most commonly occurring functions in trade centers in southern Illinois were gasoline filling stations, churches, food stores, and taverns.[4] Thus, in two spatial settings in the United States, there is agreement that the functions most commonly encountered in low order urban centers are the dispensing of automobile fuel and religious services. Is this to be taken as the basic nucleus of a low order trade center in contemporary United States? In a different cultural setting, that of southwest Wales, the four most commonly occurring functional units were, in order, place of worship, post office branch, grocery shop/general store, and public house.[5] The petrol (gasoline) filling station ranks only fifth in occurrence in Welsh communities (Table 7–1).

[2] G. Trewartha, "The Unincorporated Hamlet: One Element in the American Settlement Fabric," *Annals of the Association of American Geographers*, Vol. 33, No. 1 (March, 1943).

[3] Edwin Thomas, *Iowa Business Digest*, Vol. 31, (1960).

[4] Howard Stafford, "The Functional Bases of Small Towns," *Economic Geography*, Vol. 39, No. 2 (April, 1963).

[5] H. Carter, H. Stafford, and M. Gilbert, *Economic Geography*, Vol. 46, No. 1 (January, 1970).

The major point here is that, given favorable conditions, especially of threshold and range, a settlement cluster originates with the major overall role of providing goods and services for its tributary area and itself. This settlement has relatively few functions, regardless of its cultural setting, although the mix of functions likely is different between different cultures, if not between different regions.

Based on the number of functions performed by a trade center, the overall *order* of the center can be established. Order, as used here, has reference to the standing or level of an urban center within the context of an ordering of places in a functional hierarchy. It is assumed here that all urban centers have, to different degrees, the function of dispensing goods and services, and the notion of functional orders simply recognizes levels or degrees attained by a certain urban center in performing this general function. Reference often is made to high and low order centers, indicating extremes in performance of this function, but it should be recognized that there are several orders between these extremes. The discussion in this section has dealt only with the origin and character of the lowest order central places.

## Structural Elements of the Functional Hierarchy

Of the lowest order centers that come into being, some fail to endure, many become relatively stable and unchanging, and others become larger with a greater array of functions and larger resident populations. At any point in time, then, we have not a single order of central places in a region, but instead a hierarchy of central places. Some of the lowest order central places retain their limited number of functions, while some take on new or additional functions; these latter are, perhaps, the centers with the most favorable locations and greater degrees of cen-

trality within a region. When you consider a region in which there is a functional order of central places identified simply as $A$, there likely would develop a functional order identified as $B$. The $A$ level centers have the minimum number of functions, say six, while the $B$ level centers have all of the functions of the $A$ level centers, plus some in addition. In this region, there could be $C$ level centers as well, these being the next highest order, and each of these would have the functions of the $A$ level centers, those of the $B$ level centers, plus an additional group as well. This development of a functional hierarchy is expressed in Table 7–2. Notice that each functional order of places has the functions performed in each preceding lower order, plus an incremental number of functions. Since the incremental number of functions are those for which there is less frequency of demand than for the functions of the central places of the preceding order, it follows that each added function or group of functions calls for an increased threshold and an extended range.

**Table 7–2**  Number of Functions and Orders of Central Places

| Functional Order | Number of Functions | | | |
| --- | --- | --- | --- | --- |
| | $n$ | $n + 5$ | $n + 10$ | $n + 15$ |
| A (lowest) | X | | | |
| B | X | X | | |
| C | X | X | X | |
| D (highest) | X | X | X | X |

Regarding the functions that are added by higher order central places, there is no fixed pattern or model that applies to all cases. Each region, with its own demographic characteristics, economic structure, and cultural traits, may support functions different from those in other regions. As there is no set pattern of functions present in the lowest order central places, neither is there

**Table 7–3**  Order of Entry of Central Functions

| Score on component[a] | Central Function | Score on Component | Central Function |
|---|---|---|---|
| 5.5–6.0 | Gas and service station | | Women's clothing |
| | Automobile repair | | Supermarket |
| | Restaurant | | Dentist |
| 5.0–5.5 | Bar | | Hotel |
| | Grocery | | Jewelry |
| | Farm materials (feed, seed) | 1.5–2.0 | Extensive amusements |
| 4.5–5.0 | Church | | Liquor |
| | Farm implements | | Men's clothing |
| | Farm sales (inc. elevator) | | Men's and women's clothing |
| 4.0–4.5 | Bldg. materials, lumber | | Radio TV sales and service |
| | Barber | | Funeral |
| | Hardware | | Shoes |
| | Post office | | Motel |
| | Bank, savings and loan | | Blacksmith, sheet metal |
| | Appliances | | Fixit |
| | Local govt. facility | 1.0–1.5 | Florist |
| 3.5–4.0 | Meeting hall | | Bakery |
| | Oil fuel, bulk station | | Bus, taxi service |
| | Furniture | | Coal year |
| | Beauty | | Telegraph office |
| 3.0–3.5 | Insurance | | Telephone answering service |
| | Variety | | Job printing |
| | Other bldg. services | | Gifts |
| | Drug | | Loan |
| | Specialized auto repair | | Photographs |
| | Indoor amusements | | Private warehouse |
| | Self-service laundry | | Commercial garage |
| | Lawyer | | Pay bills, currency exchange |
| 2.5–3.0 | Doctor | 0.5–1.0 | Movers and haulers |
| | New auto sales | | Candy |
| | Real estate | | Music and records |
| | Newspaper | | Children's clothing |
| | Shoe repair | | Electrical repair |
| | Drive-in eating place | | Bldg. and Cont. |
| | Cleaners and laundry (operator) | | County government |
| | Used auto sales | | Mission |
| 2.0–2.5 | Plumbing | | Second hand |
| | Movies | | Monument sales |
| | Auto accessories | | Sporting goods |
| | Other medical | | Dairy |
| | Veterinarian | | Auto wrecking |
| | Food locker | | |

[a]Component scores are based on the incidence of central functions in a number of central places. In a matrix in which rows are central places and columns are central functions, cells are coded 1 if the function is present in the central place and 0 if it is not. Direct factor analysis summarizes variations of centers and of functions in the matrix.

SOURCE: Berry, Barnum, and Tennant, "Retail Location and Consumer Behavior," *Papers of the Regional Science Association*, Vol. 9 (1962).

a fixed sequencing of occurrence of additional functions of higher order centers. What is said here is that there is no rigid model of the first group of centralized functions, nor is there any firm pattern as to what the order of addition of new functions will be.

Within a given regional context, however, an *order of entry* can be established that presents conditions in the chosen region. Order of entry has to do with the incidence or frequency of occurrence of a particular function in a number of centers. Given a number of centers in a region, a particular specialized function or group of functions may be found in all of them, after which other functions may be found to exist in fewer of the centers, with additional functions found in a still smaller number of centers. The task is one of stating the order of frequency of different functions in a number of centers, such as what function or group of functions is the fifth most commonly

found, the sixth, seventh, tenth, twentieth, and so on through the entire array of functions and number of centers. In a study in southwestern Iowa, an order of entry of central functions was established, and the order of entry of different functions in this region is presented in Table 7–3.[6] Also, remember that other regions would exhibit somewhat different orders of entry, even different parts of the United States. In the work cited above, groups of functions of progressively lower orders of entry are associated with different functional orders of urban centers and each functional order is identified by name.

Centers with 10 to 25 functions, which are the functions with the lowest order of entry, are referred to as "villages." The

[6]Brian J. L. Berry, H. Gardiner Barnum, and Robert J. Tennant, "Retail Location and Consumer Behavior," *Papers of the Regional Science Association,* Vol. 9 (1962).

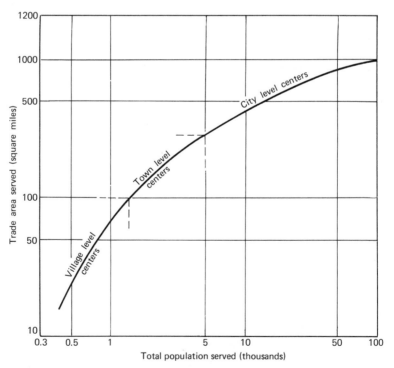

**Figure 7–1** Relationship between size of trade area and population served, by order of center. *Source.* Adapted from Berry, Barnum, and Tennant, *Papers* of the Regional Science Assoc., Vol. 9 (1962).

functions of villages are virtually ubiquitous among all cities of the region, large and small. Central places with 28 to 50 functions, a number of which have slightly higher orders of entry than village level functions, are identified as "towns." It should be remembered that, of the total number of functions of town level centers, most also characterize village level centers, while others comprise the incremental bundle peculiar to the higher order centers. Central places with more than 55 central functions are identified as "cities." The functions found in city level centers include those found in village level centers and those found in town level centers, plus an incremental group of functions unique to the highest order centers in the region.

One other aspect of the above study is that each order of central place is associated with a given population (threshold) and a maximum distance to which goods and services are distributed on a regular basis (range). Village level centers serve a population of approximately 1500 to 2000 people and have a tributary area of about 100 square miles, meaning the range of goods and services of such centers is approximately 10 miles. For town level centers, the population served is in the range of 1500–5000 and the tributary areas include about 300 square miles, thus, ranges of goods and services are about 18 miles. City level centers serve populations of 5000 to 90,000, have trade areas of over 1000 square miles, and ranges of goods and services of about 32 to 35 miles (Figure 7–1).

When we move from one order of central place to a higher order, a number of functions are added that are unique to the higher order center. These additional functions have higher thresholds, greater ranges, and a higher order of entry. Another point is that there is a greater resident population in the higher order centers, providing the work force needed to distribute the added goods and services. This is to say that higher order centers tend to have greater populations

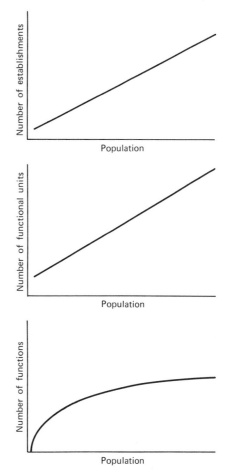

**Figure 7–2**    Population and numbers of establishments, functional units, and functions.

than do centers of lower orders, and that there is a relationship between urban center population and elements of the central place structure. One aspect of this relationship is that the number of establishments dispensing goods and services enlarges with increases in population in a linear manner; this is also true of functional units (Figure 7–2).[7] The number of functions, however, increases in a curvilinear manner. This is explained by the fact that there is a relatively fixed number of functions that urban centers can have, that is, there are only so many goods and services that can be provided. Therefore, the curve for number of functions would

[7]Edwin Thomas, *Op. Cit.*

flatten as larger cities are encountered, for example, a city of 500,000 can offer few functions that are not offered in a city of 300,000. There is, however, a duplication of functions in larger cities, with a concomitant duplication of functional units and establishments. Instead of there being a single drug store, for example, there may be sufficient population and purchasing power to provide the threshold for two or three or more establishments with this function, each with roughly the same range and threshold.

## Spatial Aspects of the Central Place Hierarchy

The point has been made repeatedly that there is a functional hierarchy of central places in a region. Also, each of the places in the hierarchy has a tributary area established by the ranges of the goods and services that the establishments of that place provide. Based on differences in ranges of goods or services, different orders in the functional hierarchy can be discerned (Figure 7–3A). With greater ranges, higher order centers have larger tributary areas than do lower order and smaller centers. Also, the higher order centers have a greater number of functions of a more specialized nature, with each of these having a greater range or threshold (Figure 7–3B).

Logically, the tributary areas of all places of a given order would be of the same areal extent.[8] Theoretically, they would have the same configuration and population. It was suggested prior to 1936 that these equivalent tributary areas were circular in form. However, if a region is blanketed with a system of circular tributary areas, there is created either (1) some unassigned area in the interstices between tributary areas when they are tangent and mutually exclusive or, (2) overlap of tributary areas when all parts of the region are included in one or another of the tributary areas (Figure 7–4).[9]

To provide a spatial framework for consideration of central place hierarchy, Walter Christaller (1933) suggested a hexagonal system of tributary areas in which all parts of the region are included in mutually exclusive tributary areas.[10] This implies, of course, a monopoly or near monopoly by a given central place in dispensing goods and services to the adjacent tributary area. In the reality of today, with the increased mobility and affluence of many people and vastly improved means of transportation, the notion of local monopoly by a trade center over adjacent population begins to prove faulty. At the time of development of Christaller's concepts, however, there likely was more validity to the notion of mutually exclusive tributary areas.

The theoretical framework of Christaller is based on a number of postulates concerning the region within which the framework exists.

Postulate 1:  The region involved is a homogeneous plain without appreciable relief throughout.

Postulate 2:  There is a homogeneous environment throughout the region, especially in terms of soil fertility, moisture supply, and the like.

Postulate 3:  There is a uniform distribution of rural population in the region.

---

[8]In reality, it would be naive to expect two or more places, though of the same functional order, to have *exactly* the same array of goods and services. Also, it would be incorrect to assume that two establishments providing the same function would have *exactly* the same range and threshold, since they could have different levels of efficiency of operations, different profit levels, different operating expenses, etc.

[9]This matter of overlap of tributary areas might not be completely unrealistic, in view of the likelihood of a "zone of indifference" between tributary areas (Chapter 6).

[10]W. Christaller, *Die zentralen Orte in Süddeutschland,* Jena: Gustav Fischer Verlag, 1933, and C. W. Baskin, "A Critique and Translation of W. Christaller's *Die zentralen Orte in Süddeutschland,*" University of Virginia, 1957.

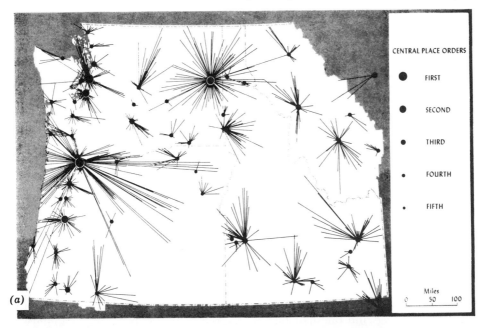

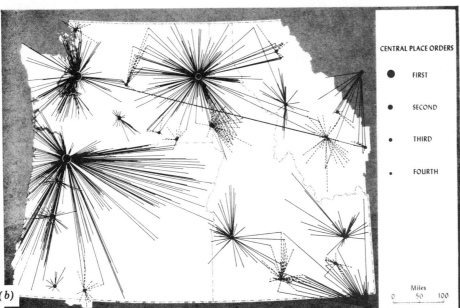

**Figure 7-3**   (*A* and *B*) Patterns of daily and Sunday newspaper dominance: Pacific Northwest. *Source.* Richard E. Preston, *Economic Geography,* Vol. 47, (1971). Reproduced by permission of *Economic Geography.*

Postulate 4: There is homogeneity throughout the region in terms of ease of movement or transportation. There are no local advantages presented by navigable waterways and the like. All movement is overland and the sole factor influencing this movement is distance.

The tendency is, in evaluating the

above postulates, to discredit them on the basis that they do not represent reality or even closely approximate the real world. One might state that the earth's surface is not without relief, that there are great differences in the physical environment, that there is not a uniform distribution of population even in small areas, and that

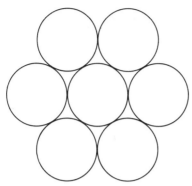
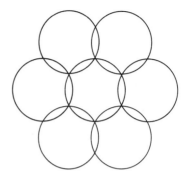

**Figure 7–4** Arrangements of circular tributary areas.

there are favored transportation routes, both over land and water. Now, absurd as it may seem, consider a world in which none of the real differences exist, as postulated by Christaller, and put on this surface about three and one-half billion people. Is it not conceivable that settlement patterns would emerge that would be at least somewhat regular and structured, as opposed to a completely random pattern? This might have been the type of question that Christaller had in mind when developing his concepts based on settlement in a homogeneous region.

With the above postulates, Christaller suggested that there would develop different orders of central places and that places of the same order would have tributary areas of the same size, with these taking on a hexagonal form.[11] The hexagonal form is the most likely conceptual form of a tributary area in that it does away with objections to the circular form mentioned above and represents a geometric form in which all points on the periphery of the tributary area are nearly equidistant from a point marking the center of the tributary area (the focal point). A network of square tributary areas falls short of meeting the last criterion, as does one made up of triangles. Thus, there is a rationale for development of a theoretical framework of

[11]The concepts of Christaller were based, not on abstract thinking, but on empirical evidence dealing with urban settlements in southern Germany.

tributary areas in a basic hexagonal pattern.

Following along with the work of Christaller, there would be in a region a number of low order centers, each centered within its hexagonal tributary area (Figure 7–5). Empirical work by Christaller disclosed that there were regularities in the spacing of the lowest order centers, which he identified as "market hamlets", and that generally, these were found to be about 4.35 miles apart, the approximate diameter also of each tributary area.

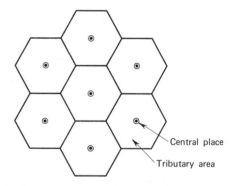

**Figure 7–5** Network of low order central places and their tributary areas.

Superimposed over the network of low order central places and their tributary areas is a network made up of central places of the next highest order, together with their tributary areas. These too would follow the hexagonal form. What is important to grasp at this point is that the tributary areas of the higher order places, say order $B$, contain the tributary

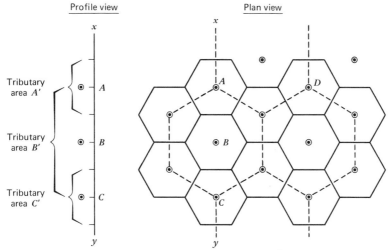

**Figure 7–6**   Nesting of central places and their tributary areas, two orders.

areas of places of the preceding lower order, say order *A*. Demonstrated here is the principle of *nesting*. In the principle of nesting, central places of a given order and their tributary areas are included within the tributary areas of the next higher order. In turn, these are included within the tributary areas of places of the next highest order, and so on throughout the hierarchy. This is logical when one remembers that each higher order center has certain specialized functions not present in centers of preceding orders, and that these added functions have higher thresholds, greater ranges, and thus, greater areal extent of tributary areas. At the same time, populations in lower order centers and their tributary areas have demands for the specialized

offerings of the higher order center, but they have not reached the threshold population or purchasing power to provide the entry of the higher order function in the lower order center. In accord with the principle of nesting, tributary areas of a given order of center are mutually exclusive of tributary areas of centers of the same order, but are included within the tributary areas of next higher order centers. (Figure 7–6).

We refer again to the work of Christaller who recognized seven hierarchical orders of urban centers, with those of higher order spaced further apart than those of the preceding order and with progressively larger tributary areas. The orders recognized are presented in Table 7–4.

**Table 7–4**   Orders of Central Places and Intercenter Distances (After W. Christaller)

| Order Number | Order Name | Intercenter Distance (Miles) |
|---|---|---|
| 1 (lowest) | Market hamlet | 4.35 |
| 2 | Township center | 7.45 |
| 3 | County seat | 13.04 |
| 4 | District seat | 22.36 |
| 5 | Small state capital | 38.50 |
| 6 | Provincial head city | 67.07 |
| 7 | Regional capital city | 115.51 |

SOURCE:   Based on W. Christaller, *Die zentralen Orte in Süddeutschland* (1933), as presented in Edward Ullman. "A Theory on Location of Cities," *American Journal of Sociology, XLVI* (May, 1941).

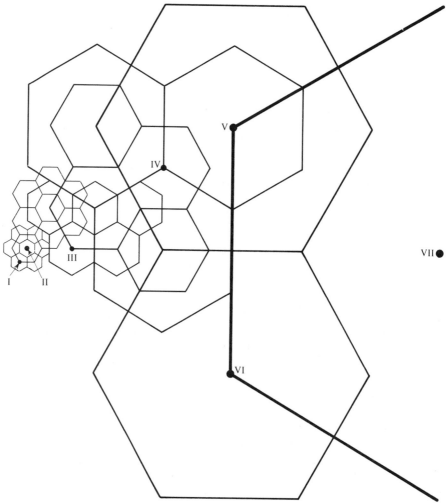

**Figure 7–7** Christaller's system of a spatial hierarchy of central places. *Order:* I market hamlet; II township center; III county seat; IV district city; V small state capital; VI provincial head city; VII regional capital city.

It is helpful to view this hierarchy in diagrammatic form since it is a spatial hierarchy (Figure 7–7). One other aspect of Christaller's work is that there appears to be a regularity, at least in a theoretical sense, in the spacing of centers of similar and different orders, and this is presented in Table 7–4. The regularity in the spacing of centers of different orders is such that the intercenter distances between centers of two consecutive orders, say order $A$ and $B$, is the intercenter distance between centers of the lowest of the two orders ($A$), times the square root of three, If the intercenter distance between places of order $A$ is 4.35 miles, the dis-

tance between places of the next highest order, order $B$, would be 4.35 × $\sqrt{3}$ or 4.35 × 1.732 or 7.5 miles. This system continues until all orders present in the region are included, with the distances between centers of higher orders becoming progressively greater, based on the greater ranges of goods and services provided by higher order centers. Eventually, there would be, at least ideally, a single center of the highest order. This, the primate city, would serve the entire region (see Chapter 6 for a discussion of primate cities).

Others besides Christaller have investigated the matter of a spatial hierarchy of

**Table 7-5**   Comparison of Spacing Patterns in Central Indiana

| Hierarchy Grouping | Mean Measured Distance (Miles) | Theoretical Distance (Miles) Based on $\sqrt{3}$) | Variation from Theoretical (%) |
|---|---|---|---|
| 2nd to 1st | 58.0 | 58.3 | −.52 |
| 2nd to 2nd | 58.6 | 58.3 | +.51 |
| 3rd to 2nd | 35.1 | 33.7 | +4.15 |
| 3rd to 3rd | 35.5 | 33.7 | +5.34 |
| 4th to 3rd | 22.6 | 20.4 | +10.78 |
| 4th to 2nd | 20.5 | 20.4 | + .49 |
| 4th to 1st | 19.6 | 20.4 | −3.92 |
| 4th to 4th | 20.7 | 20.4 | +1.47 |

SOURCE: Neil V. Weber, *Proceedings; Indiana Academy of Science,* Vol. 79, 1969.

urban centers. One investigation was an empirical study of urban center systems in southwestern Wisconsin and in southern England.[12] Different orders of centers were identified and the average distances between centers of similar order were established. Distances between higher order centers were found to average twenty one miles in both regions, and distances between lower order centers were ten miles in southwestern Wisconsin and eight miles in southern England (Table 7-5). Notice that the spacing between centers in these regions is greater than in southern Germany, Christaller's region of study. Interpolation from another study on the location of trade centers indicates that lowest order centers (villages) are approximately ten miles apart, the next highest order (towns) about twelve miles apart, and the highest order (cities) about thirty five miles apart.[13] In a recent study of a fifty-two county section of Indiana, distances between centers of the same order and between centers of successive orders were compared with theoretical distances based on Christaller's model.[14] For this

relatively homogeneous region, the spacing of urban centers was found to be in near agreement with the model (Table 7-5).

Although the studies cited above are not in absolute agreement with the work of Christaller, there are certain points of similarity. There is a functional hierarchy of urban centers established in each regional study and a spatial hierarchy of tributary areas. Further, there is a nesting of trade areas of lower order centers within those of higher order centers.

## Changes in the Nesting Principle

Concepts dealing with the spacing of urban centers and their tributary areas and the manner in which nesting is structured, appear to be predicated on a continuation of conditions of society that led to the development of the initial spatial system. In an early stage of development, the regional economy and its dispersed population provide the rationale for a functional hierarchy as suggested by Christaller, with many small market hamlets serving as the underlying stratum in a spatial hierarchy. Other strata are comprised of higher functional orders, each made up of progressively fewer centers. This spatial structure may be warranted at a certain point in time in a given regional economic setting, but times and conditions change. In today's developed society, with a greater centralization of

[12]John E. Brush and Howard E. Bracey, "Rural Service Centers in Southwestern Wisconsin and Southern England," *Geographical Review,* Vol. XLV (October, 1955).

[13]Berry, Barnum, and Tennant. *Op. Cit.*

[14]Neil V. Weber, "A Comparison of the Central Place Hierarchy Pattern of Central Indiana to the Walter Christaller Model," *Proceedings, Indiana Academy of Science,* Vol. 79, 1969.

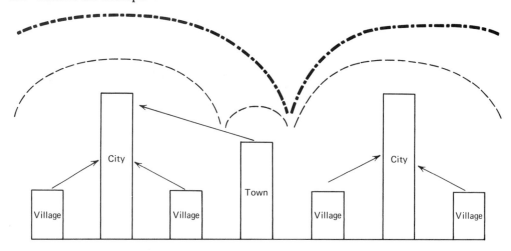

**Figure 7–8**    Altered nesting process: southwestern Iowa. *Source.* Adapted from Berry, Barnum, and Tennant, *Papers* of the Regional Science Assoc., Vol. 9, 1962 (Figure 19).

economic activity and population and changes in transportation, the viability of lower order centers is in some jeopardy. Persons in small, lower order centers may obtain the goods and services they need, not from nearby, slightly higher order centers, but from more distant and still higher order centers. This situation is well illustrated in the case of southwestern Iowa.[15] In this region, lowest order centers, villages, were within the spheres of influence, not of the nearest higher order center, towns, but were oriented to centers two orders higher, cities. Town level centers were, however, nested within the spheres of influence of city level centers, consistent with the model (Figure 7–8). Thus, the nesting process is found to be different today from what it was in the original concept put forward by Christaller. Lowest order centers are increasingly oriented toward centers several orders or levels higher, in preference to centers of the next highest order that may be in close proximity. Given three orders of centers in a region, labeled *A, B,* and *C,* with *C* level centers the lowest order, the lowest order centers (*C*) are more likely today to come under the influence of *A* level centers than they are *B* level centers, even where the *A* level

[15]Berry, Barnum, and Tennant, *Op. Cit.*

center is more distant from the *C* level center. This phenomenon has been found repeatedly to be true in various parts of the United States.

## Systems of nesting and the "*k*" Value

The system of nesting advanced in the preceding section postulates a higher order central place serving the needs of six centers of the next lowest order at equal distance intervals from the highest order center. When one considers that this arrangement results in the lower order centers being "shared" between higher order centers, this arrangement is not especially realistic. Using the same assumptions on which central place theory was developed, which was that all areas could be served from a minimum number of higher order centers, a system of nesting employing the *marketing* or *supply principle* is developed. In this system, each higher order center serves its own needs for goods and services, plus those of two adjacent lower order centers. In this manner, each higher order center is the focus of a roughly triangular area and has a virtual monopoly on distribution of goods and services in this area, that is, the notion of shared places is removed from consideration (Figure

## MARKETING PRINCIPLE

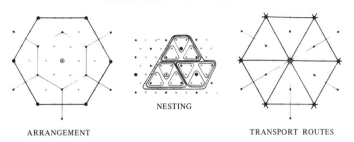

ARRANGEMENT                    NESTING                    TRANSPORT ROUTES

## ADMINISTRATIVE PRINCIPLE

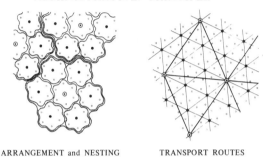

ARRANGEMENT and NESTING          TRANSPORT ROUTES

## TRANSPORTATION PRINCIPLE

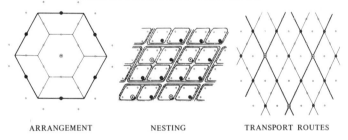

ARRANGEMENT                NESTING              TRANSPORT ROUTES

**Figure 7–9**    Systems of central places based upon the marketing, administrative, and transportation principles. Reprinted from CENTRAL PLACE STUDIES: A BIBLIOGRAPHY OF THEORY AND APPLICATIONS by B. J. L. Berry and A. Pred. Copyright 1961, 1965 by Brian J. L. Berry and Regional Science Research Institute.

7–9). This arrangement is continued, in turn, to higher order centers and in each case a given central place serves the needs of three places — itself and two centers of the next lowest order. In this system, there is optimum serving of area from a minimum of distribution centers. The relationship between numbers of central places serving themselves and lower orders is, according to the marketing principle, expressed as a constant numerical value. This value, known as the "*k*" value,

in the case of the marketing principle is three. When the distribution of goods and services is of prime significance to the number, spacing, and spatial arrangement of urban centers, this *k* value is appropriate.

If, however, the overriding principle expressing the arrangement of urban centers is to maintain political and administrative control over or contact with lowest order centers by higher order centers, a *k* value of seven is more appropriate. In this instance, the *administrative principle* applies, in which the higher order center serves itself and six adjacent lower order centers in terms of administration, protection, and dispensing political services (Figure 7–9). Again, there is a single focal point that serves as the functional center of a nodal region, but here the region is identified using criteria different from the case of the marketing principle.

If urban centers are distributed so that the more important centers or higher order places are arranged in a linear manner on one major traffic route, the nesting arrangement is in accord with the *transportation principle*. In this case, places of highest order are arranged in a linear manner and each serves itself and three other centers, thus, the $k$ value for the transportation principle is four (Figure 7–9). Note too that, in accord with this principle, a pattern of transportation routes results with the minimum amount of route connecting major centers of the spatial system. This is not the case with the other two principles of nesting we discussed.

Empirical study disputes the idea that there are any such regularities as suggested by the marketing, administrative, or transportation principles. One study conducted in southwestern Iowa presents information supporting the conclusion that places of the higher order (cities) serve themselves and four places of the third order (villages).[16] Thus, for centers of these orders, the $k$ value is five. Centers of the second order (towns), however, serve themselves and their immediate tributary areas alone and have a $k$ value of one. As stated by Berry, Barnum, and Tennant, the findings of this study ". . . militate against the development of any one of Christaller's arrangements of nests, both because at any one level, sizes of trade areas will differ, and because in the symbiosis of levels,

choice of higher order centers is always in the direction of the center with the greatest centrality."[17] This statement well reflects the difficulty of application of theoretical concepts developed in an idealized situation at an earlier time to the changed world of today with its heterogeneous character. Even in a case approximating the idealized environment of Christaller, like that of southwestern Iowa, the concepts are not suited if applied with great precision. It is important to realize, however, that the concept of a nesting process or processes is no less valid because it does not apply to all areas of the world. Indicated is a need for continued study of this type to (1) identify changes that occur in the nesting process or processes with the passage of time, and (2) identify differences in the nesting process or processes among different environments with different cultural traits and forms of development.

## Reality and Distortions of a Regular Urban Settlement Pattern

When one examines the pattern of urban settlements in the world around him, he realizes that the idealized concepts of number, spacing, sizes, and hierarchies are not duplicated in reality, nor could they be expected to since they are built on unrealistic postulates. Still, if he is an astute observer, there is the admission that the general aspects of the concepts are valid. Especially suspect, perhaps, is the concept of a regular spacing of central places of similar and different functional orders. Thus, the object at this time is to identify some of the distortions of regularity in urban settlement patterns that result from varying conditions of reality.

One type of distortion of a regular settlement pattern is *distortion by*

---

[16]Berry, Barnum, and Tennant, *Op. Cit.*

[17]Berry, Barnum, and Tennant, *Op. Cit.*

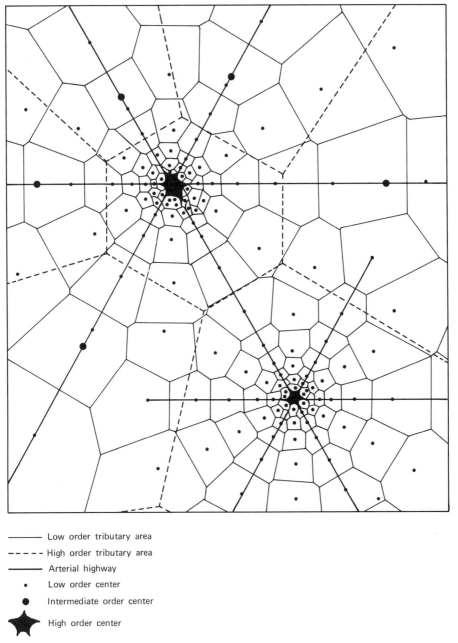

————— Low order tributary area

- - - - - High order tributary area

————— Arterial highway

•   Low order center

●   Intermediate order center

★   High order center

**Figure 7–10**  Distortion of a regular pattern of urban settlements by agglomeration. *Source.* Adapted from Waltor Isard, *Location and Space Economy,* 1956 (Figure 52).

*agglomeration.* In reality, there is a denser pattern of urban settlements in proximity to major urban centers, and the larger the major center, the greater the density of lower order centers around it. It is not uncommon in the case of large central cities that there are in the neighborhood of one hundred or more smaller and lower order centers located within 10 to 20 miles of the larger central city.[18]

[18]Examples of this situation include most large central cities in the United States, such as Chicago with 170 incorporated municipalities within its urbanized area.

Commonly, these are parts of the urbanized area of which the central city is the major component. Outward from the central city, the density of smaller population centers becomes progressively less until it begins to increase as another major center is approached, probably another central city (Figure 7–10).

In view of the above situation, it follows that the range of a good or service provided by one of the lower order centers in close proximity to the central city is less than would be true of centers of the same order but more distant from the major city. This is because a given threshold can be attained within shorter distances from the smaller central place since population densities usually are greater the nearer one is to the major city. Also, per capita disposable incomes tend to be greater in or near large metropolitan centers and this means that a smaller number of people comprise the threshold population for establishments offering centralized goods and services. The number of low order centers, then, becomes greater in the vicinity of large urban centers based on (1) higher population densities, and (2) greater per capita incomes. It follows that if goods and services offered by close-in lower order centers have shorter ranges, the tributary areas of such centers are of less area than those of similar centers more removed from the major center. Also, there would be a greater number of centers of a low order closer to the major center of the region. The manner in which centers of a lower order are nested within the spheres of influence of places of higher order is contingent on distance from the large and dominant center in a specific region.

The number, location, and spatial organization of urban centers is influenced, in addition to the above agglomeration process, by the degree of localization or dispersal of the resources on which the urban centers directly or indirectly rely. In Christaller's theory, the resource, cropland, was dispersed uniformly throughout the region with no degree of localization. In reality, there are different forms of occurrence of resources, one of which is the *uniform resource* that was considered by Christaller. As a result of different distributions of resources, or of spatial concentrations of resources, we get distortions of a regular urban settlement pattern due to *resource localization*. In a triangular or hexagonal framework of urban settlements, we assume that the resources needed to support the settlements are available everywhere to the same degree. True, some resources, such as cropland, may be relatively uniformly distributed in a region, causing a fairly regular pattern of urban settlements generally in accord with Christaller's concepts. However, other resources may be confined to only one section or zone within a region and a distortion of a regular urban settlement pattern results from the localization of a *zonal resource* (Figure 7–11). These zonal resources might include stands of sawtimber in one zone of a region, a zone of exceptionally fertile soil, or a zone including a number of outcrops of a coal seam. The distribution of urban centers in such a region would be skewed or distorted from a regular pattern, since the population involved in exploitation of the zonal resource would be oriented toward occurrence of the resource.

Another pattern of resource occurrence, still more localized, is one in which the resource occurs in a linear manner. In this case, the distribution of urban centers will be distorted from a regular pattern by the *linear resource* and will be arranged in a linear manner with elongate tributary areas (Figure 7–11). An example of this linear resource might be a stream valley in a mountainous region where most habitable land is located near the stream course, as well as routes of land transportation. In such an instance, population is concentrated in a linear fashion in the valley bottom or on nearby slopes, and central places serving this population would be likewise arranged in a linear manner. Another example of a

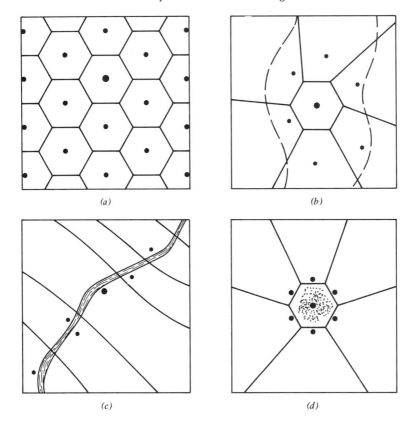

**Figure 7–11**   Types of resource localization and urban settlement patterns. *(a)* Uniform resource (example—arable land). *(b)* Zonal resource (example—sawtimber stand). *(c)* Linear resource (example—stream valley). *(d)* Point resource (example—ore deposit).

linear resource might be a navigable stream. Here, the people utilizing the stream would be concentrated along the streambanks, just like the low order central places serving this population. The many river landings and river ports would be arranged in a linear manner, duplicating the linearity of the stream.

Still another distortion of a regular settlement pattern is one involving a *point resource.* Here, the natural resource on which the human habitation is based occurs in a small area or locality, considered here as a point. Nonetheless, there is sufficient areal extent of the point resource to support a number of low order centers and one or more higher order centers, but these taken together form a

cluster in or on the periphery of the resource occurrence (Figure 7–11). Tributary areas of the central places extend away from the resource occurrence and include less densely populated areas, with the central places at or near the margins of their trade areas, and not centrally located, as suggested by Christaller. An example of a point resource and a pattern of central places that we have discussed would be the occurrence of a mineral resource, such as copper, iron, or lead ore. To serve the needs of the miners and the mining industry, central places come into existence and a multi-order system of central places develops. Perhaps, cities such as Joplin, Missouri and Butte, Montana are examples of the highest order

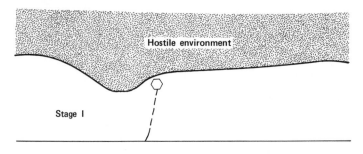

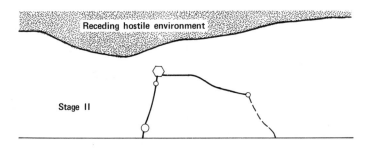

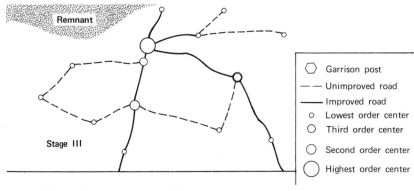

**Figure 7–12** Sequential stages in development of a settlement pattern in a hostile environment.

centers in mining districts utilizing a point resource (lead and copper respectively) but which dominate a number of lower order centers in close proximity to the higher order centers and to the point resource.

Another type or form of distortion of a regular urban settlement pattern is that due to a *time lag* in the spread of settlement. Given a settlement frontier characterized by waves of settlement occurring at different times, the pattern of settlement found in the region may represent a condition that is not destined to be long lasting. The wave of settlement may proceed to near the frontier of a hostile cultural or physical environment and may be temporarily stabilized in accordance with the frontier constraints. At a later time, the hostile environment may be overcome, subdued, or modified sufficiently for the spread of settlement beyond the original frontier, and at this time, the partial settlement pattern becomes more complete and regular in form (Figure 7–12).[19] Similarly, the existence of national boundaries, hostile or friendly, may inhibit the development of a regular settlement pattern.

## Conclusions

Numerous students, scholars, and interested parties have investigated the spatial structure of urban systems and there has developed a conceptual body of knowledge dealing with spatial hierarchies of urban centers. This includes recognition of different functional orders of centers, numbers of centers of different orders, nesting of places within the spatial system, and spatial arrangements of centers of similar or different orders. The body of theory and concept de-

veloped with these matters in mind, assuming a number of postulates, suggests regularities in number, size, and spacing of urban centers of similar or different functional orders.

In examining reality within this body of theoretical information, there were points of agreement and points of disagreement. However, one would be naive if he expects all cases taken from reality to conform to a particular theory dealing with a social phenomenon such as urban centers. If one looks at the basic elements of the theories and concepts, including the concepts of nesting, functional hierarchy, and differing numbers of centers based on different functional levels, there is general agreement that there is merit in them, and that they apply to most areal systems of urban centers. If these basic elements do not apply to a specific system, the task is to establish the reasons that serve to distort the reality from a theoretical framework that has been rationally and logically derived.

---

[19]There are numerous examples of this situation found in accounts of the spread of settlement in western United States.

# 8

# the labor force and economic base of the city

In virtually any city, regardless of its population size, there exists an array of economic activities and functions in which much of the population is regularly engaged. However, about one-third of the population generally is not involved in any economic activity and is, therefore, not in the labor force.[1] Included in this group are homemakers

[1]The labor force is defined as the civilian population that is employed, the civilian population that is unemployed but seeking employment, and members of the Armed Forces. To be included in the labor force, a person must be 16 years of age or more.

and others who do not desire to join the labor force, children and young people who are not eligible for the labor force by virtue of their age, and senior citizens who have retired from the labor force. The remaining population essentially comprises the labor force and consists of those who are regularly employed in either the private or public sector, and those who are not regularly employed but who desire employment. The wages and salaries earned by the employed labor force contribute much of the economic support and taxable wealth of the city.

It should not be assumed, however, that only the working population contributes to the city's economic support. Many thousands of persons of advanced years receive retirement and pension income that also adds to the economic support of the city. Many others receive income from investments, rents, royalties, and the like, with still more thousands of people receiving income from public assistance programs of various types, such as the American programs of welfare and aid to dependent children, and these add to the economic support of the city as well. Other income too is received by individuals, at least for relatively short periods, in the form of unemployment compensation. Additional support is received by cities and other levels of local government in the form of grants, gifts, and loans from the federal government.

Thus, there are many ways by which individuals and local governments receive economic support, though the single most important source is wages and salaries of the employed labor force. Money from this and other sources is available for acquisition of the myriad of goods and services desired by contemporary urban dwellers and their local governments.

## Employment Status of the Urban Labor Force

In the United States in 1970, the total labor force was slightly over 137 million,

**Table 8–1**  Summary of Metropolitan Employment in the U.S.: 1970

| Labor Force Status and Sex | All Races | | White | | Negro | |
|---|---|---|---|---|---|---|
| | Inside Central Cities | Outside Central Cities | Inside Central Cities | Outside Central Cities | Inside Central Cities | Outside Central Cities |
| Males: | | | | | | |
| In civilian labor | | | | | | |
| force (total) | 14,651 | 18,599 | 11,738 | 17,733 | 2,685 | 709 |
| 16–19 years | 954 | 1,338 | 743 | 1,274 | 205 | 55 |
| 20 years and over | 13,697 | 17,261 | 10,995 | 16,459 | 2,480 | 654 |
| Employed: total | 13,970 | 17,926 | 11,262 | 17,107 | 2,483 | 666 |
| 16–19 years | 810 | 1,159 | 646 | 1,100 | 158 | 48 |
| 20 years and over | 13,160 | 16,767 | 10,616 | 16,007 | 2,325 | 618 |
| Unemployed: total | 681 | 673 | 476 | 626 | 202 | 43 |
| 16–19 years | 144 | 180 | 97 | 174 | 47 | 6 |
| 20 years and over | 537 | 493 | 379 | 452 | 155 | 37 |
| Labor force partic- | | | | | | |
| ipation rates: | 75.6 | 79.1 | 75.7 | 79.7 | 76.0 | 71.8 |
| Unemployment rates: | | | | | | |
| total: | 4.6 | 3.6 | 4.1 | 3.5 | 7.5 | 6.1 |
| 16–19 years | 15.1 | 13.5 | 13.1 | 13.7 | 22.9 | — |
| 20 years and over | 3.9 | 2.9 | 3.4 | 2.7 | 6.3 | 5.7 |
| Females: | | | | | | |
| In civilian labor | | | | | | |
| force (total) | 10,181 | 10,726 | 7,837 | 10,061 | 2,198 | 556 |
| 16–19 years | 848 | 1,149 | 680 | 1,102 | 156 | 42 |
| 20 years and over | 9,333 | 9,576 | 7,157 | 8,960 | 2,042 | 514 |
| Employed: total | 9,668 | 10,166 | 7,502 | 9,560 | 2,026 | 501 |
| 16–19 years | 725 | 1,006 | 604 | 971 | 108 | 28 |
| 20 years and over | 8,943 | 9,160 | 6,898 | 8,589 | 1,918 | 473 |
| Unemployed: total | 514 | 560 | 335 | 501 | 172 | 55 |
| 16–19 years | 124 | 143 | 76 | 130 | 48 | 14 |
| 20 years and over | 390 | 417 | 259 | 371 | 124 | 41 |
| Labor force partic- | | | | | | |
| ipation rates: | 44.9 | 42.1 | 43.3 | 41.6 | 51.8 | 52.2 |
| Unemployment rates: | | | | | | |
| Total: | 5.0 | 5.2 | 4.3 | 5.0 | 7.8 | 9.9 |
| 16–19 years | 14.6 | 12.4 | 11.2 | 11.8 | 30.8 | — |
| 20 years and over | 4.2 | 4.4 | 3.6 | 4.1 | 6.1 | 8.0 |

Source: U.S. Bureau of the Census, *CURRENT POPULATION REPORTS,* Series P-23, No. 37, Government Printing Office, Washington, 1971.

with the labor force in metropolitan areas about 90 million or 66 percent of the national total.[2] The metropolitan labor force includes employees in S.M.S.A.'s only and, therefore, excludes many members of the urban labor force. If the labor force of smaller cities was included as well, the urban labor force would account for perhaps 75 to 80 percent of the nation's working population.

Males make up the largest share of the urban labor force, with the least differential between male and female employees in the case of Negro employees (Figure

[2]U.S. Bureau of the Census, *CURRENT POPU-LATION REPORTS,* Series P-23, No. 37, "Social and Economic Characteristics of the Population in Metropolitan and Nonmetropolitan Areas: 1970 and 1960", Government Printing Office, Washington, 1971.

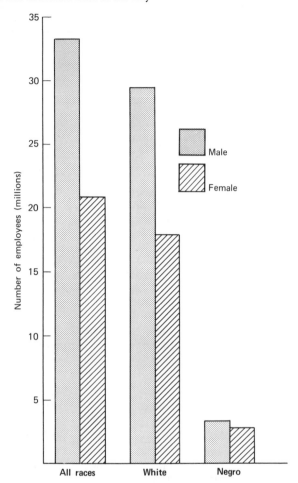

**Figure 8–1** Elements of the metropolitan labor force (by number of employees, sex, and race), United States: 1970. *Source.* Based on data in *Social and Economic Characteristics of the Population in Metropolitan and Nonmetropolitan Areas: 1970 and 1960.* Bureau of the Census (June 24, 1971).

8–1). Though females outnumber males in the population, the greater representation of males in the urban labor force is the result of differences in participation rates.[3] The participation rate of males in the labor force in 1970 was about 78 percent, a decline from the 1960 rate of 82 percent. By contrast, the participation rate for females in 1970 was about 44

[3]Participation rate has reference to the share of the population or some segment of the population that is in the labor force, either employed or unemployed.

percent, a significant increase from the 1960 rate of 38 percent.

There are other notable and important contrasts in the urban labor force, in addition to the greater participation rate of males. Another contrast is the difference in unemployment rates between sexes, between different age groups, between races, and between localities. Unemployment rates are higher for female workers than for male workers, both within central cities and within the suburban rings of S.M.S.A.'s (Table 8–1). The unemployment problem is most

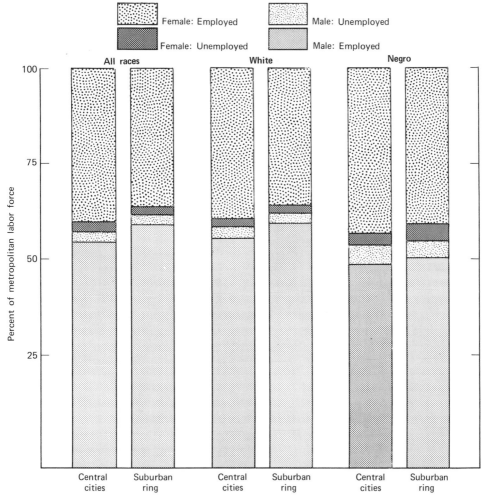

**Figure 8–2**   Structure of metropolitan labor force–1970. *Source.* Based on data in *Social and Economic Characteristics of the Population in Metropolitan and Nonmetropolitan Areas: 1970 and 1960.* Bureau of the Census (June 24, 1971).

acute for workers under 20 years of age, both male and female, and accompanying the problems of unemployment among the young and the disadvantaged are the concomitant problems of idleness, frustration, and hopelessness.

Unemployment is more chronic with black urban workers, especially the young black worker. Unemployment rates among young blacks is about 23 percent for males and 31 percent for females. For adult black workers, too, the unemployment rates are higher than for their white urban counterparts (Figure 8–2).

In addition to the individual and fam-

ily problems associated with these differences that result in less income and more idle time, there is the fact that there is less taxable income for the cities and other levels of government to provide the needed public services for the population, such as schools, streets, recreation programs, water treatment, sanitary sewers, and the like.

## Earnings and Occupations

The economic sector dealing with the distribution of goods and services is known as the *tertiary sector*. Employment in the tertiary sector is especially concen-

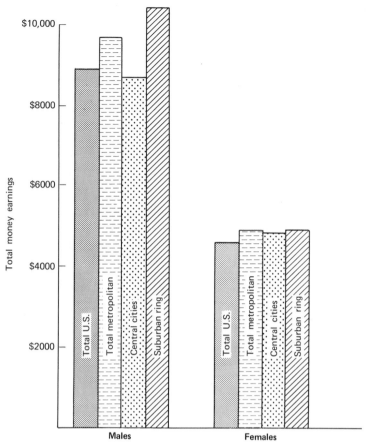

**Figure 8–3**    Average earnings of workers, by place of residence and sex, 1969. *Source.* Based on data in *Social and Economic Characteristics of the Population in Metropolitan and Nonmetropolitan Areas: 1970 and 1960.* Bureau of the Census (June 24, 1971).

trated in urban centers and earnings per capita in this sector tend to be greater than those in other economic sectors. In comparing earnings of workers in metropolitan areas, where the bulk of the tertiary activity is concentrated, with earnings of workers in the entire labor force of the United States, the former are significantly higher than the latter (Figure 8–3). Earnings of workers in the suburban rings of metropolitan areas are higher than those of workers in central cities, and the earnings of workers in total metropolitan areas are greater than those of the labor force of the entire country.

An explanation of the above differences might include the fact that a high level of skills is needed to perform the specialized jobs in the tertiary sector, such as professional services. Since earnings are assigned to the place of residence of the worker and not the place of employment, many of the more skilled workers earning incomes in the central cities reside in suburbs so that average earnings in the latter communities are higher than they otherwise might be. Those working and residing in the central cities tend to include significant numbers who possess lower levels of skills and, as a result, their incomes are less than their more highly skilled, suburban counterparts. Also, in the central city, there are higher levels of under-

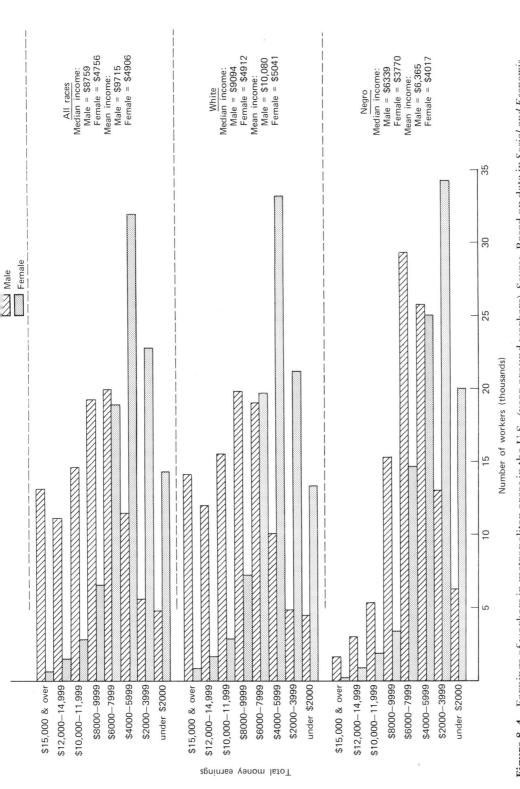

**Figure 8–4** Earnings of workers in metropolitan areas in the U.S. (year-around workers). *Source.* Based on data in *Social and Economic Characteristics of the Population in Metropolitan and Nonmetropolitan Areas: 1970 and 1960.* Bureau of the Census (June 24, 1971).

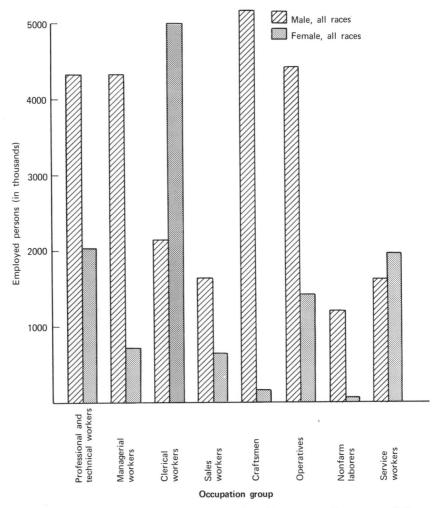

**Figure 8–5** Current occupation of the employed in metropolitan areas, U.S.—1970. *Source.* Based on data in *Social and Economic Characteristics of the Population in Metropolitan and Nonmetropolitan Areas: 1970 and 1960.* Bureau of the Census (June 24, 1971).

employment and part-time employment, especially among minority groups, than in the suburban ring, which lowers average earnings.

There also are great differences in earnings of urban workers based on locality, occupation, and demographic characteristics, such as age, sex, and race. Notice from Figure 8–4 that earnings of male urban workers are appreciably higher than those of females, in the approximate ratio of 2.0 to 1.0. Furthermore, earnings of Negroes of both sexes are lower than

those of white workers of both sexes, in the approximate ratio of 1.0 to 0.6 for males and 1.0 to 0.8 for females.

Urban workers are as we said, engaged in a wide spectrum of economic activities. It is convenient to group urban workers into similar classes or groups, either based on (1) industries, which state the economic activities in which they are engaged, or (2) occupations, which indicate the function they perform in their respective industries. To clarify the distinction between these classifications, consider two workers employed in a manufacturing establishment producing household metal utensils, one of these, an operator of a metal stamping machine, and the other, the production manager. Both of these workers are employed in the industry group known as "fabricated

technical workers, operatives, craftsmen, and managerial workers (Figure 8–5). Each of these occupation groups includes more than five million workers. Observe too that the major occupation groups are, for the most part, characteristic of the tertiary economic sector.

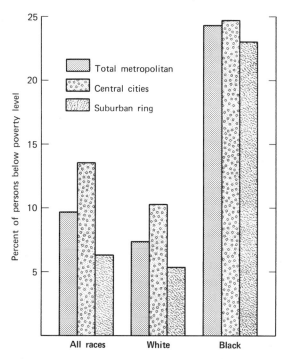

**Figure 8–6** Persons below poverty level income: by race and place of residence. *Source.* Based on data in *Social and Economic Characteristics of the Population in Metropolitan and Nonmetropolitan Areas: 1970 and 1960.* Bureau of the Census (June 24, 1971).

metal products," while one is in the occupational group or class of "operatives" and the other in the occupational group or class of "managerial workers."

With regard to occupations of urban workers, there are differences based on location of the urban area, locality within the urban area (central city or suburban ring), and demographic characteristics. The greatest share of workers in metropolitan areas in the United States are, in descending order by occupation group, clerical workers, professional and

Also remember that there are significant differences in each occupation group in the ratio between male and female workers. Only in regard to clerical workers and service workers, do females dominate in number employed. In these occupation groups, incomes are low, relative to professional and technical workers, managerial workers, operatives, and craftsmen, occupations that males dominate in number employed.

Within the urban population, with its many occupations and income levels, there are many persons whose incomes fall below an administratively based "poverty level."[4] In metropolitan areas of the United States, nearly ten percent of the workers have incomes below the poverty level, with the percentage rising to over thirteen percent in central cities, while it is appreciably less in the suburban ring with about six percent. As the percentage of the residents falling below the poverty level is considerably greater in central cities than in the more affluent suburban rings, it is also much greater among Negro residents than white residents (Figure 8–6).

## Sectors of the Urban Economy

The numerical size of the urban labor force is one aspect of the urban economy, for without this labor force, there would be no urban economy. Also significant is the output, character, and structure of the urban labor force. Character has to do with demographic characteristics, such as occupations in which the people are engaged, income levels, degrees of unemployment, composition by race and sex, and similar traits. Structure has to do more with the industrial composition of the labor force, especially the kinds of economic acitivities in which the urban workers are engaged. Character of the urban labor force has to do basically with the worker, while structure of the urban labor force essentially has to do with the economic activities or industries in which the workers find employment.

It is possible to disaggregate or divide the urban labor force into various groups, each composed of workers with

[4]The poverty level utilizes a poverty index adopted by a Federal Inter-agency Committee in 1969. This index provides a range of income cutoffs, adjusted to take into account such factors as family size, sex and age of the family head, the number of children, and nonfarm residence. The cutoffs for farm families have been set at 85 percent of the nonfarm levels. The poverty threshold for a nonfarm family of four was $3743 in 1969 and $2973 in 1959.

similar activities, tasks, or types of production. Each of these groups or the output of each group is referred to as an *economic sector*.

There are different ways of dividing the urban labor force of the urban economy into sectors. One of these is simply to group workers into *industry groups*, as recognized by the Bureau of the Census. This means that all workers in a specific industry group are engaged in similar types of productive activity. As an example, the Bureau of the Census identifies one major industry group with the name, "Transportation equipment." This implies that all workers in this industry group are engaged in production of some type of transportation equipment, although there are subdivisions that recognize the specific type of transportation equipment produced, including motor vehicles, aircraft, ships, and railroad rolling stock. Each of these subdivisions, in turn, may be subdivided as in the case of motor vehicles, where the industries include automobile production, truck production, and bus production. The point is that each of the industry groups or subdivisions of an industry group comprises an economic sector, based on groupings by industry.

Another manner of dividing the urban economy into sectors, and the one stressed in this presentation, involves consideration of spatial aspects of economic activity of the city, that is, it considers the urban economy within the context of two dimensional space. The sectoral division along industry lines is adequate for many needs, but it leaves many questions unanswered. It provides a means of inventory that allows for the recognition of the types of economic activity present in the city and the extent of involvement, usually employment, in each of the recognized types. But there are basic questions left unanswered that have to do with consumption, the remaining link in the production chain. Basic questions, then, are how large is the consumer demand, what are its' characteristics, and more important, where are the consumers located?

The reader will remember that the output of goods and services in an industry in the city is consumed by both residents of that city and by residents beyond the bounds of the city in the tributary area or service area. Certainly, the degree to which goods and services are consumed by nonlocal residents varies a great deal between different types of industry, size and nature of the city, and available transportation facilities, but there are relatively few that do not have the dual consuming population—local and nonlocal. Thus, some of the economic activity of the city goes to support the local population and some is for the support of a nonlocal population.

Therefore, there exist two production sectors of the urban economy that have to do with the spatial relationship between location of the producer and location of the consumer. The sale or distribution of goods and services beyond the bounds of the city or urban area where they are produced serves as the basis for part of the employment in production of the goods and services, for the income derived, and for the taxable wealth produced. This economic sector that consists of production of goods and services for consumers beyond the limits of the locality producing them is referred to by different names.[5] Two commonly used by

geographers, and the ones used most often in this presentation are "basic" sector or "city-forming" sector.

Once the city-forming or basic sector of the urban economy has been identified and delimited, the remaining economic activity is assumed to involve the production and distribution of goods and services to satisfy the needs of the population of the city or urban area within which the production takes place. This economic sector also is known by a variety of names, with "nonbasic" or "city-serving" preferred in this presentation. Here the distribution of goods and services is within a short distance of consumers who reside within the urban center or urban area (Figure 8–7).

We have, then, a situation where a portion of the economic activity of the city is to satisfy the needs of local residents, with the other portion going to satisfy demands of more distant, nonlocal consumers. If we use an example of a given service establishment or manufacturing firm, whose production is distributed so that 60 percent of the output goes to local consumers and 40 percent goes to nonlocal consumers, we can say that 40 percent of the output contributes to the basic or city-forming sector of the urban economy and 60 percent of the output contributes to the non-basic or city serving sector of the urban economy. It is possible to state this relationship as a ratio known as the *basic-nonbasic ratio* or the *B/N ratio*. In the above example, the *B/N* ratio is 1.0/1.5. One might also wish to establish the *B/N* ratio for a certain industry in a city, for example, retail trade, or he may wish to establish the *B/N* ratio for a number of industries, for example, retail trade, wholesale trade, and finance, insurance, and real estate. Furthermore, one might wish to establish the *B/N* ratio for all economic activities in the city which represents a summation of the overall economic structure of the city. The latter approach is the most common one and, perhaps, the most meaningful one.

[5]In the literature on economic base, numerous terms are introduced and there is an unfortunate duplication of these, with different terms used to denote the same thing. This problem is summarized in the lists of equivalent terms below.

| *Sector I* | *Sector II* |
|---|---|
| Basic | Nonbasic |
| Export | Local |
| Exportable | Internal |
| External | Service |
| Nonlocalized | Localized |
| Primary | Secondary |
| City-forming | City-serving |
| Urban growth | Ancillary |
| Independent | Dependent |
| Surplus | Residentiary |

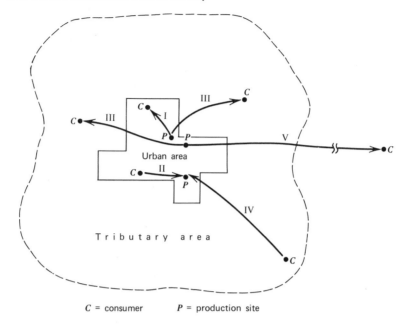

C = consumer        P = production site

**Figure 8–7**   Types of movements in the basic and nonbasic sectors of the urban economy. *Nonbasic (local) sector:* I   from production site to local consumer; II   Local consumer to production site. *Basic (export) sector.* III   from production site to nearby consumer; IV   nearby consumer to production site; V   from production site to distant consumer.

## The Problem of Measurement

In dealing with the matter of urban economic base, one has the problem of selection of suitable measurement criteria, both of economic activity and of the area where the output from this activity is forthcoming.[6]

The most commonly utilized criterion of economic output or activity is employment. The number of persons employed in a specific industry or establishment serves as a surrogate for the amount of output of the industry or establishment. It is most unlikely, however, that the labor force of this establishment is wholly engaged in production in either the basic or nonbasic sector, but more

[6]There are numerous writings on the topic of economic base and among the most complete and useful are those of Richard B. Andrews, published in *Land Economics* in the period 1953 to 1956.

likely it is producing for both local and nonlocal consumers, that is, they produce in both the basic and nonbasic sectors. For example, in an urban establishment such as a bakery, some of the output is for urban residents and some is delivered to points of consumption outside the city but within the tributary area of the city for consumption by nonlocal residents. Thus, some of the employment of the bakery is assigned to the basic sector and some to the nonbasic sector. One might assign the employment of each establishment or of each industry to derive the basic and nonbasic ratio for the entire city. This method is limited in several ways, however. Output per worker will vary between establishments and productivity of workers may increase or decrease over time. Also, it is difficult to account for sporadic and part-time employment in working with employment as a measurement criterion of sectors in the urban economy, which is true as well of fluctuating employment, such as seasonal employment.

Another criterion used is income of employees. It is said, however, that the number of employees serves as an indicator of economic opportunity, while income in the form of payrolls serves as an indicator of standard or level of living, and not necessarily the magnitude of economic activity in either of the sectors of the urban economy.

Physical production, for example, tons, units, bales, etc., might be used as a measurement criterion, but is limited since it is not suited to output involving no tangible commodity, such as government employment, educational employment, and other activities in the realm of services. Value of production and value added in the production process share the same limitations as to their suitability when dealing with nonphysical production. Of the above measurement criteria, the one utilized will be based on data sources available, purpose of the study, and resources available for the study.

A different type of problem in studying urban economic base is that of selection of the base area that (a) will be acceptable for the desired purposes and, (b) is of such a type that data can be made available. The incorporated city is the simplest area to deal with, but it often leads to inaccurate or misleading conclusions since it is often just a part of an urban complex. The county might serve as the base area, but most counties include unincorporated areas that are not urban in nature. Most urban economic base studies utilize either the S.M.S.A. or the Urbanized Area as the base area (see Chapter 2 for definitions). These studies deal with a realistic economic entity made up of many separate political entities, with this especially true of the Urbanized Area since it includes the entire area devoted to urban settlement.

## Classification of Base Types

Urban economic base deals with economic activity and production destined to serve demands of consumers in two sectors—nonlocal consumers in the basic sector and local consumers in the nonbasic sector. The former sector has a spatial dimension of a larger scale because it involves longer distance movement of goods or services over two dimensional space. Furthermore, different types of basic activities can be recognized, depending on the type of movement involved.

One type of basic activity might be termed *centrifugal* basic activities in that there is movement of goods and services produced in the urban center to consumers in the tributary area, like a steel product from a factory in the urban area or newspapers from an urban publishing plant. There may be movement of services to consumers in the tributary area, such as insurance sales, real estate services, or state legislation, in which cases, the services are dispensed from establishments in the urban area and are distributed to nonlocal residents.

Another type of basic activity can be termed *centripetal* basic activities in which goods and services are made available to consumers in the tributary area by the movement of the consumers to the source of supply (Figure 8–7). Examples of movements of this type in which the consumer acquires the good or service by coming into the urban area from the tributary area, then either carries it away or consumes it on the spot, are numerous in retail trade. Probably every commercial center or district in the city derives at least a portion of its sales volume from residents of the tributary area in which the center is located. Often, residents of the tributary area travel to the urban center to obtain medical aid of some type, especially the more specialized medical services. Also, residents of the tributary area often travel to the urban center to engage in college or university study, and in some university cities, this produces the major segment of the urban economy and is clearly a basic activity entailing the movement of the consumer to the distribution point.

## Base Ratios

After taking into account the criteria by which economic activity is to be measured and the type of urban area being considered, it is possible to present the overall structure of the urban economy as a ratio, the basic/nonbasic ratio, that we have discussed. It should not be expected, however, that the $B/N$ ratio will be the same for all cities.

Small trade and service centers of the lowest order in a functional hierarchy are primarily involved in the distribution of goods and services for their economic support, and only a small share of the output and employment goes to support the needs of the center itself. Thus, most of the economic activity of these centers is in the basic sector of the economy, and $B/N$ ratios of 1.0/0.2 or 1.0/0.5 would be characteristic of such urban centers.

When cities increase in population, the local demands for goods and services increase, in part due to greater population densities, higher disposable income, and the possibility of achieving sufficient threshold populations within relatively short distance. Thus, $B/N$ ratios of 1.0/1.5 to 1.0/2.0 are not uncommon in larger cities (Figure 8–8). Based on a number of studies of the economic base of individual cities over the years, the generalization can be made that the basic/nonbasic ratio tends to increase as a function of the population of the urban center, that is, the nonbasic sector increases, relative to the basic sector, as population increases (Table 8–2).

The question might be posed as to why the $B/N$ ratio differs among cities. There are several possible answers, in addition to population differences, for even cities

within the same population group may have notably different $B/N$ ratios. Differences in location of the cities can produce different ratios, such as suburbs and "freestanding" cities of the same general size. In suburbs, services are often lacking or deficient, producing less employment and output of services, with this reflected in the $B/N$ ratio. A freestanding" city, however, must achieve a higher level of self-sufficiency, thus, service activity is comparatively well developed and the nonbasic sector is more developed.

**Table 8–2**  Basic/Nonbasic Ratios for Selected Cities of the United States

| City | Population (at Time of Study) | $B/N$ Ratio |
|------|------|------|
| New York, N.Y. | 12,500,000 | 1.0/2.2 |
| Detroit, Michigan | 2,900,000 | 1.0/1.2 |
| Cincinnati, Ohio | 907,000 | 1.0/1.7 |
| Brockton, Mass. | 119,000 | 1.0/0.8 |
| Albuquerque, N.M. | 116,000 | 1.0/1.0 |
| Madison, Wisconsin | 110,000 | 1.0/0.8 |
| Oshkosh, Wisconsin | 42,000 | 1.0/0.6 |

SOURCE: John W. Alexander, *Economic Geography,* Vol. XXX, No. 3 (July, 1954).

There are qualitative differences in the population of cities, such as age, sex, incomes, and the like, and these too create different demands of the urban economy. Is it not unlikely that, in a city with a high proportion of its people of nonchild bearing age, the demands for such services as diaper washing, playschools, and the like would be less than in an urban center with a high proportion of people of child bearing age and with a high rate of family formation? Such differences would create variations in demand for local services that would be reflected in $B/N$ ratios.

Regional economic cycles, too, have an influence on $B/N$ ratios. If a regional economy is depressed, the personal incomes are lowered and unemployment is

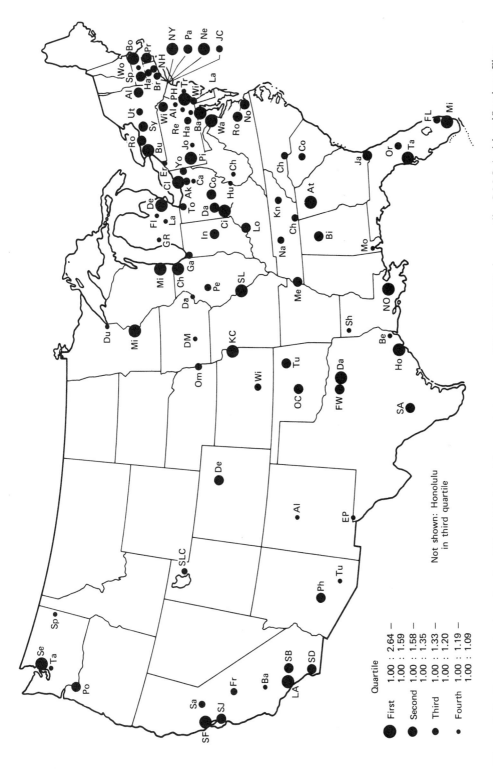

**Figure 8–8** Basic-nonbasic ratios for 101 S.M.S.A.'s with populations over 250,000 (1960), by quartile. S.M.S.A. identification: First two letters in S.M.S.A. name, e.g. De (Denver) or first letters of S.M.S.A. names of more than one word, e.g. GR (Grand Rapids). *Source.* Based on data in Ullman, Dacey, and Brodsky, *The Economic Base of American Cities* (1969).

more widespread. As a result, there would be a lowered consumption of goods and services in the cities of the region. The same situation exists with changes in the status of the national economy.

Age of the city appears to have an influence on the $B/N$ ratio. Older cities seem to have more employment and output in service industries than do newer cities. This may be attributable, however, to the fact that as cities age, they also tend to get larger.

## Methods of Base Identification

Once decisions are made concerning the type of area within which an economic base study is to be made and the measurement criterion to be utilized, there still remains the problem of how available information is to be analyzed in order to divide the urban economy into two sectors. Various means of dealing with this problem have been developed in the approximately forty years since such studies were first formally conducted.

One of the earliest methods used to identify the structure of the urban economic base is known as the *residual method*, developed by Homer Hoyt in the 1930's. In this method, all known basic activities were identified on the basis of employment, then from the number of employees not predominantly in the basic sector, were subtracted the number assumed to be necessary for meeting the needs of the local population. The size of this deduction was computed on the basis

of a ratio of 1.0/1.0 between basic and nonbasic employment, and the residual produced was then assigned to the basic sector of the local economy. For example, if the urban labor force totals 100,000, and 20,000 employees are clearly in the basic sector, the remaining 80,000 would be divided between the two sectors, with 40,000 added to each sector. This would produce 60,000 in the basic sector and 40,000 in the nonbasic sector, for a $B/N$ ratio of 1.0/0.7 for the city's economy. The adoption of an assumed ratio of 1.0/1.0 between the two sectors is a core weakness of this method, especially when this ratio has been found to vary between 1.0/0.6 and 1.0/2.6.

Another and later developed method of identifying the respective sectors of an urban economy is the *macrocosmic method*. This method is best suited to large urban areas with commensurately large employment. It makes a comparison between the employment structure of the specific urban area under study and that of the entire nation. The percentage share of the national employment in each industry is determined, as is the percentage share of the local labor force engaged in each industry. The two values derived are then compared and percentages in the national economy are subtracted from those percentages for similar industries in the local economy that are higher than those for the nation. The assumption in this procedure is that the share of the labor force of the entire nation in a given industry meets the demands of the national population, there-

**Table 8–3**  Hypothetical Example of the Application of the Macrocosmic Method of Base Measurement

| Industry | National Employment (Percent of Total) | Urban Area Employment | Urban Area Employment (Percent of Total) | Differences in Percentages | Basic Employment |
|---|---|---|---|---|---|
| A | 5.5 | 50,000 | 6.5 | 1.0 | 500 (50,000 × 1.0%) |
| B | 12.6 | 25,000 | 3.3 | −9.3 | 0 |
| C | 17.4 | 150,000 | 19.5 | 2.1 | 3,150 (150,000 × 2.1%) |
| D | 8.0 | 100,000 | 13.0 | 4.2 | 4,200 (100,000 × 4.2%) |

fore a like percentage of the local labor force is sufficient to meet local demands. Any percentage share greater than that of the nation more than meets local needs and is devoted to production for export beyond the boundaries of the given urban area (Table 8–3). As an example, if 2 percent of the national work force is involved in wholesale trade in the nation and 3 percent of the work force of a specific urban area is in this industry, it is assumed that 1 percent of the local labor force is engaged in this industry to satisfy nonlocal needs and 1 percent of the local labor force in wholesale trade is assigned to the basic sector.

There are decided shortcomings of this method, however. One is that employment in a given industry in an urban area may be below the national percentage, yet the area may be a significant exporter of the goods produced. Also, an urban area, especially those of smaller size, cannot be expected to duplicate the economic structure of an entire nation. Another objection to this method is that local consumption may vary a great deal from national consumption patterns. For example, if the per capita consumption of bottled soft drinks is exceptionally high in Atlanta, Georgia, and there is a disproportionately large number of bottling plants and production in this urban center, this cannot be taken as a significant increment to the basic sector of the economy of that city unless there is commensurately high per capita consumption of this commodity in the tributary area of Atlanta that is satisfied by producers in Atlanta. Another criticism that can be leveled at this method is that it cannot account for all types of economic activity that may influence the basic sector of the urban economy, such as cash flows between different levels of government, retirement income, and commuter activity.

An additional method of identifying the structure of a local economy is the *sales-employment conversion method*. First, a determination is made of the propor-tionate shares of sales made inside and outside the study area, then these percentages are applied to the employment of each industry or, at a smaller scale, to employment in each establishment. This method relies heavily on the use of questionnaires and field interviews and has been used mainly with regard to retail trade, and not the entire array of industries. Although it is a meaningful procedure, it is time consuming and expensive, since it involves tedious field procedures, even when conducted utilizing sampling procedures. In addition, firms may not be familiar with the distribution of their customers. An example of the use of this method might be in order. If management of a particular establishment in a given industry estimates that 60 percent of its products are sold to local residents and 40 percent are sold to nonlocal people, and the establishment employs 250 people, 150 employees are assigned to the nonbasic sector ($250 \times 60\%$) and 100 are assigned to the basic sector ($250 \times 40\%$). This is done for each establishment in turn to derive the $B/N$ ratio for an entire industry or the entire urban economy. An objection to this method, like the macrocosmic method, is that it is not suited to an accounting of all increments to the basic sector, such as cash flows, pension and retirement income, and the like. This method, as we have indicated, is probably the most time consuming of all, which serves as a handicap to its application.

Another method of base measurement is one that establishes a minimum amount of employment in a particular industry needed to support the local population and allows for assignment of greater than the minimum employment to the basic sector. This was the method developed by the Swedish geographer, Gunnar Alexandersson in 1956 (discussed in Chapter 2). Here, the researcher develops an array or ranking of cities in a given region or nation as based on the percentage share of employment in a certain industry. He then selects a value sufficiently high to omit extraneous or unusual cases, such as 5 percent from the lower end of the array as used by Alexandersson.[7] Amounts of employment greater than this value are taken as being in the city-forming or basic sector of the urban economy, while employment equal to or less than this value is taken as being in the city-serving or nonbasic sector. For example, in an array of 200 cities, with the percentage share of employment in a given industry arranged from the highest to the lowest, the city 5 percent from the lower end of the array, would be the tenth city. If the employment in the industry in question in this city is 2.2 percent of the total labor force, it is assumed that this amount is the employment necessary to provide for the needs of the local population and that any share less than this also is entirely city serving or nonbasic. If another city higher in the array has 12.2 percent of its labor force employed in the industry being considered, it is assumed that 10.0 percent of the labor force in this industry in the latter city is involved in production to serve the needs of a nonlocal population (12.2% minus 2.2%), so 10 percent of the employment total in this industry is assigned to the basic sector.

A later variation of the method of Alexandersson is the *minimum requirements method,* developed by Edward Ullman and Michael Dacey.[8] In this case, a number of cities and a number of industries are included, and the percentage employment contribution of a given industry is determined for all cities. From the array of values, the minimum percentage is identified and employment greater than this amount is taken as adding to the basic sector of the urban economy, unlike the method of Alexandersson that

selected the city 5 percent from the lower end of the array. For example, in an array of 120 cities, the minimum value of employment in industry A might be 1.0 percent of the labor force in a certain city. Assuming that 1.0 percent of the urban labor force is the minimum needed to support the urban population, any values greater than this are assigned to the basic sector. In this case, if another city has 3.5 percent of its employees in the same industry, 2.5 percent of its labor force in this industry is assigned to the basic sector of that city's economy.

There are some reservations that exist about the minimum requirements method. For one thing, it may be erroneous to consider the minimum employment in a chosen industry as a "requirement," since this implies a necessity for a city to have at least this level of employment in the specified industry. However, the city might have employment in this industry insufficient to provide the needs of the people of that city, and what it would "require" to meet its needs is beyond the minimum "requirement." Perhaps, the term "minimum employment" would be preferable to "minimum requirement," with this representing the minimum existing employment, which may or may not serve as the "minimum requirement" to meet the demands of the local population. For example, consider automobile manufacture. The likely minimum requirement disclosed from the procedure we have discussed would be 0.0 percent of the labor force, yet there would be demands present that are not satisfied by local employment and the value representing local employment in this industry cannot be taken as a "requirement" when it is, in fact, a statement of a lack of production in this industry, with unsatisfied demand being met through basic employment and production in another urban center.

Another point is that the minimum requirements vary between cities in different size groups. It is unlikely that the minimum employment in durable goods

[7]Gunnar Alexandersson, *The Industrial Structure of American Cities,* Lincoln: University of Nebraska Press, 1956.

[8]Edward L. Ullman and Michael F. Dacey, "The Minimum Requirements Approach to the Urban Economic Base," *Papers and Proceedings of the Regional Science Association,* Volume 6, 1960.

manufacture in cities of 10,000 to 25,000 is anything similar to the minimum for cities of 250,000 to 500,000.

## Special Problems of Base Identification

Most investigations of urban economic base utilize published data provided by public agencies, especially data on employment. There are some types of economic activity in the city, however, that are not treated in standard reference sources.

One difficult matter of this type has to do with commuters, especially to a central city from surrounding suburbs. The task of accounting for all regular commutation by part of the labor force of the central city is difficult, whether they commute by auto or by public conveyance. The commuter makes an economic impact to economic base, but the question is whether he makes a contribution to the economy of the central city or to that of the suburb. Taking the typical commuter as an example, he spends his working hours in the central city but makes few expenditures there, except for lunches and an occasional purchase. The greatest share of his expenditure is made in the suburb for housing, food, apparel, fuel, medical services, and the like. Therefore, he makes a far greater contribution to the economic well being of the suburb than he does to the central city. In a sense, he exports his services to the central city and in so doing, adds to the basic sector of the suburb's economy and makes only a minor addition to the basic sector of the central city.

Another situation that is difficult to deal with in economic base study is the university or college community, especially ones with large enrollments of students derived from many dispersed sources. If the bulk of the student body originates from outside the urban area where they are students and they are making expenditures for food, housing, entertainment, and the like, they are ad-

ding to the basic sector of the economic base of the community in which they reside. Students derived from within the community and making the same expenditures do not add to the basic sector in the same manner as the nonlocal students, since they would, in all likelihood, be making many of the same expenditures as local residents but nonstudents, but would not be generating wealth from sources outside the given community.

A further problem in dealing with economic base is the role of tourists. Some establishments cater almost exclusively to tourists and these can easily be assigned to the basic sector of the local economy. Other establishments, however, dispense only a small share of their goods and services to tourists, such as movie theaters, department stores, food stores, and the like. It is difficult to determine the extent of expenditure by tourists, but whatever it is, it adds to the basic sector of the local economy.

The last type of problem to be mentioned in dealing with economic base is the economic role of government employees. Here, one would disaggregate government employees by level of government served: local, state, or federal. City employees are clearly assigned to the nonbasic sector of the local economy. For other types of government employment, some form of the macrocosmic method might be utilized. This would involve the establishment of ratios between population and government employment in the city in which the employment occurs and comparison with the same ratios for a larger base area, such as the state or nation. If the percentage of the population of the base area that consists of government employees of a certain type is 2 percent, and the percentage in a chosen urban center within the base area is 4 percent, there can be the assignment of 2 percent of the city's government employment of the type being considered to the basic sector of the urban economy, on the basis that the actual employment of this type is more than warranted by a di-

**Table 8–4**  Hypothetical Example of the Assignment of State Government Employment to Respective Economic Sectors

| Political Unit | Population | State Govt. Emp. | State Govt. Emp. as % of Total Emp. | Expected State Govt. Emp. | Actual State Govt. Emp. | State Govt. Emp. in Basic Sector |
|---|---|---|---|---|---|---|
| State | 5,000,000 | 100,000 | 2.0 | 100,000 | 100,000 | |
| City A | 500,000 | 7,500 | 1.5 | 10,000 | 7,500 | 0 |
| City B | 200,000 | 3,600 | 1.8 | 4,000 | 3,600 | 0 |
| City C | 150,000 | 3,000 | 2.5 | 3,750 | 3,000 | 750 |
| City D | 50,000 | 1,050 | 2.1 | 1,000 | 1,050 | 50 |

rect correlation between population and employment. This procedure could be followed for different levels of government employment, and perhaps is the simplest manner of approaching this problem (Table 8–4).

## The Utility of Economic Base Studies

One might ask about the value of economic base study and basic/nonbasic ratios. There are several possible answers to this question that might be pointed out.

One use of economic base studies is simply to know more of the characteristics of the urban population and its economy. The gaining of knowledge is requisite to understanding of the complex entity known as the city, and acquisition of information about the economy of the city leads to an understanding of the role of the specific city in its regional setting and of the interrelationships between the city and its tributary area. How dependent is the given city on its tributary area? What forms does this dependency take? These are but two of the questions that economic base study might help to answer. In the same manner, economic base studies are of value in making comparisons among cities of the same general population or of different populations. Basic/nonbasic ratios change with population size, and economic base studies cast light on the economic structure of the chosen city as it becomes larger over time.

Another value of economic base studies is to provide information of value in implementation of tax policy. It has been established that many central cities provide places of employment for many thousands of commuters who utilize central city facilities, such as streets, public transit, and police and fire protection. At the same time, they do not appreciably contribute to the support of essential public services in the central city, so it might be considered that the city experiences a net loss in this arrangement. As a result, several cities, including New York City, have seen fit to impose a payroll tax on commuters from outside the central city so the commuter does, in fact, make a contribution to the tax revenues of the financially hard pressed central city.

Economic base studies have value in making estimations of the future economic structure and population of the city. If the B/N ratio of cities of a given population size is established, and a change is anticipated through the addition of employment in the basic sector, an estimate can be made of the change likely to occur in the nonbasic sector as well. For example, if a new establishment employs 2000 persons and the B/N ratio in the city is 1.0/2.5, the estimate of additional employment created would be 2000 in the basic sector and 5000 in the nonbasic sector, for a total of 7000 employment opportunities. This process might be carried one step further by taking the average family size in the region and, assuming that one-half of the 7000 new employees will be attracted from

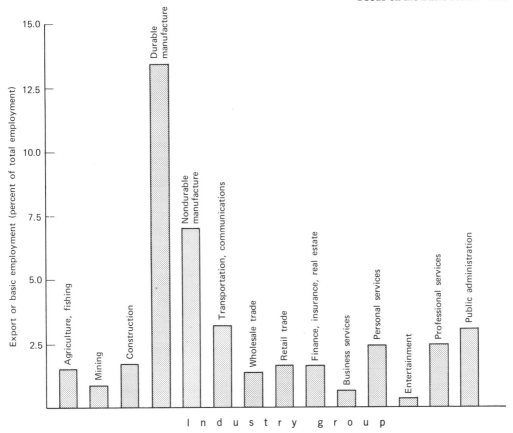

**Figure 8–9**   Export or basic employment in 101 S.M.S.A.'s over 250,000 (by industry group) 1960. *Source.* Based on data in Ullman, Dacey, and Brodsky, *The Economic Base of American Cities,* 1969.

outside the city, an estimate can be made of the additional population brought into the city through the addition of the establishment we used. If the average family size is 3.2, 2.2 dependents will be added for every employee added. There would be an addition of 7700 dependents and 3500 employees to the city's population; a total of 11,200. This estimate, in turn, can be translated into estimated needs for new dwelling units, new school classrooms, additional electric power lines, additional sewer lines, additional water mains, and additional phone installations. In planning of urban centers, it is desirable to have some notion of additional facilities needed by the addition of new employment and population, and economic base study might help in this effort. The same process in reverse might be employed as well to estimate the effect of the loss of an establishment of a

specific employment, although the reverse process would not be the exact opposite of the first outlined, for once facilities are made available, they represent a fixed investment and cannot be easily retracted or abandoned.

## Focus on the Basic Sector

Perhaps, the most vital and distinctive of the two economic sectors is the basic sector, which generates wealth for the city from outside the borders of the city. It might be considered the fundamental sector of the urban economy, with the nonbasic sector considered as ancillary. Although the two sectors are interrelated, the nonbasic sector is more dependent on the basic than is the basic sector on the nonbasic. It is important, then, to pay particular heed to the basic sector of the economies of cities.

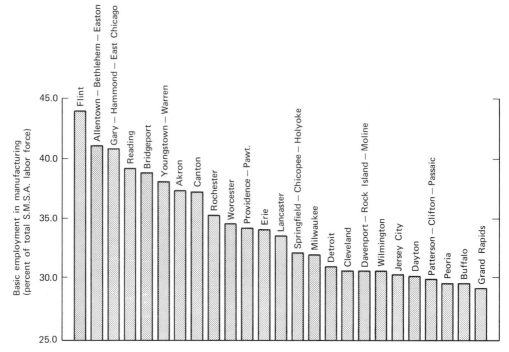

**Figure 8–10** Basic employment in manufacturing: S.M.S.A.'s in the highest quartile. *Source.* Based on data in Ullman, Dacey, and Brodsky, *The Economic Base of American Cities,* 1969.

Considering 101 S.M.S.A.'s with populations over 250,000 in the United States, the average employment in the basic sector is 41.0 percent of the S.M.S.A. labor force.[9] Thus, 59 percent of the employees are involved in the nonbasic sector. Not all industries, however, have 41 percent of their employees in the basic sector, with the average for all 101 S.M.S.A.'s ranging from 0.3 percent of the urban labor force in employment in entertainment in the basic sector, to 13.3 percent in the durable manufactures industry (Figure 8–9). The nondurable goods manufacturing industry, the transportation and communications industry, and public administration are other industries having significant shares of their employment assigned to the basic sector. If durable and nondurable manufacturing industries are combined, then

slightly over one-fifth of the employment in manufacturing is involved in the basic sector.

The S.M.S.A.'s that have a percentage of basic employment in manufacturing greater than the average for 101 S.M.S.A.'s, 20.3 percent, range in population from Los Angeles to Erie, Pa. Of the 101 largest metropolitan areas, 50 have basic employment in manufacturing greater than the average. It is possible to identify the S.M.S.A.'s where manufacturing employment is most significant to the basic sector by referring to those in the highest quartile.[10] Notice too that, with few exceptions, cities in the highest quartile are in the American Manufacturing Belt, made up of parts of the Midwest, the Middle Atlantic Region, and

[9]Edward L. Ullman, Michael F. Dacey, and Harold Bodsky, *The Economic Base of American Cities,* Seattle: University of Washington Press, 1969, Table I.

[10]Quartile refers to one-fourth of the total number in a distribution. The highest quartile refers to the one-fourth of the distribution having the greatest values. In this case, the highest quartile includes the S.M.S.A.'s with the highest percentage of basic employment in manufacturing industries.

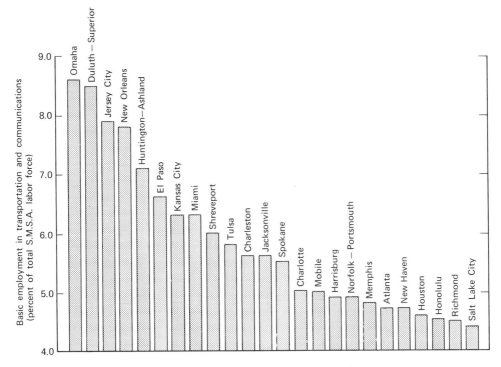

**Figure 8–11**    Basic employment in transportation and communications: S.M.S.A.'s in the highest quartile. *Source.* Based on data in Ullman, Dacey, and Brodsky, *The Economic Base of American Cities,* 1969.

New England (Figure 8–10). Also, the importance of single industries becomes apparent, such as the automobile industry in Flint, the iron and steel industry in Gary-Hammond-East Chicago, Allentown-Bethlehem-Easton, and Youngstown-Warren, the machinery industry in Bridgeport, and the rubber industry in Akron.

Of the 101 largest S.M.S.A.'s in the United States, 40 have basic employment in the transportation and communications industry greater than the average of all such areas—3.2 percent of the urban labor force. Those metropolitan areas in the highest quartile are indicated in Figure 8–11. And predictably, metropolitan centers in which transportation and communications employment has the greatest role in the basic sector of urban economies are well known railroad centers, such as Omaha, Jersey City, Huntington, El Paso, Kansas City, Tulsa, and Spokane and major ocean, river, and lake

ports, including Jacksonville, Mobile, Norfolk-Portsmouth, Honolulu, Duluth-Superior, New Orleans, Portland, and Memphis. Also included in the highest quartile are some of the major air transportation centers in the country such as Miami, Atlanta, and Honolulu.

By grouping retail and wholesale trade together, it is possible to gain some insight into which of the largest metropolitan centers these industries are more significant in the basic economic sector. Of the 101 largest S.M.S.A.'s, 51 have employment greater than the average percent, and in the highest quartile, which includes 25 S.M.S.A.'s, the greatest number are located in the southeast, especially in Florida (Figure 8–12). Five of the metropolitan areas where this is an especially significant component of basic employment are in Florida, and another 12 are in other southeastern states.

Twenty nine of the 101 largest S.M.S.A.'s in the country have greater

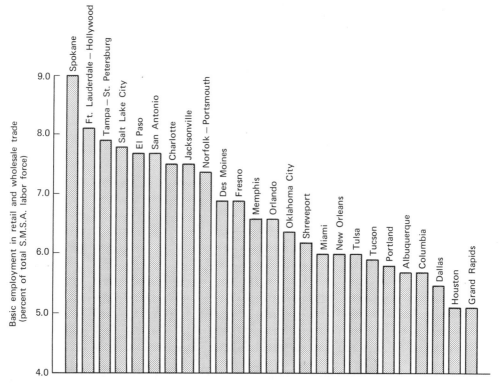

**Figure 8–12**    Basic employment in retail and wholesale trade: S.M.S.A.'s in the highest quartile. *Source.* Based on data in Ullman, Dacey, and Brodsky, *The Economic Base of American Cities,* 1969.

than average basic sector employment in public administration. Public administration's role in basic employment of S.M.S.A.'s is greatest in Washington, D.C., where it makes up nearly 24 percent of basic sector employment. Of the remaining 24 S.M.S.A.'s making up the highest quartile of employment in this industry, 11 are state capitals.

## Specialization in the Urban Economy

It is highly improbable that the characteristics of either of the sectors of the urban economy of two or more cities are exactly the same. Instead, there will be differences in the percentage contributions of even the same industry in different cities. Each city reflects in its economy, the resource base of the region where it is located, the demands of the

populations of the city and of the region it serves, historical patterns, cultural traits, and administrative decisions. As a result, certain industries in the urban economy of a specific city are developed to a greater and more prominent degree than are others.

Once again, most industries are developed to the point where at least some of the activity and production is to satisfy demands beyond the confines of the city in which the activity exists. Some of these basic industries play such an important role in the basic sector that one might attribute a distinctiveness to the city where this industry is especially prominent. This was the approach of the preceding section which identifies cities based on extreme emphasis in an urban economy of a single industry group.

To recognize the extreme conditions, however, is to focus on a single group without putting it into the perspective of

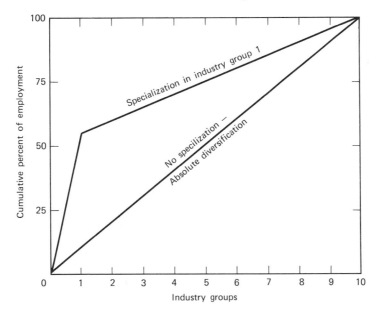

**Figure 8–13**   Specialization (diversification) curves: two hypothetical cases.

the total array of industry groups. In regard to the industries that contribute to the basic sector of the urban economy, it is important for some purposes to consider, not the extreme or unusual degree of emphasis on a given industry, but the degree of overall specialization in which all industries are considered. Are there not differences between a case where a certain urban center has a specialization in industry *A* alone, and an urban center that has an emphasis in industries *A, B,* and *C*? Is one more specialized than the other?

If we consider ten different industry groups represented in a number of cities, and each industry group contributes an equal share of basic employment in one of the cities, each industry would make up 10 percent of the basic sector employment. This would represent a complete lack of specialization in the distribution of industry groups, or absolute diversification within the basic sector of the urban economy. Of all the industry groups, none is prominent or dominant, although each is significant to the local economy (Figure 8–13). By contrast, if

eight of the ten industry groups each contributes five percent of the basic employment in the urban economy, with the other two contributing thirty five and twenty five percent respectively, there is an obvious degree of emphasis or specialization in the industry groups making up the largest share of total basic employment. One might wish to establish a measure of the degree of overall specialization in an urban economy, considering all industry groups, and such a measure has been developed and is labeled the *index of specialization.*

In essence, the index of specialization compares two values. One value represents the sum of the differences between the minimum requirement in a given industry and the actual employment in that industry. The other value represents the sum of these differences for all industries.[11] The product of this com-

[11]The details of this measurement are given in Edward L. Ullman and Michael F. Dacey, "The Minimum Requirements Approach to the Urban Economic Base," *Papers and Proceedings of the Regional Science Association,* Vol. VI (1960).

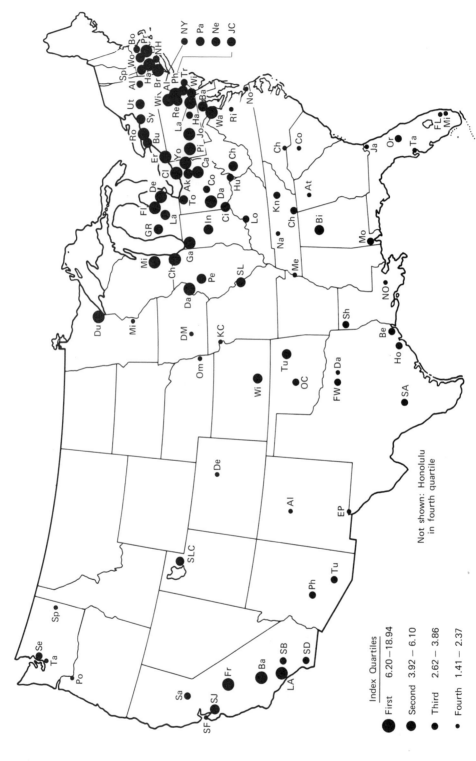

**Figure 8–14**  Indices of specialization for 101 S.M.S.A.'s with populations over 250,000 (1960) by quartile. S.M.S.A. Identification: First two letters in S.M.S.A. name, e.g. De (Denver) or first letters of S.M.S.A. names of more than one word, e.g. GR (Grand Rapids). *Source.* Based on data in Ullman, Dacey, and Brodsky, *The Economic Base of American Cities,* 1969.

parison is the index of specialization, in which the degree of overall specialization in the urban economy can be expressed numerically with 1.00 the lowest possible value, representing a case where each of the industries included has a role equal to the minimum for a number of cities.

The above procedure for the computation of the index of specialization can be formulated as follows:

$$IS = \frac{\Sigma_i \dfrac{(P_i - M_i)^2}{M_i}}{\dfrac{(\Sigma_i P_i - \Sigma_i M_i)^2}{\Sigma_i M_i}}$$

where:   $IS$ is the index of specialization
$i$ refers to each of the individual industries
$P_i$ refers to the percentage of total labor force employed in each of the industries
$M_i$ refers to the minimum requirement for each industry
$\Sigma_i$ refers to the sum of all industries

The highest indices of specialization are in the S.M.S.A.'s of Duluth-Superior (by virtue of its large areal extent), Flint, Detroit, Youngstown-Warren, Gary-Hammond-East Chicago, and Washington, D.C. (Figure 8–14). By contrast, the lowest indices of specialization are in Spokane, Denver, Tampa-St. Petersburg, Columbia, S.C., and El Paso.

Concerning the value of having an urban economy that is not highly specialized, there are arguments pro and con, although most authorities seem to find it undesirable to have exceptionally strong emphasis on one or two industries, like the auto industry in Flint and Detroit, and the aerospace industry in Seattle and Los Angeles-Long Beach. When these or other industries prosper, so do the cities in which they are localized. When these industries falter, however, so do the urban economies of cities which are specialized in these less than viable industries. This is popularly known as a "boom and bust" type of economy. Cities with lower degrees of specialization can better adjust to a faltering of one or two industries since there are others present in the urban economy to help overcome the losses. This is to say that the major industries making up the basic sector of the urban economy at any given time may not be sustained in the future and a restructuring of urban economic base is in order.

# 9

# land use in the city

The people residing and working in the city occupy, organize, and utilize space on the earth's surface. They have needs for space for different purposes and the space needed is devoted to different uses. Not only are there different uses made of urban space, there are different magnitudes of need for space for different uses. Furthermore, there are regularities in the patterns of use of urban space and in the spatial organization of urban space. The purpose of this chapter is to explore matters having to do with occupance of urban space, including

(1) land use measurement and classification, (2) land use inputs, (3) land use patterns, and (4) selected land use problems and challenges.

## Land and Land Use

In the above section, reference was made to urban space and its many uses. "Urban space" is a fairly broad designation and includes (1) land area of cities, which is to say, any ground, soil, or earth whatsoever, (2) water areas in cities, particularly those of small size, and (3) third dimensional space above the surface of the city. And, as Harland Bartholomew states, "the land we are concerned with can be described as land now used for purposes that are characteristically urban."[1] The types of urban space to be considered here, in view of this statement, are developed land devoted to urban uses, and small water bodies associated with adjacent developed land. Traditionally, urban space above the surface has not been included in the study of urban land.

The study of urban land use deals mainly with the surface utilization. Most of the land of the city is devoted to fulfilling one or more functions or types of utilization. Sometimes the use made of the land is intensive, for example, commercial land with many users per acre, and other times the use of urban land might be extensive, for example, recreational land with fewer users per acre, but in any case the land is satisfying some need of the urban residents.

## Measurement and Classification of Urban Land Use

The problem of measurement comes up once again, this time in regard to urban land use. Probably, the first aspect of the problem is the study area within

[1] Harland Bartholomew, *Land Uses in American Cities,* Harvard University Press, Cambridge, 1955, p. 14.

which urban land is to be measured. Is it to be the central or incorporated city, or is it to be the urbanized area, including the suburban ring, or is it to be a single neighborhood? There is no single scale that should be used; the selection is likely to be based on study objectives and time and funds available.

Once the study area is selected, a further aspect of the problem emerges. This has to do with the objectives of the inquiry which might be to delimit broad and fairly general zones of land use or might be concerned with the uses to which each small land parcel is put.[2] Quite often, the use of land parcels is the same throughout a given block and for a number of adjacent blocks, so there is a zonation of land use. This is not known, however, until the use of each parcel in the zone is identified. The most basic unit of measurement of urban land use is the land parcel, since it is the smallest cohesive unit of land recognizable under the control of one party and for which one party makes the decision regarding the use made of the land, often with administrative guidance or controls.

But what is a land parcel? A land parcel essentially is a cadaster, which is a registered unit stating the quantity and ownership of a unit of real property. A land parcel is a unit of real property under a single ownership or control, surveyed or platted as a separate unit of real estate. Land parcels or cadasters have legally established boundaries and are formally and legally recognized. Land parcels are cataloged by public and private agencies for real estate transactions and for tax purposes. Very often, cadastral maps are prepared which show the delimitation of each land parcel of a section of a city, and these serve as an excellent source of information on the actual delimitation and

location of land parcels. Also, they serve well as a base for the compilation and presentation of land use information at the most basic scale, the individual cadaster (Figure 9–1).

As in any body or organized knowledge, classification is vital to the study of urban land use. It is impossible to deal with the large number of land uses in the city without some grouping of similar uses, which is to say uses with similar characteristics. The groupings or classes of land uses should not be arbitrary, however, and should have some basis for their development, and they should have some measure of extended applicability, not suited only to a single city. If each city developed its own system of classification of land use, it would be virtually impossible to compare one city with another. It is realized, however, that no single land use classification suits all needs and all cities, when detailed study is desired. Still, in the general or broad context, there should be a basic structure of the classification that is applicable to many, if not most, cities.

Most urban land use classifications have originated in the field of urban planning, where the system was developed to fit the needs of a single city or a relatively small number of cities. As a result, there has not developed a generally accepted and formalized land use classification system, although attempts in this direction have been made recently.

One of the earliest attempts to formalize land use classification in the United States was made by Harland Bartholomew.[3] The elements of Bartholomew's classification are presented in Figure 9–2. Bartholomew's system was significant in itself, since it was often utilized by the planning firm headed by the originator of the system, and because it was implemented by many other planners in the United States looking for guidance in finding an applicable system of land use classification. Two related points might be mentioned with re-

---

[2]"Zone," as used here, refers to a relatively homogeneous section or district of the city developed in a spontaneous manner, and is not to be confused with a section of the city in which there has been administratively controlled development of land use, for example, "zoning" of land use.

[3]Bartholomew, *Ibid.*

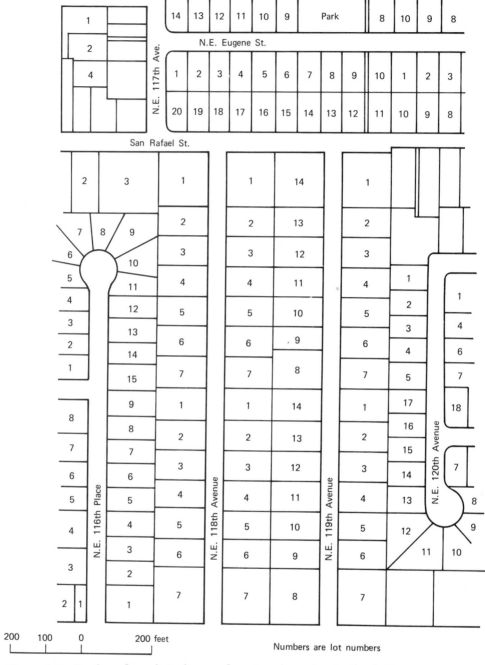

**Figure 9–1**   Portion of a cadastral map of an American city; Portland, Oregon.

gard to this system; note a distinction was made early in the system between privately developed area and publicly developed area. Here the system strayed from the matter of land use to the matter of land ownership and form of development. Also included is the land use class identified as "public and semi-public," which again confuses land use with land ownership. This land use class also is quite difficult to accept when one considers an example like an elementary school. The use to which the land is put is education regardless of whether the facility is a

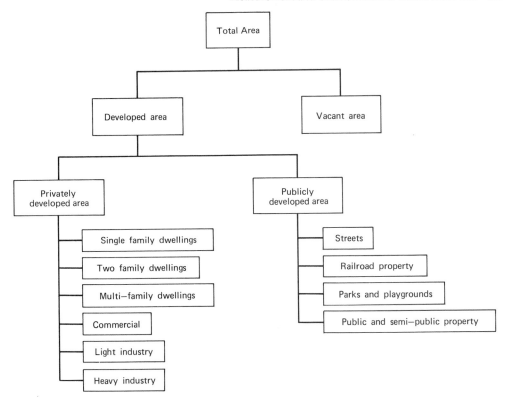

**Figure 9–2**   Classification of uses of urban land: after H. Bartholomew. *Source.* H. Bartholomew, *Land Uses in American Cities, 1955.*

public elementary school or a privately developed and funded school. Moreover, the designation of "semi-public" is troublesome and difficult to define. Cemeteries are an example of what is included in this land use class, but so are fraternal organizations such as men's and women's lodges. Is this to say that the use of land for these purposes is so similar as to include them in the same classification? Another troublesome element in the system of Bartholomew are the classes identified as "light industry" and "heavy industry." These were not explicitly defined land use classes and left much to the discretion of the individual working with the classification system, since it is very difficult to find agreement on what specific uses of land belong in each of these classes.

The purpose here is not to attempt to discredit Bartholomew's classification system, but to point out reservations and ob-

jections that have been leveled at it by others, realizing that it was not entirely applicable as presented. It did, however, have a very significant impact on land use study in the United States and on land use planning.

More recently, attempts have been made to overcome some of the objections of previous land use classification systems. An early improved system, developed by a professional planners organization, focused on land use characteristics alone as a basis for classification.[4] The elements of land use characteristics used as a basis for this classification are presented in Figure 9–3. This is similar to a dichotomous classification in which an entity is divided into its component parts.

[4]Land Use Classification Committee, North Carolina Section, Southeast Chapter,American Institute of Planners, *A Proposal For A Standardized Land-Use Classification System,* Ca. 1960.

For example, a major land use is "transportation," which is subdivided into "vehicular" and "nonvehicular" uses. Vehicular use is further divided into "routes" and "terminals." All of these land use designations are based primarily on the land use characteristics of a specific parcel.

The above classification is well organized and is applicable to most cities. It has the added advantage of being suited to data processing equipment, an important attribute in an era of utilization of vast amounts of data (Table 9–1). Notice too that there is a good bit of flexibility in the system outlined in Table 9–1. For example, if the person utilizing this system is conducting a study in a city with large numbers of motionless mobile homes, a separate class might be desirable to include all such housing units, with this identified as "mobile homes or modules"; code number 511. Another example might pertain to recreation under the broader class of social and cultural use. One might desire to form two subclasses, one "indoor recreation, code number 614", and the other "outdoor recreation, code number 615" to distinguish between such uses as indoor skating rinks and outdoor playing fields and stadiums.

**Table 9–1**  A Land Use Classification System Based on Land Use Characteristics

| Land Use Class | Data Processing Code |
| --- | --- |
| Transportation | 100 |
| Vehicular | 110 |
| Routes | 112 |
| Terminals | 113 |
| Nonvehicular | 120 |
| Routes | 121 |
| Substations | 123 |
| Production | 200 |
| Extractive | 210 |
| Agriculture | 211 |
| Forestry | 212 |
| Mining and quarrying | 213 |
| Manufacturing | 220 |
| Durable | 221 |
| Nondurable | 222 |
| Manufacturing services | 230 |
| Construction | 231 |
| Utilities | 232 |
| Miscellaneous | 233 |
| Business | 300 |
| Retail trade | 310 |
| Primary trade | 311 |
| Secondary trade | 312 |
| Convenience trade | 313 |
| Wholesale trade | 320 |
| Merchants | 321 |
| Petroleum-bulk | 322 |
| Farm products | 323 |
| Service | 400 |
| Consumer services | 410 |
| Personal | 411 |
| Amusement | 412 |
| Communication | 413 |
| Professional services | 420 |
| Administrative | 421 |
| Financial and advisory | 422 |
| Research and testing | 423 |
| Business services | 430 |
| Repair | 431 |
| Office | 432 |
| Residence | 500 |
| Single-family | 510 |
| Two-family | 520 |
| Multifamily | 530 |
| Miscellaneous | 540 |
| Social and cultural | 600 |
| Personal development | 610 |
| Educational | 611 |
| Religious | 612 |
| Recreation | 613 |
| Health and welfare | 620 |
| Medical | 621 |
| Institutional | 622 |
| Open land | 700 |
| Vacant | 710 |
| Water | 720 |

SOURCE:  Land Use Classification Committee, North Carolina Section, Southeast Chapter, American Institute of Planners, *A Proposal For A Standardized Land Use Classification System* (about 1960).

No matter how refined and systematized the land use classification, these are, nonetheless, situations that

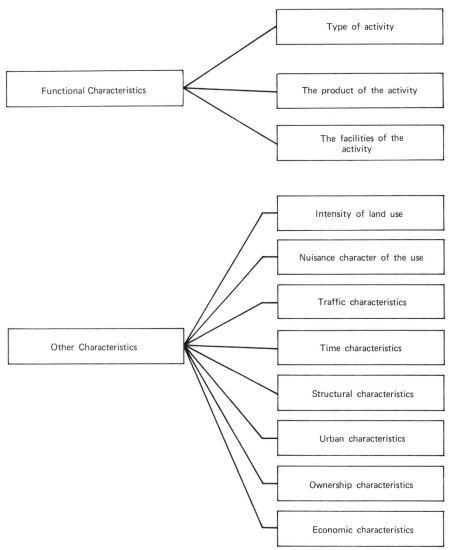

**Figure 9–3** Structure of a land use classification system based on land use characteristics. Derived from Land Use Classification Committee, North Carolina Section, Southeast Chapter, American Institute of Planners. *A Proposal for a Standardized Land-Use Classification System.*

cannot easily be accounted for. Building vacancies represent a situation that is not included in most land use classifications, although some might argue that it need not be since it represents a temporary situation. Space uses on building levels other than ground level also are difficult to provide for, especially if there is a mixture of uses on levels above ground level. Land uses which are ancillary to the major use of a land parcel also are troublesome, such as outdoor storage associated with the major use of the land parcel or parking area associated with commercial establishments or shopping centers.

There are other land use classifications that could be mentioned in this coverage, but this would not be especially profitable, since they tend to be very much the same and, therefore, redundant.

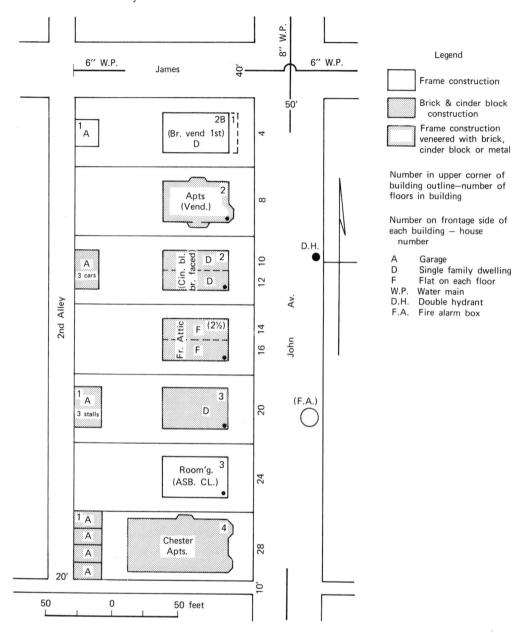

**Figure 9–4** Portion of a Sanborn map; a residential block. *Source.* Sanborn Map Co.

Reference has been made to the presentation of land use information in map form. This is a commonly used method of storing such data and from it, spatial relationships involving a given parcel can be tentatively established. More detail is presented and at a larger scale, on The Sanborn Map which is, in part, a land use map.[5] This particular map also shows details of structures occupying parcels and utilities serving the parcels (Figure 9–4).

[5] A discussion of the utility of the Sanborn Map is presented in Robert L. Wrigley, Jr., "The Sanborn Map as a Source of Land Use Information for City Planning," *Land Economics*, Vol. 24, No. 2 (May, 1949).

The Sanborn Map is made available by the Sanborn Map Company to users who subscribe to the service which provides the original maps and periodic updating and revision. Municipal governments and planning organizations often subscribe to this service, and so do fire insurance companies.

## Inputs of Urban Land in Cities of the United States

It has been difficult, and still is, to produce firm data on amounts of land used for urban purposes in the United States and other parts of the world. It is even more difficult to obtain data on amounts

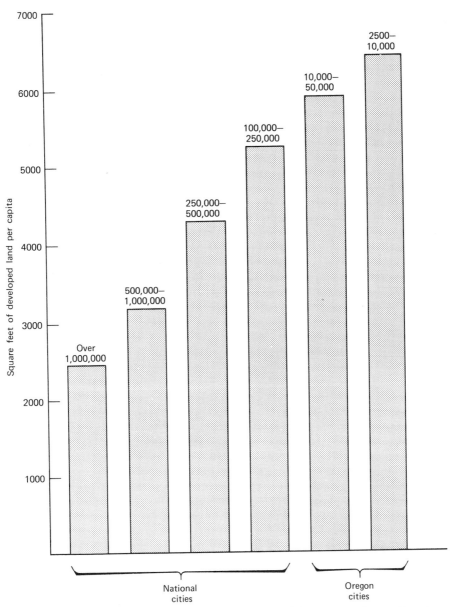

**Figure 9–5**   Land inputs per capita—cities in selected size groups. *Source.* Based on data in National Commission on Urban Problems: *Three Land Research Studies,* and Bureau of Municipal Research and Service: *Land Use in 33 Oregon Cities.*

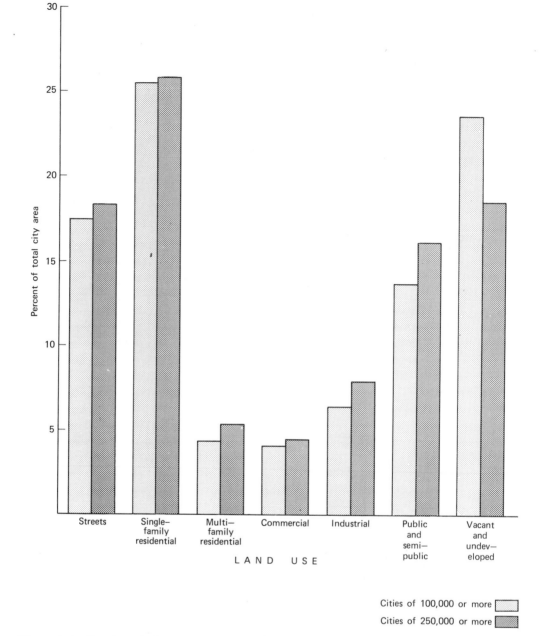

Cities of 100,000 or more ☐
Cities of 250,000 or more ▨

**Figure 9–6**   Land use in large American cities, as a percent of total city area. *Source.* Based on data in Allan D. Manuel, *Three Land Research Studies.* National Commission on Urban Problems.

of urban land used for particular urban uses. Though data may be available for a number of single cities, rarely have the data been available for a number of cities, derived in the same manner and for the same point in time. However, it is now possible to present some information on urban land inputs for a number of cities of the United States.

The average input of urban land per urban resident in cities in the United States of 100,000 or more people is 4722 sq. ft. or slightly over one-tenth of an acre per person.[6] For a sample of smaller

[6]Calculated from data in Allen D. Manvel, "Land Use in 106 Large Cities," *Three Land Research Studies,* The National Commission on Urban Problems, Research Report No. 12, Washington, GPO, 1968.

cities in Oregon with populations between 10,000 and 50,000, the per capita inputs are 5894 square feet or about one-seventh of an acre (Figure 9–5).[7] For a group of even smaller cities in Oregon with populations between 2500 and 10,000, the per capita urban land inputs are 6391 square feet, just slightly more than one-seventh of an acre.[8] Based on a per capita input of urban land of 5227 square feet or about one-eighth of an acre, it can be estimated that urban centers in the United States occupy 18 million acres of land. Observe also that there is an inverse relationship between per capita inputs of urban land and size of the city, with smaller cities having the largest per capita demands on land.

Now that estimates of the total and per capita input of land for urban uses have been presented, it is necessary to disaggregate these amounts among the various major uses to which urban land is put. This is done for major American cities and is presented in Figure 9–6. With regard to the classes of urban land included, it is with reservation that the class identified as "public and semipublic" is included, but this is the form in which useable data have been made available. Also, a land use class identified "vacant and undeveloped" land is included, which may be an error, since this land is not devoted to any urban use. It is a land type consisting of parcels not devoted to any functional use and, in fact, may not be suitable for development. This topic, however, is explored in some detail in a later chapter.

One observation about land inputs for various urban uses is that the greatest shares of urban land are devoted to uses more extensive in nature, such as land for streets, single family residences, and public and semipublic needs. By contrast, the shares of urban area devoted to more intensely used land, like those for mul-

tifamily residences, commercial, and industrial uses, are relatively small.

Consideration of the shares of city area devoted to different land uses is only one means of examining urban land use. Another way of presenting the land use mix in cities is the amount of urban land used per capita. In this manner, the amount of land used for any and all urban purposes is related to the number of people in the city where the land is being used. If percentage shares of land used for different purposes are presented, such as 20 percent for single family residences or 5 percent for commercial uses, this gives no indication of the average land need per person in the city.

Considerable differences are disclosed in amounts of land used per capita for a particular function, with this variation existing between cities of the same size class and, particularly, between cities in different size classes. For comparative purposes, the per capita inputs for a number of large cities over 100,000 distributed throughout the country and a number of smaller cities of less than 50,000 in Oregon are presented in Figure 9–7. Notice that the smaller cities in Oregon are more or less "free-standing" cities and are not incorporated suburbs of larger central cities.

## Relationships and Associations in the Land Use Mix

Another aspect of urban land use is the mixture of ways to which urban land in the city is put. An accounting of per capita inputs of land for different uses fails to take into account structural patterns and relationships that may exist with respect to the land use mix. The mean amount of land used for function $X$ may be 500 square feet per capita; the mean amount of land used for function $Y$ may be 750 square feet per person, and so on for other land uses. Is there a pronounced regularity, however, in the amount of land used for a given purpose (use $X$) relative to the amount used for a different purpose (use $Y$)? Also, is the re-

---

[7]Calculated from data in *Land Use in 33 Oregon Cities*, Bureau of Municipal Research and Service, University of Oregon, 1961.

[8]*Ibid.*

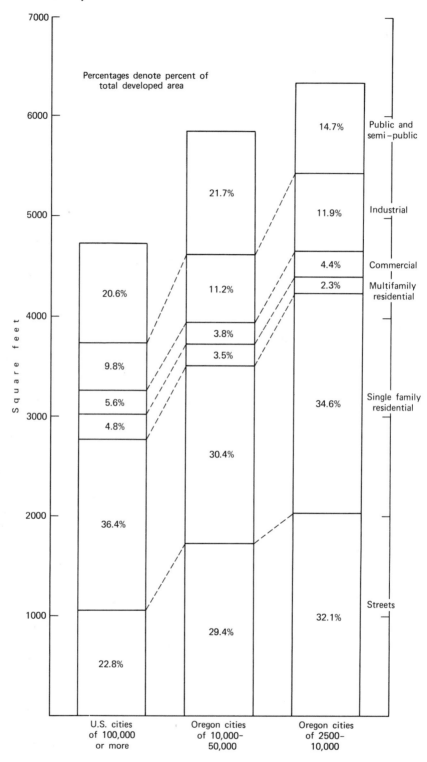

**Figure 9–7**   Average per capita land use inputs, by land use type and city size. *Source.* Ibid., Figure 9–5.

lationship such that the ratio presented in the example (1.0/1.5) applies regardless of the amount of land used for one of the functions? In addition, does the ratio remain constant if cities of different population size are considered, or does the ratio between inputs change as a function of different city size? These are some of the questions that arise concerning the land use mix in American cities, or for that matter, in cities in any part of the world.

The manner in which these questions might be approached is to derive the coefficient of correlation between per capita land needs of a certain type and per capita amounts of a different type of land need.[9] When you take six major land use classes, there is a total of fifteen of these relationships and the coefficients derived provide a means of identifying the degree of overall association between any pair of land use inputs. Going one step further, regression analysis might be utilized to provide an estimate of the manner and magnitude of variation of

[9]The coefficient of correlation is a statistical means of indicating numerically the degree and type of association between two variables. The coefficient of correlation ranges between 1.00, indicating perfect positive correlation, and −1.00, indicating perfect negative correlation.

**Table 9–2**    Land Use Associations in American Cities[a]—58 Cities of 100,000 or More and 27 Oregon Cities of 2500 to 50,000[b]

| Land Use Type | Streets Large[c] Cities | Streets Small[d] Cities | Single Family Residential Large Cities | Single Family Residential Small Cities | Other Residential Large Cities | Other Residential Small Cities | Commercial Large Cities | Commercial Small Cities | Industrial Large Cities | Industrial Small Cities | Public and Semipublic Large Cities | Public and Semipublic Small Cities |
|---|---|---|---|---|---|---|---|---|---|---|---|---|
| **Streets** | | | | | | | | | | | | |
| Large cities | — | — | .9492 | | .6827 | | .8653 | | .7980 | | .7991 | |
| Small cities | | | | .9192 | | .8034 | | .8499 | | .8011 | | .8427 |
| **Single family residential** | | | | | | | | | | | | |
| Large cities | | | | | .7312 | | .9291 | | .7565 | | .7730 | |
| Small cities | | | | | | .7896 | | 8870 | | .8095 | | .7928 |
| **Other residences** | | | | | | | | | | | | |
| Large cities | | | | | | | .7723 | | .6496 | | .5644 | |
| Small cities | | | | | | | | .7113 | | .7258 | | .8241 |
| **Commercial** | | | | | | | | | | | | |
| Large cities | | | | | | | | | .7645 | | .7170 | |
| Small cities | | | | | | | | | | .6862 | | .7675 |
| **Industrial** | | | | | | | | | | | | |
| Large cities | | | | | | | | | | | .6311 | |
| Small cities | | | | | | | | | | | | .6650 |
| **Public and semi-public** | | | | | | | | | | | | |
| Large cities | | | | | | | | | | | — | |
| Small cities | | | | | | | | | | | | — |

[a]Coefficients given are Pearsonian coefficients of correlation.
[b]Ibid., Table 9–2.
[c]58 cities with populations in excess of 100,000.
[d]27 cities in Oregon with populations between 2500 and 50,000.

land inputs of one type when compared with inputs of another type. Regression discloses that inputs of a certain type vary as do inputs of land of a different type, but by a ratio different from another pair of uses, and that generally the ratio between any two inputs is different as each changes its role in the land use mix.

The coefficients of correlation referred to are presented in matrix form in Table 9–2. Two matrices are included—one for 58 national cities over 100,000, and the other for 27 cities in Oregon with populations between 2500 and 50,000. In the former group, the cities range in size from 101,000 (Torrance, California) to 2,479,000 (Los Angeles, California).

*Land Inputs for Streets.* The per capita needs of land for streets in 58 American cities over 100,000 are 1160 square feet, compared to 1932 square feet in a sample of cities of 2500 to 50,000, the latter input 67 percent greater than the former.

Large cities having per capita land inputs for streets at least one standard deviation greater than the mean include Amarillo, Corpus Christi, Duluth, Kansas City (two standard deviations), Lincoln, Lubbock (two standard deviations), Sacramento (two standard deviations), St. Petersburg, and Tacoma.[10] Large cities having such inputs at least one standard deviation less than the mean include Buffalo, Cambridge, Hartford, Newark, Providence, Rochester, and Yonkers, all of which are in the Mid-Atlantic region or in New England.

Per capita amounts of land for streets are highly correlated with amounts used for other purposes, both in large and small cities (Table 9–2). The strongest association between amounts of land so used is with amounts used for single family residences and commercial uses. The lowest correlation is between land used for streets and for multifamily residential uses. Perhaps, these findings indicate that amounts of land used for streets are gen-

erated more to satisfy individual needs than they are to satisfy group needs. Also indicated is the fact that the major beneficiaries of these land inputs are relatively dispersed (single family residences), compared to those uses less strongly associated with land for streets—multifamily residential, industrial, and public and semi-public—which are relatively localized within the urban center.

Increased per capita amounts of land for streets are accompanied by increases in land needs of all other major types but especially for single family residences, public and semi-public uses, and industrial uses. A regression line for single family residences is at a near forty five degree angle (Figure 9–8). By contrast, a regression line for multifamily residential uses is nearly flat, indicating that increased land inputs for streets are not accompanied by commensurate increases of land for multifamily residential uses. The regression line for commercial land likewise is nearly flat. These findings indicate that amounts of land needed for streets in the large city increase fairly independent of increases in land devoted to commercial or multi-family residential uses. This condition might be explained by the fact that additional area for multifamily residences, either low-rise or high-rise, and for commercial uses is most often provided through conversion of an existing land use, rather than development of previously undeveloped area. Thus, the street pattern is established prior the emergence of the multifamily residential or commercial areas.

*Land   Inputs   for   Single   Family Residences.*   The average per capita need for single family residences in 58 large cities is 1693 square feet and in small cities it is 2056 feet, an input increase of 21 percent.

Cities with populations over 100,000 with per capita demands for land for single family residences greater than one standard deviation from the mean include Austin (two standard deviations),

---

[10]Standard deviation is explained in Chapter 2.

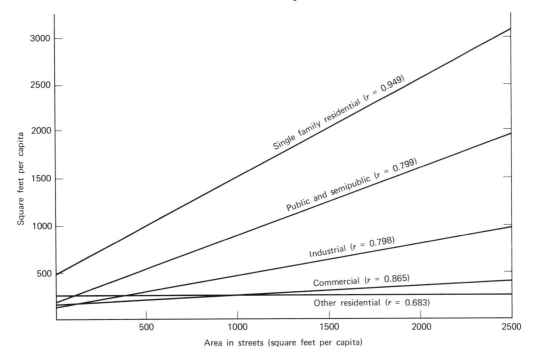

**Figure 9–8**   Relationships between land used for streets and for other major uses; 58 U.S. cities with populations over 100,000. *Source.* Ibid., Figure 9–7.

Dallas, Ft. Wayne (two standard deviations), Kansas City (two standard deviations), Mobile, Montgomery, Phoenix, Sacramento, and St. Petersburg. Cities with more than one standard deviation less than the mean include Buffalo, Cambridge, Hartford, Milwaukee, Newark, Niagara Falls, Providence, Syracuse, and Yonkers. Again, most of the cities with negative deviations are in the Mid-Atlantic region and New England.

Regarding correlation between land needs for single family residences and those for other uses, the strongest association is with land used for streets and commercial purposes. Singularly strong is the association between single family residential space needs and needs for commercial uses and for streets in large cities.

As in the case of land inputs for streets, increases in land inputs for single family residences are accompanied by increased per capita inputs for all other uses (Figure 9–9). Regression lines indicating the

magnitude of these inputs are steepest for streets and for public and semi-public uses. Demands of a certain amount of additional land for single family uses are accompanied by the greatest demands for these two uses in the approximate ratio of 1.0/0.5–0.8. The flattest of the regression lines is for multifamily residential use, indicating that increases in land used for single family dwellings are not accompanied by commensurate increases in space for other types of dwellings. There essentially is a "trade off" in land inputs here, low density, single family residences for high density, multifamily residences.

*Land Inputs for Multifamily Residences.*   Multifamily residential land inputs average 254 square feet per capita in 58 large American cities, but only 168 square feet per capita in a sample of smaller cities, or 34 percent less. This supports the impression that the larger urban center is more committed to using land for more intensive residential uses,

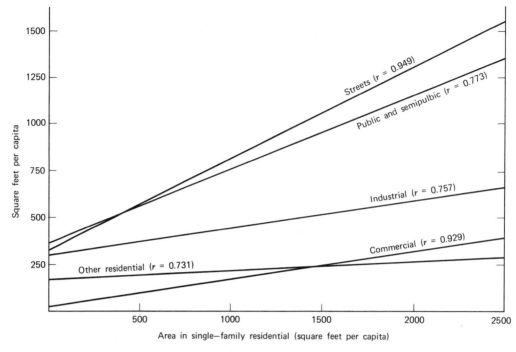

**Figure 9–9**    Relationships between land used for single family residential use and for other major uses; 58 U.S. cities with populations over 100,000. *Source.* Ibid., Figure 9–7.

such as residential hotels, high-rise apartment structures, and other multifamily structures, in contrast to the greater use of land for streets and single family dwellings in smaller cities. It bears out the general notion of spaciousness in smaller urban centers, even if the spaciousness is provided by greater per capita surface area devoted to streets.

Large cities using amounts of land for multifamily uses greater than one standard deviation from the per capita mean include Ft. Wayne, Kansas City (two standard deviations), Los Angeles (two standard deviations), Memphis, and Sacramento. Large cities at least one standard deviation below the mean include Canton and Dearborn.

Land inputs for multifamily residential uses are not as strongly correlated with other land inputs as are the individual land uses discussed earlier, with the coefficients of correlation rarely greater than .80 and, on occasion, as low as .56, indicating that, in the land use mix, this land use tends to be less an integral part of the mix.

An interesting contrast exists between the coefficients expressing the relationship between multifamily residential land and land used for public and semi-public uses. For large cities, the coefficient is only .56, while for small cities the coefficient is .82.

*Land Inputs for Commercial Uses.* For commercial uses, an average of 279 square feet of land is used per capita in large cities. For small cities, the amount is 258 square feet, or approximately 8 percent less.

Cases where amounts of land used for commercial uses exceed one standard deviation from the mean include Amarillo, Anaheim, Dallas, Ft. Wayne (two standard deviations), Kansas City (two standard deviations), Memphis (two standard deviations), New Orleans, and Sacramento. On the negative side, where the amounts per capita are at least one standard deviation less than the mean, the cities of Cambridge and Newark are included. Both of these cities are immediately adjacent to larger urban centers which serve their commercial needs to some degree, thereby lessening their inputs of commercial land to some extent.

Per capita land needs for commercial use are most strongly associated with needs for land for single family residences and, to a slightly lesser degree, with amounts used for streets. The weakest correlations are between commercial land inputs and those for industrial use and for public and semi-public use.

*Land Inputs for Industrial Uses.* Land inputs for industrial uses in large cities average 536 square feet per capita, while in small cities the average is 722 square feet per capita, or 35 percent more. Industry in small cities is more land absorbing than it is in large cities, perhaps as a function of (1) lower land costs, and (2) the more extensive type of industry in small cities.

Large cities that deserve to wear the label of "industrial" or "manufacturing" cities may be those that have per capita land inputs greater than at least one standard deviation from the mean of a number of large cities. These instances include Dearborn, Duluth, Gary (two standard deviations), Hammond, and Kansas City (two standard deviations). No large city is as much as one standard deviation below the mean, although Hartford, Miami, Pasadena, and Syracuse approach this level.

In large cities, per capita amounts of industrial land are most strongly correlated with per capita amounts used for streets and least correlated with amounts used for public and semipublic purposes. At no time, however, is the coefficient of correlation as great as .80 for large cities. For small cities, on the other hand, there is a stronger correlation between industrial land and land used for streets and for single family residences. In both instances, the coefficient is slightly over .80 (Table 9–2).

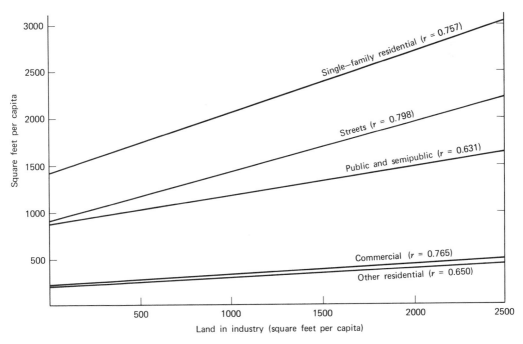

**Figure 9–10**  Relationships between land for industrial use and for other major uses; 58 U.S. cities with populations over 100,000. *Source.* Ibid., Figure 9–7.

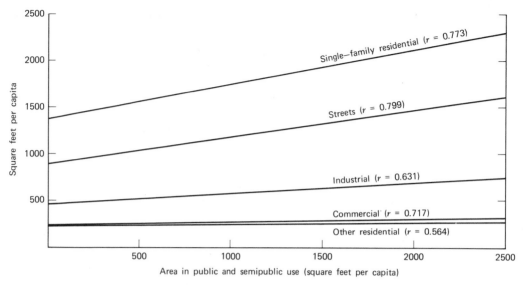

**Figure 9–11**   Relationships between land for public and semipublic use and for other major uses; 58 U.S. cities with populations over 100,000. *Source.* Ibid., Figure 9–7.

Increased amounts of land used for industrial purposes are most strongly associated with increased inputs of land for single family residences, streets, and public and semipublic uses (Figure 9–10).

*Land Inputs for Public and Semipublic uses.*   The average per capita amount of land used for public and semipublic use in large American cities is 1033 square feet, while in small cities the average amount per capita is 1069 square feet or only about 3 percent greater. Since some public and semipublic uses, such as municipal airports, civic centers, and the like are most commonly significant users of space in large cities, it would be expected that the amounts used for these purposes in large cities would be appreciably greater than in small cities. Furthermore, land used for recreational purposes also is included and inputs are small for small cities, but there is still a negligible overall difference between large and small cities.

Amounts of land used for public and semipublic purposes greater than one standard deviation from the mean for large cities characterize Amarillo, Duluth (two standard deviations), El Paso, and Phoenix. No large city is as much as one standard deviation below the mean, although Los Angeles and Miami approach this level.

Coefficents of correlation between per capita amounts of land used for public and semipublic functions and amounts used for other major purposes are not especially high for large cities and only slightly higher for small cities (Table 9–2). For public and semipublic land in large cities, the correlation coefficients are highest for streets and single family residential land and are the lowest for multifamily and industrial uses. An interesting contrast exists between amounts of land used for public and semipublic uses and for multifamily residences. The coefficient is rather low for large cities (.56), but is one of the highest for small cities (.82). Perhaps, this is due to the different nature of this housing, with high-rise and walk-up apartments more typical of large cities, and duplexes and boarding houses more typical of small cities.

Needs for land for public and semipublic uses mount as a function of increased amounts of land of each of the other major types, but mount most for single family residences and for streets. By contrast, increased needs of land for commercial and multifamily residential uses increase only negligibly as more land is used per capita for public and semipublic uses (Figure 9–11).

## Urban Population and the Land Use Mix

Reference has been made to variations in amounts of land utilized for different purposes in cities of different sizes. To examine such a relationship in greater detail, inputs of land of a specific type were compared with the populations of a number of large cities. The results of this examination are presented in Table 9–3.

**Table 9–3** Relationships Between Per Capita Land Inputs and Population of 58 Large American Cities[a]

| Land Use Type | Coefficient of Correlation |
|---|---|
| Streets | −.1885 |
| Single family residential | −.0933 |
| Multifamily residential | .6550 |
| Commercial | −.0976 |
| Industrial | −.1644 |
| Public | −.1633 |

[a]Cities over 100,000.
SOURCE: *Ibid*, Table 9–2.

Although relationships among different land use inputs are quite pronounced, that is, correlation coefficients are quite high, there is a less pronounced correlation between any single land use input in the city and the population of that city (Tables 9–2 and 9–3). Moreover, most of the coefficients expressing relationships between population and a specific land input are negative. This means, that while land input of one type increases along with input of a different type, as population of the city is increased, per capita inputs of land for streets, single-family residential, commercial, industrial, and public uses decrease. Even though the degree of negative correlation is not particularly

high in any one of these cases, there still is a general lessening of land needs per capita as a function of increased population size. Only one per capita land use input increases as does population, which is land for multifamily residential uses. So then, as population of the city becomes greater, per capita land needs of this type become greater as well.

Interpretation of the above material might include the following: (1) Increases in land needs of one type are accompanied by increases in land needs of each of the other major land use types, with a fairly high degree of correlation between any two land inputs, that is, as one land input increases, so does each of several others and, (2) while land needs mount as population increases, per capita inputs for five of six major land use types increase at a decreasing rate, with only land needs for multifamily residential purposes steadily increasing as does population. When you consider the latter situation, the indication might be that as population of the city increases at a pace greater than conversion of land to urban uses, land of most land use types is used more intensely than previously. Furthermore, the indication is that additional land for multifamily residential use might be obtained through (1) absorption of land previously vacant, (2) conversion of marginal land used for other purposes, or (3) redevelopment of land formerly used for multifamily residences, but with a higher intensity of use, that is, more dwelling units per acre.

## Land Use Specialization

As one may be interested in specialization within the urban economy, so might he be interested in specialization in the land use structure of the city. One manner of approaching the latter problem of identifying differences in the land use mix of urban centers is to identify variations in the degree to which various land uses in each city collectively comprise inputs greater than a stated base level. The

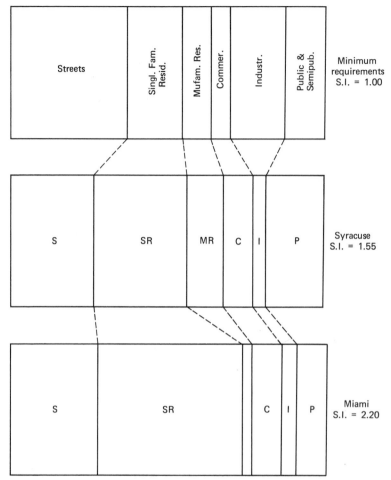

**Figure 9–12**  Graphic portrayal of different degrees of land use specialization.

minimum requirement might serve as a suitable base level for this purpose.[11] If all land use inputs equal the minimum requirement of per capita input, there obviously would be no concentration or specialization in any one land use type. If, however, there is a per capita input of land in a given land use class that is appreciably greater than the minimum requirement of that class, there would be a degree of specialization in that particular land use. Comparison of the sum of the degrees of specialization in each land use

[11]This is an adaptation of the minimum requirements approach developed by Ullman and Dacey and cited earlier. The major modification in the equation used is the substitution of data on each of the land use classes for each of the industry groups used by Ullman and Dacey.

class, relative to the respective minimum requirements in each land use class, yields a general index of the degree of land use specialization for each city. The index numbers produced will range upward from 1.00, and the greater the index number, the greater the degree of specialization in the land use mix or, conversely, the lower the index number, the greater the degree of diversification in the land use mix (Figure 9–12). Indices of land use specialization for a sample of 58 large cities are presented in Figure 9–13. Although nearly all cities have some degree of specialization in the land use mix, in terms of allocation of land among the various uses to which it might be put, there is no general agreement on what the land use specialization will be. Taking

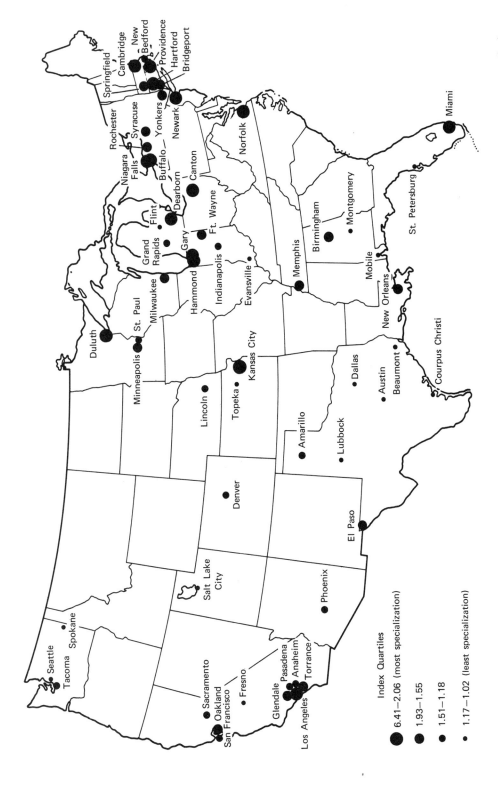

**Figure 9–13** Indices of land use specialization: selected U.S. cities. *Source.* Data from Ray M. Northam, "The Land Use Mix in American Cities." Unpublished research paper, 1970.

**Table 9–4**   Land Use Specializations, by Land Use Type and Geographic Division

| Geographic Divison | Streets | Single Family Residences | Multi-family Residences | Commer-cial | Industrial | Public and Semi-public | Number of Cities |
|---|---|---|---|---|---|---|---|
| | | | (mean rank)[a] | | | | |
| New England | 5.0 | 4.7 | 1.7 | 4.0 | 2.8 | 2.8 | 6 |
| Middle Atlantic | 4.8 | 3.3 | 3.2 | 4.7 | 2.8 | 2.3 | 6 |
| South Atlantic | 3.3 | 1.3 | 5.3 | 3.0 | 5.3 | 2.7 | 3 |
| East North Central | 3.3 | 2.2 | 3.8 | 5.4 | 2.2 | 4.1 | 10 |
| East South Central | 3.8 | 1.0 | 4.5 | 4.5 | 5.3 | 2.0 | 4 |
| West North Central | 3.2 | 2.3 | 4.5 | 5.5 | 3.2 | 2.3 | 6 |
| West South Central | 2.5 | 2.3 | 5.8 | 5.0 | 3.3 | 2.3 | 8 |
| Mountain | 3.3 | 1.7 | 5.3 | 5.3 | 4.7 | 1.3 | 3 |
| Pacific | 3.0 | 1.8 | 3.3 | 5.3 | 4.0 | 3.6 | 12 |
| Totals | 3.5 | 2.4 | 3.9 | 4.9 | 3.4 | 2.9 | 58 |

[a]For each city in each geographic division, the rank order of land use specializations was determined, these were summed for all cities in the division, and the mean rank obtained. The possible mean ranks range between 1.0 with all cities in the division having the same first ranked specialization, and 6.0 with all cities having the same sixth ranked specialization.
SOURCE:   Calculated from data in Allen D. Manvel, "Land Use in 106 Large Cities," *Three Land Research Studies,* The National Commission on Urban Problems, Research Report No. 12, Washington, GPO, 1968.

just the six most specialized cities, the land use specialization in Providence is multifamily residential land, the land use specialization in Canton, Cambridge, Buffalo, and Gary is industrial land, while that in Newark is public and semipublic land.

As there are differences in land use specialization among cities, there appear to be differences in land use specialization between regions of the United States (Table 9–4). New England cities have more specializations in multifamily housing than do those of other regions. Specialization in industrial land use is most common in cities of the upper Midwest (East North Central Division). Land devoted to public and semipublic uses comprises the most common land use specialty in cities of the Rocky Mountain and intermontane regions (Mountain Division). Single family use of urban land is the pronounced specialization in the South and Pacific Coast regions, as it is for all large cities collectively.

By contrast, for a group of cities in Oregon in the population size class of 10,000 to 50,000, industrial land use was the major specialization in four, public and semipublic land use was the specialty in three, land devoted to streets comprised the land use specialty in two, and single family residential land use dominated in only one.

One might surmise that the degree of land use specialization of urban centers is related to the population of the center. A coefficient of rank order correlation for large cities was obtained with the variables being the index of specialization and population. The coefficient obtained for large cities was .025 and for small cities it was .006, leading to the conclusion that degree of specialization in the land use mix is not particularly associated with the population of the city.

# Models of the Internal Structure of Cities

Previous sections have dealt with the array of different land uses that exist in the city and means of grouping these into a limited and workable number of groups or classes. Also, there has been coverage of the shares of city area devoted to different land uses, per capita land inputs for each of the major classes, and associations between different land uses. The matter now at hand is to put urban land uses into a spatial context. The concern here is for the spatial arrangement of different land uses or, at a more general level, of land use zones. In this broader context, three different models of land use structure have been advanced, each dealing with zonation of land uses in the city. One model deals with concentric zones based on a single nucleus, another considers sectoral zones radiating from a single nucleus, and the third recognizes an irregular zonation, based on a number of nuclei. Each of these will be reviewed in sections to follow. They all have to do with suggested patterns of land use zonation and allow a level of generalization on urban land use that would not be possible if each separate parcel was considered. Here, we focus on the general pattern and not the parcel.

width.[12] The exact dimensions, however, are not pertinent; only the spatial pattern or arrangement of the various recognized zones is pertinent. At the center of the arrangement is the central business district, and arranged in a concentric manner around this zone are, in order, the zone of transition, the zone of workingman's homes, the zone of better residences, and the commuter zone (Figure 9–14). One familiar with the city of Chicago, as was Professor Burgess of the University of Chicago, will note a similarity between the concentric zone model and Chicago if only the western half of each of the zones was considered, since the central business district of Chicago is adjacent to Lake Michigan. The central business district would be represented by the "Loop."

Regardless of some general similarities to Chicago, and perhaps to some other cities as well, there are certain land use components of the model that are questionable. There is no industrial zone recognized in the concentric zone model, except possible light manufacturing in the transition zone, much of which would

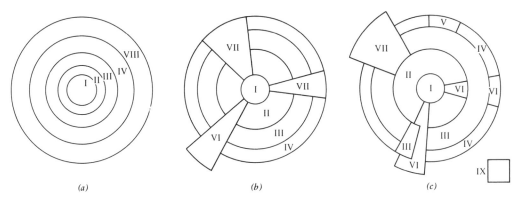

**Figure 9-14** Models of spatial patterns of urban land uses, hypothetical cases. (a) Concentric zone model. (b) Sector model. (c) Multiple-nuclei model. I CBD (central business district); II wholesale-light manufacturing; III low rent residential (multiple-family); IV medium rent residential; V high rent residential; VI commercial; VII Industrial; VIII commuter zone; IX suburb.

The *Concentric Zone Model,* developed by Ernest W. Burgess in 1925, theorized a land use pattern comprised of several concentric zones of undetermined

[12]Ernest W. Burgess, "The Growth of the City," in *The City,* ed. Robert E. Park, Ernest W. Burgess, and Roderick D. McKenzie, Chicago: University of Chicago Press, 1925.

occupy loft space. Also, in Chicago, as in many other cities, there is a concentration of high-rise luxury apartment dwellings and apartment hotels, although this is not recognized in the concentric zone model. The major reservation, however, lies in the simplistic manner in which the various land use zones are presented. One familiar with urban land use patterns realizes that zonation is, at best, difficult to identify and is subject to change, but concentric zones are even more difficult to encounter in reality. Also, the role of transportation arteries in shaping the use pattern is neglected in this model, even though it would do much to distort the concentric zone pattern.

The *Sector Model* of urban land use structure was developed by Homer Hoyt in 1939.[13] Hoyt had access to detailed housing data for 142 American cities and, therefore, the critical elements of his model were high rent and low rent residential neighborhoods. In essence, the model states that high rent residential neighborhoods are instrumental in shaping the land use structure of the city and that there is a natural succession of change in location of these neighborhoods.[14] Regarding the location of high rent neighborhoods, several general factors were found to apply:

1.    High rent residential growth tends to proceed from the given point of origin, along established lines of travel or toward another existing nucleus of buildings or trading centers.

2.    The zone of high rent housing tends to progress toward high ground which is free from the risks of floods and to spread along lake, bay, river, and ocean fronts, where such waterfronts are not used for industry.

3.    High rent residential districts tend to grow toward the section of the city which has free, open country beyond the edges and away from "dead end" sections which are limited by natural or artificial barriers to expansion.

4.    The high rent residential neighborhood tends to grow toward the homes of the leaders of the community.

5.    Trends of movement of office buildings, banks, and stores, pull the higher rent residential neighborhoods in the same general direction.

6.    High rent residential areas tend to develop along the fastest existing transportation lines.

7.    The growth of high rent neighborhoods continues in the same general direction for a long period of time.

8.    Deluxe high rent apartment areas tend to be established near the business center in old residential areas.

9.    Real estate promoters may bend the direction of high grade residential growth.

Thus, according to Hoyt's model, the high rent residential neighborhoods are basic in shaping urban land use structure and, since these neighborhoods expand and contract in a viable manner, other land use zones are located in accord with the location of high rent neighborhoods (Figure 9–14). The high rent neighborhoods, in developing with particular reference to transportation arterials (factor 6), tend to develop a sector or wedge shape zone. This sector is likely, with passage of time, to be modified by the replacement by multifamily residences in the apex of the sector (factor 8) and by widening of the sector on the outer periphery (factor 3). It was hypothesized, also, that some other land use zones developed a sector form occupying the less desirable residential lands of the city. Also, the interstices between sectors were occupied by land users with a lower rent paying ability or without the same preferences in using land as held by high rent residential users.

Although the sector model is biased in

---

[13]Homer Hoyt, *The Structure and Growth of Residential Neighborhoods in American Cities,* Washington, D.C., Federal Housing Administration, 1939.

[14]The term "rent" is used here, as it was by Hoyt, in the sense of economic rent, which refers to the capital outlay, regardless of the form, for the occupance of space. This could include purchase, lease, or "rent" in the popular sense.

regard to the location of residential zones, it does recognize the importance of transportation routes, especially arterial streets and highways, in shaping the land use pattern of the city. But whether the influence of these routes shapes city land use structure in the manner suggested by Hoyt is somewhat questionable, at least in the contemporary American city in which location near arterial highways by high rent residential land users is as much to be shunned as welcome. This would not negate the tenets of the sector model, however, although it may alter if not change the rationale for the development of a sector pattern. It is likely that sectors develop as suggested by Hoyt but that the impetus for this is provided by the nature of expansion and growth of commercial sectors, rather than high rent residential sectors. This matter is discussed in Chapter 11.

The *Multiple-Nuclei Model* was developed by Harris and Ullman and presented in 1945.[15] This model states that there is not a single nucleus of the city that shapes the land use pattern, but a number of separate nuclei, each influencing land use patterns in the city. The occurrence of separate nuclei and land use zones based on them were said to reflect a combination of four factors:

1. Certain activities require specialized facilities, such as maximum accessibility, a waterfront, large amounts of land, etc.
2. Certain like activities group together because they profit from cohesion, such as financial and office building districts.
3. Certain unlike activities are detrimental to each other, such as industrial and high rent residential districts.
4. Certain activities are unable to afford the high rents of the most desirable sites.

The multiple nuclei model is the least structured of the three basic models on the zonation of urban land use. It recognizes that there is not a single nucleus in the city in the form of the central business district, but a number of nuclei or focal points on which land uses of a similiar type are concentrated. Each zone originates in response to advantages offered by that particular district (factor 1) or the inability to use more expensive locations (factor 4). This theory does not have succession as an integral part, as do the two previous theories, but it does allow for areal growth of each of the zones and of the entire urban area, and so do the others (Figure 9–14).

In reality, there are aspects of all of these models present in most cities. The concentric zone model well may have applied to cities before the advent of the automobile and the city may have developed with something of a concentric zone land use pattern. Today, some aspects of this pattern may persist, not so much as complete concentric zones, but of arcs that are remnants of a concentric zone. This, then becomes reminiscent of the arcs provided for in the sector model, occupying the interstices between sectors. The sector model better fits the land use patterns of the modern city, with transportation arterials radiating from the central business district. The multiple nuclei model also is exemplified in the modern city, where there often has been a spontaneous or an administratively imposed segregation of land uses into specific districts, each offering advantages to the land users in that district. Is it not possible that all three models are manifested, in part, in the modern city? This, then, would represent a composite pattern of urban land use, still zonal in nature.

## Land Use Densities

Land use densities deal with the degree to which land is occupied by the users of it. Different densities exist in the use of land for residential, industrial, and

[15]Chauncy D. Harris and Edward L. Ullman, "The Nature of Cities", *Annals of the American Academy of Political and Social Science*, Vol. CCXLII (November, 1945).

commercial purposes, with densities also varying from city to city and from one point in time to another. Residential and commercial densities in large American cities both are within the general range of 60 to 80 occupants per acre, with industrial densities generally less than one-half these densities (Table 9–5). When urban populations increase, one or all of three changes in land use densities would occur: (1) the city might annex more area to accommodate the increased population resulting in densities that are essentially unchanged or that increase slightly, (2) the area of the city will be used more intensely for each use with resultant substantial increases in land use densities, or (3) available stocks of buildable or developable vacant land within the city would be converted to functional uses.[16] All of these alternatives have taken place in American cities to varying degrees.

**Table 9–5**  Changes in Land Use Densities in American Cities*

| Land Use | 22 cities early data | 22 cities late data | 12 constant area cities early data | 12 constant area cities late data |
|---|---|---|---|---|
| Residential | 63.2 | 53.3 | 76.8 | 67.3 |
| Industrial | 28.4 | 25.4 | 36.2 | 30.9 |
| Commercial | 65.8 | 62.0 | 81.4 | 81.8 |

*Residential densities are based on population of the city and amount of land used for residential use. Industrial and commercial densities are based on respective amounts of employment and land used for these purposes.
SOURCES:  Niedercorn, John H. and Edward F. R. Hearle, *Recent Land Use Trends in Forty-Eight Large American Cities,* Santa Monica, California, The Rand Corporation, Memorandum RM-3665-FF (June, 1963).

After considering differences in density between various major land uses, we should consider changes in land use densities. The intensity of use of land a specific type at a certain point in time can

[16]The matter of absorption of vacant urban land is discussed at greater length in Chapter 15.

be expected to change by a later point in time. This change results from a variety of causes, including changes in life styles and living preferences, changes in the means of production of urban enterprises, and changes in the use of urban space. During the late nineteenth and early twentieth centuries, larger cities in the United States and Western Europe experienced increased densities, but these have been falling since about 1950 in many cities.

For consideration of changing land use densities, one considers the total population or employment of a chosen type divided by the land area devoted to residences or employment of this certain type; for example, the employment in industrial establishments divided by the land area used by industrial establishments. Changes in residential, industrial, and commercial densities are presented in Table 9–5. Two sets of data are presented, one for 22 large cities regardless of boundary changes, and one for 12 large constant area cities. It is obvious that densities of use may change with time simply because of expansion of the city borders which would have the effect of reducing densities, since land parcels in annexed areas would tend to be large and without a commensurately high density of use.

Notice too that residential densities in both cases have declined. This likely results from more value placed on single family residences as opposed to multifamily, the more spacious nature of newly developed single family residences and the larger size of land parcels used for single family dwellings.

Industrial land use densities have likewise declined in both expanding cities and in constant area cities, probably resulting from horizontal line production in manufacturing, greater space needs for materials handling, and greater space needs for parking and landscaping.

By contrast, commercial land use densities have remained the least changed, although they are slightly lower in constant area cities. Greater use of high-rise structures for commercial purposes would tend to increase the density, but increased land needs for customer and employee parking would lessen the density, as would operational changes involving more automation, self-service, and machine processing of data.

## The Special Case of the Transition Zone

The models of land use patterns in the city all consider a zonal pattern in which identifiable sections or zones of the city are primarily devoted to a discrete land use. One land use is dominant in a given zone, for example, residential, commercial, industrial, etc., although some land parcels may be used in ways different from the dominant one in a specific zone. One zone of the city, however, is not so characterized by a single land use or a land use that is relatively static and unchanging. This is the zone of transition, which is identified in the concentric zone model of Burgess.[17]

This is the land use zone located between the central business district and the innermost of the residential zones. In a sense, it is a buffer zone and has been subject to occupance by various minority groups in the past and has experienced a continuing succession of land uses.[18] Realizing there is a rationale for the zonal aspect of other land uses, there is little rationale for the development of the transition zone. This is a land use zone that is, in some ways, similar to the outermost zone of the city where there is an admixture of urban and rural land uses. Changes in land use in the latter zone, however, tend to be relatively perma-

nent, while continued change characterizes the transition zone.

The transition zone, as viewed by Burgess, is a relatively heterogeneous concentric zone of indeterminate width. More likely, the transition zone is a belt-like zone encircling the CBD and is divided into various sectors. Broadly speaking, there are one or more sectors of active assimilation, sectors of passive assimilation, and sectors of general inactivity which are between two sectors of assimilation (Figure 9–15).[19] The transition zone is characterized by concentrations of certain types of activities and establishments, particularly (1) wholesaling, private and commercial storage, transporation facilities, and industrial establishments, (2) automobile sales and servicing, and parking, (3) public, organizational, and headquarters office establishments, (4) food, service trade, and miscellaneous retail establishments, (5) financial establishments, general offices, variety stores and transient residences, frequently grouped spatially with establishments of type 4, and (6) homogeneous heavy industrial districts.[20]

The sector of active assimilation represents the "growing edge" of the zone of transition in that the land uses characteristic of this sector are invading areas of older, higher quality residential uses. Encroaching into this residential zone are nuclei of public and institutional offices, and high-quality commercial uses adjacent to major arterial streets (Figure 9–15). It is not uncommon to find urban renewal projects within this sector, which often provide the impetus for the dynamic nature for the transformation of this sector that may earlier have been a sector of general inactivity or a zone of discard.[21]

The sector of passive assimilation is characterized by change that is less

[17]Burgess, *Op. Cit.*

[18]For excellent discussions of the transition zone one might read Donald W. Griffin and Richard E. Preston, "A Restatement of the 'Transition Zone' Concept," *Annals of the AAG,* Vol. 56, No. 2 (June, 1966) and Richard E. Preston, "The Zone in Transition: A Study of Urban Land Use Patterns," *Economic Geography,* Vol. 42, No. 3 (July, 1966).

[19]Griffin and Preston, *Ibid.*

[20]Griffin and Preston, *Ibid.*

[21]The concept of the "zone of discard" is discussed in Chapter 11 in conjunction with the central business district.

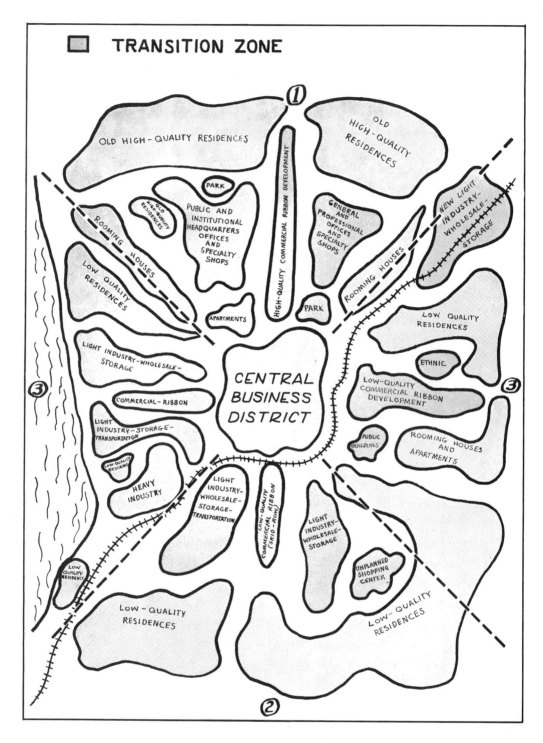

**Figure 9–15**   Sectors of the transition zone. (1) Sector of active assimilation, (2) sector of passive assimilation, (3) sector(s) of general inactivity. Donald W. Griffin and Richard E. Preston, "A Restatement of the 'Transition Zone' Concept," *Annals of AAG*, Vol. 56, No. 2 (June, 1966). Reprinted by permission.

dynamic than in the zone of active assimilation. Although growth and change are characteristic of this sector, there are qualitative differences in the form. The new establishments in this sector are of lower quality and often are intermixed with older high quality establishments. Land use types found in this sector include low quality commercial establishments, light industry, wholesaling, and storage, all of which represent incursions into an existing zone of low quality residences (Figure 9–15). Very often, the establishments in this sector have a short life span and rapid turnover in the management of establishments is common.

The sector of general inactivity is difficult to define and separates the sectors of active assimilation and passive assimilation (Figure 9–15). In this sector, change does occur but at a relatively slower pace than in the other sectors. This sector is typified by nuclei of heavy industry oriented to harbor facilities or railroad terminals, older public facilities, such as fire stations and police stations, and low quality multifamily residences and rooming houses. Additional land use types in this sector include low quality commercial ribbons, light industry, wholesaling and storage, and ethnic residential ghettos, particularly Negro, Puerto Rican, and Oriental. In an earlier era, the minority groups residing in this general sector included Irish, Polish, and Jewish groups. Even though change occurs in the uses of land in this sector, and in the population residing in the sector, there is a general lack of conversion of land uses. The lack of viability of commercial enterprises and the lack of vitality of residential neighborhoods found here tends to characterize the sector.

There is, therefore, strong evidence that a transition zone exists in the land use pattern of the city. Instead of this being a continuous, homogeneous zone, however, it is found that it has a sub-zonal structure of its own, with different degrees of viability and different forms of transition. The heterogeneity of land uses is the common characteristic of this zone, with the land use mix different in different sectors of the zone and with the form of change different as well.

## Special Topics in Urban Land Use

As demands mount for the utilization of two dimensional space in the city, especially for land at prime locations, there has been a trend underway toward the increased use of space above ground level. Multistory structures date back at least to the Roman Empire, with the building of wooden insula or thermal baths of several stories in height. With the development of improved building construction using first brick and masonry, later cast iron, and still later, steel beams, plus the development of the electric elevator about 1887, the matter of multistory building construction was expedited to where these buildings, or "skyscrapers," became commonplace in many world cities.[22]

The use of urban space above ground level has now been carried to extremes in the form of the well known Empire State Building (102 stories, 1250 feet), and the World Trade Center (twin towers of 110 stories each, 1350 feet high) in the borough of Manhattan in New York City, and the Hancock Building (1127 feet) and the Sears Tower (110 stories, 1450 feet) in Chicago. Skyscrapers are not unique to the United States, however, with one or more in metropolises all over the world.

The point here is that it has been found that space utilization can be more nearly maximized with development of structures of many stories with high speed elevators. Such structures today

[22]An excellent review of the development and acceptance of the skyscraper, and construction of skyscrapers in major world cities, is presented in Jean Gottmann, "Why the Skyscraper?", *Geographical Review*, Vol. LVI, No. 2 (April, 1966).

accommodate many service and administrative activities, especially industries in the industry group of finance, insurance, and real estate. Some skyscrapers, such as the twin towers of Marina City in Chicago, are mainly devoted to residential use on the top levels, with parking, shopping facilities, and even schools on the lower levels. Although the skyscraper is often criticized because of the sterile, antiseptic lines of a number of these monoliths, and the interference with an aesthetically pleasing skyline, they do represent an economy in terms of space use. For example, the twin towers of the World Trade Center in New York, built on a sixteen acre site, will contain about ten million square feet of rentable floor space. The same sixteen acre site, if developed with one story buildings covering the entire site, would contain only about 500,000 to 600,000 square feet of rentable space.

The advantages of development of urban space above ground level include greater accessibility to the centers of activity of the city and to transportation foci of the city. The disadvantages include greater congestion and higher land or space costs. In the process of "trade-offs," the high intensity space users in skyscrapers obviously find it to their advantage to occupy this urban space.

A related matter in the consideration of urban space above ground level is the utilization of *air rights*. Air rights can be defined as "the rights to inclusive and undisturbed use and control of a designated space within delineated boundaries, either at the surface or above a stated elevation. Such rights may be purchased or leased."[23] Implementation of this concept entails obtaining of legal rights to airspace over the surface or a surface use and the development of this space, usually with a structure of some type.

Use of air rights began in Italy in

Roman times, but the notion did not enjoy widespread acceptance until the beginning of the twentieth century. In the United States, the term "air rights" probably was first applied with the commercial use of space over railroad terminals and tracks, beginning with the development of the Grand Central Terminal area in New York City in 1902. This was followed by the New York Central Railroad's Grand Central and Park Avenue project initiated in 1913. Gradually, the term acquired a broader and more general application and is no longer used solely with regard to airspace over railroads.

In the period around 1930, railroad airspace projects were built in Chicago, with these including the 25 story Daily News Building (now Riverside Plaza) and the Merchandise Mart. Other major air rights developments occurred in the 1950's. These included the 40 story Prudential Mid-America Building over the Illinois Central tracks, the Twin Tower Marina City (896 apartments) over the railroad right-of-way alongside the Chicago River, and the 59 story PanAm Building over and adjoining the Grand Central Terminal in New York City.

Significant air rights projects in the early 1960's included the luxury 40 story Outer Drive Apartments over the Illinois Central Railroad Yard on the edge of Lake Michigan and downtown Chicago and the seven high-rise towers of Concourse Village built over the Mott Haven Railroad in the lower Bronx of New York City.[24] More recently, air rights were utilized in development of the new Madison Square Garden over Pennsylvania Station in midtown Manhattan. There are many other examples of air rights utilization on a lesser scale in smaller cities. The potential for use of air rights, however, is far greater than is presently being realized. The use of this space could be considered a means of relieving pressure on space demands as

[23]Urban Land Institute, *Air Rights and Highways,* Technical Bulletin 64, 1964.

[24]Urban Land Institute, *Ibid.*

needs mount and of using present urban space more efficiently.

An interesting paradox is presented in the use of urban land and of urban space above ground level. There has been a trend toward the development of sky-scrapers with their intervening urban can-yons, and the development of airspace above surface uses of land. Both ap-proaches have contributed to a more compact and, perhaps, a more confining urban atmosphere. On the other hand, there is increased concern for the provi-sion of *open space* in cities. The mean-ing of open space is somewhat unclear, since some may use the term in reference to preservation of undeveloped land on the periphery of the city or in the outer zones of the city. These lands are open preserves, undeveloped and serving no tangible function. Others would have this land left relatively undeveloped, except for bridle paths, hiking trails, and nature trails. A different concept of open space might be more confined to lands main-tained in a state of idleness in the core area of the city, mainly to provide some relief from the crowdedness and conges-tion there.

In any case, the objective is to retain some urban lands as open space, most likely public lands. Also, such lands should have maximum accessibility to the people of the city for their use and en-joyment. There are, then, two seeming-ly opposing objectives: one to create a greater intensity of use of urban space and the other to provide a lesser intensity of use of urban space. Is it possible to reach both objectives? Perhaps so, through the development of high density use zones, even in the central business district, surrounded by discontinuous cells of open space with low density use. These cells, for an optimum location, would be within walking distance of the users and would be improved only to the point of insuring human safety and a minimum of human comfort. By doing this, sections of the city that provide the working space and the living space for people could also become sections that provide space for leisure activities.

# 10

# land values and land use zoning

Once again, there are spatial patterns of land use in the city, not just a random distribution of land parcels used for various purposes. There are numerous factors that influence the use to which a parcel might be put, including (1) physical characteristics of the parcel, (2) administrative policies of the city, (3) location of the parcel within the spatial context of the city, and (4) value of the parcel. There is a dilemma here, however, in that the last factor, value, is determined essentially by the other factors. Therefore, it is difficult to separate land values from other attributes or liabilities of the land parcel. In this context, it is also difficult to establish a causal relationship between land use and land values, when land values are in fact, essentially established by such factors as physical characteristics, administrative policies, and spatial setting. A reasonable approach might be, then, to first consider the variables that influence land values.

## The Meaning and Expression of Land Values

The common notion of the meaning of land value is its monetary worth—the value of land in the market place. Land value can be considered in two contexts. One is the market value, which is the price of a land parcel negotiated at the time of sale of the parcel, and the other is the assessed value, which is the estimated worth of the parcel made by a competent private or public assessor. The true or market value of a parcel may be different from the assessed value, although attempts are made to keep the two in accord.

A parcel of urban real estate sometimes, but rarely, consists of land alone. More commonly, there are improvements made to the land parcel, such as structures of some sort. Therefore, the public records, made by local tax assessors for taxation purposes, will list the specific location of the land parcel, the assessed value of the land, and the value of improvements. One dealing with land values must be careful to include values of land alone, and not land plus improvements.

In urban real estate transactions, it is not uncommon to have land values quoted on the basis of the cost per front foot, especially for parcels used for commercial purposes where street frontage is especially desirable and valuable. For larger parcels, like those used by manufacturing industries, prices are more likely to be quoted on the basis of price per acre.

## Factors Influencing Urban Land Values

An anonymous real estate expert once stated that there are three tests of a "good" piece of real estate: its location, its location, and its location. This was not an attempt to be facetious or redundant, but was a means of stressing the importance of location of the parcel in establishing its value. Serious studies on the topic of land values have reinforced this judgment concerning relative location. For example, in the case of residential land values in Los Angeles County, California, several variables were included and of these the most significant was the accessibility of the parcel, especially to places of employment.[1] A study of land values in Chicago tested the influence of a number of variables, including distance from the central business district, distance from the nearest regional shopping center, and distance to the nearest elevated subway system.[2] All of these variables proved significant in a negative manner, but supported the proposition that location of a land parcel is important in influencing its value, which is to say, the greater the distance the lower the land values.

Thus, a number of distance relationships between a specific land use parcel and other parcels used for different uses are instrumental in determining urban land values. Relative location with respect to other activities, then, influences land values. There are, of course, physical influences on land values as well, although there are spatial implications to the effect of these. For example, a land parcel at a certain location and at a certain time may have a degree of slope that is restrictive to conversion to a given use, such as residential and, therefore, the value of the parcel would be low. When pressure mounts on available space for residential uses, this parcel may become more attractive for residential purposes and may be converted to this use. The value of the parcel would appreciate considerably as a result, al-though the physical setting of it has not changed; only conditions of the urban land market have changed. The point is that a physical constraint on use of an urban land parcel can be modified or overcome so the limiting effect of the constraint is lessened. This will depend, to a great degree, on the spatial setting of the parcel and the nature of the market for urban land.

## The Centrality of Urban Land Values

The argument is made that variations in urban land values are based on a number of factors, principal of which are (1) locational or spatial differences, and (2) physical differences of respective land parcels. For the developed sections of the city, which tend to occupy land that is relatively homogeneous in character, the physical variations would tend to be less important in shaping land values than would the spatial factors. At least, this would be true of the more intensely developed sections of the city. If an area of the city is subject to physical limitations that are not extreme, they can be overcome through modern technology such as flood protection by levees, dikes and storage reservoirs, by land drainage, and by land leveling.

If we can consider, then, that urban land values are influenced primarily by location of land parcels, this suggests the matter of optimum location of urban land parcels. In a spatial context, there is considered to be a single location or site in the city that has the highest land value and that all other sites have a value that is some fraction of that of the site of highest land value. This site or location of highest land value is often referred to as the "hundred percent corner" or the "hundred percent location," or the "peak land value intersection."[3] If the term

[1] Eugene F. Brigham, "The Determinants of Residential Land Values," *Land Economics,* Vol. XLI, No. 4 (November, 1965).
[2] Maurice H. Yeates, "Some Factors Affecting the Spatial Distribution of Chicago Land Values, 1910–1960," *Economic Geography,* Vol. 41, No. 1 (January, 1965).

[3] The dominance of the 100 per cent corner is likely becoming lessened, however, as suggested by Richard Lawrence Nelson, "Land Values in the United States", *Urban Land,* Vol. 28, No. 2 (February, 1969). Nelson states, "The downtown 100 percent retail corner has become largely a fiction." This is based on the fact that central business district values have been stable for 40 years, while values in outlying shopping centers have increased significantly.

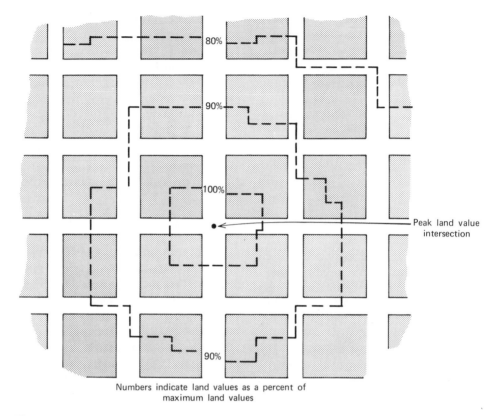

Numbers indicate land values as a percent of
maximum land values

**Figure 10–1**   Representation of the "hundred percent location."

hundred percent corner is used it may refer to the highest value land parcel of those surrounding the intersection of two major streets. If the term hundred percent location is used, it may refer to the average value per square foot of the land parcels surrounding the intersection of highest land values (Figure 10–1). Most often, the point of maximum land value occurs adjacent to a major street intersection in the central business district.

If land values are the highest at a single, identifiable point in the city, logically all other points or locations enjoy land values that are less than that of the hundred percent location. One could assume, however, that from the point of maximum value, land values steadily and uniformly decrease outward in all directions from this point. This is not the case. There is a pronounced curvilinear relationship between decreases in land values and distance from

the point of maximum value where land values decrease at a decreasing rate with greater distance from the point of peak value.

Generally, land values, outward from the point of maximum value, decline sharply within a short distance, only a few city blocks, of the hundred percent location, and then gradually the change with each increment of distance becomes less. This pattern has been existing for many decades in American cities, as indicated by maps of land values in a sample of major cities at the end of the nineteenth century (Figure 10–2).[4] Studies made more recently show the same basic curvilinear relationship between decreasing land values with increased distance outward from the point of highest values for the cities of

[4]Richard M. Hurd, *Principles of City Land Values,* Real Estate Record Association, New York, 1903.

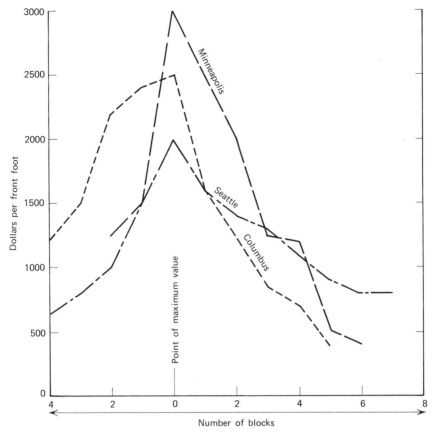

**Figure 10–2**   Spatial distribution of land values; Minneapolis, Seattle, and Columbus (Ohio): About 1900. *Source.* Adapted from data in Richard M. Hurd, *Principles of City Land Values,* 1903.

Seattle and Topeka.[5] If there is any difference in the land value curves after an interval of over half a century, it would be that the steepness of the upper section of the curve is greater, as indicated by the curves for the city of Seattle (Figure 10–2). In each of the cases referred to the curves represent land values along a major commercial street where values would tend to be especially high. If curves were constructed for other rays outward from the location of maximum values, they would have the same configuration, although there would

be differences in the steepness of slope. But they would all tend to be concave.

When land values decline outward from the hundred percent location in all directions, the general statistical surface of the city would take on the same basic configuration (Figure 10–3).[6] Near the center of the city, there would be a relatively small area of high land values surmounted by a single peak of highest land values. This steep sided "island" of high values would abruptly merge into a surface of gradually less slope and elevation.

This statistical surface would not be per-

[5]Warren R. Seyfried, "The Centrality of Urban Land Values," *Land Economics,* Vol. XXXIX, No. 3 (August, 1963).

Duane S. Knos, *Distribution of Land Values in Topeka, Kansas,* Center for Research in Business, The University of Kansas, Lawrence, Kansas, May, 1962.

[6]A statistical surface is one based on computed values and usually involves more than one variable, for example, persons per square mile, dollar value per square foot.

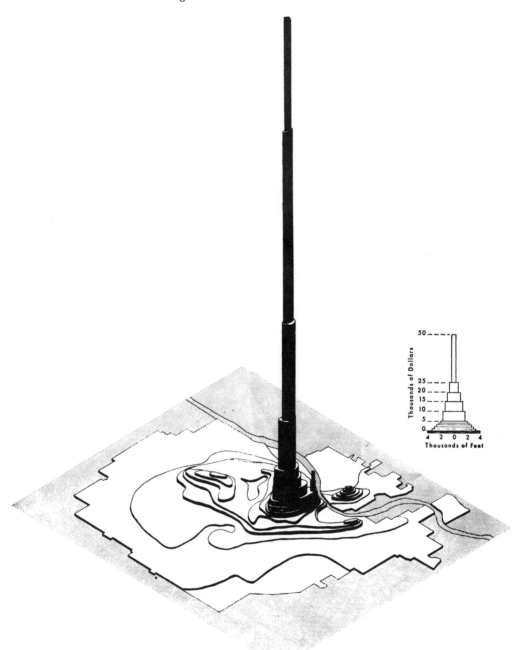

**Figure 10-3** Isometric land values: Topeka, Kansas. Duane S. Knos, *Distribution of Land Values in Topeka, Kansas.* Center for Research in Business. Reprinted by permission.

fectly smooth, however. There would be small areas resembling hills, which would represent a small area of higher land values surrounded by a lower surface of relatively low land values. In reality, these secondary peaks could be outlying commer-

cial centers, high quality residential areas, or small professional enclaves. Besides the secondary peaks, there likely would be relatively small depressions in the generally smooth statistical surface (Figure 10–3). These would represent blighted commercial or industrial areas or pockets of substandard housing that are characteristic of many ghettos housing minority groups. Examination of Figure 10–3 reveals certain similarities to the models of urban land use discussed in Chapter 9. The depressions and indentations in the statistical surface of land values tend to be in the zone of transition found on the outer margin of the central business district. The secondary peaks of higher land values are consistent with the multiple nuclei model of urban land use, with each peak representing a secondary nucleus of higher values that could coincide with a secondary nucleus of a certain land use.

## A Theory of Urban Land Values

In developing a general theory on urban land values, there are certain points to keep in mind. One of these is that, in a capitalistic society, different potential land users might bid on a given land parcel, but the one in the better position to afford the price of the land parcel is the one likely to obtain and use it. The term used in reference to this economic policy is "bid-rent," meaning the amount of capital one is willing to bid or offer for use of a specific land parcel. In other words, a theory of urban land values, in many cases, will be shaped by the actions of the market place for urban land.

In the United States, this is the usual major criterion determining land values, which in turn influence land use. The value of a land parcel is established by the amount a land user is prepared to pay for it. This is modified in many cases, however, by local planning agencies which control land use and, therefore, land values. Also, public agencies may use the power of eminent domain and condemnation proceedings to shape land use and land values. In other countries, such as Australia, the doctrine essentially is that a certain land parcel will be used for the "highest, and best use," thus, land values will be determined not only by the use made of the parcel, but by the best use to which the parcel may be put

in the judgment of the professional staffs of public agencies. As an extreme example of the difference in these doctrines, a land parcel may be valuable to a user for low income or "slum" housing. The potential monetary returns may be thought to be high, therefore, this individual is prepared to outbid other potential users of the land parcel. In a different situation, a similar use made of an urban parcel would be judged undesirable and untenable with general public desires. This would not, then, be considered the highest and best use to be made of the parcel and such a move would not be tolerated; the preference would be for a more generally desired use, such as a high-rise residential structure. Under the first doctrine, the monetary value of the land parcel would be considered low, based on its use for substandard housing, while under the second doctrine, the value of the land parcel would be relatively high. Other aspects of these different policies will be discussed in a later chapter.

An accepted theory of urban land values is patterned after an older theory of values of agricultural land.[7] The theory on agricultural land states that a farmer will attempt to maximize profits which are established by the market value of production minus the cost of production and minus costs of shipping his produce to the market. As a result, the farmers producing commodities of higher market value are in a position to outbid those raising crops of lower market value for locations nearer the market center (Figure 10–4). Based on the spatial variations of rural land use and land values we conclude that:[8]

1. Land uses determine land values through competitive bidding among farmers.

[7]William Alonso, "A Theory of the Urban Land Market," *Papers and Proceedings of the Regional Science Association*, Vol. VI, 1960. In the introduction of the article by Alonso, there is a discussion of the model for agricultural land by Johan Von Thunen, *Der Isolierte Staat in Beziehung Auf Landwirtschaft Und National ekonomie*, 1863.

[8]Alonso. *Ibid.*

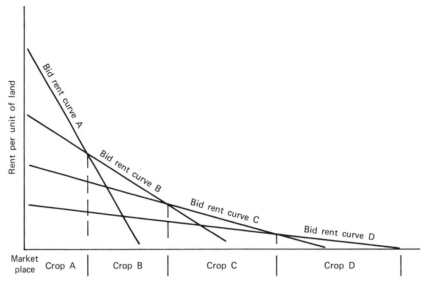

**Figure 10–4**   Bid rent curves for four crops, based upon a single market place.

2.   Land values distribute land uses according to their ability to pay.

3.   The steeper bid rent curves capture the central locations.

In considering urban land, we have different land users competing for the use of urban land parcels, and these potential users have different abilities to pay, just as do different farmers in von Thunen's model. Because of these different abilities to pay, they have different levels of the amount they are prepared to bid for use of an urban parcel. But what is the rent paying ability of different land users? The answer to this question depends on a number of factors, including (1) the size of the city involved, (2) the degree of viability of the urban economy, (3) the specific nature of the use to be made of the land parcel, (4) individual preferences and desires, and (5) the extent of available land stocks in the particular city. In view of these factors, it is impossible to produce firm estimates on the amount of rent paying ability of different land users. As early as 1903, however, estimates were made regarding the range of values of high quality land of different types in different cities in the United States.[9] These values provide

some insight into rent paying abilities, since they refer to developed and occupied land. Absolute amounts from this period are of little contemporary value since land values have appreciated greatly in about one-half century. Even today, absolute values are not as meaningful as are relative values, since we are concerned with the rent paying ability of one land user, relative to others.

The ratios between rent paying abilities of three land users, retail, wholesale, and residential, were in the order of 1.0 for land used for retail purposes, .12–.40 for land used for wholesaling, and .01–.05 for land used for residential purposes. This means that rent paying ability of retail users was from two to eight times greater than for wholesale trade, and from twenty to over one hundred times greater than for residential uses.

In the contemporary city, it is the bid rent curve for urban business users of land that reaches the greatest levels (Figure 10–5). This level would be greatest at the point of greatest desirability which coincides with the point of maximum land value. The willingness to buy locations away from this point gradually diminishes and the bid rent curve gradually slopes downward, although it remains higher than those of other potential users.

[9] Hurd, *Principles of Urban Land Values, Op. Cit.*

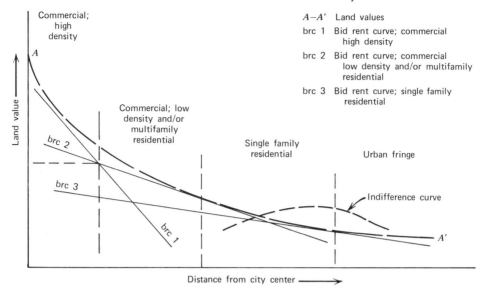

**Figure 10–5**   Bid rent curves for selected urban land uses and the indifference curve.

Another potential land user, such as wholesale trade, desirous of urban land but with less rent paying ability, would be represented by a bid rent curve that would originate at a lower level. This land user would not place such a high premium on location near the point of greatest accessibility in the city and, therefore, would not be willing to pay the higher price of such close-in sites, though could outbid potential users for land in the zone around the central business district. Another land user, the residential user, is willing to pay less than either of the preceding users and his bid rent curve originates at a still lower level (Figure 10–5). The residential user is less concerned with locating at or very near the point of maximum accessibility, so his bid rent curve is flatter and covers a greater area of the city.

A major point here is that the distribution of land values has a logical basis which is based on ability and willingness to pay for land at prime locations. Also, there are certain points that relate to theories on land use structure of the city. If the central business district outgrows its existing borders and needs room for expansion, it has little difficulty in expanding into the adjacent transition zone where wholesale trade is a major user of

land, since the user of land for retail trade can outbid the wholesale trade user. The user of land for wholesale trade, in turn can outbid land users in the adjacent zone of residential uses if faced with additional space needs.

The residential user of land can, in turn, outbid the agricultural user of land on the outer margin of the city as population of the city increases and as residential land needs mount. Within the context of the theory presented, then, we can identify the zone of active assimilation in an expanding central business district, and elements of land conversion in the urban-rural fringe.

One element of the theory has not been included thus far. This has to do with the residential user of land. The theory of urban land values we discussed has to do with a market economy where a land parcel is put to a particular use in order to maximize profits from activities existent on that parcel. Residential land users value land for purposes different from commercial and industrial interests in that they attempt to maximize benefits which are not to be considered the same as profits. The rationale for establishing the value of residential land may be diametrically opposite from that of the commercial user of land. The retail and wholesale user of land benefits from a location at or near to the point of maximum accessibility, while the residential user may value locations removed from this point. At more distant locations, the residential land user can (1) avoid congestion associated with close-in sites, (2) avoid the social turmoil often associated with close-in sites, and (3) obtain larger land parcels that generally have larger, more modern residences, at lower cost per square foot. Also, the residential land user may value land parcels that are removed from major transportation arterials, rather than along such routes, as sought by the profit motivated land user.

The situation here is one where the value of urban residential land is less determined by the bid rent curve than it is by the *indifference curve* implying that this land user competes for land on a different basis than other land users, in which he is, at least to a degree, indifferent to distance from the hundred percent location. At some distance from the city center, the land values are less, yet these are the land parcels that are most desirable for the single family residential user. The lower value of land is based on monetary worth, not the value of the land in terms of livability—a point of prime importance to the residential user. The bid rent curve for residential users of land has a different configuration than those of other land users, since it is more bell-shaped and skewed to the right (Figure 10–5).

An interesting situation arises in view of the above situation. If the willingness to acquire land for residential use is greater at some distance from the center of activity of the city and the point of highest land values, the residential population becomes increasingly dispersed in these more distant areas and the value of land tends to increase as a result and residential population becomes more dispersed. To serve this residential population, commercial centers come into existence and industrial concerns locate in proxim-

ity to the residential neighborhoods to be nearer to potential customers and potential workers. This, then, has the effect of placing a higher than usual value on locations other than those in or near the prime area of the city. Land values go up as well, which tends to create a distortion in the bid rent curves for all land users. Instead of smooth curves, the bid rent curves take on a wavelike appearance with the crest of each wave being a commercial or industrial complex in the outer margins of the city or in suburbia (Figure 10–5). The height of these waves is less, however, than that of the hundred percent location in the central business district. These waves do not represent an indifference to distance from the central area, as does the indifference curve for residential land. The users of higher value land represented by these waves are as conscious of distance as are tenants of the central business district. For their purpose, they are maximizing accessibility to customers or workers and, in the process, create distortions in the bid rent curves and in the spatial distribution of land values.

## Trends and Changes in Land Values

Previous sections have dealt with spatial distributions and theory of urban land values. It is implied, perhaps, that there is an inherent stability to both and it is now necessary to discuss changes in urban land values. These are subject to change because of (1) changing individual preferences and life styles, (2) continued areal expansion of urbanized areas, (3) increased spatial mobility of the urban population, especially in the more developed nations, and (4) changes in the urban economy and increased propensity to consume.

It is a cliché to say that nearly all land values have appreciated. It is meaningful, however, to consider the increases in value of land of one type relative to values of land of other types. Data in a re-

**Table 10–1**  Changes in Real Estate Values and Selected Economic Indicators, 1956–1966

| Economic Indicator or Type of Property | Percent Increase Total | Per Year |
|---|---|---|
| Total U.S. population | | 1.5 |
| Gross National Product | | 6.0 |
| National income | | 5.9 |
| Personal income | | 5.8 |
| All taxable real estate | 95 | 6.9 |
| Acreage and farms | 81 | 6.1 |
| Urban property | 104 | 7.4 |

SOURCE:  Manvel, *Ibid.*

cent study of land values in the United States indicate that urban land values have increased by an annual rate greater than other land values and selected economic indicators (Table 10–1).[10] Urban land values in the period 1956 to 1966 have increased by a rate greater than personal incomes, all taxable real property, and rural property. Not all urban property has increased in value at the same rate, however. Residential property, both single family and multifamily, has increased in value at a rate

[10] Factual information is supplied by Allen D. Manvel, "Trends in the Value of Real Estate and Land, 1956–1966," *Three Land Research Studies,* The National Commission on Urban Problems, Research Report No. 12, Washington, D.C., 1968.

greater than has commercial or industrial property (Table 10–2). Singling out land values from value of land and structures combined, it will be noted that urban land values are increasing at a greater rate than rural land values, regardless of the type of urban land. Of the types of urban land included in Table 10–2, the greatest rates of increase are for residential land of all types, and for vacant land parcels.

If we place these data within the context of the theory of land values discussed in a preceding section that involves a series of bid rent curves, several points come to light. The bid rent concept results in the most intensely used land parcels and the most costly being located at or near the center of activity of the city. By contrast, the less intensively used and lower value lands are located at some distance from this center, with variations a function of distance from the center or hundred percent location.

The data on changes in land values indicate that the most rapidly appreciating land parcels are, however, of types that are located in the outer zones of the city, specifically residential land and vacant land. Although all urban land values are appreciating, bringing the points of origin on the bid rent curves to a higher level, the slopes of the curves would be altered in a different manner. The curve

**Table 10–2**  Average Annual Percentage Change in Values, 1956–1966, by Type of Property

| Type of Property | Assessed Valuations | Total Value | Land Value | Structural Value |
|---|---|---|---|---|
| Total: all real property | 6.6 | 6.1 | 6.9 | 5.6 |
| Acreage and farms | 4.2 | 5.5 | 6.1 | 2.5 |
| All urban property | 7.0 | 6.3 | 7.4 | 5.8 |
|   All residential | 7.6 | 6.5 | 7.7 | 6.1 |
|     Single family | 7.6 | 6.2 | 7.5 | 5.8 |
|     Multifamily | 7.7 | 8.1 | 9.2 | 7.8 |
| Commercial | 5.7 | 5.7 | 6.8 | 5.0 |
| Industrial | 5.3 | 5.3 | 6.6 | 4.9 |
| Vacant lots | 8.0 | 7.6 | 7.6 | — |

SOURCE:  Manvel, *Ibid.*

for residential land would be at a higher level with a steeper slope than before. If this trend were to continue, it is conceivable that the bid rent value of land at some distance from the point of maximum accessibility would approach that of land near the center of activity (Figure 10–5). This raises several questions concerning the pattern of urban land values. Does the theory that applied in the past suit the pattern of land values in the modern city? Does the pattern change appreciably as a result of continued urban spatial expansion, in which a single point of accessibility is no longer as valid in shaping or influencing land values? Consistent with the multiple nuclei concept of land use patterns, are there now a number of points of accessibility to be considered, each producing its own influence on land values in adjacent parts of the city? In any case, the theory of land values appears to be quite generalized and likely does not fit the modern, expanding city with an affluent and highly mobile population.

## Land Values, Land Taxation, and Land Use

There are several reasons why values are placed on parcels of land, including (1) the obvious need to have some basis for real estate transactions, especially change in ownership, and (2) as a means of deriving tax revenue based on the assessed valuation of a land parcel with or without improvements. Revenue collected from taxation of real property provides much, if not most, of the financial resources of the city to provide needed public services, especially public schools. For tax purposes, a tax rate is applied to the assessed valuation of the land parcel, with rates and assessment levels different between various regions and cities within a given region.

With regard to regional differences in property taxes, the lowest rates are found in the southeast and intermontane reg-

ions (Figure 10–6). The highest tax rates occur in New England, the mid-Atlantic region, and some states of the upper Midwest and Great Plains. In New England, two thirds of the urban and metropolitan counties experience tax levels "above average" or higher, in East North Central states, about two thirds of the counties are in the "average" category and 30 percent are "above average" or higher.[11] In the East South Central states (Alabama, Mississippi, Kentucky, and Tennessee), over four fifths of the urban and metropolitan counties have tax levels below average (Figure 10–7). The greatest variation in property tax levels are between the Southeast and the Northeast, with these far greater than differences in income or wealth. Property tax levels tend to be highest in at least some of the most developed and wealthiest regions of the country.

Besides property taxes varying between regions, they also vary among metropolitan areas within larger scale regions consisting of a number of states. Much of the variation from metropolitan area to metropolitan area is a function of population size (Table 10–3). There is a strong linear trend between per capita property taxes and population of the metropolitan area, with the tax levels lower in nonmetropolitan areas than in metropolitan areas. These higher tax levels could be a function of fewer alternate forms of taxation or increased demands for revenue for operation of local governments in metropolitan areas.

Changing the scale again, there are variations in property tax levels within a given metropolitan area comprised of many different taxing units. The tendency is toward lower per capita taxable real property in the core areas than in suburban rings, but a higher effective tax rate, that is, less taxable wealth per person in core areas to which the same or

[11]Jerome P. Pickard, *Property Taxation in the United States, 1957, Per Capita Levels and Regional Variation*, Urban Land Institute, Research Monograph 6, 1962.

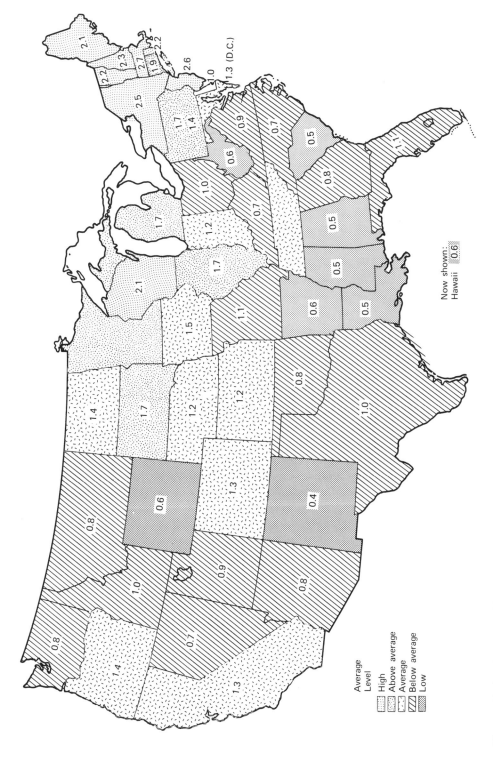

**Figure 10–6** Average effective rate of property taxation; by state: 1961–62. *Source.* Adapted from Jerome P. Pickard. Urban Land Institute, Research Monograph 12; 1966, pp. 20–21.

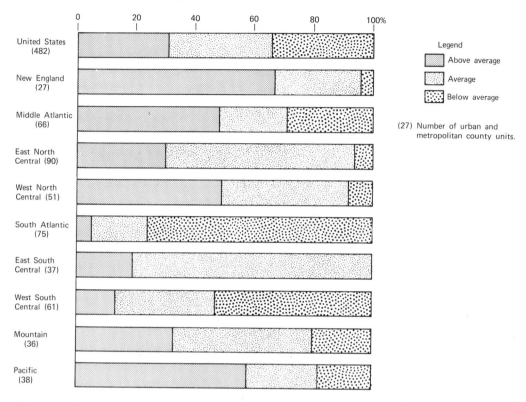

**Figure 10–7**   Levels of property taxes per capita: urban and metropolitan county units. *Source.* Based upon data in Jerome P. Pickard, Urban Land Institute, Research Monograph 6. 1962.

similar tax rates are applied, resulting in a higher percent per person (Table 10–4). This situation has proven increasingly troublesome in urban regions, for the property tax is considered regressive as applied in the manner described above. The effective tax rates for older, more deteriorated sections of the city are higher than those for newer, more appealing sections of the urban area. The

**Table 10–3**   Property Tax Payments per Capita, United States: Metropolitan Areas by Size Grouping and Nonmetropolitan Areas—Fiscal Year 1962

| Metropolitan Area Population, 1962 | Number of Local Governments[a] | Total Property Tax Revenues, Fiscal Year 1962 | Per Capita Property Taxes |
|---|---|---|---|
| | | (Millions of $) | |
| Over 5 million | 1,893 | $3,671 | $150 |
| 2.5 to 5 million | 1,345 | 1,822 | 134 |
| 1.2 to 2.4 million | 2,190 | 2,220 | 120 |
| 1.0 to 1.19 million | 1,162 | 866 | 101 |
| 500,000 to 999,000 | 1,176 | 919 | 100 |
| Smaller metropolitan areas | 8,416 | 3,847 | 90 |
| Nonmetropolitan areas | 66,138 | 5,069 | 75 |
| United States total | 82,320 | 18,424 | 100 |

[a]Local governments with property-taxing power.
SOURCE:   Jerome P. Pickard, *Taxation and Land Use in Metropolitan and Urban America,* Urban Land Institute, Research Monograph 12 (April, 1966).

**Table 10–4**  Selected Characteristics of Urban Subregions in Northeastern New Jersey, 1960

| Subregion | Number of Municipalities | Population Density | Taxable Real Property | | | Mean Effective Property Tax Rate |
|---|---|---|---|---|---|---|
| | | | Total | Per Square Mile | Per Person | |
| | | | (millions) | (millions) | | |
| Core A | 22 | 15,190 | $ 4,845 | $46.9 | $3,088 | 3.96% |
| Core B | 48 | 6,371 | 4,661 | 34.5 | 5,413 | 2.47 |
| Inner ring A | 53 | 4,526 | 4,443 | 25.6 | 5,655 | 2.44 |
| Inner ring B | 107 | 1,550 | 5,465 | 9.3 | 6,021 | 2.32 |
| Outer ring | 49 | 217 | 1,727 | 1.4 | 6,263 | 2.08 |
| Region | 279 | 1,939 | $21,141 | $ 9.3 | $4,806 | 2.46% |

SOURCE:  Jerome P. Pickard, *Ibid.*

older sections are the ones most in need of funds for renovation, upgrading, and maintenance by the owners, yet they are the ones subject to the highest effective rates of taxation.

Once again, property taxation varies widely and in a complex manner in the United States. There is great variation between taxing jurisdictions; state, county, and local governments. Also, there is variation within a given taxing jurisdiction, with different practices and methods of assessing different land uses and condition. Furthermore, trends in property taxation over time vary greatly from place to place. When you take the complexity of property taxation and its variations, it becomes difficult to determine relationships between local property taxation and urban development and land use change.

Various researchers have studied possible relationships between property taxes and urban growth or land use change, but most of these have dealt with interregional levels of property taxation, especially pertaining to industrial site selection. In this context, property taxes sometimes have been structured to attract industries to particular areas, usually states, although some local taxing jurisdictions have altered taxation practices to achieve the same end. Lowered property taxes are not necessarily attractive to industry, however, since this often is accompanied by a lower level of public services.

Regarding the more general or widespread relationship between property taxes and land use structure or change, there is little agreement as yet. Conclusions reached in a study by the Urban Land Institute pertaining to this matter include the following:[12]

1.  Property taxes exert an effect upon land uses, especially where there are marked differences in the effective tax rate within close geographic proximity.

2.  Property taxation and present land use policies subsidize horizontal expansion, while penalizing vertical growth in American metropolitan areas. Horizontal urban growth does not provide inherently superior benefits, especially at the low densities prevalent in urban fringes.

3.  Planning goals and taxation policies need to be coordinated by local governments. Not every community needs to have a balance of land uses in order to enjoy fiscal health.

This is one view of the role of property taxes as they effect urban land use. A somewhat different or modified view is presented by another study on the sub-

[12]Jerome P. Pickard, *Ibid.*

ject of property taxes and the spatial growth patterns of urban areas.[13] Of a number of variables considered in the analysis of the Syracuse, New York area, the property tax was found to be a relatively unimportant variable, with property density, surface features, and location being more important in shaping the pattern of urban growth.[14] It follows from this study that property taxes would not be a principal factor in shaping or restructuring urban land uses in the city, with other factors being more significant in this role.

In actuality, there would appear to be two different settings in which property taxation could exert an influence on land use. On the fringes of the urban area on the interface between land used for urban purposes and land used for nonurban uses, especially agriculture, property taxes are relatively low which has the effect of encouraging, along with other factors, conversion of land to urban use. This adds to the spatial expansion of the urban area, that is, horizontal expansion. In this context, property taxation well might have an effect on land use. In a different setting, the already largely developed urban area, restructuring of land use is more commonly the case than is absorption of undeveloped land and conversion to urban uses. Change in use of urban land is more widespread in the developed city, but this change is more likely influenced by economic conditions, obsolescence of structures, changes in distribution of the urban population, changes in consumer behavior, and existing zoning policies and practices, moreso than property taxation. Acting as a principal deterrent to land use change is land use zoning, for once the zoning of land uses is established, it is less likely that land use change will occur. This stability in

land use, in turn, is reflected in a relative stability of property taxation.

## Land Use Zoning

Previous sections on land use patterns, concepts of land use zonation, patterns of urban land values, and theoretical aspects of land values deal, for the most part, with a spontaneous development of the city. That is to say, development that is the result of gradual evolution and metamorphosis of the city, with the market place and the profit motive being the principal criteria on which land use and land values were established, and without benefit of any general guidance, framework, or control. Decisions on the use of a specific land parcel, influenced by the value of the land parcel, have largely been the sole responsibility of the individual landowner and not that of the total citizenry of the city. Along with cities becoming more complex spatially, economically, and socially, many problems have arisen in the general realm of land use conflicts. This has tended to result in a city where the land is used in a less than optimal and satisfying manner, which early gave rise to the need for some level of restriction and control on urban land use.

There is, however, a traditional attitude, especially in English speaking countries, that a certain sanctity and inviolability are inherent in regard to private property. The feeling has long been that the owner of property must be protected against any act that would curtail his enjoyment or profit from the management of his property, regardless of the effects on others.

In continental Europe, however, aesthetic regulations have long been accepted as a matter of policy. By 1911, a considerable number of cities in Germany had regulations dealing with sanitary conditions.[15] Classes of streets were

---

[13]William Joseph Beeman, *The Property Tax and the Spatial Pattern of Growth Within Urban Areas,* Urban Land Institute, Research Monograph 16, (1969).

[14]Beeman, *Ibid.*

[15]Harold MacLean Lewis, *Planning the Modern City,* Volume 1, New York, John Wiley and Sons, 1949.

regulated in Munich and Karlsruhe and the proportion of a lot that could be covered by buildings was regulated in Berlin, as were building heights.

As a prelude to comprehensive zoning in the United States, by 1916 a number of cities, including New York and Chicago, had enacted restrictions on the proportion of lots that could be covered by buildings, although the restrictions were not as stringent as in the European cities. Building heights were regulated in New York, Chicago, Boston, New Orleans, Cleveland, Fort Wayne, Buffalo, and Rochester, plus Toronto, Canada.

The concept of district or area zoning of the U.S. city with regulations on land use in each district, likely originated in Los Angeles with an ordinance in 1909 in which the entire city was divided into industrial and residential districts. Here, there were twenty-five types of industrial districts, but one type of residential district. Seattle adopted an ordinance in 1913 regulating land use on private property, and so did other cities in turn. Also in 1913, New York City initiated comprehensive regulations on use of land, height of buildings, and proportion of lot area covered by structures, with this effort culminating in the first legal status of "zoning" in 1916. The concept of zoning land use in American cities, once implemented, spread quite rapidly, although zoning was often used as a substitute for planning. Zoning only provides the framework within which planning is to be undertaken, and is an essential part of any comprehensive plan but is not a substitute.

Many of the early attempts at zoning were unclearly stated and, in an effort to make them flexible, ample provision was made for appeal through variances and special exceptions to zoning codes.[16] The quandry lingered concerning rights of the individual property owner in the use

[16]Stephen Sussna, "Zoning Boards: In Theory and In Practice," *Land Economics*, Vol. XXXVII, No. 1 (February, 1961).

of his land and the rights of the general public in overseeing the use of the individual's land parcel. Questioned was the acceptability of having private land ownership, but with some measures of public control.

To reconcile this quandry, if the landowner believed himself to be unfairly treated on the basis that the zoning ordinance resulted in "undue difficulty or unnecessary hardship," he could be granted a variance to the zoning ordinance and his land parcel could be deemed a "nonconforming land use." Perhaps, it was inevitable then that the administrative boards responsible for zoning became, in effect, boards of appeals. The ultimate decisions having to do with zoning often were made by the judiciary branch of government rather than by the zoning administrators who were responsible to the legislative branch of government. In the 1950's in the United States, consideration turned more to performance standards, rather than a particular land use. Thus a nonconforming land use became acceptable if its level of performance was acceptable.

Today, most major cities of the world have some type of public zoning policy, some more restrictive than others, and some more effective than others. In general, land use zoning is a practice where the area of the city is divided into subareas, districts, or neighborhoods. Within each of these smaller areas, the quantitative and qualitative aspects of land use are prescribed within accepted levels, such as residential lot size, and the uses made of the land are prescribed as well, such as single family residential. At a smaller scale, however, within any given district or area, even a single block, there may be one or more nonconforming land uses. Thus, the city is blanketed by a number of general land use zones that are administratively controlled by a zoning board or commission. Each of these zones, however, is likely to have small enclaves of nonconforming land use within it, providing some aspect of heterogeneity within an otherwise homogeneous land use zone.

One matter pertinent to zoning is the extent of the area to be included within a single planning and zoning jurisdiction. The use of land for urban purposes does not stop at municipal boundaries, but continues into peripheral urban areas and urbanizing areas as well. This urbanized area is comprised of many political jurisdictions and, for maximum benefit of zoning, all should be brought into the zoning process. Not only should land currently devoted to urban use be subject to zoning, but so should lands on the growing edges of the urbanized area, for only then can zoning take on a prescriptive nature, not just a remedial nature. The logical manner in which areawide zoning can be implemented is on a county basis or, in the case of larger cities, a multicounty zoning district.

It should be pointed out that today there is not but one type of zoning as discussed above, but least six types and these can be grouped under the major headings of "flexible zoning" and "fixed zoning."[17] Distinctions between these groups are based on the approach, objectives, and scale of the zoning policy. Rezoning through amendment of existing zoning to accommodate proposed new developments or renewal projects is one type of flexible zoning. Other types of flexible zoning include floating zoning in which zoning districts are not rigidly fixed, and special exemptions by which, at the discretion of an administrative body, large-scale developments are allowed in areas not previously zoned in such a manner. There are at least three types of fixed zoning, one of which is the widely adopted gridiron or lot zoning we already mentioned. This type of fixed zoning was based on the assumption that development would take place one lot at a time and by separate owners. Community unit zoning, as implied, is a type of fixed zoning in which regulations on land use and development are applied, not to the individual lot, but to large tracts with the expectation that the total tract development would adhere to the regulations of the general zoning ordinances. Density zoning is the newest type of fixed zoning and differs from other zoning types in that the others tended to establish standards for the single building or single lot, while density zoning deals with density controls on the use of land in zoning districts of the city. Density zoning differs from community unit zoning in that the former is generally applied to larger areas and is an on-going zoning program, whereas community unit planning and zoning is applied more to exceptional cases requiring special treatment.

Expanding on the concept of density zoning, this approach calls for zoning regulations based on the number of residents or employees per unit of area, usually an acre. This can also be interpreted as the share of land area covered by structures. Using an example of density controls for an area to be developed within the context of zoning, the number of dwelling units permitted is determined by dividing the net development area by the minimum lot area per family.[18] Net development area was determined by subtracting the area set aside for churches, schools, or commercial use from the gross development area and deducting fifteen percent of the remainder for streets. The amount deducted for streets should vary somewhat with density (Table 10–5). For zoning of commercial use, for each one hundred dwelling units in the development, one acre is set aside for commercial use, which conforms with standards of the neighborhood. The usual focus of density control zoning is residential land use, with other uses planned around the residential

[17]Eldridge Lovelace and William L. Weismantel, Density Zoning: Organic Zoning for Planned Residential Developments, Urban Land Institute, Technical Bulletin No. 42 (1961).

[18]Urban Land Institute, Density Zoning, Technical Bulletin, No. 42 (July, 1961). One might also read Byron Hanke, "Land Use Intensity, A New Approach to Land Use Controls", Urban Land, (November, 1969).

# AN EXAMPLE OF DENSITY CONTROL ZONING

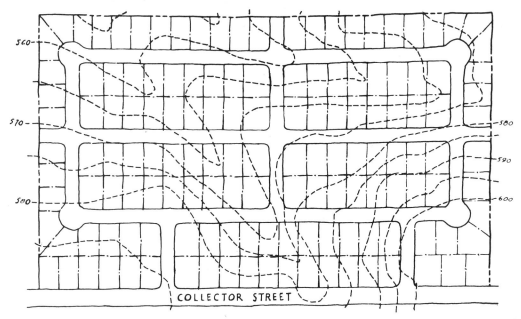

THIS TRACT OF LAND CONTAINS 40 ACRES AND IS ZONED 8500 SQ FT
SINGLE FAMILY LOTS. MAXIMUM USE OF LAND YIELDS 143 LOTS

*(a)*

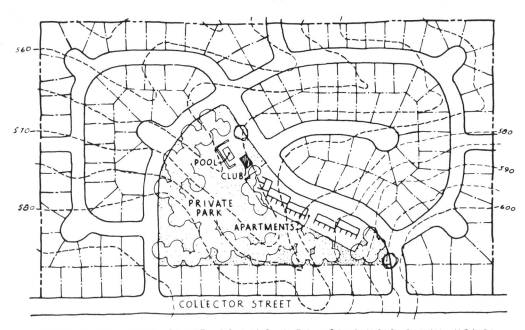

THIS IS THE SAME TRACT OF LAND WITH 125 SINGLE FAMILY HOMES
ON LOTS WITH A MINIMUM AREA OF 7500 SQ. FT, 18 UNITS IN
APARTMENTS (ROW HOUSES) AND 45 ACRES OF COMMUNITY PARK.

*(b)*

**Figure 10-8**  An example of density control zoning. *Source.* Eldridge Lovelace and William L. Weismantel. Urban Land Institute, Technical Bulletin No. 42. Reprinted by permission.

needs. The workings of density control zoning are exemplified in Figure 10–8. With density control zoning, the concern is broadened from just the use made of land, to include the intensity to which the land is used.

**Table 10–5** Area Deductions for Streets, Related to Lot Size

| Average Lot Size | Percentage Deduction for Streets |
|---|---|
| One acre–30,000 sq. ft. | 15 |
| 20,000 sq. ft. | 20 |
| 15,000–12,000 sq. ft. | 25 |
| 10,000–7,500 sq. ft. | 30 |

SOURCE: Urban Land Institute, *Density Zoning,* Technical Bulletin No. 42 (1961).

There is not yet any general agreement on the "best" or "proper" type of zoning to employ, in part because each administrative jurisdiction is, at least to some degree, unique so that not one approach to zoning suffices for all cities. Density zoning has been implemented in many cases in new residential areas and is thought desirable because it allows for a heterogeneity of dwelling units and a greater variety of land uses in a particular section of the city. Thus, there is avoidance of the sterile, antiseptic appearance and structure that characterizes many residential areas. One aspect of zoning that is not commonly incorporated into density zoning is provision for zoning of industrial areas on a density basis. Density zoning lends itself especially to residential areas and ancilliary commercial areas and less so to zoning of industrial areas. Today, land use zoning is increasingly modified by consideration of *performance standards* which have to do with establishment of acceptable levels of performance of the use of a given land parcel.

In essence, zoning of some type has been adopted in many of the world cities and, most often, has been generally accepted. The implementation of zoning concept has not produced instant perfection, however, nor could it be expected to. Zoning has to be considered an ongoing process, not a static procedure that is done once and for all times. As more knowledge of cities becomes available, as the benefits of zoning are better known and appreciated, as more tangible support is allocated in support of zoning, and as the problems become more critical, perhaps the means and incentive will be provided for the adoption of the zoning concept in all cities.

# 11

# commercial activities and centers in the city

We mentioned in previous chapters that much of the economic activity of the city is concerned with dispensing of goods and services to the resident population of the city and to the population of the tributary area of the city. And if you remember, the places from which these goods and services are dispensed are "establishments," and the offering of each type of good or service constitutes a function of the city providing it. There are numerous commercial establishments performing commercial functions, with these distributed in various ways, creating different spatial patterns. The purpose here is to discuss the role of commercial activity in the city and the spatial patterns of commercial establishments performing the various commercial functions.

The absolute number of people engaged in commercial activities or the dispensing of goods and services in the city is, of course, a function of its population. A more meaningful way of considering the role of trade and service industries in the urban center is to deal with the share of total labor force that is engaged in commercial activities, that is, the relative role. The share of total urban labor force that is in commercial activities in cities of the U.S. varies among specific industries and between cities of different sizes (Figure 11–1). Invariably, however, the greater the population of the city, the greater the relative employment in commercial activities. The industries considered here as being commercial in nature are (1) retail trade, (2) wholesale trade, (3) finance, insurance, and real estate, (4) professional services, (5) personal services, and (6) business services. As a group, these industries may be referred to as *tertiary activities*. When the city forming or basic employment in these activities is added to the city serving or nonbasic employment in the same industries, the average employment in commercial activities in metropolitan areas of the United States is approximately 15 percent in retail trade, 3 percent in wholesale trade, 4 percent in finance, insurance, and real estate, 12 percent in professional services, 6 percent in personal services, and 3 percent in business services, or a total of about 43 percent of the urban labor force of metropolitan areas.[1] The role of commercial

---

[1]Edward Ullman and Michael Dacy, *The Economic Base of American Cities*, University of Washington Press (1969). This value is somewhat higher than the one presented in James Simmons, *The Changing Pattern of Retail Location*, University of Chicago Press, Department of Geography, Research Paper No. 92, (1964).

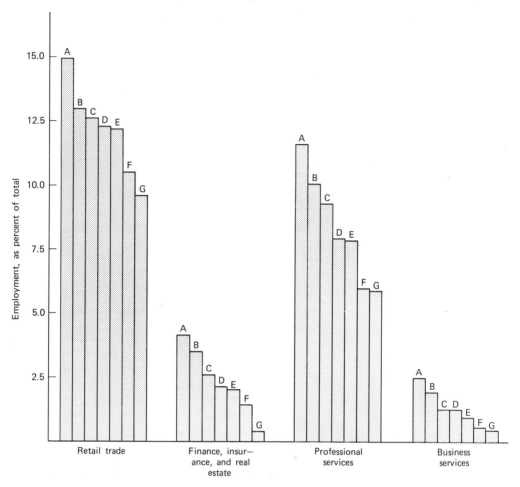

*Minimum employment in cities included

**Figure 11-1**   National and urban employment in selected trade and service industries: 1960*. (A) National; (B) metropolitan areas over 1 million; (C) metropolitan areas: 300–800,000; (D) metropolitan areas 100–150,000; (E) cities: 25–40,000; (F) cities: 10–12,500; (G) cities: 2500–3000. *Source.* Based on data in Ullman, Dacey, and Brodsky. *The Economic Base of American Cities,* Univ. of Washington Press, 1969.

activities in the urban labor force could be somewhat different by inclusion of more industries than the six used here, but if this were done the role of commercial activities would become greater in any case.

Thus, we have something approximating 40 percent of the urban labor force of metropolitan areas engaged in commercial activity that occupies only about 4 percent of the land area. This gives an indication of (1) the intensity of use made of commercial land, or (2) the use made of

urban space other than at ground level. Both conditions are characteristic of commercial centers of the city.

## Localization of Commercial Activities

With much of the commercial activity of the city occupying relatively little of the land area, it follows that there will be a high degree of concentration of such activities, with commensurately high levels of land use intensity. Questions

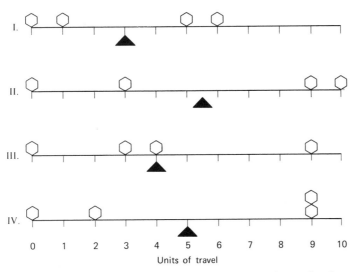

**Figure 11-2**   Points of minimum aggregate travel (▲) for four linear distributions.

arise, however, as to whether this commercial activity is concentrated in one clustering or whether there are a number of commercial concentrations. If there is a dispersal of commercial activity into a number of concentrations, are these all basically the same or are there structural and functional differences between them?

As stated in the discussion of land values, commercial activities tend to benefit from occupance of sites at or near the point or points of maximum accessibility within the city or a part thereof. The benefits from occupance of such sites are that the commercial establishment (1) has greater access to pedestrian traffic, (2) has greater access to transportation terminals located in the central part of the city, such as bus and streetcar stops, subway stations, and railroad stations, (3) has a high level of access to wholesale suppliers and other supporting industries, and (4) has a considerable degree of proximity to complementary commercial establishments. It follows that only one small area of the city can enjoy these benefits of maximum accessibility, however, and this is in the vicinity of the *point of minimum aggregate travel*.

The concept of the point of minimum aggregate travel deals with the total minimum travel distance incurred by a population in reaching a given point.[2] It is the point of greatest centrality, not within an areal unit, but within a given population distribution. To illustrate, we begin with a certain distribution of people in an area, all of whom wish to reach a certain point or location in the area with a minimum of travel distance (Figure 11–2). However, the minimum travel distance for one likely is greater than the minimum for another. The consideration here is with the location of the point that minimizes the travel distance for *all* of the population collectively, hence the term "point of minimum aggregate travel." Of course, if there are changes in the distribution of the population of the area, there will be a change in the location of the point of minimum aggregate travel (Figure 11–2). At a chosen point in time, there will be a certain distribution of population in the city with its own point of minimum aggregate travel which

[2] Philip W. Porter. "What is the Point of Minimum Aggregate Travel?," *Annals of the Association of American Geographers*, Vol. 53, No. 2 (June, 1963).

maximizes accessibility of that aggregate population to a particular point.[3] At the time of city formation, this point generally became the commercial pivot of the city, tempered, of course, by physical conditions that may have restricted development of a commercial center at the exact point of minimum aggregate travel, even if its location was known. With fairly restricted areal extent of the city and travel methods that were slow, difficult, and often torturous, it served the commercial establishments well to locate at or near such a location so as to provide the greatest measure of access to the population of the city as it existed at that time. From this embryonic beginning at or near the point of minimum aggregate travel, there evolved the commercial core of the city of today, which is referred to as the *central business district* or the CBD.

[With continuous areal growth of the city, an increasingly dispersed population, and a redistribution of the population, the ease of travel to a single point became lessened, especially in terms of time spent in intracity travel. It developed that the central business district was often no longer centrally located within the city as population was redistributed. This is to say, the point of minimum aggregate travel had shifted to a new position within the city. Even without this population redistribution, the CBD, which included the point of minimum aggregate travel, was not so centrally located that it could serve the population of the city in terms of supplying the people with goods and services needed, mainly because it was too distant from the consumers. This provided the impetus for development of other commercial centers situated at locations that would more nearly minimize travel distances and time to segments of the population desiring goods and services. For example, the residents of an urban neighborhood several miles distant from the CBD would be unlikely to make a daily trip to the CBD for purchase of food staples]

For the entire city, then, there would be a single point of minimum aggregate travel for the entire population (Figure 11–3). If the city is divided into districts or other major subareas, there is a point of minimum aggregate travel for each. If the districts are divided into still smaller subareas, such as communities or neighborhoods, each of these would have a point of minimum aggregate travel for the population of that particular subarea. In each case, there is a point that represents the maximum accessibility to the population of a unit of area and this accessibility is essential to the existence of a commercial establishment or concentration. If all such points of minimum aggregate travel, that is, maximum accessibility, are utilized for commercial activities we have, then, the basis for a number of commercial centers in the city, not just the central business district that once might have served virtually all of the city's commercial needs (Figure 11–3). Figure 11–3 presents an hypothetical city divided into districts which, in turn, are divided into communities. It is possible to establish the point of minimum aggregate travel for the population of the entire city in terms of the district where it would be located (district II). In actuality, one could establish a more precise location by considering basic population areas such as census tracts or blocks, instead of large scale districts. Within each district shown in Figure 11–3, the community within which the point of minimum aggregate travel for the population of the district is located can be established (communities B, F, H, M, and O). Again, more precise locations of the points of greatest accessibility to the population of the subarea could be obtained by dealing with smaller areal units. Notice also that the points established are

---

[3]An application of the concept of the point of minimum aggregate travel is employed by the Bureau of the Census which, based upon each decennial census of population, locates the geographic center of the population of the United States. This point changes location every ten years, as would be expected, and now is in the vicinity of Mascoutah, Illinois.

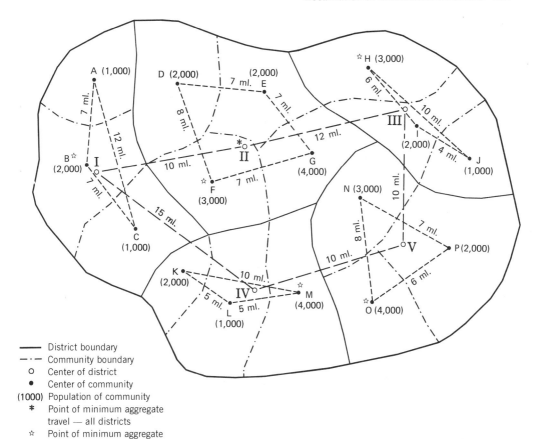

**Figure 11-3** Hypothetical city, divided into districts and communities, with points of minimum aggregate travel indicated.

based on populations of each areal unit and the distance from one to each of the others. When you take the example of the community containing the point of minimum aggregate travel in district IV, the calculations are as follows:

Community $K =$
$$(5)(1000) + (10)(4000) = 45,000$$
Community $L =$
$$(5)(2000) + (5)(4000) = 30,000$$
Community $M =$
$$(10)(2000) + (5)(1000) = 25,000$$

In district IV, then, the community with the greatest accessibility and the lowest measure of aggregate travel to the population of the entire district is community

$M$ and this would appear to be the most logical of the communities for development of a commercial center, considering the number of people to be served and the distance to which they would have to travel.

It is obvious at this point that the commercial centers that might arise to take advantage of points of maximum accessibility would be serving population of different sizes and likely of different characteristics and would not be of the same types or structure and have the same commercial functions. This is to say that the centers would not be of the same magnitudes or orders.

A means by which the point of minimum aggregate travel might be esta-

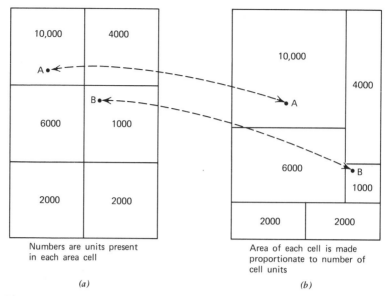

Numbers are units present
in each area cell

Area of each cell is made
proportionate to number of
cell units

*(a)*                                    *(b)*

**Figure 11-4**   Elements of a map transformation. *(a)* Map area and area cells. *(b)* Map area with cells transformed.

blished is through the employment of a *map transformation*.[4] This involves changing the map area, in which a unit of map area is proportionate to earth area, to map area in which a unit of area of the map is made proportionate to some other variable, most likely, population (Figure 11–4). In this event, the geometric center of the transformed map represents the point of minimum aggregate travel between the cells of map area. This point can then be relocated on the original map of earth area, giving the location of the point of minimum aggregate travel. In Figure 11–4, a map of earth area is shown and divided into equal area cells with variable populations. A second map of the same earth area is shown, with each cell area transformed to an area proportionate to the population of the cell in question. On the second map, the shapes of the cells are changed somewhat, but

[4]Donald A. Blome, *A Map Transformation: Lansing Tri-County Area*, Michigan State University, Institute for Community Development and Services, 1963, and Arthur Getis, "The Determination of the Location of Retail Activities With the Use of a Map Transformation," *Economic Geography*, Vol. 39, No. 1, January, 1963.

adjacent cells remain adjacent on both maps. The geometric center of the transformed map is then transferred to the original map, giving the location of the point of minimum aggregate travel in addition to the identification of the cell within which this point is located.

## A Functional Hierarchy of Urban Commercial Centers

Aspects of a hierarchy of urban centers as trade centers were discussed in Chapter 7. It serves to reiterate that each trade center performs a number of functions and that the greater the number of functions, the higher the order or standing of the trade center. Also, it was pointed out that successively higher order centers serve populations in tributary areas of progressively greater area, based on higher threshold populations required for the good or service to be offered and the greater range of the good or service offered. These concepts were presented within a regional system of urban centers, with the region including considerable area. Elements of these concepts apply, however, to the urban area or the single

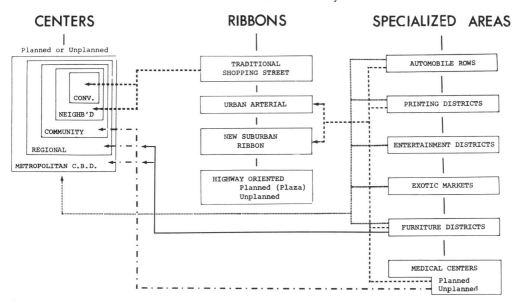

**Figure 11-5** A typology of commercial centers in the city. The University of Chicago Department of Geography, Research Papers. Reprinted by permission.

city as well. The basic difference is only the change of scale from a regional one to a local one.

One point that needs clarification at this time is the use of the term "commercial center." In this book, the term includes groupings of commercial establishments, as well as free-standing or isolated establishments. The groupings or clusterings may have arisen spontaneously without benefit of any single or integrated development plan. The cases are numerous where a single establishment is built and begins operations, after which one or more establishments of different types are established in proximity to the first. Other groupings or clusters of commercial establishments may originate at the same general time, but with benefit of a development plan and generally with a continuity of architecture and with common-wall construction. The entire grouping is planned to operate as a unit, with all establishments subject to the same controls and management decisions of the developers of the center. In essence, then, we have the unplanned commercial center and the planned commercial center. When placed in the context of a hierarchy of commercial centers, both types are to be included.

Before considering the various orders in a hierarchy of commercial centers, it should be recognized that some groups of establishments are considerably different from others with regard to location, structure, function, and form. There are those commercial agglomerations that have an array of functions which comprise a cluster with a relatively compact form. These are often referred to as shopping centers (Figure 11–5). There are other agglomerations of commercial establishments that tend to be arranged in an attenuated manner along major transportation arterials, and these are known as commercial ribbons. A third type of commercial agglomeration, the specialized district or area, includes a number of establishments that all perform basically the same function, for example, the furniture district, banking district, etc., and they tend to be arranged in a relatively compact cluster.

It is difficult to include these various types of commercial centers in a single hierarchy, since they differ significantly, especially in function and form. The shopping center has a compact form and an array of functions, while the specialized area has a compact form and an emphasis on a single function. The following functional hierarchy deals mainly with shopping centers, planned or unplanned, and with commercial ribbons.

Within the context of a functional hierarchy, the free-standing or isolated commercial establishment would represent the lowest order commercial center. Examples might be the small grocery store, often called the "mom and pop grocery," the isolated eating place, or the unattached furniture store. Such establishments generally have one functional offering, and serve a relatively small number of people derived from a fairly small area. This is to say that they have a low threshold, a short range of their goods or services, and a small market area.

The next higher order commercial center would be an agglomeration of contiguous or adjacent establishments, each performing a different function. In an unplanned commercial center, this order of center would consist of a ribbon development along a major arterial or an unplanned cluster of establishments at some point of intersection of major arterials. The planned equivalent of this order of center is referred to as a *neighborhood shopping center*.[5] The neighborhood shopping center contains a number of tenants, generally between ten and twenty, with a chain supermarket or drug store being the leading tenant (Table 11–1). The tenant composition of an average neighborhood shopping center is such that convenience goods establishments dominate over shoppers goods establishments. Once again, convenience goods refer to those that are most fre-

[5]Terminology and data referring to planned shopping centers are taken mostly from Urban Land Institute, *The Dollars and Cents of Shopping Centers*, (1963).

**Table 11–1**   Characteristics and Tenant Composition of Neighborhood Shopping Centers

| *Characteristics* | |
| --- | --- |
| Average gross floor area | 40,000 square feet |
| Average minimum site area | 4 acres |
| Minimum support (threshold) | 1000 families or 7000–20,000 people |
| Leading tenant | Supermarket or drug store |
| *Tenant composition* | *Gross leaseable areas* (square feet) |
| Food and service | |
| Supermarket | 18,000 |
| Bakery | 1,600 |
| Restaurant | 2,000 |
| General merchandise | |
| Variety store | 10,400 |
| Ladies wear | 2,900 |
| Children's wear | 1,900 |
| Family shoes | 2,300 |
| Drugs | 5,400 |
| Services | |
| Beauty shop | 1,000 |
| Barber shop | 600 |
| Cleaners and dyers | 1,400 |
| Coin operated laundry | 1,600 |

SOURCE:   Urban Land Institute, *The Dollars and Cents of Shopping Centers* (1963).

quently acquired by consumers, where the individual purchase is relatively low in cost, and where selective buying is not commonly practiced. Shoppers goods, by contrast, include those that are less frequently acquired, where the cost of individual purchase is relatively high, and where comparative buying is common.

Although specific establishments included in such commercial centers vary between individual centers and between cities, the number and types of establishments are, in general, in accord with the concept of *order of entry*. In Chapter 7, order of entry of commercial functions was discussed in regard to differing functions of central places; order of entry, we said, had to do with the degree of ubiquity of a particular function. Commercial centers within the single city contain functions with different orders of entry

as well. If every commercial center includes a foodstore as a functional unit, the degree of ubiquity of this function could be no greater and one could conclude that this functional unit is the most likely to "enter" a commercial center, with the likelihood of other functions entering the center being somewhat less.

We have already said that the order of entry of a particular function depends on the culture area, the preferences of the population, the disposable income available, and other factors, but in cities the order of entry would be fairly much the same from city to city. In assessing order of entry into commercial centers, remember that in planned shopping centers it is true that many, if not most, of the functional units enter at the same time. This means concepts of a spontane-

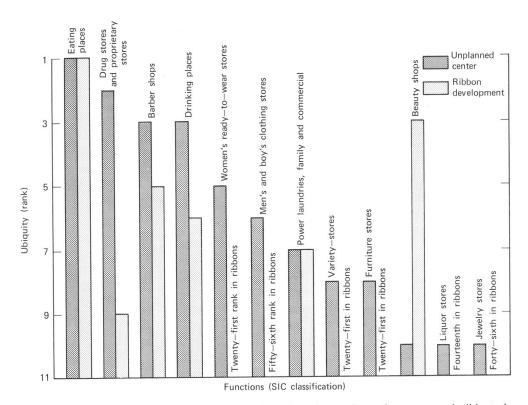

**Figure 11-6** Order of entry of commercial functions in unplanned centers and ribbon developments. Ubiquity ranking of major functions in unplanned centers and ranking of same functions in ribbon developments. *Source.* Based on data in Brian J.L. Berry, *Commercial Structure and Commercial Blight,* 1963.

ous order of entry do not apply, that is, a number of functional units begin operations at the same time. In the unplanned commercial centers and the commercial ribbons, the order of entry likely is applicable. In Chicago, the order of entry of functional units in unplanned centers, based on ubiquity measurement and of commercial ribbons, is such that the tenant composition based on the twelve functional units with the highest ubiquity measures (lowest order of entry) are approximately the same as the tenant composition of the planned neighborhood center (Figure 11–6).[6] Major differences are drinking places and liquor stores in both the unplanned and ribbon center, when they are not commonly present in the neighborhood center, and foodstores that are not common to the unplanned center, when they are in the planned neighborhood center.

Perhaps, then, the functional structure of the planned commercial center is, to a high degree, a duplication of that of the unplanned center or the commercial ribbon but without the less desirable functions and with a modern and more convenient facility. The concept of order of entry, in general, applies to the commercial centers of the city, regardless of their types. Further, there are similarities between the order of entry of commercial centers in the large city and their small urban center counterparts.

The rationale for inclusion of a low order of entry function in a neighborhood shopping center is that the good offered by the convenience goods outlet is fairly frequently acquired and the total annual expenditure per family is relatively large, although each purchase is relatively low in value (Table 11–2). Because of this, the threshold for neighborhood shopping centers can be attained within a relatively small area, such as an urban neighborhood. Thus, this type of

commercial center has a relatively low threshold that can be attained within a fairly short distance of the establishments in the center, that is, a short range for the goods and services offered, and a relatively small tributary area (Figure 11–7).

A commercial center of higher order than the one previously discussed, is one of third order, with the free-standing establishment the first. A center of this level includes higher order of entry functions

**Table 11–2**    Annual Retail Expenditures Per Family Unit: By Type

| Type of Expenditure | Percentage Per Year Per Family |
|---|---|
| Convenience goods | |
| Drugs | 2.6 |
| Grocery and combination | 35.5 |
| Other food | 6.0 |
| Liquor | 1.5 |
| Hardware | 1.3 |
| Filling stations and accessories | 6.7 |
| Other stores | 2.6 |
| Total | 56.2 |
| Primary shoppers goods: | |
| Department stores | 12.0 |
| Family and other apparel | 1.5 |
| Men's clothing and furnishings | 2.6 |
| Shoes–men's and family | .8 |
| Shoes–women's | 1.0 |
| Women's apparel | 4.9 |
| Variety stores | 1.6 |
| Jewelry | .3 |
| Total | 24.7 |
| Secondary shopper's goods | |
| Furniture and household furnishings | 3.2 |
| Household appliances and radio | 2.1 |
| Eating and drinking places | 4.5 |
| Total | 9.8 |
| General purchases | |
| Auto dealers | 8.3 |
| Auto parts and accessories | 1.0 |
| Total | 9.3 |
| Grand Total | 100.0 |

[6]Berry, Brian J. L., *Commercial Structure and Commercial Blight*, University of Chicago Press, Research Paper No. 85, (1963).

SOURCE:    Urban Land Institute, *Conservation and Rehabilitation of Major Shopping Districts*, Technical Bulletin No. 22.

not found in the lower order centers. This order of center may exist as an unplanned agglomeration adjacent to an older residential district, a longer ribbon development along a major arterial but still largely confined to the two sides of the arterial, or around a major intersection of arterial routes that may be commonly known as a "five-points," or a "six-points" district, depending on the number of interesecting arterials. A planned commercial agglomeration of this order could be referred to as a *community shopping center,* and generally would have in the order of twenty to forty functional units, with a variety store or junior department store normally the dominant tenant in such centers. In commercial centers of this order, there is a duplication of functions, that is, there may be more than one functional unit performing the same function (Table 11–3).

In community level shopping centers, there is more emphasis on establishments dispensing shoppers goods than was true of the neighborhood shopping center. However, as with the hierarchy of central places, each commercial center of a given order or level includes all of the functions of centers of the preceding order. Thus, community shopping centers usually contain all of the functions of the neighborhood shopping centers plus an incremental group not found in the lower order centers. All of the convenience goods establishments present in the neighborhood centers usually are also present in the community level centers. However, there is the addition of more functions, these primarily in the realm of shoppers goods outlets, for example, jewelry, ladies specialty shops, paint and wallpaper, and a bank. Notice too that each establishment in the community shopping center is larger in floor space than the same type of establishment in the neighborhood shopping center (Tables 11–1 and 11–3). The supermarket is larger, as are the variety store, the restaurant, and the drug store, among

others. In the community level shopping center, then, there are more functions and more functional units, plus establishments that are larger in size than their counterparts in centers of the preceding order. The latter is a point to remember,

**Table 11–3**   Characteristics and Tenant Composition of Community Shopping Centers

| Characteristics | |
| --- | --- |
| Average gross floor area | 150,000 square feet |
| Average minimum site area | Ten acres |
| Minimum support (threshold) | 5000 families or 20,000–100,000 people |
| Leading tenant | Variety or junior department store |

| Tenant composition | Gross leaseable area (square feet) |
| --- | --- |
| Food and service | |
| Supermarket | 19,500 |
| Bakery | 1,800 |
| Restaurant | 3,800 |
| General merchandise | |
| Junior department store | 34,900 |
| Variety store | 16,000 |
| Clothing and shoes | |
| Ladies specialty | 4,300 |
| Ladies wear[a] | 4,300 |
| Children's wear | 2,400 |
| Men's wear | 3,300 |
| Family shoes | 3,300 |
| Paint and wallpaper | 1,900 |
| Other retail | |
| Drugs | 8,000 |
| Jewelry | 1,500 |
| Cards and gifts | 1,900 |
| Bank | 3,800 |
| Services | |
| Beauty shop | 1,300 |
| Barber shop | 800 |
| Shoe repair | 800 |
| Cleaners and dyers | 2,300 |

[a]Includes two tenants of this classification.
SOURCE:   Urban Land Institute, *The Dollars and Cents of Shopping Centers* (1963).

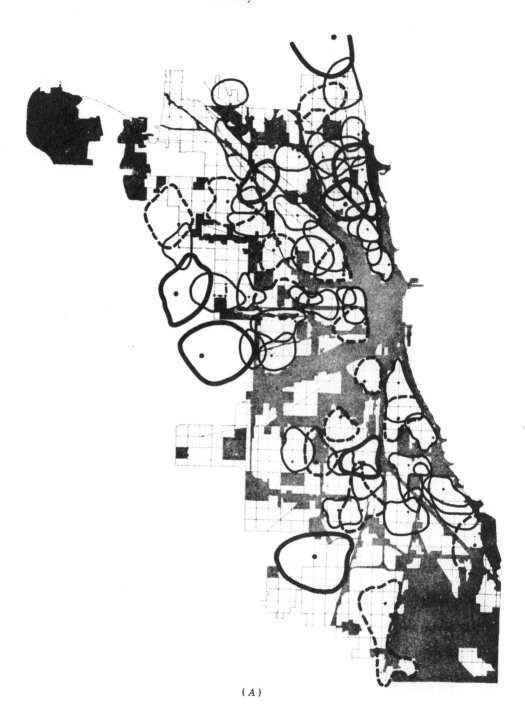

( A )

**Figure 11-7** Convenience goods and shoppers goods trade areas: Chicago. (A) The three different lines used to delineate the trade areas of centers for the convenience goods they provide are intended to differentiate between the major regional centers, the smaller shoppers goods centers —, and the community and larger neighborhood centers —. (B) Shoppers goods trade areas. The solid line shows the outer limit of the "intensive" trade areas of the major

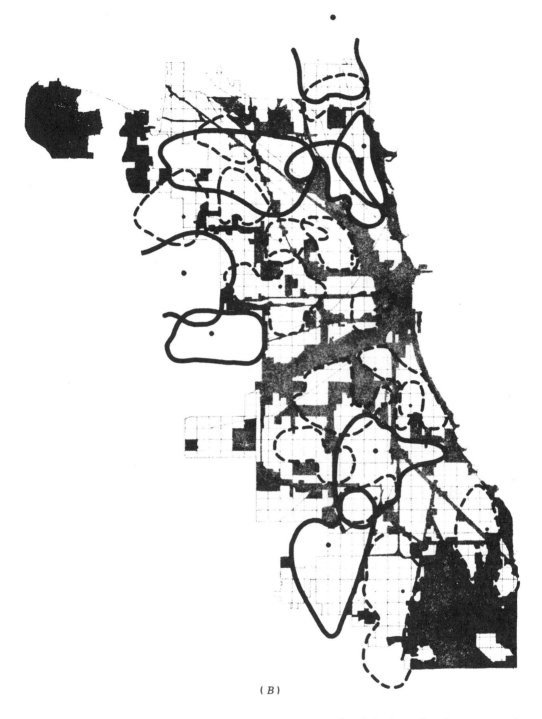

( B )

regional centers, whereas the dotted line refers to the margin of the intensive shoppers goods trade area of the smaller shoppers goods centers. Shaded areas show nonresidential land uses. *Source.* Brian J. L. Berry. *Commercial Structure and Commercial Blight,* 1963. The University of Chicago Department of Georgaphy, Research Papers. Reprinted by permission.

since it is not necessary for two establishments of the same type to provide for two times the threshold population as for one; one larger establishment might do the job as well and benefit from economies of scale. The concept of threshold treats only the *minimum* level needed for the support of a given function or functional unit, but does not deal with any upper limit on the size or extent of the establishment.

Of course, with a higher order commercial center, the threshold is greater than that of preceding orders. Most likely, this would mean a greater range of at least some of the goods and services of the center which, in turn, would result in a market or service area of greater areal extent than those of centers or preceding orders.

A further type and higher order commercial center (order IV) is one having still more functions, functional units, and establishments. In an unplanned agglomeration, this order of center might be represented by a major traditional commercial district within the central city or by the CBD of a suburban community within the urbanized area. In a planned agglomeration, this order would be represented by the *regional shopping center*, including a number of functional units in the range of forty to two hundred or more. In a regional shopping center, there are additional functions not found in centers of the preceding order, and greater duplication of functional units, both of convenience goods and shoppers goods as well as of service establishments. In general, services take on a greater role in the regional shopping center than they do in centers of low orders (Table 11–4). The sizes of establishments in a regional shopping center are generally greater than comparable types of establishments in lower order centers.

Observe that the square footage of floor area and the size of the site of regional shopping centers is on the order of four times that of the community shop-

**Table 11–4**   Characteristics and Tenant Composition of Regional Shopping Centers

| Characteristics | |
| --- | --- |
| Average gross floor area | 400,000 square feet |
| Average minimum site area | Forty acres |
| Minimum support (threshold) | 70,000–300,000 families or 100,000 or more people |
| Leading tenant | one or two department stores |

| Tenant composition | Gross leaseable area (square feet) |
| --- | --- |
| Food and service | |
| Supermarket | 26,700 |
| Bakery | 1,800 |
| Candy, nuts | 1,100 |
| Restaurant | 5,800 |
| General merchandise | |
| Department store | 181,300 |
| Junior department store | 44,100 |
| Variety store | 25,200 |
| Clothing and shoes | |
| Ladies specialty[a] | 4,200 |
| Ladies wear[a] | 7,000 |
| Children's wear | 3,400 |
| Men's wear[a] | 5,300 |
| Family shoes[a] | 4,400 |
| Ladies shoes | 6,000 |
| Other retail | |
| Furniture | 12,500 |
| Drugs | 11,100 |
| Jewelry | 2,000 |
| Cards and gifts | 1,600 |
| Bank | 5,400 |
| Services | |
| Beauty shop | 1,700 |
| Barber shop | 800 |
| Shoe repair | 900 |
| Cleaners and dyers | 1,600 |
| Optometrist | 800 |

[a]Includes two or more tenants of this classification.
SOURCE: Urban Land Institute, *The Dollars and Cents of Shopping Centers* (1963).

ping center, while the center's threshold is many times greater. With a higher minimum threshold, the ranges of the goods and services offered are extended considerably as well and the service or trade area is likewise larger in areal extent. The leading tenant of centers of this order is a major department store or perhaps two such establishments.

er array of functions, a more diverse mix of functions (especially in the CBD of large cities), more functional units, and a larger trade or service area. The central business district in the city might be considered as analogous to the primate city in the interurban hierarchy. It is unique in the city in that there is only one such center and, by definition, there can only

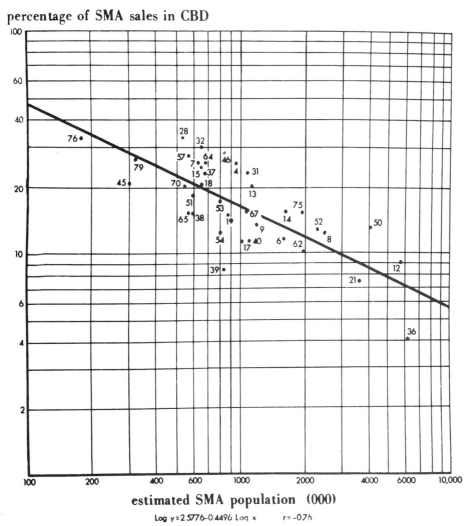

percentage of SMA sales in CBD

estimated SMA population (000)

Log y = 2.5776−0.4496 Log x        r = −0.76

**Figure 11-8** Central business district sales and metropolitan area population. *Source.* Ronald R. Boyce and W. A. V. Clark, "Selected Spatial Variables and Central Business District Retail Sales"; *Papers,* Regional Science Assoc. Vol. 11, 1963.

The highest order commercial center in the city is the *central business district* (CBD). This commercial center is dominant over all others because it has a great-

be one. Every city has such a center, although it is obvious that the size, structure, and role of the CBD of a small city is not equal to that of a large city. The composition of the CBD of a small city of about 10,000 people is about the same as a community shopping center in a city of 250,000. Therefore, the degree to which the CBD dominates the commercial structure of a city has meaning mainly within the context of that city. It is not meaningful to present definite statements regarding the number of functions, functional units, or establishments

ing height and commercial use of floors above ground level are important variables included.[7]

Once again, the highest land values in the city occur in proximity to the point of maximum accessibility and land users with the greatest rent paying ability can outbid other potential users of this space. By and large, these are commercial users of space in the CBD who pay high prices

**Table 11–5**   Hierarchy of CBD Land Uses and Land Values

| Location | Land Value (per Square Foot) | Land Uses |
|---|---|---|
| Core (office) | $50–$25 | Prime multi-tenant office |
| | | Prime single occupancy office (prestige) |
| | | Prestige retail |
| | | Financial |
| | | Other mixed uses (not free-standing) |
| | |    Service |
| | |    Food (eating and drinking) |
| Core (retail) | $25–$15 | Large comparison retail (department stores) |
| | | Specialty and chain retail |
| | | Multi- and single-tenant office |
| | | Hotel |
| | | Entertainment |
| | | Banks |
| | | Service and support uses |
| | | Luxury high-rise residential apartments |
| Fringe | $15–$5 | Secondary retail |
| | | Other centrally oriented commercial |
| | | Secondary office |
| Fringe | $5–$1 | Wholesale |
| | | Middle-income residential apartments |
| | | Neighborhood-convenience retail |
| | | Loft industrial |

SOURCE:   Larry Smith, "Space for the CBD's Functions," Table 3 in *Internal Structure of the City*, ed. Larry S. Bourne, New York, Oxford University Press (1971).

in the CBD, since these will vary as a function of the city's population.

It should be mentioned though, that when talking about space use in the CBD, prime value is put on space use above ground level as well as on surface use. High-rise buildings used for commercial purposes are commonplace in the CBD, providing a serrated skyline and urban canyons in these areas. In a formalized procedure for delimiting the CBD, build-

for the use of their locations, both at ground level and above, and use the space intensely as a result. The general types of tenants of the CBD's of larger cities are indicated in Table 11–5.

One manner of examining the role of the CBD in the commercial structure of

[7]Raymond E. Murphy and J. E. Vance, Jr. "Delimiting the CBD," *Economic Geography*, Vol. 30 (July, 1954).

**Table 11–6** Selected Variables and CBD Sales

| Variable Examined | Volume of Retail Sales | CBD Sales as a Share of SMSA Sales |
|---|---|---|
| | Type of Relationship | |
| Degree of CBD centrality | Positive | Negative |
| Floor space in planned shopping center | Slightly positive | Negative |
| CBD office space | Slightly positive | Slightly negative |

SOURCE: Based on Boyce and Clark, *Ibid.*

the city is to consider the volume of sales made by CBD establishments. The percentage of total SMSA retail sales accounted for by the CBD has been found to decrease with increases in the population of the metropolitan center, which is logical since urban centers of greater population tend to have greater areal extent, resulting in an increased proportion of the population being more distant from the CBD. For SMSA's of about 500,000 people, about 20 percent of the total retail sales are made by the CBD, while in SMSA's of about 5,000,000, less than 10 percent of all SMSA retail sales are made by the CBD (Figure 11–8).[8] In examination of CBD retail sales, Boyce and Clark, considered a number of spatial variables that might have a bearing on the volume of CBD sales and of CBD sales as a share of total sales of a metropolitan area, with the findings summarized in Table 11–6. When the degree of centrality of the CBD is greater, the volume of retail sales increases, but CBD sales as a proportion of total metropolitan area sales declines. Also, when more floor space exists in planned shopping centers, the volume of sales increases slightly, but the share of metropolitan areas sales made by the CBD declines. Further, as there is more office space in the CBD, the volume of retail sales increases slightly, while the share of total sales made by the CBD declines.

In general, the degree of dominance of the CBD in the commercial structure of the city is influenced by the population size, by the degree of centrality of the CBD within the city, by the extent of competition in the form of planned shopping centers (and perhaps unplanned centers), and to a lesser extent, by the amount of complementary office space in the CBD.

In viewing change in the sales mix of retail establishments in the CBD, many conflicting statements have been made. Some say that the CBD is losing strength as a retail center, while others say it is holding its own or gaining ground slightly with the passage of time. In a study of this matter over the time span 1948 to 1958, the CBD sales mix was established for SMSA's in 1958, as were changes in major retail groups, specifically general merchandise, apparel, furniture, and eating-drinking places.[9] In the aggregate, these groups are referred to as the GAFE group. GAFE sales made up sixty to seventy-five percent of total CBD retail sales, with the percentage increasing as SMSA population increased. It is stated that "it is this group which will determine the business health of the CBD."[10] Within the GAFE

[8]Ronald R. Boyce and W. A. V. Clark, "Selected Spatial Variables and Central Business District Retail Sales," *Papers of the Regional Science Association*, Vol. 11, (1963).

[9]Lorne H. Russwurm, "The Central Business District Retail Sales Mix, 1948–1958," *Annals of the AAG*, Vol. 54, No. 4, (December, 1964).

[10]Russwurm, *Ibid*, p. 529.

# CBD GAFE SALES, 1958

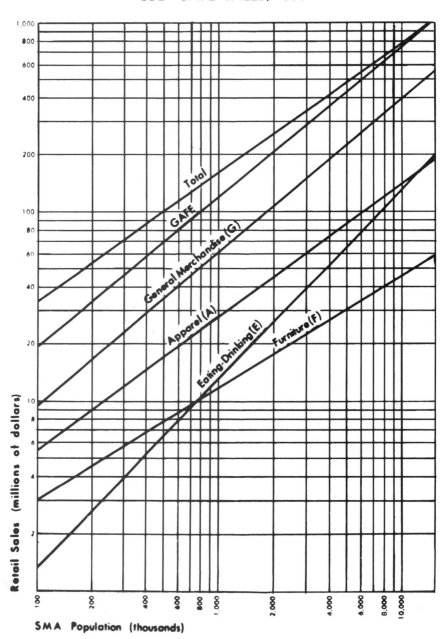

**Figure 11-9**   Central business district GAFE sales and metropolitan area population. Lorne H. Russwurm. "The Central Business District Retail Sales Mix, 1948–1958." Reproduced by permission from the *Annals* of the Association of American Geographers. Vol. 54, No. 4 (December, 1964).

group, general merchandise (G) is the singlemost important in total sales, regardless of SMSA population, followed by apparel (A). For SMSA's up to about 850,000, furniture (F) is the third most important, followed by eating and drinking places (E). For SMSA's over this size, eating and drinking places are third most

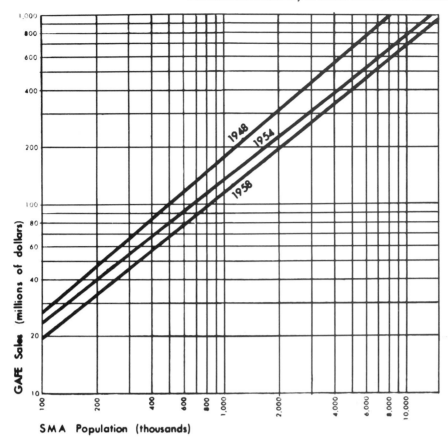

**SMA  Population  (thousands)**

**Figure 11-10**  Changes in central business district GAFE sales: 1948–1958. Lorne H. Russwurm. "The Central Business District Retail Sales Mix, 1948–1958." Reproduced by permission from the *Annals* of the Association of American Geographers Vol. 54, No. 4 (December, 1964).

important, nearly equaling apparel in retail sales, followed by furniture (Figure 11–9).

With regard to changing roles or levels of importance of retail sales with the GAFE group, there was an overall decline over the decade 1948 to 1958 (Figure 11–10). This trend characterized each of the components of the GAFE group as well. Evidence indicates that this trend has continued since the completion of the study cited, in spite of sometimes elaborate attempts to bolster CBD sales, such as expansion of offstreet parking facilities, development of pedestrian malls, and nighttime store hours. The volume of sales over the decade noted is lower at the end of the decade than at the beginning for general merchandise (department stores), apparel stores, and furniture stores, with the volume of sales for eating and drinking places experiencing less of a relative decline. Contrasts exist, however, in sales behavior of each of the components in the GAFE group, depending on populations of the metropolitan areas. Declines in sales have been experienced most sharply in larger SMSA's in general merchandise, apparel, and furniture outlets, while the smaller SMSA's have experienced the sharpest declines in sales by eating and drinking places.

Concerning the loss of retail sales by the CBD, especially in the GAFE group, this is most likely due to the development

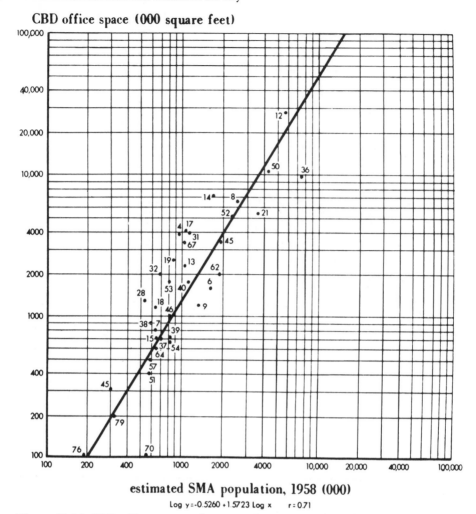

**CBD office space (000 square feet)**

**estimated SMA population, 1958 (000)**

Log y =-0.5260 + 1.5723 Log x    r = 0.71

**Figure 11-11** CBD office space and metropolitan area population. *Source.* Ronald R. Boyce and W. A. V. Clark. "Selected Spatial Variables and Central Business District Retail Sales"; *Papers,* Regional Science Assoc. Vol. 11, 1963. Reprinted by permission.

of competing outlets in planned and un-planned shopping centers which, as pointed out earlier, have greater accessibility to the clientele of retail establishments. These centers have greater provision for offstreet parking, have more modern facilities, and tend to have greater aesthetic value, with malls, plantings, and overhead protection from the elements. That the shopping center has had an impact on the commercial sales in the CBD, seems to be beyond question. One study, including thirty-five metropolitan areas in the U.S., indicated that there is a distinct negative relationship between the share of metropolitan area sales made in the CBD and the floor area in planned shopping centers.[11] This is to say, that as shopping center square footage was greater, the share of metropolitan area sales made in the CBD decreased.

Does this indicate that the CBD is losing its viability and shortly may be doomed as the major commercial center in the city? This is not at all likely. What does appear to be underway is a metamorphosis of the CBD involving a change in functions from the ones that have been dominant in the past. The dominant functions of the CBD have

[11]Boyce and Clark, *Op. Cit.*

traditionally been to serve as a commercial center and a transportation hub. With a population expanding outward, however, it appears to have lost its vitality as a commercial center in the sense of dispensing retail goods, having forfeited much of its advantage to outlying centers. The CBD is still, though, a center of many urban activities which attract a nonresident population consisting of visitors and businessmen. Further, many group assemblies, such as conferences, conventions, and professional meetings, are held in the CBD of the city. Many administrative functions profit, as well, from locations in the CBD. For these reasons, two types of demand for urban space in the CBD have increased greatly, these being visitor lodging (hotels and downtown motels) and office space. Neither of these uses of urban space is confined to street level, as retail outlets largely are, and do not benefit particularly from access to pedestrian traffic. These uses are more suited to high rise buildings which have come to dominate much of the CBD at present.

Hotel and motor hotel construction in the CBD, as well as along major arterial highways, has proceeded at an accelerated rate in recent years, but even more striking is the increase in office space in the CBD, especially in larger metropolitan areas (Figure 11–11). In many respects, this may be considered a more efficient use of urban space in the CBD. In any case, with changes in the use of CBD space in the ways mentioned, there is a gradual change from the traditional commercial functions of the CBD to new types of functional emphasis as an administrative and lodging center.

## Commercial Space Above Ground Level

We have mentioned the utilization of urban space above ground level for commercial purposes, moreso in the central business district than in other types of commercial centers, although such space is increasingly used in regional shopping centers. The rationale for the use of this type of urban space is essentially the same as for the use of ground level space—accessibility to the population served. In this manner, the benefits of prime locations enjoyed by ground level establishments can be shared with establishments of the same or other types above ground level. Second level and higher establishments have nearly the same degree of accessibility or convenience as do ground level ones by virtue of stairs, escalators, or elevators. They do not, however, enjoy the benefits of visual contact that are important to retail trade.

The tendency is for upper floor establishments to be much more involved in the provision of services than of retail goods, with retail outlets uncommonly found above ground level. In outlying shopping centers, the types of service functions most often found on upper floors are medical services, other professional services (lawyers, architects, insurance, real estate, etc.), schools (dance and language schools), and business offices. Establishments providing medical services account for the greatest share of upper level establishments in regional, community, and neighborhood centers in Chicago, as they most likely do in upper levels of such centers in other cities (Figure 11–12).[12] A considerable share of the floor space available in upper levels of all types of commercial centers remains vacant, however, indicating that the potential of such space is not being fully realized. In shopping centers in Chicago, one study disclosed that about 13 percent of upper level establishments in regional centers were vacant, 22 percent in community centers, 34 percent in neighborhood centers, and 31 percent in ribbon developments.[13]

Related to demands for commercial space above ground level in outlying centers are the demands for office space in

[12]Berry, *Op. Cit.*
[13]Berry, *Ibid.*

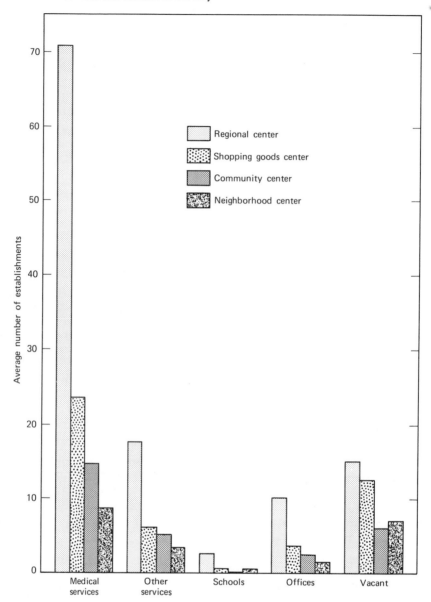

**Figure 11-12**   Number of establishments on upper floors of commercial centers, Chicago, Illinois. *Source.* Based on data by Brian J. L. Berry, *Commercial Structure and Commercial Blight,* 1963. Table 8. Reprinted by permission.

the city as a whole, be it in the CBD, outlying commercial center, or commercial ribbon. Much, if not most of the office space of the large city is above ground level, with retail trade outlets and service establishments preempting most of the ground floor area where they have greater access to pedestrian traffic and enjoy the benefits of visual contact with passersby. Office functions have somewhat different needs and can function on floors above street level.

The demands for office space in the city have been steadily mounting for over a decade and have, with the exception of the period 1969 to 1970, been adequately met (Figure 11–13). Demands for office space have increased several fold in the

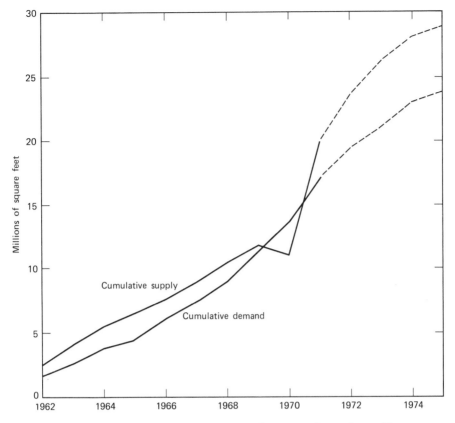

**Figure 11-13**  Cumulative demand and supply curves for prime office space, major Western city: 1962–1975. *Source.* Adapted from *Urban Land,* June 1972, Figure 4.

decade 1962 to 1972 and most of these have been accommodated by additonal supplies of office space in the CBD, where the administrative function takes on increasing significance, such that the CBD may well become a district of office workers and managers, rather than shopkeepers and clerks.

Demands for office space are not existent for all economic activities, as pointed out previously. In the CBD, the major demands for office space are by insurance, legal, and business services, which, together, make up about 51 percent of the total demand for office space in the CBD of a major West Coast city (Figure 11–14).

Observe too, with respect to the demand and supply of office space in the large city, that if a shortage of such space

exists, there is an inducement for the provision of additional facilities of this type. This unsatisfied demand can be met, however, by one or a very few new high rise structures and this may result in a temporary surplus of such space. The size of the investments needed to meet such demands is very large and the time lag between original conception and final occupance of office buildings is fairly long. Because of the magnitude of financial resources needed, the problems associated with financing such structures, and the length of the construction period, a lengthy period of shortage exists. When the facilities, as with a sky-scraper, are ready for occupance, there may be an oversupply of office space, which replaces a period of shortage. Thus, there tends to be a cyclic nature in

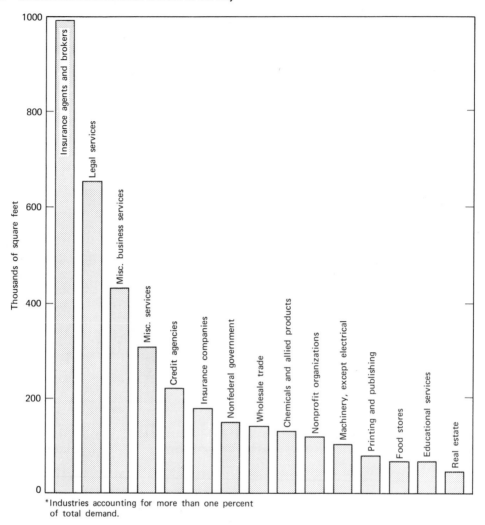

**Figure 11-14** Office space demanded by selected industries*, major West Coast C.B.D. *Source.* Adapted from data in Charles J. Detoy and Sol L. Rabin. "Office Space: Calculating the Demand." *Urban Land,* June, 1972. The Urban Land Institute.

the supply and demand structure of such facilities, perhaps moreso than with other types of commercial establishments. The high proportions of vacant office space in outlying commercial centers and ribbon developments might, therefore, reflect a short term oversupply, rather than a permanent lack of demand.

## A Spatial Hierarchy of Intraurban Commercial Centers

As a working framework for the concept of size, spacing, and functioning of

central places, Walter Christaller developed a number of postulates (Chapter 7). The same could be done for development of a spatial hierarchy, not of cities as trade foci, but of commercial centers within the individual city. The postulates adopted at this time are as follows:

*Postulate 1:*    There is an even distribution of population of the city.

*Postulate 2:* There is a uniform distribution of purchasing power within the city, and of basic needs for goods and services.

*Postulate 3:* There are no physical impediments to consumer travel within the city.

*Postulate 4:* There is equal mobility of all people residing in the city.

Even a casual observer would recognize that the above postulates are far removed from reality. Residential population is not at all uniformly distributed, nor is disposable income; there are physical impediments to intraurban travel, such as rivers, and not all people have equal means or ease of travel in the city. Still, these postulates serve for the purpose of developing a spatial hierarchy of commercial centers.

The most basic of commercial needs of the urban population likely is food supply. In the modern American society, this is dispensed by the supermarket most commonly, and to a lesser degree, by the "mom and pop" grocery. The supermar-

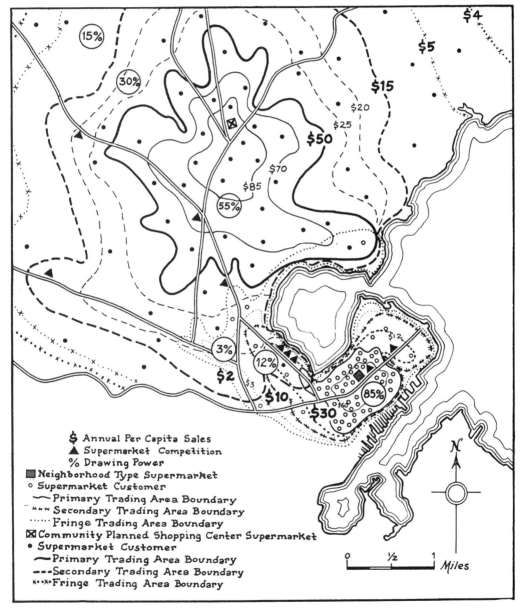

$ Annual Per Capita Sales
▲ Supermarket Competition
% Drawing Power
▦ Neighborhood Type Supermarket
○ Supermarket Customer
⌒ Primary Trading Area Boundary
ᴧ⸱ᴧ⸱ᴧ Secondary Trading Area Boundary
⋯⋯ Fringe Trading Area Boundary
⊠ Community Planned Shopping Center Supermarket
• Supermarket Customer
⌒ Primary Trading Area Boundary
––– Secondary Trading Area Boundary
×⸱×⸱× Fringe Trading Area Boundary

N

0   ½   1
⊢———⊢———⊣ Miles

**Figure 11-15**   Sales penetration and drawing power of two supermarkets. *Source.* William Applebaum and Saul B. Cohen. *Annals* of the Association of American Geographers. Vol. 51, 1961. Reprinted by permission.

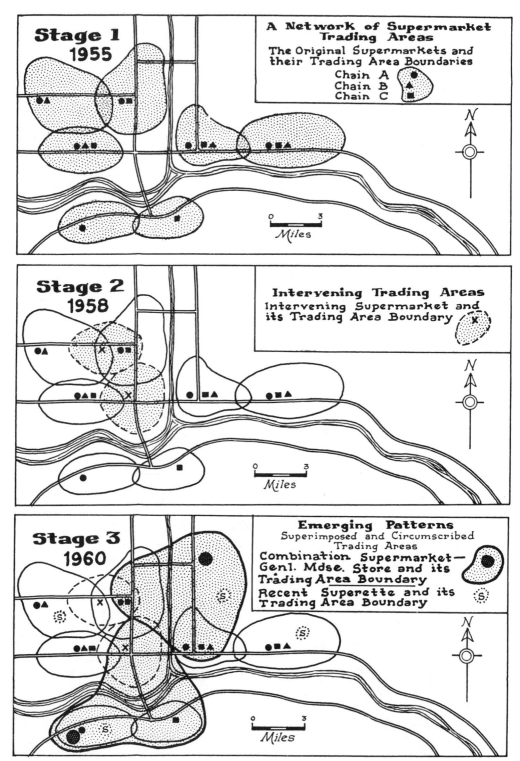

**Figure 11-16** Stages in the development of a system of supermarkets and their trading areas. *Source. Ibid.,* Figure 11-15. Reprinted by permission.

ket may be a free-standing functional unit or may be a tenant in a shopping center.

In the order of entry, the foodstore is one of the very first to come into being and seeks to gain immediate proximity to the threshold population needed for its support. These establishments tend to have a relatively low threshold: low range of its goods, and fairly small service areas. When distance increases from the establishment, its drawing power is lessened (Figure 11–15).

To serve the needs of the population, a number of free-standing foodstores may be developed, each serving a relatively small market area. Each establishment does not, however, enjoy a monopolistic position in its trade area, with the potential clientele on the outer margin of the service area often being shared with a competing establishment. Hence, the trading areas of two competing establishments of this order tend to overlap (Figure 11–16). Thus, theoretically there would be a uniform distribution of foodstores within the urban area, each serving small trading areas of the same general size. In reality, however, the population served by these foodstores is not uniformly distributed, that is, postulate 1 is not applicable, but does this indicate the lack of validity of statements concerning the distribution of free-standing foodstores? A study, involving a large part of the city of Tacoma, Washington, approached this question through use of a map transformation, as discussed earlier in this chapter.[14] The procedure here consisted of dividing the study area into equal area cells, with the dollar amount of expenditures for groceries as a function of population, established for each cell. Next, the area of each cell was transformed so that map area of the cell was proportionate to the expenditure for

[14]Arthur Getis, "The Determination of the Location of Retail Activities With the Use of a Map Transformation," *Economic Geography*, Vol. 39, No.1(January 1, 1963).

groceries in that cell (Figure 11–17 *A–E*, see pages 244–248). Then, a grid of regular size hexagonal trading area was constructed, with the center of each being the theoretical location of a supermarket. The size of each cell in the hexagonal grid was established to include an amount of consumer expenditure equal to the average sales of supermarkets, approximately $1.5 million at the time of study. Finally, the locations of the centers of the hexagons were transferred to the distorted map of consumer expenditures by superimposition of the theoretical hexagonal trade areas over the distorted map. The final step consisted of adjusting the theoretical locations of supermarkets to the nearest area of commercially zoned land. It was found, as a result of this study, that there is considerable regularity in the spacing of free-standing supermarkets, not within the urban area *per se*, but within the distribution of population and purchasing power within the area under consideration. The free-standing supermarket or other isolated establishment, as the major representative of the lowest order commercial center (order I), exhibits a number of spatial characteristics of the lowest order trade center in central place theory.

The next highest order (order II) in the spatial hierarchy of urban commercial centers is exemplified by the neighborhood shopping center or its unplanned equivalent. Rather than a single function or maybe two or three functions, these centers include a number on the order of 15 to 18 as noted earlier. With a higher threshold for such centers and consistent with the postulates mentioned previously, these centers would derive customers from a greater area than would the free-standing units. This is to say that the ranges of goods and services dispensed by such centers and the tributary or service areas would be larger. With the inclusion of a few establishments offering shoppers goods, however, the frequency of visits to such centers

|    | 10  | 11  | 12  | 13  | 14  | 15   |
|----|-----|-----|-----|-----|-----|------|
| 10 | 235 | 321 | 611 | 449 | 462 | 496  |
| 11 | 543 | 663 | 764 | 472 | 612 | 400  |
| 12 | 457 | 827 | 940 | 535 | 264 | 1023 |
| 13 | 345 | 827 | 823 | 420 | 288 | 162  |
| 14 | 194 | 515 | 680 | 265 | 298 | 46   |
| 15 | 24  | 397 | 508 | 336 | 153 | 99   |
| 16 | 35  | 312 | 300 | 31  |     |      |
| 17 | 43  | 251 | 263 | 169 |     |      |
| 18 | 87  | 147 | 175 | 88  |     |      |

(a)

**Figure 11-17** *(A to E)* Theoretical and actual locations of supermarkets using a map transformation: Tacoma, Washington. *(A)* Location of consumption expenditures available for groceries in study area (in thousands of dollars). *Source.* Arthur Getis. *Economic Geography.* Vol. 39, 1963. Reprinted by permission.

would be less, even though the drawing power would be extended over greater area.

A still higher order commercial center (order III) would be the community shopping center or its unplanned equivalent. All of the functions performed by the two preceding orders are present in centers of this order, plus an incremental group, especially in the shoppers goods realm. The orders of entry of this incremental group are, as would be expected, higher than those of functions represented in lower order centers, for example, men's wear, ladies specialty, and a bank. The threshold of centers of this order is still higher than that of lower order centers, the ranges of goods and

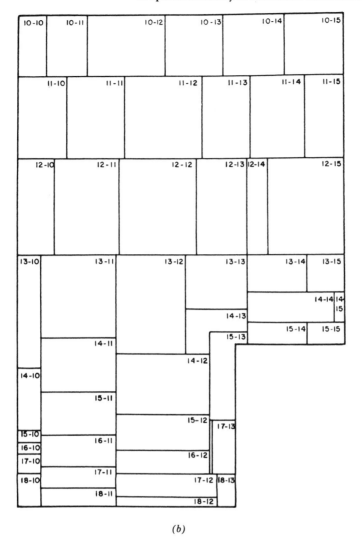

*(b)*

**Figure 11-17** *(B)* Map distortion of consumption expenditures for groceries in study area.

services offered are greater, and the tributary or service areas served are larger. And, just as with central places of the equivalent order, there is the first duplication of functions with this order of commercial center.

The next higher order of commercial center (order IV) is the regional shopping center or the unplanned agglomeration with an equivalent role in urban commercial structure. In centers of this order, the number of functions is greater than in centers of lower orders and, since duplication of functions is still greater,

the increase in number of functional units is greater than is the increase in number of functions. All of the functions of lower order centers are characteristic of this order, plus the incremental group, again mostly of shoppers goods establishments. The ranges of such goods are greater than those found in lower order centers, and the thresholds of such centers are greater as well. With stated thresholds of 100,000 or more people, the tributary or service area would include a large segment of the population of the city and would explain why (1) few

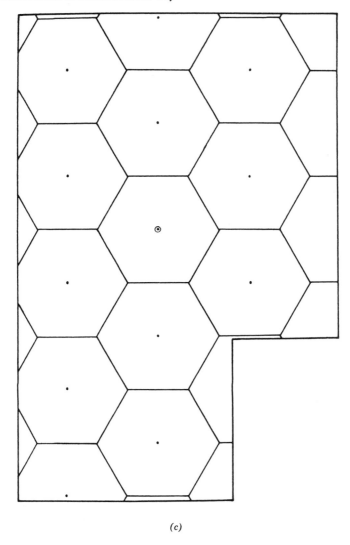

*(c)*

**Figure 11-17** *(C)*  Theoretical trade areas.

centers of this order are found in larger cities, and (2) why no centers of this order are found in smaller cities, since they would rival or duplicate the CBD.

The next and highest order of commercial center (order V) would be the central business district. As stated before, there is only one center of this order in the city and it contains more functions, functional units, and establishments than any other order of commercial center. There are functions well represented in the CBD, such as lodging and administration, that not only exist but that are very prominent in the CBD, as mentioned in

an earlier section. The thresholds of many of the goods and services of the CBD are greater than for other centers and their ranges are greatly extended. In fact, the range of many of the services includes the entire city, the urbanized area, or the region within which the city is located. For example, a state employment office located in the CBD serves the entire state, as a federal regional office of the Department of Housing and Urban Development serves a multistate region.

If all of the population of the city is to be included within the service areas of each order of commercial center, the

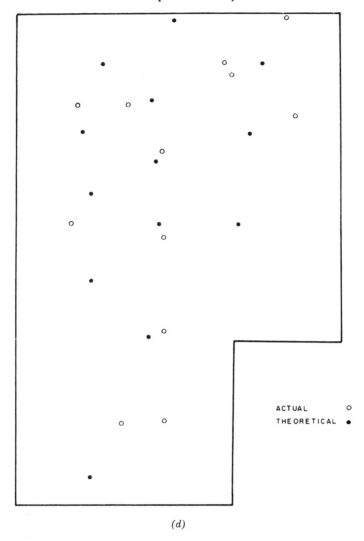

*(d)*

**Figure 11-17** *(D)* Theoretical and actual locations of largest
centers of grocery store sales in study area.

lowest order centers, together with their
service areas, would be nested or contained within the service areas of the next
higher order centers, which, in turn,
would be contained within the service
areas of the next higher order. This process of nesting would continue from the
lowest order to the highest order centers
within the city (Figure 11–18).

If the concepts of threshold, range,
and functional order apply to a commercial hierarchy within the city in a manner
similar to the hierarchy of a system of
central places, it would be logical that the
concept of nesting would apply as well,
and this is the suggestion made at this
point. In a city with a specific land area, if
each of these orders of commercial centers is represented, and the threshold,
ranges, and service areas of each order
are different from other orders, it would
follow that the number of centers of each
order would be progressively less the
higher the order of the centers. Further,
the spacing between equal order centers
would be about the same, while the spacing between centers of successively
higher order would be greater, in the

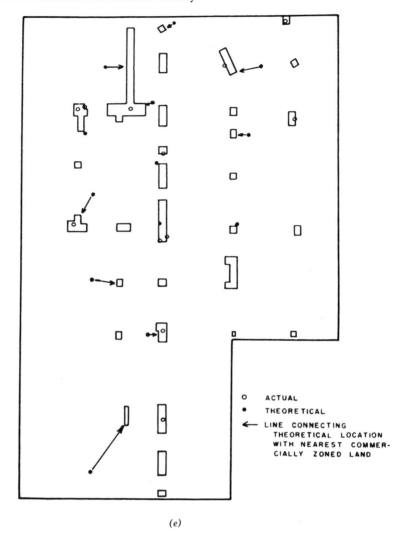

(e)

**Figure 11-17** *(E)* Theoretical locations adjusted to nearest commercially-zoned land, and actual locations of supermarkets in study area.

same manner that the spacing between towns usually is greater than between villages (Figure 11–18).

There is a similarity, then, between the hierarchy and spatial ordering of centers within the city and that of a regional system of cities. There is one incongruity, however, that does not exist in the latter case. This is the case of the ribbon development of commercial facilities following major transportation arteries.

In the attempt to maximize access to vehicular traffic, rather than pedestrian traffic, many commercial establishments seek locations providing a high degree of direct access, but with lower land costs than encountered within the CBD or planned shopping centers. Some of these commercial strip or ribbon developments are fingerlike extensions of the CBD along major streets radiating from the CBD. Other ribbon developments are along thoroughfares at some distance from the CBD, even on the outer margins of the urbanized areas and beyond. Some ribbon developments are but a few

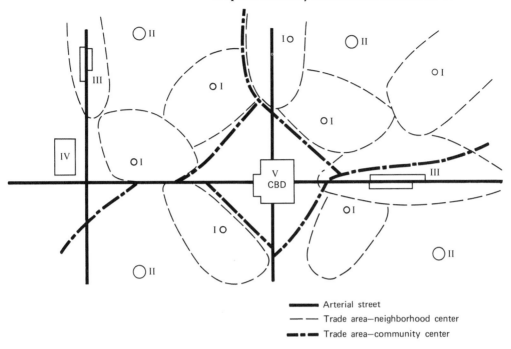

**Figure 11-18**  Schematic representation of the spatial arrangement of commercial centers in the city. I  neighborhood shopping center; II  community shopping center; III  ribbon development; IV  regional shopping center; V  central business district.

blocks in length, while others are miles in length. Generally, such developments are but a half-block or full block in depth on each side of the street or highway, although sometimes they may take on a somewhat bulbous appearance with depth on each side of the street or highway of two or three blocks. Ribbon developments tend to serve customers that might be considered as more casual or irregular patrons, as compared to patrons that seek out an establishment or commercial center and patronize it on a regular basis.

In regard to the functions of these commercial developments, there are certain similarities from city to city. By and large, the tenants of such ribbon developments have reatively low thresholds, but extended ranges, since the bulk of the customers arrive by auto. It would be difficult to delimit the service areas of ribbon developments, since they cater to nearby residents as well as people en-

route between points in the city or beyond.

Regarding specific types of commercial activity in ribbon developments, there are similarities among those catering to vehicular traffic that are different from similarities among those catering more to pedestrian traffic. One study indicated relationships between the structure of ribbon developments and traffic volume, direction of traffic flow, and extent of adjacent residential neighborhoods.[15] For a major thoroughfare in Denver, Colorado, it was mentioned that traffic volumes were greater inbound, and on this side, there was a greater incidence of gas stations and automobile dealers. Population

[15]Paul R. Merry, "An Inquiry Into the Nature and Function of a String Retail Development: A Case Study of East Colfax Avenue, Denver, Colorado," Unpublished Pd.D. thesis, Northwestern University. Cited in Brian J. L. Berry, "Ribbon Developments in the Urban Business Pattern," *Annals of the AAG*, Vol. 49, No. 2 (June, 1959).

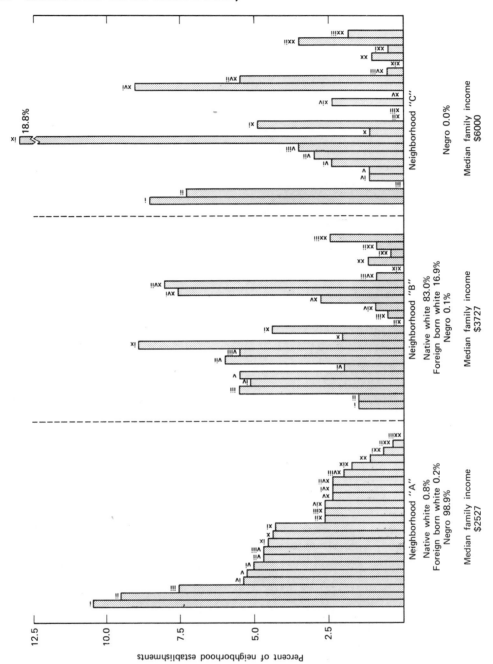

**Figure 11-19**   Contrasts in tenant composition of three urban commercial ribbon developments in Chicago. ((i) Beauty and barber shops; (ii) dry cleaners; (iii) shops advertising credit; (iv) cheap restaurants; (v) bars; (vi) independent groceries; (vii) jewelers and optometrists; (viii) shoe stores; (ix) women's clothing; (x) liquor stores; (xi) miscellaneous business services; (vii) billiard parlors; (xiii) store-front churches and spiritual consultants; (xiv) drug stores; (xv) loan and pawn establishments; (xvi) confectionaries, gift shops florists, and cigar stores; (xvii) vacant or for rent; (xviii) record stores; (xix) tailor-made men's clothing; (xx) automatic laundromats; (xxi) gas stations; (xxii) "presentable" restaurants; (xxiii) bakeries. *Source.* Based on data in Allan Pred, *Economic Geography.* Vol. 39, 1963.

density was greater on the outbound side where there were relatively more beauty shops, bakeries, groceries, taverns, and hardware stores. Also, within ribbon developments, there are differences in density of establishments. In the example in Denver, high density zones included beauty and barber shops, and grocery, clothing, shoe, hardware, and dry goods stores, florist shops, and bars. The low density zones were more characterized by automobile dealers, auto repair, gas stations, chain groceries, and ice cream shops. Notice too that the above commercial establishments tend to (1) have relatively low orders of entry and (2) relatively low thresholds. They could have, however, fairly large service areas.

An interesting study involving three commercial ribbon developments in Chicago provides insight on differences in the structure of ribbon developments in white communities and Negro communities (Figure 11–19).[16] In the Negro neighborhood and in one with a large white, foreign born population, largely Puerto Rican, there is decided emphasis on personal services and consumer finances, including pawn shops, loan establishments, and credit establishments. There is, in general, an emphasis on establishments catering to foot traffic and low income families. In the neighborhoods with higher family incomes, there is more emphasis on establishments catering to vehicular traffic, as well as foot traffic. The establishments in such neighborhoods tend to be of slightly higher quality and have higher thresholds and larger service areas, such as "presentable" restaurants, women's clothing stores, and specialty stores, such as gift shops, florists, and confectionaries.

The above statements and others derived from the literature indicate that the functional units included in commercial

ribbon developments are dependent on a number of factors: (1) the location of the ribbon development within the urban area; along a core area arterial or along an arterial on the outskirts of the city, (2) the volume, type, and direction of traffic on the arterial, vehicular or pedestrian, inbound or outbound, high volume or low volume, (3) the income levels of the neighborhood containing the ribbon development, and (4) the culture group served by the ribbon development.

In contrast to the compact, convenient, and often aesthetically pleasing planned shopping centers and some of the unplanned commercial clusters, the phenomenon of the commercial ribbon is not always held in high regard by residents. A major newspaper states, "Opposition is welling up across the nation to the garish signs, flamboyant buildings, harsh lights, flapping pennants, and circus colors of the commercial strips that have seized the busiest traffic arteries in thousands of cities and towns. In an age fraught with ecological concern and consumerism, the strip has become a prime target for some of the new catchwords and phrases, such as 'uglification,' 'cluster-vision,' and 'visual pollution'."[17] This fairly well sums up public reaction to many, if not most, of the commercial ribbons in the city. Although the article goes on to associate the undesirable aspects of ribbon developments with the spread of franchised commercial establishments, it could well have included the proliferation of automobile dealerships and the spread of "automobile row." Although commercial ribbons serve functions or they wouldn't exist, it is the form in which they appear to the passerby that is being criticized. Also, these ribbons include a great number of generators of vehicular traffic and as a result of numerous points of exit and entrance to

---

[16]Allan Pred, "Business Thoroughfares as Expressions of Urban Negro Culture," *Economic Geography*, Vol. 39, No. 3, (July, 1963).

[17]*The New York Times*, November 28, 1971, Byline, Douglas E. Kneeland.

the traffic artery, there are potential traffic hazards along the extent of the ribbon.

## Blight and Succession of Commercial Centers

Conditions that lead to the development of a commercial center, planned or unplanned, compact or ribbon, are constantly changing. The character of the population may change, as might their demands, and the functional attractiveness of the commercial center may lessen as time passes. These conditions can lead

to the obsolescence or malfunctioning of the commercial center that serves to impair its viability or stability. This situation, where there is a lessening of the desirability of the commercial center, might be termed "commercial blight." Berry recognizes, in a study of the Chicago area, four different types of commercial blight: economic, physical, functional, and frictional.[18]

Economic blight occurs when there are changes in the demand structure, such as from population losses in the market

[18]Berry, *Op. Cit.*

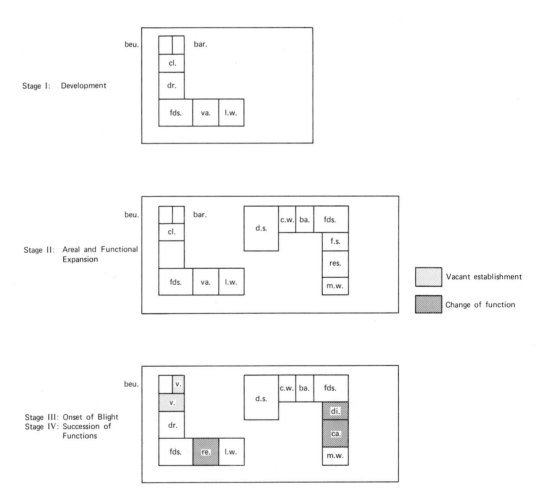

**Figure 11-20** Development and succession in a shopping center. Type of function: (beu.) beauty shop; (bar.) barber shop; (cl.) cleaners; (dr.) drugs; (fds.) foodstore; (va.) variety store; (l.w.) ladies wear; (d.s.) jr. dept. store; (c.w.) childrens wear; (ba.) bakery; (f.s.) family shoes; (res.) restaurant; (m.w.) mens wear; (v.) vacant; (re.) record store; (di.) discount store; (ca.) cafeteria.

area, losses to competing centers, or changes in the economic structure of the threshold population. The evidence of economic blight might come in the form of increased vacancies, a loss of higher order establishments, or changes in merchandise lines in remaining retail establishments.

Physical blight refers to the deterioration of the structures occupied by business concerns, probably as a function of age. Buildings that are deteriorated become unsightly and unsafe, as well as being undesirable to the people comprising the body of customers. Functional blight has to do with the inability of a given establishment to engage in efficient operations due to changes of a technological nature. A small food store that has its stock displayed on floor-to-ceiling shelves may be less desirable to shoppers than a modern supermarket with eye level display racks. Frictional blight or environmental blight exists when the commercial establishment exists within an area that reflects unfavorably on the business operation. Examples might include a neighborhood that has experienced the gradual deterioration of residential structures, a mounting incidence of crime and vandalism, or a situation in which access to the commercial establishments is stifled by traffic congestion.

It is possible to hypothesize the development and period of operation of a commercial center in terms of different stages (Figure 11–20). The first stage would be inauguration of commercial activities in a number of establishments. Upon the initial success of the first establishments, others would be added to the center, which would add additional functions and the center would expand areally (stage 2). With the onset of commercial blight in one form or another, the viability of the center is lessened and no new establishments are added, although some may change their functions, and the center ceases to expand areally (stage 3). The next stage would consist of a period in which there is increased loss of viability and many commercial operations become marginal in terms of profitability (stage 4). Vacancies begin to occur, first above ground level and then at ground level. Physical blight begins to occur noticeably and the establishments of the center begin to be less attractive. Finally, the commercial center may be faced with collapse or deterioration of the point where it is, as a unit, quite marginal and attracts but a small share of the customers it did previously. There may be, in this stage, the removal of some of the structures in the center (stage 5).

In the above process, there is a succession, not so much of land uses, since the land area of the center is used for commercial purposes throughout, but a succession in terms of functions performed by the center. The number of functions becomes less, as does the array of functions. Further, there is the replacement of some functions of a higher order with those of a lower order, making the desirability of the center less. Also, the service area of the center may experience contraction. Developers of commercial centers must guard against the first signs of commercial blight to protect the commercial center from passing to the last, and least desirable, stage.

# 12

# residential land in the city: its charac- teristics and its use

We have said residential land comprises a greater share of the developed land area in the city than does any other single land use type. In American cities, with populations of over 100,000, approximately 41 percent of the developed area is devoted to residential use, with the proportion becoming greater in smaller cities. This share of urban area is devoted to housing the population of the city and includes dwelling units of different types, with varied characteristics, and in different locational settings.

The single family residence usually is the most common type of housing unit in the city, ranging from the near palatial in appearance to those that are virtual shanties. A second type of housing in the city is the multifamily residential unit, each including a number of separate house- holds. Again, there are differences in the form of this type of housing, from the simple duplex or triplex units, to the high rise complexes including a consider- able number of individual households, to the dwelling units providing single-room housing for a transient population. Each of these types of housing provides resi- dential space for different sectors of the urban population, each has its identifiable social and physical charac- teristics, and each has its place in a spatial pattern of zonation of residential areas. Also, there are differences in the inten- sity to which each type of residential area is utilized.

With urban housing, it is important to realize that the type of housing charac- teristics of a given locational setting in the city may change with the passage of time, that is, the locational pattern is dynamic. Further, the occupants of a specific type of housing are prone to exercise their mobility and change places of residence so there tends to be a continued change in the population group that is housed in a certain residential area. The housing stocks in the area are in a constant state of flux, but even more pronounced is the state of flux of the population of that area (Figure 12–1).

## Zonation of Residential Areas of the City

With regard to the location of resi- dences within the city and the land oc- cupied by dwellings of urban residents, it is apparent that (1) they are not evenly distributed within the urban area, (2) there are spatial differences in their density within the city, (3) there are phys- ical and structural differences in residen-

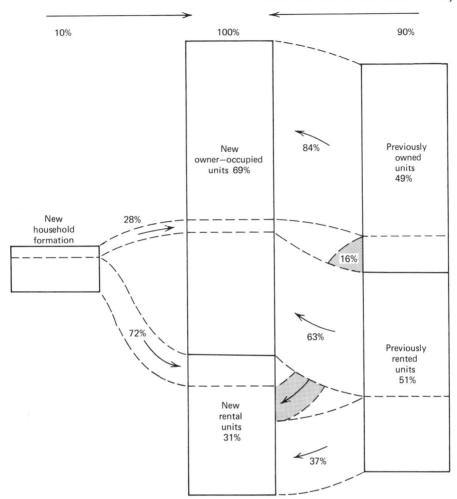

10%                         100%                    90%

New owner—occupied units 69%         84%        Previously owned units 49%

New household formation         28%

16%

72%         63%         Previously rented units 51%

New rental units 31%

37%

**Figure 12-1**   Flow of households: October 1965 through March 1966 into new housing units. *Source.* Adapted from *Housing Surveys, Parts 1 and 2;* Housing and Urban Development, 1969.

tial areas within the city, and (4) there are quality variations of dwelling units in the city. This section addresses the first of these points — spatial distribution of residential areas.

To place this matter in the perspective of time during which the city increased in population and expanded in areal dimensions, we first have to consider the locations of residential areas within the city as it first developed. Characteristically, the first node of residential development was in close proximity to the business core of the city, usually within walking distance of the compact cluster of busi-

ness establishments in the embryonic central business district (Figure 12–2). The major reason for this early development of a roughly concentric residential zone was that it provided ready access for all urban dwellers to the centers of urban activity at a time when systems of private and public transportation were essentially nonexistent. All residents were, therefore, near the point of minimum aggregate travel of the youthful city. Sometimes, physical constraints inhibited development of a complete concentric zone, as in the case of a lakefront or riverfront, and the zone of early residen-

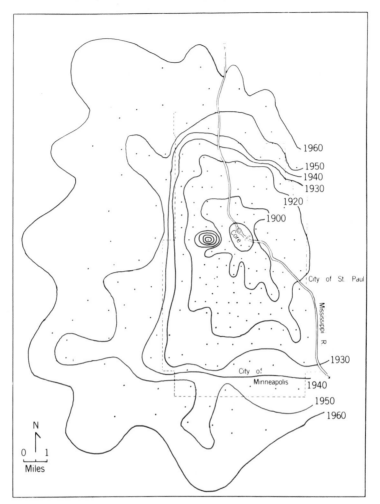

**Figure 12-2**   Spatial expansion of urban housing: Minneapolis, Minnesota. *Source.* John S. Adams "Residential Structure of Midwestern Cities." Reproduced by permission from the *Annals* of the Association of American Geographers. Vol. 60, No. 1 (March, 1970).

tial development was incomplete and existed as an arc of a concentric zone.

When the population of the urban center increased with time, residential sites were developed to accommodate the additional inhabitants. Some of this expansion of residential areas came in the form of areal expansion of the already established concentric zone around the commercial core of the city, with this resulting in some residents being relatively distant from places of urban employment and business activities, that is, further from the point of minimum aggregate travel. In response to this circumstance, improved transportation routes were constructed, linking the more distant residents with the core of the city. These improved routes were graded, drained, and sometimes surfaced with stone, brick, logs, or planks to facilitate movement by horsecar and wagons. Still, these wagonroads did not suffice completely to provide access to residents on the margin of the growing city to the commercial core.

Still more sophisticated forms of urban transport came into being, but the ones

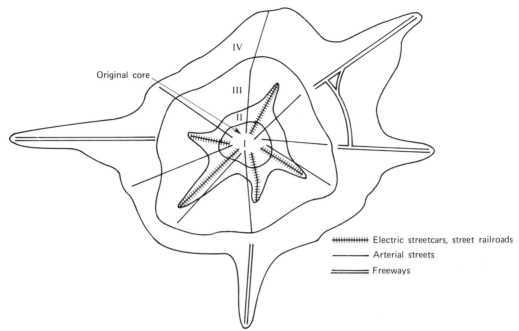

**Figure 12-3**   Changes in spatial forms of urban residential areas and in types of urban transportation. *Source.* Adapted from John S. Adams; *Annals* of the Assoc. of Amer. Geographers, March 1970.

having the greatest impact on spread of residential population were those that could move the greatest number of people with greatest convenience and lowest cost, and with reliable and rapid service. This period was marked by the advent of the mechanized, motorized, and electrified forms of urban transport. The trolley, the streetcar, and the steam railroad all extended lines outward to and beyond the margins of the city, opening new areas for residential settlement. In order to minimize travel time to the center of the city, the land adjacent to the newly established lines of mass transportation was especially desired, was the first developed, and was the most densely populated.

In terms of zonation of residential areas, the original concentric residential zone became altered by extension of residential settlement outward following the major transportation routes. Hence, there was developed more of a sectoral pattern of residential areas of the city,

with each transport artery serving as the focus of a given residential sector (Figure 12–3).

Much of the demand for housing in the city at this general period of city development came from new arrivals from abroad or from rural areas who provided the work force for the expanding and flourishing urban industries. Many new types of manufacturing were being developed, such as the iron and steel industries, and factory enterprises were becoming commonplace. To man the production lines in the factories, new social elements were being drawn to the city in ever increasing numbers. The unskilled and relatively poor workers came to the city and provided demands for housing somewhat different from those of the monied groups largely involved in trade and commerce. These demands tended to be met by housing in residential areas adjacent to major mass transport lines, especially those connected to factory districts on the margin of the city. With thousands of such workers housed in these residential sectors, and having a high degree of dependence on the transportation available, the density of inhabitants in such zones became very great. This, in turn, resulted in many walk-up apartment structures or tenements in these sectors. Therefore, the form of this residential zone was and is quite different from that of the original concentric residential zone with its free-standing dwelling units, each of which was for single family occupance, most of which were spacious and comfortable.

With more elapsed time and greatly increased population, still another type of residential zone came into being. This was the residential area toward the outer margin of the city and even beyond. This was the zone of modest single family dwellings. The formation of this zone was based on the coming of the privately owned automobile and the development of a network of arterial streets for their use. Also, basic to formation of this zone was a degree of decentralization of work places, so that not all workers were directed to one or a few small districts of the city. Contingent on development of this zone were increases in family incomes so that home ownership became widespread; at least the financial structure changed to encourage acquisition of home mortgages, if not homes. Extensive zones of single family dwellings characterize most present day American cities and have, in a somewhat more affluent form, come to characterize many incorporated and unincorporated suburbs as well—the "bedroom" communities housing middle-income commuters.

It is possible to recognize three general residential zones in the contemporary American city.[1] Near the center of the city is an areally restricted, roughly concentric zone of multifamily dwelling units

with this zone having a high density of settlement (Zone I). Outward from this zone is a more extensive zone of "workingmen's homes" (Zone II).[2] The outer margin of this zone may have a somewhat asterisklike form in response to residential expansion along major transportation arterials. In this zone, there is a lower density of dwelling units and of population than in Zone I. Still further removed from the center of the city is the zone of more affluent housing (Zone III). Single family dwellings predominate in this zone, but they tend to be larger than in other zones and on larger parcels of land. Thus, the density of dwelling units and population is still less than in other zones. This is the residential zone of the commuter and included within it are residential suburban concentrations.

## The Process of Succession of Residential Areas

Residential areas, perhaps more than other land use zones, are dynamic and subject to change. Some changes are physical in nature, especially structural changes in the dwellings in residential areas. Also, there are different types of social or demographic change, such as changes in density, in age of residents, in income levels of the residents, in occupational structure, and in ethnic and racial composition of the population.

The major point here is that a given residential zone may be characterized in a certain manner at the time of its inception, but these characteristics often are replaced by a different set of traits later, resulting in a residential zone appreciably different from the first. The residential zone may go through still other gradual stages in a cycle of change, in a continued succession of stages in the development and transformation of residential areas,

[1]Although the same general residential zones might exist in other societies, the spatial arrangement of them is strikingly different as mentioned at a later point in this chapter.

[2]Robert E. Park, Earnest W. Burgess, and Roderick D. McKenzie, *The City*, Chicago: University of Chicago Press; (1925).

each a replacement in whole or in part of the one before. For example, the stately and spacious dwellings in the concentric zone developed early around the business core of the city are likely to be replaced in part by expansion of the commercial core, while others in the outer portion of this zone are abandoned as living places by the original residents who acquire new dwellings further removed from the core of the city. The remaining dwellings, faced with increased levels of taxation, often are divided into a number of smaller dwelling units through conversion to apartments, rooming houses, and boarding houses. This type of dwelling unit is sought by the less affluent and more transient segment of the urban population who rent living quarters in these converted structures. As a result, the density of population increases substantially over what it had been originally, the socio-economic nature of the residential area changes, and the general complexion of the residential neighborhood changes. At still a later time, efforts may be made to refurbish or replace the substandard dwelling units of these residential areas through public housing and renewal programs. The residential area then may become characterized by modern, high-rise apartment structures designed to house the lower income groups. In this example, the residential area has experienced three distinct stages in a process of succession of the area, although the residential function has been the dominant use of the area in each stage.

In the succession of residential areas, numerous factors characterized each stage in the succession process. The densities of the population changed, the morphology of the areas changes, and the ethnic nature of the areas quite likely changed. The pattern appears to be that an original population group becomes more affluent, has greater needs for living space, or the area in which it resides becomes less desirable due to congestion, environmental degradation, or obsoles-

cence of dwelling units. The original group tends to gradually leave the older residential area, seeking different and, hopefully, improved housing elsewhere in the city. Upon abandonment of the residential area, ownership passes to new owners, many of whom are absentee owners. They may elect to raze the original residential structures and rebuild with tenement type structures or they may choose to subdivide the older existing structures, creating a number of dwelling units from each of the original ones.

Created in the above process are many additional dwelling units, each of limited space and with limited conveniences, but each one of which is available to tenants at relatively low cost. In exchange for the lower rents, the tenants seek and find residences that are substandard in many ways, are in congested environments in which the inhabitants are subject to personal overcrowding and which, in the extreme, are hazardous as a result of vermin, rodents, and lack of structural integrity. Such is the genesis of the urban slum; an evolved residential zone, not a constructed one.

## The Inner Residential Zone

Moving into such residential areas in American cities have been representatives of two different groups; first, the immigrants from abroad, then the migrants from rural areas of the country. In the nineteenth century, streams of immigrants arrived in America, often with little or no personal wealth or possessions, with no assured employment, and often with a culture and language different from those dominant in the country at that time. The major source areas of these immigrants in the nineteenth century who were added to the urban populations were Russia, Poland, Germany, Ireland, and Italy (Figure 12–4).[3]

[3]David Ward, *Cities and Immigrants: A Geography of Change in Nineteenth Century America*, New York, Oxford University Press, 1971.

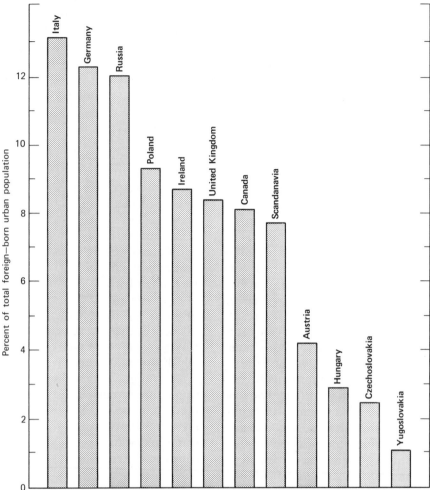

**Figure 12-4**  Urban residence of foreign-born white population: 1920. *Source.* Adapted from data in David Ward, *Cities and Immigrants,* 1971.

The bulk of the immigrants tended to settle in larger cities, especially the port cities at which they disembarked from foreign shores. The cities to which early immigrant groups gravitated attracted later immigrant groups of the same national origin, whether they were port cities or inland cities. As a result, there developed a regionalization of immigrant groups where cities in a certain region of the country tended to reflect the presence of similar immigrant groups. Some large cities, such as New York, drew large number of immigrants of a variety of national origins with each group tending to settle in a district of the city. Other cities attracted one immigrant group in par-

ticular, however, with this particular group reflecting its culture in the city of today. The German immigrants came to characterize cities of the Middle West, while Irish immigrants were more commonly identified with cities of New England (Figure 12–5). The Italian and Russian immigrants tended to settle in cities of the Northeastern seaboard, with the Austro-Hungarian immigrants more inclined to settle in cities of the Ohio Valley and the upper Midwest.

After each immigrant group settled in the city, it leaned toward a particular type of economic activity that was localized in a particular section of the city, for example, the retail trade district, the wholesale

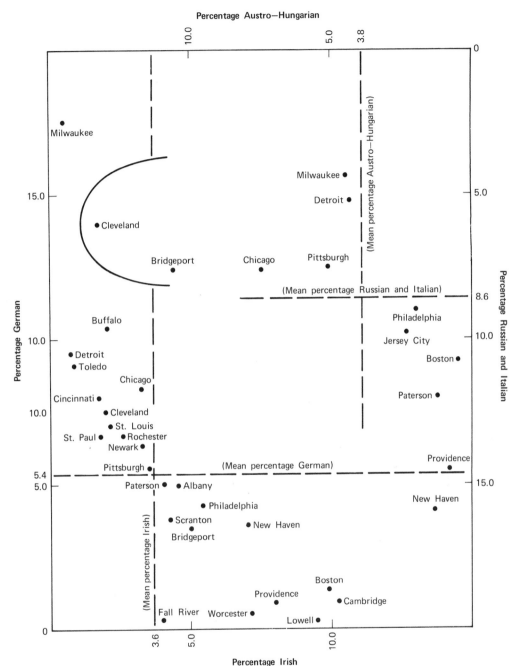

**Figure 12-5** Irish, German, Austro-Hungarian and combined Russian and Italian proportions of large American city population: 1910. *Source.* Adapted from David Ward, *Cities and Immigrants,* Oxford University Press, 1971.

foods district, the garment district, etc. In order to maximize access to employment opportunities, they tried to settle in residential areas in proximity to the industrial activity with which they were associated and, at the same time, maintain cultural ties with others of the same ethnic background. Thus, there developed a settlement pattern in which each immigrant group of similar ethnic background formed a node of residential settlement distinctive from others, that is, an early form of urban ghetto originated in cities of the country.[4]

conditions. To illustrate this point, a descriptive model of the spatial implications of immigrant districts has been developed (Figure 12–6).[5] Each immigrant

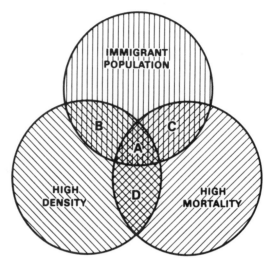

Probable Occupants:  **A** Italian  **B** Russian-Jewish  **C** Irish  **D** Remnant Native

**Figure 12-6** Model of the internal spatial structure of immigrant residential districts. *Source.* From *Cities and Immigrants: A Geography of Change in Ninteenth Century America* by David Ward. Copyright © 1971 by Oxford University Press, Inc. Reprinted by permission.

To be sure, the immigrant concentrations did not form into nodes that were mutually exclusive of others, since they all were in competition for the same basic type of housing and were in the same general economic group. The developing immigrant residential district associated with a part of the city in which a substandard living environment prevailed would, logically, share in the impact of this objectionable condition. If the developing immigrant district was located in a section where a number of different demographic problems existed, it would then share all of the undesirable living

district, as indicated by the historical record, became characterized by the various larger districts which tended to overlap spatially. It is suggested that the worst conditions characterized the worst sections of the Italian ghetto, with large immigrant populations, high densities, and high mortality. The Russian-Jewish immigrant district was typified by high immigrant populations and high densities, but low death rates; and the Irish ghetto had less crowdedness, but large immigrant populations and high mortality rates.

As the nineteenth century merged into the first decades of the twentieth, the immigrants slowly assumed a measure of affluence and social adjustment and had attained sufficient social mobility, especially the second and third generation residents, that they could and did abandon the residential districts into which

---

[4]The term "ghetto" is often misused. In the original sense, it referred to a cloistered, isolated, and often persecuted minority group segregated from the population at large, either through choice or by force, especially in the cities of eastern Europe. In the U.S. today, the term is used by some exclusively in reference to compact concentrations of Negro residents. In this context, the term "black ghetto" is preferable.

[5]Ward, *Op. Cit,* Chapter 4.

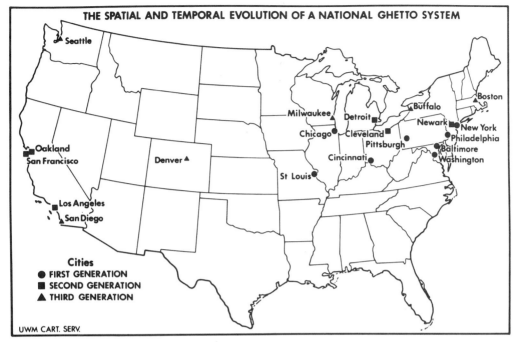

**Figure 12-7** The spatial and temporal evolution of a national ghetto system. *Source.* Harold M. Rose. Association of American Geographers, Comm. on College Geography; Resource Paper No. 6, 1969. Reprinted by permission.

they were concentrated earlier. However, although the ghetto dwellers gradually became assimilated into the general urban populations, the ghettos remained. In spite of renovation, demolition, and reconstruction, the same low cost housing areas remained to be occupied by still new waves of residents.

The first surge of new arrivals to major cities after the influx of immigrants from abroad were nonwhites migrating from regions of the nation that were experiencing accelerated economic change from an agrarian base to an industrialized base, particularly in the Deep South. In 1900, about 34 percent of the blacks of the U.S. resided in the South but an exodus began from this area in the decade 1910 to 1920, especially to urban centers in the North Central region.[6] By 1920, there were sizeable concentrations of American blacks, large enough to be termed ghettos (25,000), in seven cities in the North Central region. These early black ghettos might be termed the "old ghettos" (Figure 12–7).

The wave of nonwhite migrants to major cities outside the South continued to mount, strengthening the old ghettos and leading to the formation of new or second generation ghettos (Figure 12–7), as well as the expansion of black ghettos in cities of the Deep South. The black migrants tended to fill the void created by restrictive legislation of 1921 and 1924 which limited the number of European immigrants.[7] The pace of black migration quickened in the period 1940 to 1960, leading to the statement that " . . . it should be recognized that today's nonwhite urban in-migrant is the counterpart of yesteryear's European immigrant."[8] The paths of movement of the black migrant became more varied,

[6]Commission on College Geography, *Social Process in the City: Race and Urban Residential Choice*, Resource Paper No. 6, AAG, Washington (1969).

[7]Commission on College Geography, Resource Paper No. 6, *Ibid*.

[8]Paul F. Coe, "The Nonwhite Population Surge to Our Cities," *Land Economics*, Vol. XXV, No. 3 (August, 1959), p. 199.

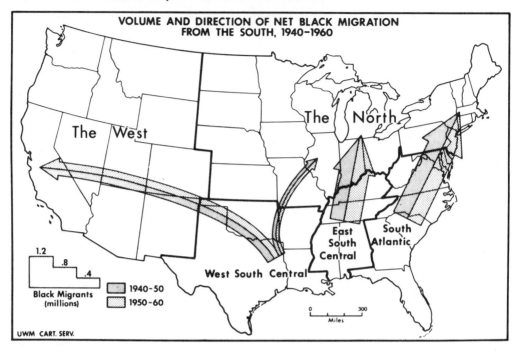

**Figure 12-8**    Volume and direction of net black migration from the South: 1940–1960. *Source. Ibid.,* Figure 12-7. Reprinted by permission.

with a considerable volume moving to cities of the West. As a result, the black ghetto came to characterize most large American cities, and the rise of third generation ghettos (Figure 12–8).

The black ghetto was, at least initially, located in one or more of the low-income, low-rent zones on the margin of the central business district that might be referred to as slums or blighted areas. In this spatial setting, the black migrants competed for the same housing with the earlier immigrant groups who often prevailed. There was, however, a common unwillingness of the white socio-eonomic groups of the same level to share the same living areas with the more recently arrived black residents. This produced a somewhat polynucleated system of ghettos in the same general roughly concentric zone ringing the central business district and provided for some of the chronic social unrest there. It has been stated that the black ghetto

gains its foothold in zones originally occupied by the Jewish ethnic group which has gained the social and economic mobility to move out of the original ghetto situation.[9] It also has been disclosed that the black ghetto dweller occupied housing that was more costly than comparable housing for his white counterpart and that his housing was more likely to be located in a poverty area and be of substandard quality (Figure 12–9).

In the 1960's and 1970's, several additional culture groups came to the larger cities in significant numbers. These groups tended to concentrate in the same general zone as did the earlier arrived groups, marginal to the CBD, shared the same low-cost and substandard housing, and formed ghetto concentrations. The Mexican immigrant was inclined to settle in a nucleated manner in cities of the Far

[9]Commission on College Geography, Resource Paper No. 6, *Op. Cit.*

West, especially Los Angeles.[10] The Puerto Rican immigrants were attracted in the 1960's especially to New York and Chicago, while in the late 1960's and 1970's, the Cuban refugees, arriving in

such, however, that before one group could vacate the ghetto situation, a further immigrant wave emerged, destined for the same residential zone and the same general types of housing. As a

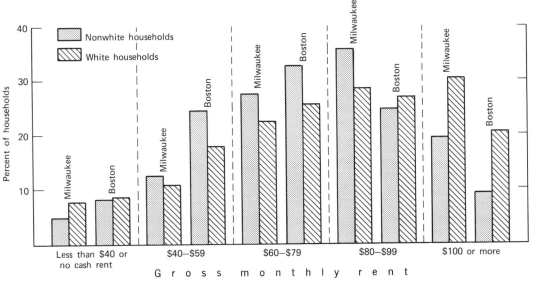

**Figure 12-9**  Race and rent in Milwaukee, Wisconsin and Boston, Massachusetts: 1960. *Source.* Based on data in Harold Rose, *Assoc. of Amer. Geographers Resource Paper No. 6.,* 1969.

the United States, formed nucleated settlement clusters in Miami.

The major point here is that the residential zone of the city roughly encircling the central business district, characterized by overcrowding and high population densities, substandard housing, and low cost housing, has served as the urban home in larger cities of a series of diverse groups in the historical development of the city. One group settled in this zone originally but gradually was replaced in whole or part by a different group of migrants destined for the urban center. This process of replacement and succession has been experienced a number of times and has taken on different forms involving different culture groups in different cities. The pace of migration of urban migrants became

result, there is not a culturally uniform zone of low income and high density housing peripheral to the CBD, but a zone made up entirely or in part of a series of nucleated clusters or ghettos each providing residence for a given cultural or ethnic group. Programs have been adopted and attempts have been made to break down this ghetto structure, but the conditions that led to it in the first place tend to persist to the present.

Succession of different residential groups in the zone peripheral to the central business core involves the housing of different demographic groups of diverse culture, backgrounds, national origin, employment patterns, and race. Succession, as we have said, is also an ongoing process involving the replacement, in total or in part, of one population group with another in the same general zone or sector. It is meaningful to identify the factors that stimulate, encourage, and in-

[10]Richard L. Morrill, "The Negro Ghetto: Problems and Alternatives," *Geographical Review*, Vol. LV, No. 3 (July, 1965).

itiate this process. These can be associated with two forces at play in the city: *centripetal forces* that provide a rationale for localization or concentration of population groups and *centrifugal forces* that underlay the decentralization of the population groups inhabiting this residential zone.[11]

Centripetal forces that tend to stimulate the early concentration and continued maintenance of this zone with its polynucleated ghetto structure very often do not apply equally to all sectors of the residential population of this zone, but in the aggregate, apply to most (Table 12–1).

**Table 12–1** Centripetal and Centrifugal Forces in the Succession of Population Groups in the Zone Marginal to the Central Business District

Centripetal forces
1.  Stocks of available, low-cost housing
2.  Association with others of the same cultural group
3.  Nearness to places of employment
4.  Proximity to mass transportation
5.  Personal security and safety

Centrifugal forces
1.  Increased affluence
2.  Improved social mobility
3.  Upgraded occupational levels
4.  Increased residential space needs
5.  Fears and social conflict
6.  Decentralization of employment opportunities

Centrifugal forces exert an influence on the residential population of the inner residential zone, such as to draw residents from the zone to other residential zones of the city. However, they do not apply to the same degree to all groups in the zone, like blacks, but have applied significantly to other groups, for in-

[11]Charles C. Colby, "Centrifugal and Centripetal Forces in Urban Geography," *Annals of the AAG*, Vol. XXIII (March, 1933). The terms "centrifugal forces" and "centripetal forces" were used here in reference to users of land in the commercial core, not residential land users. The concepts are applicable to various types of urban land users, however.

stance, the Jewish ghetto groups. Also, because of different local attitudes, the centrifugal factors do not apply equally to all metropolitan areas and they may not apply equally to all urban centers at a specific time. They do, in the aggregate, indicate some of the basic factors underlaying the metamorphosis and succession of the residential zone in question.

## Other Residential Zones

With regard to acquisition of housing in the United States, the attitude has long prevailed that home ownership is desirable with this idea supported by a recent housing survey in which fifty-five percent of former renters gave this as a reason for moving from rented dwellings to owner-occupied dwelling units (Figure 12-10).[12] Home ownership likely is equated with more rooms in the dwelling unit and more living space. Twenty percent of new home owners, moving to new residential locations, moved to obtain a better home or better neighborhood. Among current renters, the reasons for moving were more varied and included new family formation (11 percent), new job (8 percent), reduction in family size of older households (8 percent), and a desire for smaller living quarters (7 percent) (Figure 12–10). For the residents in the mid-age range, major reasons for a move were a growth in family size, an increase in income, and a desire for a larger or better housing unit in a better neighborhood.

A profile of the residents occupying new dwelling units beyond the inner residential zone, then, discloses that they are in middle and lower-middle income groups, with many in the process of family formation. Most of this group seek more living and housing space, most are young (median age of 32 years for rental units and 42 years for owner occupied

[12]Department of Housing and Urban Development, *Housing Surveys, Parts 1 and 2*, Washington, Government Printing Office, 1969.

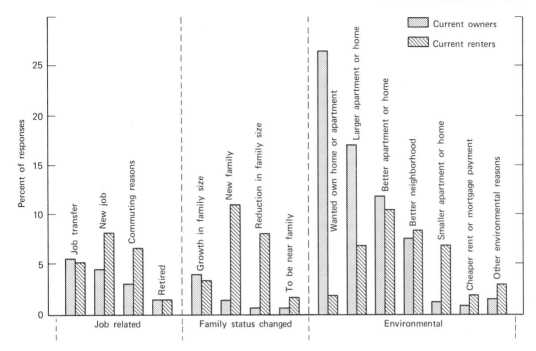

**Figure 12-10** Reasons for moving to new dwelling units. *Source.* Based on data in *Housing Surveys*, HUD; Parts 1 and 2 (1969).

homes), and almost all desire living in a better neighborhood in a better home that they purchase.[13] The mobility of residents in the housing market is not extended to all population groups, however. The residents of the ghettos of the inner residential zone, many of whom live at or slightly above the poverty level and who concentrate by choice or pressure into compact clusters, and the low income residents outside the ghettos, many of whom are elderly, are not the common beneficiaries of the improved housing opportunities in the broad zone of owner-occupied homes in residential neighborhoods in the middle and outer portions of the central city and extending into suburbia (Figure 12–11).

The pattern with regard to residential zonation and interzonal movement of urban residents appears to be shaped by several variable circumstances. There is a strong desire on the part of urban residents to acquire more spacious living

quarters or to purchase their own dwelling, preferably an upgraded dwelling in a better neighborhood. The types of dwelling units most desired are newer and more costly than ones presently occupied, and these are more frequently encountered in the middle and outer portions of the city. After the social and economic mobility of the residents increases and their space needs mount, especially through family formation, there is a tendency to abandon the former dwelling unit, particularly in the inner residential zone and acquire housing in the zone adjacent, the middle residential zone. In turn, residents of the middle zone often move to the outer residential zone as their mobility increases or as they desire a different life style. In the above process, there is continued movement from one residential zone to another as means become available, as needs mount for living space, and as desires change. The mobility needed for movement is not enjoyed by all, however, and many residents remain "locked into" ghetto living in the inner zone.

[13]Department of Housing and Urban Development, *Ibid.*

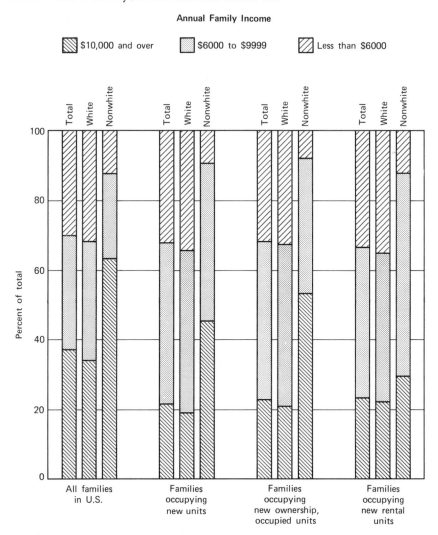

Figure 12-11   Annual income: all United States families and families occupying new dwelling units. *Source.* Based on data in HUD, *Housing Surveys:* Parts 1 and 2, Table 2 (1969).

Many have moved from this zone and continue to do so, but their places are generally taken by others migrating to the urban center from rural areas and smaller urban centers.

## Urban Population Densities

It is a truism to state that population is not evenly distributed within the city. Since, however, the urban population is not evenly distributed, how does it vary from an even distribution? In what parts of the city are densities the greatest and

in which parts are they the least? Further, are there regularities in the manner in which population distribution varies from an even distribution so that general conclusions can be made?

Before we approach these questions, however, one should be clear about the meaning of "population density." One expression of urban population density, or any population density for that matter, is the number of residents per unit of area, in this case, unit of urban area, without considering whether the area is devoted to residential uses. The concern here is simply for unit of urban area, regardless of the function to which the unit area is put. This expression of urban population density is referred to as *gross density (GD)* of population and is derived according to the equation $GD = P/GA$. In this equation, the number of people comprising the population of the city $(P)$ is divided by the total number of units of gross area of the city, whether they are number of acres, square miles, or some other unit of gross area $(GA)$.

A more refined measure of population density involves the number of people per unit of area devoted to a specified use, such as number of persons per acre of arable land. When you consider urban residential population densities, the comparison is between number of persons per unit of area devoted to residential uses, again, in acres, square miles, or some suitable areal unit. In this measure, land area devoted to uses other than residential are omitted from gross land

area of the city. The residual is the land area that is devoted to residential use $(RA)$, and it is used for deriving the *net density (ND)* of the urban population according to the equation $ND = P/RA$.

There will, of course, be differences in density values, depending on whether they express gross density or net density (Table 12–2). In several respects, net density is preferable to gross density, but is more difficult to obtain since land use data often are not disaggregated into discrete land use classes, one of which is residential use. For large cities, the ratio between gross and net densities tends to fall in the range of 1:2 to 1:4, with the greatest differentials reflecting disproportionate amounts of land used for nonresidential uses, expecially industry as in the case of Chicago, for public and institutional use, as with San Diego, or large amounts of land that remain vacant and unpopulated, such as Phoenix.

For comparative purposes, it may be

**Table 12–2**  Gross and Net Population Densities for Selected American Cities[a]

| City | Gross Density (GD) | Net Density (ND) | GD/ND Ratio |
|------|--------------------|--------------------|-------------|
| Akron, Ohio | 5,387 | 14,010 | 1:2.60 |
| Atlanta, Georgia | 3,802 | 8,514 | 1:224 |
| Bridgeport, Connecticut | 10,381 | 23,088 | 1:2.22 |
| Buffalo, New York | 13,552 | 39,191 | 1:2.89 |
| Chicago, Illinois | 15,836 | 50,000 | 1:3.16 |
| Dallas, Texas | 2,428 | 9,354 | 1:3.85 |
| Denver, Colorado | 6,956 | 12,538 | 1:1.80 |
| Des Moines, Iowa | 3,240 | 9,812 | 1:3.03 |
| Detroit, Michigan | 11,964 | 28,694 | 1:2.40 |
| Miami, Florida | 8,529 | 18,961 | 1:2.22 |
| Oakland, California | 6,935 | 21,272 | 1:3.07 |
| Phoenix, Arizona | 2,343 | 9,165 | 1:3.91 |
| Providence, Rhode Island | 11,592 | 35,690 | 1:3.08 |
| San Diego, California | 2,979 | 14,470 | 1:4.86 |
| San Francisco, California | 16,599 | 52,482 | 1:3.16 |
| Seattle, Washington | 6,295 | 17,683 | 1:2.81 |
| Springfield, Massachusetts | 5,271 | 15,398 | 1:2.92 |
| Torrance, California | 5,050 | 14,853 | 1:2.94 |

[a]Density, as used here, refers to number of people per square mile.
Source:   Population data from 1960 Census of Population. Land use data from Allen D. Manvel, "Land Use in 106 Large Cities," *Three Land Research Studies*, The National Commission on Urban Problems, Research Report No. 12, 1968.

necessary to deal with gross densities, rather than net densities, but the seriousness of this is lessened when one considers that residential land accounts for the greatest share of the land area of the city.

## Urban Population Density Models

Turning again to questions posed in the preceding section having to do with spatial differences and patterns in the density of population within the city,

**Table 12–3**  Gross Population Densities in Cities of Different Size Groups: Selected Cities in Illinois, 1970

| City | Population | Gross Density |
| --- | --- | --- |
| Chicago | 3,366,957 | 15,126 |
| Rockford | 147,370 | 4,309 |
| Peoria | 126,963 | 3,395 |
| Springfield | 91,753 | 3,641 |
| Rock Island | 50,166 | 3,609 |
| Danville | 42,570 | 3,300 |
| Galesburg | 36,290 | 2,975 |
| Highland Park | 32,263 | 2,689 |
| Streator | 15,600 | 2,644 |
| St. Charles | 12,928 | 2,085 |
| Peru | 11,772 | 2,402 |
| Woodstock | 10,226 | 2,176 |
| Murphysboro | 10,013 | 2,329 |
| Benton | 6,833 | 1,708 |
| Cairo | 6,277 | 1,846 |
| Salem | 6,187 | 1,406 |
| Galena | 3,930 | 1,404 |
| Fulton | 3,630 | 1,650 |
| Hamilton | 2,764 | 953 |

SOURCE:  Bureau of the Census, *1970 Census of Population*, Number of Inhabitants, United States Summary, December, 1971.

these vary a great deal among cities. The culture area within which the city is located, the age of the city, the economic functions performed by the city, the size of the city's population, and the physical setting in which the city exists all have a bearing on spatial patterns of population densities within cities (Table 12–3).

Still, those who have studied urban population densities have found simi-

larities and regularities in urban densities such that models have been developed that express the statistical relationships between population densities and urban distance. Models here, as elsewhere, allow for the expression of general relationships, associations, and/or regularities. They may not apply to each individual case, but do express a condition of normalcy pertaining to the type of entities included in development of the model. In a sense, a model is a formalized manner of expressing a general situation or condition.

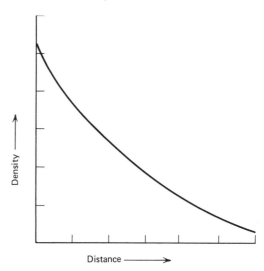

**Figure 12-12**   First degree negative exponential curve, as recognized by Clark.

One of the earlier models dealing with urban population densities stated that urban population densities, outward from the center of the city, decline exponentially with distance and graphically take on the form of a first degree negative exponential curve.[14,15] This is to say that the population density is highest at the center of the city and gradually de-

[14]Colin Clark, "Urban Population Densities," *Journal of the Royal Statistical Society*, Vol. 114, Part 4, 1951.

[15]A first degree curve is one that has only one basic change in slope; a negative curve is one that trends from upper left to the lower right on a graph; and an exponential curve is one that changes slope in accordance with application of an exponent to one of the variables plotted on the graph.

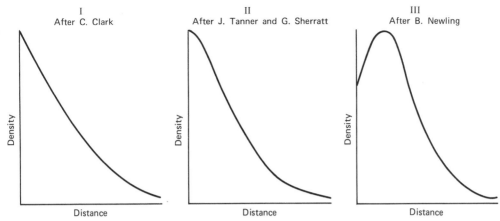

I
After C. Clark

II
After J. Tanner and G. Sherratt

III
After B. Newling

Density

Distance

Density

Distance

Density

Distance

**Figure 12-13**   Different suggested density profiles.

creases until the outer limits of the city or urban area are reached. However, since this is an exponential decline in density, it proceeds at a much greater rate nearer the city center, with the density declining at a gradually lower rate as the margins of the city or urban area are approached (Figure 12–12).

An alternate model of urban population densities was developed independently by J. Tanner and by G. Sherratt.[16] This model suggests that densities decrease rather slowly in the first incremental distance zone outward from the city center, then the decline accelerates appreciably until the outer margins of the city are approached at which distance the decrease in density slows again (Figure 12–13).

Still later, another alternate formulation of urban population densities was developed. This concept of B. Newling is a further extension of the model of Tanner and of Sherratt because it suggests a relatively low density near the core of the city, with densities increasing in the incremental zone nearest the city center and reaching maximum density levels some distance from the center of the city

(Figure 12–13).[17] Just beyond the outer margin of the central district, there exists a *density rim or crest* which surrounds the *density crater* of the central business district. Outward from the density rim, the densities decline in a negative exponential manner to the urban fringe (Figure 12–14).

It may be possible to incorporate the above models, each somewhat different from the others, into one concept of spatial variation in urban population densities. This is done by recognizing that densities expressed by one or another of the models represent the situation at a certain stage in the developmental process of the city during which there is areal expansion of the city as well as a redistribution of the city's people. Four distinct stages in urban development can be recognized, each with a different structure of population densities.[18] The first of these stages is identified as the stage of *youth* during which the population is relatively restricted areally. The densities during this stage are closely approximated by the model of Clark (Figure 12–15). During this stage, the population is especially concentrated near the business core of the city, reflecting the lack of means of mass or rapid transportation. The next stage in the develop-

[16]J. D. Tanner, "Factors Affecting the Amount of Travel," *Road Research Technical Paper*, No. 51, Department of Scientific and Technical Research, London, 1961.
G. G. Sherratt, "A Model for General Urban Growth," *Management Science, Models and Techniques*, New York, 1960.

[17]Bruce Newling, "The Spatial Variation of Urban Population Densities," *Geographical Review*, Vol. 59, No. 2 (April, 1969).
[18]Newling, *Ibid*.

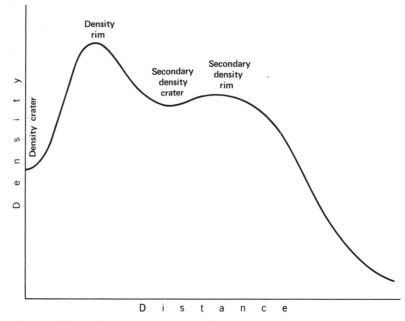

**Figure 12-14**   Idealized density profile.

mental process is *early maturity* which is characterized by areal expansion of the city beyond its earlier margins and a greatly increased density adjacent to the commercial core. The close-in zone is being more densely settled at the same time that urban settlement is spreading outward. A model of population densities at this stage is in general accord with the concepts of Tanner and Sherratt. At a later time, the stage of *late maturity* is reached and is typified by still greater

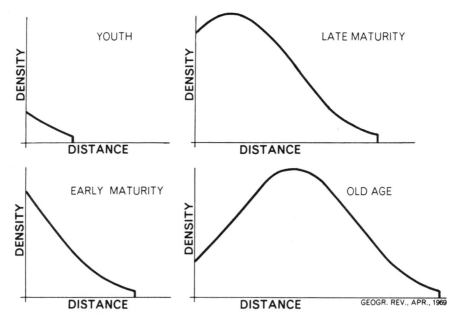

**Figure 12-15**   Urban density profiles at different stages in the development process. *Source.* Bruce Newling, "The Spatial Variation of Urban Population Densities". 'Reprinted from the *Geographical Review, Vol. 59,* 1969, copyrighted © by the American Geographical Society of New York'.

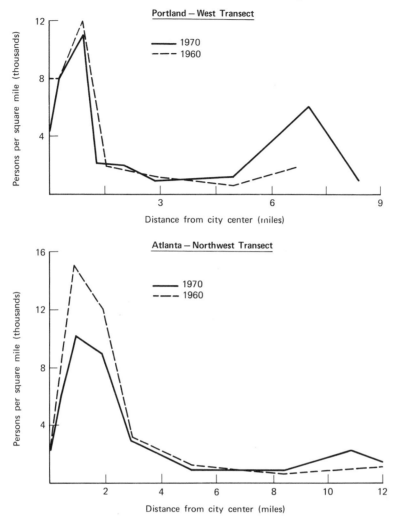

**Figure 12-16** Changes in urban residential density profiles: Portland, Oregon and Atlanta, Georgia.

peak densities and areal extent of the population. Also, there emerges at this stage a density crater that is accounted for by the lowered desirability of residence in the commercial core and the ability of commercial users of close-in land to outbid residential users, reflecting the areal expansion of the central business district. Around the density crater that emerges in this stage, there exists a density rim representing high population densities in areas adjacent to the central business district (Figure 12–15).

A still later stage of urban development is characterized by a somewhat altered density curve expressing still greater areal expansion of the city, by a deepened density crater, and by a density rim that is still further removed from the commercial core of the city. This stage is identified as the *old age* stage of urban development, and a model of population densities during this stage closely approximate the model suggested by Newling (Figure 12–15).

The basic elements of population densities in the development of the city are, then, (1) the early negative linear or near linear relationship between distance from the center of the city and population densities, (2) a later curvilinear relationship of a negative exponential type,

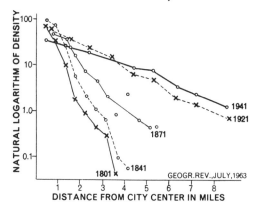

**Figure 12-17** Changes in the urban density curve of London: 1801–1941. *Source.* 'Reprinted from the *Geographical Review, Vol. 53,* 1963, copyrighted © by the American Geographical Society of New York'.

(3) the later emergence of a density crater and a density rim along with increased areal expansion of the city, and (4) the continued outward movement of the density rim and a broadening and deepening of the density crater (Figure 12–16).

Changes in the pattern of urban population densities through time are illustrated in Figure 12–17. Over nearly a century and a half, the city of London has experienced a flattening of the density curve, has become progressively less compact, and has expanded areally, with densities becoming greater as a function of increased distance from the city center.

Change in urban density curves can be also discerned over a relatively short span of time, as well as over an extended time span. A study of densities of the Toronto Metropolitan Area for 1951, 1956, 1962, and 1963 (twelve years) reveals a continued outward shift of peak population densities and of the density rim.[19] Based on statistical treatment of density data, the authors were able to predict density curves for 1966 and 1971, demonstrating the utility of models of urban population densities, not only to describe the past and present conditions and patterns, but to predict future situations as well (Figure 12–18).

## Urban Population Densities in Different Culture Areas

According to Clark, spatial variation in population density generally conforms to the empirically based equation $d_x = d_o e^{-bx}$,

where: $d_x$ is the population density ($d$) at distance ($x$) from the city center;

$d_o$ is the central density as extrapolated;

and    $b$ is the density gradient.

[19]Robert F. Latham and Maurice H. Yeates, "Population Density Growth in Metropolitan Toronto," *Geographical Analysis*, Vol. 2, No. 2, Ohio State University Press (April, 1970).

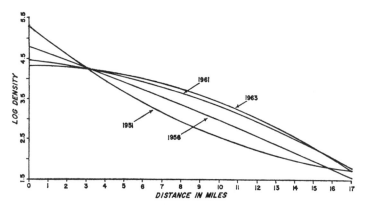

**Figure 12-18** Changes in the urban density curve of Toronto: actual and predicted, 1951–1971. *Source.* Reprinted from "Population Density Growth in Metropolitan Toronto," by Robert F. Latham and Maurice H. Yeates, in *Geographical Analysis*, Vol. 2 (April, 1970), Copyright © 1970 by the Ohio State University Press.

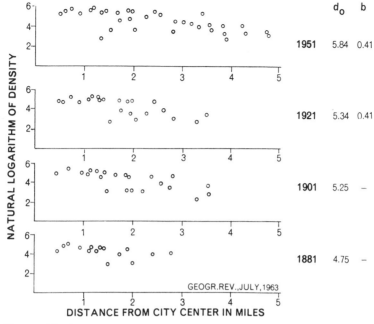

**Figure 12-19**   Urban population density curves of Calcutta: 1881–1951. *Source.* 'Reprinted from the *Geographical Review, Vol. 53,* 1963, copyrighted © by the American Geographical Society of New York'.

This indicates a lessening of density with distance from the city center in a negative exponential manner. For a number of cities considered in Clark's study, this equation was said to describe the spatial variation of population density for Western cities, but not for non-Western cities where density gradients remained relatively constant (Figure 12–19).

In contrasting population densities in Western and non-Western cultures, significant differences emerge. Western cities experience steady decrease in density gradients and degree of compactness at the same time that central densities first increase and later decrease. The same conditions of change do not, however, characterize non-Western cities. In the case of Calcutta, central densities increased steadily during the period 1881 to 1951 and, although there was areal expansion of the urbanized area, the density gradient remained relatively constant.[20] This characteristic of

continued overcrowding and maintenance of a high degree of compactness appears to be representative, not only of the rest of India, but of the bulk of the non-Western world as well.

Alonso has shown that the rich in Western cities tend to live on the periphery of the city on relatively inexpensive land, but consume more of it, with resultant lower densities than the poor who live in the central area of the city.[21] If, in Western cities, the poor live near the city center and the mobile and affluent at the periphery, in non-Western cities, the reverse is true. The groups with the least spatial mobility reside on land at the periphery and improvement of income levels leads to greater demands for central locations, with resulting increases in overcrowding. The degree of compactness of non-Western cities remains relatively unchanged. As stated by Berry, Simmons, and Tennant, "In spite of reductions of transportation costs in non-Western cities, the groups located

[20]Brian J. L. Berry, James W. Simmons, and Robert J. Tennant, "Urban Population Densities: Structure and Change," *Geographical Review*, Vol. LIII, No. 3 (July, 1963).

[21]William Alonso, "A Theory of the Urban Land Market," *Papers and Proceedings of the Regional Science Association*, Vol. 6, 1960.

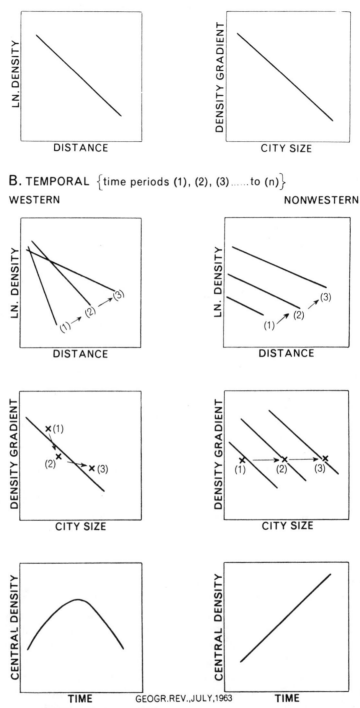

**Figure 12-20**  Comparison of density curves: western and nonwestern cities. *Source.* Reprinted from the *Geographical Review, Vol. 53,* 1963, copyright © by the American Geographical Society of New York.

where the possibilities of saving are greatest are the groups least able to take advantage of the possibilities".[22]

Western and non-Western cities differ in the manner in which population densities change, then, with differences in change of two parameters, central density $(d_o)$ and density gradient $(b)$. In Western cities, central densities increase, then decrease, while the density gradient drops steadily (Figure 12–20). Still later in the developmental process, the central density decreases, while suburbanization occurs and is manifested in a falling density gradient. Non-Western cities experience a continued increase in central densities and a relatively constant density gradient.

## Population Densities and Size and Age of Cities

The models of urban population densities discussed in previous sections apply, for the most part, to large cities of metropolitan status that have experienced spatial growth in a relatively uniform manner in all directions outward

from the city center. They do not take into account different ages of cities, each developing under different types of constraints and influences, even though located within the same culture area. It is most likely, however, that size and age of cities have a bearing on spatial aspects of population densities of urban centers, which is true of sectoral spatial growth of the city, as opposed to an inferred uniform spatial growth.

A recent study discloses that there are, in a single culture area, variations in central densities between large and small cities, as there are between old and new cities.[23] Further, there are variations in density gradients between small and large cities and old and new cities.

Because of regularities found in urban population densities in Midwestern cities of the United States, distinct density profiles can be established for large and for small cities of different age classes. Larger cities have greater central densities than do small ones, but small cities have steeper density gradients than do larger cities in each age class (Figure

[22]Berry, Simmons, and Tennant, *Op. Cit*, p. 404.

[23]John S. Adams, "Residential Structure of Midwestern Cities," *Annals of the Association of American Geographers*, Vol. 60, No. 1 (March, 1970).

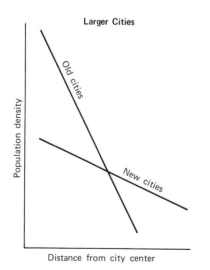

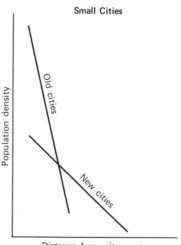

**Figure 12-21**  Density profiles for cities of different sizes and different ages. *Source.* Adapted from John S. Adams, *Annals* of the Assoc. of American Geographers, March 1970.

12–21). Midwestern cities are in an intermediate position between the density profiles of the older cities of the eastern seaboard and New England and the newer cities of the southeast and the southwest. Thus, it can be said that, though the same models might apply to cities of different sizes and ages within the same basic culture region, the manner in which they can be applied is variable.

An interesting association is made between urban population densities in cities of different ages and different eras in the development of urban transportation. It is suggested that with each significant improvement or change in urban transportation, there is a distinct burst of housing construction in zones outward from the city center to take advantage of this improved transportation and mobility. Four distinct transport eras can be recognized as follows:[24]

   I. The walking/horsecar era: to the 1880's
  II. The electric streetcar era: 1880's to World War I
 III. The recreational auto era: 1920's to 1941
 IV. The freeway era: post World War II

Each transport era experienced during the life span of the cities and developed during the period covered, was associated with a different spatial form of residential growth. Eras I and III were relatively restrictive and produced a generally circular form of residential growth as concentric zones with fairly uniform density gradients outward in all directions from the city center Eras II and IV led to an articulated form of residential growth with lower density gradients in the directions of extensions of streetcar lines or, later, in the direction of the axes of urban freeways. Perhaps, the same distortion would result, but in a modified manner, from lesser highway improvements, such as widening, straightening,

[24]Adams, *Ibid.*

or limited access. The point to be made here is that, in addition to the size and age of the city as influences on urban population densities, the specific form taken by the city, as it expands areally in response to improved transportation, has a significant bearing on the nature of urban population densities.

## Spatial Variation in Quality of Urban Housing

It has been inferred that differences exist in the quality of housing with individual cities; furthermore, it can be suggested that there are regional variations in residential quality as well. In a study of 209 American cities with populations of 50,000 or more, it was found that there is considerable variation in quality of urban housing, based on the criterion of rent or housing cost as an indicator of quality.[25] Variation in housing quality was more pronounced in central cities than in non-central cities (Figure 12–22). Also, it was indicated that regional differences exist in quality of urban housing. Regions with especially high measures of intraurban variation in residential quality are (1) southeastern United States, with the exception of Florida, and (2) southern New England. In these regions, there is a greater likelihood of a wider range in quality of urban housing in a given city.

## Concepts of Blight, Slums, and Substandard Housing

In writings dealing with urban housing, there is a virtual plethora of terms used to identify housing of different

[25]Roland J. Fuchs, "Intraurban Variation in Residential Quality," *Economic Geography*, Vol. 36, No. 4 (October, 1960). Fuchs considered other indicators of housing quality, as had earlier investigators, but concluded that rent or housing cost served quite well as an indicator of housing quality.

An earlier, but similar study was conducted by George W. Hartman and John C. Hook, "Substandard Urban Housing in the United States: A Quantitative Analysis," *Economic Geography*, Vol. 32, No. 2 (April, 1956).

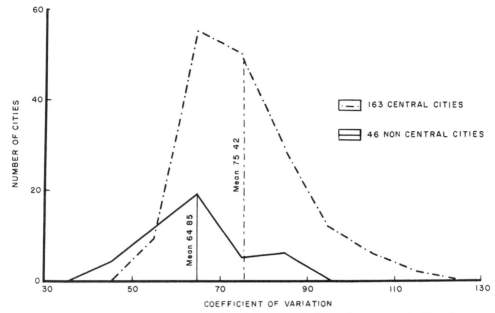

**Figure 12-22**   Variations in quality of housing: central city and noncentral cities. *Source.* Roland J. Fuchs, "Intraurban Variation in Residential Quality," *Economic Geography,* Vol. 36, No. 4 (October, 1960).

quality types. With regard to lower quality housing or to areas of such housing, there are a number of terms used, although no precise meanings are accepted for them.

It appears that the term "slum" originally was used in reference to social group as much as to a particular section of the city where the 'social pathologies' of alcoholism, disordered family life, prostitution, and the like are common occurrences. In addition, slums are neighborhoods with given structural characteristics. They are old, the houses are aesthetically displeasing to the slum definer, the rents are relatively low, and the houses are crowded.[26] Consistent with this concept of slums, the term has both physical and social connotations—a particular social group occupying a discrete housing setting.

The term "urban blight" often is used interchangeably with 'slum,' yet there appear to be differences between the terms. Blight is a somewhat less inclusive term, referring to physical characteristics of urban housing, more than to the social

characteristics of the occupants of such housing. One author states that "urban blight designates a critical stage in the functional or social depreciation of real property beyond which its existing condition or use is unacceptable to the community."[27] In this sense, the major concern is the functional depreciation of real property (loss of productivity) of the area involved. To be sure, the concept of blight can be extended to nonresidential areas, since they too can experience a lowering of functional attributes and value.

The term "substandard housing" is quite often used in regard to low quality housing, but is probably the least acceptable. If reference is made to substandard housing, the inference is that there is, in fact, a standard housing against which the substandard housing is compared. This is conceptually difficult to accept.

Blight, then, might be associated with selected variables pertaining to urban housing. A study of urban blight in cities in California of populations over 10,000

[26]Scott Greer, *Urban Renewal and American Cities,* The Bobbs-Merrill Company, 1965, p. 21–22.

[27]G. E. Breger, "The Concept and Causes of Urban Blight," *Land Economics,* Vol. XLIII, No. 4 (November, 1967), p. 372.

in 1960 disclosed that the incidence of blight was most closely correlated with (1) percent of the dwelling units that were renter occupied, (2) percent of nonwhite owner occupied units, and (3) median number of rooms in the dwelling unit.[28] Thus, blight is most closely associated with areas where there is a high incidence of rental units, a high proportion of dwelling units occupied by nonwhites, and a tendency toward relatively small dwelling units, all of which are fairly characteristic of residential units in the inner residential zone of the city, either within or without ghettos. A blighted area is one in which the housing units are predominately dilapidated or suffering deterioration; physical conditions of the structures involved.

## From Slum Clearance to Urban Renewal

In the latter years of the Great Depression of the 1930's, there arose increasing dissatisfaction with housing conditions in the United States, especially in urban centers. Slums existent at the time were viewed as undesirable and out of this attitude came the Housing Act of 1937, which provided for slum clearance and replacement with subsidized public housing. Eventually, this resulted in construction of approximately three million public housing units for the low income segment of the population, and the demolition of a similar number of dilapidated dwelling units.[29] Often, the public housing units were constructed on the sites where slums had been razed, thus the slum dwellers settled in the same areas as before in residential structures that were not appreciably improved, as indicated by the reference made by critics that public housing was "slums with hot running water."[30]

[28]Fred E. Case, "Prediction of the Incidence of Urban Residential Blight," *Papers of the Regional Science Association*, Vol. 11, (1963).

[29]Greer, *Op. Cit.*

[30]Housing and Home Finance Agency, *Federal Laws: Urban Renewal*, Washington, GPO, (1961).

Public housing programs proved unpopular as originally structured and in 1949, a Housing Act was passed by Congress that authorized Federal assistance to slum clearance and urban renewal. A subsequent Housing Act in 1954 broadened the provisions of sections of the Act to authorize Federal assistance in the prevention of the spread of slums and urban blight through the rehabilitation and conservation of blighted and deteriorating areas, in addition to the clearance and redevelopment of slums.[31] This, then, paved the way for urban renewal, and not just slum clearance. The Housing Act of 1956 again broadened the scope of Federal assistance by authorizing relocation payments to parties displaced by an urban renewal project, and making funds available for the preparation of "General Neighborhood Renewal Plans." The Housing Act of 1957 approved greater capital funds with which urban renewal projects were undertaken. The Housing Act that was passed in 1961 provided for still more Federal grants to cities, and a greater share of project costs to be borne by the Federal government. Several facets of urban housing emerged in this series of Housing Acts: (1) there developed a national housing policy, (2) the federal government assumed a greater role in administering and funding programs to upgrade low quality or blighted housing, and (3) planning was necessitated that not only would remove pockets of undesirable housing (blighted areas), but would assure that the same condition did not reemerge or spread.

## Elements of the Urban Renewal Process

Urban renewal, as it exists in the United States, might be viewed as a process consisting of stages undertaken in a successive manner. The process begins with the establishment of eligibility of the

[31]Housing and Home Finance Agency, *Ibid.*

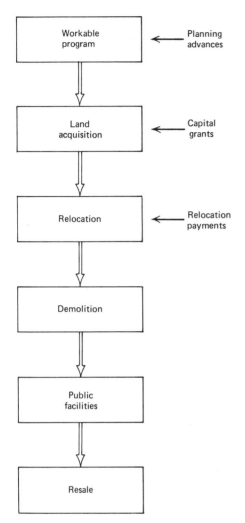

**Figure 12-23** Stages in the urban renewal process.

city to participate in federally assisted programs, (Figure 12–23).

Eligible communities must have a "workable program" of community improvement designed to prevent as well as eliminate the spread of blight. This workable program consists of a number of objectives: (1) adequate local codes and ordinances effectively enforced, (2) a comprehensive plan for development of the community, (3) analysis of blighted neighborhoods to determine treatment needed, (4) adequate urban renewal administrative organization, (5) ability to finance local share of costs, (6) plan for rehousing displaced persons, and (7)

community citizen participation.[32] Notice too the need for local planning, funding, organization and citizen involvement. For the development of a workable program, the federal government may advance funds or provide loans to local public agencies, such as a local urban renewal or redevelopment agency.

After eligibility has been established and a workable program developed, the local community, through its public agencies, can begin the next stage in the urban renewal process. This involves acquisition of land in the area of blight, at this stage known as the urban renewal project, through direct purchase at "fair market prices." Many times, this can only come about through public condemnation of structures in the project. The funds for this purpose are made available to local governments in the form of capital grants to help defray the net project cost. The net project cost or deficit is the difference between the return from the eventual disposition of project land and the cost of carrying out the project. The federal government is authorized to contribute, in the form of capital grants, up to two-thirds of net project costs in most instances, and up to three-fourths in others. This stage often is a slow process involving the acquisition of many land parcels and transfer of title to the urban renewal agency.

As lands in the project area are acquired, residents, businesses, and other tenants of the area are displaced. Under urban renewal authority, the displaced tenants must be given aid in relocation and this is provided in several ways: (1) outright payments to the displaced person, family, or business concern to cover costs incurred in a move or for losses experienced in the move, (2) provision of special mortgage insurance on housing obtained in the private sector, and (3) aid in obtaining alternate housing in existing low rent, public housing projects in

[32]Department of Commerce, Area Redevelopment Administration, *Handbook of Federal Aid to Communities*, Washington, GPO, (June, 1961).

the community. The parties, displaced by an urban renewal project, must be provided for in terms of their relocation to new sites.

Upon completion of the relocation stage, there begins the stage of demolition. The project area is cleared of blighted buildings, residential or otherwise. Certain structures included in the area may, however, be judged structurally sound and consistent with the workable plan developed for the project area and may, therefore, be left intact.

After completion of the demolition stage, the land area is improved through grading and leveling and public facilities constructed. These include such things as new streets, widened streets, water mains, trunk sewer lines, street lighting, and gas and electric lines (the latter may be underground), all consistent with the workable program and the comprehensive plan for development of the urban renewal area.

Once the land is cleared and improved, and the public facilities are in place, the land in the project is made available to private parties for purchase and redevelopment in accord with the comprehensive plan for the project. It happens that there is sometimes a considerable time lag between the time urban renewal land is made available and the time it is purchased by parties in the private sector. Many times, the land is retained in public ownership and utilized for low income rental housing in high-rise structures under the administration of a local housing authority. If the land is acquired by a private party, the use made of it must be in accord with the comprehensive plan for the redevelopment of the project area. Further, private parties may offer a purchase amount that is substantially below the project costs, for example, the private buyer may offer $2 per square foot for a land parcel in an urban renewal site, and the project costs of making it available might be $3. In such an event, the difference is borne by the capital grant provided by the federal government. This course might be considered desirable since (1) the blighted area has been removed, (2) the area will be developed in a way that guards against the reoccurrence of blight, (3) the land in the project area is returned to the private sector, and (4) the land once again is placed on the tax rolls, restoring a source of tax revenue to the city.

There are urban renewal programs designed to deal with specific renewal problems in relatively uncommon urban settings. These have to do with renewal of blighted areas in the vicinity of urban colleges and universities and of major hospitals. The aim is to provide a cohesive neighborhood environment compatible with the functions and needs of these urban facilities.

## Some Emerging Problems Having to Do With Urban Renewal

Of the persons displaced by construction of urban renewal projects, many are elderly persons in less than good health subsisting on very low incomes. Formerly, they resided in low quality hotels and rooming houses that, if little else, provided low cost shelter. It was reported that in an urban renewal project in Portland, Oregon, of 392 individuals living in the area, 16 had incomes of about $40 per month, 280 had incomes of less than $100, and 110 less than $150.[33] There were found to be 230 dwelling units available in nearby areas that were of standard quality and priced within the financial reach of the tenants; an inadequate number considering the need. Perhaps more important was the fact that the displaced persons did not wish to abandon their former lodging places and resented having to move. This is not an uncommon attitude with regard to the people who are most directly affected by

[33]The Sunday Oregonian, *Urban Affairs Report*, June 4, 1967.

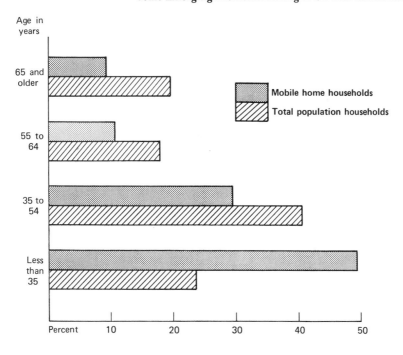

**Figure 12-24**  Comparison of age distributions: mobile home household heads and total population household heads. *Source.* Based on data in Dept. of Housing & Urban Development. *Housing Surveys,* 1969, Table 3, p. 82.

urban renewal, the residents of the blighted area to be renewed.

Another problem related to urban renewal programs is that new high-rise residential structures built under urban renewal programs have been only partially occupied, completely unoccupied, or never continued to completion. This is part of the phenomenon of abandoned housing that has reached serious proportions in some central cities, such as New York where 2 percent of the housing stocks are now said to be abandoned, and St. Louis where 6 percent of the stocks are in the same state of non-use.[34] Some, but not all, of this abandoned housing is within urban renewal areas.

Urban renewal projects in the inner city in the form of high-rise apartment complexes have not been successful in many instances, and private parties developing them have been confronted with financial difficulties so severe that they have had to default on mortgage payments and the Department of Housing and Urban Development has had to reassume ownership of the affected properties. A federal spokesman recently stated that HUD was contracting for the management of 45,000 to 50,000 apartment units that had been foreclosed.[35] In Dallas, of a total of 179 projects developed over three years, 1 in every 15 was in default. The same situation characterizes urban renewal projects in a number of other large central cities as well, indicating that urban renewal projects do not have the desirability for housing and the overall viability that was originally thought. The success of urban renewal is not yet established, although it has been as successful as planned in some cities. In the questionable cases, there has

[34]Reported on television documentary: *First Tuesday*, July 6, 1971.

[35]The New York Times, January 2, 1972.

been general upgrading of urban residences, though often at a higher cost to the dweller than they had been accustomed to paying, but there has not been a striking change in the urban environment within which the urban renewal dweller lives. In these cases, perhaps there has been formed a higher priced, more modern, antiseptic, and structurally sound slum—the old problem with a facelift.

## The Motionless Mobile Home and Modular Housing

A relatively recent housing phenomenon in urban centers, especially those of moderate and small size, is the development of mobile home clusters in a nucleated pattern in a discontinuous zone on the periphery of the city. They tend to serve the housing needs of two population groups, the younger couples in the beginning stages of family formation and the elderly and retired. A recent survey stated that mobile home output equalled about 18 percent of total conventionally built housing units and over 28 percent of the new conventionally built single family homes in 1967.[36]

One might consider the type of housing, urban or otherwise, that is provided for by the mobile home. The resident, as we have said, in a mobile home unit is younger than residents of conventional housing units (Figure 12–24). Further, the family size in these units is smaller (2.85 the median for conventional hous-

[36]Department of Housing and Urban Development, *Op. Cit.*

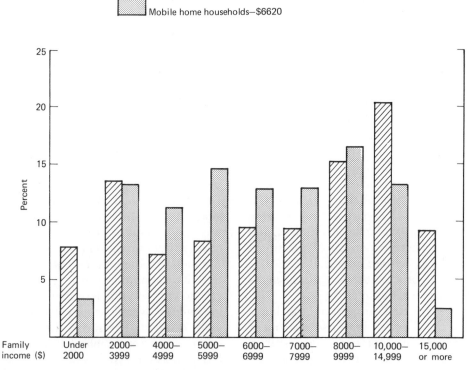

Median income

////  All families, 1967      −$7440

Mobile home households−$6620

| Family income ($) | Under 2000 | 2000– 3999 | 4000– 4999 | 5000– 5999 | 6000– 6999 | 7000– 7999 | 8000– 9999 | 10,000– 14,999 | 15,000 or more |

**Figure 12-25**  Incomes of all families and incomes of two or more persons mobile home households. *Source.* Based on data in Dept. of Housing & Urban Development. *Housing Surveys,* 1969, Table 12. p. 91.

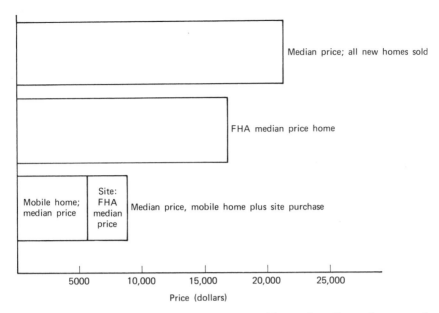

**Figure 12-26** Costs of new single-family dwelling units: all new homes and mobile homes. *Source.* Based on data in Department of Housing and Urban Development. *Housing Surveys,* Parts 1 and 2; Washington, 1969, p. 70.

ing and 2.49 the median for mobile homes), and the size of the unit, as based on number of bedrooms, is less for mobile home dwellers.[37] Also, the income levels of mobile home dwellers tend to be less than for residents in conventional housing units (Figure 12–25).

In a survey of mobile home dwellers, the most common reason given for a preference for this type of housing was the small cost of obtaining and living in mobile home units (45 percent of respondents). This raises the point of cost of housing in mobile home units, relative to costs of conventional housing units. Considering both the cost of the mobile home and the site it occupies, the capital outlay for this type of housing is approximately one-half to one-third that of conventional single family homes (Figure 12–26).[38] Remembering that income

levels of many urban households are relatively low at the same time that family size is small, the mobile home provides an alternative in obtaining urban housing, which means that low-cost housing for low income groups can be and is made available in this form. In addition to provision of lower cost housing, mobile homes appear to provide greater access of occupants to places of employment. The use of private automobiles to get to work is more common among residents of mobile homes than other workers (Figure 12–27). The combination of lower cost housing and housing more convenient to places of employment serve, then, as a dual stimulus for the trend toward occupance of housing of this type.

Regarding the matter of location of mobile homes, they are less associated with SMSA's than they are with smaller cities outside of metropolitan areas (Figure 12–28). The pattern is one in which mobile homes form clusters of dwelling units on the outer margin of the urban center, often beyond the corporate limits,

[37]Department of Housing and Urban Development, *Op. Cit.*

[38]Department of Housing and Urban Development, *Op. Cit.*

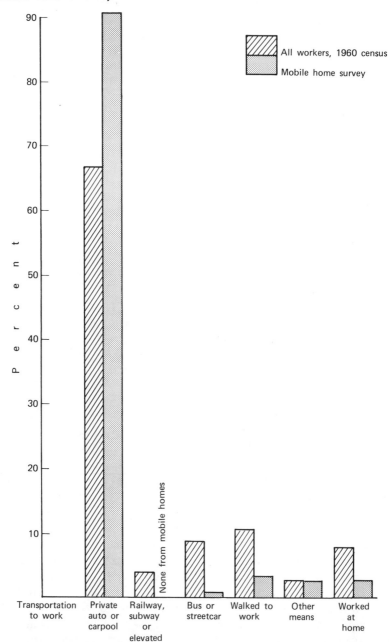

**Figure 12-27**  Means of transportation to work: all workers and mobile home household heads. *Source.* Based on data in Dept. of Housing & Urban Development, *Housing Surveys,* 1969, Table 13, p. 93.

constituting nodes of residential settlement of relatively high density and in proximity to other land uses of types that are conducive to the reduction of use and social conflicts. The distribution of mobile homes in the metropolitan area is of two different types, a clustering in a compact grouping, commonly referred to as a *mobile home park*, and a dispersed pattern of freestanding mobile homes

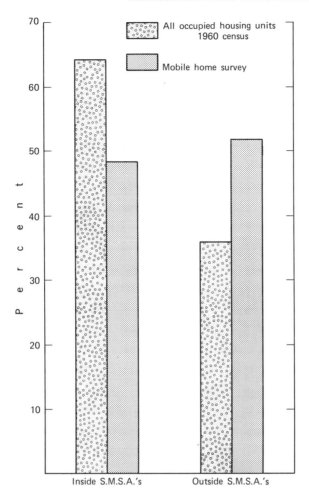

**Figure 12-28**  Location of housing units: all housing units and mobile homes. *Source.* Based on data in Dept. of Housing & Urban Development, *Housing Surveys*, 1969, Table 13, p. 93.

outside of mobile home parks. The more usual pattern is one of mobile homes located in mobile home parks on sites rented by the occupant (Figure 12–29). The mobile home parks include the greater number of dwelling units and the greater share of residential population, even with smaller family size per dwelling unit.

A still more recent advent in urban housing types is the housing module. These housing units are constructed in units in an industrial operation, such as individual room units, then transported by truck or rail to a development site where the individual units are assembled into a finished residence. This type of housing has the advantage of providing modern, somewhat individualized housing at relatively low cost and assembled on the site at great speed. The Department of Housing and Urban Development has funded several demonstration projects of this type in various cities of the country. In one instance, modular townhouse units, produced in Battle Creek, Michigan, will be transported 2300 miles to a demonstration site in

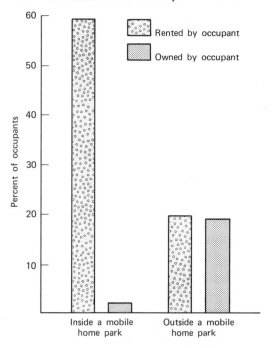

Seattle.[39] Other modular developments of single family homes and townhouses are to be undertaken in Kalamazoo, Michigan; Macon, Georgia; Sacramento, California, and Indianapolis, Indiana. There are problems, however, of adjusting this type of housing to local building codes, but if such obstacles can be overcome, this type of housing can aid in providing housing, especially low income housing, in urban areas.

[39]The New York Times, August 6, 1971.

**Figure 12-29**   Sites occupied by mobile homes. *Source.* Ibid., Figure 12-29, Table A-9.

# 13
# manufacturing in the city

Manufacturing has to do with the conversion of raw materials through inputs of capital, labor, and energy into higher value products to meet anticipated demands. Industry can be considered as any productive effort of man, one of which is the manufacturing industry. There are many types of manufacturing industries and, for clarification, it is desirable to group similar types into a common designation. The Bureau of the Census has developed a digital system of Standard Industrial Classification in which the broadest classes are named and

identified with two digit numbers, for example, textile mill products, SIC 22. A greater degree of specificity is gained by adding refinements to the name and by addition of a third digit, for example, cotton broad woven fabrics, SIC 221 or knitting mills, SIC 225. Still more detail can be added with use of a four digit classification. The major manufacturing groups that serve as points of reference in this chapter are two digit classifications, as presented in Table 13–1.

Each of the major manufacturing groups, subgroups, and individual establishments has its own distinguishing characteristics and mode of operation. Each has its own needs in terms of locational attributes and is influenced in selection of a site by different factors and combinations of factors. Various theories of industrial location have been developed and place major emphasis on transportation, raw materials, market, and labor (availability and cost).[1] Other locational factors that have a bearing on the location of manufacturing industries are, perhaps, not of such wide applicability, but do influence greatly specific types of manufacturing firms or single establishments. These include water supply, electricity supplies and cost, land availability and cost, administrative and tax policy, and a number of intangible factors, such as physical and cultural amenities.

Some manufacturing industries are geared to processing of bulky, relatively inexpensive raw materials with considerable weight loss in the industrial process, such as in lumber milling. Others process raw materials that are perishable and that experience considerable weight loss, such as many food products manufacturing plants. In both cases, such manufacturing establishments are most likely to be lo-

[1]These theories are reviewed in Melvin L. Greenhut, *Plant Location in Theory and Practice,* Chapel Hill, University of North Carolina Press, 1956 and in Walter isard, *Location and Space Economy,* Cambridge, Massachusettes Institute of Technology, 1956.

**Table 13–1**   Digital Classification of Manufacturing Industries

*Two-Digit SIC Codes for Major Industry Groups*

| SIC Code | Major Industry Group |
|---|---|
| 20 | Food and kindred products |
| 21 | Tobacco manufactures |
| 22 | Textile mill products |
| 23 | Apparel and related products |
| 24 | Lumber and wood products |
| 25 | Furniture and fixtures |
| 26 | Paper and allied products |
| 27 | Printing and publishing |
| 28 | Chemicals and allied products |
| 29 | Petroleum and coal products |
| 30 | Rubber and plastics products, n.e.c. |
| 31 | Leather and leather products |
| 32 | Stone, glass, and clay products |
| 33 | Primary metals industries |
| 34 | Fabricated metal products |
| 35 | Machinery, except electrical |
| 36 | Electrical machinery |
| 37 | Transportation equipment |
| 38 | Instruments and related products |
| 39 | Miscellaneous manufacturing |

*Seven-Digit SIC Codes, with SIC 20 as the Major Industry Group*

| SIC Code | Industry Breakdown | Industry Products, etc. |
|---|---|---|
| 20 | Major industry group | Food and kindred products |
| 203 | Industry group | Canned and frozen foods |
| 2033 | Industry | Fruits and vegetables, etc. |
| 20331 | Product class | Fruits |
| 2033113 | Product | Applesauce |

cated in areas with supplies of needed raw materials. Other manufacturing establishments are more influenced by other locational factors than raw materials obtained from industries in the primary economic sector, which includes agriculture, mining, forestry, and commercial fishing. They may have need for relatively large supplies of semi-skilled workers or for maximum proximity to consumers of the products manufactured. Such establishments would not be consumers of large amounts of raw materials that experience high proportions of weight loss. Indeed, there may not be any appreciable loss of weight in the manufacturing process so nearly all of the material transported to the manufacturing site appears in the final product, that is, there is little material of no value being received at the manufacturing site. These are the types of manufacturing that are usually located in or near major population centers where they take advantage of available supplies of workers, nearness to potential customers, and a number of other advantages of urban locations. For example, a bakery benefits by locating in a large city that provides ready access to the buyers of its products, food stores, which are concentrated in larger population centers.

Of the two digit industry groups, some are more characteristically found in urban areas than are others. In one large section of the United States, the East North Central Division, comprised of the states of Wisconsin, Illinois, Indiana, Ohio, and Michigan, differences are disclosed in the degree to which individual

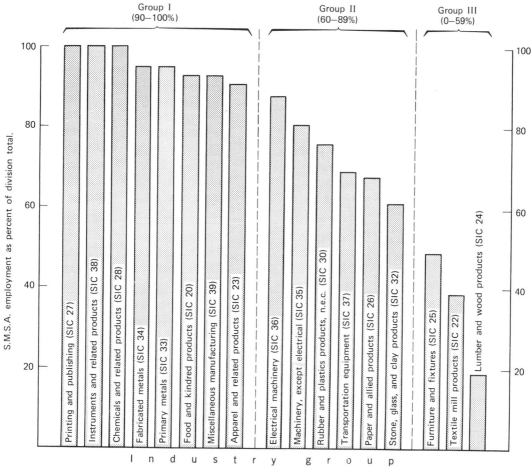

**Figure 13–1** Employment included in S.M.S.A.'s in the east-north-central division: Two digit industry groups. *Source.* Based on data in Department of Commerce, *Annual Survey of Manufactures: 1969*, Part 3 (March 1972).

industry groups are associated with large metropolitan areas. This association is based on the share of total divisional employment in a specific industry group that exists in S.M.S.A.'s in the region. The industry groups can be placed into three different groups, based on the degree to which they are associated with metropolitan areas, (Figure 13–1). The two-digit industry groups most associated with metropolitan areas in the geographic division are printing and publishing, chemicals and allied products, and instruments and related products, each of which have their entire reported employment in S.M.S.A.'s of the region.

The data presented in Figure 13–1 indicate the different degrees of association between various industry groups and metropolitan areas, that is, the importance of metropolitan area locations for certain industry groups. They do not indicate, however, the role of particular industry groups in metropolitan centers in terms of the industry mix. Most employment in a given industry group may be in metropolitan areas, but this may not make up a particularly large share of manufacturing employment in metropolitan areas. To provide some insight into this matter, the industrial structure of several large S.M.S.A.'s is considered, with the role of each industry group based on the employment in that group

(Figure 13–2). While all industry groups are found in urban areas, the ones most characteristic of large metropolitan areas are indicated in Figure 13–2. These are the manufacturing industries that most nearly satisfy the criteria mentioned for industries in urban areas.

One point to remember here is that manufacturing establishments may locate in a nonurban setting at a certain point in time, and the city may essentially grow up around them. Further, the locational or technological advantage offered by the

original location may be diminished or lost with the passage of time, yet the capital investment may be of such magnitude that the manufacturing operation continues with a lower level of profitability, even though other locations may offer greater advantages. This condition is referred to as *industrial inertia* which is the tendency to remain in place even though the advantages of that place are lessened. The presence of a chosen manufacturing establishment or a number of similar establishments in a city today may not ex-

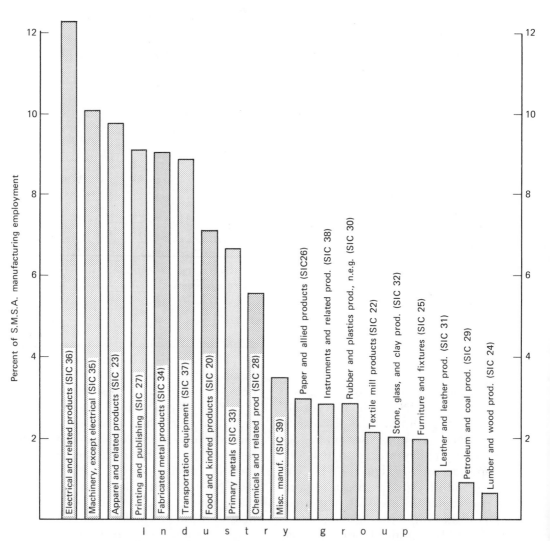

**Figure 13–2**    The industry mix of eight large S.M.S.A.'s, based upon employment: 1969. S.M.S.A.'s included are New York-NE New Jersey, Philadelphia, Los Angeles, Cleveland, Chicago-NW Indiana, Minneapolis-St. Paul, Kansas City, and St. Louis. *Source.* Department of Commerce, *Annual Survey of Manufactures: 1969,* (March, 1972).

press any particular locational advantage of that location, although it did offer an advantage at the time of inauguration of the manufacturing enterprise.

Another point to ponder is whether manufacturing enterprises are attracted to cities with their large populations, or whether people are attracted to manufacturing employment in the city where they add to the development and growth of the city in the process. Historically, the latter seems to have been the case, as in eighteenth century England during the Industrial Revolution and in nineteenth century America when waves of immigrants were attracted to large American cities.[2] Today, the reverse may be more common, with manufacturing concerns seeking population centers to gain access to larger consumer and industrial markets.

## Factors Influencing the Location of Urban Manufacturing Industries

A host of factors have a role in influencing the location of manufacturing industries and the role of any single factor varies between different industry groups, as well as between single establishments within a given industry group. Some of the factors apply more to a regional unit because they characterize a region more than any particular locality in that region. Other location factors apply more at the local level and recognize some locational advantage of a particular locality within the region. There are, then, *regional factors* of location and factors that influence *site location*. These distinctions were formalized in a classic theory of industrial location that assigns prime importance to labor, transportation, and raw material availability, and considers these as "regional factors of location".[3] Other factors, such as water supply, distribution facilities, public utilities, land availability and costs, mass transportation, electricity availability and cost, and tax structure are more in the realm of site location factors. With regard to location of manufacturing in urban areas, the site factors are especially important, since they influence the location of a manufacturing enterprise in a specific urban area as opposed to other urban centers in the same general region. The choice of the region is based largely on one set of factors, the choice of the urban area on another set of factors.

Of the various location factors, regional or local, the ones stated as being the most important to all industry groups are distribution facilities, transportation facilities, and tax structure.[4] In addition, availability of industrial sites, water supply, labor, and access to raw material supplies are given as important locational factors for food processing (SIC 20), and lumber and wood products (SIC 24). Labor supply is a prime locational factor for textile mill products (SIC 22), apparel and related products (SIC 23), and instruments and related products (SIC 38). Industrial fuel and power supply are of special significance to production of chemicals and chemical products (SIC 28), stone, glass, and clay products (SIC 32), primary metals (SIC 33), and machinery and metal products (SIC 34, 35, and 36). Illustrated here is the fact that the factors of location of manufacturing vary greatly between different industry groups, as stated earlier. There is perhaps more general applicability of the regional factors of location to all types of manufacturing than there is of the factors of site location. In this regard, all manufacturing enterprises produce tan-

---

[2] An interesting account of the English experience is presented in James Morris, *The Road to Huddersfield: A Journey to Five Continents*, New York, Pantheon Books (1963).

[3] Alfred Weber, *Ueber den Standort der Industrien*, Tubingen, 1909, translated by C. J. Fredrich as *Alfred Weber's Theory of the Location of Industries*, University of Chicago Press, Chicago, 1928.

[4] U.S. Department of Commerce, *Basic Industrial Location Factors*, Industrial Series No. 74 (June, 1947).

gible goods to serve a market that is are-ally distributed, they all utilize means of transportation to assemble raw materials and distribute their products, and they all have needs for workers who are areally distributed. However, the other location factors are quite variable with regard to their importance and do not apply generally or to the same degree to all manufacturing efforts. The urban center is the focus of a large number of consumers and transportation systems. Also, it is the place of residence of large numbers of workers, so it enjoys many of the regional attributes favorable to the location of manufacturing, plus some or all of the local advantages. Perhaps, one might consider which of the locational attributes are *not* provided by the urban center on the basis that the city can provide the remaining ones. Following this line of thinking, the location factors that are not generally provided by the urban center are raw material supplies and supplies of industrial fuels. For manufacturing industries, other than ones needing access to raw materials and industrial fuels, the urban center provides a favorable location based on both regional and site factors.

One means of attempting an evaluation of locational factors important to manufacturing concerns in urban centers is to consider the reasons given by industrial concerns for locating in a major American city. The results of such a survey are presented in Table 13–2. It can be noted that some factors are more important than others and that the degree of importance varies among industry groups. One can note, for example, the differences in importance to different industry groups of rail access, of a deep water dock facility, of systems of mass transit, and of proximity to the central business district. One aspect, not illustrated by surveys of what influenced the location of manufacturing concerns in a city, are the factors that influenced the rejection by other concerns of locations in

the same city. Until such a step is included, there cannot be many conclusive generalizations concerning industrial location in urban centers.

## Linkages in Manufacturing

We have said that each manufacturing concern operates on a site thought to offer locational advantages, and that concerns in the same general industrial group tend to be influenced in location by the same set of locational factors. The number of basic locational factors may be limited for some concerns or types of concerns, but more numerous for others, for example, two factors may be instrumental in site selection of establishments in one manufacturing group, while six factors may be basic in site selection of establishments in another manufacturing group.

One factor that bears on the location, distribution, and functioning of manufacturing firms in an urban area is that of *linkages* between manufacturing concerns. Linkages refer to the degree of dependence of a specific manufacturing concern on another, that is, the functional relationship between manufacturing concerns. Linkages can be expressed and measured on the basis of whether one establishment obtains materials and services from other industrial concerns in the same prescribed area and whether the output of one concern is sold to other industrial concerns in the area. Linkages deal with the interdependence of manufacturing concerns in the same area.

It follows, then, that the location of one manufacturing establishment and consideration of the factors underlying that location cannot necessarily be taken from the broader context of the total industrial structure of the area. Manufacturing plant $A$ may locate in region $X$ on the basis of two principal locational advantages. Subsequently, manufacturing plant $B$ also may locate in region $X$, but

**Table 13–2**  Factors Influencing the Location of Manufacturing Establishments: Portland, Oregon (1370 Concerns)

Location Factor
(Percent Considering Factor of Primary Importance)

| Industry Group SIC Code | Cost of Land | Rail Access | Near to Freeway or Four Lane Expressway | Deep Water Dock Facility | Proximity to CBD | Proximity to other Manufacturing or Service Process | Proximity to Minerals, Timber, or Agriculture | Short Home to Work Travel Time | Bus or Other Mass Transit | Availability of Sewer |
|---|---|---|---|---|---|---|---|---|---|---|
| Food and kindred products (20) | 47 | 53 | 30 | 10 | 14 | 9 | 16 | 15 | 21 | 82 |
| Textile mill products (22) | 62 | 42 | 0 | 8 | 8 | 17 | 8 | 42 | 33 | 62 |
| Apparel and textile fabrics (23) | 55 | 13 | 21 | 5 | 26 | 4 | 0 | 64 | 84 | 63 |
| Lumber and wood products (24) | 59 | 72 | 18 | 15 | 5 | 12 | 50 | 25 | 9 | 20 |
| Furniture and fixtures (25) | 66 | 48 | 41 | 4 | 11 | 8 | 4 | 27 | 12 | 37 |
| Paper and allied products (26) | 53 | 53 | 31 | 20 | 0 | 14 | 8 | 29 | 29 | 46 |
| Printing, publishing, etc. (27) | 60 | 2 | 18 | 2 | 48 | 28 | 0 | 31 | 26 | 62 |
| Chemicals and allied products (28) | 56 | 69 | 17 | 11 | 11 | 16 | 6 | 16 | 16 | 54 |
| Petroleum products (29) | 25 | 100 | 0 | 33 | 0 | 0 | 0 | 25 | 0 | 33 |
| Rubber products (30) | 33 | 33 | 17 | 0 | 0 | 17 | 0 | 50 | 50 | 66 |
| Leather and leather products (31) | 31 | 20 | 25 | 0 | 0 | 0 | 0 | 50 | 50 | 40 |
| Stone, clay, and glass products (32) | 46 | 38 | 47 | 11 | 15 | 20 | 20 | 31 | 4 | 35 |
| Primary metals (33) | 79 | 61 | 23 | 4 | 0 | 17 | 0 | 9 | 13 | 52 |
| Fabric, metal products (34) | 60 | 37 | 26 | 3 | 7 | 27 | 3 | 34 | 18 | 54 |
| Machinery, ex. electrical (35) | 68 | 20 | 15 | 6 | 16 | 27 | 2 | 25 | 16 | 50 |
| Elect. machinery and equipment (36) | 55 | 25 | 55 | 0 | 5 | 10 | 0 | 35 | 20 | 50 |
| Transportation equipment (37) | 75 | 5 | 37 | 14 | 0 | 14 | 0 | 38 | 5 | 52 |
| Prof. and scientific equipment (38) | 55 | 18 | 36 | 0 | 36 | 10 | 0 | 27 | 40 | 64 |

SOURCE:  Metropolitan Planning Commission, *Land For Industry*, Portland, Oregon (July, 1960).

not on the basis of the prime locational factors influencing the location of plant $A$. Plant $B$ may be functionally linked to plant $A$ in that it may use, as raw materials, products produced by plant $A$; this makes the location of plant $B$ contingent on the linkage to plant $A$, and to others that it may be linked to as well. An aluminum plant might serve as an example of the former (plant $A$) and a metal products plant producing aluminum luggage, an example of the latter (plant $B$). The products of the aluminum plant include sheet aluminum that might be marketed in the plant producing the aluminum luggage. In this case, there is a functional linkage between the two. The plant making the aluminum luggage, in turn, might also receive raw materials from other manufacturing concerns in the form of fabric components, metal or plastic hardware, paint, etc. (plants $C, D$, etc.) The latter firms are linked then to plant $B$, just as is plant $A$. Plants $C, D$, etc. may be more firmly linked to plant $B$ than is plant $A$, however, since plant $A$ was the first to locate in the region and before plant $B$, whereas plants $C, D$, etc. followed the location of plant $B$.

The linkages in manufacturing have been studied in a number of areas, one of which is Kane County, Illinois, just west of Chicago and including Elgin, Illinois.[5] Nearly all major industry groups were represented in the county and all had linkages with other major groups to varying degrees (Table 13–3). There are particularly strong functional production-consumption linkages in this area between certain types of manufacturing industries, especially involving (1) furniture and fixtures, (2) paper and allied products, (3) printing and publishing, (4) primary metals industries, (5) fabricated metal products, (6) non-electrical machinery and, (7) electrical machinery. These are the manufacturing industries that supply raw materials to other local industries, as well as to each other, and that consume some or all of the output of other local industries. This study provides insights into the existence of functional relationships between manufacturing concerns, but does not measure the magnitude of degree or strength of linkages or the role of different linkages in the industrial structure of the urban center. These questions are approached in a somewhat more rigorous manner through use of input-output analysis. The input-output matrix is similar to Table 13–3, except that monetary values are included rather than simple production and consumption occurrences, that is, in the latter case, a linkage may exist between industry groups, but no measurement is made of the dollar value of this linkage and, thus, the value to the local industrial economy. Input-output study is concerned with tracing the output or production of a given industry to other industries where it becomes an input. An outstanding example of input-output analysis of an urban economy is the Philadelphia Region Input-Output Study, which generated a number of related studies as well.[6] One of these studies dealt with manufacturing in the Phildadelphia economy and measured directly the supply linkages and indirectly the demand linkages.[7] In the latter case, the linkage identifies those local industries which experience large demand from the local economy, as measured by the number of times a local firm sells to a local industry and the value of the local sales.

Considering only two digit industry groups in the Philadelphia area, it can be seen that some are more firmly linked to

[5]John R. McGregor, *Manufacturing Linkages Within the Kane County Area*, Kane County Planning Department, 1967.

[6]Isard, Walter, T. W. Langford, Jr., and E. Romanoff, *Philadelphia Region Input-Output Study: Working Papers,* Regional Science Institute, Philadelphia, 1967.

[7]Gerald J. Karaska, "Manufacturing Linkages in the Philadelphia Economy: Some Evidence of External Agglomeration Forces," *Geographical Analysis*, Vol. 1, No. 4 (October, 1969).

**Table 13–3**   Number of Linkages Between Industry Groups: Kane County, Illinois

| Producing Group and SIC Code | Consuming Group, by SIC Code | | | | | | | | | | | | | | Totals by Group |
|---|---|---|---|---|---|---|---|---|---|---|---|---|---|---|---|
| | 20 | 23 | 25 | 26 | 27 | 28 | 30 | 32 | 33 | 34 | 35 | 36 | 37 | 39 | |
| Food and kindred products (20) | 2 | | | | | | | | | | | | | | 2 |
| Apparel and related products (23) | | 1 | | | | | | | | | | | | | 1 |
| Furniture and fixtures (25) | | | 5 | | | | | | | | | | | | 5 |
| Paper and allied products (26) | 8 | | 13 | 1 | 6 | 2 | 4 | 1 | 1 | 14 | 14 | 5 | 2 | 8 | 79 |
| Printing and publishing, etc., (27) | 3 | | 3 | 3 | 6 | 5 | 1 | 1 | | 6 | 7 | 3 | 1 | 3 | 42 |
| Chemicals and allied products (28) | | | 4 | | | | 1 | | | | 2 | 1 | | 1 | 9 |
| Rubber and plastics products (30) | | | 5 | | | | 2 | | | 2 | 2 | 1 | | 1 | 14 |
| Stone, clay, and glass products (32) | | | | | | | | 2 | | 4 | 5 | 1 | | | 12 |
| Primary metals (33) | | | 1 | | | | | | 5 | 5 | 18 | 10 | 3 | 1 | 43 |
| Fabricated metal products (34) | | | 15 | 2 | 1 | | 3 | 3 | 8 | 25 | 28 | 17 | 12 | 3 | 117 |
| Machinery, ex. elec. (35) | | | 1 | | | | | | | | 9 | | 1 | 1 | 12 |
| Electrical machinery (36) | | | 1 | | | | | | | | 6 | 5 | | | 12 |
| Transportation equipment (37) | | | | | | | | | | | 2 | | | | 2 |
| Miscellaneous manufacturing (39) | | | | | 4 | | | | | | | | | 5 | 9 |
| Totals; by consuming group | 13 | 1 | 48 | 7 | 17 | 7 | 11 | 7 | 14 | 56 | 93 | 43 | 19 | 23 | 360 |

SOURCE:   Adapted from John R. McGregor, *Manufacturing Linkages Within the Kane County Area* (1967).

other local industries than are others on the basis that a greater monetary share of their needed inputs is provided locally (Figure 13–3). The industry groups with the strongest local linkages include (1) apparel and related products (SIC 23), (2) lumber and wood products (SIC 24), (3) printing and publishing (SIC 27), (4) primary metals industries (SIC 33), (5) fabricated metal products (SIC 34), and (6) instruments and related products (SIC 38). Notice too that there are great differences in the value of purchased inputs by each of the major industry groups, which have different effects on the industrial sector of the economy.

Of the inputs acquired by Philadelphia manufacturing industries from local sources, some are acquired more frequently than are others. Thus, the magnitude of nonlocal inputs must be considered together with the frequency of acquisition of local inputs. The frequency of local purchases made by Philadelphia manufacturing firms in each two digit SIC groups is presented in Figure 13–4. The point here is that the impact on the manufacturing sector of the economy is different if one large purchase is made from one local supplier as compared with a number of smaller purchases made from a number of local suppliers. This

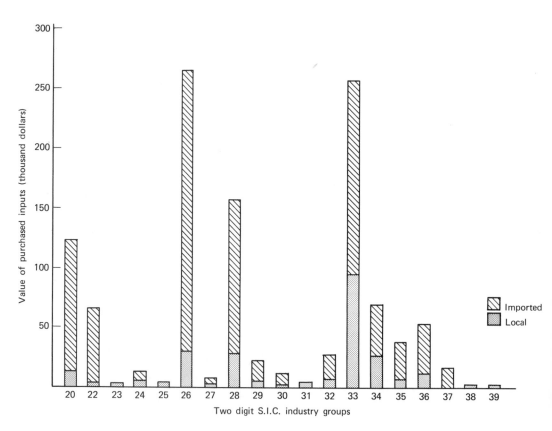

**Figure 13–3**   Value of locally purchased and imported inputs: the Philadelphia region. (20) Food and kindred products; (22) textile mill products; (23) apparel and related products; (24) lumber and wood products; (25) furniture and fixtures; (26) paper and allied products; (27) printing and publishing; (28) chemicals and allied products; (29) petroleum and coal products; (30) rubber and plastics products; (31) leather and leather products; (32) stone, clay, and glass products; (33) primary metal industries; (34) fabricated metal products; (35) machinery, except electrical; (36) electrical machinery; (37) transportation equipment; (38) instruments and related products; (39) miscellaneous manufacturing. *Source.* Data from Gerald J. Karaska, *Geographical Analysis,* October 1969.

will effect the industrial mix of the city involved and the employment structure as well.

In the Philadelphia region, the two digit SIC industries with the strongest local demand linkages are, in order, printing and publishing, lumber and wood products, fabricated metal products, and machinery.[8] The weakest local demand linkages are, in order, miscellaneous manufacturing, apparel, rubber and plastics products, and food. The largest inputs are obtained from nonlocal sources and the inputs that are purchased locally are small in size. Although the frequency of inputs from local sources is greater than from nonlocal sources, the value of the nonlocal inputs is considerably greater.

The effect of linkages, such as those discussed above, on the extent of agglomeration of manufacturing industries of similar types and within the same major group, is that a number of manufacturing establishments may obtain needed inputs from local sources and, in turn, supply other local industrial concerns. This produces a beneficial situation for all establishments involved in a complex system of linkages in manufac-

[8] Karaska, *Ibid*.

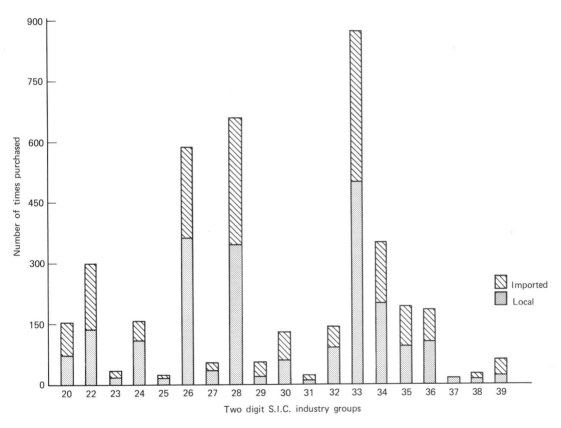

**Figure 13–4**   Frequency of local and imported input purchases: the Philadelphia region. (20) food and kindred products; (22) textile mill products; (23) apparel and related products; (24) lumber and wood products; (25) furniture and fixtures; (26) paper and allied products; (27) printing and publishing; (28) chemicals and allied products; (29) petroleum and coal products; (30) rubber and plastics products; (31) leather and leather products; (32) stone, clay, and glass products; (33) primary metal industries; (34) fabricated metal products; (35) machinery, except electrical; (36) electrical machinery; (37) transportation equipment; (38) instruments and related products; (39) miscellaneous manufacturing. *Source.* Data from Gerald J. Karaska, *Geographical Analysis,* October 1969.

turing. This provides a rationale for the existence of agglomerations of manufacturers of similar types. The location of a specific firm in a particular setting, then, may be explained by *agglomeration economies* as much as by any other factor. The presence of a given establishment in a given urban center may stimulate the coming of other firms that provide some or all of the inputs to the first or consume some or all of the output of the first. The impact of manufacturing linkages should be considered when attempting to understand the industrial structure of the urban area and the factors that provide a basis for its existence.

## Localization of Manufacturing in Urban Settings

Each urban manufacturing establishment occupies a discrete site in the city, determined by the decision makers responsible for the inauguration of the business enterprise. The objectives of such decisions are not clearly identified in all cases, however. One theory of industrial location holds that profit maximization underlies such decisions, while another contends that cost minimization is basic to such decisions. In any case, decisions as to location are made and manufacturing enterprises are begun. The sites of such operations are not, however, evenly distributed or randomly distributed within the urban setting. The existing advantages for location of one manufacturing establishment also influence the location of others. A chosen site may be not only desirable for a single establishment, but equally desirable for others with similar locational needs. Therefore, it is not uncommon to find agglomerations for manufacturing establishments in the city, with each sharing to some degree in the locational advantages. These agglomerations might be termed *industrial districts*. They are areal groupings or concentrations of a number of manufacturing establishments where manufacturing is the dominant use made

of the land, but not necessarily the sole use.

Different districts may be the setting of different types of manufacturing establishments, and different districts most likely originated at different times in response to different locational advantages and needs. With different commercial and residential districts originating at different times, and as commercial districts developed a polynucleated pattern, so did industrial districts. It can be said that the pattern of manufacturing districts developed in a series of stages. Because of the large investments involved and the greater inflexibility of manufacturing establishments, industrial inertia is more characteristic than is the inertia of commercial and residential districts. Succession and replacement are not as often encountered in manufacturing districts.

Three distinct stages can be recognized in the development of the distributional pattern of manufacturing districts in the large city of today. Each stage saw the development of industrial districts without benefit of planning and land use controls of today, that is, a spontaneous development pattern existed for the most part. A fourth stage of development of industrial districts has emerged more recently than the original three, but exists essentially as an overlay of the existing fabric and is not so much a discrete type. This stage, resulting in the development of the *planned industrial district*, is discussed separately.

The development of each of the three stages is based primarily on (1) existing energy sources or (2) available means of transportation for movement of raw materials, fuels, and finished goods. The stages and major characteristics of each are as follows:

Stage I:  Waterfront Districts—water transportation dominant; water and coal prime energy sources.

Stage II: Railroad Districts—rail transportation gaining in prominence; coal and petroleum prime energy sources.

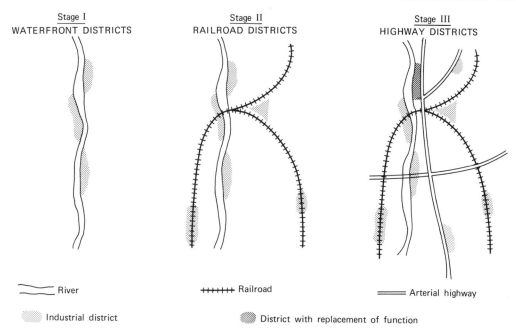

Stage I
WATERFRONT DISTRICTS     Stage II
RAILROAD DISTRICTS     Stage III
HIGHWAY DISTRICTS

~~~~~ River     ++++++ Railroad     ===== Arterial highway

▒ Industrial district     ▒ District with replacement of function

**Figure 13-5** Stages in the development of urban manufacturing districts.

Stage III: Highway Districts—motor vehicle transportation dominant, especially for short distance movements; petroleum and natural gas rising in importance as energy sources; increased use of electrical energy.

## Waterfront Districts

Major requirements of early factory type operations that replaced the earlier homecraft and cottage industries were the need for energy sources to power the newly developed industrial machinery, together with a means of transportation that lent itself to large volume and inexpensive shipments.

Early, the major sources of inanimate energy for this purpose were fast flowing streams, making streambank sites particularly desirable; especially if they could be used for shallow draft water transportation as well. Water could be harnessed at small waterfalls and could be diverted via millrace from the streams to overshot or undershot waterwheels which, through systems of belts, shafts, and pulleys, could activate the simple industrial machinery. Many of the early manufacturing operations in urban centers of Western Europe used water as a basic energy source. In the United States, waterpower was used for operation of sawmills and gristmills in New England in the seventeenth and eighteenth centuries and later was utilized in other sections of the Atlantic seaboard and in interior river valleys.[9] Development of manufacturing that used water as an energy source was especially great in the valleys of the Merrimack, Passaic, Connecticut, Susquehanna, Miami, Fox, and Rock Rivers. On some of the deeper waterways of the Atlantic Seaboard, shipbuilding, sailmaking, and ropemaking became prominent manufacturing industries.[10]

The earliest of manufacturing plants utilized riverside, lakeside, and bayside

[9]Edward P. Hamilton, *The Village Mill in Early New England*, Meriden, Connecticut, Old Sturbridge Village Booklet Series, 1964.
[10]Allan R. Pred, "The Intrametropolitan Location of American Manufacturing," *Annals of the AAG*, Vol. 54, No. 2 (June, 1964).

sites, and then, clusterings of establishments using the same power source and means of transportation came into being and the first of the industrial districts emerged. Somewhat later, steam engines came into use and coal became the major energy source. Again, waterfront sites were advantageous, since they provided a means of transportation for the needed fuel at low cost, plus providing water to be used in the boilers of steam engines if the manufacturing site was adjacent to fresh water supplies. This technological advance did not greatly alter the spatial pattern that was early established; it tended to reinforce it so that waterfront manufacturing districts became more widespread and the navigable waterways of the urban center became lined with such operations on one or both banks (Figure 13–5).

## Railroad Districts

In the nineteenth century, the railroad became commonplace as a means of transportation for raw materials and finished products and provided an alternative to waterborne shipments. Further, the railroad provided a means of moving the mineral fuel, coal, that was in increasing demand by manufacturing establishments.

Since the early developed waterfront sites tended to be adjacent to the commercial core of the city and relatively large scale operations were begun in this district, the major railroad terminal facilities were developed in this district as well. Further, the rise of wholesaling took place at this same general time and in the same general area, and this activity had functional linkages with manufacturing. Therefore, the juxtaposition of wholesaling and manufacturing served as an additional stimulus for continued dominance of waterfront districts after the coming of the railroad.

The manufacturing establishments became oriented to rail lines as well as to dockside as a result. When manufacturing industries expanded and grew in number, industrial sites in waterfront districts became less abundant and more costly. The railroads could serve non-waterfront sites, however, as well as those on the waterfront, so manufacturing operations came to be established in sections of the city more distant from the commercial core where large tracts of land could be purchased at lower cost. Quite commonly, manufacturing establishments came to line the major railroad lines converging on the urban center and formed attenuated railroad manufacturing districts.

Thus, a pattern began to emerge where the city developed a ribbonlike pattern of industrial districts along the waterfront, and along the major trunk railroads in the city. These were not so much continuous ribbons of uninterrupted manufacturing establishments, especially those of large size (Figure 13–5). Notice also that a greater degree of locational flexibility was effected with the onset of stage II, since alternative locations were possible for many, if not all, types of manufacturing establishments. The locational needs could be satisfied by different locational settings; orientation to waterfronts and to railroads.

## Highway Districts

In the twentieth century, with the coming of the truck and improved systems of highways, still more flexibility was offered in the location of manufacturing establishments. Intersections of major highways within the urban area became prime sites for manufacturing concerns, as well as for complementary warehousing, and many small nodes of manufacturing came into existence at such locations. With the coming of the freeway systems in the post World War II period, such as the Interstate Highway System, the advantages of sites with maximum access to a highway system became even more pronounced.

There were changes, too, in energy

needs of manufacturing, with electrical energy gradually replacing earlier types. This energy was transmitted via high voltage transmission lines, negating the need to import energy minerals, especially coal. Electricity could be produced hundreds of miles from the urban center and transmitted, rather than being produced on-site as before. During this stage, there also were significant changes in industrial operations, with horizontal line factories replacing the several story factories that dominated in previous stages. As a result, there were greater demands for larger land parcels which could be obtained more cheaply outside more intensely developed parts of the city with higher land costs.

The relationship between highway oriented manufacturing and overall manufacturing growth has been studied and it appears, for the United States, that proximity to the Interstate Highway System did not significantly influence manufacturing growth.[11] In this study, the number of new jobs per 1000 persons was 19 for freeway cities, while it was 16 for non-freeway cities. The same study indicated, however, that there are regional differences in the relationship between urban freeways and growth of manufacturing, with the association greatest in the Southeast, the East Midwest, and the Northwest. Further, it was disclosed that the 16,000 population level was the optimal breaking point for differentiation between cities which respond to freeways and those that do not, that is, larger cities react most to manufacturing growth and freeway development. Nationally, freeway cities above 16,000 outgrew nonfreeway cities in population to the ratio of 14 to 5.[12] The relationship between urban freeways and manufacturing growth is particularly pronounced for cities that have well developed com-

plementary air service and for smaller manufacturing establishments. Establishments with large work forces are not especially attracted to freeway locations as are smaller concerns.

In several respects, it is not surprising that manufacturing growth is associated more with freeway development in large cities, for in larger cities there has been more of an areal expansion of population and, therefore, of employees. Freeways developed to link the outlying areas with the core area of the city also become avenues of movement for workers in manufacturing establishments in districts at key intersections and at locations along frontage roads peripheral to freeway routes. As railroad industrial districts reflected to some degree the outward growth of the city, highway districts reflect even more this phenomenon. This stage was and still is characterized by development of industrial districts with ready access to major highway networks, especially on the outskirts of the urban area.

## The Pattern Today

In the city of today, we can find elements of each of the above stages in the development of manufacturing districts, each with its own locational pattern (Figure 13–6). The waterfront locations (stage I) are still utilized for manufacturing as they were in years past, for they still are advantageous for those types of manufacturing that require large inputs of low value, bulky raw materials and which ship large volumes of finished products. The railroad districts (stage II) are still existent and even expanding, for they too continue to offer locational advantages to some manufacturing concerns. In addition, they are actively promoted by the railroad companies who own much of the land adjacent to the railroad rights-of-way, as well as large tracts of land removed from the railroad line that were acquired through the system of land grants to railroads in the Un-

[11]Leonard F. Wheat, *The Effect of Modern Highways on Urban Manufacturing Growth*, Presented at the 48th Annual Meeting of the Highway Research Board, January 13–17, 1969.
[12]Wheat, *Ibid*.

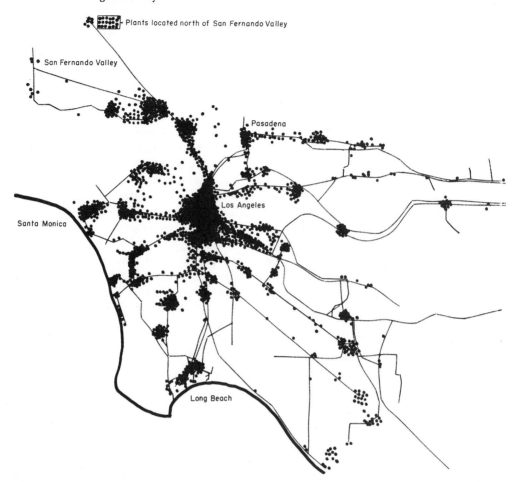

**Figure 13–6**  Manufacturing plants and locations on railroad lines: Los Angeles Basin. *Source.* Dudley F. Pegrum, "Urban Transport and the Location of Industry in Metropolitan Los Angeles." © *The Regents of the University of California, 1963.*

ited States. Highway manufacturing districts (stage III) are increasingly common in large and small cities and also are promoted and planned actively by developers of such districts and by local government agencies.

One might assume that waterfront districts active today utilize the waterways on which they are fronted, and that railroad districts include tenants that take advantage of railroad transportation. Here again, industrial inertia comes into play, for many sites on waterfronts do not utilize water transport to any significant degree and many located on rail lines do not use this form of transport. The initial advantage offered by each form of transportation has not endured, but the estab-

lishment has, especially in cases where the capital investment is significantly large and where other locational attributes are present. As an example of this circumstance, the association between manufacturing establishments in railroad districts and the use of railroads immediately adjacent to the establishments was investigated in Atlanta, Georgia by the author. It was found that relatively few establishments did, in fact, use the railroad even though it passed beside one edge of the manufacturing establishments. Often the tracks of spur lines were rusty, overgrown with weeds indicating nonuse, and sometimes rails were even removed. New truck loading docks had been constructed in some cases on the side of the establishment facing away from the railroad tracks, indicating a reversal of orientation to newer forms of transportation.

## The Planned Industrial District

The industrial districts recognized in a preceding section tend to have one common characteristic, other than the fact the area involved is devoted to industrial use. They were developed in a disorganized and unplanned manner, based on a number of individual or small group decisions. Consequently, many establishments came into being and formed a cluster or concentration befitting the term "district." There was little or no consideration given to (1) the effect of one establishment on others in the district, (2) the compatibility of the industrial district with adjacent land users, and (3) the total impact on the urban community. There were few controls exercised with regard to the spatial entity developed and the operation of the establishments included. Many times, there developed an unpleasant, disagreeable, and untenable industrial concentration, suffering from progressive deterioration and not operating as a viable unit might have.

To overcome these problems, toward the end of the nineteenth century in Western Europe and the United States, "a few organizations were set up for the purpose of assembling, improving, and subdividing tracts of land, and frequently for erecting factory buildings, according to a comprehensive plan, in advance of, or on demand, either for sale or lease to prospective industrial occupants. The plan provided for streets, rail lead tracks, and utilities and sewers, which were usually installed before the sites were sold or leased, or were otherwise assured to the prospective occupants. Control over the area and buildings was exerted by the developing agency through zoning and restrictive covenants incorporated in the deeds of sale or leases, with a view of pro-

tecting the investments of both developers and occupants and ensuring compatibility among the industrial activities of the latter."[13]

The above features are characteristic of the entities known today as planned or organized industrial tracts, districts or parks in the United States, trading estates or industrial estates in the United Kingdom, industrial zones in Italy, industrial subdivisions in Puerto Rico, and industrial estates in India and other countries. These industrial communities are differentiated from portions of a city reserved for industrial use by city zoning ordinances, from unimproved and unplanned tracts of land offered for sale as suitable for industry, or from sites improved for the use of an individual industrial establishment or of a very small number of industries. Thus, the concept of the planned industrial district developed, the first of which was established in 1896 in the United Kingdom in Manchester. The first such district in the United States was developed near Chicago in 1899 which, like the one in Manchester, was developed by private interests. The first public development of such a district was the industrial zone of Naples, founded in 1904 and managed by the city.[14]

Although the concept of the planned industrial district or estate originated and was implemented many decades ago, the number of such districts increased very slowly until the 1940's. The ones developed were mainly in the United States, the United Kingdom, and Italy. After World War II, however, the pace of growth of industrial districts in these countries accelerated greatly and they were developed as well in Canada, India, Brazil, and other countries. In Anglo-America, there are over 1200 industrial districts at present, most of them in the

[13]United Nations, *Establishment of Industrial Estates in Under-Developed Countries*, Department of Economic and Social Affairs, New York, 1961, p. 1.
[14]United Nations, *Ibid.*

United States. Of these, over 95 percent came into existence in the post World War II period (Table 13–4). In the United States, there is an uneven distribution of industrial districts, with states in the South, such as Georgia, Florida, and Texas, plus Ohio and Illinois in the Midwest, and California in the Far West having the greatest numbers (Figure 13–7). In the United States, most industrial districts are of small size; 68 percent include less than 200 acres and have a relatively small share of this area occupied by industrial tenants (Figures 13–8 and 13–9).[15]

The fact that many industrial districts in the United States have not been fully occupied reflects, in part, the objectives behind their development. Often, industrial districts are developed to encourage, promote, or stimulate industrial growth in a community in advance of actual demand for new industrial sites. In this sense, they are not developed to solve or alleviate existing problems, but to keep future problems from occurring. Therefore, industrial districts developed as growth outlets experience a time lag between the offering of sites in the district and actual occupance of the sites by industrial firms.

It is reported that the greatest share, approximately 70 percent, of industrial districts in the United States have been developed by profit-motivated private interests—industrial corporations, railroads, landowners, real-estate brokers, and contractors, with about one-fourth developed by nonprofit organizations, such as industrial foundations, chambers of commerce, and development commissions.[16] A smaller share is developed by local governments and by port and airport authorities. In any case, there usually are restrictions put on the tenants that are permitted to acquire sites

**Table 13–4**   Planned Industrial Districts in Anglo–America: 1965 by Year of Origin

| Year of Origin | Number of Districts | | |
| --- | --- | --- | --- |
| | United States | Canada | Total |
| 1965 | 35 | 0 | 35 |
| 1964 | 152 | 2 | 154 |
| 1963 | 119 | 2 | 121 |
| 1962 | 134 | 1 | 135 |
| 1961 | 94 | 4 | 98 |
| 1960 | 124 | 1 | 125 |
| 1959 | 91 | 4 | 95 |
| 1958 | 62 | 1 | 63 |
| 1957 | 55 | 2 | 57 |
| 1956 | 63 | 0 | 63 |
| 1955 | 46 | 2 | 48 |
| 1954 | 40 | 0 | 40 |
| 1953 | 13 | 0 | 13 |
| 1952 | 25 | 0 | 25 |
| 1951 | 13 | 1 | 14 |
| 1950 | 11 | 0 | 11 |
| 1949 | 4 | 0 | 4 |
| 1948 | 12 | 0 | 12 |
| 1947 | 4 | 0 | 4 |
| 1946 | 4 | 1 | 5 |
| 1945 | 2 | 0 | 2 |
| Before 1945 | 14 | 0 | 14 |
| Total | 1117 | 21 | 1138 |
| Not accounted for | 104 | 0 | 104 |
| | 1221 | 21 | 1242 |

Source: Compiled from *Industrial Development and Manufacture's Record* (March, 1965).

in the industrial district, based on the nature of their operation and compatibility with other tenants, plus controls put on their operations, such as issuance of pollutants, creation of vehicular congestion, and disruption of adjacent residential areas. In some districts, more properly known as "parks," there are controls placed on the aesthetic aspects of the district, with mandatory acceptance of landscaping, setbacks, controls on display signs, and structure design.

There is no consistent pattern developed with respect to the location of planned industrial districts. They are

[15]Ray M. Northam, "The Planned Industrial District in Anglo-America," *Yearbook of the Assoc. of Pacific Coast Geographers*, Vol. 27, 1965.

[16]United Nations, *op. cit.*

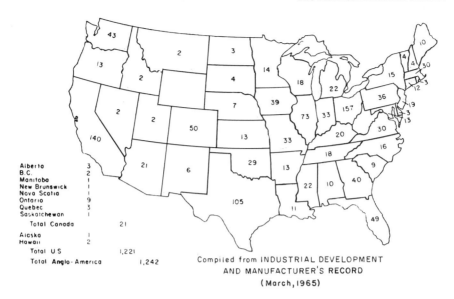

Compiled from INDUSTRIAL DEVELOPMENT
AND MANUFACTURER'S RECORD
(March, 1965)

**Figure 13–7** Planned industrial districts in Anglo-America. *Source.* Ray M. Northam, "The Planned Industrial District in Anglo-America," *Yearbook of the Assoc. of Pacific Coast Geographers,* Vol. 27, 1965. © Oregon State University Press, 1965.

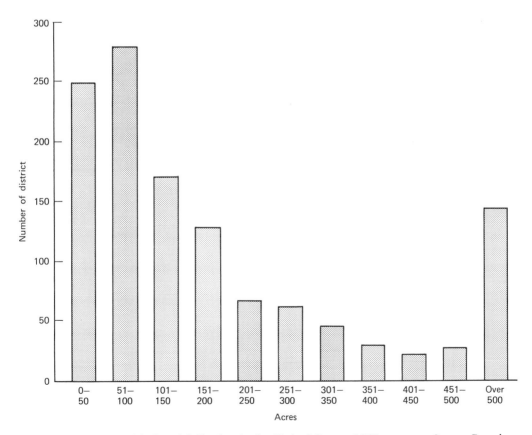

**Figure 13–8**   Planned industrial districts in the United States; 1965: acreage. *Source.* Based on data in *Industrial Development and Manufacturer's Record* (March 1965).

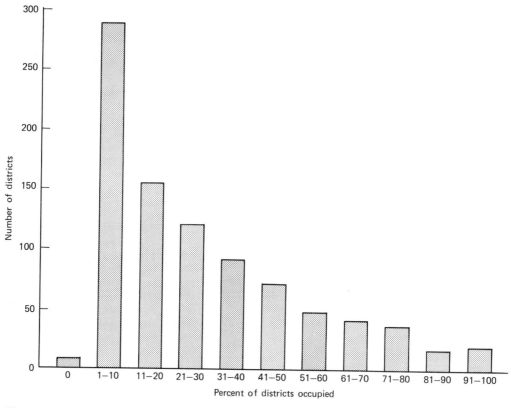

**Figure 13–9**  Planned industrial districts in the United States; 1965: degree of occupance. *Source.* Based on data in *Industrial Development and Manufacturer's Record* (March 1965).

found in large cities and in small ones, especially the latter. The development may include actual construction of multi-purpose buildings offered for sale or lease, or may involve the offering of sites only. Their location may be within the central city or, more commonly, on the outer margins of the city, based on lower land costs and greater land availability. If there is a common characteristic, it would appear to be that all industrial districts seek to maximize access to one or more means of transportation. Sometimes, the districts provide ready access to highway and rail transportation, at other times, to highway and air transportation (the "air parks").

Another general characteristic of industrial districts is that they are the site of operation of smaller industrial concerns of a more "footloose" nature, that is, they are not tied to a single locational factor, such as raw material supply. This tends to

be true in both developed countries and underdeveloped countries.

The notion that a planned industrial district is a "community of industries" recognizes linkages between different industrial operations and their general compatability. Thus, manufacturing establishments may be found in industrial districts along with warehousing operations and trucking depots. This concept fails to recognize, however, linkages between industrial operations and commercial operations needed for the functioning of the industrial tenants. For example, one or more gas stations in the industrial district or a branch post office might complement the industrial operations. There has been some recognition of this matter in some of the industrial parks in the United States, and acceptable tenants have come to include restaurants, motels, meeting facilities, the virtually ubiquitous gas station and, in at least one case, a golf course (Table 13–5). In these cases, there is not so much a community of industries, as there is a combination industrial-commercial district, with residential tenants excluded.

**Table 13–5** Tenant Composition: Swan Island Industrial Park; Portland, Oregon (as of March, 1964)

| Tenant Group | Number of Employees | Percent of Total Employment |
|---|---|---|
| Manufacturing | 907 | 29.3 |
| Trucking | 715 | 23.1 |
| Ship repair | 630 | 20.4 |
| Wholesaling–distribution | 507 | 16.4 |
| Government–administration | 217 | 7.0 |
| Other | 117 | 3.8 |
| Totals | 3093 | 100.0 |

SOURCE: Adapted from Columbian Research Institute, *Commercial Study: Swan Island Industrial Park* (April 1, 1964).

The planned industrial district, park, or estate represents a striking change in the development, management, and operation of industrial districts. There is concern given to the planning and spatial organization of such districts, where it has often been lacking in the past. The development of planned industrial districts supports the general decentralization of manufacturing in the urban center toward the outer margins and, in this regard, adds to the role of the outer zone of manufacturing. Regardless of the zone affected, however, it represents a new approach to the location and operation of manufacturing establishments in the city.

## Zonation of Manufacturing in the City

Reference has been made to different types of manufacturing districts in the city, based on different locational settings and advantages. These districts have not been considered within the context of a spatial organization, however, and any one of the districts mentioned could occur in different general areas of the city, for example, a waterfront district may be near the center of the city, on the outskirts of the city, or both. To provide a spatial context within which manufacturing exists in the city, zones can be recognized, with these based on distance increments outward from the center of the city. Any type of manufacturing district may exist within any one of the recognized zones.

In this presentation, three general zones are recognized and these are not based on regular distance increments, but general ones. The three general zones considered are (1) a central zone, (2) an intermediate zone, and (3) an outer zone (Figure 13–10). The central zone occurs in proximity to the central business district, the intermediate zone exists in the midsection of the city and includes more area than the central zone, and the outer zone includes the outer portions of the city and may extend into adjacent and contiguous suburban areas. It is logical to expect that each zone may be characterized by different types of manufacturing and that a specific major industry group may be concentrated in a particular zone.[17] By, contrast, a given major industry group may be dispersed fairly uniformly among all zones.

One major concentration of manufacturing plants and manufacturing employment in the city is an arc or concentric circle around the central business district. In this, the central manufacturing zone, the parcels of land used for industrial purposes tend to be intermixed with others characteristic of the transition zone discussed earlier (Chapter 9). If not within the transition zone, the industrial parcels are just outward from it. These

---

[17]This topic is discussed in Raymond J. Struyk, "Spatial Concentrations of Manufacturing Employment in Metropolitan Areas: Some Empirical Evidence," *Economic Geography*, Vol. 48, No. 2 (April, 1972).

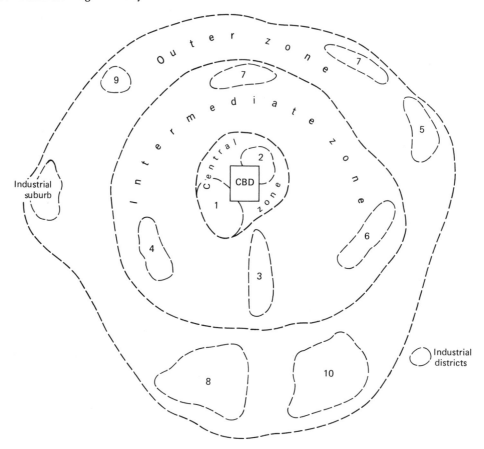

**Figure 13–10** Spatial pattern of manufacturing zones and districts in the city. Principal industry groups represented: (1) apparel; (2) printing and publishing; (3) food products; (4) textile mill products; (5) furniture and fixtures; (6) fabricated metals; (7) machinery; (8) primary metals; (9) chemical products; (10) petroleum and coal products.

sites enjoy the benefits of a waterfront location or of access to focal points of railroad systems and were devoted to manufacturing use early in the development of the city. On sites in the core area of the city, these establishments are subject to extreme congestion and conflict with other land uses, these serving as centrifugal forces for movement outward from the central zone for certain types of manufacturing. Employment in manufacturing establishments in this zone seems to be high in the aggregate, but low per establishment, that is, many smaller concerns each with relatively low employment (Table 13–6). Further, the land area of the average site in this zone tends to be small, with most of the site occupied by structures with little space devoted to ancillary use such as landscaping, offstreet parking, etc. (Table 13–6). The original sites tended to be small and little possibility was offered for expansion due to the competition for land for other uses in this zone. In general, this zone is one of numerous older and smaller industrial establishments on congested sites. Many of the manufacturing structures in this zone are in a state of dilapidation, deterioration, and abandonment, all characteristic of *industrial blight.*

But what are the types of manufacturing characterizing this zone today? The answer to this question depends on the particular city and the industrial structure of that city. However, some general

**Table 13–6**   Zonal Characteristics: The Central Zone, Selected Cities

| Characteristic | Portland[a] | Chicago[b,c] | Cleveland[d] | Minneapolis[d] |
|---|---|---|---|---|
| Number of establishments | 591 | 416 | — | — |
| Percent of total establishments | 48 | 24 | — | — |
| Manufacturing employment (zone) | 22,152 | 85,145 | — | — |
| Percent of total manufacturing employment | 38.1 | 19.4 | 14.82 | 11.10 |
| Mean employment per establishment | 37 | 205 | — | — |
| Area used for manufacturing (acres) | 376 | — | — | |
| Mean area per establishment (acres) | .64 | — | — | |

[a]Metropolitan Planning Commission, Portland, Oregon, *Land for Industry* (July, 1960).

[b]Department of City Planning, Research Division, Chicago, Illinois, *Locational Patterns of Major Manufacturing Industries* (November, 1960).

[c]Includes only firms of 50 employees or more.

[d]Raymond J. Struyk, *Economic Geography*, Vol. 48, No. 2 (April, 1972).

observations can be made. The establishments best represented in this zone are those that have lower space needs per worker, higher value of output per worker, and minimal needs of bulky, low value raw materials or finished product. This is to say that the use made of the land must be intensive and productivity must be high to offset the higher land costs and taxes. Also, the establishments seeking locations in this zone often have functional needs of other core area tenants, such as business and professional services. For some central zone manufacturing occupants, proximity to visitors, buyers, and suppliers from out of town is essential. The specific types of manufacturers concentrated in this zone include (1) food and kindred products, based on the inclusion of beverage industries, such as soft drink bottling plants and breweries (SIC 20), (2) apparel and related products (SIC 23), (3) printing and publishing (SIC 27), and (4) instruments and related products (SIC 38). With regard to the concentration of apparel and related products manufacture in the central zone, much of this activity occurs in "loft" space in stories of buildings above street level. Here, there is a high density of employees and relatively small allocations of land area per worker. Printing and publishing industries in the central zone share the same characteristic to some degree.

Outward from the central zone of manufacturing is the intermediate zone. This is a more polynucleated zone, comprised of a number of industrial districts that are intermixed with residential and commercial districts of the city. The advantages for manufacturing in this zone are that (1) there are more abundant stocks of land available for manufacturing use, (2) land costs are less than in the central zone, as is taxation, (3) there is less congestion and conflict with other land users, (4) there is less likelihood that other land users will outbid the manufacturing user of land, (5) there is adequate access to major rail lines and to arterial highways, and (6) there is greater proximity to residential areas from which workers are derived. Considering the perspective of time, as the city expanded areally, the only industrial sites available were in what was to become the intermediate zone, although at the time of development, this well might have been the outer margin of the city. When the city expanded still more, the manufacturing establishments were no longer in the outer zone, yet the inertia is such that they continue to operate.

The number of manufacturing establishments operating in the intermediate zone is comparable to that in the inner zone, largely the result of greater land area included in the intermediate zone. The number of manufacturing employees tends to be greater, however, indicating a greater number of employees per establishment (Table 13–7). Also, the average land area occupied by establishments in this zone is considerably greater than in the central zone. The greater land area is necessitated by greater storage space for materials and for warehousing, newer horizontal line plants, larger industrial structures, more space needed for materials handling, and greater allocations for employee parking (offstreet parking replacing onstreet). Also, provision is often made for plant expansion by acquisition of larger sites.

The major industry groups that are especially represented in the intermediate zone include those prominent in the central zone as well, such as food products, apparel and textiles, printing and publishing, and instruments. The greatest concentration of industrial operations, though, include industry groups not especially representative of the central zone—fabricated metal products (SIC 34) and machinery (SIC 35). In this zone are considerable numbers of establishments and employees involved in the production of such items as household appliances, fixtures, plumbing and electrical equipment, internal combustion engines and their components, and a wide variety of electrical motors and their components. In actuality, there is a wide variety of products produced in establishments in these industry groups. Employment in these establishments is rela-

tively high, often in the hundreds and thousands working in vast, sprawling structures on large sites.

Another characteristic of manufacturing in this zone is that there tends to be a nucleated pattern of manufacturing concentrations comprised of a number of discontinuous districts. Each district tends to include a number of firms engaged in the same major industry group, such as food processing in the now defunct stockyards district of Chicago. Likewise, there may be a district that includes a number of firms producing electrical machinery of different types or the components of electrical machinery, such as shafts, housings, armatures, etc. This degree of district specialization results, at least in part, from linkages between the different establishments in the same major industry groups and the sharing of common locational attributes.

Moving outward still further toward the outer parts of the city, there is another zone of manufacturing, the outer zone. This zone also has a polynucleated character, with the number of industrial districts comprising it tending to be less than in the intermediate zone. Each district seems to be larger, however, than those in the previous zone. Again, there is a tendency toward a district specialization, with each district representing a concentration of establishments in the same major industry group, that is, a district largely of paper mills, of steel mills, of oil refineries, etc.

**Table 13–7**  Zonal Characteristics: The Intermediate Zone, Selected Cities

| Characteristic | Portland | Chicago | Cleveland |
|---|---|---|---|
| Number of establishments | 403 | 861 | — |
| Percent of total establishments | 33 | 67 | — |
| Manufacturing employment (zone) | 19,161 | 221,249 | — |
| Percent of total manufacturing employment | 33 | 67 | 42 |
| Mean employment per establishment | 48 | 257 | — |
| Area used for manufacturing (acres) | 1,251 | — | — |
| Mean area per establishment (acres) | 3.1 | — | — |

SOURCE: *Op. cit.*, Table 13–6.

**Table 13–8**   Zonal Characteristics: The Outer Zone, Selected Cities

| Characteristic | Portland | Chicago | Cleveland |
|---|---|---|---|
| Number of establishments | 227 | 14 | — |
| Percent of total establishments | 19 | 1 | — |
| Manufacturing employment (zone) | 16,779 | 21,265 | — |
| Percent of total manufacturing employment | 29 | 6 | 25 |
| Mean employment per establishment | 74 | 1,519 | — |
| Area used for manufacturing (acres) | 1,162 | — | — |
| Mean area per establishment (acres) | 5.1 | — | — |

SOURCE: *Op. Cit.*, Table 13–6.

The establishments in this zone tend to occupy large sites so lower land costs and greater availability of land serve as locational attributes. Similarly, industrial operations in this zone tend to be those with lower levels of public acceptance and compatability with other land uses, in the context of general livability. By being in this zone, the industrial establishments experience less conflict with other land users, especially residential. Also, there is less congestion in this zone and provision of considerable access to major transportation terminals and routes.

This zone is characterized by large industrial establishments on large sites, with high employment per establishment (Table 13–8). Often, the output of establishments in this zone is destined for regional or national markets, rather than local markets, and the firms involved are large national corporations. Therefore, the land area necessary for such operations is great, since the establishments are of greater size and the area needed for ancillary facets of the industrial enterprise, such as materials handling, warehousing, and outdoor storage, is considerable.

There is less consistency regarding the industry groups common to this zone, except that they generally fall within the type known as "heavy industry." The specific types depend on the economic structure of the city and region. In Portland, the dominant industry group in this zone is paper and allied products (SIC

26), while in Chicago, it is primary metals industries SIC 33). In other cities, industries in the general class of "light industry" will dominate this zone, such as machinery manufacture (SIC 35 and SIC 36) in Boston, where heavy industry is not an integral part of the industrial structure.

The above section deals with the zonation of manufacturing in the city, differences between different general zones, and elements of the manufacturing structure of respective zones. It should be borne in mind, however, that a clear zonation of manufacturing may not exist in some cities, at least not in the manner presented. There could be a sectoral pattern, rather than a roughly concentric zonal pattern, especially in smaller cities. Also, the details as to role and structure of each zone could be expected to vary among cities as it likely would if cities in different world regions are considered. Any pattern of zonation in American cities may not be duplicated in cities in other nations of the world, developed or underdeveloped. Thus, there are many unanswered questions relating to the zonation of manufacturing in the city.

## Trends in Spatial Change of Urban Manufacturing

Much has been said and written about movement of manufacturing concerns and the development of new manufacturing enterprises in the suburban sections of the urban area, that is, the outer portion of the outer zone. The concern has been that this has served to the detriment of the central city and especially the core area of the central city. The record for the United States seems to support such statements and questions might be asked as to what advantages suburban locations offer that are not shared by the central city.

There is a generalization that the choice between an inner city or a suburban site for an industrial firm involves a trade-off between access and space.[18] Each of these factors deserves elaboration.

Access is directly related to the development of specialization that has come to characterize modern industry during its existence. Each manufacturing concern came to specialize in economic tasks in the most efficient units. Although each firm could produce more efficiently, the need remained to have access to other specialized functions for an integrated operation. Access to customers, suppliers, banks, utilities, transport facilities, employees and other supporting economic units was necessary for the particular firm to specialize in a single economic task. The main advantage of an inner city location for manufacturing is that it offers the least-cost access to each of the supporting specialized functions, such as those mentioned above. These locations were sought by many firms, however, leading to one of the main disadvantages of such sites—high cost of space and lack of available space. The demand for existing space was so great that a high degree of space utilization came about, and all available space was used intensely with little, if any, space allocated to off-street parking, truck loading docks, landscaping, and the like.

The result has been that old and new firms have tended to trade off some of the access advantage for more attractive sites at lower cost and in a better environment away from the urban core. Also, with improvements in communications and transportation, the suburban sites can offer much of the same access formerly provided by the inner city. A popular reason in surveys for site selection in suburban areas was the availability of land at low cost, but the partial loss of access was not commonly mentioned. But is this to say that future growth of urban manufacturing is likely to continue to take place in the suburban areas, with a commensurate decline in manufacturing in the central area? Is the latter area to become even more an area of "industrial blight?" Is the central city going to experience a continued loss of the tax base provided by manufacturing?

Several points bear on these questions. In a 1968 survey in San Francisco, the major reasons given by firms for locating within the city limits were fire protection, police protection, and public transportation.[19] Also, the importance of governmental services influences the location of manufacturing firms. The availability of city services, then, has a strong influence on the location of manufacturing firms, although the importance will vary among them. The desired services just mentioned can usually be offered at considerably less cost than they can in smaller suburban centers, which provides a distinct advantage for manufacturing sites in the inner city.

If blighted industrial areas in the inner city can be renewed or redeveloped, this, together with stated advantages of such locations, could serve as the impetus for a reversal or slowing of the trend toward zonal shifts of manufacturing, especially from the central to outer zones of the city. In fact, one writer states, "Since few central cities have 'good' sites available, it remains to create them by investing in programs of urban industrial renewal."[20] The major point is that the blighted industrial areas in the inner city have in-

[18]Leland F. Smith, "Inner City Industrial Districts: Is There a Future?," *Urban Land*, May, 1971.

[19]Leland F. Smith, *Ibid*.
[20]Leland F. Smith, *Ibid*, p. 8.

herent advantages for location of manufacturing. If there is renewal of these areas so that their desirability is enhanced, there could be a surge of manufacturing development in the inner city.

# 14
# transportation in the city

Transportation in the city can be viewed in two ways. One is the movement of people and commodities from points of origin, over fixed routes, to points of destination. The other deals with a type of land utilization in the urban center. The two contexts are not mutually exclusive, however, since transportation routes utilize urban land. In this presentation, transportation is examined in both contexts. A further distinction can be made in urban transportation between movement involving vehicles and that involving foot traffic, that is, vehicular traffic

and pedestrian traffic. These might be viewed as two distinct systems of transportation, each existing at a different scale and utilizing different modes of transportation, and often following different routes. In fact, however, the system of pedestrian movement is most often a subsystem within the major system of vehicular movement, since most pedestrian trips originate or terminate as vehicular trips.

The greatest share of trips made in the urban center involve movement of people rather than goods and the major problems of urban transportation revolve around people movement and the vehicles used. With the population of the city relatively dispersed and the existence of a multitude of possible destinations of trips made, the matter of generalizing about urban transportation is made difficult.

## Space Used for Transportation

Urban space for transportation exists in a variety of forms.[1] Urban space is needed in large amounts for transportation routes, public or private, and for terminals, whether for commercial vehicles such as bus depots, railroad stations and air terminals, or for private vehicles, like parking lots or above ground parking structures.

We have already said that about 23 percent of the land area of American cities over 100,000 is used for streets and roads, while in cities of smaller size, the proportion of the urban space used for this purpose is even greater. Added to this is the amount of area used for off-street parking in either public or private facilities. Each auto that enters the city and becomes a "vehicle at rest" necessitates about 300 square feet of space for parking, either onstreet or offstreet.

[1]"Urban space" is used here, in preference to "urban land," since transportation facilities utilize ground level space, space above ground level, and subsurface space as well.

When this is multiplied by the thousands of vehicles entering the CBD each day, there is need for many acres for vehicle parking. Surely, this necessary area can be reduced by underground parking or by above ground multilevel parking structures; both alternatives incidentally are taken as pressure on urban land mounts, and the potential user of urban space for parking can be outbid by other users of the same space. Another point about space for vehicle parking is that it is largely used for only portions of the day. The bulk of vehicle parking is for durations of four to eight hours, after which the space allocated to this use is not utilized at near capacity.

Another interesting alternative to lessen the need for vehicle parking came with enactment of the Federal-Aid Highway Act of 1961 which allowed states to permit use of airspace above and below interstate highways for parking of

vehicles, among other uses.[2] This alternative has not been widely adopted, but it may in the future as urban space problems become more critical. Concerning space needs for routes used by vehicles, the amount of land used for streets and highways in the city has grown in direct proportion to the number of vehicles operated. Presently, there is still an increase in amount of land used for this purpose through new route construction and route widening, and at the same time, there is little contraction of the amount of land so used, such as through street closure or abandonment. It appears to be very difficult to implement a street closure even today, even though strong arguments can be made for such action.

Another way in which urban land is

---

[2] Dana E. Low, "Air Rights and Urban Expressways," *Traffic Quarterly*, Vol. XX, No. 4 (October, 1966).

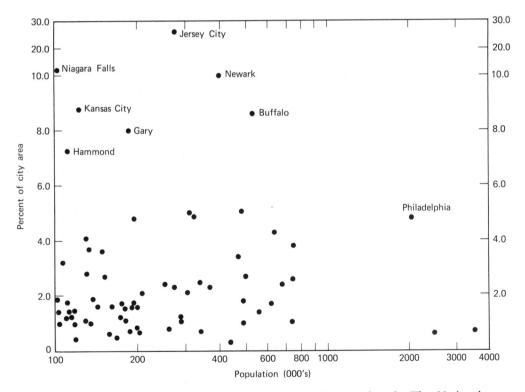

**Figure 14-1** Land used for railroads. *Source.* Based upon data in The National Commission on Urban Problems, *Three Land Research Studies,* Research Report No. 12 (1968).

needed for transportation is in the form of land needs for railroad lines, yards, and terminals. Most likely, greater amounts of land are used for rail tracks than for freight yards and terminals. For 72 cities of 100,000 or more people in the United States, the average proportion of land area of the city used for railroads is 1.7 percent; for cities of populations of 250,000 or more the proportion is 2.4 percent. For specific cities, however, there is considerable variation from the means mentioned above (Figure 14–1). Extreme percentages of urban land used for railroads occur in Jersey City (26 percent), Niagara Falls (11 percent), and Newark (10 percent). There is relatively low correlation between the amount of land used for railroads and the populations of large cities with the amounts greatest for established rail centers and transportation hubs. Certainly, those cities that enjoy locations in productive areas of little topographic limitation, and

which gained dominance as rail centers early in the history of rail carriers, have had larger amounts of land preempted for railroad use. One point to remember is that all land designated as railroad use is not necessarily devoted to the functional use of providing transportation. Large parcels of land so designated are in railroad ownership, but are devoted to other uses, especially industry.

In addition to the land occupied by railroad track or considered as railroad right-of-way, there are considerable amounts used for terminals. These terminals may be on interurban trunk lines, on elevated train lines, or on interurban commuter surface lines, but each calls for parcels of land used for terminal facilities. The premier terminal facility or facilities, since larger cities tend to have more than one major rail terminal, occupies land near the center of the city that is of high value. With declining railroad revenue, such stations are not com-

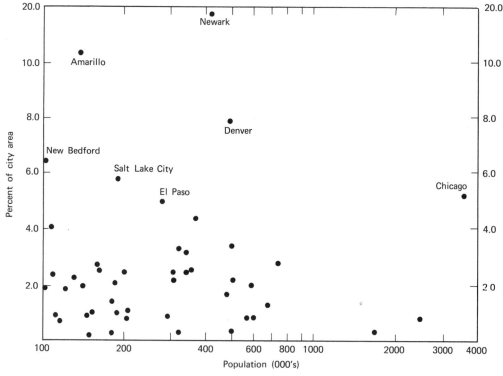

**Figure 14–2**  Land used for airports. *Source.* Based upon data in The National Commission on Urban Problems, *Three Land Research Studies,* Research Report No. 12 (1968).

monly maintained as in the past and are often in disrepair and unsightly, and eligible for renewal that is slow in coming. In the United States, there are probably no railroad stations that equal the subway stations of Moscow in attractiveness or the stations of Japan in terms of congestion and crowding. The railroad terminals in each country seem to reflect the role and status of rail transportation in that particular culture.

Air transportation creates needs for urban space as do other forms of transportation, but with some differences. With other modes of transportation serving or emanating from the city, land is needed for routes and for terminals. Air transportation creates need for land used for terminals but only indirectly for routes. For forty-five cities of 100,000 or more people in the United States, the average proportion of city area devoted to airport use is 2.0 percent; for cities of 250,000 or more the average proportion is 2.5 percent.[3] There is less variation in the amount of airport land in large cities than with railroad land, although there are some extreme cases (Figure 14–2). Cities with unusually high proportions of city land for airports include Amarillo (11.8 percent), Denver (7.9 percent), and Newark (19.2 percent). Newark presents an interesting case in that 45 percent of the city area is devoted to transportation, streets, railroads, and airports, leaving just slightly more than one-half of the city area for all other uses.

Airport land, like railroad land, is not used exclusively for air transportation functions. An air terminal consists of the terminal building or buildings, runways, taxiways, adjacent vehicular parking areas, baggage handling facilities, air freight handling facilities, and other ancillary facilities. Also occupying land on airport property may be commercial establishments and industrial operations,

with the latter including both "air-oriented" and nonair oriented operations. Not uncommonly today, industrial parks are developed on airport property in the expectation or hope that this will generate a desired volume of air traffic, both freight and passenger. The general success of such developments is somewhat unclear at present, although some have been very successful.

There are indirect needs for land used for transportation that are created by airports, and they have to do with access to airports. Each trip by air consists of two parts, the surface journey to or from the airport from some point in the city or from some point on the city's periphery, and the air trip to or from the airport facility. The shorter trips to or from an airport are, of course, generally by means of transportation other than air and utilize routes used for other trip purposes as well. Still, the pressures put on surface routes to and from airports is increased and the use made of various modes of transit is increased as well. Further, there may be need for additional surface routes essentially to serve the complementary needs of the airport facility with these adding to the land needed for transportation use.

People traveling to or from airports include airline passengers, airport employees, and visitors (Table 14–1). The passengers travel to and from airports largely by auto, especially passengers from outside the core area of the central

**Table 14–1** Trips Generated by Kennedy Airport, New York City (Daily One-way Person Trips)

| Tripmakers | Person Trips | Percent of Total |
|---|---|---|
| Airline passengers | 20,250 | 27 |
| Employees | 26,500 | 36 |
| Visitors and others | 27,000 | 37 |
| Totals | 73,750 | 100 |

SOURCE: David K. Witheford, "Airports and Accessibility," *Traffic Quarterly*, Vol. 23, No. 2 (April, 1969).

[3]Allen D. Manvel, "Land Use in 106 Large Cities," *Three Land Research Studies*, National Commission on Urban Problems, Research Report No. 12, Washington, D.C. (1968).

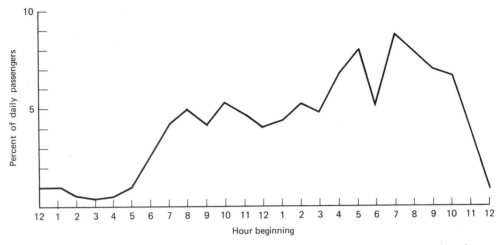

**Figure 14-3**  Hourly passenger arrivals and departures combined: six composite airports. *Source.* Adapted from Figure 2, David K. Witheford. "Airports and Accessibility" *Traffic Quarterly,* April, 1967.

city, and produce a bimodal distribution of vehicle traffic, with one peak in early morning and another in late afternoon (Figure 14-3). Regarding the areas of origin of people traveling to airports, the employees largely are from within the city served by the airport. Passengers, on the other hand, are derived from dispersed areas of origin (Figure 14-4). The specific areas of origin of air passengers depends on the nature of the air terminal facility, the service offered, and alternatives available at other locations. The airport facility in a particular city may largely serve the needs of that city, but not the needs of other cities. In these instances, the major area of origin of air travelers is the central business district of the city (Figure 14-4). In other cases, the airport facility in a major city may serve a regional function as well as a local one and will draw considerable numbers of air travelers from outside the city where the airport is located. With regard to the latter, consider a large, higher order city where a large commercial airport is developed. Outward from this city at distances of up to about one-hundred miles, there are a number of moderate size cities of lower order. Each of the lower order cities is the place of origin of a number of air trips, but not of sufficient

number to support the same type of air facility as in the larger city. Rather than attempt to duplicate a substantial part of the air facility of the larger city, the smaller cities may be content to utilize the airport facilities of the larger city, with the latter taking on more of a role of a regional airport. This condition in which smaller urban centers are dominated by a larger city in terms of air transportation is referred to as the *traffic shadow* concept.[4] For example, consider a large city with a population of around one million, such as San Francisco, that has an airport to serve its needs. This airport likely would have a wide range of air services and schedules available. Other, nearby cities with populations in the range of 250,000 to 500,000 may rely on the airport facility of the larger city, and air travelers originating in them will travel by surface transportation to the regional airport facility. In this case, the smaller cities would be within the traffic shadow of the city with the regional airport (Figure 14-5). If any one of the smaller, lower order cities was a freestanding one more distant from a larger

[4]Edward J. Taaffe, "The Urban Hierarchy: An Air Passenger Definition," *Economic Geography*, Vol. 38, No. 1 (January, 1962).

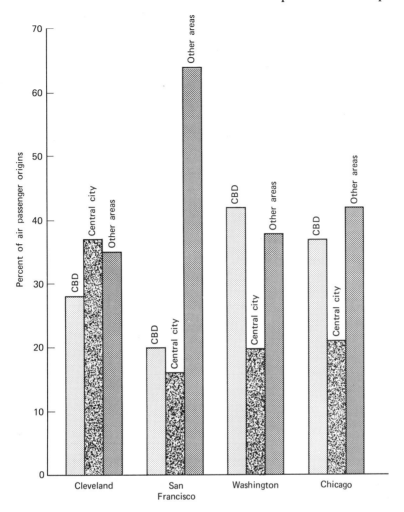

**Figure 14–4** Distribution of air passenger origins: selected cities. *Source.* Based upon data in David K. Witheford, "Airports and Accessibility," *Traffic Quarterly,* April, 1969.

city, it is likely that its commercial airport facility would be expanded beyond what it is in cities of the same order within the traffic shadow of a larger facility.

The major point here is that the demands for urban land to support one or more airports in a large city, both for air transportation and for complementary surface transportation, may be considered disproportionately large until one realizes that the facilities involved are regional in nature, rather than solely local. When space needs for regional airports continue to mount, and as technology of air transportation changes, there is in-

creasing conflict between large, jet airports and, particularly, their expansion within the central city. Although the bulk of air travelers are derived from the central city, space problems and environmental concerns are such that regional airports are quite often developed in outlying sections of the urban area, thereby reducing the amounts of land used for airport functions in the central city. Examples of this are O'Hare Airport in the Chicago area which replaced much of airport function of Midway Airport on a close-in site, and the Dulles International Airport between Washington and Balti-

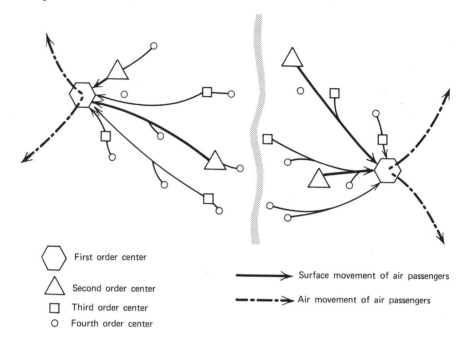

First order center

Second order center

Third order center

Fourth order center

→ Surface movement of air passengers

– · – · → Air movement of air passengers

**Figure 14–5**    Hypothetical situation illustrating the concept of traffic shadow.

more which replaced much of the function of the closer in Washington National Airport.

The traffic shadow concept was developed in study of air transportation but it may also apply to other forms of urban transportation, especially intercity railroad passenger transport. Many rail passenger terminals in smaller cities have been abandoned, so that this type of transportation service is available only in larger cities. In this sense, the smaller cities may be within the traffic shadow of the larger ones and the passenger railroad terminals may be more regional in scope than solely local.

## Principles of Urban Transportation

Urban transportation, like transportation elsewhere, generally takes place in accord with certain underlying principles of spatial behavior. Three principles in particular apply to the movement of people and commodities over two-dimensional space: *complementarity, trans-*

*ferability,* and *intervening opportunity*.[5] These principles help to explain movements of people and of commodities in the aggregate or of some segment of the total movement, although they do not explain each individual movement.

Complementarity refers to the spatial separation of areas of supply and demand. In the context of urban transportaiton, this would likely be the separation of points of supply of tripmakers (supply) and points of attraction for tripmakers (demand). This situation would apply to the movement of people as well as to the movement of commodities, for in each case, there is an origin of the trip or movement and a destination, with the two separated by distance. The greater the distance between trip origin and trip destination, the less the likelihood of the trip occurring and the lower the frequency of trips. Under conditions of complementarity, distance exerts a frictional effect on movement, although the *friction of distance* is variable for different

[5]Edward L. Ullman, *American Commodity Flow*, Seattle; University of Washington Press (1957).

types of trips. For example, it has been found that trips made to school are the most sensitive to distance, and trips for recreational purposes are the least sensitive (Table 14–2).[6] Other variables, besides trip purpose, that influence the sensitivity to distance include sex, age, occupation, and income of the tripmakers and density of settlement.

the greater the combined magnitude of two masses, the greater will be the spatial interaction between them, that is, there is a direct relationship between the two. Further, the model considers an inverse relationship between the mutual interaction of two masses at two locations and the distance between them. In this respect, the model incorporates the notion

**Table 14–2**   Trip Purpose and Distance in Four States

| Purpose | Average Trip Length (Miles) | Vehicle Miles (Percent) | Number of Trips (Percent) |
|---|---|---|---|
| Shopping | 3.7 | 6.0 | 13.4 |
| Education, civic, religious | 5.0 | 2.8 | 4.6 |
| To and from work | 5.9 | 22.7 | 32.2 |
| Business and farming | 10.4 | 21.3 | 17.0 |
| Pleasure riding | 13.0 | 14.1 | 9.0 |
| Medical and dental | 15.5 | 2.5 | 1.3 |
| Vacation | 249.7 | 4.8 | 0.2 |
| Other purposes | | 25.8 | 22.3 |

SOURCE:   William L. Garrison, et al *Studies of Highway Development and Geographic Change*, Seattle: University of Washington Press (1959).

The principle of complementarity can be expressed by the equation $I = \dfrac{(P_1)(P_2)}{d}$ in which:

$I$ is the relative interaction or movement between two locations or areas,

$P_1$ is population or some other measure of mass at one location or in one area,

$P_2$ is the population or some other measure of mass at a second location or in a second area,

and $d$ is the linear or route distance separating the two areas or locations considered.

This equation is based on Newtonian physics and was first formalized by Carey in 1858, with significant modifications made in the years that followed.[7] The model is predicated on the notion that

of friction of distance. There have been several reformulations of the interaction model, but the two variables essentially remain, mass and distance. For application to urban transportation, one might wish to let one measure of mass $(P_1)$ be represented by the number of households or dwelling units in a chosen subarea of the city, with the other measure of mass $(P_2)$ being the number of trip attractions in a second subarea, with these being shopping attractions, employment opportunities, etc. In this sense, one subarea has a mass that can be expressed as trip origins and the other subarea has a mass that can be expressed as potential trip destinations. Further, if one is interested in describing or estimating the movement from a given area of trip origins, such as a residential neighborhood, to a number of areas of trip destination, the first measure of mass (trip origins) is held constant and the only influences are the masses of alternate areas of attraction and the distances to

[6]This matter is discussed in Gunnar Olsson, *Distance and Human Interaction: A Review and Bibliography*, Regional Science Research Institute, Bibliography Series Number 2, Philadelphia (1965).

[7]Gunnar Olsson, *Ibid*.

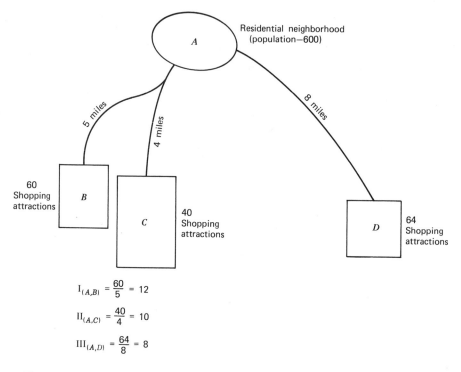

$$I_{(A,B)} = \frac{60}{5} = 12$$

$$II_{(A,C)} = \frac{40}{4} = 10$$

$$III_{(A,D)} = \frac{64}{8} = 8$$

**Figure 14–6** Hypothetical conditions of spatial interaction.

each (Figure 14–6). Figure 14–6 is a simple case involving a single subarea of trip origins and only three subareas of trip destination for trips of the same type. An urban center is, in fact, made up of a multitude of points of trip origin that is comprised of each person in the population and a host of points of trip destination. It is desirable, therefore, to systematically divide the city into subareas so that the interaction can be estimated from each subarea to each of the other subareas. This is accomplished by use of a rectangular grid of equal area cells, with each cell having a known population or mass of potential tripmakers. Further, each cell has some attractiveness for trip destination, depending on the trip purpose considered. A specific area cell might include dwelling units alone with these comprising potential trip origins for that cell. Each dwelling unit is, as well, a potential trip destination for social trips made by persons in other cells. The cell referred to may have no commercial

facilities, however, and would have no potential as a trip destination for shopping trips, the same as if it contained no employment opportunities. The point is that the attractiveness of the cell to stimulate spatial interaction with other cells in the urban area is variable with the type of trip. For this reason, researchers have often disaggregated trip data to account for different trip purpose, such as journey to work, shopping trip, etc. It would be possible to consider the attractiveness of a specific cell for each type of trip, and then combine the measures of attractiveness into a single measure, but this serves to obscure the nature of the interaction between areas of the city. For example, the CBD serves as the destination for many trips. Most of these are trips to places of employment or are shopping trips, with social and recreational trips and trips to school relatively uncommon to this subarea. If all trips having the CBD as their destination were combined, it would not be possible to discern the purpose for which the trips were made and the nature of the attraction of the CBD would be obscured.

One item that might be pointed out here is that with numerous subareas, points, or cells of trip origin in the city, and a similar number of places of trip destination, the volume of data to be considered in any analysis of complementarity between areas becomes staggering. If the analysis is to include the entire city, commuter usage is virtually essential. The tasks of data collection and tabulation alone are formidable, especially in large cities.

There is a point concerning the interaction model that applies especially to urban transportation. And that is, that travel time, rather than travel distance, often is more critical in influencing movement between different locations in the city. This would be especially true of daily commuters, traveling by private auto. A shorter travel distance might be via narrow, circuitous routes with many impediments to smooth traffic flow along the route. In some cases, there are points of *route friction* which impede travel such as stop signs, traffic lights, hazardous intersections, pitted road surface, and the like. In other cases, there may be points of *lateral friction* that also slow movement of traffic, such as private driveways, distracting signs or lights beside the route, and entrances and exits of parking lots and shopping centers. Points of route friction are impediments in the route and points of lateral friction are peripheral to the route. The result of such frictional impediments is that time of travel over these routes may be lengthened over what it would be on routes longer in distance, but faster in elapsed time. In an urban setting, where commuting effort is often expressed as a matter of time rather than of distance, it would be appropriate to substitute time ($t$) for distance ($d$) in the interaction model to study or estimate the complementarity between two locations in the city—one of trip

origins and the other of trip destination.

Use of models of the type discussed above is valuable in making forecasts of travel, especially in an urban area. When new subdivisions come into being and new neighborhoods are created, it is desirable to anticipate the effect of these on the direction and magnitude of urban travel. Once new needs are estimated, planning of new facilities can be undertaken, and new routes can be established or older ones improved to accommodate the needs.

The condition of complementarity is, in itself, not sufficient to implement the movements suggested. The existence of potential trip origins in one area and trip destinations in another more or less sets the stage for movement, but this will not occur unless the means of making the trips are provided. Here, the principle of transferability comes into play, for this principle considers the ability of the tripmakers to make a particular trip and the means of completing it. Before a trip can be made, there must be a route connecting points of origin and destination and there must be a means of conveyance over this route. Furthermore, transferability takes into account the cost of making this trip, for this too must be considered in evaluating the ability of tripmakers to complete a specific trip. For example, the complementarity may be great between two areas, yet the costs incurred in making the trip may be prohibitively high and enough so that the trip is not made. There may not be a means of conveyance available that is within the cost limitations imposed on the tripmaker. A person of low income may have a desire to make a trip to a chosen destination, but can do so only by some means of public transit, such as a bus or subway. If those means of making the trip are unavailable, the trip will not be made.

Regarding the means of transportation of people in the urban area in the U.S., the most common ones are the private automobile and the bus. Subways and elevated trains are used intensely wherever they are available, but only the largest of metropolitan areas enjoy the benefits of this means of transportation. Other means of urban conveyance are less common and less utilized, although there are experimental types that may hold promise in the future, such as the skybus or the monorail. In other world regions, the means of urban transport reflect the needs and cultures of the area, such as the rickshaw, the pedicab, and the bicycle. Because of cultural differences, it is very difficult, if not meaningless, to generalize concerning the ones used most commonly the world over and the relative costs of different forms of urban transport.

In reference to the United States alone, it also is difficult to generalize about the most common forms of urban transit and their respective costs, since the entire array of alternate transport means may not be available, that is, in smaller cities the only form of urban transport may be the private automobile. Further, the means of transport used by one sector of the population may not be used to nearly the same degree by another. Taking a metropolitan area that has the entire array of transportation means available, New York City, the most frequently used means of transport of workers are, in order, the subway, the bus, the auto, and the railroad.[8] Even for workers traveling to places of employment in mid-

[8]Martin Wohl, "Users of Urban Transportation Services and Their Income Circumstances," *Traffic Quarterly*, Vol. XXIV, No. 1 (January, 1970).

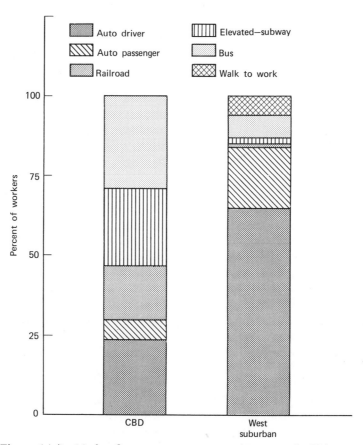

**Figure 14–7**  Mode of commuter transportation to work: Chicago. *Source.* Adapted from Table II–1, Edward J. Taaffe, Barry J. Garner and Maurice H. Yeates, *The Peripheral Journey to Work,* Northwestern University Press, 1963.

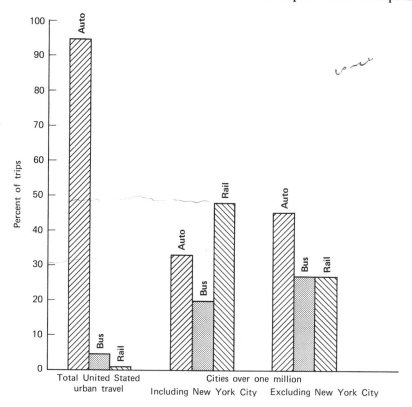

**Figure 14–8** Urban person travel; by mode: total United States and cities over 1,000,000. *Source.* Based upon data in Francis C. Turner, "Moving People on Urban Highways," *Traffic Quarterly* (July, 1970).

Manhattan, there are striking differences in their means of transportation, based mainly on the relative availability and service provided (Figure 14–7). The same pattern existing in New York holds true as well for Chicago, although the private auto makes up a greater share of total trips. Considering the most common form of urban transport in the United States in total, the private auto is the dominant form of urban transport for all cities grouped together (Figure 14–8).[9]

There are differences in the principal mode of urban travel used by various segments of the population, as there are differences from city to city. One of the

[9]Francis C. Turner, "Moving People on Urban Highways," *Traffic Quarterly*, Vol. 24, No. 3 (July, 1970).

significant differences in mode of travel is based on household income, with a general tendency for lower income groups to use bus and subway transportation, while higher income groups utilize private automobiles and railroads more than do lower income groups (Figure 14–9). It is not clear whether these differences reflect differing abilities to pay for more expensive types of transportation or whether they reflect spatial variations in the areas of residence of different income groups. Very likely, the latter case holds true much of the time, since higher income groups tend to live further from their places of work, as indicated by the fact that 54 percent of workers with family income over $15,000 travel over six miles to work, while 42 percent of workers with family incomes less than $2,000 travel this distance to

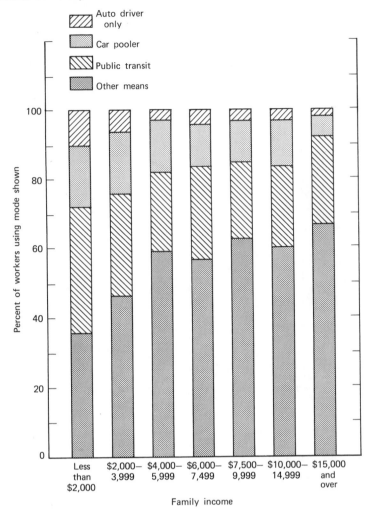

**Figure 14–9** Distribution of work trips by mode. *Source.* Based upon data in Martin Wohl, "Users of Urban Transportation Services and Their Income Circumstances," *Traffic Quarterly,* (January, 1970).

work.[10] Also, white workers travel further to work than do nonwhite workers, perhaps as a function of differences in income or in areas of residence. In regard to the distance workers travel from home to work place, it generally is true that in recent decades greater distances have come to separate the two, especially in larger cities (Figure 14–10).

A third principle of transportation, the principle of intervening opportunities, also provides insight into the likelihood

and magnitude of travel between different locations or areas in the city. Complementarity and transferability both focus on the resistance to travel in the form of distance or cost. Intervening opportunity focuses more on attractions for trip making. Basically, this principle deals with the alternative opportunities available to the tripmaker in terms of alternate destinations. A trip destination may be possible five miles from the point of origin and another termination may exist within two miles of the same trip origin. Here, the second termination represents

[10]Martin Wohl, *Op. Cit.*

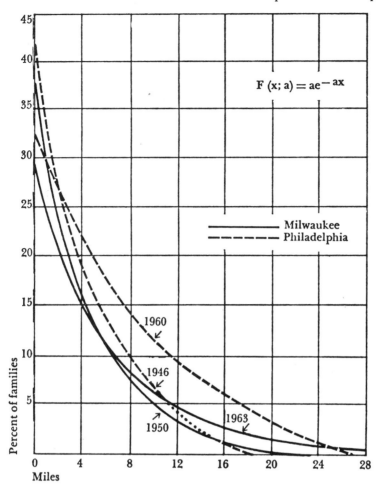

**Figure 14–10** Changes in home-work distances: Philadelphia and Milwaukee. *Source.* Reprinted by permission of the ENO Foundation. Anthony J. Catanese, "Community Behavior Patterns of Family." *Traffic Quarterly,* Vol. 24, No. 3, July, 1970.

an intervening opportunity, relative to the first and, if it did not exist, the trip would likely be made to the more distant termination.

The intervening opportunities principle is used for traffic analysis as an alternative to the gravity model. For this, the destinations of all traffic are tabulated and destinations of traffic from a specific area are placed in order of time or distance required to reach a particular destination.[11] The analysis of the traffic generated by the area under study, then,

takes place in accord with the equation $V_{ij} = V_i \ P(S_j)$ where:

$V_i$ is the number of trip origins from area $i$

$V_{ij}$ is the number of trips from area $i$ that terminate in area $j$

and $P(S_j)$ is the probability of a trip from area $i$ terminating in area $j$.[12]

It was found that the $P(S_j)$ factor was more closely related to the total number of opportunities available in areas closer to area $i$, the area of origin, than in area $j$. The likelihood of a particular trip to a specific destination, then, is greatly influenced by the number of oppor-

[11] Colin Clark and G. H. Peters, "The 'Intervening Opportunities' Method of Traffic Analysis," *Traffic Quarterly,* Vol. XIX, No. 1 (January, 1965).

[12] Colin Clark and G. H. Peters, *Ibid.*

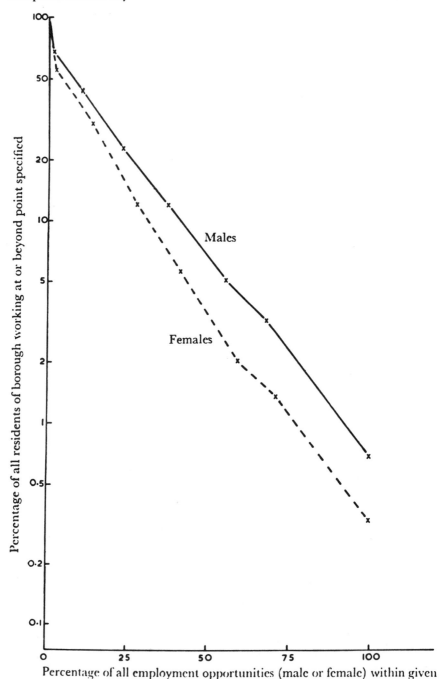

Percentage of all employment opportunities (male or female) within given distance

**Figure 14-11**   Alternate employment opportunities: Greater London. *Source.* Colin Clark and G. H. Peters. *Traffic Quarterly.* Vol. 19, 1965. Reprinted by permission of the ENO Foundation.

tunities available for a successful trip termination and the likelihood increases as these opportunities are available nearer to the point of trip origin, that is, as intervening opportunities are presented. Studies undertaken in London,

Copenhagen, and Chicago support the contention that opportunities have a greater bearing on trip making than does distance, *per se*. It might be said that the influence is exerted by opportunities at a distance. This influence has been shown to hold true for urban travel of different types: for employment, and for goods delivery (Figure 14–11).

## Origin and Destination

It is important, in studying urban transportation, to assemble and tabulate a great deal of data dealing with the movements within or through the city. These data include number of trips originating at different locations, the number of trips terminating at different localities, the purpose of trips made, and characteristics of the movement, such as routes followed, stops enroute, and turns made. In the United States, much of the data needed in urban transportation study of physical movements is provided by *origin and destination* studies funded by the Bureau of Public Roads and undertaken by respective state highway departments. In these studies, the city is divided into subareas, as is the surrounding area, and the number of trips originating in each subarea is established (Figure 14–12). The bulk of the trips originating in one subarea will be terminated in subareas within the city or outside the city and the number of trip destinations is established for each of these. Of the total volume of vehicular traffic moving within the specific urban area, there are four basic types of trips that can be identified on the basis of origin and destination and data are gathered for each. The four trip types are (1) trips originating and terminating within the urban area, (2) trips originating within the urban area but terminating outside the urban area, (3) trips originating outside the urban area but terminating within the urban area, and (4) trips neither originating nor terminating in the urban area that com-

prise through traffic. These different types of trips all contribute to the aggregate movement of the traffic of the city and must be accounted for in an $O$ and $D$ study.

It might be pointed out that $O$ and $D$ studies deal mainly with vehicular traffic, as opposed to pedestrian traffic. Moreover, the vehicular traffic moving on major arterial public roads and streets is of major concern, with rail and air traffic not generally included in $O$ and $D$ studies. Distinctions are usually made, however, between private passenger vehicles and commercial vehicles.

Considering that there are large numbers of trips made daily in the urban area and that these involve innumerable origins and destinations, the data which are accumulated dealing with these trips essentially must be obtained through sampling procedures. In an $O$ and $D$ study, a number of checkpoints is established in the city, with the number depending on the population of the city and the nature of transportation network. For example, in an $O$ and $D$ study of Boise, Idaho with a population of approximately 75,000, there were seventeen such checkpoints established within the city.[13] At each of these, automatic recording and counting devices were employed to record the volume of traffic passing that particular point. Also, each checkpoint was an interview station and traffic was halted so that interviews could be conducted and information obtained as to the trip origin, destination, and purpose. These checkpoints and interview stations are usually manned for relatively short periods. For the Boise $O$ and $D$ study, automatic recording counters were operated for periods of 48 hours or more, and interviews were conducted from 6 a.m. to 10 p.m. at five checkpoints and at twelve checkpoints from 6 a.m. to

[13]Idaho Department of Highways, in cooperation with the Bureau of Public Roads, *1960 Origin-Destination Traffic Study: City of Boise, Idaho.*

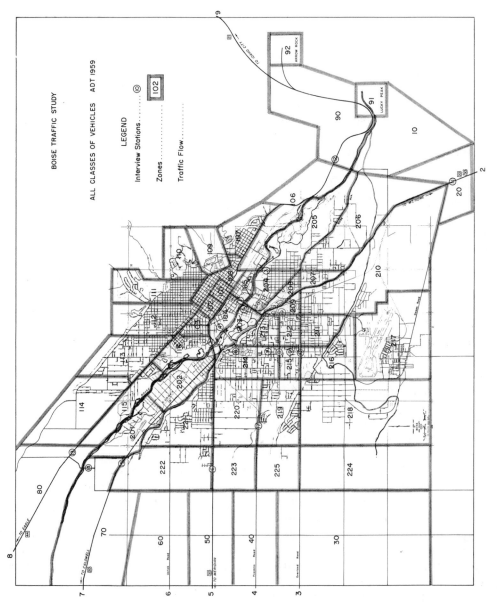

**Figure 14-12**  Subareas for an O and D study: Boise, Idaho. *Source.* Idaho Dept. of Highways, 1959. Used by permission.

2 p.m. during weekdays in the month of June, 1959.[14]

Notice that sampling was employed in three different instances in completion of the above study: in the number and placement of the checkpoints, in the time of day during which interviews were made, and in the months of the year during which interviews were made. In each case, the sample was established in a manner that included the maximum number of trips within or through the urban center, with the realization that vehicular trips tend to peak in daylight hours and in the summer months.

The results of $O$ and $D$ studies are presented in various ways. Commonly, a series of maps are prepared showing the spatial pattern of traffic movements, with separate maps for through nonstop trips, through trips with a stop, and trips terminating in each of the zones or subareas of the urban area (Figure 14–13). Often, the results of $O$ and $D$ studies are presented in matrix form in which trip origins are noted on one axis and trip destinations on the other. Another type of output of $O$ and $D$ studies, derived from the interview stage, is information on trip purpose. This can be gained for each checkpoint included in the study and these can be aggregated for all trips to or within the urban center (Figure 14–14). Information can also be gained about the purpose of different types of trips, internal, external with a stop, or external through traffic. These are some of the types of information provided by a thorough origin and destination study.

## Traffic Generators

It has been suggested that the city can be broken down into zones of trip origin and trip destination, with these serving as the framework for origin and destination study. Questions might be asked as to what stimulates or attracts traffic,

pedestrian and vehicular, to a particular destination. Given the desire to make a trip of short or long duration and distance, and a mode of transportation by which the trip can be made and an improved route on which the conveyance can operate, what, then, attracts the trip-maker to a particular destination at a specific location in preference to alternative destinations at different locations? What, also, generates the trip being made to its destination?

Traffic generation can be considered on the basis of (1) distance of the trip to a particular traffic generator, or (2) the frequency of trips made to a traffic generator. Both factors provide a measure of the attractiveness or drawing power of a traffic generator at a specific trip destination. For example, in a sample of households in Cedar Rapids, Iowa, the average distance of multiple purpose shopping trips was 3 to 4 miles, while the average distance of single purpose trips was less than three miles, with the latter characterized by more variance in frequency of trips made.[15]

Some trips are made in response to the attraction of a single traffic generator, that is, the single purpose trip, while others result from attraction of more than one traffic generator, that is, the multiple purpose trip. Single purpose trips tend to be of shorter distances than do multiple purpose trips, but likely are made more frequently (Figure 14–15). Shopping trips, in particular, are combined with work trips and with social-recreational trips, both of which involve trips of about the same distances, but the latter occur less frequently (Figure 14–16). An interesting point with regard to trip generation is that a certain type of commercial establishment, which is a traffic generator in a certain locational setting, may not generate traffic to the

[14]Idaho Department of Highways, *Ibid*.

[15]William L. Garrison, et. al., *Studies of Highway Development and Geographic Change*, Seattle, University of Washington (1959).

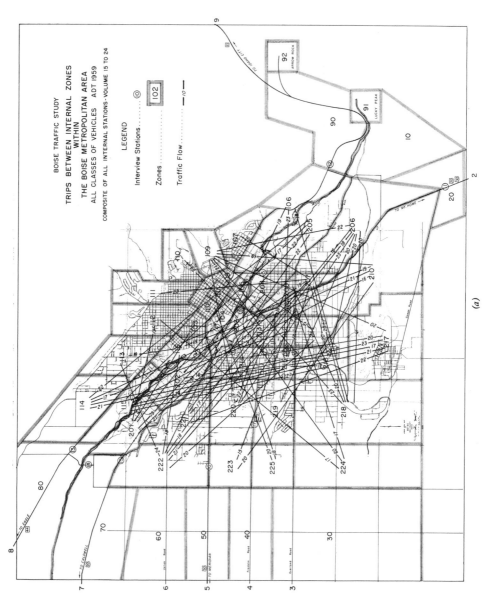

**Figure 14–13** Interzonal vehicular travel patterns: Boise, Idaho. *Source.* Idaho Dept. of High-ways, 1959. Used by permission.

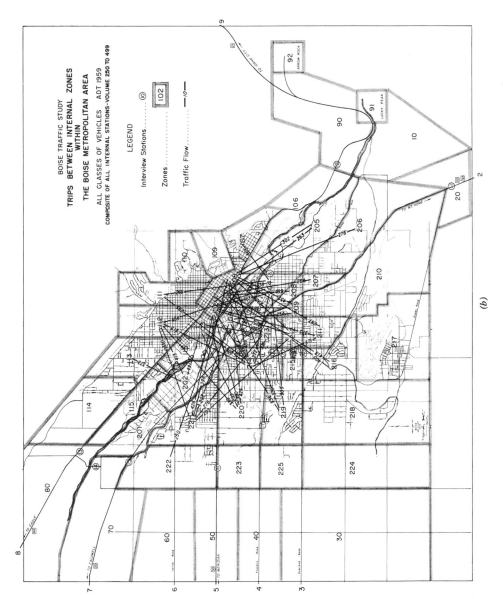

**Figure 14–13B** Interzonal vehicular travel patterns: Boise, Idaho. *Source.* Idaho Dept. of Highways, 1959. Used by permission.

(*b*)

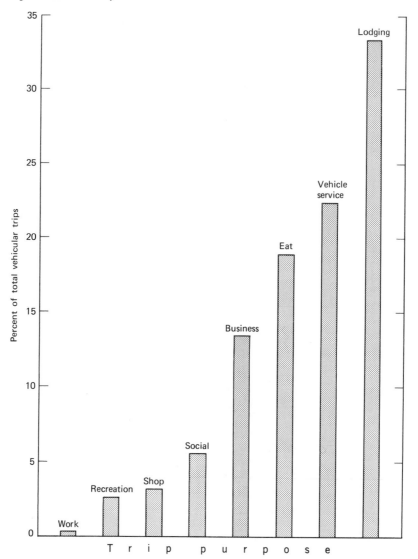

**Figure 14–14** Percentage distribution of trip purposes: Boise, Idaho. *Source.* Based upon data in State of Idaho—Department of Highway; *Origin—Destination Traffic Study: Boise, Idaho,* 1959.

same degree when in a different locational setting. In a study of Cedar Rapids, Iowa, furniture stores in the CBD generated 90 percent of the single purpose trips generated by all furniture stores in the city, yet only about 50 percent of all these stores were located in the CBD.[16] Furniture stores in large or medium size shopping districts generated but 10 percent of the trips, but included about 35

percent of the stores of this type. By contrast, drug stores as traffic generators in large and medium size shopping districts, accounted for 28 percent of all trips made to these establishments, and had 65 percent of the stores. Drug stores in small size shopping districts attracted 21 percent of the trips, while having only 10 percent of stores of this type.

A question could be posed as to what exactly is the nature of a traffic generator? Is it a particular, but general

[16]Garrison, et. al, *Ibid.*

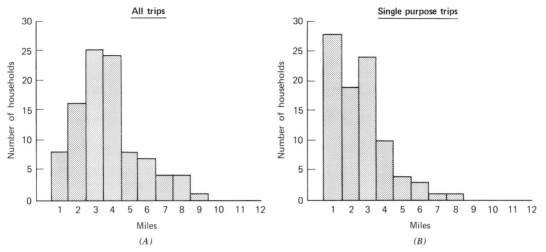

**Figure 14–15**  Average distance traveled, by trip type. (A) All trips. (B) Single purpose trips. *Source.* Adapted from William L. Garrison, et al., *Studies of Highway Development and Geographic Change,* University of Washington Press, 1959.

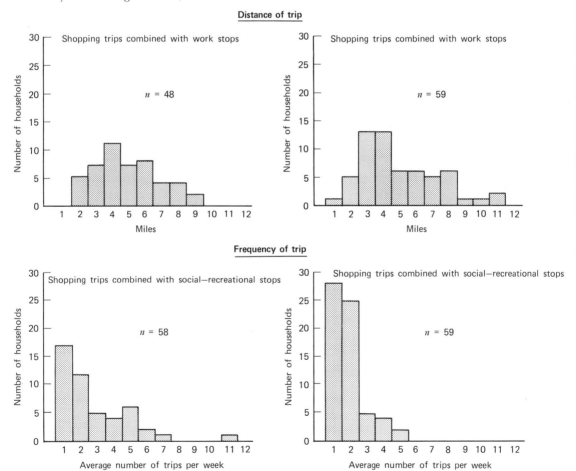

**Figure 14–16**  Distances traveled and frequency of trips of different types. *Source.* Adapted from William L. Garrison et al., *Studies of Highway Development and Geographic Change,* University of Washington Press, 1959.

land use? Is it a concentration of land uses of specific types? Or is it a particular type of establishment? Most studies have dealt with land use as the measure of trip generation, with the land use becoming the trip generator. Rarely are other than broad land use classes employed in such studies of traffic generators in the city, with residential, commercial, industrial, and public and semipublic very commonly employed. In some studies, a broad land use category, such as commercial, might be disaggregated to identify more specific commercial land use generators. In studies of generators of pedestrian traffic, more specific types of land use are generally considered rather than broader land use classes, which is a logical step when one considers that most pedestrian traffic movement is in the central business district where commercial land uses are dominant and other land use classes are not represented to any major degree.

An important consideration when dealing with traffic generation is the matter of peak and slack periods during which traffic is generated. This would tend to hold true regardless of how a traffic generator is defined. Certain land uses and establishments in the central business district may be substantial traffic generators, and peak generation would be experienced in this area around midday on weekdays. By contrast, slack periods would be experienced in nighttime hours and weekends. The same contrast likely would occur with regard to industrial traffic generators, as well, although the hours of peak traffic generation would be different from what they are in the CBD. There are differences in the rates of traffic generation between different times of the year, as there are between hours of the day and days of the week. For example, recreation and social traffic generation tends to peak in the summer months and experience slack periods in the winter.

In attempts to change the pattern of peak traffic generation, when streets and intersections are clogged with vehicles, staggered work hours have been implemented, but with less than maximum results. Shopping hours have been extended and weekend shopping periods have been inaugurated in the CBD with somewhat better results. Modern society seems to be so locked into a regular schedule that to alter one part puts it out of phase with the others. A change in the work day of one family member puts it out of phase with the shopping pattern of another family member and with the school regime of one or more other family members. If, however, all parts of the schedule are changed together, nothing is gained with regard to movement and traffic generation.

Considering seven different land uses as traffic generators, there are considerable differences in the rates of traffic generation, both of vehicular trips and person trips. For a group of ten metropolitan areas in the United States, the major generator of vehicular trips was commercial land, followed by transportation (most likely terminals), public buildings, and residential uses (Figure 14–17).[17] Each of the land uses serving as a traffic generator is summarized below:

*Residential Land.* The vehicle trips generated by attraction to residential areas range from about 12 to 26 per acre of residential land.[18] The trip generation rate for person trips ranges from 18 to 49 per acre per day, indicating about two persons per vehicle attracted to such areas. The trip generation rate will, of course, vary between cities, and even more, between sections with different residential densities in the city, especially between single family dwelling areas and multifamily dwelling areas. Very likely, a curve of traffic generation for such areas would have less pronounced peaks and troughs than would others for different

[17]Paul W. Shuldiner, *Non-Residential Trip Generation Analysis,* The Transportation Center, Northwestern University, Evanston (November, 1965).

[18]Paul W. Shuldiner, *Ibid.* Similar values that follow are taken from the same source.

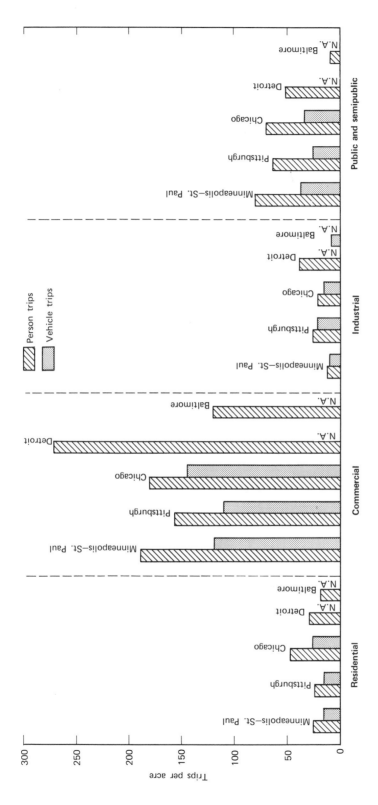

**Figure 14-17**  Summary of trip generation rates for five metropolitan areas, by land-use type. *Source.* Based upon data in Paul W. Shuldiner, *Non-Residential Trip Generation Analysis*, November, 1965.

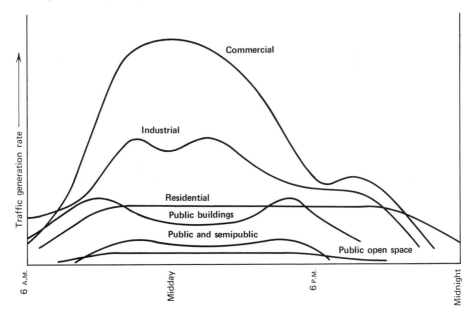

**Figure 14–18**   Daily pattern of urban trip generation rates; major land uses.

land uses, and would extend over a greater portion of the day (Figure 14–18).

*Commercial Land.* This is the land use with the highest traffic generation rates, both for vehicular trips and person trips. The trip generation rates for vehicular trips range between 63 and 144, and person trips range between 121 and 271, indicating somewhat less than two persons per vehicle attracted to such areas. The rate of trip generation for this land use tends to increase steadily during the morning hours, reaching a peak around noon, after which it declines, reaching a trough in the late afternoon. In many cities, there is a secondary peak in the evening hours with trips generated by outlying shopping centers, rather than the central business district. There would, then, be a bimodal distribution of trips, generated by commercial land (Figure 14–18).

Evidence supports the contention that planned shopping centers have greater trip generation rates than do commercial areas collectively. In a study in the Los Angeles area, six shopping centers (five regional centers and one community center) had an average trip generation rate of 296 trips per acre.[19] Futhermore, particular establishments within shopping centers exhibit variances in trips generated, with drug stores, grocery stores and variety stores having the highest trip generation rates.

*Industrial Land.* Trip generation rates for industrial land are lower than for residential and commercial land, tending to approximate 5 to 40 person trips per acre and 3 to 20 vehicular trips per acre. Employees, going to work, contribute to a surge of trips in the early morning hours, followed by commercial vehicles which are attracted to industrial districts. There tends to be a trough in midday, followed by an afternoon peak, that is, a bimodal distribution exists (Figure 14–18).

*Public and semi-public land.* The land use class "public and semi-public land" includes a great variety of different ways in which public land is used. In the aggregate, such land has high trip generation rates, likely second only to commer-

[19]Walter D. Stoll, "Charactersitics of Shopping Centers," *Traffic Quarterly*, Vol. XXI, No. 2 (April, 1967).

cial land. Trip-generation rates approximate 20 to 90 person trips per acre and 25 to 60 vehicular trips per acre. Public buildings exhibit a trip generation curve that has peaks in midmorning and in midafternoon, with a midday trough. The trip generation curve for public buildings would extend into the evening hours due to the trips generated by public facilities such as auditoriums, coliseums, arenas, and the like. Other public and semipublic land, including schools, parks, and cemeteries, have lower trip generation rates than do public buildings, generating about 10 to 40 person trips per day and 5 to 30 vehicular trips. The trips generated mostly are during the daytime hours, with a slight tendency for a bimodal distribution of trips with minor peaks in midmorning and in midafternoon.

Contrasts exist with regard to traffic generators in different world regions. In the United States, commercial and industrial land are major traffic generators. In South Africa, the major traffic generators in large cities are railway stations and bus terminals, which reflects the characteristic of mass transit in other cultures.[20]

## Transit Systems

There are numerous ways by which people travel within urban areas. Each mode of transit incorporates a network of routes, stations, and destinations which, together, constitute a transit system. A certain system may serve only part of the city or the urban area, or may be more regional in scope serving the entirety of the urban area. In some cases, one transit system may complement another, while in other cases, one may compete with another. The emphasis today is on transit systems that complement one another, and which are developed on a regional basis with much of the planning effort in

urban transportation directed toward these ends.

It is useful to recognize the various types of transit systems that exist in the city today, especially the larger cities. Smaller cities often have but one or two alternatives available for the transportation of people, while large cities may have four or five alternative systems. Distinctions between transit systems can be based on ownership and management, on the mode of transportation involved, or on characteristics of the operation. A typology of transit systems is presented in Table 14–3. Of the different transit systems, those dealing with individualized transit tend to be a combination of privately owned and publicly owned, that is, privately owned vehicles operating on publicly owned routes. Systems of group transit, by contrast, tend to be publicly owned, that is, publicly owned vehicles operating on publicly owned routes.

**Table 14–3** A Typology of Urban Transit Systems.

I. Individualized transit
    A. Private automobiles and other private vehicles
    B. Taxicabs, pedicabs, and other commercial vehicles for individual hire

II. Group transit
    A. Mass transit, especially by bus, streetcar, trolley, ferry, and cablecar
    B. Rapid transit, especially by train, monorail, and subway

In cities of the United States, the major transit system is the one involving private automobiles, with this type accounting for the bulk of people and vehicles focusing on the city. This has led to serious problems for the city, as well as for the tripmaker. Serious problems have arisen from emission of exhaust from autos on city streets that have contributed to overall seriousness of environmental degradation. There has developed an increasingly serious problem of traffic congestion on city streets and conflicts between

[20] E. W. N. Mallows and Julian Beinart, "Planning in the CBD: The Potential of the Periphery." *Traffic Quarterly,* Vol. XX, No. 2 (April, 1966).

vehicles and pedestrians. Furthermore, increased amounts of urban land have to be utilized for vehicle parking, which may not be the highest or best use to make of urban space. Due to these and other problems, many large cities have reached or nearly reached the saturation levels with respect to capacities of city streets and downtown parking facilities, and have begun to seriously explore alternative means of urban transit.

The earliest form of mass transit in American cities was in the form of horse-drawn cars operating on tracks, which began operation in New York City in 1832 to provide for the needs of low income workers in the city.[21] Other cities followed with development of street railroads with the same type of locomotion in the 1840's and 1850's. Somewhat later, electricity provided the motive power for street railroads, and by the 1880's, street railroad lines had been extended into outlying sections of American cities. This was followed, in turn, by development of steam railroads to transport commuters in urban areas, especially in the early decades of the twentieth century (Figure 14–19).

Street railroads in American cities were extended until about World War I, after which tracks were gradually torn up or abandoned. By 1955, the trackage of street railroads was only about one-sixth what it had been at its peak in 1917.[22] Accompanying the contraction of street railroads, there was a lower volume of passengers taking advantage of this type of urban transit (Figure 14–19).

The decline of the street railroad was the result, not of lowered demand for urban transportation, but the rise of alternative methods of transit, both individualized and group transit. After World War I, the private automobile came into widespread use for individual

movements in the city. Further, new types of urban mass transit rose in acceptance and use and these contributed to the decline of the street railroad. The motor bus steadily increased in importance, as did the subway and elevated train, and the trolley coach (Figure 14–19). When urban population became increasingly dispersed and outlying densities became less, the greater convenience was afforded by the private auto and the motor bus, neither of which was tied to a fixed route as was the street railroad. The use of systems of mass transit is based on convenience of schedules and a fairly high density of population, and neither condition seems to underlay mass transit systems today.

In recent decades, the private auto has come to dominate urban transportation in virtually all American cities and many in other world regions as well. At the same time, large volumes of passengers are moved by subways or elevated trains, and by motor buses in those cities that have these transit systems.

The economic viability of systems of mass transit is, however, in jeopardy today. Operating costs of such systems has increased greatly in recent decades and the alternative of raising transit fares is not acceptable to those low income travelers most dependent on mass transit. Private companies have gradually been liquidating their investments in mass transit systems, selling their holdings to the public sector, usually a city government or a city or regional transportation authority. Therefore, motor bus systems, subway systems, and elevated train systems in American cities are today usually operated by a public agency. The conditions that led to the lack of profitability when such systems were operated by the private sector remain today, however. There are several reasons for the lack of economic viability of mass transit systems, and each is significant. One reason is the travel patterns of users of mass transit systems. There are, as pointed out earlier, diurnal differences in demand for urban transportation, whether it is indi-

[21]George M. Smerk, "The Streetcar: Shaper of American Cities," *Traffic Quarterly,* Vol. XXI, No. 4 (October, 1967).

[22]Donald N. Dewees, "The Decline of the American Street Railways," *Traffic Quarterly,* Vol. XXIV, No. 4 (October, 1970).

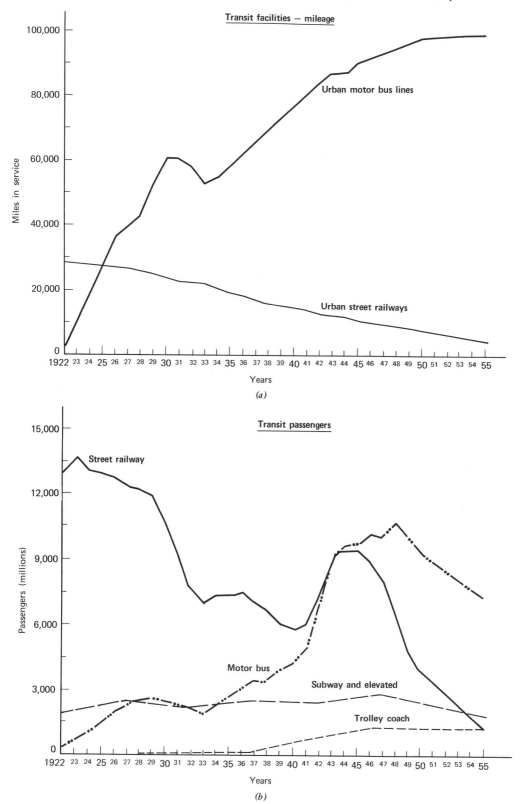

**Figure 14–19** (A) Transit facilities—mileage. (B) Transit passengers. *Source.* Based on data in Donald N. Dewees, *Traffic Quaterly,* Vol. XXIV, No. 4 (October, 1970).

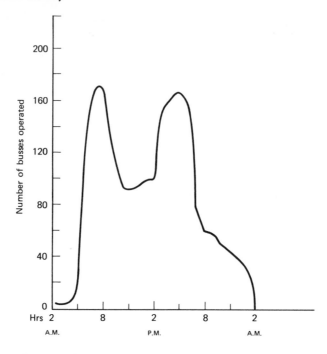

**Figure 14-20**   Hourly variation in bus flow. *Source.* Rose
City Transit Co.; Portland, Oregon (November, 1964).

vidualized or group transit. There are
pronounced peaks in demand, one in
mid-morning and one in mid-afternoon
(Figure 14–20). If the transit system is to
satisfy these peak demands adequately,
there will be a large number of vehicles
and operating personnel left idle in the
slack periods of the day and night.
Further, the vehicles needed to satisfy
peak demands create a congestion on the
routes followed, and especially in the
core area of the city, the most spatially
concentrated area of passenger destination and origin. Another important factor underlying the difficulty of mass
transit is that the urban population con-
tinually expands outward, creating
longer transit runs and many more places
of origins of potential passengers. It is
difficult and expensive to provide the
frequency, flexibility, and nearness of
service desired, so the traveler is inclined
toward urban travel by private automobile, thereby adding to the problems
associated with air pollution, clogged city
streets, and high accident rates.

When systems of mass transit are reduced and service is curtailed, it is the
segment of the population most dependent on mass transit that suffers the
most, specifically the low income groups,
the elderly, and school age youth. The
alternatives are not available to them as
they are to others. It might be considered, then, that an urban system of mass
transit should be considered as an urban
service, in the same manner as provision
of water distribution, streets, police protection and fire protection, and not as a
facility that would generate a profit or
even be operated at no financial loss, that
is, it should not be considered solely
within economic parameters. Such an argument has often been made, and in
some large American cities, this is the approach taken to support continuation
and expansion of urban mass transit systems.

But what are alternatives in urban
transportation to a system of individualized vehicular traffic that has
reached near saturation levels and a mass

transit system that is not economically viable or socially acceptable? Such questions often are asked and transportation planners have long sought answers. The alternative of developing more and more freeways in and around the city does not seem to be a realistic long-term alternative because it allows still more vehicles on city streets, adding to already difficult problems of congestion, parking, and pollution. Subways offer another alternative, as do elevated trains or some combination of the two, but these are, however, expensive alternatives. It is suggested that rail rapid transit systems have been successful in urban areas with populations greater than one million.[23] Also, it is suggested that rail rapid transit construction becomes less costly than expressways when gross population densities are over 25,000 to 30,000 per square mile.[24] However, some large cities with populations or densities less than these mentioned are planning subway systems based upon need rather than economic feasibility (Table 14–4).

An expanded system of rail rapid transit, in itself, is not likely to provide for the urban transportation needs of the urban area for there is still the matter of getting passengers to rapid transit stations. A suggested solution to this problem is to develop a bus system that would transport passengers from points of trip origin in outlying areas to rapid transit stations where they would transfer to rapid transit trains, destined for the core area of the city. The bus routes would be feeder lines and the subway or elevated routes would be trunk lines. In this manner, different modes or transportation are used in combination. Another combination presently utilized in Chicago is the operation of rapid transit commuter trains on a right-of-way shared with major freeways. A further combination is

[23]Armando M. Lago, "United States Subway Requirements 1968–1990: Projections and Benefits," *Traffic Quarterly*, Vol. XXIII, No. 1 (January, 1969).
[24]Lago, *Ibid.*

**Table 14–4** Projections of Subway Tunnel Miles to be Constructed, 1968–1990 (at Present Costs)

| City | 1968–1975 | 1976–1980 | 1981–1990 |
|---|---|---|---|
| Cleveland | — | 4.0 | — |
| Baltimore | 8.8 | — | — |
| Atlanta | 3.0 | — | — |
| Los Angeles | 2.3 | — | — |
| Philadelphia | 7.3 | 3.0 | 7.0 |
| San Francisco | 19.5 | — | 4.0 |
| Seattle | 4.6 | 2.4 | — |
| Washington | 13.1 | — | — |
| Boston | 3.9 | — | 4.0 |
| Chicago | 2.8 | 1.4 | 2.8 |
| New York | 10–20 | — | 10.0 |
| New Orleans | — | 1.0 | — |
| Detroit | — | 7.0 | — |
| Pittsburgh | — | 4.4 | — |
| St. Louis | — | 7.8 | — |
| Miami | — | 4.5 | — |
| Minneapolis | — | — | 2.1 |
| Houston | — | — | 1.6 |
| Milwaukee | — | — | 5.9 |
| Providence | — | — | 1.9 |
| Denver | — | — | 1.8 |
| Buffalo | — | — | 4.2 |
| Indianapolis | — | — | 1.3 |
| Dallas | — | — | 1.3 |
| San Diego | — | — | 1.1 |
| Cincinnati | — | — | 2.1 |
| Rochester | — | — | 1.5 |
| Kansas City | — | — | 2.0 |
| San Antonio | — | — | 0.9 |
| Totals | 75.3–85.3 | 35.5 | 55.5 |

SOURCE: Armando M. Lago, "United States Subway Requirements 1968 to 1990: Projections and Benefits," *Traffic Quarterly*, Vol. 23, No. 1 (January, 1969).

the development of large auto parking lots on the periphery of the core area from which passengers are transported into the core area by shuttle buses, thus keeping a large number of vehicles out of the congested core area.

Another alternative suggested for urban transportation is the jitney, a five to eight passenger vehicle operated on a fixed or semifixed route. They serve as a cross between individual-service taxi operations and scheduled bus operations. Jitneys are used in many countries in the world and first appeared in the United States in 1914 in Los Angeles and were later adopted in a number of other cities.[25] They suffered a decline due to dispersal of the urban population, changing shopping habits, the building of freeways, and the need for vehicles with larger capacities for use during peak hours, among other factors. It is suggested that several prospects are likely for revival of the jitney including (1) small cities (approx. 50,000 to 150,000) faced with loss of its bus service, (2) use on marginal routes in large cities that are unprofitable, (3) smaller cities that do not have a public transit system at present, and (4) private city and suburban bus lines in financial difficulty.[26]

An example of an integrated rapid transit system, regional in scope and involving several means of transportation that is being developed at present, is the Bay Area Rapid Transit (BART) system. With nearly 900,000 persons passing through six major gateways in the San

Francisco Bay area, on trips of over five miles during an average 24 hour day, there was need for a rapid transit system that would serve the population in all parts of the region.[27] The system developed includes about 52 miles of surface trackage for high speed trains, 44 miles of elevated trackage, and 24 miles of subways and tunnels. The latter includes a tunnel beneath San Francisco Bay between Oakland and San Francisco and a subway beneath the CBD's of San Francisco and Oakland.

When complete, the BART system will include a total of 52 stations. Of these, 14 are central or downtown stations without parking facilities, but these are not essential, since the stations are in close proximity to major central city traffic generators. The 38 stations outside central core areas are provided with adequate parking facilities for the vehicles of passengers.

The regional BART system, then, incorporates private vehicles for collection of passengers at outlying stations, high speed transit by surface and aerial tracks, and subsurface transit by tunnel and subway between the foci of the system,

[25]Richard N. Farmer, "Whatever Happened to the Jitney?," *Traffic Quarterly*, Vol. XIX, Number 2 (April, 1965).
[26]Farmer, *Ibid*.

[27]Stone and Youngberg, Municipal Financing Consultants, *Rapid Transit for the Bay Area*, (September, 1961).

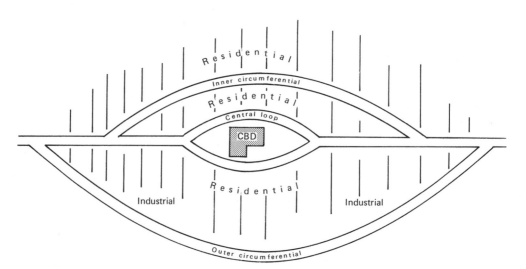

**Figure 14-21**  Hypothetical urban region and different types of freeway bypasses.

the CBD's of San Francisco and Oakland. In this manner, passengers can be provided with fast, convenient, and relatively inexpensive transportation in the urban region, relieving many of the problems that have existed. If the BART system proves successful, it may serve as a model of an integrated regional transportation system for employment in other urban areas of the country. The costs are very great, but the possible benefits are even greater.

## Urban Effects of Route Development

Development or redevelopment of transportation routes in the city does not take place without there being some impact on sections of the city through which they pass or on the city as a whole. In addition to having an effect on the transportation systems of the city, there are economic, social, and environmental effects as well. Each development or redevelopment is undertaken with hope that the transportation network will be improved. The economic, social, and environmental effects are another matter and may actually be in conflict with transportation objectives, and the population of the urban center may protest route development on the grounds of adverse ramifications.

The most commonly encountered transportation route in the city is the street or highway and these are the ones experiencing most sustained development or redevelopment. There are two forms taken in these processes: route improvement and route construction. Route improvement includes resurfacing, but the greater impact is through route improvement by widening, straightening, depression, elevation, or extension. A certain city street may originally be two lanes and a decision is made, based on increased traffic volumes, to widen the route to four lanes and to straighten the route somewhat, but there

is a sufficiently wide right-of-way so that no peripheral land will be converted to street use. A similar situation might involve the extension of an existing street to some distance beyond its present end, but following a right-of-way that has been previously acquired. It might be assumed in both cases that the route improvement would have adverse economic effects on land and land users adjacent to the improved route and environmental effects on the population living adjacent to the improved route. The adverse economic effects might be (1) that the value of land immediately adjacent to the route would be lessened, (2) there would be an increase in real estate sales in the adjacent area, and (3) there would be an increase in number of vacant commercial establishments and private dwellings in the adjacent area. A detailed study, examining these possible effects of urban street improvement through widening from two to four lanes, disclosed that there is little evidence to support these contentions.[28] Over a period of about ten years, land values of parcels adjacent to the improved route appreciated at about the same rate as did other parcels in the urban area. Further, there was no greater rate of real estate transactions than in the urban area as a whole, and vacancy rates also were not appreciably different. Other cases in other cities might produce different results, but the assumption that highway or street improvements have an adverse economic effect on the areas through which they pass is questionable.

The environmental or social effects of such developments are more clearly nonbeneficial to the areas involved. The improved routes, designed to accommodate greater volumes of vehicular traffic, present a greater barrier to easy and safe movement of pedestrian traffic. This especially applies to foot movement of

[28]Columbian Research Institute, *Swan Island Industrial Park: Access 1969*, Portland, Oregon (February, 1970). The author was co-director of this study.

children en route to schools and to persons traveling to parks and other pedestrian traffic generators in the area, where the pedestrian has to cross the improved route. Further, the records indicate a higher incidence of traffic accidents on improvement of the street and movement at greater vehicle speeds. If the route improvement calls for public acquisition of wider right-of-way, a swath of demolition and clearance of buildings, including private homes, may be necessary. These procedures tend to create a barrier within residential neighborhoods which destroys or impairs their cohesiveness and results in an aesthetically less desirable area of the city.

A different type of effect of highway improvement is found in the form of the highway bypass, a route designed to expedite vehicular traffic movement. There are different types of bypasses that have been constructed in or around cities, with the differences based on their locations

within the urban area and the objectives of the route construction. Circumventing the core area of the city is a *central* or *inner distributor loop* which includes the "business routes" found in many cities. The central loop commonly skirts the central business district, either as a surface street or a depressed freeway, and provides ready access to established business establishments (Figure 14–21). It is designed to channel previous core area traffic away from central business district streets. Outward from the central loop, there often is an *inner circumferential* bypass that passes through developed sections of the city or urban area, but avoids the CBD and most of the core area. It has limited access to established businesses and tends to disrupt residential areas through which it commonly passes. It is designed basically to provide improved linkages between different districts and subareas of the city, such as between a residential neighborhood and an

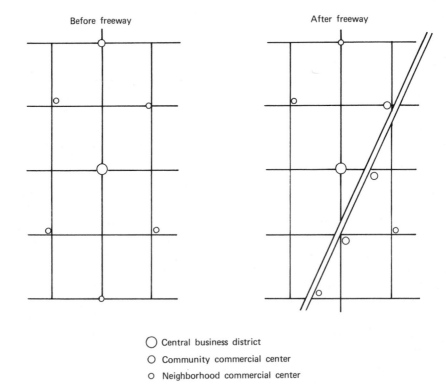

○ Central business district

○ Community commercial center

○ Neighborhood commercial center

**Figure 14–22**  Spatial adjustment of commercial centers to freeway development.

industrial district, or a suburb and an out-lying commercial district. The environ-mental impact of this type of bypass is perhaps greater than for other types, since it basically is superimposed over an existing development pattern. Still further out from the center of the city is the *outer circumferential* bypass, which passes through presently undeveloped sections of the urban area. This type of bypass is designed more to bypass the en-tire developed area of the city, more than to bypass any particular part, as do the other types. In this regard, the outer cir-cumferential is more to expedite the free flow of through traffic and is likely to be developed on what is currently rural land. Urban expansion being what it is, however, the developed area eventually may extend to the outer circumferential or beyond.

Each of the types of bypasses discussed above includes segments of the Interstate Highway System, although many by-passes constructed are not incorporat-ed into this system.

The effects of highway improvements of the above types have been examined in a number of localities and there are sev-eral generalizations possible as a result. One possible and expected effect would be a reduction of traffic volume on city streets as a result of bypass construction. Traffic volumes on city streets have been reduced from 5 to 50 percent after bypasses are constructed, at the same time that population in the cities involved

has increased. The specific reduction in traffic, however, depends on the location of the bypass, the type or types of bypass involved, and the locations of work and living places relative to the location of the bypass.

Another effect of highway bypasses often discussed is the economic impact on established businesses. Here, there are differences that should be recognized be-tween the impact of a bypass on a small urban center and on a larger urban center. The generalization is that small urban centers are more reliant on basic or export activity, which includes the dis-pensing of goods and services to non-local population, such as tourists and through-travelers. If access to these peo-ple is reduced, the establishments cater-ing to their needs might be impaired with their viability lessened in the process. In looking at the evidence dealing with sev-eral small urban centers in Montana, with populations less than 1500 that have had bypasses built around them, there is no clear pattern as to the effect of the bypass.[29] Using various economic indi-cators, there was an increase in some cases, and a decline in others, except for personal incomes which increased in all cases (Table 14-5). Specific declines in other indicators may have been due to circumstances other than the bypass and

[29]Bureau of Business and Economic Research, *Effects of Highway Bypasses on Five Montana Communities*, University of Montana (1964).

**Table 14-5** Economic Changes in Four Bypassed Montana Communities with Popula-tions Less Than 1500

| | Economic Indicator | | | | |
| | Gross Receipts | | | | |
| Community | Highway Oriented | Not Highway Oriented | Gallonage of Gasoline | Bank Deposits | Personal Income |
| --- | --- | --- | --- | --- | --- |
| Cascade (population 604) | down | down | down | up | up 15% |
| Lima(population 397) | — | down | up | — | up 6% |
| Saint Ignatius (population 948) | — | — | down | up | up 27% |
| Superior (population 1242) | down | up | up | up | up 1% |

SOURCE: University of Montana, *Effects of Highway Bypasses on Five Montana Communities*, 1964.

it is difficult to establish a cause and effect relationship between the bypass and a faltering economic sector in these small urban centers.

When one examines the effect of bypasses on somewhat larger urban centers, the situation is somewhat clearer. For this purpose, two urban areas in Washington in the size group 10,000 to 25,000 that have been bypassed are considered, as is a comparably sized city that has not been bypassed. In this manner, a control area is included to better evaluate any changes experienced in the bypassed areas.[30] In this instance, changes in measures of sales of commercial establishments located along the major business route and of those in the total trade area were derived for each of the three urban areas (Table 14–6). From this study, it can be observed that declines in sales were most pronounced in the city that was not bypassed (the control area) and that no consistent pattern of increases or decreases exists with regard to the two bypassed cities. Furthermore, where declines occurred in the bypassed city, they tended also to occur in the county containing the bypassed city.

The cases cited in previous sections that concern the impact of highway improvements in the form of bypasses deal with small urban centers. In dealing with the impact of highway improvement on large metropolitan centers, the task is much more difficult, since there is a host of variables that might affect economic, social, or spatial change in the metropolitan center that would not be associated with highway development. It has been suggested that variables inherent to an assessment of the impact of urban freeway development include the following: (1) extent of the freeway network and its degree of completion, (2) degree of development and completion of the inner distributor loop, (3) extent of central space used for highways, (4) extent of freeway interference with business linkages, (5) time required to construct the system, (6) extent of changes in trade area structure, and (7) extent of centralization of activities.[31] In addition, there are noninherent variables bearing on the impact of urban freeway development on the CBD. These include (8) planning and urban redevelopment, (9) provision of off-street parking near the core; and (10) development of mass transit. To be sure, the time-frame within which each of these variables applies is different; variables having to do with the engineering and construction of the route encompass a shorter time span than do those dealing with a more lasting impression such as interference with business linkages, amount of land used for freeways, and change in trade area structure. Each of these variables make it difficult, however, to assess the impact of highway improvements on an entire urban area or even a major part of such areas.

In terms of spatial impact of redevelopment or realignment of highways in a region, it is possible to develop a number of generalizations based on studies that have been completed. For one thing, there are desired reductions of vehicular traffic on core area streets. Also, some businesses located on bypassed routes are adversely effected in regard to volume of sales, while others at different locations appear to be relatively uneffected or even bettered somewhat, depending on the specific type of business. Another effect of highway improvement appears to be a greater degree of centralization of commercial establishments. This is to say, less dispersion of such establishments in the urban area. New commercial concentrations may be formed at prime locations, such as interchanges of freeways and at prime intersections of major arterials. Further, commercial clusters in proximity to the

---

[30]Washington State Highway Commission, *The Effect of a Bypass on Retail Trade* (1965).

[31]Edgar M. Horwood and Ronald R. Boyce, *Studies of the Central Business District and Urban Freeway Development*, Seattle: University of Washington Press (1959).

**Table 14–6**  Some Measures of the Impact of Highway Bypass: Two Washington Communities

| | Changes in Index of Aggregate Sales | | | | | |
| | Olympia–Tumwater (Three years After) Bypass) | | Centralia–Chehalis (Six years After) Bypass) | | Puyallup (Not Bypassed) | |
| Business Type | Business Route Only | Total Area | Business Route Only | Total Area | Business Route Only | Total Area |
|---|---|---|---|---|---|---|
| More oriented to motorists and tourists | | | | | | |
| Service stations | −14 | −5 | 11 | 23 | −19 | 24 |
| Eating and drinking places | −15 | 4 | 4 | 4 | −21 | −21 |
| Hotels, motels, transient lodging | −3 | 21 | −9 | 8 | −12 | −12 |
| More oriented to area residents | | | | | | |
| Food group | 1 | −1 | −7 | −4 | −40 | −39 |
| General merchandise | 13 | 12 | 22 | 3 | −15 | 2 |
| Apparel group | −13 | −18 | 13 | −7 | −25 | −22 |
| Furniture and appliances | 3 | −1 | −22 | −8 | −62 | −35 |
| Building materials | −1 | −5 | 28 | −7 | −31 | −20 |
| Automotive group | −11 | −11 | −15 | 4 | 36 | 40 |
| General services | 4 | 5 | 24 | −3 | −36 | 51 |
| Professional services | 17 | 17 | 8 | 0 | 23 | −5 |

SOURCE:   Washington State Highway Commission, *The Effect of a Bypass on Retail Trade* (1965).

improved route tend to be enlarged. In essence, this produces a rearrangement of commercial clusters that reflects, to some degree, the development of highway improvements (Figure 14–22). There is a tendency toward a number of commercial nucleations arranged in a linear pattern, which duplicates the pattern of major highway arterials, especially in smaller urban centers with a high proportion of highway oriented business concerns. The degree to which this centralization proceeds will depend on the nature and orientation of the improvements provided. The result, though, is a revision of the spatial structure of commercial centers that are associated with vehicular movement on highways, and there are very few of these clusters that do not benefit somewhat, at least, from such as association.

# 15
# other land components of the city

Previous chapters have dealt with the land in the city that is used for work places, for residential sites, for commercial purposes, and for transportation. Collectively, amounts of land for these purposes account for the greatest share of total city area, and each of the amounts of land used in these ways is characterized by a relatively high intensity of use or occupance. They are the uses of urban land that play a near daily role in the lives of urban dwellers and are, therefore the uses of which we are most aware. There are, however, large amounts of urban space that are often overlooked in

urban awareness and in urban studies; these typified by a low intensity of use or by nonuse. Attention in this chapter is drawn to such components of urban structure.

There are several different types of land that are devoted to low intensity use or to non-use and it is necessary to clarify the meanings of terms used to designate these. We referred in Chapter 9 to public and semipublic land and the difficulty in developing a clear definition of the meaning of this land use designation. The name, public and semipublic, refers to the form of ownership or administration and not to land use *per se*. So in actuality, this is not a land use, although the inference is that it can be applied to land that is owned or administered by public agencies and used in a manner that is in accord with the desires of the public. Public land is used for a variety of purposes, although the common characteristic is that such land is used for the benefit of the public or some segment of the public. Semipublic land, as a land use designation, is more difficult to define, for there is no possibility of land being partially owned by the public or by private parties. Here, the distinction seems to be based on land that is privately owned but available for use by all of the people or by sizeable segments of the general population.

Vacant land is a type of open space that is not devoted to any functional use, that is, it is not a land use type, but a type of nonuse. For this presentation, vacant land is used in reference to land area that is not devoted to any functional use, but not to vacated or razed buildings. Vacant land is considered as not performing any urban function and possibly never did, and in this sense, it is idle urban land.

Open space is a term of reference that has different interpretations for different people. For some, open space refers to land within the urban area that is not devoted to usual types of development. For others, open space implies land on the margin of the urban area that also is undeveloped. To say that such lands are undeveloped is not completely accurate, however, since if this were the case, there would be little or no distinction between open space and vacant urban land. Although vacant land is not devoted to any functional use, open space provides a function of creating an openness in the urban expanse and a deviation from the crowdedness characteristic of most urban communities.

## Public and Semipublic Land

Some of the types of public and semipublic land have been discussed previously, such as land devoted to streets, public housing, and airports. These account for the greatest share of publicly owned lands in the city, but there remain some significant users of public land for the functioning of urban society, although these use relatively small amounts of urban space—likely less than ten percent of the total. There are four additional types of public and semipublic land considered at this time: recreational land

in the city, land for schools and colleges, land for cemeteries, and land for churches.

Of these four types, recreational areas account for the largest demands for urban land. Based on eighty-two cities in the United States with populations of 100,000 or more, the average amount of land used for recreational purposes in the city is approximately 2,600 acres or just over five percent of total city area. There is a great deal of variance in the proportion of area of large cities devoted to recreational use, however (Figure 15-1). The highest proportions of recreational land are in New York City (17.3 percent), Allentown, Pa. (12.4 percent), Phoenix (12.2 percent), San Francisco (10.5 percent), and Hartford (9.9 percent).[1] There appears to be no pronounced relationship between popula-

[1]National Commission on Urban Problems, *Three Land Research Studies,* Research Report No. 12 (1968).

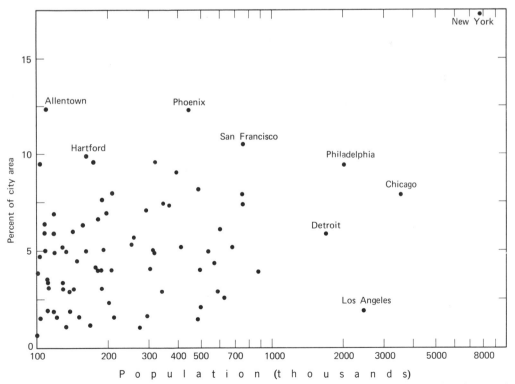

**Figure 15–1** Land used for recreational purposes. *Source.* Based on data in the National Commission on Urban Problems Research Report No. 12. 1968.

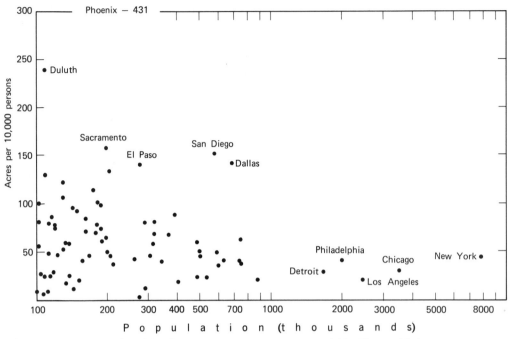

**Figure 15–2**    Recreational land per 10,000 persons. *Source.* Ibid., Figure 15–1.

tion of the urban center and the proportion of city area used for recreational purposes. A high proportion of recreational land seems to accompany the presence of outstanding recreational sites, as in the cases of San Francisco and Niagara Falls, but it may also accompany an active program of recreational development in cities without great natural or scenic attributes. A measure of the adequacy of amounts of recreational land in the city is the amount available per 10,000 residents. In this case, the best endowed cities tend to be those of smaller populations, although there is considerable variation here too (Figure 15-2).

Recreational land in the city is devoted to a variety of functions. This land can be divided between (1) land for active recreation, that is, sports and games, and (2) land for passive recreation, that is, relaxation, sightseeing, etc. In essence, this distinction is between participant recreation and spectator recreation. These distinctions bring to mind the difficulty of defining precisely what is meant by recreation; for some it may mean some type

of competition, for others a form of amusement, and for others it may mean relaxation. For the most part, the use of land for such recreational purposes deals with outdoor recreation on sites with some types of facilities that provide for both active recreation, such as outdoor swimming pools and tennis courts, as well as passive recreation, such as contemplation at an artistic fountain or on a park bench.

Once again, the share of city area used for recreational purposes of all types varies a great deal among cities, but for cities of 100,000 or more people, the average is about five percent. Standards have been established by different cities and organizations regarding the share of city area that should be devoted to recreation, one of which is ten percent of city area devoted to recreation and open space. Notice that this standard is well above the average of major cities in the United States. Another proposed standard is based, not on proportion of city area, but on a specified area per unit of population. In this case, ten acres per 10,000 people is the standard often employed, but this does not provide for differences in needs of cities of different populations.[2] As a result, this overall standard has been revised to state a standard for cities of less than 500,000 of ten acres per 10,000 people, for cities of 500,000 to 1,000,000 ten acres per 2,000 people, and for cities over 1,000,000 ten acres per 3,000 residents. There still is no generally accepted standard for amount of recreation area desired in the city as a share of city area or as a ratio to population, although more refined standards of a different type have been suggested and employed. These take into account user characteristics and the facilities of a particular recreation site.

The urban parks that comprise most of the land put to recreational use in the city exhibit considerable variation in size, form of development, facilities provided, location within the city, and extent of the service area. It is meaningful, therefore, to disaggregate the recreational land of the city into its identifiable parts and consider the characteristics and development standards for each. There are several identifiable types or orders of recreation sites in the city and each could be evaluated or developed according to standards established for that particular order. Further, based on the differences between orders or types of urban parks and suggested standards for each, it is possible to develop a functional and spatial hierarchy of urban parks. Fundamental to this organization is the realization that no single park serves the entire array of recreational needs of the population of the city, and that a number of parks is essential in the city. Total or per capita acreage does not indicate the adequacy of a multi-order city park system to serve the needs of the population.

In a functional and spatial hierarchy of urban parks, the lowest order would include the smallest of urban parks (order I). These have been termed "tot-lots," "vest-pocket parks," or "play lots" and serve a few hundred persons located within short distance of the recreation site, generally 4 to 5 blocks at the maximum. These parks have a limited number of facilities and may include nothing but a fenced and leveled area, a pile of sand, or a bench or two. The range of the recreational services provided by these low order recreation sites is low, as is the size of the service area and the population served. If all of the urban population is to be served by this level of recreational area, the number of them would be large, however. Vacant land parcels could easily be converted to this use and would serve to keep city streets from becoming playgrounds.

The next order of urban park in a hierarchy would be represented by the urban playground (order II). Parks of this order are of larger size and include the basic facilities of lower order parks, plus a number in addition. The suggested size of playgrounds is in the order of one acre per 800 to 1000 population. Further, the population in the service area of playgrounds is roughly 4000 to 8000, meaning that these sites would include approximately five to ten acres.[3] It is considered that the population utilizing such a facility would be derived from a radius of about one-half mile, well within walking distance. The playground or neighborhood park often is found in conjunction with an elementary school and includes general purpose areas for different age groups: a paved area for games of younger children, a sports field for team sports by older children, and a grassed area for adults.

The community park, the next highest order of urban park (order III), includes facilities not found in those of lower order and has a duplication of facilities found in parks of lower order as well, for example, several sports fields instead of one. Community parks are characterized

---

[2]National Recreation Association, *Outdoor Recreation: Space Standards*, New York (July, 1965).

[3]National Recreation Association, *Ibid.*

by serving a larger number of people, in the realm of about 20,000. These parks include larger areas than do those of lower order, with the standard about two acres per 1000 population in areas of multifamily housing and one to one and one-half acres per 1000 in areas of single family housing. The service areas of parks of this order have a radius of about three-fourths mile to one mile, making them somewhat less accessible to small children whose needs are provided for by parks of lower order. The facilities, found in such parks, include those common to lower order parks, such as playground equipment, paved surfaces for games, etc., but also include some more specialized facilities as well. These might include shallow pools used for outdoor skating rinks in winter, one or more shelters, a public restroom, or a tennis court.

The next highest order of park is the district park (order IV) that serves a larger number of people, on the order of 40,000 to 50,000, and which includes facilities not found in lower order parks, that is, the array of facilities is extended. Such parks have an area/population ratio of about 2.5 to 4.0 acres per 1000 people and have a service area with a radius of about 2½ to 3 miles. These parks are accessible by foot for those living nearby, but necessitate use of mass transit or automobile by those on the fringe of the service area.

The regional park (order V) is the highest order of urban park and is the least commonly found. The regional park includes facilities that are fairly specialized, such as swimming pools, duck ponds, or a small zoo, plus those more common to lower order parks. These parks are regional in the sense that they serve an entire urban area or a major portion thereof, as well as attracting users from outside the urban region but within the sphere of influence of the city where the regional park is located. There are no firm standards developed for regional parks in regard to area and size of population served. Generally, regional parks include hundreds of acres and serve tens of thousands of people on a regular basis and additional tens of thousands on an irregular basis. The radius of the service areas of regional parks is given as ten miles or one hour driving time. Certainly, this indicates that the users of these parks are dependent on mass transit or private automobiles for access to the facility. Regional parks tend to have a number of specialized facilities not found in parks of lower orders, such as skating rinks, swimming pools, tennis courts, race tracks, formal gardens, zoos, hiking trails, etc. Very often, these regional parks include considerable area that is better categorized as open space than purely recreational area in that the level of development is minimal and there is a low intensity of use.

Aspects of a functional hierarchy have been already mentioned, with each order or level of park having identifiable functions or facilities, and with higher order parks providing services or facilities not found in those of lower order at the same time that they have those services or facilities offered by those of lower order. The concept of a functional hierarchy applies to urban parks, while it would not apply as well to state or national parks since recreation in urban areas is mainly dependent on man-made facilities, utilizing urban space. State and national park systems are more influenced by unique or outstanding features of the natural environment, such as waterfalls, ski slopes, geologic formations, and white-water rivers. The urban area likely does not include such features, but still the need for recreation exists and is provided for by urban park systems, comprised of different functional orders.

A spatial hierarchy is implied in sections above as well. Each order of urban park discussed has a threshold population, a range within which the recreation service is extended, and a service area. It can be seen that the lowest order parks with a small array of facilities serves a relatively small number of people and a limited service area. With each succeeding order of park, the population served and the size of the service area becomes greater, and at the same time, the service area of a higher order park includes the service areas of a number of lower order parks (Figure 15-3). This is logical, since the recreational opportunities of the lower order parks are limited, and if the individual is to obtain a more specialized recreational service, he must travel to a more distant and higher order park where such a service is available. For example, a playlot may provide the need for play space, such as throwing a ball, but the neighborhood park would be the recreational unit offering a surfaced ball diamond, a somewhat more specialized form of recreational facility. Implicit in the notion of a spatial hierarchy of urban parks and their service areas is the concept of nesting. The service area of a lower order park is nested within the service area of an urban park of the next highest order, with this in turn nested

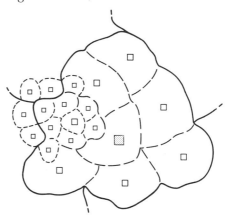

○ Urban playground and service area boundary
□ Community park and service area boundary
▦ District park and service area boundary

**Figure 15-3** Hypothetical spatial hierarchy of urban parks: three orders.

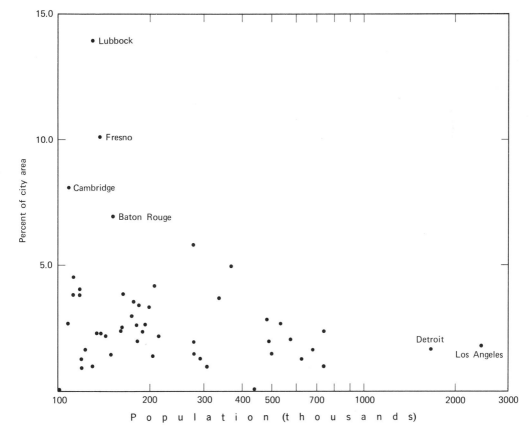

**Figure 15-4** Land used for schools and colleges. *Source.* Ibid., Figure 15-1.

within the service area of a park of the next higher order. In this manner, the system of parks blankets the entire urban area, and each person in the urban area has access to an urban park of each level or order.

One value of considering urban recreation within the context of a functional and spatial hierachy has to do with formulation of a developmental plan. Public officials responsible for urban recreation systems might consider an urban park plan in that way. In a specific urban community, a certain number of playgrounds may be desired to serve the needs of the people, as would be true of playlots, neighborhood parks, and each of the other orders in a functional hierarchy. Once these needs were determined, it would be a relatively simple task to compare the existing recreational system with the needed system. The planning of needed parks of each order, then, could be undertaken within a planning framework in the hope that funding would be provided and development undertaken. This procedure was followed by a research team dealing with recreation sites in a community in Portland, Oregon in which they (1) estimated the number of parks of different orders that were needed, and (2) estimated the needed acreage in parks of each order.[4] By comparing number and acreage of existing parks with necessary park sites, they provided valuable insights into unsatisfied needs for recreation in the community and identified the specific types of recreation areas that were needed beyond those developed at the time. In addition, they estimated the space needs for recreation areas of different orders.

Land used for schools and colleges is another type of public and semipublic land in the city. Many of these facilities

are publicly financed and operated, while others are financed and operated by organized groups such as religious orders. In the latter case, the term semipublic is appropriate with regard to the manner in which the land is used. Public and private educational facilities of different levels, from kindergartens to universities, are included in this discussion.

Based on a group of fifty-three American cities with populations over 100,000, the average amount of land used for schools and colleges is nearly 1100 acres or 2.88 percent of the area of the cities included (approximately one-half the percent of city area devoted to recreation). There is considerable variance too in the proportion of city area used for educational purposes (Figure 15-4). Cities with the highest percentages of their area used for these purposes include Lubbock (13.8 percent), Fresno (10.7 percent), Cambridge (8.3 percent), and Baton Rouge (6.9 percent). These lands tend to be distributed throughout the city in a manner roughly approximating the distribution of urban population. In cases where the city is the home of a major college or university with a sprawling campus, the greatest share of land used for educational purposes would be accounted for by this single institution, which may be sited without particular regard to the distribution of population of that city. Of the average acreage of land used for schools and colleges in large cities in the U.S., about six-tenths is used for public schools, or about 1.72 percent of total city area, leaving an average of approximately 1.0 percent for use by denominational and other semipublic schools.

With regard to location of elementary and secondary schools, there is continued controversy as to which of two courses is best followed. Should schools be located on the growing edge of the city or beyond, or should schools be located and built in the wake of spatial expansion of residential developments? In the first instance, with school location preceding

[4]Robert Vining, Jeanne Newton, Ronald Weinkauf, and Helen Jane Armstrong. *A Recreational Plan for the St. Johns Community of Portland, Oregon,* Unpublished Research paper, (March, 1971).

residential growth, the direction of growth is essentially fixed as residential areas come into existence in proximity to the schools. Surely, land costs may be less in this case, but provision of utilities, such as water, sewers, electricity, etc. is more costly. Further, provision of essential services, such as police and fire protection, is made more difficult. The alternative course in location of new schools involves their development in a manner that reflects a need to serve established residential areas, not ones that are planned or projected. This course is made difficult if possible school sites are preempted by residential construction, or if land parcels sufficient in size to accommodate a school are few in number and more costly as a result. An alternative in the latter instance would be the reservation of school sites at the time of development of new subdivisions, with school construction phased in as needs arise from residential growth in the subdivision.

Concerning school site needs, certain key factors should be considered. These include (1) community characteristics, such as the pattern of population growth and directions of growth or quiescence, (2) population trends, including population projections, population distribution, and economic structure of the population, (3) school board policies involving such items as school consolidation, bussing, etc., (4) educational philosophy of the community and school administrators, and (5) evaluation of present plants and proposed sites.[5] Once the decision is made that new school sites are needed, certain criteria are suggested for selection of a school site.[6] These are as follows:

1.   The site should be large enough to accommodate necessary buildings and provide ample space for outdoor instruction and recreation, for parking, and for future expansion.

2.   The site should be readily accessible not only to children who will attend the school, but also to the general public for community use.

3.   The site should be so located that water, sewers, electricity, and other utilities can be provided at reasonable cost.

4.   The site should have an elevation that will insure good drainage, and a subsoil that will provide a good base for building foundations.

5.   The site should be selected with due regard to its proximity to public, recreational, educational, and cultural facilities in the community.

6.   The site should be one that lends itself to landscaping and a pleasing natural environment.

Once the rationale for new school sites is provided and the criteria established and met as to the attributes the school site should possess, the matter of size of school site remains. In the United States, there is no national standard on this matter, with any standards left to the individual states. There is a set of suggested standards, however, and these often have been adopted or approximated by respective states. The guidelines suggest minimum sizes for school sites for different types of schools as follows: elementary schools—five acres, junior high schools—twenty acres, and senior high schools—thirty acres.[7] These are minimum suggested sizes and would be increased according to enrollment in the following manner: an additional acre for each one-hundred students of predicted ultimate enrollment for each type of school. In actuality, these suggested site sizes have been fairly well implemented and, in many cases, exceeded, with forty-three reporting states (plus the District of Columbia) having a minimum site size for elementary schools of five acres

[5]Department of Health, Education, and Welfare, *School Sites: Selection, Development, and Utilization,* Special Publication No. 7 (1958).

[6]Department of Health, Education, and Welfare, *Ibid.*

[7]National Council on Schoolhouse Construction, *Guide for Planning School Plants* (1958).

or more (Table 15–1). For secondary schools, forty-four of the reporting states and the District of Columbia have a standard minimum site size of ten acres or more. In the majority of cases, the addition of one acre for every one-hundred students is adopted as well. Considering then the magnitude of school-age youth in cities, large and small, there is a considerable amount of urban land needed for use by schools and colleges.

**Table 15–1** Minimum Size of School Sites: By Number of Reporting States

| Site Size (Acres) | Number of States |
|---|---|
| Elementary Schools | |
| Less than 5 | 5 |
| 5 | 34 |
| More than 5 | 9 |
| Secondary Schools | |
| Less than 10 | 4 |
| 10 | 27 |
| More than 10 | 17 |

SOURCE: Department of Health, Education, and Welfare, *School Sites: Selection, Development, and Utilization*, Special Publication No. 7. (1958).

The major activity occurring on land occupied by schools and colleges is, of course, the provision of instruction for the young and, to a lesser degree, services to the community at large. In the conduct of these functions, there is an economic impact in various forms. The role of education in the economic structure of the city has been discussed briefly in Chapter 8, but it serves here to reiterate and expand on earlier comments. It was mentioned that employment in schools, serving a local population, adds to the city serving or nonbasic sector of the urban economy, that is, the employment is based on serving a local market for educational services. By contrast, employment in colleges and universities that draw students from a larger area than just the local community contributes to the city forming or basic sector of the urban economy.

The economic impact of schools and colleges is manifested in ways other than employment, however. One manner of assessing the role of educational functions is to consider the different types of expenditures connected with their operation, in this case, focusing on the way in which money is expended, rather than how it is earned. Taking the example of the Berkeley Campus of the University of California and tracing through its expenditures, a total of $318 million was expended in 1966.[8] The major share of this expenditure was made for nonhousing needs by students and faculty, with housing being the second largest expenditure (Table 15–2). Of the total expenditure, 43.9 percent was made in the city of Berkeley, with an additional 13.3 percent made in Alameda County (the county containing Berkeley), and another 27.3 percent made elsewhere in the San Francisco Bay area. The bulk of the personal expenditure for housing and for nonhousing was made in the city of Berkeley, which had an obvious and significant impact on the economy of that city.

In addition to the expenditures itemized in Table 15–2, there are indirect economic effects of a major educational facility. For example, there is often an increase in property values associated with institutions of higher education, as well as with primary and secondary schools. These effects are felt most in parts of the city in close proximity to the educational facilities and tend to diminish as a function of distance away from the facilities. The matter of contract maintenance of the educational facility also adds to the economic impact on the city. In these examples, most likely there is an addition to the nonbasic sector, but in any case, there is an increment to the economic vitality of the community.

[8]University of California, Office of the Vice-President, *The Community Impact of the University of California's Berkeley and Santa Cruz Campuses* (April, 1967).

**Table 15–2**  Expenditures in the City of Berkeley Attributable to the University of California–Berkeley Campus, 1966

| Type of Expenditure | Percent of Total |
| --- | --- |
| Students: nonhousing | 31.7 |
| Faculty-staff: nonhousing | 31.5 |
| Students: housing | 14.5 |
| Faculty-staff: housing | 7.3 |
| Miscellaneous vendor | 6.2 |
| Construction | 4.6 |
| Visitors | 2.6 |
| Auxiliary enterprises | .9 |
| University-wide | .6 |

SOURCE:  University of California, *The Community Impact of the University of California's Berkeley and Santa Cruz Campuses* (April, 1967).

Educational values of schools and colleges in a community are fairly obvious. The economic values have been discussed in the preceding section. Other values of schools and colleges are manifested to the community in addition. These include the provision of social or cultural amenities in the city in the form of exhibits, theater, creative arts, and athletic events. Also, there is an upgrading of the abilities of the potential or existing labor force, especially in communities with a college or university. Related to the presence of a college or university in a community is a betterment of the general cultural level of the community in terms of involvement, interests, and awareness. All in all, there are many types of impact from schools and colleges in the community; some of them are direct benefits fairly easily to identify, and others, indirect or intangible benefits that tend to be more obscure and difficult to recognize.

The next type of land in the general category of public and semipublic is land put to use as cemeteries. For a group of fifty-five cities in the United States with populations over 100,000, the average amount of land so used is about 457 acres or 1.32 percent of the total area of the city. Thus, cemeteries are relatively small users of urban land, although their roles are greater when assessed in ways other than as occupants of urban space.

Cities with exceptionally large shares of their area devoted to cemeteries include Richmond, Pittsburgh, New Bedford, and Providence, with 8.6, 3.7, 3.2, and 3.0 percent respectively (Figure 15–5).[9] It is likely that many cities of smaller size have

----

[9]National Commission on Urban Problems, *Op. Cit.*

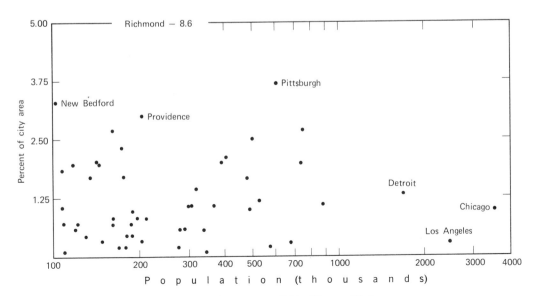

**Figure 15–5**  Land used for cemeteries. *Source.* Ibid., Figure 15–1.

still higher proportions of their area devoted to cemeteries.

Urban cemeteries are owned by different groups, such as in the city of Chicago. Of seventy cemeteries in the Chicago urban area, thirty-nine are owned by corporations on a profit making basis, twenty-six by churches, three by fraternal societies, and two by nonprofit cemetery associations.[10] In other cities, cemeteries are often owned and administered by the municipal government. Not only are there cemeteries developed for different religious groups, there are cemeteries developed for different ethnic groups. Thus, there is segregation even after death, especially in cemeteries developed by churches.

The first developed cemeteries were soon followed by others as well and by expansion of existing ones, mainly as a function of increasing number of deaths in the urban population. Due to these demands, the exclusion policies of established cemeteries, and other reasons, there was an increase in the number of cemeteries in urban areas. For example, from 1900 to 1950 in Chicago, the number of cemeteries increased from 27 to 70.[11] This led to development at new locations in and on the margin of the city.

The first cemeteries in the city tended to be located on close-in sites on the margin of the city that were physically acceptable with regard to drainage, soil materials, slope, etc. Prime sites were on hilltops or on hilly land, as suggested by studies in the Willamette Valley in Oregon and in southern Illinois.[12] When the city expanded areally, the early cemeteries became surrounded by urban developments and were not especially ac-

cessible to the patrons. Opposition began to mount with regard to additional cemeteries in the city based on the impediments they comprised to urban development, to the supposed health hazard presented by them, and to the fact that land used for burial purposes was not subject to property taxes.

Ordinances were passed in a number of major cities that curtailed expansion of existing cemeteries or development of new ones. In 1930, an ordinance was passed in Chicago that prohibited the establishment, enlargement, or alteration of the boundaries of any cemetery within the city or within one mile of the city.[13] Burials were prohibited in San Francisco in 1901, except for the Presidio.[14] The response to this opposition, since nobody calls a moratorium on death and the need for burial space continued, was to select large expanses of land for cemeteries outside the limits of the city and in fringe areas where cemeteries would be more acceptable. Cemetery founders sought more remote locations, but at the same time, they desired sites near major transportation lines. The remoteness sought often was to disappear as urban expansion continued to and beyond the fringe area cemeteries. In the Chicago area, locations with access to railroad lines were especially desirable and cemeteries came to be located in the interstices or wedges between rail lines radiating outward from Chicago.[15] In the San Francisco area, cemeteries were developed on the peninsula to the south of the city and in the San Jose area after the turn of the century to provide for the burial needs of San Francisco. In the latter case, the city of Colma, adjacent to the cities of Broadmoor, Daly City, and South San Francisco, was incorporated for the protection of several cemetery owners.[16] Today, the special-function city of Colma has a population

[10] William D. Pattison, "The Cemeteries of Chicago: A Phase of Land Utilization," *Annals of the AAG*, Vol. XLV, No. 3 (September, 1955).

[11] Pattison, *Ibid*.

[12] Richard V. Francaviglia, "The Cemetery as an Evolving Cultural Landscape," *Annals of the AAG*, Vol. 61, No. 3 (September, 1971). Larry W. Price, "Some Results and Implications of a Cemetery Study," *The Professional Geographer*, Vol. 18, No. 4 (July, 1966).

[13] Pattison, *Op. Cit.*

[14] Gerry A. Hale and Lay James Gibson, "A City Designed to Keep People In," *Yearbook*, Assoc. of Pacific Coast Geographers, Vol. 33 (1971).

[15] Pattison, *Op. Cit.*

[16] Hale and Gibson, *Op. Cit.*

of about 500 living persons and over 300,000 bodies in thirteen cemeteries. This response to need for burial space is unusual, however. Regarding the early developed cemeteries within a city, most of them remain, although there are exceptions. In the case of Chicago, several cemeteries were evacuated and removed to more remote locations. There is considerable ambivalence, however, concerning the removal of cemeteries and in most cases, such an alternative is neither feasible nor possible.

Two different types of urban cemeteries can be recognized based on form and location. The cemeteries developed early in conjunction with a church or by a religious group tend to endure on sites within the central city. These cemeteries tend toward ornate landscaping and tombstones and often have a grid pattern of layout. These cemeteries likely are surrounded by other urban land users and have little if any possibility for expansion. By contrast, the cemeteries developed later tend to be on hilly sites outside of the central city. These cemeteries tend toward a sinuous layout and have gravemarkers flush with ground level to expedite care and maintenance. Further, these cemeteries are of larger size than their earlier counterparts and have ample land for burials in the future. Examples include Olivet cemetery in Colma, which has 82,000 bodies at present and an ultimate capacity of 200,000, and Cypress Lawn, also in Colma, has 230,000 bodies and a capacity of 600,000.[17] Hale and Gibson state, "If estimates of burial capacity approximate future reality, Colma will have a long life after death".[18]

The demand for burial space continues to increase as time passes. Efforts to ease the pressure on land for cemeteries by cremation have met with but modest success, since such an alternative is unacceptable to certain religious and cultural groups. Likewise, reuse of burial plots

and multilevel stacking of coffins in a single grave have not met with any widespread success. Cemeteries will persist as a land use in the future, but the amount of land devoted to them in the central city is not likely to increase to any significant degree. Cemeteries are, however, likely to become a more prominent land use component in the urban fringe.

If the cemeteries remaining as artifacts in the central city are judged to be an impediment to orderly development and more of a hindrance than a benefit, the use of air rights over the cemeteries might be considered. In this case, the cemetery could be maintained and improved with landscaping and fountains creating a park like atmosphere. At the same time, the air space above the cemetery could accommodate many-storied buildings used for commercial purposes. Office space, in particular, could be provided in this manner.

Still another type of public and semipublic land in the city is the type devoted to churches. There is no complete accounting of the amount of land so used, but it would vary greatly among cities. Also, there is a paucity of material available in the literature dealing with the location of churches. The tendency is for the greatest share of this land to be near the core of the city, since many church facilities in the core area have a long standing heritage and date from early in the history of the city. These often imposing edifices have withstood the years and continue to occupy prime parcels of land near the heart of the city. If these parcels were taxed as other parcels are, it is unlikely they could continue as religious facilities. Newer churches have tended to be constructed on the margins of the city where land costs and access to patrons is greater. It is not uncommon either, as we will mention later, for religious organizations to purchase tracts of vacant land on the growing edge of the city in advance of residential development; the objective here is to construct a church on the parcel at a time that residential growth seems to warrant it. Again, this procedure is

---

[17]Hale and Gibson, *Op Cit.*
[18]Hale and Gibson, *Op Cit*, p. 171.

aided a great deal by the tax structure that allows land of this type to remain virtually tax-free, even before church construction occurs.

## Vacant Urban Land

While public and semipublic uses of urban space make up about ten percent of the land area of large cities in the United States, for a group of eighty-six cities over 100,000, vacant land accounts for about one-fifth of the land area of the city. Although the public and semipublic lands are put to some functional use of low intensity, even though it is difficult to assess the intensity of land use of urban cemeteries, vacant land is put to no functional use whatsoever. Included as vacant urban land are parcels that have been bypassed by areal expansion of the urban area and that exist as enclaves surrounded by parcels that have been converted to one or more types of urban use. It should be recognized that there are different types of vacant urban land in the city. Type I vacant land consists of remnant parcels that are the bits and pieces left after platting and development have taken place.[19] Vacant parcels of this type are the most numerous of all types of vacant parcels, although each parcel tends to be smaller than those of other types. In addition to small size, these vacant parcels are often characterized by irregular shape. Type II vacant urban land consists of parcels that are unbuildable, based on slopes in excess of 10 to 15 percent, danger of flooding, or unstable subsurface materials. Of these physical impediments to development in the usual urban manner, excessive slope is the most often cited by authorities in major cities, although there is no concensus as to the degree of slope

beyond which development would be curbed. The working definition of excessive slope varies in different cities, depending on local living standards and market conditions. Of the other physical constraints on land that may render it unbuildable, a less frequently cited reason is unstable subsurface materials, including poor compaction of earth materials, unstable foundation materials, or an overabundance of soil moisture. The hazard posed by recurrent flooding is still less frequently given as a reason for rendering vacant urban land unbuildable, largely due to flood control works that have lessened the severity and frequency of floods affecting major metropolitan areas. In addition to the physical factors that serve to render a vacant land parcel unbuildable, there are societal or institutional factors that bear on the matter. Size of vacant land parcel can inhibit conversion to an urban use. For example, in Portland, Oregon, there are hundreds of miniparcels of vacant land that are zoned for single family residential use. If the vacant parcel includes an area of 2,000 to 3,000 square feet and the zoning calls for single family dwellings on parcels of 7000 square feet or more, the possibility of conversion of the vacant parcels in question to the designated use, single family residential, is not great, that is, they could be considered unbuildable. These parcels tend to remain as vacant lots overgrown with weeds and strewn with litter and serve no functional use. Closely associated with the above situation are the miniparcels of vacant land that remain vacant by virtue of small size and irregular shape. The marketability of elongate parcels, many-sided parcels, or those with any other unusual geometric configuration, tends to be low, and for all practical purposes, such parcels are unbuildable. An institutional factor that has a bearing on the buildability of a vacant parcel is the desire to provide "open space" in the city. It is difficult to establish the degree to which this attitude prevails today, but it is equally difficult to envision

---

[19]Ray M. Northam, "Vacant Urban Land in the American City," *Land Economics*, Vol. 47, No. 4 (November, 1971). Most of the material in this section dealing with vacant urban land comes from the source stated.

a garbage strewn vacant lot in a residential area as desirable open space. Perhaps, the open space is provided and could be maintained in the form of large, unbuildable parcels that are rendered unbuildable due to physical limitations, especially steep slope. These and other unbuildable vacant parcels in the city are less numerous than are remnant parcels, but each tends to be larger in area.

Type III vacant urban land includes those parcels that comprise corporate reserves. These are less numerous than are remnant parcels or unbuildable parcels, though they seem to be larger in size, often including tens or hundreds of acres. These are land parcels acquired in the past by business concerns with the notion that they eventually would be used for relocation of the concern or for an expanded operation of the concern. In this sense, they constitute a land reserve in which the land is retained in a state of vacancy, but only temporarily until it is needed for a functional use.

Type IV vacant urban land consists of land parcels of modest size held for speculation in the expectation that they will eventually be sold for a profit. Type V vacant land parcels include those held as institutional reserves, such as future school sites, religious facilities, public service organizations, such as Red Cross or Boy Scouts, or fraternal organizations, such as lodges.

Each of the types of vacant urban land has a distributional pattern somewhat different from others. Remnant parcels are found throughout the city, as tends to be true of unbuildable parcels. Corporate reserves tend to be found nearer the core area of the city than do others. Institutional reserves tend more to be found in the outer portions of the city, while vacant parcels held for speculation are most common on the periphery of the city. Regarding the overall spatial setting where vacant parcels are found, one might consider the location of vacant parcels relative to different types of developed urban land. These spatial rela-

**Table 15–3**  Amount of Buildable Vacant Land and Selected Distance Variables.

| Distance | Distance to 100 Percent Corner | Distance to Nearest Industrial District | Distance to Nearest Commercial Center |
|---|---|---|---|
| | *(Coefficients of Correlation)* | | |
| Portland study[a] | .2431 | .2871 | .3215 |
| Tulsa study[b] | .3999 | — | .4398 |

[a]Ray M. Northam, *The Distribution and Potential of Vacant Urban Land,* unpublished research paper (1968).

[b]Robert C. Brown, *Spatial Variations of Idle Land in Tulsa, Oklahoma*, unpublished doctoral dissertation (1967).

tionships can be expressed by means of coefficients of correlation between (1) the amount of buildable vacant land in an area cell, such as a quarter-section, and (2) the distance to a specific major center or focus in the urban center, such as the 100 percent corner in the CBD, a major commercial center, or an industrial district. Once again, land at or near some point that tends to minimize travel time and distance, is the most sought after by urban land users, and the nearer a land parcel is to such a point, the more intense the use made of it. In this context, land near a major urban focus of the types mentioned above, would be most in demand for some functional use. Therefore, based on this conceptual framework, the incidence of buildable vacant land would be greater as distance from an urban focus increases. This proposition was examined in Portland, Oregon, as well as in Tulsa, Oklahoma, and the results do not support the above hypothesis concerning the spatial distribution of buildable vacant land in the city (Table 15–3).[20]

There appears to be little relationship between the two variables, with distance

[20]Ray M. Northam, *The Distribution and Potential of Vacant Urban Land*, An unpublished research paper (1968).

not especially influencing the incidence or location of vacant urban land parcels. The existence of these parcels tends to be continued for reasons other than those suggested by theories of land use in the city. Quite likely, they have to do with specific aspects of the land parcel, such as size and shape, or with ownership, such as estates and trusts. Further, vacant parcels that constitute corporate reserves or institutional reserves would logically be located in the core area of the city in fairly close proximity to major urban foci, and not at great distance from such focal points. Also, there is no particular reason why remnant parcels, the most numerous of all types, would be fewer in number near to commercial and industrial focal points. One can note, however, that there is a greater correlation betwen distance from commercial centers and amount of buildable vacant land than there is for other urban foci, such as the CBD or industrial districts. Perhaps, ways are being found to convert vacant parcels near shopping centers to functional uses that do not apply to those adjacent to the other urban foci.

The proportion of land of the city that is vacant varies with size of the city. For cities of over 1,000,000, the proportion is about 9 percent, for cities of 100,000 to 250,000 it is 27 percent, and for cities of 2500 to 10,000, it rises to about 37 percent (Table 15–4). Even within a specific population group, there is considerable variation in the proportion of vacant urban land in the city (Table 15–5). When the amount of vacant urban land per capita is considered, the amounts in cities over 100,000 ranges from a high of over 14,000 square feet (about one-third of an acre) in Corpus Christi to a low of 26 square feet in Cambridge, Massachusetts. There is a relationship between the per capita amount of vacant land in the city and the population of the city that can be expressed by the equation $Y_c = 3243 - 1.446X - .0003X^2$ in which $Y_c$ is the estimated per capita amount of vacant land in a city and $X$ is the population of the city. This regression equation indicates there is not a negative *linear* relationship between the two variables, but a slight tendency for a negative *curvilinear* relationship (Figure 15–6).

**Table 15–4**   Vacant Urban Land as a Percent of Total City Area

| Population Group | Average Amount of Vacant Area as a Percent of Total City Area |
|---|---|
| National cities | |
| Over 1,000,000 (*n* = 4, of 5) | 8.7 |
| 500,000–1,000,000 (*n* = 12, of 16) | 23.9 |
| 250,000–500,000 (*n* = 21, of 30) | 18.6 |
| 100,000–250,000 (*n* =49, 0f 79) | 27.4 |
| Subtotal: cities over 100,000 | 19.7 |
| Oregon cities | |
| 10,000–50,000 (*n* = 10, of 14) | 30.5 |
| 2500–10,000 (*n* = 17, of 45) | 36.7 |
| Less than 2500 (*n* = 6, of 163) | 53.8 |
| Subtotal: cities of less than 50,000 | 37.9 |

SOURCE:   Ray M. Northam, "Vacant Urban Land in the American City," *Land Economics*, Vol. XLVII, No. 4 (November, 1971). Copyright © 1971 by the Regents of the University of Wisconsin.

**Table 15–5**  Extremes in Proportions of Vacant Land in 86 Cities with Populations of 100,000 or More

| Population Group | Number of Cities | Highest Proportion of Vacant Land | City with Highest Proportion | Lowest Proportion of Vacant Land | Cities with Lowest Proportion | Inter-Group Range |
|---|---|---|---|---|---|---|
| 1,000,000 plus | 4 | 12.5% | New York | 5.9% | Detroit | 6.6% |
| 500,000–1,000,000 | 12 | 53.6 | San Diego | 4.7 | San Francisco | 48.9 |
| 250,000–500,000 | 21 | 49.4 | Phoenix | 4.8 | Minneapolis | 44.6 |
| 100,000–250,000 | 49 | 68.3 | Beaumont | 1.8 | Cambridge | 66.5 |

SOURCE:  Northam, *ibid*, Table 15–4.

This is to say that per capita amounts of vacant land decrease with increases in city population.

In addition to differences in amounts of vacant urban land per capita among cities, based on population, there are regional differences. Per capita amounts are least in cities of the northeastern section of the country, with cities in the lower Great Lakes and upper Mississippi River Valley having only modest amounts of vacant urban land per capita (Table 15–6). By contrast, cities in the South Atlantic region and the Far West have intermediate amounts of such land per capita, with cities of the lower Mississippi area, through the Southwest, and in the Rocky Mountains having the greatest amounts of vacant land per capita.

There are over 1.3 million acres of vacant urban land in 86 large cities of the United States, and the average proportion of the city that is comprised of vacant land is 24.5 percent. As indicated previously, not all of this land is buildable, in that it is not physically suited to the accommodation of structures. The average proportion of vacant land in the city that is buildable is slightly greater than 78 percent. The cities of Buffalo, Corpus Christi, Fresno, Jersey City, Kansas City (Kansas), Los Angeles, Miami, Norfolk, and St. Petersburg report that all of their vacant land is buildable (Figure 15–7). On the other hand, the cities of Camden, Glendale, Louisville, and Syracuse consider that one-third or less of their vacant land is buildable.

Since the vacant land considered here is largely within the private sector, the monetary value of the roughly one million acres of buildable vacant land might be considered. The value of vacant land in 86 of the larger urban centers of the country (over 100,000) can be estimated at $4 billion. Using the same estimating procedure for all 130 cities in the country of more than 100,000, the value of vacant urban land in major cities is slightly over $6 billion. Further, the value of all vacant land in an urban setting—central city and urban fringe, and large cities and small cities—is estimated at $13.3 billion in 1970. Thus, there are sizeable stocks of

**Tables 15–6**  Vacant Land per Capita by Geographic Division

| Geographic division | Number of Included Cities of over 100,000 | Square Feet of Vacant Land per Capita: Mean of Divisional Cities |
|---|---|---|
| New England | 7 | 540 |
| Middle Atlantic | 13 | 360 |
| South Atlantic | 5 | 2,923 |
| East North Central | 15 | 1,142 |
| East South Central | 7 | 3,129 |
| West North Central | 9 | 1,764 |
| West South Central | 10 | 6,276 |
| Mountain | 5 | 4,055 |
| Pacific | 15 | 2,329 |
| U. S. | 86 | 2,279 |

SOURCE:  Northam, *ibid*, Table 15–4.

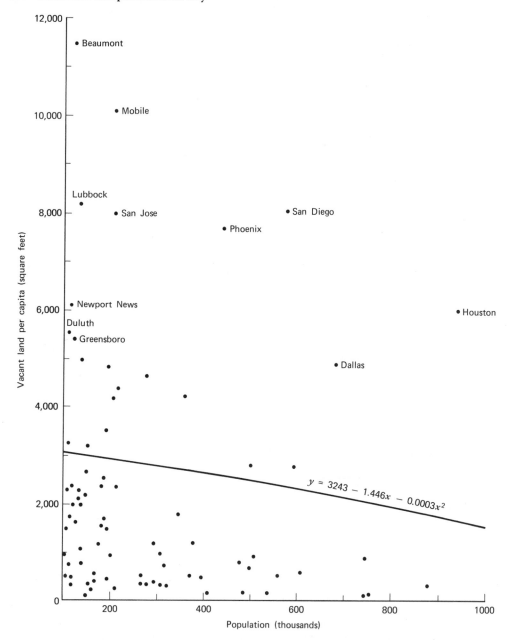

**Figure 15–6**   Per capita amounts of vacant urban land and city population: major United States cities.

vacant land in the city, the greatest portion of which is buildable in terms of accommodating some type of urban use. Further, this resource has a multi-billion dollar value, most of which is taxable. The land parcels comprising this resource have no functional use at the same time that demands for urban land continue to mount. The amounts of land needed commonly are provided by continued areal expansion of the city into the rural-urban fringe, creating conflicts among land users, yet at the same time, large amounts of vacant urban land present in the central cities remain in a state of nonuse. The efficiency of this pattern of land use might be seriously questioned.

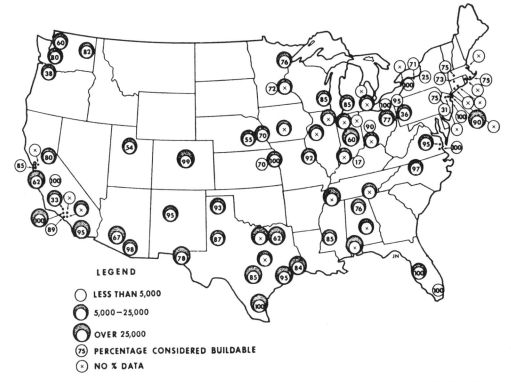

**Figure 15–7**   Vacant urban land: total acreage and percentage considered buildable. *Source.* Ray M. Northam, "Vacant Urban Land in the American City." *Land Economics*, Vol. XLVII, No. 4 (November, 1971), University of Wisconsin Press. Copyright © 1971 by the Regents of the University of Wisconsin. Reprinted by permission.

Having made the point that buildable vacant land in the city is a neglected resource of considerable value, the question might be posed as to what use such land might be put, that is, in what ways are the potentials of vacant urban land to be realized? This problem was approached in a study of vacant urban land in Portland, Oregon.[21] By using data in map form and from computer printouts, it was possible to complete an inventory of vacant land and to determine the use for which each vacant parcel was zoned (Table 15–7). If the vacant parcel was to be converted to a functional use, it normally would be of the type indicated by the zoning applicable to the parcel in question. By applying existing land use densities to vacant land parcels of each type, it was possible to estimate the

amount of growth that could be accommodated by vacant land of each zoned type. The potentials established were

**Table 15–7**   Zoning Designation, Number of Vacant Buildable Parcels, Area in Vacant Parcels, and Mean Parcel Size: Portland, Oregon

| Zone Designation | Number of Vacant Buildable Parcels | Total Area in Vacant Buildable Parcels (Acres) | Mean Parcel Size (Acres) |
|---|---|---|---|
| Apartments | 985 | 505 | .51 |
| Single-family residential | 2397 | 1982 | .83 |
| Commercial | 515 | 329 | .64 |
| Industrial | 951 | 897 | .94 |
| Totals | 4848 | 3713 | .77 |

SOURCE: Ray M. Northam, *The Distribution and Potential of Vacant Urban Land,* unpublished research paper, 1968.

[21]Northam, *Ibid.*

**Table 15–8**   Current Demand and Projected Demand for Land in 1980, and Stocks of Vacant Land: Portland, Oregon

| Land Use | Currently Occupied (Acres) | Projected Demand-1980 (Acres) | Needed Increment (Acres) | Available Stocks of Buildable Vacant Land (Acres) | Surplus Beyond 1980 Needs (Acres) |
|---|---|---|---|---|---|
| Residential (gross)[a] | 24,600 | 25,800 | 1200 | 3714 | 2514 |
| Commercial | 1700 | 1800 | 100 | 329 | 229 |
| Industrial | 3000 | 3700 | 700 | 897 | 197 |

[a]Includes area for residential streets.
SOURCE: Northam, *ibid.*, Table 15–7.

compared with estimated demands for the future for land of different types, disclosing that conversion of buildable vacant land parcels to the uses for which they are zoned would provide for land needs beyond 1980 in the city of Portland (Table 15–8). The amounts of buildable vacant land that are zoned for residential use are especially in excess of estimated demands for 1980, with the more favorable situation existing for needs of land for single family residences. The challenge for the future might be to find means of implementation of a policy and program to encourage conversion of vacant urban land to the use for which it is zoned as a way of relieving or countering the continued areal expansion of the city.

## Open Space

Open space may be found as small, isolated tracts of land within the city or as larger tracts on the margins of the city. The objective in both instances is essentially to provide unmolested, undeveloped, and near-natural areas, characterized by openness in a rustic setting. This interpretation of open space sees the areas as virtual oases in an urban desert where one might enjoy a respite from the day-to-day pace of urban living. There is, however, no generally accepted definition of open space and the perception of open space by one person may not be shared by another. Rather than considering open space in the aggregate, one might do well to consider different types of open space, and these are: (1) subdivision open space, (2) agricultural open space, and (3) recreational open space.[22] Each of these types is discussed below.

The provision of open space for some segments of the population of the city is achieved in the form of the open space community. This involves development of a residential community in which man-made lakes, golf courses, numerous wooded and grassed areas, bicycle paths, and swimming pools are integral parts of the community that is laid out in a freeform, curvilinear plan. The open space areas are owned collectively, with access and use available to members of the community only.

A number of open space communities have come into being in the United States in all parts of the country, especially on the east and west coasts. Invariably, these communities have a combination of open space, recreational facilities, and community facilities, and it is difficult to separate open space from other community attractions. One thing that should be noted from the beginning is that living in open space communities is costly. In a survey of open space communities, it was disclosed that 62 percent of those buying housing in such developments paid

[22]Metropolitan Planning Commission, Portland, Oregon, *Planning for Open Space* (July, 1964).

$20,000 or more (Figure 15–8).[23] The greatest share of the buyers are middle-aged, well educated, and in professional occupations. Concerning the reasons why parties purchased homes in open space communities, the survey did not identify the importance of open space as such, very likely because this attraction is difficult to separate from others, that is, the identity and definition of open space is difficult. Still, in the survey, several factors mentioned prominently as reasons for movement to an open space community are in the realm of open space, no matter how it might be defined (Table 15–9).

**Table 15–9** Reasons Given for Move to an Open Space Community

| Reason | Percent of Respondents |
| --- | --- |
| Desirable and enjoyable community | 27.9 |
| Recreation facilities | 23.6 |
| Good area to raise children | 15.4 |
| Location convenient to job | 14.7 |
| Nice, friendly, better class of people | 13.3 |
| Quiet, rural neighborhood | 11.0 |
| Well planned | 9.3 |
| Good schools | 6.7 |
| No maintenance necessary | 6.0 |
| Enjoy this type of atmosphere | 5.6 |
| Individuality of home | 3.5 |
| Location | 3.3 |
| Good resale value | 3.2 |
| Less congested | 3.2 |
| Better home or apartment for the money | 3.0 |

SOURCE: Urban Land Institute, Technical Bulletin 57 (December, 1966).

One feature that is an attraction for open space communities is the pattern by which they are laid out and developed. Cul-de-sacs, sinuous streets, a variety of

[23]Carl Norcross, *Open Space Communities in the Market Place*, Urban Land Institute, Technical Bulletin 57 (December, 1966).

homes, clustering of homes, and green-belts typify such developments and these appear to add greatly to the attractions of such communities (Figure 15–9).

Agricultural open space involves crop-land that is located on the margins of the urban area and in danger of being absorbed into urban uses with a commensurate loss of open space. With conversion of farmland to subdivisions or other urban uses, taxes on the converted land and the remaining farmland inevitably increase. When property taxes continue to increase, the profitability of the farming operation may be substantially lessened, eventually reaching the point where the most profitable course is to sell the farmland for conversion to urban uses. This process is stimulated by tax assessing policies whereby the assessor values land at its highest and best use as expressed by the land market. If the highest and best use is judged to be single family residential, the tax load on such land will be based on this use and not on agricultural use. The agricultural landowner is a loser in another respect in that his demand for urban services is considerably less, considering the nature of the areas taxed, than is his urban counterpart. This applies to less need for streets, schools, police protection, etc. The result, then, has often been the sale and subdivision of farmland adjacent to the city due to the loss of economic viability. In the process, the urban center may lose part of its food supply and a great deal of open space.

Under certain conditions, it may be thought advisable to develop a land policy where agricultural open space can be preserved. These conditions include (1) the uniqueness of the agricultural products produced on such land based on physical or economic conditions that would preclude the products being grown elsewhere, (2) the degree to which the urban center is dependent on local producers for its food supply, (3) the degree to which urban residents are employed on a seasonal basis on nearby

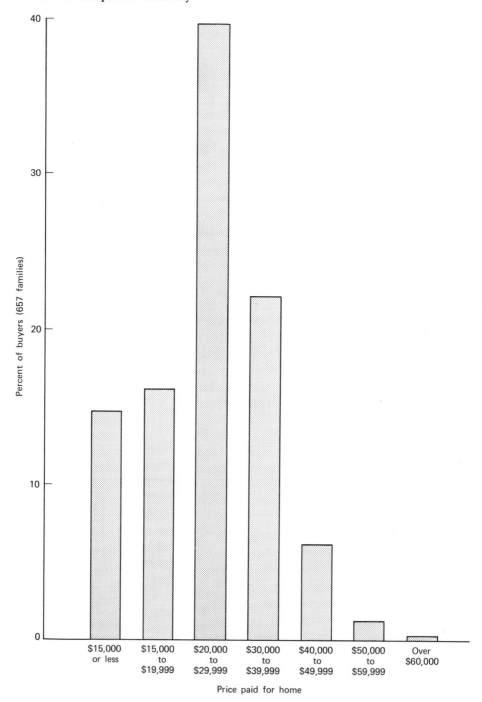

**Figure 15–8**   Prices paid for housing in open space communities. *Source.* Based on data in Urban Land Institute; Technical Bulletin 57; December, 1966.

farms and the ramifications of the loss of such employment opportunities, and (4) the effect produced by reduction of local farm output on local food processing industries.

If local farmland is considered essential and desirable based on the above conditions, steps may be taken to insure its preservation. One course sometimes taken is a revision of tax policy, such that

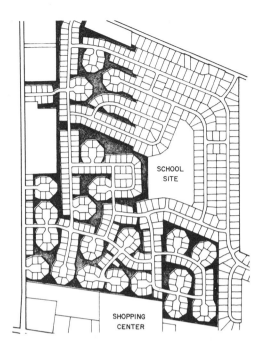

**Figure 15–9** Alternate forms of plotting and development in an urban community. *Source.* Carl Norcross. *Open Space Communities in the Market Place.* Urban Land Institute, Technical Bulletin No. 57; December, 1966. Reprinted by permission.

farmland is taxed as farmland and not as potential urban land, that is, taxation based on existing use, rather than a potential use. The taxing authority must protect itself, however, against a situation where a farm may enjoy the benefits of lower taxation for a number of years after which the land is converted to urban use. In the meantime, the farm operator would enjoy the benefits of tax reduction and then reap a profit from eventual sale of the farmland, so the taxing authority would lose revenue and the urban area would lose farmland and open space. To guard against such possibilities, the tax policy might state that such considerations on revised assessments would (1) continue so long as the land remains as productive farmland, and (2) that taxes would be collected on a retroactive basis for a number of years prior to the sale of the farmland and its conversion to a nonfarm use. This has proven to be an effective way of continuing the existence of agricultural open space in the urban area.

Recreational open space consists of large tracts of land held in a relatively undeveloped state with a limited number of facilities and improvements, such as access roads, culverts, and walkways. Areas that might be especially suited to recreational open space would include floodplains with a hazard of recurrent flooding and areas with slopes so steep as to render them unsuited to urban development. These tracts of recreational open space could be combined with other nonurban uses such as wildlife sanctuaries, and these tracts could be incorporated into an urban park system, although they would not include the facilities of other parks in the system, nor would they have the intensity of use of other parks. The prime objective would be to preserve an undeveloped and unmolested area of open space for personal enjoyment, but not for the amusement or enjoyment of people seeking constructed forms of recreational facilities.

One of the significant differences between the types of open space discussed above is ownership of land used for open space. In open space communities, the land is owned by the residential community for their collective use and administered by a community group, such as a homeowners association. The open space of this type, being in the private sector, is subject to property taxes. Agricultural open space also is privately owned, usually by individuals and is, therefore, subject to property taxation. Recreational open space generally is publicly owned, usually by the municipal governments in which the open space tracts are found. Quite often, recreational open space is administered by park departments of the city involved. Since this land is in the public sector, it is not subject to property taxation.

## Summary

This chapter has dealt with the ways in which large amounts of urban land are (1) utilized in a less intensive manner, if used at all, and (2) developed and administered by the public sector. Land types included are, in some cases, of a dynamic nature because their present role likely will change with passage of time, such as vacant urban land being utilized for functional uses. Other land types discussed are of a more static nature and are not likely to change their functions in the near future, such as land used for educational purposes, for recreational uses, land for cemeteries, and land devoted to open space. In this regard, the land types are somewhat different from those discussed in previous chapters in that the latter are more subject to change in use, such as commercial establishments razed to make way for high rise apartments, single family homes removed to allow for street construction, and industrial establishments removed to allow for transportation needs. The uses of urban space discussed in this chapter are more of a public trust and are not likely to be absorbed, altered, or compromised to perform a different use, while vacant urban land, which does not fulfill a functional need, hopefully will be absorbed into the fabric of the land use structure of the city.

# 16
# spatial movements, areal expansion, sion, and urban governments

There are certain general trends that have been mentioned earlier in this book and others that will be discussed at this time. With regard to world population in general, there has been an implosion at the same time that there has been an explosion. What we mean is that the overall population in most parts of the world has increased greatly in recent times as birth rates have increased and mortality rates have been reduced. At the same time that populations of nations have increased greatly (explosion), there has been increased localization of the population, with more and more people taking up residence in urban centers (implosion).

When more people become part of the urban population, and if the city does not expand areally in accordance with increased number of inhabitants, the only result can be an increase in population density in existing urban centers. To a considerable degree, this has happened in the larger metropolitan centers, with the less mobile and less affluent segments of the urban population in particular taking up residence in high density areas. Partly as a result, social conflicts have more frequently occurred within larger urban centers.[1] Also, the financial situation of the city has been impaired as needs for social services increase and taxable wealth is reduced through the replacement of higher income groups by those of lower means.

Urban residents of higher incomes and mobility have tended to desert the central city to take up residence in outlying areas, giving rise to population increases in suburban cities and communities with which they are poorly prepared to cope. Not only do the more affluent and mobile groups of original central city residents gravitate to suburbs in the urban fringe, so do new arrivals to the urban area who share the same advantages. Thus, the suburban communities have experienced phenomenal population increases and transformation and have become less capable of accommodating still more arrivals to the urban area. In view of this, there have been significant incursions of urban dwellers into rural areas adjacent to the city, contributing to urban sprawl in an unchecked, unrestricted, and perhaps, unwise manner. This process of invasion and succession has been particularly pronounced in the United States, but has taken place in other nations as well.

[1] On the topic of social conflict in cities, one might refer to Kevin B. Cox, *Conflict, Power, and Politics in the City: A Geographic View,* New York: McGraw-Hill, Inc., 1973.

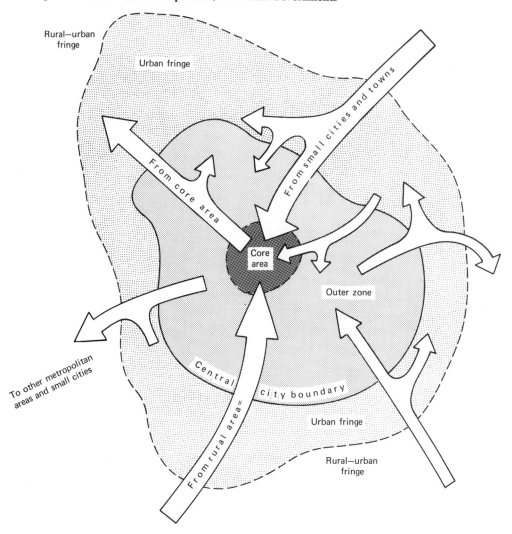

**Figure 16–1**   Migration paths in urban areas.

## Urban Migration Paths

Consider the above process as being comprised of movement along a number of different migration paths of different lengths. One of these, an external path, is comprised of movements into the urban area from rural areas or smaller cities, some distance from the larger city (Figure 16-1). Of the various paths in this section, this is the longest, with many of the individual movements consisting of interregional moves. This migration path bifurcates on arrival of the newcomers to the urban area, one branch directed to

the urban fringe and the suburbs therein and to the outer, less densely populated zone of the central city. The other branch is directed to the core area of the central city, with this branch largely comprised of low income or minority groups seeking low cost housing that generally is available there. Another prominent migration path, this one occurring within the urban area, is made up of short distance outward movements of inhabitants of the core area and less desirable sections of the city. This migration path also divides, with one branch directed to desirable suburbs, another to the outer zone of the central city, and still another to the zone beyond the outer margin of the existing urban area where the people comprising this path contribute to areal expansion of the urban area and to urban sprawl. There is some indication that a counter-migration path exists in some metropolitan areas, this comprised of people leaving the urban fringe or outer zone of the central city and seeking residence in the core area, particularly in more desirable sections or those that have been renewed. Further, there is a migration path, generally minor, of people leaving the urban area in question, with this path directed to another metropolitan center or, to some degree, to smaller cities in a rural setting. One factor that is apparent is that the migration paths directed to the urban area are much greater in magnitude of people than those leading away from the urban area. Further, the migration path from central city to urban fringe is greater than that to the central city, as evidenced by the fact that in the metropolitan areas of the United States there was, in the period 1960 to 1970, an increase in population of 10.3 percent in central cities and 44.0 percent in metropolitan areas outside of central cities.[2] Of 252 cities that serve, either singly or jointly, as central cities of metropolitan areas, 139 or 55 percent experienced population gains in the period mentioned, while 113 or 45 percent had population losses in the same period. Central cities with population losses included many of the larger cities in the country, such as Baltimore, Boston, Chicago, Cleveland, Detroit, Minneapolis, Philadelphia, St. Louis, San Francisco, Seattle, and Washington, D.C. By contrast, in the same period all but a very few of the fringe areas of metropolitan areas increased in population. The recipients of this population growth mainly have been the residential and industrial sub-

urbs, both incorporated and unincorporated, plus new developments beyond the existing margins of the urban area. In any case, there is a resultant areal expansion of the urban area and dispersal of its population.

Areal expansion of the urban area usually proceeds, unfortunately, without benefit of established policy and guidelines on the growth process. The direction, magnitude, and timing of the areal expansion are mainly influenced or shaped by the actions of the urban land market and its major representatives, the financiers and developers. This often results in a less than desirable pattern of urban expansion. Thus, there are many questions that might be asked as to the merit of uncontrolled or unchecked areal expansion, in which the urban area becomes increasingly sprawled over the landscape at the same time it accommodates an increasingly larger population. Perhaps, there should be greater concern given to planning within existing metropolitan areas and development of additional urban centers to accommodate the spillover from major existing metropolitan centers.

## Urban Sprawl

Given the situation in recent decades in which increasing numbers of people have taken up residence in a relatively fixed number of small areas, there are three possible circumstances that can result: (1) more land area can be converted to urban use by areal expansion of existing urban areas, (2) the densities of population in existing cities can increase substantially, or (3) new urban communities can be formed. In actuality, all three circumstances have come to pass, but to different degrees, and the one discussed at this time is the first—urban sprawl associated with existing metropolitan areas and smaller cities.

Very simply, urban sprawl refers to the areal expansion of urban concentrations beyond what they have been. Urban

[2]U.S. Bureau of the Census, *Census of Population: 1970, Number of Inhabitants,* Final Report PC(1)–A1, United States Summary, 1971.

sprawl involves the conversion of land peripheral to urban centers that has previously been used for nonurban uses to one or more urban uses. In the process, the land absorbed by the urban center becomes a functional part of the urban agglomeration and is occupied by people who in attitude, behavior, and activity are integrated into the urban society. This process of areal expansion has been in effect for centuries, yet the term "urban sprawl" has been used mainly in reference to fairly recent times. It would appear, perhaps, that urban sprawl has a meaning beyond the mere occupance of land on the periphery of cities or the areal expansion of cities, for this process has been taking place for millennia. It seems that urban sprawl refers to the pace of land conversion to urban use and the magnitude of areal expansion of the city, that is, it likely is a matter of degree. It should come as no surprise, however, that the land needs and areal expansion of cities have increased greatly in fairly recent times, when one recalls that the greatest surge of migration to cities and increases in urban population have taken place in the recent past, and if people increasingly take up residence in cities, they will occupy land area in or near those cities.

## The Situation in Cities of the United States

Has there been areal expansion of American cities, that is, has urban sprawl taken place, especially in the decade from 1960 to 1970? The answer to this question, for the most part, is yes, with areal expansion being experienced by cities large and small in this country. A recent report states that farm land being converted to urban uses approximated 750,000 acres per year in the past decade.[3]. As an indication of this circum-

stance, consider the change in land area of urbanized areas of the country, with the reminder that urbanized areas essentially include built-up areas with central cities as their foci. Each urbanized area includes land that has residential densities characteristic of urban concentrations, plus other land uses characteristically urban.

In 1960, there were nearly 25,000 square miles included within urbanized areas, and in 1970, this total had risen to just over 35,000 square miles. This comparison cannot be accepted at face value, however, since the number of urbanized areas increased from 213 in 1960 to 248 in 1970. Considering only the land area of the 213 urbanized areas that existed in both 1960 and 1970, the total land area included was 33,848 square miles in 1970, compared with 24,979 square miles in 1960. This represents an increase of 8869 square miles (5.7 million acres) or 35.5 percent, which supports the statement that urban sprawl has characterized recent growth patterns of major American metropolitan areas in the aggregate.

Not all urbanized areas have experienced increases in land area in the decade mentioned, however. Of the 213 urbanized areas existent in both 1960 and 1970, 197 (92.4 percent of the total) had increases in land area, 2 (1.0 percent) remained unchanged in land area, and 14 (6.5 percent) experienced decreases in land area, indicating that urban sprawl or areal expansion is not a universal condition of large American metropolitan areas. One might surmise that urbanized areas that have had contractions in land area are ones that are losing population, but such is not the case. Of the fourteen urbanized areas in this group, only five have experienced population as well as area loss, while nine that have smaller urban areas have experienced population increases. All fourteen of the urbanized areas of decreased area have had increases in population density, whether or not they had a commensurate increase in population. These findings indicate that

[3]Economic Research Service, Department of Agriculture, reported in the Portland *Oregonian*, December 10, 1972.

**Table 16-1**   Urbanized Areas with a Decrease in Land Area 1960–1970

| Urbanized Area | Decrease in Population | Increase in Density |
|---|---|---|
| Bridgeport, Connecticut | No | Yes |
| Erie, Pennsylvania | Yes | Yes |
| Fall River, Massachusetts | No | Yes |
| Harlington–San Benito, Texas | Yes | Yes |
| Hartford, Connecticut | No | Yes |
| Lewiston-Auburn, Maine | Yes | Yes |
| New Orleans, Louisiana | No | Yes |
| Oklahoma City, Oklahoma | No | Yes |
| Port Arthur, Texas | No | Yes |
| Scranton, Pennsylvania | Yes | Yes |
| Springfield-Chicopee-Holyoke, Massachusetts and Connecticut | No | Yes |
| Stamford, Connecticut | No | Yes |
| Trenton, New Jersey-Pennsylvania | No | Yes |
| Utica-Rome, New York | Yes | Yes |

SOURCE:   Based on data in Bureau of the Census, 1970 Census of Population, *United States Summary,* December, 1971.

some urbanized areas are absorbing more people without increasing the land area occupied and, in fact, occupy less land area than they did previously. Further, the increase in densities indicates that urban land is being used more intensely than in the past. The fourteen urbanized areas that have experienced contractions in area are not peculiar to any one section of the country, since six are in New England, four are in the Middle Atlantic region, and four are in the south central section of the country (Table 16-1).

Regardless, however, of the growth characteristics of the fourteen urbanized areas identified in Table 16-1, the majority of large metropolitan areas and smaller urban centers in the country have experienced urban sprawl to varying degrees and with it exist a number of problems.

## Problems Associated With Urban Sprawl

To state simply that urban sprawl generates problems is to state very little until one is aware of the specific forms these problems may take. Perhaps, the most significant problem associated with urban sprawl is in the realm of inefficiency of land use. A not uncommon procedure followed in the areal expansion of urban areas is one in which the expansion takes place in the form of new residential subdivisions, new commercial and industrial districts, and other types of development beyond the existing margin of the city. These developments tend to occupy sites that are most physically acceptable to development, most accessible, and those on which the development can be made with a minimum of cost. In this context, residential developments may preempt gently rolling lands with good drainage and pleasant surroundings, while commercial and industrial developments tend to occupy flatter sites of lower per acre costs than similar sites within the built-up area. Many new developments have been made on large tracts of land, five, ten, fifteen or more miles from the urban area with which the development is functionally linked, with the intervening area used for farming operations. Although the residential inhabitants may enjoy the "country atmosphere" of these developments, objections to uses made of adjacent tracts of land may be raised, which is to say that real or perceived conflicts between land users may result. Further, there may be impediments to freedom of daily movement through the nonurban zone that exists. Also, there are problems for the agriculturalists caught up in the squeeze of two advancing fronts of urban development, in that his operations can be inhibited, the value of the farm land may increase substantially, and the tax load may become excessive as in the manner discussed in Chapter 15. All in all, such a pattern of growth may well serve to the detriment of the inhabitants of the new development and to those residing in the trough between two waves of urban development. It is this "leap frog" growth pattern that often creates a problem, for the behavior pattern, activities, and life style of those on each of the urban fronts often is different from those caught in the middle of this type of urban growth.

The above developments represent a type of urban growth in which *urban exclaves* are formed, which is to say, urban territory detached from the main body of the urban area. Not only are urban exclaves formed in this process, but so are *urban enclaves* consisting of areas or tracts of vacant urban land bypassed by the developmental process in favor of more distant tracts beyond the leading edge of the urban area. It could be considered unwise to sanction development of land for urban use beyond the existing margins of urban areas at the same time that sizeable stocks of land remain undeveloped within the city, which likely could be developed at less cost than land in the urban exclaves. The wisdom of absorbing nearly 9000 square miles into urbanized areas within a decade at the same time that thousands of square miles of vacant urban land exist within present urbanized area is to be questioned. A growth pattern, where a number of exclaves and enclaves are created, is not as efficient as one consisting of continued or

progressive outward expansion of the urban center in which little or no area is left in the wake of the advancing urban front and no area is developed far in advance of the growing edge of the urban area. If there is to be areal expansion of the city, that is, urban sprawl, there will be less conflict in land use and a more efficient growth pattern if there is progressive and orderly growth replacing the leap-frogging so common today.

Another of the problems arising from urban sprawl is the progressive loss of farmlands, especially those of highest quality (land capability classes I, II, and III). The farmers occupying this agricultural land on the growing edge of the urban area are of different types: (1) professional farmers, (2) capital gains speculators, and (3) those using the farm largely as a place of residence.[4] Farmers of each type are affected differently by urban sprawl. The farmers who use their farms on the urban fringe basically as a place of residence earn much more of their income from employment in nonfarm pursuits than from farming. These "pseudo-farmers," as they are referred to by Higbee, are less affected by the agricultural economy than they are by the urban economy, and the absorption of their farmlands into the urban sphere would represent no serious loss of agricultural output. The same general situation holds true with regard to farmers or investors who hold farm land for speculation and eventual sale when market conditions are favorable.

The real loss of farm output, as a result of urban sprawl, comes from commercial farmers whose operations are threatened by urban expansion and the tax structure that accompanies it. Commercial farms on the urban fringe tend to be relatively small, but still the bulk of the income of

[4]Edward Higbee, "Agricultural Land On The Urban Fringe," *Metropolis on The Move: Geographers Look At Urban Sprawl,* Eds. Jean Gottmann and Robert A. Harper, New York, John Wiley & Sons, Inc., 1967.

the operators is derived from sale of specialty items, such as fluid milk, vegetables, berries, small fruits, and poultry. One alternative followed by these commercial farmers, faced with the wave of urban sprawl, is to sell their holdings near the city and reinvest in farm operations further removed from the urban area, but not so distant that the farm operation cannot remain viable and retain its local market advantages.

It follows from the preceding discussion that the effects of urban sprawl on agriculture are different, depending on the type of farmers and farms involved. For the speculator and the "pseudo-farmer" who receives little of his income from farming and who contributes little in the way of agricultural output, there is the loss of farm land, of the farming operation, and the farmer, as such land is absorbed into the urban area. For the commercial farmer, there is a loss of the farm output, of farm land, and a viable farm operation, but not necessarily the loss of the farmer who may relocate to a farm further removed from the surge of urban sprawl. The key point, however, is that the loss of the farm land to urban uses in each of the cases is of an irreversible type. Once farm land is lost, it cannot easily be reclaimed as such if the need arises, although at this point in time, there is no pressing demand for this land. Who is to say, however, that the demand will not exist in the next decade or next half-century?

Thus far, two problems associated with urban sprawl have been recognized: "leap frog" growth patterns with accompanying land use conflicts, and real or potential loss of prime farm land.[5] There are other problems too, that result from urban sprawl, and these have to do with inefficiencies and shortcomings in de-velopment of settlement clusters in the urban-rural fringe that is removed from the main body of urban settlement.

Consider a new residential development that is constructed about ten or fifteen miles from the growing edge of the urban concentration in an area that is essentially farm land. This development of single-family homes and some multifamily units will house about 5000 people when fully developed. These families, though removed from the major urban focal point, depend on incomes derived from within the central city of the urban area, that is, they are a functional part of the urban area, although they live in an exclave of the urban area. These people have demands for utilities and services, private and public, just as do their counterparts within the urban area *per se*. They must have access to modern utilities, such as electricity, telephone lines, gas lines, water mains, and sewage lines which necessitates extension of all of these utilities over ten or fifteen miles of intervening distance to meet the needs in the new development, and this can only be achieved at considerable cost. In addition to provision of utilities of these types, there are needs for other urban facilities and services, such as widened or improved streets and roads. Also, school bus runs will be lengthened, at least until new schools are constructed, and fire and police protection are more difficult and costly as well. Even parcel and mail delivery are more costly and time consuming when the needs of the new development are met.

All in all, the costs of this type of development to both the public and private sectors would be lessened considerably, if the new development had been located immediately adjacent to the growing edge of the urban area, thereby reducing appreciably the distances to which urban facilities, utilities, and services would have to be extended. A related problem of urban sprawl exists in the form of tax inequities in which the entire taxing jurisdiction (county, special district, or

[5]An interesting discussion of the theoretical aspects of land absorbed by urban sprawl is provided by Robert Sinclair, "Von Thunen and Urban Sprawl," *Annals* of the AAG, Vol. 57, No. 1 (March, 1967).

others) bears the cost of providing for the needs of outlying developments. The bulk of those paying taxes or levies may, in fact, be subsidizing development and operation of the urban exclave.

Regarding solutions for the problems of urban sprawl, three might be mentioned: (1) formation of a governmental unit of larger size than the corporate city, such as the metropolitan area, within which planning could be effectuated, (2) adoption and enforcement of an area-wide planning policy that would channel the directions of urban growth, and (3) revision of tax policy so as to restrict the piecemeal, leap frog growth that has been experienced. These points are examined in greater detail in the following section and in the following chapter.

## Fragmentation of Metropolitan Governments

It was suggested in the previous section that controls and guidance be extended to the areal expansion of urban areas. Such controls and guidelines would have to be imposed by a unit of government with area-wide jurisdiction and, for the most part, such governmental units do not exist in the United States. Rather, metropolitan areas are governed by a number of different governmental units, each with its own limited area of jurisdiction and with its own designated powers. Rarely, is there a unit of government with authority over the areal growth of the entire metropolitan area so that problems of urban sprawl might be identified and controlled.

In the United States, there was a total of 81,248 local governments of all types in 1967, of which 20,703 or 25 percent were within S.M.S.A.'s.[6] Five years earlier in 1962, there were 21,817 local governments within metropolitan areas or 24 percent of the total of 91,185. In the

[6]U.S. Bureau of Census, Census of Governments: 1967, Volume 1, *Governmental Organization*, Washington, D.C., GPO, 1968.

half-decade from 1962 to 1967, then, there was an overall decrease of 5.1 percent in number of local governments within metropolitan areas, but these constituted an increased share of total local governments in the country (Figure 16-2)

These governmental units that exist within metropolitan areas are of various types, including (1) school districts, (2) special districts, (3) municipalities, (4) townships, and (5) counties (Figure 16-2). Let us consider a metropolitan area over which there is an overlay of local governmental units in the form of municipal or city governments, which consist of the central city or central cities and all incorporated cities within the urban fringe. In most urbanized areas in the country, the number of municipal governments is considerable, such as the New York-N.E. New Jersey urbanized area with 306 municipal governments and the Chicago-N.W. Indiana urbanized area with 170 municipal governments. In the entire U.S., in the five year period between 1962 and 1967, there was an increase in number of municipal governments within metropolitan areas and a slight decrease outside metropolitan areas. The former situation results from incorporation of previously unincorporated places in urban fringes as their populations have increased, as well as from annexation of additional places as urban sprawl has taken place. Today, most of the municipal governments within metropolitan areas include populations of less than 5000 people, especially those in the outer portions, with local governments of greater populations more concentrated in the inner portion of the S.M.S.A. (Figure 16–3). Many of the problems faced and tasks performed by municipal departments in the respective corporate cities are common to all of them, yet there is little or no integration of governmental agencies in the municipalities in the metropolitan area, and quite often, there is, in fact, conflict among them.

Going back to the metropolitan area

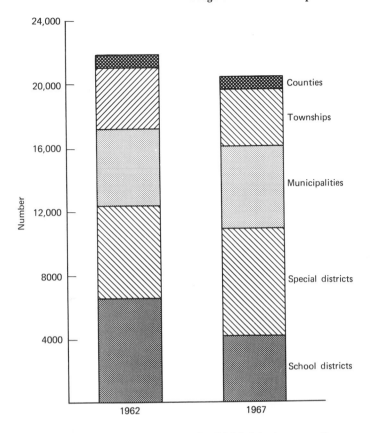

**Figure 16–2** Local governments in S.M.S.A.'s, by type. *Source.* Adapted from Bureau of Census, *Government Organization,* Vol. 1, 1968.

with an overlay of municipal governmental units, we next insert another overlay of local governments, this one consisting of school districts. In the period 1962 to 1967, there was a significant increase in the number of school districts within metropolitan areas (20 percent of the total in 1962 and 23 percent in 1967), and an equally significant decrease outside of metropolitan areas (82 percent compared to 77 percent). More likely than not, this is due to formation of new school districts and division of existing ones within metropolitan areas and consolidation of school districts with small enrollments so that those that remain are fewer in number, but include larger enrollments (Figure 16-4A). This trend has characterized public school systems in metropolitan areas as well as those in the country as a whole (Figure 16-4B).

Of the various types of local governments in metropolitan areas, special districts account for the greatest share of the total. These are governmental jurisdictions formed to serve a particular function within specified areal bounds, which may include several counties, a single county, a small drainage basin, or a portion of an urbanized area, as examples. In the United States, there is a considerable number of different special districts, but the most numerous are for fire protection, soil conservation, drainage, and urban water supply.

Of the over 7000 special districts in metropolitan areas of the United States, just over 55 percent have property taxing power, although there are regional variations in the proportion of special districts having such authority. The regional percentages of special districts having taxing

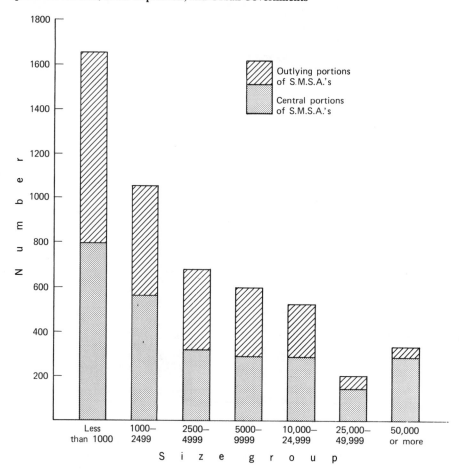

**Figure 16-3** Municipal governments in S.M.S.A.'s, by population size: 1967. *Source.* Ibid, Figure 16-1.

authority are as follows: Northeast-34 percent, North Central-62 percent, South-41 percent, and West-76 percent. Special districts, with or without taxing power, are most numerous in the West with 2223, while the Northeast has 2033, the North Central region has 1765, and the South has 1,028.[7]

Special districts in metropolitan areas perform functions that are often different from those performed outside of metropolitan areas. The most numerous single-function special districts within metropolitan areas are for, in order, fire protection, water supply, sewerage, education (school buildings), housing and

[7]U.S. Bureau of Census, *Ibid,* Table 15, p. 72.

urban renewal, and drainage (Figure 16-5). Although the majority of special districts are single-function districts, some are multiple-function districts in which two functions are combined for administrative purposes within a prescribed jurisdiction, such as sewerage and water supply or natural resources and water supply.

## The Alternative of Metropolitan Government

In response to metropolitan problems that result from action or inaction in a setting of numerous governmental units, it often has been proposed that there be

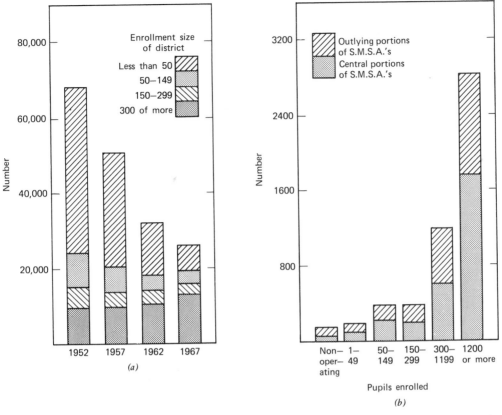

**Figure 16–4**   School districts and public school systems. (*A*) School districts by enrollment size: selected years 1952–1967. (*B*) Public school systems in S.M.S.A.'s by enrollment size: 1967. *Source.* Ibid, Figure 16–2.

formed a single governmental authority encompassing the entire metropolitan area—a metropolitan government. The objectives of such a procedure is to reduce duplication and inefficiency and to better offer governmental services on a comprehensive and equitable basis.

Before continuing with aspects of metropolitan government, we might profit from identification of factors that have a bearing on political integration. Of the total array of integrative factors, only some have a bearing on metropolitan government and these are identified below.[8]

[8]The factors considered here are based on a more lengthy treatment by Philip E. Jacob and Henry Teune in *The Integration of Political Communities*, Eds. Philip E. Jacob and James V. Toscano, New York: J. B. Lippincott Company, 1964.

1. Proximity. The hypothesis is that the closer people live together geographically the greater the likelihood of integrative relationships.

2. Homogeneity. The hypothesis is that social homogeneity will contribute greatly to the feasibility of political integration.

3. Transactions. The hypothesis is that cohesiveness among individuals and among communities of individuals is promoted by the extent of mutual relationships or interaction among them. Included for consideration under this factor are communications, trade, and mobility.

4. Mutual knowledge. The hypothesis is that mutual knowledge or understanding among people and groups of people is essential to their functioning together as a political community.

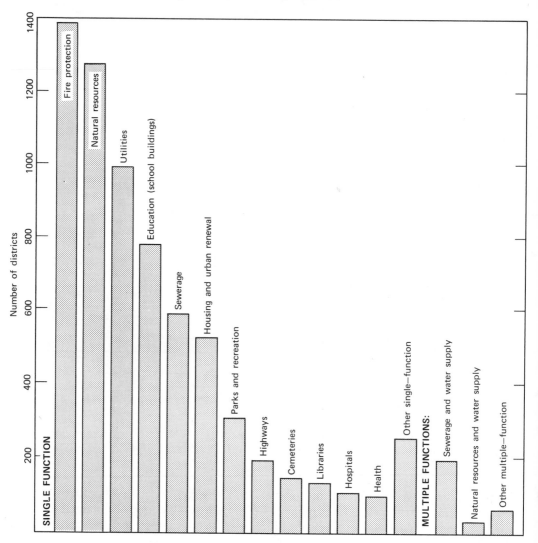

**Figure 16–5**   Special districts, by function or functions: S.M.S.A.'s, 1967. *Source.* Ibid., Figure 16–2.

5. Functional interest. The hypothesis is that the functional interests of the bulk of a community are sufficiently similar so that they will be advanced by the development of common political ties.

6. Governmental effectiveness. The hypothesis is that cohesion of a political community is related to the effectiveness of its government in meeting demands and expectations of its citizens.

Without benefit of formalized hypothesis testing, one may intuitively assume that all six of the above hypotheses

hold true for metropolitan areas. Certainly, the people live and operate in close proximity to one another; there are common aims, problems, and challenges among urban dwellers at the same time there are social differences; and there is a phenomenal array and volume of transactions among residents of metropolitan areas. Further, there is mutual knowledge among people in metropolitan areas, although often without understanding or appreciation; there are similar functional interests among urban dwellers, if no more than those resulting from similar economic interests; and these people will be more likely to function as members of the urban community if they perceive that the local government operates in an efficient manner and is responsive to the needs and interests of the people.

From the above, one might conclude that the situation in major metropolitan agglomerations is favorable to formation of metropolitan government, since metropolitan areas meet, although to different degrees, the conditions thought favorable to such an action. The question may be posed, however, if this is such a desirable course of action, why is it not taken? The answer to this question is highly complex and it would be presumptuous of the writer to suggest one, since most likely there is no single answer. Two points that bear on an answer, however, are the desire to preserve local autonomy by individuals, both urban and rural, and the long standing tradition of local governments in urban areas (political inertia). Also to be considered is the point that it has not been proven conclusively that metropolitan government is a decided improvement over existing political structure.

Still, a few metropolitan areas have undertaken the bold step of formation of metropolitan governments. In North America, forms of metropolitan government have been implemented in Miami, Florida (Dade County), and in Toronto, Ontario. The attempt toward a metropolitan government in Dade County was the first in the United States, with voter approval coming in 1957[9] The "metro" government of Dade County includes Miami and twenty-five other cities in Dade County and has been reaffirmed by voters in several elections, but not strongly so until 1964. The concept has had only modest success, however, since the various cities included operate essentially as they did before the formation of

metro government; each has its own police and fire departments, its own housing program, its own water supply and sewage disposal system, and each collects its own taxes.[10] The governing body of the Miami metropolitan government is a board of nine part-time commissioners and this board appoints a professional county manager. The benefits of formation of this metropolitan government are not clear as yet, due to its infancy and the lack of overwhelming support by the citizens of the county.

Another metropolitan government formed in North America is the Municipality of Metropolitan Toronto, established by the provincial government in 1953.[11] The functions of this governmental body are numerous, and include responsibilities for construction and maintenance of a water system to serve all municipalities, construction and maintenance of trunk sewer lines to serve the region, and preparation of an official plan for the metropolitan area and all adjoining townships, including land use. Within the context of this governmental unit, the individual communities retain control over local matters and are directly represented in the Metropolitan Council, which has control over area-wide matters. The Toronto metropolitan government has been somewhat more successful than Miami's, partly due to the fact that home rule is not so deeply instilled in Canadian voters as in voters in the United States.

A level of governmental reorganization that provides some aspects of metropolitan government, but without the formalized and centralized control, is an inter-county agency made up of representatives of counties comprising a single metropolitan area. The aim here is to have a local jurisdiction empowered to work on problems common to all parts of the metropolitan area, and to create a channel of communications among vari-

[9]Edward C. Banfield, *Big City Politics*, New York: Random House, Inc., 1965.

[10]Banfield, *Ibid.*

[11]Webb S. Fiser, *Mastery of the Metropolis*, Englewood Cliffs, N.J.: Prentice-Hall, Inc., 1962.

ous local governmental units and agencies in the area. This is not so much a governmental unit as such, but an advisory agency with a minimum of collaborative programs pertaining to the entire metropolitan area. This concept of political integration is exemplified by the Inter-County Supervisors Committee in the Detroit Metropolitan Area and the New York Metropolitan Council.

Thus, there have been attempts toward some form of metropolitan government in a few metropolitan areas, but there has not been widespread acceptance of this concept as yet. Essentially the problems associated with a multiplicity of local governments in metropolitan areas remain and only slowly are they being resolved.

Based on what we have said, certain conclusions might be formed, one of which is that problems of urban sprawl do indeed exist, but that this problem is, to a great extent, inevitable as more of the population resides in urban areas. Still, the matter of directing, guiding, and planning areal expansion of urban agglomerations might be a reasonable course as an alternative to current patterns of urban sprawl. In the face of such objectives, the multiplicity of urban governments serves as an impediment to area-wide goal realization and attempts at formation of a jurisdictional entity, such as metropolitan government, have not as yet offered a viable solution to problems as they exist.

# 17
# urban land policy, urban planning, and new towns

Cities are the creations of man for the benefit of man; therefore, it is the responsibility of man to administer his creations in such a manner as to optimize the benefits of them for the people who live in them and for those who are dependent on them. Before administration can be implemented, there must be the formulation of policies by the leadership of the urban center to aid in its operation and for the well being of its residents. Since these policies or guidelines are designed for the mutual benefit of the people, they fall into the realm of public policy, and so now we concern ourselves with the various types of public policy that pertain especially or exclusively to urban centers. There are many different facets of the city of today and a single policy is insufficient to provide adequately for the array of needs and concerns of urban dwellers. Rather, a particular policy tends to apply to one aspect of urban living, while cities today operate with the guidance of a number of public policies. Within our framework, policy refers to a formalized set of guidelines of a fairly general and broad nature.

## Urban Land Policy

Since one aspect of urban centers that is stressed more than others in this book is the occupance and spatial organization of urban land, the following discussion has mostly to do with this matter. Other types of policy pertain more to such aspects of urban centers as social services, economic development, or provision of facilities, although these aspects are not separable from public land use policy.

The first urban land policies, although not rigidly formalized, were developed in the earliest of cities of Mesopotamia and the lower Nile Valley, where the use of urban land and the guidance of such use was overseen by the religious leadership or kings and their equivalents. Still later, with the rise of cities in Europe, policies pertaining to urban land were within the realm of the sovereign. With the rise of the mercantile city, privately owned land increased in proportion to the lowered influence of absolute monarchies, and today private land ownership is an entrenched institution in much of the western world.

At present, social and political attitudes toward land ownership are extremely important in affecting public land policies in most of the western world, and there has been, since World War II, increased emphasis on the public interest and greater public influence and control over land use. Commissions to consider the necessity and propriety of public control over privately owned land were established in Norway (1958), Spain (1959), the Netherlands (1961), and Denmark (1961).[1] These changes in approach to urban land recognize that man as an urban animal has many of the same requirements and is confronted with many of the same types of problems, regardless of where he lives: he shares the same requirements for space, light, clean air, safety, movement, tranquility, and social unity. In spite of cultural differences among countries and people, there still is an underlying similarity in the fundamental behavior patterns of urban man and his needs.

There are widespread and increasing pressures on urban land resources, and a scarcity of urban land exists in some parts of the world today, especially in western Europe and in some portions of North America.[2] With regard to the scarcity of urban land, several factors have been suggested in producing this situation. There is increased pressure for urban land resulting from population increases, smaller households, and more people in urban areas. Also, there is greater affluence and changing life styles in the population, which results in more land per household. Speculation by owners of strategic properties has resulted in an artificial shortage, and there often is a time lag in providing needed utilities by municipal authorities to sites suited to development.

There are several problems, resulting from an urban land scarcity, and one of these is higher land prices and valuations, often at increasing rates (Table 17-1). Furthermore, landowners who monopolize important holdings, often

get the advantage of publically owned and financed improvements and reap gains in value of their holdings, arising from growth in population, industry, and general productivity. Another problem arising from a scarcity of urban land is that there is greater difficulty in obtaining large parcels suitable for development due to complex ownership patterns, and this tends to impede provision of building sites for low and moderate income groups. Moreover, with higher land prices in the central city and along transportation routes, there is a shift of development to outlying areas (urban sprawl) that serves as a burden to the community.

In view of problems of urban land scarcity, several methods of alleviation have been suggested, with these having the objective of controlling urban land use to attain maximum efficiency in the urban structure.[3] One means of negating these problems is advance land acquisition in the public sector. Publicly owned land reserves have long been a tradition in Europe since the Middle Ages, and have been extended into recent times as well. During the 1920's, land for improved housing was acquired in no fewer than fourteen countries of Europe. Sweden, in particular, urges municipalities to acquire land reserves in advance of need. In Stockholm by 1935, 20,000 acres located within a radius of nine miles of the urban center had been acquired and much of the housing, both public and private, by 1962, had been built on these lands.[4] In Norway, in the early 1960's 15 to 20 percent of all real estate transactions involving land for urban housing, dealt with sites acquired by municipalities in advance of use. Many municipalities in western Europe make sites available for development in land reserves on a leasehold basis for periods of 75 to 99 years.

---

[1]Department of Housing and Urban Development, *Urban Land Policy: Selected Aspects of the European Experience,* Washington: GPO, March, 1969.

[2]"Scarcity," as used here, has reference to lack of availability in an economic sense, more than to nonexistence. Stocks of land can exist in an urban area, yet not be made available to persons desirous of acquiring such land.

[3]Department of Housing and Urban Development, *Ibid.*

[4]Department of Housing and Urban Development, *Ibid.*

**Table 17-1**  Increases in Land Prices in Selected Countries and Years (Base of 100 Applies to First Year Given)

| Country | Period | Typical Costs | Cost of Living Index |
|---|---|---|---|
| Belgium | 1953–1960<br>1953–1963 | 125 (private sales)<br>124 (public sales) | — |
| Denmark | 1957–1964<br>1960–1964 | 309<br>188 | 124 |
| Finland, Helsinki | 1954–1960 | 820 | 132 |
| West Germany | 1961<br>1964 | 123 (developed land)<br>175 (undeveloped land) | — |
| Italy | 1956–1961/62 | 200 | — |
| Israel | 1953–1963 | 1500 (central sites) | 280 |
| Netherlands | 1953–1960<br>1953–1962 | 136 (undeveloped sites)<br>185 | — |
| Norway | 1939–1958 | 200–300 | 250 |
| Spain | 1950–1963 | 1000 (developed areas) | 194 |
| Yugoslavia | 1956–1959 to<br>1962/1963 | 175–200 | — |

SOURCE: Department of Housing and Urban Development, *Urban Land Policy: Selected Aspects of the European Experience,* Washington: GPO, March, 1969.

Another means of controlling scarcities of urban land is to control prices. This has several aims, including (1) provision of housing at a moderate cost, (2) encouragement of industrial development, (3) avoidance of overcrowding of structures, which tends to occur if land prices are exceptionally high, and (4) to hold down business operating expenses. A policy of control of land prices has rarely been implemented, however.

A further means of regulating urban land is by means of the tax mechanism, which can discourage monopoly and restrict socially useless or harmful types of speculation. The objective here is to regain for the public the values by publicly instituted improvements. If the value of a land parcel is increased as a result of construction of a public improvement, such as a street or water main, the increase in value is taxed, which results in some of the initial cost that is borne by the public being reclaimed by the public. Another form of taxation on urban land that is employed in several European countries is a transfer tax, even on long-term leases. In this procedure, each real estate transaction is taxed, with the rate being from four to fifteen percent when the real estate is transferred from one owner or leaseholder to another. A further type of tax that is employed for urban land in some European nations is a capital gains or betterment tax. Rather than such a tax with a fixed rate, in Sweden, the capital gains tax has a sliding scale related to the length of time the property has been held in one ownership—the longer the period, the lower the capital gains tax. In France, this tax is called a "Land value regularization tax," and is levied when public agencies have provided all of the improvements that make the land ready for building. In this way, the public cost of improving private land is reclaimed. In Great Britain, such taxes are known as "betterment levies" or "development charges."

When different urban land policies are adopted in Europe, the usual procedure is that they be applied within the context of development plans. In the United Kingdom, all authorities are required to base development plans on a survey covering "the physical features of the area, water supply, soil fertility, minerals and so forth, the growth of the population, the industries that are expanding and those that are declining, housing, open spaces, public buildings. . . .".[5] In Scandinavia, especially Sweden, local governments have been combined on a broad scale to permit more effective physical planning and urban development.

There are contrasts, however, between urban land policy in western Europe and in the United States. After World War II, efforts in western Europe were directed more to peripheral development and new towns, while in the United States, the thrust was concentrated on the improvement and restructuring of the central city. The dominant urban land policy in the U.S. was urban renewal, in which this country is ahead of Europe with the exception of the clearance and rebuilding of war damaged areas and programs of preservation of historical and cultural areas. In the United States, there is little in the way of national urban land policy, with the exception of urban renewal, and policies that exist usually have been developed and implemented at the local level. Since each locality develops its own policy, there is little similarity between those of different cities. In general, there are several policies pertaining to cities that are developed at the local level, such as policies for (1) zoning and land use control, (2) building and housing policies,

(3) taxation policies, (4) transportation and communications policies, and (5) utilities and facilities policy.[6] These various policies do not stand alone, however, and each has relationships with the others.

At this point, a distinction should be made between urban land policy and urban land planning, although there often is not a clear separation of the two. Urban land policy usually involves the establishment and adoption of guidelines, objectives, and goals relating to the manner in which urban land is to be used. As examples, there may be a policy adopted with the aim of providing each urban dweller with a safe, abundant, and reliable water supply from public sources, or a policy that would have urban land used in such a manner as to avoid adjacent land uses that are incompatible or that are in conflict. Each of the examples cited is a statement of a particular goal or objective in a rather broad sense, and after such goals or objectives are set, it then is the task of the planning process to explore means of implementing each policy, of organizing and administering the effort, and establishing the feasibility and timing of each policy implementation. Following up with one of the above examples, involving incompatible land uses and land use conflicts, it is the task of the planning process to identify incompatible land uses by type and location, and the particular characteristics that make them incompatible within a particular local setting. Not only must there be concern for the land uses that are incompatible or that result in land use conflicts, there would be attention given to possible remedial measures to reduce or remove the problems and to possible acceptable locations for the land uses involved.

In essence, then, urban land policy sets general goals and objectives for management of urban land, while urban land planning involves the detailed treatment

---

[5]Department of Housing and Urban Development, *Ibid*.

[6]Richard B. Andrews (Ed.) *Urban Land Use Policy: The Central City,* New York: The Free Press, 1972.

of urban land so that the goals and objectives can be realized. Policy states what needs to be accomplished and planning deals with the ways of doing it. In many, if not most, American cities, planning is undertaken without benefit of any established long term policy as to what type of city or what type of urban environment is desired. A decision, pertaining to the use of one urban land parcel, does not constitute a policy; such a decision should be in accord with an urban land policy that pertains to the given land parcel within the context of all other parcels. Although the cities in the United States often have no formalized land policy or have limited land policies, and there is a general lack of national land policies, there is a relative abundance of land use planning in urban areas, large and small.

## Planning and Cities

When the term "planning" is used in regard to cities, different notions come to mind. In cities of the United States and many other nations, city planning usually connotes an action program to aid in the operation of existing cities. Urban planning dealing with such programs is of different types, however, and distinctions can be made between ongoing or *operational planning, developmental planning,* and *restorative planning.* Operational planning essentially has to do with means of planning for better operation of the component parts of the existing city, that is, a more efficient and livable existing city. Planning of this type is an ongoing process in that as one operational problem is solved, others take its place so that the planning process is continuous. Examples of this type of planning might include planning of changes in vehicular traffic flow, planning of land use on a group of contiguous land parcels, planning of acceptable levels of air pollution, or planning of a neighborhood for possible annexation to the central city.

Developmental planning is concerned with development of an area of the city not previously put to urban uses, or the redevelopment of a designated blighted area in the city, such as an urban renewal area. Restorative planning is of a similar nature in that it deals with redevelopment, but through restoration of existing facilities, rather than through reconstruction or replacement of facilities. Examples of this type of planning might include restoration of a neighborhood containing facilities and structures of unusual historical, aesthetic, or cultural value, such as a number of waterfront facilities in San Francisco. The challenge of this type of planning is to restore the facility in such a manner that it is viable and safe and performs a desired function.

Planning of the types mentioned above deals with organization, development, or restoration of components of the existing city, ranging from land use planning in a new development in the city to conversion of an old, abandoned warehouse area into a complex of high quality shops and restaurants.

In other instances, city planning means the planning, layout, design, and location of completely new urban agglomerations on large land areas removed from any existing urban center. This type of planning is not as commonly practiced in the United States and other nations as is operational planning, with the possible exceptions of the Soviet Union and Israel. *New town* planning, of the type mentioned above, deals with the planning of new centers and, although not common at present, this approach offers considerable possibility for the future.

## City Planning

Planning of new cities in the United States had its beginning in colonial America in Philadelphia (1682), Williamsburg, Virginia (1699), and Savannah, Georgia (1733), in which cases, the basic pattern of streets was laid out in mainly a grid pattern.[7] After these and other early but ill-fated attempts at city planning in colonial America, city planning fell out of favor and continued so until about 1900 to 1930, but by this time much of the needed planning was of restorative nature to revitalize large cities of the nation that were showing signs of decay, dilapidation, and disorder. After the beginning of the twentieth century, the City Beautiful movement came into focus, and this was the beginning of comprehensive planning, encompassing a number of cities, the main one of which was Chicago that developed the plan of Daniel Burnham in 1905. In the period after the 1930's, city planning reached a higher level of acceptance, and comprehensive planning, which by this time was more than just city beautification, was extended to numerous cities, large and small. In recent decades, city planning has become much more refined and analytical than it was previously and has been more widely accepted and has been implemented in more cities.

Still, there is no general agreement as to what exactly city planning is, with different definitions developed to suit different areas, different cities, and different culture groups. Some definitions basically deal with aesthetic and design characteristics, often of public facilities and buildings alone, which tended to be true with the City Beautiful movement. Other definitions consider planning to be concerned with the spatial organization of all the component parts of the urban complex. One definition that has been developed states that "city planning simply means getting ready for the future in city growth."[8] In the constitution of the

American Institute of Planners, as amended in 1946, it is said of city planning that "Its particular sphere of activity shall be the planning of the unified development of urban communities and their environs, and of states, regions, and the nation, as expressed through determination of the comprehensive arrangement of land uses and land occupancy and the regulation thereof."[9]

Regardless of the explicit definition of city planning, it might be pointed out that it occurs within two different contexts; there is remedial planning that essentially attempts to overcome past mistakes, as contrasted with preventative planning which attempts to keep mistakes from occurring. Much of the urban planning in the United States is of the former type, since there was no widespread heritage or acceptance of urban planning during the periods of formation and growth of most American cities. A good deal of the planning effort of cities in Europe also has been of a remedial nature, with preventative planning only recently given serious consideration.

## Elements of the City Plan

Since there is no general acceptance of a definition of city planning, there is no universal pattern followed in formulation and development of a city plan, although there are certain component elements that are present in most city plans in the United States. These elements consist of studies done on single facets of the city or of single-purpose plans developed for one aspect of the city. Quite often, the studies conducted are basic inventories that provide the basis for making future projections which, in turn, provide the rationale for plans that are developed. Component elements, valuable in development of a city plan, are indicated below, although different cities in different settings may use inputs in formation

[7]William I. Goodman and Eric C. Freund (Eds.), *Principles and Practice of Urban Planning,* International City Managers' Association, 1968. This volume presents an outstanding coverage of the elements and development of city planning, especially in the United States.

[8]Developed by Nelson P. Lewis and presented in Harold MacLean Lewis, *Planning the Modern City,* New York: John Wiley & Sons, Inc. 1949, p. 7.

[9]Harold MacLean Lewis, *Ibid.* P. 8.

of a city plan other than those mentioned.

1. *Population Studies.*[10] Population studies are needed in planning, both for knowledge of existing conditions and for making future projections.

Such studies should disaggregate the general population so that independent projections can be made for each component population group, based on age, sex, income group, or other pertinent criteria. Furthermore, in making such studies, care must be exercised in using the best projection method and one suited to the data on which the projection is based. Also, population studies should be suited to consideration of migration, not just natural reproduction, and should be structured so that information and projections for small areas within the city are forthcoming. Such studies also should be suited to the exercise of a certain amount of personal judgement and insight to modify strictly standard procedures.

2. *Housing Studies.* Housing studies are related to population studies in that the latter provide measures of the number of people for which housing must be provided in the future. In addition, housing studies include consideration of demands for different types of housing (single family, multifamily) in different price ranges in different sections of the city. Also, housing studies often include study and planning of low income public housing in terms of feasibility, need, types, location, and time when needed.

3. *Economic Studies.* Included in this type of study are aspects of the economic structure of the city, directions to be taken in economic development, and the economic base of the city. The latter facet provides a perspective as to how the economy of the city is interrelated with that of the region and of the nation. Another direction the economic study of

the city might take deals with disaggregation and inventory of the labor force and development of projections of the individual segments of the labor force.

4. *Land Use Studies.* This is a key element of any city plan, for all of the urban residents and activities occupy urban space. An inventory of existing land use is essential to development of a city plan that is based on formulation or acceptance of a suitable land use classification. Of value also is study of land use trends in the city, land use densities, and land absorption, for in this way, estimates of future land needs can better be developed. Once a land use inventory is made, public controls on land use can be implemented so as to avoid nuisances, conflicts, and incompatible situations, in addition to providing a basis for urban land being used in a more efficient manner.

5. *Transportation Studies.* Consideration here is for the development, planning, and administration of the transportation network consisting of both public and private facilities, plus ancillary works of this network. Planning of the street and highway network is a basic part of such planning, which also includes such facets as planning and development of mass transit systems, planning of airport facilities, and planning of rail and bus terminals. Ancillary works considered in transportation planning might include offstreet parking facilities (surface, above-ground, below-ground) and transportation facilities for other than motor vehicles.

6. *Open Space and Recreation Planning.* This element includes the planning of outdoor recreation facilities and less intensely used open space areas that serve a recreational function. Planning as applied here, encompasses the scale of operation, location, and functional types of needed recreational areas and specific types of open space needed: recreational, residential, or agricultural.

7. *Governmental and Community Facilities.* In any city, there must be concern

---

[10] International City Managers' Association, *Op.Cit.* The matter of population studies for city planning is discussed at some length in this volume.

for planning of facilities to serve governmental needs, plus those of the community. There is a great variety of these facilities that must be incorporated into a city plan, with consideration given to scale of operations, type of facility, time of development, and location of facilities. The facilities referred to include schools, health facilities, administrative structures, libraries, fire stations, police stations, and water systems, among others.

## The Comprehensive Plan

Each of the component elements above, in the form of a study or a plan, deals with but one facet of the city, yet policy cannot be based on only one element when each is related to others. The various studies and single-purpose plans ultimately must be coordinated into a common single framework and this is the role of the comprehensive plan. The comprehensive plan has been defined as "an official public document adopted by a local government as a policy guide to decisions about the physical development of the community."[11] It has the properties of being comprehensive in that all geographical areas of the community and all functional elements that bear on its development are included, it is general and does not deal with specific locations and regulations, and it is long range, since it deals with the city twenty years or more in the future. In a general way, it provides the community with a format of how the city is to develop two or three decades in the future.

Once developed, the comprehensive plan is presented in printed form, often in several volumes for larger cities, and is summarized in map form. Whatever the form of presentation, the comprehensive plan hopefully serves as the basic guide for physical development of the city in years to come.

[11]International City Managers' Association, *Ibid*, p. 349.

## New Towns

The preceding discussion dealt with planning of existing cities, and attention now is directed to the planning and development of entirely new urban settlements. Ebenezer Howard (1850 to 1928) developed the concept that there was a functional limit to the growth of the city and proposed that centers be developed with limited areas and populations to relieve the overgrowth of London. The optimum population mentioned by Howard was 30,000 and these planned urban centers were to embody four basic principles: limitation in population and area, growth by colonization, variety and self sufficiency in economic opportunities and social offerings, and control of the land in the public interest.[12] The implementation of these concepts has been realized, in various forms, in new towns today in various parts of the world.

The new towns of today, which result from deliberate planning and construction, had antecedents as early as about 3000 B.C. with Kahune (Kahun) in ancient Egypt. The first new towns developed for special purposes in Europe were creations of Greeks about 3000 years ago. These were built for colonization, commerce, and absorption of population increases in larger cities. Hippodamus is credited with the planning of a number of new towns in the fifth century in Greece and about sixty new towns were built in the Macedonian period, mostly as military posts and for settlement of conquered territories. During the Roman era, many new towns were founded, often as military outposts, and during the Medieval period, the bastides (discussed in Chapter 3) were a form of new town developed especially in southern France. In the same period, new town development took place in England, but lagged somewhat behind that of Fr-

[12]Frederic J. Osborn and Arnold Whittick, *The New Towns: An Answer to Megalopolis*, London: Leonard Hill, 1963.

ance. Although there was a decline in new town building during the Renaissance, there were some notable exceptions of new towns built in the baroque format, such as Karlsruhe, Germany and Richelieu, France. Some early settlements in the United States took on many aspects of European new towns as well.

By the end of the nineteenth century, the burst of formation of new towns and cities had waned and growth of existing cities became the major phenomenon. Areal expansion and population growth of existing cities began to reach serious levels and in this context, Ebenezer Howard spearheaded the movement for development of "modern" new towns. Howard originated the concept of the Garden City, which was to combine the best aspects of town and country life. The Garden City, as envisioned by Howard, included certain basic elements including (1) a greenbelt that would provide a physical boundary for the city, (2) division into wards or neighborhoods that faced inward on parks containing a school at its center, that is, a neighborhood "superblock," (3) bounding of the wards by radial boulevards and a circumferential railway, and (4) location of industries on the periphery of the town, with ready access provided to residential neighborhoods and the circumferential railroad. An interesting aspect of the Garden City, as envisioned by Howard, is the way in which the land occupied by the city would be treated. The occupied land was to be held in trust for the community, that is, rents and leaseholdings rather than purchase, and unearned increment in value of land would become the property of the community rather than of individuals. As a result of the writings and actions of Howard, the first Garden City, Letchworth, was built in 1903 about thirty-five miles from London. Although this effort experienced financial difficulties and grew only slowly, a second Garden City, Welwyn, was built in 1920, approximately twenty miles from London.[13] The impact of the Garden City experience of England was such that, by 1913, there were forms of Garden Cities considered or constructed in seven other countries. More recently, new towns have been built or are under construction in the Soviet Union, the United States, Canada, Germany, France, Israel, the Netherlands, South Africa, Sweden, and India. Of these, the Soviet Union has witnessed the development of the greatest number of new towns, with over 800 reportedly built in the period 1926 to 1963, with about one-third located in wholly undeveloped areas.[14] There is a national new towns policy in the Soviet Union and in Israel, just as there is in Great Britain.

*The Definitional Problem.* Having discussed the early beginnings of new towns and the revival of new town thinking and building during and after the life of Ebenezer Howard, it serves now, perhaps belatedly, to attempt some clarification of the term "new town." As with the word "city," the term "new town" can be viewed from different perspectives, and there is no general agreement about meaning, with different people defining the term to suit their particular viewpoint and need. A definition may stress physical, social, environmental, legal, or administrative factors, but a single definition has yet to be adopted. The task is made more difficult by the fact that different terms may be used to describe the urban entity known as the new town, such as "new community," "planned community," "satellite town," "new city," "greenbelt town," or "garden city."[15] Drawing from a number of definitions of new towns that have been presented, the

[13] James A. Clapp, *New Towns and Urban Policy,* New York: Dunellen Publishing Co., 1971.

[14] Clapp, *Ibid.*

[15] The definitional problem is discussed by Harold Brodsky, *"Land Development and the Expanding City," Annals* of the AAC, Vol. 63, No. 2 (June, 1973).

more frequently mentioned elements include (1) an urban settlement form that is completely planned, designed, and built with the inclusion of all elements of a complete urban settlement, regardless of size, (2) planning for a community of an optimal size and density, perhaps with restraints on expansion beyond general guidelines, (3) a single ownership, public or private, of the land included, (4) a high degree of self-sufficiency and social and economic balance, and (5) development in accord with design concepts, procedures, and standards. These elements, included in definitions of new towns, are expanded on below.

*Planning of New Towns.* Before building of a new town commences, a master plan is developed and the new town is developed in accordance with this plan. In a sense, this represents "pre-planning" of new towns, in contrast to "replanning" of existing cities. The planning of new towns is desired to be in accord with modern concepts of city planning, but not necessarily planned in all respects. Furthermore, plans for new towns are based on a thorough analysis of the towns location, physical characteristics of its site, relationship to transporation networks, projected population size and land needs, and relationships to other communities. A measure of flexibility is retained, however, in the planning of new towns to allow for innovation in pattern or layout, structures, and morphology.

*New Town Size and Density.* Generally, there is some consideration given to population size of new towns as they are originally conceived, but there is no agreement as to what maximum or minimum populations should be. Minimum populations of 20,000 to 25,000 and 50,000 have been suggested, however questionable such values may be. Consideration of optimum population size for new towns also is fairly common, with such sizes in the order of

50,000 to 100,000, depending on the specific new town considered. Five of the eight new towns in the London area of England, as one example, have proposed populations in the range of 80,000 to 120,000 persons, and five have existing populations in the range of 59,000 to 70,000.[16] Statements concerning maximum and minimum populations of new towns are questionable, however, since each situation must be considered in the context of the purpose of the new town and its location.

Perhaps, more significant in new town development than rigid values as to allowable population is the density of the population which takes up residence in the new town. Howard felt that new towns would have densities lower than those prevailing in major cities of the time. At present, thinking suggests that densities in new towns should be higher than those in typical American suburbs that contribute to inefficiency of land use and to urban sprawl.

*Sponsorship and Ownership.* Sponsorship of new towns tends to reflect the purpose for which the new town is developed, such as Brasilia, the new capital of Brazil, that was sponsored entirely by the public sector, and Oak Ridge, Tennessee, sponsored by the federal government for strategic purposes. The new towns proposed or being built in the United States at present are sponsored by single developers and development corporations, large landholders, and large financial and industrial corporations, all in the private sector.[17]

*Self-Sufficiency.* Terms such as "self-sufficient," "self-contained," or "balanced" often are applied to new towns, although one familiar with urban systems knows that no urban center is entirely

[16]Clapp, *Op. Cit.*

[17]This is borne out by Richard W. Helbock, "New Towns in the United States," *The Professional Geographer,* Vol. 20, No. 4 (July, 1968), Table 1.

self-sufficient or self-contained, with each having linkages with other centers and localities. When one considers that new towns in Great Britain and in the United States, nearly all are located near major metropolitan areas, the conclusion may be reached that they are intended to absorb the "spill-over" population, industries, and commercial activities from the metropolis. New towns of the Soviet Union are different in that many of them are located in remote areas far from major urban concentrations. Moreover, there are contrasts between new towns in Britain and the United States, in that a higher degree of self-sufficiency is attained by British policy, which provides that the greatest share of new town workers have local employment. New towns are not intended to be populated by commuters as are typical suburbs, but some in the United States have taken on the role of a commuter suburb to some degree. New towns are intended to be relatively self-sufficient in terms of employment of the local work force and are not to be totally dependent on a larger parent city.

New towns are often mentioned as balanced communities, which applies to a variety of desired relationships of a physical, social, and structural nature, more than to economic structure. It is desired that new towns not become "bedroom" suburbs or residential satellites, and that they include a fairly wide spectrum of economic levels, rather than becoming white collar, middle-income ghettos. Also, there should be in new towns, a land use mix that includes residential areas of different types, commercial centers, parks and other public facilities, office complexes, and perhaps manufacturing of acceptable types. Basically, new towns are not to be single-class or single-function communities, but such objectives seem to be rarely achieved.

## New Towns in the United States

A number of settlements have been founded in the United States that might be considered new towns, but these have not been developed in the same manner as other new towns of recent times; their nature is different, as is their structure. Most people are familiar with "company towns" built to house workers employed in large industrial operations. Some of these towns have been considered as positive contributions, while others have been strongly criticized, and of the former type, Kitimat, British Columbia (though not in the United States) is an outstanding example. In addition to towns founded by industry, there are some that have been founded by government, such as Oak Ridge, Tennessee; Los Alamos, New Mexico; and Richland, Washington. These towns were founded for special purposes often associated with defense efforts, and are not to be equated with modern new towns, developed to perform a variety of functions.

The number of new towns in the United States meeting the criteria discussed in earlier sections, as of 1970 and with an area of 1000 acres or more, is one-hundred and thirty.[18] An earlier statement gives the number of "new communities" in the country in the planning or development stages and a with an area of 1000 acres or more as being greater than one-hundred and sixty.[19] In any case, there are in excess of one-hundred new towns being developed in the nation, yet the regions with the greatest numbers of new towns are not necessarily the regions with the greatest number of metropolitan centers or those in which the bulk of the population resides. Rather, they are regions with the most desirable year-around climates, and in these regions, oceanfront locations are the most often selected (Figure 17–1).

There is a wide variation in the populations, residing in reported new towns in the United States, ranging from 4000 (Kearny, Arizona) to 500,000 (Irvine Ranch, California). Of the 97 new towns

---

[18]Clapp, *Op. Cit.* Appendix I.
[19]Thomas McDade, "New Communities in America," *Urban Land,* January, 1965.

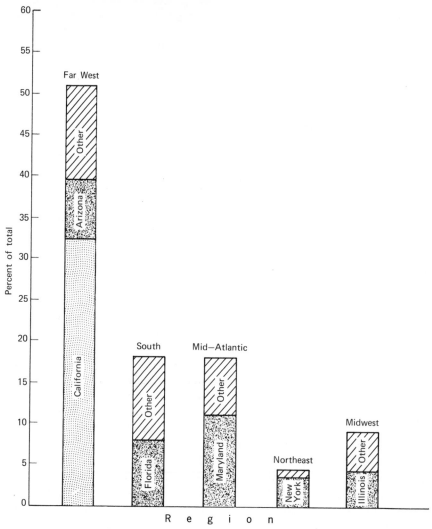

**Figure 17–1**   Regional location of new towns in the United States: 1970. *Source.* Based upon data in James A. Clapp, *New Towns and Urban Policy* (1971). Appendix I.

with reported populations, 14 (14.4 percent) have populations of 100,000 or more and 77 (79.4 percent) have populations of 20,000 or greater (Figure 17-2A). As with population, there is considerable variation in land area included in new towns in the U.S., with extremes of 700 acres (San Manuel, Arizona) and 101,000 acres (California City, California). Of 109 new towns with reported area, 52 or 47.7 percent have areas of less than 5000 acres and 97 or 89.0 percent reported areas of less than 25,000 acres (Figure 17-2B). Popula-

tion densities in new towns in the U.S. generally are in the range of two to fourteen persons per acre, although such values are difficult to determine until one knows how much of the area of each new town is devoted to greenways, open space, and the like, that is, to derive net densities.

Concerning the success of new towns in the United States, it is difficult to make generalizations, since none of the new towns is as yet completely developed, and there has not been a sufficient period to establish long term impact and viability.

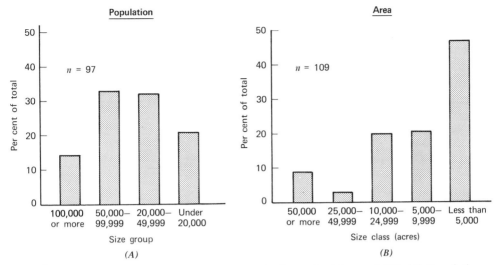

**Figure 17–2**   Population and area of new towns in the United States: 1970. *(A)* Population. *(B)* Area. *Source.* Based upon data in James A. Clapps, *New Towns and Urban Policy* (1971). Appendix I.

There are unanswered questions dealing with the marketability of land in new towns and the livability of new towns. On the first point, incomplete information indicates that real estate sales have seriously lagged in some larger new towns, such as Reston, Virginia, eighteen miles west of Washington, D.C., which has encountered serious financial difficulties. One factor that seems to have emerged from the limited U.S. experience with new towns is that scale of size is related to problems that develop. It is reported that new town projects up to 3,000 to 4,000 acres in size are successful, but that new towns over 6000 acres are questionable in terms of financial success for the developer. There are logical reasons for this situation, since large tracts of developable land for new town sites that can be acquired at reasonable cost are quite distant from existing margins of nearby metropolitan areas. In the initial stage of new town occupance, a large share of the labor force commutes to jobs in the nearby urban center and large new towns may well be beyond a reasonable commuting distance. Therefore, many potential residents of new towns cannot take advantage of them due to the prohibitively long journey to work. Also, the more remote new towns cannot take advantage of pre-existing facilities, such as water supply and distribution lines, sewer lines, and access roads, and if these facilities have to be constructed on the new town site, this adds appreciably to the cost of the development. Another point, related to scale of new town development, is the need to absorb the cost of undeveloped land in the new town site, until additional phases of the development are complete and occupied. A great deal of investment may be made in these developments before any return on the investment is realized from much of the area, included in the new town site. For example, it is reported that Reston, Virginia with an investment of about $60 million, and Columbia, Maryland with an investment of approximately $50 million have very large continuing costs, including $10,000 per day in interest alone on each development.[20]

The above statements refer to the financial success of new towns; the livability of new towns and the price people are willing to pay for a more livable environment are questions that might be asked,

[20]Roy Drachman, "The High Cost of Holding Land," *Urban Land*, October, 1968.

but there is even less information on which to base answers than there is for questions on the financial success of new towns. With greater elapsed time and greater experience with new towns, perhaps answers will be forthcoming.

## New Towns and Urban Policy

New towns cannot be taken as the panacea for metropolitan problems that beset different parts of the world. Modern new towns have only recently been developed, and then only in a limited number, yet based on a short span of time and a limited number of cases, the success of new towns is questionable in those areas where the private sector is involved, and somewhat less so where new town development is a part of national policy, such as in the Soviet Union and Great Britain. To date, new town development is not part of national policy in the United States, although there are some aspects of new town development in this country that are now included in national legislation.[21] More specifically, there is a program of mortgage insurance for new towns (1966), one providing guarantees for financing new community development (1968), and another providing for urban growth and new community development (1970). The latter Act recognized four different geographical settings for new towns that are to be federally supported, including (1) a free-standing new town, (2) a new town near an existing small town growth center, (3) a new town as a satellite of an existing city, and (4) a new town within an existing city—a new-town-in-town (Figure 17-3). No fewer than eleven new communities have been or are being funded under the 1970 Act, of which nine are satellites, one is a new-town-in-town, and one is a free-standing new town.[22] As yet, there is no broad new town or new community policy

[21]Policy implications of new towns are discussed by Herman G. Berkman in "New Towns and Urban Change Form," *Land Economics,* Vol. XLVIII, No. 2, May, 1972.

[22]Harold Brodsky, *Op. Cit.*

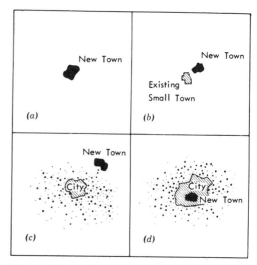

**Figure 17–3**  Types of new towns. (*A*) Free-standing new town. (*B*) New town near existing small town growth center. (*C*) New town as satellite to existing city. (*D*) New town within existing city. *Source.* Harold Brodsky. *Annals of the Association of American Geographers.* Vol. 63, 1973. Reprinted by permission.

that would incude such factors as (1) determination of need for new towns and communities, (2) location of new towns, once need has been established, (3) size, design, and structure of new towns, and (4) livability of new towns and communities. Although the new town has found its way into the urban settlement fabric of the United States, it is still a fairly unknown and perplexing phenomenon. Perhaps, the philosophy and objectives of Ebenezer Howard have as yet not been fairly tested, and the new towns experience in the United States should not be taken as conclusive evidence of the success or failure of the concept. Perhaps, sometime in the future, new towns, as envisioned by Howard, will be commonplace and will assume a role in the urban structure of the United States and other nations. In the meantime, we have the task of dealing with the complex problems of existing cities that already contain about one-third of the world's people, and before we can better cope with the problems and affairs of existing cities, we must more thoroughly understand and identify them.

# Epilogue

The content of this book has come full circle. Considered early was the origin of cities and the gradual dispersal of the city forming process to various parts of the world. Next was discussion of the rapid and fairly recent surge of urbanization in the world and its impact on the livability of the urban environment. The content of the book then dealt with aspects of spatial and hierarchical systems of contemporary cities, followed by material having to do with the occupance of the contemporary city that involved the interplay of people and urban space. The fabric and functions of the modern city have resulted in creation of urban problems and these were the focus of material toward the end of the book. To solve some of the existing urban problems, material on planning of existing cities and on development of new urban agglomerations, has been presented.

The book has proceeded, then, from birth of cities, through their early establishment, their maturity, and the first signs of decay and infirmity. The final stage is not, however, suggested to be decline, abandonment, and eventual death of the city as some might suggest, for there are means of therapy by which the city can be revitalized to remain as the viable habitat of much of the world's human population. The city proves to be a little understood phenomenon, although its role is becoming increasingly appreciated. Many parties have helped in providing greater understanding and appreciation of the urban phenomenon, and have communicated, in one way or another, knowledge, insights, and information on this topic. It is in this spirit that this book has been written and toward this end that the effort has been undertaken.

# index